The ABCs of Workflow

for E-Business Suite Release 11i and Release 12

Shining a Light on Oracle Workflow

Published by Reed-Matthews, Inc.
Cover Art © Copyright 2008 by Hope Malone, Solution Beacon. All Rights Reserved.

Solution Beacon, LLC
14419 Greenwood Ave N #332
Seattle, WA 98133

Phone 206 366-6606

http://www.solutionbeacon.com

Reed-Matthews, Inc.
41 Sycamore Ridge
Honeoye Falls, NY 14472

Phone 585 624-2402

http://www.oncalldba.com

Oracle is a registered trademark of Oracle Corporation.

HP is a trademark or a registered trademark of Hewlett Packard Company.

Sun is a trademark or registered trademark of Sun Microsystems, Inc. in the United States and other countries.

Other trade and service marks are the property of their respective owners.

Order additional copies at http://stores.lulu.com/store.php?fAcctID=83172

Meet the Authors

If you have questions about Oracle Workflow, send a note to Solution Beacon's Oracle Workflow Team at workflow@solutionbeacon.com

Karen Brownfield of Solution Beacon has 35+ years experience programming, installing, and managing applications used in various industries including Chemicals, Entertainment, Defense, Recruitment, Telecommunications, and Hospitality. The past 18 years she has focused on Oracle Applications, specializing in Financials and Workflow as a functional specialist, Workflow Administrator, trainer, programmer, team lead, and/or project manager. An expert in Workflow since its inception in 1998, Karen says that Workflow "put the fun back in being an E-Business Suite developer". Karen is also a member of the OAUG Board of Directors, serving in multiple capacities in the last 15 years, including President, Past President, and other committee roles. She has presented many papers and training sessions at the various OAUG and user group conferences locally, regionally, and internationally. For fun, Karen reads, gardens, golfs, researches genealogy, travels, and enjoys spending time with her grown children and her grandchildren. Karen dedicates this book to her mother who taught her that nothing is impossible if you believe in yourself and to her husband who showed her that love could be real and lasting.

Susan Behn has 23+ years experience developing, implementing, upgrading, customizing and managing enterprise applications for government and commercial industries. Susan has worked with Oracle Applications since 1993 in many technical and functional roles. Susan enjoys Oracle Workflow due to the combination of functional and technical skills utilized in working with this product. Since joining Solution Beacon, LLC five years ago, Susan has also enjoyed working in management and sales support while staying involved in technical roles to keep skills current. Susan presents frequently at local, regional and national conferences on both functional and technical topics. Many thanks go to Susan's husband of 21 years and three children who have been incredibly supportive during the hours working on this book. When Susan is not living and breathing Oracle, her preference is to be almost anywhere outside – preferably walking on a nature trail or hiking up a mountain. Susan's long-term dream is to retire and become a hike master in the Rocky Mountains.

Special thanks to **Gerald Jones**, of Solution Beacon. *Chapter 14, Approvals Management Engine (AME),* was based on Gerald's *AME Case Studies* paper. Gerald K. Jones has 15+ years developing, customizing and implementing ERP applications in a variety of industries including telecommunications, publishing, manufacturing, medical insurance and hotel management. Since 1994, Gerald has worked primarily as a technical resource developing extensions and customizations for Oracle Manufacturing and Financials modules. For the past couple of years, Gerald has become focused on Oracle's Approvals Management Engine (AME) application. He enjoys working with AME because of the unique blend of functional and technical skills that are utilized working with the application. Although AME is primarily functional in nature, the ability to incorporate SQL programming still allows him to exercise his "techie" side. As a consultant, he has helped design and develop complex programming to integrate AME with Oracle Payables, *i*Procurement and a third party application. Gerald has presented topics on AME at local, regional and national conferences. These topics include the basics of AME and migration of AME setups using the FNDLOAD utility. Gerald dedicates this book to his mother whose unconditional love, support and encouragement throughout the years has always been the primary motivation and driving force behind his will to achieve and be a better today than yesterday. In his spare time, Gerald enjoys a great workout at the gym, reading, music and good conversation with his family and friends.

Special thanks to **Jerry Ireland**, of Rightsizing, Inc. The BPEL chapter was based on Jerry's *BPEL for Workflow Developers* paper. Jerry Ireland first started working with Oracle in 1981 and as a co-founder of RIGHTSIZING, Inc., has earned a reputation as a leading architect and developer of high-performance Oracle applications. With almost thirty years of consulting experience, Jerry has considerable experience with implementation and development of Oracle's E-Business Suite, including complex customizations and extensions using Application Object Library and Workflow. He has designed and developed one of the more advanced "Vendor Managed Replenishment" systems with EDI interfaces to major retail chains such as Wal-Mart, Kmart and Target. He has also designed web store systems interfaced to Oracle's Order Entry. Jerry has extensive development experience with large databases. He has a thorough knowledge of Oracle development tools. He has also participated in beta testing as far back as CASE 5.0, CASE 5.1 and ReportWriter 2.0, and as recently as the 11*g* database. Jerry has served on the board of directors of the Oracle Development Tools User Group from its infancy and is a regular speaker and panel member at the ODTUG and OAUG conferences. He has chaired several ODTUG conferences and has been a driving force behind collaboration between OAUG and ODTUG at OAUG conferences. When Jerry is not trying to keep up with the latest Oracle technology, he spends time outdoors and on the sometimes more challenging joy of keeping up with his four children and three grandchildren.

Dedication

Solution Beacon employees donate the proceeds from the sales of this book to the Solution Beacon Foundation. The Solution Beacon Foundation is a charitable organization whose mission is "Feeding Children's Bodies and Minds" by delivering aid and assistance to others less fortunate.

http://www.solutionbeaconfoundation.org/stevepeifer.htm

Solution Beacon's Workflow Team are experts on the inner workings of Oracle Workflow. The team regularly configures and tunes Workflow environments. They also research problems reported by users of Solution Beacon's free E-Business Suite Release 11i and Release 12 Vision Instances and our clients' E-Business Suite environments.

As preparation for this book, team members developed a set of presentations about topics covered in several of the chapters. The team delivered these presentations around the country at various OAUG venues. You can see all of Solution Beacon's presentations, including those about other topics, at www.solutionbeacon.com

Special Thanks

The ABCs of Workflow is a collaborative effort between Solution Beacon and the Oracle Applications User Group. We appreciate OAUG's support in helping us publish this book.

Acknowledgements

There are many people who enabled us to amass the knowledge contained in this book. Our apologies to any that may be omitted from this list.

All things have a beginning. When Workflow was released in 1998 White Sands Test Facility (WFSF) in Las Cruces, NM contacted us and asked if we could customize Purchasing to do approvals via Workflow. They knew it was a new product and that no one knew it. However, everyone was willing to take a chance. So our first acknowledgement is for the people who made that engagement a possibility and a success. Thanks to Alicia Hoekstra, who selected Karen for the assignment, Barbara Headrick and Ed Whaling, who worked for WSTF, Kevin Bailey, who helped with Karen's fledgling PL/SQL skills, and Joe Rock, who was the Support Analyst at Oracle who worked with Karen on all the installation issues.

The development staff at Oracle also provided much help and has worked tirelessly over the years to improve the product. Thanks to Kevin Hudson, Mark Craig, Robert Wunderlich, and Cliff Godwin, as well as all their staff. A special thanks goes to the Oracle Support team who provides all the knowledge contained on MetaLink.

Solution Beacon has provided Workflow assistance for many customers. The names mentioned are just a few of the wonderful people that we've worked with: Dave Filecia, Alex Katsevman, Lisa Kramer, Lura Langley, Prashant Sahgal (ADP Dealer Services); Glenna McDonald, Sarah Porter (AMC Theatres); Prameela Burugu, Kieu Oanh Carter, Debra Cooksey, Jennifer Drapeau, Laura Haney, Lucy Lew Harris, Suresh Nookala, Ali Rahim, Andrew Richard, Kelly Ryan, Bill Schuchardt, Elizabeth Scott–Fox, Jim Srock, Pamela Wells (American Tower); Guna Bellampalli, Cris Crockett, Nick Desai, Grant Gasson, Patrick McCormick, Chetan Nayak, Joseph Stroka (Apollo Group); Laura Yang, Mark Rudolph (aQuantive); Pat Bare, Neil Brown, Jim Corder, Ken Humphries, Peggy Lund (Avista Corporation); Dave Moot (BAE Systems); Melanie Cameron (Blood Systems); Alison Campbell, Jamie Christner, Brett Rebischke–Smith, Carol Rigdon, Robert Rittiger (Carnegie Mellon University); Collin Ghosh, Kevin McManus (City of Chandler); Brigitte Byers, Victoria Forbes, Carl Frey, Aparna Gupta, Unaiza Jafri, Ravi Kadiam, Linda Laird, Donna Montagna, Jeanie Platt, Mike Trevino, Dave Truzinski, Allen Tsai, Susan Xing (Cricket Communications); Srini Chavali, Nancy Fox, Bill Waller (Cummins); Arvind Govindarajulu, Bryan Haakenson, Vickie Muse, Robery Myers, Kathy Van Abel (Cummins Filtration); Meryl Fisher , Jennifer Harris, Kelly Tuggle (DFW Airport); Kim Anderson, Tonya Fox, Edwin Ghahramani, Kathy Hageman, Michelle Harrington, David Horkey (Eaton Trucks); Karen Brown, Martha Cerny, Vivian Pemberton, Linda Westland (General Dynamics C4 Systems); Robert Moore (Haworth); Katie Tougas, Jeff Vold (Hazelden); Mark Montgomery, Alan Tu (Jet Propulsion Laboratory); LaRae McCartney, Reggie Thurn (Larimer County); Dwain Istre, Randy McKay, Tammy Miller, Ronda Sachnowitz, Mike Towery, Dewayne Treadway (Lone Star Steel); Mike Laubach, Teri Nelson, Kimberly Pratt, Cathy Sampson, Maureen Simon, Scott Williamson (Mactec); Elizabeth Carver (Mark Andy); Leisa Cagle, Don Lastine, Phil Pritchard, Tim Lawson (McKee Foods); Troy Dawson, Rhonda Stonaker, (Microtune); Sherri Wilkins (Mitre); Lori Kamer, James Lovell, Carrielyn Weber Hamann (NCR); Ron Batra, Kathy Brown, Johnny Guzman, Matt Lewis (National Instruments); Lura Langley (Nystrom); Prasad Katragadda (Progressive); Anjan Dutta, Eric Knutson, Tracey Morales, Lori Pearce, Sharmila Perumal, Eduardo Renteria, Trang Tran, Mike Zill (ResMed); Dave Spaller (RF Monolithics); Sheri Adkins, Gene Gysin (R+L Carriers); Elizabeth O'Connor, Scott Wright, Jim Srock, Scott Wright (Skidmore College); Amy Eaton, Frank Scobby (Southern Illinois University); Sirish Dandamudi (Southern Union); Al Dhalla (Sun Life); Dave Griebl, Brian Post, Bob Scott (TMP Worldwide); Natalee Ash, Chris Bittakis, Mischelle Harmon, Izabela Sobik (Trustreet Properties, GE Capital Solutions); Marcia Frampton, Tara Poleski, Robert Remsbert, Bob Shiflett, Teresa Wimmer (University of Virginia);

Paulette Hamilton, Doug Sparks (Vical); Rattan D'Souza (Worthington Industries); Rick Hill, Betty Montgomery, and Jill Reese (Zale Corporation).

Our DBA, System Administration, and fellow Workflow friends have answered our questions and applied our patches: Peter Adamson, Brian Bent, Michael Brown, Kevin Dahl, Mark Farnham, Randy Giefer, Jeff Holt, Vicki Howard, Kelly Johnson, Chuck Kennedy, Kirby Kraft, James Jones, James Morrow, Rich Niemic, Amit Singh, John Stouffer, and Lon White. Solution Beacon is indebted to John Peters of JRPJR, Incorporated, for his presentation *Deferred Workflow Context Issues*, located at http://jrpjr.com/paper_archive/collab07_wf_context.ppt, which he presented at Collaborate 07.

And because it truly does take a village, our friends, OAUG associates, and co–workers: Stacy Atkison, Kim Autrey, Shameeka Ayers, Dawn Bachmann, Rick Bardy, Susan Beals, Aaronica Bell, Vince Benz, Jalene Bermudez, Melanie Bock, Larry Bowers, Bob Braden, Shelly Burton, John Bushell, Marie Caradonna, Brenda Carlton, Mark Clark, Geordie Coates, Carol Conine, Ken Conway, Laura Cox, Paul Cyphers, Robin Dahlen, Faun deHenry, Jeannie Dobney, Les Dougherty, Don Driggs, Pat Dues, Bill Dunham, Cindy Force, Clinton Frank, Don Grons, John Faucher, John Garnett, Peter Gee, Daryl Geryol, George Govathoti, Don Grons, Earl Guynes, Paul Harrison, Todd Hess, Bob Hester, Christine Hilgert, Tim Hillard, James Hobbs, Craig Hobson, Joel Howard, Steven Hughes, Art Hunt, Joe Imbimbo, Pam Irwin, Connie Johnson, Erin Kirshtein, Nanda Kishore, Matt McDonough, Jamie Molesky, Basheer Khan, Nancy Lane, Debra Lilley, Mike Levin, Hope Malone, Debbie Marsh, Bruce Masters, Jeanne McDonald, Bryan Meyer, Marcia Michalik, Ronan Miles, Steve Miranda, John Nicholson, Alex O'Keefe, Brian O'Neil, Don Payne, Ray Payne, Steve Peifer, Kathy Ponder, Martin Power, Denise Quashie, Jeff Rausch, Anne Ristau, Tracy Robertson, Steve Romeo, Donna Rosentrator, Betsy Rothwell, John Schindler, Karen Settembrino, Tim Sharpe, Joey Simmons, Jagan Singam, Vinita Singh, Goetz Schmitz, Andrew Snyder, Sheryl Stein, Jay Suryadevara, Cyndie Sutherland, Floyd Teter, Naren Thota, Becky Tipton, SallyAnn Ulm, Jan Wagner, Gwen Walker, Lynne Weil, Mary Lou Weiss, Jeff Wells, Suzanne Williams, Jacqueline Woods, John Wookey, Margaret Wright, Jeremy and Kate Young, and Kandi Zastro.

And last, but not least, our editors. This book would not have happened without them: Alysha Behn, Alyssa Johnson, Chuck Kennedy, Barbara Matthews, and Coy Weems.

A Note from the Editors

Early into the final editing stage for this book, we began calling it "the 700 pound gorilla" due to our necessary efforts to keep it below a 700 page limit. We started calling Karen and Susan "The Workflow Girls". We began to make disparaging remarks about Karen and her use of Microsoft Word 2000. We proclaimed that we would demand that Karen upgrade her version of Word as a condition of employment. Then we shrunk the font from a readable 12 point to 11 point, widened the margins by more than an inch, and ran off to Wal-Mart to buy some reading glasses.

The Workflow Girls poured their hearts, souls and minds into this book. It includes everything they think you should know about Workflow. It is not a manual, nor is it a reference guide. It is a manual and a reference guide filled with real-life examples. It captures Karen and Susan's encyclopedic knowledge of the inner workings and outer manifestations of Oracle Workflow.

Now, you may wonder how The Workflow Girls gained all this Workflow knowledge. Surely their time spent in the trenches dealing with customers' Workflow problems has had an important impact. But Karen revealed another trade secret recently – she has MetaLink set to automatically email her with any new information about Workflow or AME. Karen spends her mornings basking in information about Workflow. For those of you who think that Workflow is 'dead', we have to demur. Workflow is a critical part of Release 11*i* and Release 12, neither of which will be going away too soon.

While every precaution has been taken in the preparation of this book, the authors, editors, publishers, and Solution Beacon, LLC assume no responsibility for errors or omissions, or for damages resulting from the use of the information contained herein.

Give us a call when you need guidance on Oracle Workflow.

We have the knowledge and experience that you need. We are Your Trusted Advisors.

TABLE OF CONTENTS

PREFACE .... **XXIII**

WHAT THIS BOOK COVERS XXIII
    1   Introduction .... *xxiii*
    2   Setup .... *xxiii*
    3   Builder Basics .... *xxiii*
    4   PL/SQL in Workflow .... *xxiv*
    5   Business Events .... *xxiv*
    6   Testing Workflows .... *xxiv*
    7   Account Generators .... *xxiv*
    8   Administration .... *xxiv*
    9   Diagnostics .... *xxiv*
    10   Workflow Tables .... *xxiv*
    11   Advanced Builder and PL/SQL .... *xxiv*
    12   Most Commonly Used Workflows .... *xxiv*
    13   New Features .... *xxiv*
    14   Approvals Management Engine (AME) .... *xxv*
    15   What's on the Horizon? .... *xxv*
    16   BPEL for Workflow Developers .... *xxv*
    Appendix A – Sample BR110 .... *xxv*
CONVENTIONS USED IN THIS BOOK XXV
    Screen Shots .... *xxv*
    Lower Case vs. Upper Case for SQL and PL/SQL .... *xxv*
    <your token names> .... *xxvi*
    RUPs, CPUs, CUs, ATGs, and Their Importance .... *xxvi*
        Release 11*i* xxvi
        Release 12 xxviii
    Reader Feedback and Questions .... *xxviii*
    Errata .... *xxviii*

INTRODUCTION **1**

WORKFLOW – IT'S A TECHNOLOGY ALL BY ITSELF 1
WORKFLOW – SOME DEFINITIONS 2
ROLES AND RESPONSIBILITIES 5
    Workflow Administration Tasks 5
    The Workflow Administrator 7
    The Junior Workflow Administrator 9
    The Database Administrator (Apps DBA) 10
    The Applications System Administrator 10
    Developers 10
    Functional SuperUsers 11
    All Users 11
    Summary 11

SETUP **13**

ASSUMPTIONS AND ENVIRONMENT 13
WORKFLOW BUILDER (CLIENT) 13
    Finding the Most Recent Workflow Builder Client 13
    Installing the Workflow Builder Client 15
ORACLE WORKFLOW (SERVER) 18

Finding the Most Recent Workflow Server Patch *18*

Finding the Latest Workflow Information on MetaLink *20*

Major Workflow Changes Starting with Family Pack OWF.G *20*

Major Workflow Changes Starting with 11i.ATG_PF.H.delta.3 (Rollup 3) *20*

Major Workflow Changes Starting with 11i.ATG_PF.H.delta.4 (Rollup 4) *20*

Major Workflow Changes Starting with 11i.ATG_PF.H.delta.5 (Rollup 5) *21*

Major Workflow Changes Starting with 11i.ATG_PF.H.delta.6 (Rollup 6) *21*

Major Workflow Changes Starting in Release 12 .... *21*

Important Workflow MetaLink Doc. IDs *21*

ORACLE WORKFLOW (SERVER) SETUP 22

Prerequisites *22*

Required Steps *22*

Workflow Configuration 22

Workflow System Administrator 23

LDAP 24

Business Event Local System 24

Global Preferences 25

Profile Options 26

Directory Services 28

Verify Directory Services 29

Background Engines 34

Setting Up Background Engines from the Concurrent Manager 34

Setting up Background Engines in the Oracle Applications Manager (OAM) 36

Start Listeners 38

Business Event System 40

Set up and Verify Queues 40

Business Event System Parameters 41

Synchronize License Statuses 41

Schedule Queue Cleanup 41

Optional Steps *42*

Partition Tables 42

Additional Languages 44

Set Up the Notification Mailer 44

Prerequisites 44

Mailer Setup in Oracle Applications Manager (OAM) 44

Setting an Override Notification Mailer Address 56

Responsibility Functions and Request Groups 58

Vacation Rules 58

Customize Logo 59

Custom Icons 59

Verification Scripts *59*

wfver.sql 59

WHAT'S NEXT 66

BUILDER BASICS 67

A SAMPLE WORKFLOW – BUSINESS RULES 67

BUILDER TERMINOLOGY AND SYMBOLS 68

GETTING STARTED 69

Determine the Item Key *69*

Open the Builder, Verify Access Level *70*

Define the Item Type and the Top Process – The Quick Start Wizard *71*

Save Your Work FREQUENTLY *74*

PROCESS MODELING PHILOSOPHY 76

ACTIVITIES 76

Function Without a Result *76*

Function With a Result *78*
Notifications – FYI vs. Response Required *79*
Custom Lookup Type and Lookup Code(s) *80*
Notification With a Result *82*
Time to Save Again *84*
CONNECT THE DOTS – TRANSITIONS 84
THE DIAGRAM IS COMPLETE, BUT IS THE PROCESS? 87
PROPERTY PAGE – NAVIGATOR VS DIAGRAMMER WINDOW 87
STANDARD ACTIVITIES – COMPARE 87
Be Careful Not to Add Activities to Standard *89*
RESULTS <DEFAULT> AND <ANY> 89
STANDARD ACTIVITIES – AND VS. OR 91
TIMEOUTS 92
STANDARD ACTIVITY – LOOP COUNTER 93
STANDARD ACTIVITY – WAIT 98
ITEM ATTRIBUTES 99
COMPLETING NOTIFICATIONS – MESSAGES 101
COMPLETING NOTIFICATIONS – PERFORMERS 110
COMPLETING FUNCTION ACTIVITIES – FUNCTION NAMES 115
COMPLETING THE WAIT ACTIVITY – NODE ATTRIBUTES 116
COMPLETING THE LOOP ACTIVITY – NODE ATTRIBUTES 119
COMPLETE THE COMPARE TEXT ACTIVITY – NODE ATTRIBUTES 120
VALIDATE YOUR DESIGN 122
OPTIONAL (BUT FUN) – CHOOSE ICONS 123
SOME ADDITIONAL BUILDER FEATURES 124
Cost *124*
On Revisit *125*
Error Handling *126*
THERE'S ALWAYS MORE STUFF 127

USING PL/SQL IN WORKFLOW **129**

SPECIAL CONSIDERATIONS REQUIRED BY WORKFLOW 129
Starting Workflow *129*
Maintaining Context *130*
No Commits *131*
Error Handling *134*
WF_CORE.Context *135*
STARTING OUR WORKFLOW 136
PROCEDURE CALLED WITHIN WORKFLOW – NO RESULT 142
PROCEDURE CALLED WITHIN WORKFLOW – WITH RESULT 151
ANOTHER "NO RESULT" PROCEDURE 154
RESETTING THE LOOP COUNTER LOOP COUNT 156
SET_CTX AND TEST_CTX 158
SOME ADDITIONAL NOTES 165
What to Do if you Choose the Incorrect Attribute Type in the Builder *165*
What if the Diagram Contains More than One Loop Counter? *166*
VERSIONING 166
WHAT'S NEXT 167

BUSINESS EVENTS **169**

BUSINESS EVENTS – TERMINOLOGY 169
AN ANALOGY 170
THE QUEUES 171

EVENT MENU STRUCTURE 172
DEFINING BUSINESS EVENTS 173
    Naming Standard 173
    Query Existing Event 174
    Create New Event 174
EVENT GROUPS 177
    Edit/Create Subscription 179
    Action Type – Launch Workflow 182
    Action Type – Custom 185
    Action Type – Send Notification 186
PROGRAMMATICALLY START EVENTS 186
USING EVENTS IN WORKFLOW 188
OTHER USES OF THE RECEIVE ACTIVITY 191
EVENT STANDARD ACTIVITIES 192
WHAT'S NEXT 192

TESTING WORKFLOWS **193**

TEST CASES 193
ADJUST TIMEOUTS AND WAITS AND LOOP COUNTS 195
DEVELOPER STUDIO 195
    Errors Detected Before the Workflow is Initiated 198
    Required and Optional Fields 199
STARTING WORKFLOWS USING THE RAISE EVENT PAGE 201
    Why Workflow Didn't Start 203
VIEWING THE RESULTS 205
    Notification with a Result Type 205
    Notification Without a Result Type but With a Response Attribute 206
    'FYI' Notification – no Result Type nor Response Attribute 207
TEST RESULTS – EXAMPLES OF ERRORS 208
    PL/SQL Procedure is Missing or Mistyped 208
    "Expected" Error 210
    Unexpected Error 212
    "Existing state of has been invalidated ORA-04601" 213
    "Attribute <attribute name> does not exist" 214
    Completes Successfully, but Data is Incomplete 216
STARTING WORKFLOWS USING A TRIGGER OR OTHER PROCEDURE 217
ONCE TESTING IS COMPLETE 218
    Kill the Associated WFERROR 218
    Remove Runtime Data and Old Designs 221
    Migration 222
WHAT'S NEXT 223

ACCOUNT GENERATORS **225**

SEEDED ACCOUNT GENERATORS 225
CUSTOMIZATION RULES 227
HOW ACCOUNT GENERATORS WORK 229
STANDARD FLEXFIELD ACTIVITIES 230
REGISTER YOUR CUSTOMIZATION 234
HOW TO SEND A NOTIFICATION WHEN NOTIFICATIONS ARE PROHIBITED? ... 235
PROJECTS ACCOUNT GENERATORS 236
DEBUGGING 238
RELEASE 12 CHANGES 239
CONCLUSION 239

WHAT'S NEXT 239

ADMINISTRATION...**241**

WHEN TO USE OAM VERSUS THE WORKFLOW ADMINISTRATION MENUS 241
USING ORACLE APPLICATIONS MANAGER (OAM) TO ADMINISTER WORKFLOW...............242
   Workflow Manager Page Overview...242
   Notification Mailer 244
   Agent Listeners..244
   Service Components 244
   Containers 245
   Background Engines...245
   Purge 246
   Control Queue Cleanup 248
   Related Database Parameters 248
   Workflow Metrics 248
      Work Items...249
      Agent Activity 253
   Related Links 254
   Throughput 255
USING THE WORKFLOW ADMINISTRATION MENU STRUCTURE TO ADMINISTER WORKFLOW 257
   The Home Page Tab 257
   The Developer Studio Tab 258
   The Business Events Tab 258
   The Status Monitor Tab 258
      Results..259
      Error Details 260
      The Activity History Button 261
      The Status Monitor Button 262
      The Participant Responses Button 263
      The Workflow Details Button 264
   The Notifications Tab 266
   The Administration Tab 267
      Workflow Configuration 267
      Workflow Configuration for Cloned Database Instances 268
         Set the Global Notification Preference to 'Do not send me mail'.......................269
         Change the email Address in the Employee and User Tables (optional) 269
         Update the FND_USER_PREFERENCES Table 270
         Update the FND_CONCURRENT_REQUESTS Table 271
         Update the FND_FORM_FUNCTIONS Table...271
         Update the FND_SVC_COMP_PARAM_VALS Table....................................272
         Update the ICX_PARAMETERS Table 272
         Update the WF_AGENTS Table 272
         Update the WF_ITEM_ATTRIBUTE_VALUES Table.....................................272
         Update the WF_NOTIFICATION_ATTRIBUTES Table 273
         Update the WF_SYSTEMS Table 273
         Run the Script to Rebuild the WF_NOTIFICATION_OUT Queue.....................274
         Setting an Override Notification Mailer Address 274
      The Vacation Rules Tab 274
      Notification Search 275
WHEN ALL ELSE FAILS – SOME SQL QUERIES 276
   To Count Errors by Error Message...276
   To Determine Which Workflow/Event Invoked WFERROR 277
   WFERRORs Still Not Closed...278
   WFERROR is not the only error–invoked Workflow 278
HOW TO RESEND NOTIFICATIONS 279

Option to Resend Notifications with mail_status = 'ERROR' 280
Don't Email Closed Notifications 281
Know Your Data – FYI Notifications vs. Response Notifications 281
Rebuild WF_NOTIFICATION_OUT 282
RECOMMENDATIONS 284
WHAT'S NEXT 284

DIAGNOSTICS **285**
THE BASICS 285
What is Oracle Diagnostics? 285
Access to Diagnostics and Security 286
Grouping of Diagnostic Tests 287
Running Diagnostic Tests 287
Viewing Test Results 289
Finding the Diagnostic Version and Date 289
Administration Workflow Tests 289
Other Workflow Tests 294
SUMMARY 294
WHAT'S NEXT 294

WORKFLOW TABLES **295**
WORKFLOW IS LANGUAGE ENABLED 295
DESIGN VS. RUN-TIME 295
_TL Tables 298
PROTECT_LEVEL and CUSTOM_LEVEL 301
READ_ROLE, WRITE_ROLE and EXECUTE_ROLE 301
Characteristics Common to All Design/Runtime Tables 301
WF_ITEM_TYPES – design 302
WF_ITEM_ATTRIBUTES – design 305
WF_ACTIVITIES – design 306
WF_ACTIVITY_ATTRIBUTES – design 311
WF_ACTIVITY_ATTR_VALUES – predominately design 312
WF_MESSAGES – design 316
WF_MESSAGE_ATTRIBUTES – design 318
WF_LOOKUP_TYPES_TL – design 321
WF_LOOKUPS_TL – design 322
WF_PROCESS_ACTIVITIES – design 323
WF_ACTIVITY_TRANSITIONS – design 326
WF_ITEMS – runtime 326
WF_ITEM_ATTRIBUTE_VALUES – runtime 327
WF_NOTIFICATIONS – runtime 327
WF_NOTIFICATION_ATTRIBUTES – runtime 331
WF_COMMENTS – runtime 331
WF_ITEM_ACTIVITY_STATUSES – runtime 332
WF_ITEM_ACTIVITY_STATUSES_V – runtime View 333
SAMPLE QUERIES – RUNTIME AND DESIGN 334
Open and Closed Workflow Counts 334
Errored Workflow Counts 335
Notification Counts 336
EVENT TABLES 337
WF_SYSTEMS 337
WF_AGENTS 337
WF_EVENTS 338

WF_EVENT_GROUPS..*339*
WF_SUBSCRIPTIONS...*339*
QUEUE TABLES 340
The Event Data Structure – WF_EVENT_T *341*
The Event Data Structure – SYS.AQ$_JMS_TEXT_MESSAGE *342*
The WF_DEFERRED_TABLE_M Structure – WF_PAYLOAD_T.....................*343*
USING SQL TO ACCESS THE DATA IN THE QUEUES 344
DIRECTORY SERVICES TABLES 345
WF_LOCAL_ROLES...*345*
WF_LOCAL_USER_ROLES *350*
WF_ROLES and WF_USER_ROLES *350*
WF_ROLE_HIERARCHY and WF_USER_ROLE_ASSIGNMENTS.................*351*
WF_ROUTING_RULES and WF_ROUTING_RULE_ATTRIBUTES *352*
Worklist Access..*353*
FND_USER_PREFERENCES...*354*
MISCELLANEOUS 355
WHAT'S NEXT 355

ADVANCED BUILDER AND PL/SQL **357**

COMMENTS AND LABELS 357
DIAGRAMMER DISPLAY BUTTONS 357
START AND END NODES 358
ACCESS LEVEL 360
Making Changes in the Diagrammer Window..*363*
How to Customize Objects Oracle has Locked *363*
Using the Builder to Save to the Database *364*
Changing an Object's Access Level...*364*
AND OTHER MESSAGE ATTRIBUTES 364
WF_NOTE *365*
#HIDE_REASSIGN *365*
#WF_REASSIGN_LOV *365*
#HIDE_MOREINFO *365*
#FROM_ROLE *366*
#WF_SECURITY_POLICY *366*
#RELATED_HISTORY *366*
#WFM_FROM, #WFM_REPLYTO, #WFM_NODENAME...................................*366*
#WFM_LANGUAGE..*367*
#WFM_RESET_NLS...*367*
#WFM_HTML_DELIMITER *367*
#WFM_CC and #WFM_BCC *367*
ITEM ATTRIBUTE TYPES – URL, FORM, DOCUMENT 368
URL *368*
FORM..*370*
DOCUMENT..*371*
PL/SQL USED TO GENERATE A DOCUMENT ATTRIBUTE 372
Anomalies and PL/SQL Document Procedure Errors *379*
POST NOTIFICATION FUNCTIONS 381
A SAMPLE PROCEDURE TO VALIDATE DATA RETURNED IN A NOTIFICATION............382
EXPAND ROLES – VOTING 385
A SAMPLE PROCEDURE TO COUNT VOTES 387
OTHER NOTIFICATION APIS 389
CONCURRENT MANAGER FUNCTIONS 391
Execute Concurrent Program Activity..*391*

Submit Concurrent Program Activity 392
Wait for Concurrent Program Activity 392
MASTER / DETAIL PROCESSES 392
MISCELLANEOUS APIs 397
WF_ENGINE.CompleteActivity or WF_ENGINE.CompleteActivityInternalName 397
WF_ENGINE.CreateForkProcess and WF_ENGINE.StartForkProcess 398
WF_DIRECTORY.GetUserName 399
WF_DIRECTORY.CreateAdHocUser 399
WF_DIRECTORY.CreateAdHocRole 400
WF_DIRECTORY.CreateAdHocRole2 401
WF_DIRECTORY.AddUsersToAdHocRole 401
WF_DIRECTORY.AddUsersToAdHocRole 401
WF_DIRECTORY.RemoveUsersFromAdHocRole 401
SQL SCRIPTS 401
Change Internal Name of a component 402
Forcibly Delete Design or Run-time data 402
WHAT'S NEXT 403

SOME COMMONLY USED WORKFLOW SETUPS **405**

SETUPS THAT REQUIRE WORKFLOW BUILDER 406
Timeouts 406
Performers 408
Activity Attributes 412
Item Attributes (not used as Performers) 413
JOURNAL BATCH – GLBATCH 413
The Applications Part 414
    Release 11.5.10 414
    Release 12 415
    Profile Options 418
    Approval Hierarchy and Limits 418
    Restrict Assignee and Notification Reassignment Approval Lists 419
The Builder Part 419
EXPENSES – APEXP 423
The Builder Part 423
Activity Attributes 424
Timeouts 426
Performers 427
Defer Workflow to Background Engine When Workflow Starts 429
Saving the Workflow 430
REQUISITION AND PURCHASE ORDER APPROVALS 431
Background vs. Online Processing 432
Replacing Oracle Workflow or Process with Custom Workflow or Process 432
Document Types Attributes 433
Start the Document Approval Manager 435
PO REQUISITION APPROVAL – REQAPPRV 435
Item Attributes 436
Timeouts 436
Special Note 437
PO APPROVAL – POAPPRV 437
Timeouts 438
Item Attributes 438
Special Note 439
REQUESTOR CHANGE ORDER APPROVALS 440

Function Security..*440*
Item Attributes..*441*
PO CREATE DOCUMENTS – CREATEPO..442
Item Attributes..*442*
PO APPROVAL ERROR – POERROR..443
Item Attributes..*444*
Performers...*445*
Activity Attributes..*445*
Possible Customization..*446*
PO SEND NOTIFICATIONS...447
OM ORDER HEADER – OEOH AND OM ORDER LINE – OEOL 447
OTL WORKFLOWS FOR EMPLOYEES – HXCEMP...449
Define Approval Style..*450*
Assign Approval Styles Using Preference *455*
The Builder Part...*460*
Item Attributes..461
Validation Errors for HXCEMP 461
Approval Style of Workflow Requires Workflow Builder and Custom Workflow.......*465*
SOME NOTES ON PROJECTS WORKFLOWS..467
PASYSADMIN *467*
PA: HR Related Updates Workflow – PAXWFHRU..*467*
SUMMARY AND WHAT'S NEXT..468

NEW FEATURES..**469**

PATCHING CURRENT IS IMPORTANT 469
RETRY ERRORED WORKFLOW ACTIVITIES 471
JUNIOR ADMINISTRATOR 472
One-Time Setups..*472*
Restrict by Item Type – Create Object Instance Set 472
Restrict by Item Attribute Value – Create Object Instance Set...............................475
Restrict by Action – Create Action Permission Sets 478
Restrict by Action – Create Role 479
User/Responsibility Setup..*483*
Grant Object Instance Set 483
Assign Roles 489
Final Step..492
NEW LOOK FOR ACTIVITY HISTORY 493
NOTIFICATION SEARCH SCREEN AVAILABLE FOR END USERS 494
WORKFLOW MAILER NOW REQUIRED FOR ORACLE ALERT 494
WORKFLOW MAILER PARAMETER CHANGES 494
New Patches *494*
Setting the Workflow Mailer Framework User (and Other Selected Mailer Parameters) *494*
Schedule Startup and Shutdown of Mailer *498*
SET PROFILE OPTION VALUES FOR THE USER ASSIGNED TO THE MAILER 501
RESPONSE VALUE DELIMITER 502
ADDITIONAL MAILER FEATURES 502
WORKFLOW DIRECTORY SERVICES USER/ROLE VALIDATION...................................503
OTHER DIRECTORY SERVICES NOTES 504
ADDITIONAL SECURITY FEATURE FOR GRANT WORKLIST 504
WORKLIST FLEXFIELDS 505
Assign Personal Worklist to a Menu..*505*
Create Flexfield Rule(s)..*506*
Create Worklist View..*510*
WFERROR – Errored Item Type Query 513

WFERROR – Errored Event Query 514
TWO IMPORTANT ONE–OFF PATCHES 514
   Bulk Close of FYI and Bulk Response *514*
   Blackberry HTML Response Fix *515*
SUMMARY AND WHAT'S NEXT 516

APPROVALS MANAGEMENT ENGINE (AME) **517**

AME BASICS 517
   Advantages of AME *518*
   AME Components *518*
      Transaction Types 518
      Configuration Variables 519
      Attributes 522
         Attribute Types 522
         Mandatory Attributes 523
         Required Attributes 524
      Conditions 527
         Types of Conditions 527
         Condition Definition Formats 528
      Action Types and Actions 528
      Action Type Hierarchies 530
         Chain-of-Authority Action Types 530
         List-Modification Action Types 532
         Substitution Action Types 533
         Pre List and Post List Approver Group Action Types 533
      Approver Groups 533
      Rules 538
   AME Integration with Workflow *542*
      Invoice Approval Workflow and AME 543
      Approval Logic 543
   AME Implementation *545*
      AME Installation 545
      AME Security Setup 545
         Predefined Roles 546
         Custom Roles 546
         Assigning Roles 546
      Integrated Application AME Setup 551
         AP Invoice Approval Workflow 552
         Payables Expense Report Approval Workflow 552
         Purchase Requisition Approval Workflow 553
         *i*Recruitment Vacancy Approval Setup 553
      Configuring AME Transaction Types 555
         AME Configuration Dashboard 556
         Transaction Type Analysis 556
         AME Rule Development Planning 557
         Business Case #1 558
         Business Case #2 568
         Business Case #3 575
         Business Case #4 578
   AME Testing Workbench *579*
      Executing a Test 581
   Migrating AME Components *586*
      Transaction Types 587
      Attributes 587
      Conditions 588
      Approval Groups 589
      Action Type Configurations 590

Rules 591
CONCLUSION 592

WHAT'S ON THE HORIZON? **593**

WHAT DESUPPORT ENTAILS 593
WHAT HAPPENS TO MY EXISTING WORKFLOWS? 594
WHAT ABOUT THE APPROVALS MANAGER ENGINE (AME) 595
SHOULD I PANIC? 595
SHOULD I MAKE PLANS TO LEARN AND USE BPEL? 595
HOW DO I LEARN MORE ABOUT BPEL? 596
WHAT OTHER SKILLS ARE NECESSARY? 597
WHAT NOW? 597

BPEL FOR WORKFLOW DEVELOPERS **599**

WHAT IS BPEL? 600
BPEL PROCESS MANAGER COMPONENTS 600
WORKFLOW COMPONENTS 601
BPEL DESIGNER (JDEVELOPER) 602
    Application Navigator 603
    Diagram Window 603
    Structure Window 603
    Component Palette 603
    Property Inspector 604
    Log Window 604
SOA CONSOLE 604
    Dashboard 604
    Component Details 604
    Instances Detail 605
PROCESS OVERVIEW 606
    Workflow 606
    BPEL 607
PROCESS DETAILS 610
    Create an Application to Contain the Process from the Application Navigator 610
    Create a BPEL Project for a Process 611
    Create Item Type and Process 614
    Check the Employee for Valid Setup for BPEL 616
        Add a Database Connection 616
        Add Database Adaptor Service 617
        Add Invoke Activity to Diagram 619
    Check the Employee for Valid Setup for Workflow 620
        Add Function to Call Procedure 621
    HR Validation Notification for BPEL 622
        Add a Human Task to the Employee Validation Process 622
        Add Human Task to Diagram 625
    HR Validation Notification for Workflow 626
        Create a Lookup Type 626
        Create Message 627
        Create the Notification on the Diagram 629
VALIDATING AND RUNNING THE EMPLOYEE VALIDATION PROCESS IN BPEL 631
    Validating the Process 631
    Running the Process 631
DEPLOYING THE EMPLOYEE VALIDATION PROCESS IN WORKFLOW 634
ADDITIONAL OBSERVATIONS 634
CONCLUSIONS 635

SAMPLE BR110 .... **637**

OVERVIEW AND JUSTIFICATION 637
   Basic Business Need 637
   Business Process 637
   Notification Layout – Email Address is Missing 638
   Notification Layout – HR Data is Incomplete 638
   Notification Layout – Escalation to HR Manager 639
IMPLEMENTATION (INCLUDING REQUIRED SETUPS) 640
   Resources Needed 640
   Compile Program 640
   Install Workflow 641
   Create Profile Options 641
   Assign Value to New Profile Options 642
TECHNICAL OVERVIEW 643
   Overview of Process 643
   Create Workflow from Scratch 644
      Verify Access Level 644
      QuickStart Wizard 644
      Define Lookup Types / Codes 645
      Define Attributes 645
      Define Messages 646
      Define Functions / Notifications/Events 648
      Add Timeouts, Performers, Messages, Event Details, Node Attributes to Functions/Notifications/Events 650
      Transitions 651
   Code for Program 652
      Package Spec 652
      Package Body 652

INDEX **653**

Preface

Workflow has evolved extensively since its introduction in 1998. In 2003, Solution Beacon published *Installing, Upgrading and Maintaining Oracle Applications 11i*. That book contained three chapters on Workflow entitled *Workflow Setup*, *Using Workflow Builder*, and *Workflow Care and Feeding*. It covered the information needed to manage Workflow through Release 11.5.8.

Then Oracle got busy. Business Events, optional in Release 11.5.8, became required. Oracle introduced Workflow Administration in Oracle Applications Manager (OAM) and re-wrote all the administration forms in Java. Oracle created Diagnostics for many products, including Workflow. The Mailer became a Java Mailer. New types of Attributes were introduced. The documentation increased from a single manual of 1192 pages to six (Release 11.5.10) manuals or five manuals (Release 12) totaling more than 1350 pages.

Therefore, since Workflow became such an expansive topic, we chose to omit Workflow from the 2007 Solution Beacon book *Installing, Upgrading and Maintaining Oracle E-Business Suite Applications Release 11.5.10+* so we could write a separate book. The writing of this book, which started 18 months ago, is finally complete. Interestingly, separating Workflow out from our other books allowed the book to cover not only Release 11.5.10+, but also Release 12, thus facilitating a discussion of the releases covered by Oracle's Applications Unlimited Policy and the releases serving as a jumping point to Fusion.

The intent of this book is not to cover all 1350+ pages of documentation, but to cover the basics (hence the title *The ABCs of Workflow*) and provide the information necessary to keep your Workflow environment from getting out of control (or to bring it back into control).

WHAT THIS BOOK COVERS

1   Introduction

This chapter identifies the various components of Workflow and provides definitions for many of the terms used when using Workflow. It discusses the duties of the Workflow Administrator and provides guidelines on how these duties can be allocated to the various roles in the organization.

2   Setup

This chapter provides the information necessary to set up Workflow, including the Business Event System and Notification Mailer.

3   Builder Basics

This chapter explains how to use the Builder tool. As an example, a Workflow is created to improve the Business Process of setting up new employees in Oracle HR. Readers can practice using Builder by following the steps outlined in this chapter to recreate the same Workflow.

THE ABCS OF WORKFLOW

4 PL/SQL in Workflow

This chapter explains the basic APIs required for Workflow Procedures used by Workflow Function activities. Sample Procedures are provided to explain how these APIs can be utilized and are used to complete the Workflow designed in *Chapter 3*.

5 Business Events

This chapter clarifies the terminology used in Business Events, discusses the queues used by Workflow, and explains how to define Events and Subscriptions. The chapter then explains how to use PL/SQL to start an Event and how to use Events in the Builder. The Workflow from *Chapter 3* is modified to start from an Event.

6 Testing Workflows

This chapter explains how to use both the Developer Studio and the 'Raise Events' page to test Workflows. Common errors and troubleshooting techniques are also demonstrated.

7 Account Generators

This chapter explains the difference between Account Generators and "normal" Workflows, how to use the special Functions designed for Account Generators, and how to bypass some of the restrictions such as the inability to send Notifications.

8 Administration

This chapter explains how to use the forms provided in the Workflow Administrator responsibilities, including the 'Workflow Manager' section of Oracle Applications Manager (OAM), to troubleshoot problems and monitor the health of the Workflow and Business Event Systems.

9 Diagnostics

This chapter introduces Oracle E–Business Suite Diagnostics. It explains how to access the various scripts, and demonstrates some of the scripts used in Workflow.

10 Workflow Tables

This chapter explains the Workflow design and runtime tables, the Business Event tables, the Directory Services tables, and a few of the miscellaneous tables.

11 Advanced Builder and PL/SQL

This chapter is a continuation of *Chapters 3, 4, 5*, and *6*. It discusses Access Levels and shows how to utilize advanced features such as Document, Form, and URL Attributes, # Attributes, post Notification Functions, Voting, Concurrent Manager functions, and master/detail activities to further enhance Workflows.

12 Most Commonly Used Workflows

This chapter explains how to set up many of the Workflows used in General Ledger, Purchasing, Payables, Time and Labor, and Order Management. The chapter shows the setups that must be performed from the forms and those that must be performed using the Workflow Builder.

13 New Features

This chapter is a continuation of *Chapters 2* and *8* and explains the new functionality in Release 12 and 11i.ATG_PF.H.delta.5 (Rollup 5) and 11i.ATG_PF.H.delta.6 (Rollup 6). This new functionality includes setting up Junior Administrators, Worklist Flexfields, and new settings for the Notification Mailer.

14 Approvals Management Engine (AME)

This chapter provides examples based on case studies for Purchasing, Payables and Human Resources on how to set up a variety of Approvals Management Engine (AME) Approval Rules.

15 What's on the Horizon?

This chapter talks about the future of Workflow and provides a list of resources for learning BPEL.

16 BPEL for Workflow Developers

Using a version of the Workflow from *Chapter 3*, this chapter shows how developers can create the same Business Process in BPEL.

Appendix A – Sample BR110

Because the authors strongly believe in documenting all setups, configurations, and customizations, this appendix is provided to present a format example for documenting the creation of a Workflow and any required setups. The Workflow documented is the Workflow utilized throughout the entire book.

CONVENTIONS USED IN THIS BOOK

This section discusses the conventions used to present the material in the various chapters.

Screen Shots

The book covers functionality used in Release 11.5.10 and Release 12. Wherever possible, Release 12 screen shots are used. If the functionality or screen is markedly different, screen shots from both releases are shown.

In order to show as much of the content of the screens as possible, the headers (see FIGURE 1), the repeat of the buttons, and the navigation links at the bottom of the screen (see FIGURE 2) are often omitted.

FIGURE 1

FIGURE 2

Lower Case vs. Upper Case for SQL and PL/SQL

When SQL or PL/SQL code is listed, it is indented and shown in Courier New font. Reserved words are capitalized and Procedures, tables, and column names are in lower case. The exception to this rule is the references to ItemType, ItemKey, ResultOut, and the names of the APIs such as SetItemAttrText. Mixed case is used for readability.

Table and column names used in sentences, and bulleted lists, are capitalized. This will distinguish Oracle objects from the text used to describe them.

Internal Names of Workflows are always capitalized as that is the way the data appears in the table WF_ITEM_TYPES.

<your token names>

Brackets are used to identify tokens where the reader can substitute text. If this token is used in a SQL statement, it is usually enclosed in single quotes, since it represents text.

RUPs, CPUs, CUs, ATGs, and Their Importance

Throughout the book, we talk about patches that your Applications DBA may apply to your E-Business Suite environment.

Release 11*i*

For Release 11*i* major patches that we reference include

- **Critical Patch Updates (CPUs)** – Critical Patch Updates are the primary means of releasing security fixes for Oracle products. They are released on the Tuesday closest to the 15th day of January, April, July and October. Thus, as of this writing, the next four dates are:

    - 15 July 2008

    - 14 October 2008

    - 13 January 2009

    - 14 April 2009

    Oracle recommends that customers apply CPU patches within 30 to 60 days of their release. Note that certain parts of CPU patches are now included in ATG RUPs, but not all. Check the ATG RUP Readme for details. In addition to security patches, CPUs can include functionality and performance patches, so it is worthwhile to stay current.

- **Consolidated Updates (CUs)** – Since the time between E-Business Suite releases is significant, Oracle releases a number of patches, Mini-packs and Family Packs between releases. A Consolidated Update is a consolidation of the recommended patches that have been released up to the date of the release of the Consolidated Update. A Consolidated Update brings the entire Oracle E-Business Suite environment to the latest recommended patch level. For example, E-Business Suite 11.5.10 had two Consolidated Updates, 1 (patch number 3140000) and 2 (patch number 3480000), with CU2 being the last available Consolidated Update patch. Due to the sheer number of patches included in a Consolidated Update, the Readme for a Consolidated Update patch is a separate MetaLink Note with detailed and relatively lengthy instructions

- **Release Update Patches (RUPs)** – The RUPs, in the context of Release 11*i*, refer to Rollup Patches or Release Patches. A Release Update Patch (also called a Rollup Patch) targets a family. When used in the context of E-Business Suite HR, a RUP requires a base level to already exist in Release 11*i*. For example, Oracle HRMS Family Pack K Rollup 2 or RUP2 (11i.HR_PF.K Rollup 2) Patch 5337777, can be applied only to an existing Oracle E-Business Suite Release 11*i* system running Oracle HRMS Family Pack K (11i.HR_PF.K). If you do not already have a running 11i.HR_PF.K system, then you must first install 11i.HR_PF.K (Patch 3500000). As with HR, ATG also uses the RUP acronym to mean both Rollup and Release Update Patch. ATG patches are cumulative from ATG RUP3 forward with the Oracle Applications Technology Family Pack 11i.ATG_PF.H.

- **Applications Technology Group (ATG) patches** – An ATG RUP patch is a collection of technology-stack patches that can be safely applied on top of the ATG Family Pack H. ATG Rollup Patch 6, for example, is cumulative: all previous patches released for Family Pack H since the initial 11.5.10 release, including Rollup 5, are included in this latest patch. Rollup 5 is superseded by this latest Rollup.

  Note that an ATG RUP targets ATG but touches other products considered to be a part of the ATG group. Modules included in ATG RUP 6 are: FND, OAM, OWF, FWK, JTT, JTA, TXK, XDO, ECX, EC, AK, ALR, UMX, BNE, and FRM. This particular rollup includes new features and fixes for: Oracle Applications Framework (OAF), Oracle Application Object Library (AOL), AutoConfig, and Oracle Workflow (OWF). To be sure, the type of fixes and enhancements does not include every technology-stack product. For example, 11i.ATG_F.H.delta.5 (Rollup5) included new features and fixes for other technology-stack products such as: Oracle Report Manager, Oracle Alert, Cloning, configuration changes for the Oracle database, and XML publisher changes. Note that there is a relationship between ATG and CPU patches. 11i.ATG_F.H.delta.3 (Rollup 3) is the minimum requirement for the October 2006 Critical Patch Update. Starting with the July 2007 CPU, you must be running at least RUPn-1 (where n is the current RUP).

- **Mini-pack** – A collection of patches that fix bugs, improve performance and add new features for a single product. Mini-packs can introduce changes to any aspect of products contained in a product, but must work with lower levels of products in the same family and other families. Mini-packs must be able to use the technology and operating system certified for the corresponding CU or Point Release. For example, Release 11i Payables Mini-pack O (11i.AP.O), released on top of FIN_PF.G must work with all Financials products in FIN_PF.G as well as all products outside of Financials that are still on the Family Pack released in Release 11.5.10 CU2.

- **Point Release** – A collection of patches that fix bugs, improve performance, and add new features across all products in the E-Business Suite. Point Releases can introduce major changes to any aspect of the application (forms, tables, reports, etc.). Point Releases may require upgrading the underlying technology stack and/or operating system. Point Releases are usually designated as the first number after the first decimal. Release 11i is an exception to this rule as Release 11i is also called Release 11.5. Release 11.5.10 is therefore the 10th Point Release of Release 11i. The first Point Release for Release 12, due sometime in 2008, will be 12.1. Dates for the various levels of support (Premier, Extended, and Sustaining) are based on the date a Point Release becomes commercially available.

- **Family Pack** – A collection of patches that fix bugs, improve performance and add new features across a group of products in E-Business Suite. Family Packs can introduce changes to any aspect of products contained in a family, but must work with lower levels of products in other families. Family Packs must be able to use the technology stack and operating system certified for corresponding CUs or Point Releases. For example, Release 11i.10 CU2 (11.5.10.2) contains Financials Family Pack F (FIN_PF.F) and Projects Family Pack L (PA_PF.L). Oracle later released Financials Family Pack G (FIN_PF.G) and Projects Family Pack M (PA_PF.M). FIN_PF.G must work with PA_PF.L and PA_PF.L must work with FIN_PF.F.

Release 12

For Release 12 major patches that we reference include

- **Critical Patches** – If Oracle detects that a one-off or collection of one-offs for a particular product needs to be released prior to the scheduled release of a RUP, a Critical Patch will be issued. These patches are for a particular product and address issues raised in Priority 1 (P1) Service Requests (SRs). Release 12 Critical Patches can be tracked from the 'Knowledge Browser' page of MetaLink. Click the 'Critical Patches Update' link. Read the notes applicable to each product. Alternatively, access MetaLink Doc. ID: 394692.1, *Oracle Applications Documentation Resources, Release 12*, click on the link to the desired product, then click on the 'Known Issues' link.

- **Critical Patch Updates (CPUs)** – See the CPU description for Release 11*i*. The main difference between Release 12 CPUs and Release 11*i* CPUs is that CPUs for Release 12 are cumulative. They are not cumulative for Release 11*i*.

- **Release Update Packs (RUPs)** – In the context of Release 12, RUP means something different than RUP did in Release 11*i*. In Release 12, RUP stands for Release Update *Pack* (rather than Release Update Patch or Rollup Patch). Also, a Release Update Pack targets multiple products rather than just one product – thus, the patches are typically very large. Release 12 RUPs are released on a quarterly schedule and are cumulative. Also, Release 12 RUPs contain CPUs. Check the Readme MetaLink Note for a given RUP for details

- **Applications Technology Group (ATG) patches** – In Release 12, ATG patches follow RUPs. So, when a quarterly RUP is released, a complementary ATG patch should be released. ATG patches in Release 12 focus on the technology stack. The Readme MetaLink note for a given release will detail what is being addressed.

- **Point Release** – See the Point Release description for Release 11*i*.

- **Family Pack** – See the Family Pack description for Release 11*i*.

Reader Feedback and Questions

We wrote this book to enable more people to utilize Workflow effectively. We welcome your comments on what you found useful and what you wish had also been included or further explained. These comments will help us determine future topics for papers and newsletters. Comments and questions can be sent to workflow@solutionbeacon.com.

Errata

Our editors spent many days editing this book. Everyone has worked hard to ensure there are no errors in the text. However, mistakes do happen. Additionally, new patches or MetaLink Doc. IDs may be released at any time that might invalidate some statement. If you see a mistake or find incorrect information, please contact us at workflow@solutionbeacon.com.

Introduction

Workflow is now an integral part of the Oracle database and especially the E-Business Suite Release 11*i* and Release 12. Like any other technology, it requires understanding and management. This chapter will introduce Workflow, explain the Workflow terminology, discuss some of the technology components and finish by describing the tasks that must be performed to effectively manage Workflow.

Workflow can function as a standalone product atop Oracle database Versions 8 through 10*g*. The chapters on the Builder and PL/SQL are applicable to this version of Oracle Workflow as well as the "Workflow embedded in Oracle E-Business Suite" version. However, other chapters assume you are running "Workflow embedded in Oracle E-Business Suite", either Release 11.5.10.2 with ATG_PF.H.delta.6 (Rollup or RUP 6), or Release 12. See *Chapter 15, What's on the Horizon*, for a discussion of Workflow beyond Release 12 and the RDBMS Version 10*g*R2 database.

While this book is written from the perspective of an administrator and developer, sections have been included to describe Workflow-specific tasks that Applications DBAs must perform to ensure a properly working environment, as well as an environment in which Workflow can flourish. This book assumes that the reader has a working knowledge of the various technologies that Workflow utilizes, such as PL/SQL and E-Business Suite navigation. This book is not meant to replace the Workflow documentation provided by Oracle. In fact, a great deal of the knowledge in this book is gleaned from E-Business Suite Release 11*i* and Release 12 documentation and the articles found in the 'Knowledge Browser' section of MetaLink. Therefore, efforts will not be made to try to explain every API, every 'Standard' Function,or every nuance of this exciting technology. Readers are encouraged to read Oracle documentation, MetaLink Doc. IDs and, most importantly, to experiment with writing Workflows and administering the results.

Oracle is constantly updating their technologies and adding functionality to the E-Business Suite. Patches, releases, and MetaLink Doc. IDs referenced in this book may be superseded, updated, replaced, or made obsolete at any time. Later chapters will discuss the various resources that the Workflow Administrator can use to stay current.

WORKFLOW – IT'S A TECHNOLOGY ALL BY ITSELF

Workflow is a tool that allows the modeling of Business Processes combining Procedures performed by the computer with a system of Notifications that allow humans to better direct the computer how to proceed.

Workflow consists of the following:

- **Engine** – now an integral part of the database, the Engine starts the Workflow, audits the Workflow's progress, interacts with the Notification System to send/receive Messages, manages deferring/execution of all Function activities, detects error conditions and starts error Processes.

- **Builder** – the PC-based graphical tool used to diagram Business Processes and define Attributes and activities. The Builder requires a Windows operating system.

- **Notification System** – the screens within Oracle Applications that allow viewing/responding to Messages and allow the Notification Mailer to deliver Messages through SendMail or any MAPI-compliant email system.

- **Monitor** – A graphical tool that allows users to view the progress of Workflows they "own" and the Workflow Administrator to view/update the progress of all Workflows.

- **Loader** – A utility that moves Workflow definitions from the Builder to the database, from the database to the Builder, from the database to a flat file, or from a flat file to the database.

- **Directory Services** – A list of users, Roles, and users within Roles that Workflow accesses to manage Notifications. It allows users/administrators to set up rules to allow automatic responses or re-direction of Notifications.

- **Business Event System** – A system that allows interaction via Oracle Advanced Queuing (AQ) to your own system or other systems through Agents, Subscriptions, and Events.

Workflow utilizes and requires many Oracle technology components. The obvious components are the Workflow Builder, PL/SQL, SQL, the database, the E-Business Suite, JInitiator (for Release 11.5.10), and Sun's JRE (for Release 12). The following components may be considered optional by some companies; however, they are not:

- **Oracle Applications Manager (OAM)** – A set of dashboards and configuration pages that monitor the health of the E-Business Suite. The Workflow Manager is the section in OAM provided for Workflow Administration.

- **Generic Services Manager** – An extension of Concurrent Processing that provides a framework for managing Java Processes such as Oracle Reports Server, Apache Web Listener and Workflow Business Event containers (Listeners and the Notification Mailer) across multiple instances.

Additionally, Oracle has released Oracle Diagnostics, which is a collection of programs that can be secured by responsibility. While the Workflow technology will function without the Diagnostics, the scripts provide an additional means of ensuring the Workflow environment is correctly configured and managed. Because of the value of these scripts, we consider Oracle Diagnostics to be a required technology component and have dedicated *Chapter 9, Diagnostics*, to discussing its features.

WORKFLOW – SOME DEFINITIONS

Workflow introduced some new terms to Oracle. In order to better understand the following chapters, some (not all) of the terms defined in the *Oracle Workflow Administrator's Guide, Release 2.6.4, Part B15852-05, July 2006* or the *Oracle Workflow Administrator's Guide, Release 12, Part B31431-01, December 2006* are (with minor changes for clarification):

ACCESS LEVEL – see PROTECTION LEVEL

ACTIVITY – a unit of work performed in a business process; either a NOTIFICATION, a FUNCTION, an EVENT, or a PROCESS

AGENT – a named point of communication within a system that has a unique name. Agents translate between standard Workflow format and the format required by the queue. A specific Agent either listens for inbound Messages or sends outbound Messages, not both

AGENT LISTENER – a SERVICE COMPONENT that processes event Messages for inbound AGENTs

ATTRIBUTE – a piece of data needed by a Workflow to supply information in a MESSAGE, determine the path in the Workflow to follow, pass configurable information to a FUNCTION, or store some custom piece of information applicable to the specific instance of a Workflow. Attributes are defined at the ITEM TYPE level (ITEM ATTRIBUTE), the ACTIVITY level (ACTIVITY ATTRIBUTE), or the MESSAGE level (MESSAGE ATTRIBUTE)

BACKGROUND ENGINE – a program that progresses timed-out or deferred activities. It also detects activities that are stuck and invokes the appropriate error routine

BUSINESS EVENT – see EVENT

COST – the relative value you can assign to a FUNCTION to tell the Workflow Engine whether to process the FUNCTION immediately, or to defer the FUNCTION until the appropriate BACKGROUND ENGINE runs

DATASTORE – a database connection whereby multiple ITEM TYPEs can be loaded, or a grouping of ITEM TYPEs that are stored together in a .wft file

DEFERRED ACTIVITY – an ACTIVITY with a cost greater than the Workflow Engine deferral cost (default Workflow Engine deferral cost = 50)

DIRECTORY SERVICES – a method of loading users or roles into an ITEM TYPE for use as PERFORMERs in NOTIFICATIONs as well as a mapping of users and roles to a site's directory repository

EVENT – an occurrence in an internet application, intranet application or program that might be significant to other system objects or to external agents

EVENT DATA – a set of additional details describing an EVENT. Event Data may include a list of (up to) 100 parameters and/or a XML document

EVENT KEY – a string that uniquely identifies an EVENT. When it is used to start a Workflow, it becomes the ITEM KEY

EVENT SUBSCRIPTION – see SUBSCRIPTION

EXTERNAL JAVA FUNCTIONS – Java programs executed outside of the Oracle Database by the Java Function Activity Agent

FUNCTION – a PL/SQL stored procedure that can execute business rules, retrieve application information and/or return a result that indicates the path to the next activity

ITEM TYPE – a grouping of ACTIVITYs, ATTRIBUTEs, MESSAGEs and LOOKUP TYPEs that define a business process. The item type is the Workflow, these two terms are interchangeable

ITEM KEY – a string that uniquely identifies a particular instance of an ITEM TYPE (Workflow)

LOOKUP TYPE – another name for a List of Values

LOOKUP CODE – a specific value for a LOOKUP TYPE

MESSAGE – the information sent by a NOTIFICATION activity

NAVIGATOR TREE – a hierarchical structure that shows all ITEM TYPEs,

ATTRIBUTEs, NOTIFICATIONs, MESSAGEs, LOOKUP TYPEs, FUNCTIONs, EVENTs, PROCESSes, and a DIRECTORY SERVICES branch

NODE – an instance of an ACTIVITY in a process diagram shown in the PROCESS DIAGRAMMER window

NOTIFICATION – a unit of work that requires human intervention or information passed to a human in the middle of a Workflow

NOTIFICATION MAILER – a program that passes NOTIFICATIONs to an email system

PERFORMER – a user or role to which a NOTIFICATION is sent

PROCESS – a group of FUNCTIONs, EVENTs, NOTIFICATIONs, and sub-PROCESSes that model a business process

PROCESS DIAGRAMMER – the "pretty picture" or pictorial representation of a PROCESS in the Workflow Builder or Monitor, which is also referred to as the Diagrammer window or the Process window

PROTECTION LEVEL – a numeric value from 0 to 1000 that governs who can modify a component in the Workflow Builder

RESULT CODE – the internal name of the RESULT VALUE

RESULT TYPE – the name of the LOOKUP TYPE that contains the possible RESULT VALUEs for an ACTIVITY

RESULT VALUE – the value returned by a NOTIFICATION, FUNCTION or sub-PROCESS that the Workflow Engine uses to determine which path in a PROCESS to follow. It can also be the final value assigned by the Workflow Engine for the main (top) PROCESS

ROLE – an individual, user, group of individuals or users defined in the DIRECTORY SERVICES tables. Roles also provide the value for the PERFORMER in a NOTIFICATION

SERVICE COMPONENT – an instance of a Java program that is defined according to Generic Service Component Framework standards

SERVICE COMPONENT CONTAINER – an instance of a service or servlet that manages the running of its individual SERVICE COMPONENTs. A Service Component Container monitors the status of its components and handles control events for itself and its components. In the E-Business Suite, a Service Component Container is a Java Concurrent Manager

SUBSCRIPTION – a record or set of records that govern the actions that should occur when an EVENT is raised

SYSTEM – a logically isolated software environment such as a host machine or a database instance

TIMEOUT – the amount of time the Workflow Engine will wait for a response to a NOTIFICAITON, or wait for an ACTIVITY to complete before proceeding down the path marked with the RESULT VALUE of 'Timeout' or to the error process if no timeout path is specified

TRANSITION – the relationship that defines the completion of one ACTIVITY and the activation of another ACTIVITY within a process. In the process diagram; this is represented by the arrow between activities

ROLES AND RESPONSIBILITIES

Workflow Administration Tasks

The setup and administration of Workflow must be done by a person or persons designated as the Workflow Administrator. *Chapter 2, Setup*, will provide detail on how to set up the Workflow Administrator Roles. This discussion is about the skills and attributes required for the Role of Workflow Administrator.

The primary Workflow Administrator can be an individual or a responsibility. Prior to 11i.ATG_PF.H.delta.5 (Rollup 5) (released April 30, 2007), a working subset of the Workflow Administration screens that would allow limited administration responsibilities could not be created. Responsibilities and menus could be created, but since the name of the responsibility did not match the responsibility assigned to the Workflow Administrator, the screens would not function in administrator mode. If an individual belongs to the Role assigned as the Workflow Administrator, but does not have access to a responsibility with the appropriate administrator screens, he or she will be unable to function as the administrator. In other words, the responsibility menus, assignment of responsibilities to users and participation in the Role assigned as the administrator are required.

In Release 12 and beginning with Release 11.5.10 with 11i.ATG_PF.H.delta.5 (Rollup 5), users may be allowed to administer a subset of the Workflows, such as Purchasing or Order Management. This Junior Administrator Role allows access to the 'Status Monitor' only and prohibits administering Workflows owned by that user. Access can be restricted by Workflow name or by the value of an Item Attribute such as ORG_ID. Administration rights can be restricted to view only (monitor) or any combination of monitor administration activities such as skip, retry, rewind, or cancel. See *Chapter 12, New Features*, for a detailed explanation of setting up this functionality.

Administration of Workflow requires periodic execution of the following tasks:

- Ensure that the technology (database, Advanced Queuing, Propagation, Notification Mailer, Agent Listeners) is working, and ensure patches are applied as directed by Oracle Support or the business management team

- Ensure that current Oracle Diagnostics patches are applied quarterly or per Oracle's published release schedule

- Ensure that the Workflow Administrator Role is properly reset after each execution of AutoConfig

- Ensure that all aspects of cloned environments accurately point to the cloned instance

- Develop and enforce the methodology for maintaining and testing the Notification Mailer in cloned instances

- Ensure that the parameters on the 'Global Administration' page remain accurate

- Finish Workflow technology setups not completed by any upgrade, patch, or install process

- Configure and maintain Workflow Administrator security

- Assist SuperUsers in understanding the Workflows in each module and the setups that are required to make them work correctly. Ensure any required setups are determined, documented, and applied in all instances

- Monitor MetaLink for new patches and ensure patches are applied and tested at both the database and PC level

- Monitor the WFSTD.wft Workflow for additions added by developers that should either be placed in a specific company or application standard library Workflow

- Set up and maintain the scheduling of the Background Engine(s)

- Set up and maintain the purge schedule(s) for runtime history (completed Workflows)

- Ensure appropriate Directory Services synchronization programs are scheduled

- Monitor Concurrent Programs, Concurrent Managers, Concurrent Requests and Containers to ensure all required Workflow Processes are scheduled and run at appropriate intervals. These programs include but are not limited to:

  ♦ 'Control Queue Cleanup'

  ♦ Oracle Application Manager statistics programs:

    ○ 'Workflow Agent Activity Statistics' Concurrent Program

    ○ 'Workflow Mailer Statistics' Concurrent Program

    ○ 'Workflow Work Items Statistics' Concurrent Program

- Monitor Business Event Queues to ensure Listeners and Propagations are scheduled and Messages are moving through the Queues

- Ensure the 'Synchronize Product Licenses and BES' Concurrent Program is executed whenever a Family Pack, Point Release, or Cumulative Update (CU) is installed or whenever a new product is implemented

- Monitor status of running Workflows and overdue Notifications

- Monitor status of the Notification Mailer and ensure Notifications are delivered. In the event of failure, ensure the appropriate Notifications are rescheduled for email delivery

- Troubleshoot Workflows that are stuck or in error status

- Ensure that the issues raised in Notifications to SYSADMIN are resolved and that the Notifications are subsequently closed

- Ensure Notifications sent to SYSADMIN are available to Workflow Administrators through various methods such as assigning a group email address to SYSADMIN, setting up Vacation Rulesand/or Worklist access.

- Ensure folders used by the Workflow Mailer are periodically cleaned and that Messages sent to the Discard Folder are not sent there in error

- Ensure that the Notification Mailer tags are complete and that they handle Messages from out-of-office assistants or email servers bouncing emails due to invalid server or invalid email addresses

- Periodically run the Workflow Diagnostics and other administrative scripts, and report/repair any issues

- Assist users/developers in the use of the Workflow Builder tool

- Develop original or customize Oracle-supplied Workflows as necessary to enable optimization of Business Processes

- Ensure Workflow customizations (Workflows and associated PL/SQL Packages) are accurately migrated from instance to instance according to policy

- Ensure custom Workflows are documented

- Ensure Workflow development standards are followed for Events, Workflows, PL/SQL Procedures and other components

- Ensure that the Directory Services remains clean (no assignment of multiple users to the same employee)

- Work with HR to ensure email addresses are specified for each employee linked to a user and that appropriate hierarchies and approval limits are set up with respect to established control procedures

- Re-assign Notifications and/or establish Vacation Rules for persons unavailable to act on pending Workflow tasks such as sick time, leave of absence, or vacation

- Provide feedback to management if there are any issues in the management or operation of any aspect of the Workflow application

All this is usually more than a single person has either the skill set, time or security access to perform. The following list assigns the Applications DBA tasks that are necessary to the smooth running of the technology. The tasks that require knowledge of individual applications are assigned to the functional SuperUsers. The tasks that require access to the Define Users screen are assigned to the System Administrator. Ultimately, someone has to be responsible for ensuring that all groups are performing their assigned tasks. That person is referred to here as the Workflow Administrator. Companies that do not utilize a large support staff can certainly reallocate the tasks. The individual who is assigned the task is not as important as making sure all the tasks are performed.

Some of the following tasks require SQL access to the tables and/or the APPS password. Therefore, when assigning tasks to individuals, the required access to perform the task must be considered. For example, the developers may have the APPS password in a development environment and thus be able to load/save Workflows using the Builder. Applications DBAs will probably be tasked with saving Workflows and required Workflow code in other environments. Therefore, tasks below that are assigned to developers assume that these tasks are performed in a development environment and movement to other environments is performed in accordance with established change management processes and controls.

The Workflow Administrator

This can be an Applications DBA, Applications System Administrator or developer, but needs to be someone who is ultimately responsible for ensuring everything is working correctly.

- Work with the Applications DBA to ensure that the Workflow Administrator Role is properly reset after each execution of AutoConfig

- Work with the Applications DBA to ensure all aspects of the cloned environment accurately point to the cloned instance

- Work with the Applications DBA to develop and enforce the methodology for maintaining and testing the Notification Mailer in cloned instances

- Determine the methodology for maintaining and testing the Notification Mailer in cloned instances

- Work with the Applications DBA to ensure the parameters on the 'Global Administration' page in the Workflow Administration screens remain accurate

- Finish Workflow technology setups not completed by any upgrade, patch or install process

- Work with the System Administrator to configure and maintain Workflow Administration security

- Assist the Functional SuperUsers to understand the Workflows in each module and ensure any required setups are determined, documented, and applied in all instances

- Assist the Applications DBA in monitoring MetaLink for new patches and ensuring the patches are applied and tested at both the database and PC level

- Monitor the WFSTD.wft Workflow for additions added by developers that should either be in a specific, company or application standard library Workflow

- Setup and maintain the scheduling of the Background Engine(s)

- Setup and maintain the purge schedule(s) for runtime history (completed Workflows)

- Ensure that the appropriate Directory Services synchronization programs are scheduled

- Monitor Concurrent Programs, Concurrent Managers, Concurrent Requests and Containers to ensure all required Workflow Processes are scheduled and run at appropriate intervals. These programs include, but are not limited to:

  - 'Control Queue Cleanup'

  - Oracle Application Manager statistics programs:

    o 'Workflow Agent Activity Statistics' Concurrent Program

    o 'Workflow Mailer Statistics' Concurrent Program

    o 'Workflow Work Items Statistics' Concurrent Program

- Monitor the Business Events queues to ensure Listeners are scheduled, Propagations are scheduled, and Messages are moving through the queues

- Ensure that the 'Synchronize Product Licenses and Workflow BES License' Concurrent Program is executed whenever a Family Pack, Point Release, or Cumulative Update (CU) is installed or whenever a new product is implemented

- Monitor the status of running Workflows and overdue Notifications

- Monitor the status of the Notification Mailer and ensure Notifications are delivered. In the event of failure, ensure the appropriate Notifications are rescheduled for email delivery

- Assist the Junior Administrators in troubleshooting Workflows that are stuck or in error status

- Ensure that the issues raised in Notifications to SYSADMIN are resolved and that these Notifications are subsequently closed

- Work with the Applications System Administrator to ensure that Notifications sent to SYSADMIN are available to Workflow Administrators through various methods such as assigning a group email address to SYSADMIN, setting up Vacation Rules, and/or Worklist access

- Work with the Applications DBA to ensure that the folders used by the Workflow Mailer are periodically cleaned and that Messages sent to the Discard Folder are not sent there in error

- Ensure that the Notification Mailer tags are complete and that they handle Messages from out-of-office assistants or email servers bouncing emails due to invalid server or email addresses

- Periodically run the Workflow Diagnostics and other administrative scripts, and report/repair any issues

- Assist users / developers in the use of the Workflow Builder tool

- Work with the Developers to ensure custom and/or customized Workflows are documented

- Work with the Developers to ensure Workflow development standards are followed for Events, Workflows, PL/SQL Procedures and other components

- Work with Applications System Administrators to ensure the Directory Services remains clean (no assignment of multiple users to same employee)

- Work with Applications System Administrator and HR to ensure email addresses are specified for each employee linked to a user and that appropriate hierarchies and approval limits are set up and do not violate control procedures

- Re-assign Notifications and/or establish Vacation Rules for persons unavailable to act on pending Workflow tasks due to sick time, leave of absence, termination, or vacation

- Provide feedback to management if there are any issues in the management or operation of Workflow

The Junior Workflow Administrator

- Understand the Workflows in all assigned modules and ensure any required setups are determined, documented, and applied in all instances

- For assigned modules, monitor the status of running Workflows and overdue Notifications

- For assigned modules, troubleshoot Workflows that are stuck or in error status

- For assigned modules, ensure that the issues raised in Notifications to SYSADMIN are resolved and that these Notifications are subsequently closed

- Periodically run the Workflow Diagnostics and other administrative scripts, and report/repair any issues

- For assigned modules, assist users / developers in the use of the Workflow Builder tool

- For assigned modules, work with the Developers to ensure custom and/or customized Workflows are documented

- For assigned modules, work with the Developers to ensure Workflow development standards are followed for Events, Workflows, PL/SQL Procedures and other components

- For assigned modules provide feedback to management and the Workflow Administrator if there are any issues in the management or operation of Workflow

The Database Administrator (Apps DBA)

- Ensure that the technology (database, Advanced Queuing, Propagation, Notification Mailer, Agent Listeners) is working, and apply patches as directed by Oracle Support or the business management team

- Apply current Oracle Diagnostics patches quarterly or per Oracle's published release schedule

- Ensure that the Workflow Administrator Role is properly reset after each execution of AutoConfig

- Ensure all aspects of cloned environments accurately point to the cloned instance

- Work with the Workflow Administrator to develop and enforce the methodology for maintaining and testing the Notification Mailer in cloned instances

- Work with the Workflow Administrator to ensure that the parameters on the 'Global Administration' page remain accurate

- Migrate Workflow customizations (Workflows and associated PL/SQL Packages) from instance to instance according to policy

- Work with the Workflow Administrator to ensure the folders used by the Workflow Mailer are periodically cleaned and that Messages sent to the Discard Folder are not sent there in error.

- Monitor MetaLink for new patches and ensure patches are applied and tested at both the database and PC level

The Applications System Administrator

- Ensure that the Directory Services remains clean (no assignment of multiple users to same employee)

- Work with HR to ensure email addresses are specified for each employee linked to a user and that appropriate hierarchies and approval limits are set up and do not violate control procedures

- Review setups for all utilized Workflows to ensure compliance with contractual and legal obligations

- Provide backup to the Workflow Administrator for re-assigning Notifications and/or establishing Vacation Rules for persons unavailable to act on pending Workflow tasks due to sick time, leave of absence, termination, or vacation

Developers

- Work with the functional SuperUsers or the Workflow Administrator as requested to determine the cause of Workflow errors

- Troubleshoot errors in Workflows developed internally

- Develop custom Workflows or customize Oracle-supplied Workflows following approved standards for Events, Workflows, PL/SQL Procedures and other components

- Document custom Workflows

Functional SuperUsers

- Understand the Workflow Processes for their respective areas and ensure any required setups are determined, documented and applied in all instances

- Validate that the Workflows in their assigned functional area are operating without error, are not stuck, and are progressing in accordance with Business Process guidelines

- Monitor the status of running Workflows and overdue Notifications in their assigned functional area

- Troubleshoot Workflows in their assigned functional area that are stuck or in error status

All Users

Administrators are not the only individuals who need to ensure certain tasks are performed. Every user of the applications has certain tasks they should be required to perform. These tasks can be performed from any responsibility that has a 'Worklist' screen, such as 'Workflow User'. This responsibility will allow end users to view Workflows they own, view and respond to Notifications, as well as perform the following recommended functions:

- Set up Worklist access for their immediate supervisor to ensure Notifications can be processed in the event of illness

- Set up Vacation Rules and ensure effective dates are changed whenever vacation or leave of absence is scheduled

- Inform the Help Desk whenever a Workflow problem is detected

Summary

Except for help desk, security, and end users, persons involved in the administration/development of Workflow must be able to define components in the Workflow Builder, must have access to MetaLink, must know how to research issues and must understand how to file Support Requests (SRs) with Oracle Support.

Developers, the Workflow Administrator, and Applications DBAs should have strong SQL and PL/SQL skills, and knowledge of the Directory Services tables, the queue tables, and the Workflow design and runtime tables.

Functional SuperUsers and Junior Administrators must have a good knowledge of their assigned area and be able to facilitate discussions about the setups required to configure the seeded Workflows.

This book will not attempt to teach SQL or PL/SQL, although it will discuss techniques and coding rules required by Workflow. This book is not meant to replace the numerous product user/setup guides, where instructions on the setups of the product Workflows are discussed; however, selected Workflows will be described in detail so that the reader can understand the types of setups product Workflows may require. The focus will be more on the Workflow technology, techniques and guidelines that can be applied to all Workflows.

But before we can talk about developing or administering Workflows, the reader needs to ensure that Workflow is correctly set up.

Setup

This chapter covers the following topics:

- Workflow components

- Steps to set up the Workflow environment using Oracle Applications Manager (OAM)

- Scripts and steps required to verify that the Workflow environment is configured correctly

- Steps to set up the Workflow Notification Mailer

- Optional setup steps

We will focus on setup steps required to run Workflow in the Oracle E-Business Suite environment. Additional steps required to run Workflow as a standalone application are not covered.

ASSUMPTIONS AND ENVIRONMENT

This book assumes readers are running E-Business Suite Release 11.5.10.2 with Applications Technology Patch 11i.ATG_PF.H.delta.6 (Rollup 6) or Release 12.0.4 or higher. Differences between the current environment and earlier Workflow environments will be identified where significant.

WORKFLOW BUILDER (CLIENT)

Workflow Builder is a developer tool used to create or modify specific Workflows. Some products require you to make changes in Workflow Builder. For example, if you are using Oracle Projects, you must modify the Purchasing Account Generator. The Workflow Builder is not needed for Workflow users.

Finding the Most Recent Workflow Builder Client

To find the most recent Workflow Client patches for releases prior to RDBMS Version 10gR2, use the Advanced Search on the 'Patches' tab on MetaLink. Choose Product Family 'Workflow Client (wf)', Release 'Applications 11i' or 'Applications R12' and Patch Type 'Any'. Click the Go button (see FIGURE 2.1).

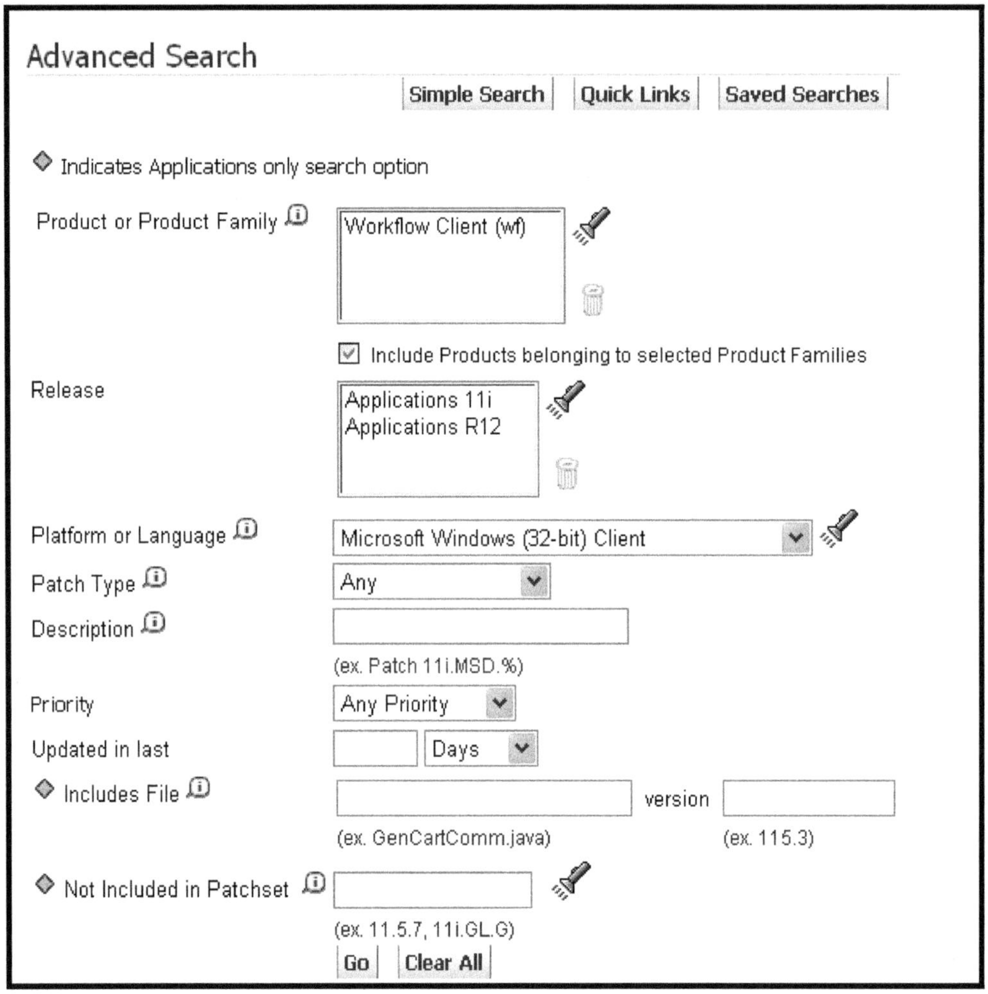

Advanced Search

Simple Search | Quick Links | Saved Searches

◇ Indicates Applications only search option

Product or Product Family ⓘ   Workflow Client (wf)

☑ Include Products belonging to selected Product Families

Release   Applications 11i
Applications R12

Platform or Language ⓘ   Microsoft Windows (32-bit) Client

Patch Type ⓘ   Any

Description ⓘ
(ex. Patch 11i.MSD.%)

Priority   Any Priority

Updated in last   Days

◇ Includes File ⓘ   version
(ex. GenCartComm.java)   (ex. 115.3)

◇ Not Included in Patchset ⓘ
(ex. 11.5.7, 11i.GL.G)
Go | Clear All

FIGURE 2. 1

As of June, 2007, the most recent patches for Workflow are shown in FIGURE 2.2. Although there is a different patch listed for Release 11.5.10, we have not observed any problem with using Patch 4066964 for Releases 11.5.9 or 11.5.10, so we recommend choosing the most recent patch.

Patch	Description	Release	Updated ▽	Size		
4066964	Workflow Client: Patch Workflow Client for Apps 11i10	11i	27-JAN-2005	81M		
3031420	Workflow Client: Patch Workflow Builder 2.6.3.0.1	11i	04-DEC-2003	81M		

FIGURE 2. 2

If you expect to upgrade to RDBMS Version 10*g*R2 in the near term, consider installing the Workflow Client for RDBMS Version 10*g*R2. It will also work with other 11*i* releases on the Oracle9*i* database. The only disadvantage to loading this version is that it will install a Version 10*g* ORACLE_HOME on the client. If you have no other need for a Version 10*g* ORACLE_HOME, we advise against using the additional space on your client and having another ORACLE_HOME to manage.

Either version can be used with Release 12 as well.

The RDBMS Version 10*g*R2 version is not available on MetaLink. You must download this release from the OTN website at the following link:

http://www.oracle.com/technology/software/products/Workflow/index.html

Choose the 'Oracle Workflow Client Release 2.6.3.5 for Microsoft Windows' (see FIGURE 2.3):

Oracle Workflow Client Downloads

☒ Oracle Workflow Client Release 2.6.3.5 for Microsoft Windows

FIGURE 2. 3

MetaLink Doc. ID 551484.1, *Unable to Install Workflow Builder on Microsoft Vista*, states that Workflow Builder is only certified against the following Desktop Operating Systems: Microsoft Windows 2000 with Service Pack 1 or higher, Windows Server 2003, or Windows XP Professional. MetaLink Doc. ID 563350.1, *Installing Oracle Workflow Builder 2.6.3 On Windows Vista Fails,* provides the following workaround that enables the installation on Vista PCs

- Navigate to the WF Builder installer (setup.exe) in the file system

- Right–Click on "setup.exe", then choose Properties

- Check Compatibility Mode and select "Windows XP (Service Pack 2)"

- Restart the Installer for the Workflow Builder

Installing the Workflow Builder Client

Prior to installing Workflow Builder Client, it <u>might</u> be necessary to disable firewall products such as Norton or McAfee. Some client product installations, particularly those installing an RDBMS 8*i* ORACLE_HOME, will actually require you to <u>de-install</u> McAfee, however, we have not yet observed this problem with the Workflow Builder Client. If you have problems connecting to the database after you have completed the installation process, you should look at potential conflicts with your firewall software.

- After your download is complete and you have extracted the files, go to Disk1 → Install → win32 → setup.exe. This will start the Oracle Universal Installer as shown in FIGURE 2.4:

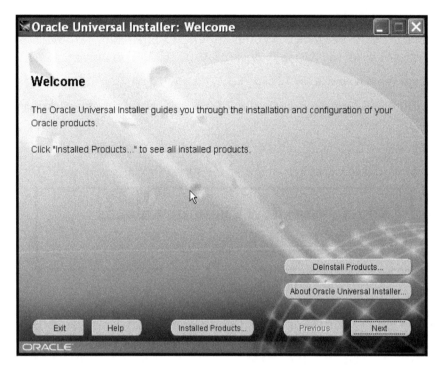

FIGURE 2. 4

- Click Next. Do not install Workflow Builder in an existing ORACLE_HOME used for other client products. Workflow is very selfish. It wants its own ORACLE_HOME. See FIGURE 2.5.

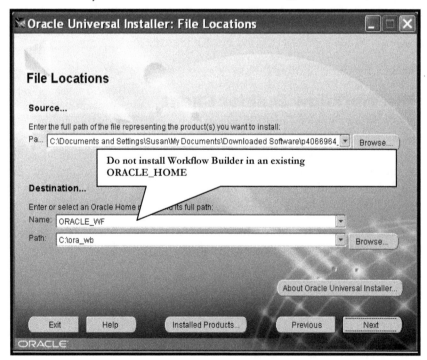

FIGURE 2. 5

- Accept the defaults or change as desired, then click Next (see FIGURE 2.6).

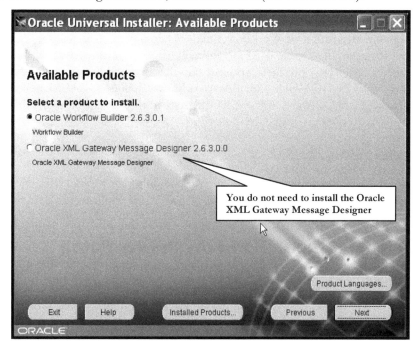

FIGURE 2. 6

- Click Next. The 'Summary' page details what will be installed (see FIGURE 2.7). You do not need to install the Oracle XML Gateway Message Designer.

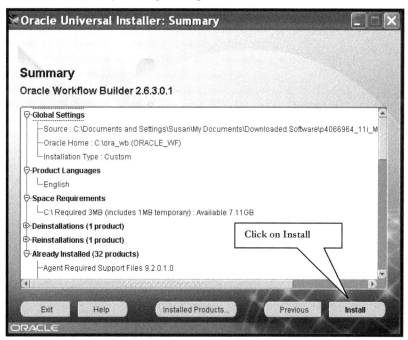

FIGURE 2. 7

- Click Install to install Workflow Builder.

- If this is the first time you have installed Oracle Workflow Builder, the Configuration Tools window will appear after the installation of Workflow Builder is complete. This will help you install the net services needed to access the Oracle database and will help you set up your TNSNAMES.ORA file. If you have other Oracle client products, you can skip this step and copy the TNSNAMES.ORA file from another ORACLE_HOME to the new Workflow Builder ORACLE_HOME, or get the appropriate TNSNAMES.ORA and SQLNET.ORA files from your Applications DBA.

ORACLE WORKFLOW (SERVER)

Oracle Workflow (OWF) is the Applications Technology module that provides functionality to execute Workflows created using the Workflow Builder (Client) tool. Your Applications DBA will apply patches to the server when appropriate.

Finding the Most Recent Workflow Server Patch

To find the latest Oracle Workflow (OWF) patch, use the Advanced Search on the 'Patches' tab on MetaLink. Choose Product Family 'Workflow (owf))', Release 'Applications 11i' or 'Applications R12' and Patch Type 'Patchset/Minipack'. Also choose your server platform (Platform or Language) where you have installed Oracle Applications. Click the Go button (see FIGURE 2.8).

Advanced Search

| Simple Search | Quick Links | Saved Searches |

◇ Indicates Applications only search option

Product or Product Family ⓘ

Workflow (owf)

☑ Include Products belonging to selected Product Families

Release

Applications 11i
Applications R12

Platform or Language ⓘ   Linux x86 ▾

Patch Type ⓘ   Patchset/Minipack ▾

Description ⓘ

(ex. Patch 11i.MSD.%)

Priority   Any Priority ▾

Updated in last   Days ▾

◇ Includes File ⓘ   version

(ex. GenCartComm.java)   (ex. 115.3)

◇ Not Included in Patchset ⓘ

(ex. 11.5.7, 11i.GL.G)

| Go | Clear All |

Results for Platform : *Microsoft Windows (32-bit) Client*

☑ **Tip** Consider Saving the search to make it easy to run again. | Save Search |

Patch	Description	Release	Updated	Size		
4066964	**Workflow Client**: Patch Workflow Client for Apps 11i10	11i	27-JAN-2005	81M		
3031420	**Workflow Client**: Patch Workflow Builder 2.6.3.0.1	11i	04-DEC-2003	81M		

FIGURE 2. 8

Finding the Latest Workflow Information on MetaLink

To find the latest updates regarding Workflow Builder or Workflow on the server, go to the Knowledge Browser on MetaLink, choose E-Business Suite → Workflow in the alphabetical list of categories, and click the Go button (see FIGURE 2.9).

FIGURE 2. 9

Major Workflow Changes Starting with Family Pack OWF.G

Release 11.5.9 was a transitional release for Workflow. Family Pack OWF.G was introduced in Release 11.5.9, which included major changes to Workflow. Some of the most significant changes were:

- The Java Mailer was introduced replacing the c-based Mailer in earlier releases.

- The Inbound Mailer was required to be IMAP4 compliant.

- Oracle Applications Manager (OAM) was incorporated for Workflow setup and administration, including the Workflow Mailer.

- Family Pack OWF.G with Patch 3409889 introduced the SMTP Outbound Mailer in the database. Client software setup for Outbound Mail is no longer required.

- Workflow forms migrated to the OA Framework (Java) format. The old grey forms are gone.

Major Workflow Changes Starting with 11i.ATG_PF.H.delta.3 (Rollup 3)

- A new page for Mailer Override Address and Verification of Address was added

- A new program to resend Notifications was added

- An important bug was fixed, allowing Workflow Administrator to be set to a responsibility

- Worklist Flexfields were introduced (see *Chapter 13, New Features*)

Major Workflow Changes Starting with 11i.ATG_PF.H.delta.4 (Rollup 4)

- Directory Services corruption was fixed

- Oracle Alert began to leverage the Workflow Notification Mailer

- A 'Refresh' button for statistics was added to improve performance

Major Workflow Changes Starting with 11i.ATG_PF.H.delta.5 (Rollup 5)

- Specialized Workflow Administrators by Item Type was added

- Improved drill down functionality for administrators was added

- The ability to grant access functionality by Item Type was added

- Workflow Administrators were given the ability to attach their own digital signature when responding on behalf of another recipient

Major Workflow Changes Starting with 11i.ATG_PF.H.delta.6 (Rollup 6)

- New 'Retry Errored Workflow Activities' (FNDWFRET) Concurrent Program was added to allow retrying activities of an Item Type with a status of ERROR

Major Workflow Changes Starting in Release 12

- Bulk Synchronization was added to rebuild partitions rather than only make incremental updates

- The ability to publish Message Attributes to the Worklist was added

- Several Digital Signature enhancements were made

Important Workflow MetaLink Doc. IDs

The following MetaLink Doc. IDs regarding Workflow should be reviewed.

- 268085.1 – Configuring the Mailer

- 225947.1 – OWF.G – Known issues

- 260393.1 – OWF.G Java Mailer issues

- 258312.1 – OWF.H – Mailer changes

- 299974.1 – Mailer won't start after upgrade

- 242941.1 – Troubleshooting in OWF.G

- 316352.1 – Check if Mailer running without using OAM

- 274764.1 – Java Mailer Setup Test

- 332152.1 – OWF.H Diagnostics

- 337274.1 – About Oracle Applications Technology 11i.ATG_PF.H Rollup 3 (RUP 3)

- 406892.1 – Missing/Corrupted User-Role Responsibilities

- 365228.1 – About Oracle Applications Technology 11i.ATG_PF.H Rollup 4 (RUP 4)

- 412709.1 – Oracle Workflow Documentation Updates for 11i.ATG_PF.H.delta.5 (RUP 5)

- 275379.1 – Script To Check What Workflow Related Patches Are Installed In EBusiness Suite 11i

- 453137.1 – Oracle Workflow Best Practices Release 12 and Release 11i

ORACLE WORKFLOW (SERVER) SETUP

Prerequisites

- Multi-org may be required depending on installed products. See MetaLink Doc. ID: 272292.1, *Expense Report Errors in Workflow With ORA-20001 Error Occurred During Product Initialization for MO*

- Generic Services Manager (GSM) must be running

- A user's web browser must support JavaScript and Frames

Required Steps

Workflow Configuration

Workflow Configuration is accessed via Workflow → Administer Workflow→ Administration (see FIGURE 2.10). This page is available from multiple responsibilities, including the Workflow Administrator Web Applications, Workflow Administrator Web (New) and System Administrator; however, only users with Workflow Administrator privileges can make changes to this page. The following sections describe how to set the values on this page.

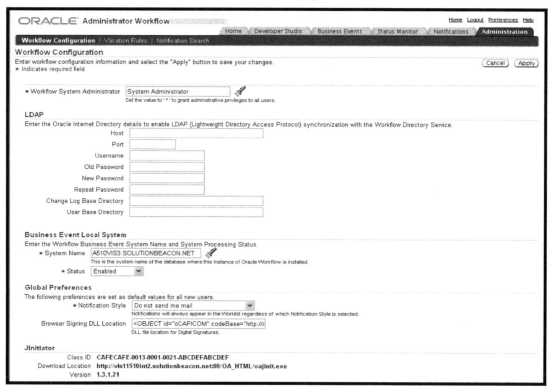

FIGURE 2. 10

Workflow System Administrator

We recommend setting the Workflow Administrator to a responsibility. If the Workflow Administrator is set to a responsibility, any user with that responsibility can update the fields on the 'Workflow Configuration' page from any responsibility that includes this page. If the Workflow Administrator is set to a user, only that user can make changes. Other users with access to this page, but without Workflow Administrator privileges, can still view the page.

To identify the Workflow Administrator via SQL, execute the following statement:

```
select text from wf_resources where name = 'WF_ADMIN_ROLE';
```

Release 11.5.10 and above will return a result similar to the following:

```
TEXT
---------------
FND_RESP|FND|FNDWF_ADMIN_WEB|STANDARD
```

Security Groups are now part of the WF_ADMIN_ROLE. Therefore, in these releases, make sure the correct value (one that includes the security group) is selected when updating the Workflow Administrator.

Prior to 11i.ATG_PF.H.delta.3 (Rollup 3), there was a bug on the 'Workflow Configuration' page preventing updates to the Workflow Administrator from the 'Workflow Configuration' form. Additionally, the default value was set to an invalid value. Therefore, prior to applying this patch, a SQL update is required to update the Workflow Administrator. This SQL statement and additional details are in MetaLink Doc. ID: 308160.1, *11.5.10 Workflow System Administrator field LOV uneditable after setting it to system administrator responsibility*. The SQL statements are also included here for your reference.

To set the Workflow Administrator Role to the 'Workflow Administrator Web Applications' responsibility, execute the following SQL statement:

```
UPDATE wf_resources
  SET text = 'FND_RESP|FND|FNDWF_ADMIN_WEB|STANDARD'
 WHERE name = 'WF_ADMIN_ROLE';
```

OR

To set the Workflow Administrator Role to the 'System Administrator' responsibility, execute the following SQL statement:

```
UPDATE wf_resources
  SET text = 'FND_RESP|SYSADMIN|SYSTEM_ADMINISTRATOR|STANDARD'
 WHERE name = 'WF_ADMIN_ROLE';
```

If an 11i.ATG_PF.H.delta.3 (Rollup 3) or later patch has been applied, click the flashlight next to the 'Workflow System Administrator' field (see FIGURE 2.11).

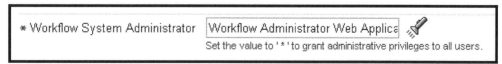

FIGURE 2. 11

Enter your search criteria and click the Go button. Then choose a responsibility that includes the Security Group (see FIGURE 2.12).

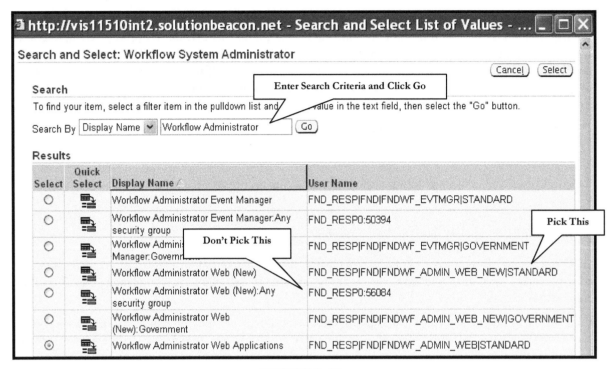

FIGURE 2. 12

LDAP

LDAP settings are for systems using Single Sign On. This allows the directories used by Single Sign On to sync with Directory Services. Enter the following information for LDAP (refer back to FIGURE 2.10):

- **Host** – Database name where the LDAP directory resides

- **Port** – Port of above database

- **Username** – LDAP user account used to connect to the LDAP host

- **Old Password** – Current LDAP password

- **New Password** – New LDAP password you want to use

- **Repeat Password** – New LDAP password you want to use

- **Change Log Base Directory** – LDAP node for change logs

    ♦ cn=changelog

- **User Base Directory** – LDAP node where user records are found

    ♦ cn=Users, dc=oracle, dc=com

Business Event Local System

The System Name is the name of the database where Workflow Server is installed. After completing Business Event System setups, the status must be Enabled until the Business Event System setups are complete (see FIGURE 2.13). After completion, come back to this page and change this status if necessary.

Business Event Local System

Enter the Workflow Business Event System Name and System Processing Status.

∗ System Name `A510VIS3.SOLUTIONBEACON.NET`

This is the system name of the database where this instance of Oracle Workflow is installed.

∗ Status `Enabled` ⌄

Disabled
Enabled
External Only
Local Only

Global Preferences

The following preference   t values for all new users.

∗ Noti   not send me mail ⌄

FIGURE 2. 13

Valid status options include:

- **Disabled** – all Business Events are disabled

- **Enabled** – all Business Events are enabled

- **External Only** – only external Business Events are enabled

- **Local Only** – only internal Business Events are enabled

 The only valid values for E-Business Suite are Enabled and Local Only

Global Preferences

Notification Style

The Notification Style specifies how Workflow Notifications should be sent. The user can override these defaults in their individual preferences (see FIGURE 2.14). For this reason, the Workflow Administrator should periodically check user records for valid preferences. For example, if you have chosen not to email Workflow Notifications, users should not change their Notification Style to one of the email options. This will cause Workflow Notification errors.

Additionally, if you choose one of the email options, users must have a valid email address and the Notification Mailer must be set up. Setup of the Notification Mailer is covered later.

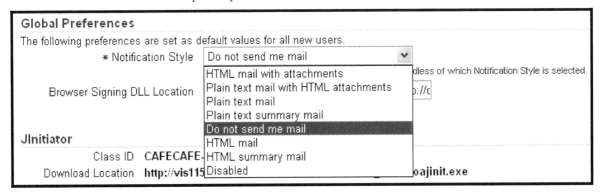

Global Preferences

The following preferences are set as default values for all new users.

∗ Notification Style `Do not send me mail` ⌄   dless of which Notification Style is selected.

HTML mail with attachments
Plain text mail with HTML attachments
Plain text mail
Plain text summary mail
Do not send me mail
HTML mail
HTML summary mail
Disabled

Browser Signing DLL Location   b://c

JInitiator

Class ID **CAFECAFE-**

Download Location **http://vis115**   **oajinit.exe**

FIGURE 2. 14

- **HTML mail with attachments** – Notifications are in HTML format and include an attached link to the 'Notification Details' page. Users must read their email using an HTML email client. Users can click buttons in the email to provide responses.

- **Plain text mail with HTML attachments** – Notifications are in plain text format and include an attached link to the 'Notification Details' page and an attachment with the HTML-formatted version of the Notification. Users must type the exact text to respond. Comments that are more than one line must be enclosed in double quotes. Text of the original email must be excluded from the response. Details of Notifications written using OA Framework are not visible.

- **Plain text mail** – Notifications are in plain text format. Users must type the exact text to respond. Comments longer than one line must be enclosed in double quotes. The text of the original email must be excluded from the response. Details of Notifications written using OA Framework are not visible.

- **Plain text summary mail** – Send a summary of all Notifications as a plain text email. Users must use the 'Worklist' pages to view and respond to Notifications.

- **Do not send me mail** – Do not send the Notifications as email. Users must use the 'Worklist' pages to view and respond to Notifications. Use this setting until the Workflow Notification Mailer is set up.

- **HTML mail** – Notifications are in HTML format but do not include the attached link to the 'Notification Details' page. Users must read their email using an HTML email client. Users can click buttons in the email to provide responses.

- **HTML summary mail** – Send a summary of all Notifications in HTML format with a link to the 'Worklist' page and links to each Notification in the 'Notification Details' page. Users must use the 'Worklist' pages to view or respond to Notifications.

- **Disabled** – Do not use this value for Global Preferences. Individual user preferences will be set to Disabled when Workflow tries to send a Notification but does not find an email address.

Note: Starting with 11i.ATG_PF.H.delta.3 (Rollup 3), Workflow puts the Notification in your Worklist if there is no email address without recording an error. Previously, a Notification would be sent to SYSADMIN stating the Event failed and error records would exist even if the Notification was acted upon properly via the Worklist. If a Notification to SYSADMIN is desired when emails fail to deliver, MetaLink Doc. ID: 456378.1, *How to notify SYSADMIN if a notification failed to deliver*, explains how to re-enable this feature without causing the Workflow to error.

Browser Signing DLL Location

The Browser Signing DLL Location is the location of the Capicom.dll file that is used for Web page operations with encryption in the Microsoft Internet Explorer browser. This preference is required when using electronic signatures for Notifications and using Internet Explorer to access the E-Business Suite. Update this value if Microsoft changes this location or if you choose to point to a local copy of this file.

Profile Options

- **Concurrent: GSM Enabled** – This Profile Option should be set to 'Y' at the site level for Workflow to perform efficiently. The Generic Services Manager (GSM) automates the management of Java Processes. It will automatically start and stop various services.

- **Server Timezone** – Set the 'Server Timezone' at the Site level (see FIGURE 2.15). Failure to set this Profile Option will prevent the Workflow Monitor from opening.

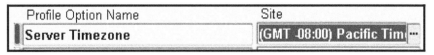

Profile Option Name	Site
Server Timezone	**(GMT -08:00) Pacific Tim** ···

FIGURE 2. 15

- **WF: Notification Reassign Mode** – This Profile Option specifies how you will allow recipients of Notifications to pass responsibility for that Notification to other users. Valid values for 'WF: Notification Reassign Mode' are Delegate, Transfer or Reassign.

  - ♦ **Delegate** – You can delegate Notifications to other users, but you cannot reassign Notifications. Delegate allows another user to respond to a Notification, but the original user will retain ownership. Use this option to delegate authority while you are away from your job.

  - ♦ **Transfer** – You can transfer Workflow Notifications, which will sometimes also change the hierarchy, but you cannot delegate. This options transfers ownership of the Notification. Use this option when you have received a Notification for an Action that falls outside your area of responsibility.

  - ♦ **Reassign** – You can choose to Delegate or Transfer. Prior to Release 11.5.10, this Profile Option was called 'FND: Notification Reassign Mode'.

- **WF: Vacation Rules – Allow all**. Valid values are Enabled or Disabled. If enabled, this Profile Option allows the user to specify All for Vacation Rules. If you are using Human Resources fully installed, enabling this feature is not recommended. You should force the user to specify delegation or transfer of HR Notifications separately for privacy reasons. Note: Prior to Release 11.5.10, this Profile Option was called 'WF: Routing Rules – Allow All'.

- **WF: Plain text sign-on** – Set this Profile Option to 'Yes' to allow electronic signing to occur only on Plain Text Notifications.

- **WF: GUEST Access to Notification** – You can set the 'WF: GUEST Access to Notification' Profile Option to Enabled at the site level to allow users to access the Worklist from the email Notification without logging in to the Oracle E-Business Suite. This feature is not recommended due to security considerations.

  MetaLink Doc. ID: 258312.1, *About Oracle Workflow Mini-pack 11i.OWF.H*, provides further instructions on setting up guest access.

- **WF: Workflow Mailer Framework Web Agent** – This Profile Option must be set to a specific physical server address if the Application Framework Agent Profile Option is set to a virtual or load balancing server. You may need to consult with your Applications Database Administrator to determine your Application Framework Agent setup.

- **WF: ICX Session Mode** – This Profile Option specifies the mode to use when accessing a Notification that was sent without the Access Key. Valid values are Personal Home Page (PHP) or Portal.

- **Socket Listener Port** – This Profile Option was introduced in Release 11.5.6 and is standard in Release 11.5.10. Set the 'Socket Listener Port' to a different value for each database to allow a user to open multiple Forms sessions where each session is connected to a different database. MetaLink

Doc. ID: 272585.1, *Users Cannot Open Multiple Forms Sessions On The Same PC In Application 11i*, provides additional information about this functionality.

Directory Services

This Process synchronizes data from specific applications such as Human Resources, TCA, Marketing, Engineering, Federal HR, and FND, with the WF_LOCAL_ROLES and WF_LOCAL_USER_ROLES tables. Run the 'Synchronize WF LOCAL tables' Concurrent Program daily for sources of data that are not automatically synchronized (see FIGURE 2.16). Automatic synchronization was introduced in Release 11.5.9 and completed in Release 11.5.10.

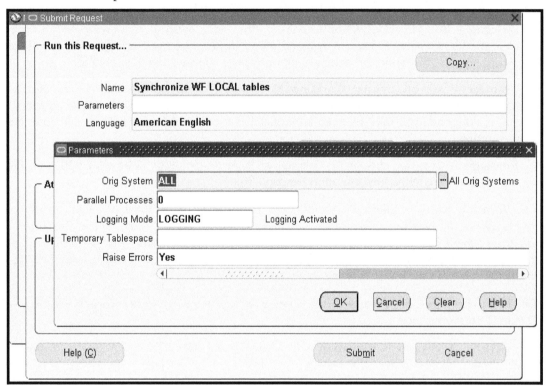

FIGURE 2. 16

Prior to upgrading to Release 11.5.10, you should run this Concurrent Program and resolve all synchronization errors. This Process will not run in Release 11.5.10 for systems that are synchronized. If you do not run this Process prior to upgrading, errors must be manually resolved by updating data in the source record. In Release 12, the 'WF Bulk Synchronize Local Tables' Concurrent Program will re-sync a directory partition in its entirety.

MetaLink Doc. ID: 171703.1, *11.5.x: Implementing Oracle Workflow Directory Service Synchronization*, provides the latest patches and additional information on Directory Service Synchronization.

To set up the 'Synchronize WF LOCAL tables' Concurrent Program:

- Choose the original system data to be synchronized or 'ALL'. If you are unsure which systems must be synchronized, choose 'ALL'. The process will only synchronize systems that are not automatically synchronized.

- If you have sufficient hardware resources, the number of Parallel Processes can be increased. Otherwise, set this value to 1. You should consult with your Applications Database Administrator to decide how many parallel processes you could use.

- Set the Logging mode to NOLOGGING to increase performance, but if the process fails, you will need to rerun it. NOLOGGING means that changes will not be saved to the database's redo logs. Since the program can easily be re-run, NOLOGGING can be used without any risk.

- Family Pack OWF.G added the option to choose a Temporary Tablespace. If this process fails with ORA-1652 – unable to extend temp segment by %s in tablespace %s, choose a larger Temporary Tablespace. You may need to work with your Applications Database Administer to determine the best Temporary Tablespace to use.

- Set 'Raise Errors' to 'Yes' to allow errors to be reported to the users.

Verify Directory Services

The wfdirchk.sql script, located in $FND_TOP/sql, will provide information associated with Directory Services. Run this script as the APPS user and resolve errors prior to upgrades and prior to opening Service Requests (SRs) if possible.

A partial sample output file is shown here. This script will typically return hundreds of pages depending on the number of Roles defined in your database.

The information in this report is also contained in a combination of Diagnostic Reports located in the Application Object Library Group. Refer to *Chapter 9, Diagnostics,* for additional details.

```
Workflow Tests - Notification Preference Validation Test
Data Collection - Workflow Directory Services
Data Collection → Workflow Directory Services.
```

Workflow Patch Version

```
--------------------Workflow Directory Services Version
Version of WFDS : V3
PL/SQL procedure successfully completed.
```

Originating Systems for Partitions

```
-------------------- Originating System -----------
Valid Originating Systems
Apps Install
----------------------
AMV_APPR
AMV_CHN
ECX
ENG_LIST
FND_RESP
FND_USR
GBX
HZ_GROUP0
```

```
HZ_PARTY
PER
PER_ROLE
POS
PQH_ROLE
PL/SQL procedure successfully completed.
```

Partitions and Views

```
ROLE / USER - DIRECTORY PARTITIONS TABLE AND VIEW Information
Orig System    : UMX
-----------------------------------------
Partition id   : 13
.
Orig System    : WF_LOCAL_ROLES
-----------------------------------------
Partition id   : 0
.
Orig System    : FND_USR
-----------------------------------------
Partition id   : 1
Role view      : NOBS
Migration of user/role data successful
User/Role view : NOBS
```

Bogus error

```
ERROR : Seeded view NOBS does not exist
Migration of user-role data successful
Role TL view NOBS
.
.
Orig System    : PER_ROLE
-----------------------------------------
Partition id   : 3
Role view      : PER_ROLE_ROLES_V
```

Migration error – rerun 'Bulk Synchronization' Concurrent Program

```
ERROR : Migration of user/role data unsuccessful : Please rerun Bulk
Synchronization for this Orig System and reverify
No User_Role view is defined for Orig System PER_ROLE
Orig System not MLS Enabled
.
.
Orig System    : POS
-----------------------------------------
Partition id   : 4
Role view      : PQH_POS_ROLES
Migration of user/role data successful
User/Role view : PQH_POS_UR
Migration of user-role data successful
Orig System not MLS Enabled
.
.
```

```
Orig System    : AMV_CHN
------------------------------------------
Partition id   : 6
Role view      : WF_AMV_CHN_ROLES
Migration of user/role data successful
User/Role view : WF_AMV_CHN_UR
Migration of user-role data successful
Orig System not MLS Enabled
.
```

Tables and Indexes

```
---------------- WFDS Tables and Indexes ---------
WFDS Table and Index Details
Table Info
---------------------------------
Table name  : WF_LOCAL_ROLES
Partitioned : YES
Table Space : APPS_TS_TX_DATA
Index Info
-----------
Index name  : WF_LOCAL_ROLES_N2
Partitioned : YES
Table Space : APPS_TS_TX_IDX
Uniqueness  : NONUNIQUE
.

.
…lots of additional pages
.
```

Invalid names (#,/,length > 30)

```
------------------ Roles (Includes users) --------
prompt
-- WF_ROLES: Invalid names

ERROR

1 row selected.

NAME                                 ORIG_SYSTEM       Orig S-ID
---------------------------          -----------------
ARC/PUR                              FND_USR                1774
BENEFITS/AWARDS                      GBX                     191
FND_RESP|GMS|PA/GA BUDGETS|STANDARD FND_RESP              57577

3 rows selected.
```

Invalid compound names

```
-- WF_ROLES: Invalid compound names
--   NAME <> <orig_system>:<orig_system_id>

ERROR :

1 row selected.
```

```
NAME                           ORIG_SYSTEM            Orig S-ID
------------------------------ ---------------------- ---------
EBUSINESS:MANUFACTURING        PER                         5541
```

1 row selected.

Duplicate roles

```
-- WF_ROLES: Duplicated Roles
```

no rows selected

no rows selected

Roles linked to the same original id

> The first two records listed are false errors, as it is OK to have two responsibilities with the same ID as long as either the Application is different (characters after the first pipe) or the Security Group is different (characters after the last pipe)

```
WF_ROLES: Multiple WF ROLES linked to same re      original system

ORIG_SYSTEM Orig S-ID  NAME                                         display_name
----------- ---------  -------------------------------------------- ----------------
FND_RESP    20419      FND_RESP|FND|APPLICATION_DEVELOPER|GOVERNMENT Application
                                                                    Developer:Government
FND_RESP    20419      FND_RESP|FND|APPLICATION_DEVELOPER|STANDARD  Application Developer
PER         25                                                      OPERATIONS
                                                                    Stock, Ms. Pat
PER         25                                                      DDRIGGS
                                                                    Stock, Ms. Pat
PER         855                                                     4JDAUGHERTY
                                                                    Daugherty, Mr. John
PER         855                                                     JDAUGHERTY
                                                                    Daugherty, Mr. John
.
.
.
1261 rows selected.
```

No email address with a preference for mail. If you are linked to an employee record, the email must be in the employee record, not just the user record.

```
-- WF_ROLES: Invalid Notification Preference
-- Preference not in ('MAILTEXT', 'MAILHTML', 'MAILATTH', 'SUMMARY', 'QUERY', -
-- 'MAILHTM2')
-- Preference is in this list but EMAIL_ADDRESS is null

NAME                   notification_preference  PARTITION_ID
---------------------- ------------------------ ------------
4JDAUGHERTY            MAILHTML                            1
4RABBOTT              MAILHTML                            1
4RBROOKS              MAILHTML                            1
```

Invalid user roles

```
--------------------- User Roles ---------------------
-- WF_USER_ROLES Invalid (User / Role) Foreign Key
```

User Name	User Sys	U.System ID	Role Name	Role Sys	R.System ID	PARTITION_ID
COMMS_ISTORE	PER	5131	~WF_ADHOC-460	WF_LOCAL_ROLES	0	0
COMMS_ISTORE	PER	5131	~WF_ADHOC-461	WF_LOCAL_ROLES	0	0
CONTAPPROVER	PER	11215	~WF_ADHOC-365	WF_LOCAL_ROLES	0	0

Ignore the JRES errors. Oracle broke their own rules and has code to deal with it.

JRES_IND:100001382	JRES_IND	100001382	JRES_IND:100001382	JRES_IND	100001382	0
JRES_IND:100001383	JRES_IND	100001383	JRES_IND:100001383	JRES_IND	100001383	0
JRES_IND:848	JRES_IND	848	JRES_IND:848	JRES_IND	848	0

Missing user roles
They are in wf_local_roles but not in wf_local_user_roles where the user name and role name are the same

```
-- WF_USER_ROLES: Missing user role

--      Every User must Participate in their own role

NAME
------------------------------
ECX_SA

1 row selected.
```

Duplicate Roles

```
-- WF_USER_ROLES - Duplicate Rows
no rows selected
```

Expired roles – This is an inaccurate count. Patch 4483634, MetaLink Doc. ID: 329500.1 will provide a new query in the wfdirchk.sql. (Not available on all platforms yet.)

```
--Number of roles that qualify for purging (Make sure you run --purge
regularly!

  COUNT(*)
----------
      1385
```

```
1 row selected.

--Number of userroles that qualify for purging (Make sure you --run purge
regularly!

   COUNT(*)
----------
      2425

1 row selected.
```

Background Engines

The 'Workflow Background Engine' is a Concurrent Program that runs periodically on a schedule that the Workflow Administrator defines. The Background Engine processes outstanding Workflow Processes. At least one Background Engine must be started to run Workflow Processes in the E-Business Suite. However, Workflow will run more efficiently with additional Background Engines.

Background Engines can be started through the Concurrent Manager or through Oracle Applications Manager (OAM).

Setting Up Background Engines from the Concurrent Manager

To set up a Background Engine from the Concurrent Manager, enter the following parameters (see FIGURE 2.17):

- **Item type** – Choose an Item Type or leave blank for all.

- **Minimum and Maximum Threshold** – If you have Workflows that are long running, the threshold can be set to a high number in the Workflow Builder. You can run a separate Background Engine during slower processing times for those Workflows with a higher threshold.

- **Process Deferred** – Enter 'Yes' to process deferred Workflows

- **Process Timeout** – Enter 'Yes' to process timed out Notifications

- **Process Stuck** – Enter 'Yes' to process stuck Workflows

  Stuck Workflows occur when the Workflow Engine cannot determine what Workflow activity should be next. This is usually due to: a PL/SQL Package returns a non–modeled result; an End Node is not marked as an End Node; or the first node in a loop has 'On Revisit' set to Ignore. If the error occurs in the PL/SQL Package, the Workflow can be restarted once the Package is recompiled. If the error is due to a bad End Node or bad 'On Revisit', the Workflow cannot be restarted, as any running copies of a Workflow do not recognize changes in the Workflow design. If continuing these Workflows is a requirement, file a Service Request (SR) with Oracle Support and ask for a script to fix the design using SQL.

  It is not recommended that Process Stuck be set to 'Yes' for the Background Engine you have set to run every 5–20 minutes, as the code that identifies Stuck Workflows runs slowly and places any Workflow identified as Stuck into error status. This can cause performance issues. Stuck Workflows are rare as long as companies are administering Workflows and fixing any design errors. A separate background engine should be set up to run less frequently (once a day is sufficient) for Stuck Processes.

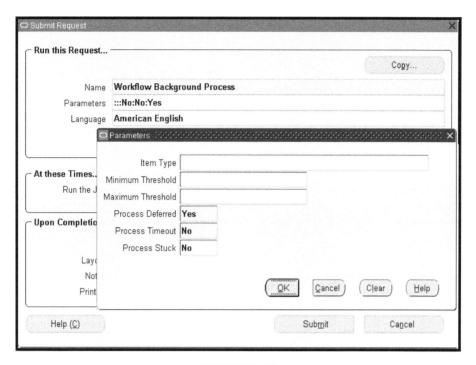

FIGURE 2. 17

- At a minimum, start two Workflow Background Processes. One should run every 5-20 minutes with the parameters null, null, null, yes, no, no. The second engine should run daily with the parameters null, null, null, no, yes, yes. Add other Background Engines to manage throughput as necessary depending on your installed products.

- Schedule the request to run as needed (see FIGURE 2.18).

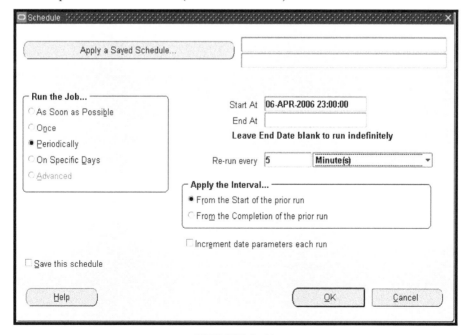

FIGURE 2. 18

Setting up Background Engines in the Oracle Applications Manager (OAM)

To start a Background Engine in OAM:

• Click on the Go button next to 'Submit Request for' 'Background Engine' (see FIGURE 2.19):

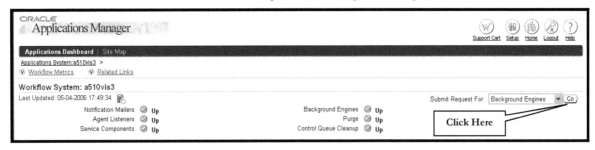

FIGURE 2. 19

• Name the request and click Next (see FIGURE 2.20):

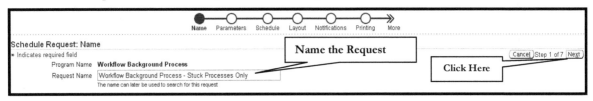

FIGURE 2. 20

• Enter the parameter values and click Next (see FIGURE 2.21):

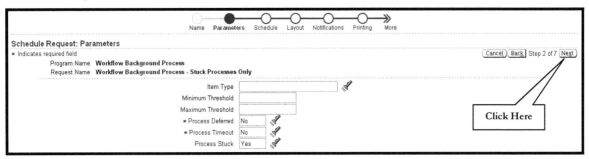

FIGURE 2. 21

• Schedule the Background Engine to run daily and click Next (see FIGURE 2.22):

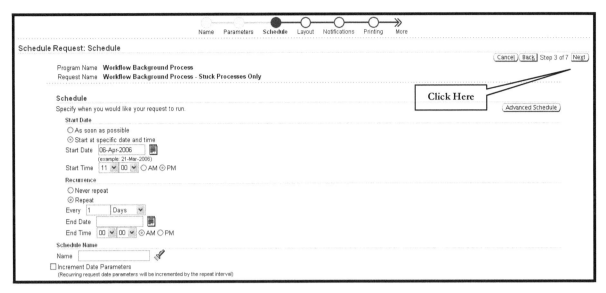

FIGURE 2. 22

- Optionally schedule Notifications and click Next (see FIGURE 2.23):

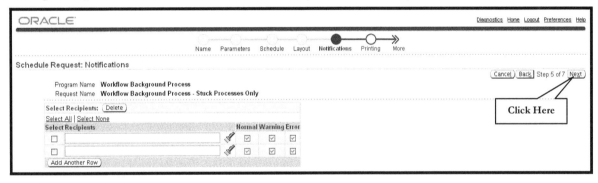

FIGURE 2. 23

- Optionally change printing preferences and click Next (see FIGURE 2.24).

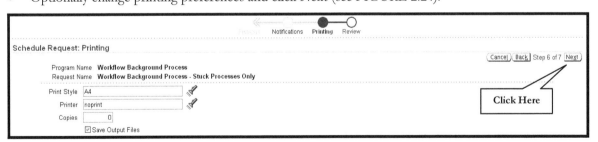

FIGURE 2. 24

- Review your settings and click 'Submit' (see FIGURE 2.25).

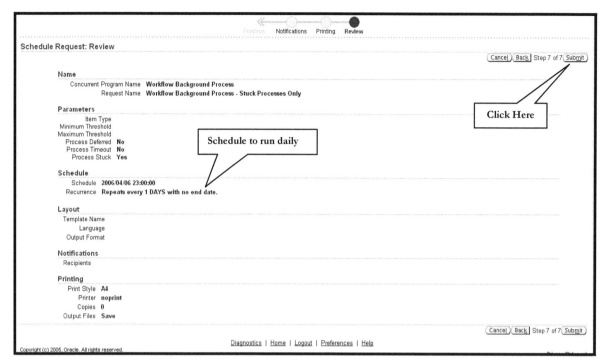

FIGURE 2. 25

- Your Concurrent Request is processed (see FIGURE 2.26).

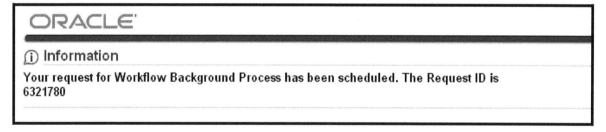

FIGURE 2. 26

Start Listeners

Start the 'Workflow Agent Listener Service' container the first time you use Workflow. Listeners start Workflow Events and send Notifications. The 'Workflow Agent Listener Services is the container for several other Listeners. These other Listeners listed in FIGURE 2.27 will start automatically when you start the 'Workflow Agent Listener Service' container. The Listeners in FIGURE 2.27 with a Status of Running are the Listeners automatically started by the 'Workflow Agent Listener Service' container. The startup mode for the running Listeners will be set to Automatic. Do not change this setting.

If a listener is assigned a Startup mode of Manual, this indicates that the listener is not used by the E-Business Suite, or that the application that requires this listener is not installed. The ECX listeners are examples of listeners that are only required when XML Gateway is installed. If this application is not installed, the Startup mode is set to Manual to avoid wasting processor cycles on unneeded listeners.

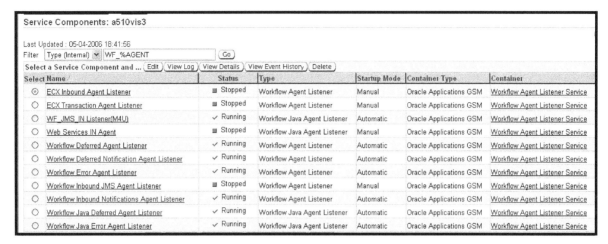

FIGURE 2. 27

To start the 'Workflow Agent Listener Service' container:

● Go to OAM → Workflow. Click on the icon next to Agent Listeners or Service Components (see FIGURE 2.28).

FIGURE 2. 28

● Click on the 'Workflow Agent Listener Service' link (see FIGURE 2.29).

FIGURE 2. 29

- Select the 'Workflow Agent Listener Service', choose 'Start' from the Actions drop down list and click Go.

- If you plan to use the Workflow Notification Mailer to email Notifications, return to this page and start the Workflow Mailer Services after configuration of the Workflow Notification Mailer is complete (see FIGURE 2.30).

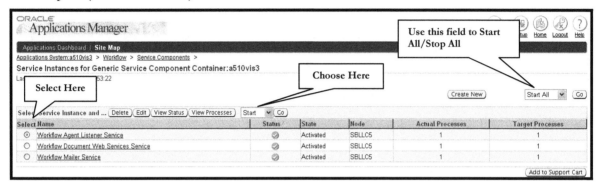

FIGURE 2. 30

Business Event System

Set up and Verify Queues

A Queue is like a mailbox. The Queue holds Events or Notifications. If it is an Event, the Subscription will process the Event. If it is a Notification, the Notification Mailer will process the Notification. A Queue is assigned to each Agent Listener. Oracle now sets up these Queues automatically. You should verify that the required Queues are active in OAM. To check the Queue assigned to an Agent Listener, go to OAM and click on the icon next to Agent Listeners. Choose an Agent and click the 'Edit' button (see FIGURE 2.31).

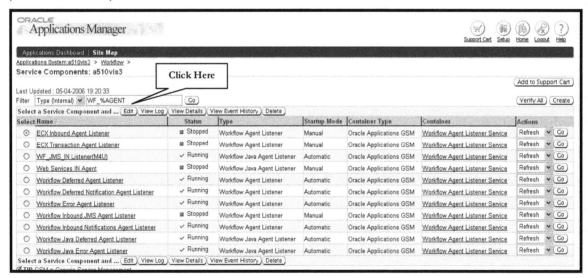

FIGURE 2. 31

The Inbound Agent is the Queue (see FIGURE 2.32).

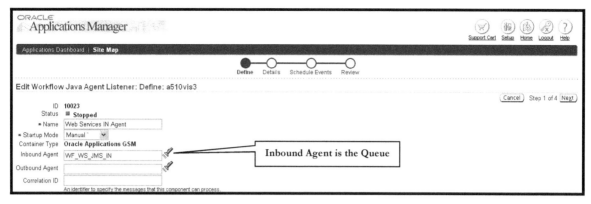

FIGURE 2. 32

Business Event System Parameters

Certain parameters affect Workflow performance. You can see the current value as well as the recommended value for Related Database Parameters from the Applications Dashboard screen in FIGURE 2.33. If the values don't match the recommended values, you'll need to work with your Applications DBA to determine if he should change those parameters, which are stored in your database's init.ora file. Your Applications DBA should check the following parameters:

- **aq_tm_processes** - monitors delayed Events such as Wait Activities. When set to a value greater than 0, this parameter sets Time Monitoring for Queue Messages.

- **job_queue_processes** - handles Propagation of the Business Event System Event Messages. The default value is 2; however, the recommended value is 10.

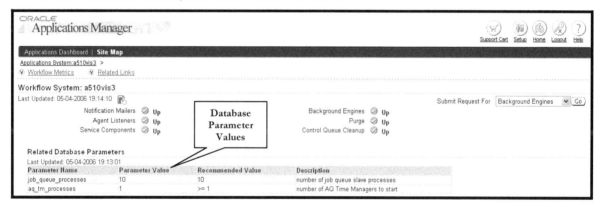

FIGURE 2. 33

Synchronize License Statuses

Run the Concurrent Program 'Synchronize Product License and Workflow BES License' to disable any Business Events for products not licensed at your site. If you are using the 'System Administrator' responsibility as the Workflow Administrator, add this Concurrent Program to the System Administrator Request Group.

Schedule Queue Cleanup

If the 'Control Queue Cleanup' Concurrent Program is scheduled, the icon next to 'Control Queue Cleanup' in OAM will be green (see FIGURE 2.34). If not, schedule this Concurrent Program to run every 12 hours. 'Control Queue Cleanup' removes Subscribers from the WF_CONTROL Queue for

Processes that are not active. Processes become inactive when a middle tier process dies. This will make the Business Event System run more efficiently.

FIGURE 2. 34

Optional Steps

Partition Tables

Partitioning Workflow tables can increase the performance of Workflow Processes. Partitioning is a task for your Applications Database Administrator. Partitioning a table creates subsets of the table based on the value of a specified column. The column used for the Workflow tables is ITEM_TYPE. For companies whose runtime tables contain millions of rows, this step will increase performance because the code used to access these tables will only have to read through a particular subset of the data instead of the whole table.

To prepare to partition, run the 'Purge Obsolete Workflow Runtime Data' Concurrent Program to purge the maximum amount of data possible in the Workflow tables prior to partitioning (see FIGURE 2.35). This will speed up the partitioning process. Choose the following parameters:

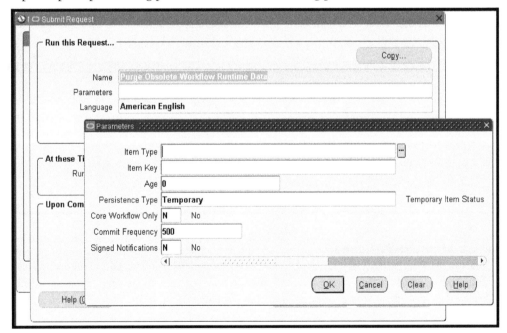

FIGURE 2. 35

- **Item Type** – null

- **Item Key** – null

- **Age** – this is the age since the Workflow was completed plus the number of days specified for retention for the Item Type (from Workflow Builder)

- **Persistence Type** – Run once for Temporary and once for Permanent to eliminate the maximum amount of data. (This is determined by Item Type in Workflow Builder)

- **Core Workflow Only** – Enter 'Y' to purge only obsolete runtime data associated with Work Items, or 'N' to purge all obsolete runtime data as well as obsolete design data

- **Commit Frequency** – 500. Commit Frequency is how many Workflows should be purged before issuing a commit. This parameter can be increased to speed performance as long as there is sufficient disk space for the redo logs. You should consult your Applications DBA to decide on the best value for Commit Frequency.

- **Signed Notifications** – 'Y' will purge Notifications with electronic signatures

Your Applications DBA must backup the following tables prior to starting the partition process. Note that according to the documentation in the script, the script runs with logging turned on. Still, it is a good practice to backup the following tables in case something goes wrong.

- WF_ITEM_ACTIVITY_STATUSES

- WF_ITEM_ACTIVITY_STATUSES_H

- WF_ITEM_ATTRIBUTE_VALUES

- WF_ITEMS

Your Applications DBA should verify that the free space in the tablespace that contains these Workflow tables is slightly more that what is currently in use, including indices. The main reason the partitioning process might fail is due to lack of space.

The Oracle documentation references a blank script, wfupartb.sql. MetaLink Doc. ID: 260884.1, *How to Partition tables in OWF.G*, states that the current script is wfpart.sql and that the script is located in $FND_TOP/patch/115/sql. The script should be run as follows:

```
sqlplus apps/appspw @wfupart <fnd_user> <fndusr pw> <apps_user> <apps_pw> <utl_dir>
```

Example:

```
sqlplus apps/appspw @wfupartb.sql applsys applsyspw apps appspw /home/utl
```

According to the remarks in the script: "This script will generate the script wfpart.sql to partition the tables in the location of your utl directory. The script can be customized and run for enhancing performance. Logging is turned on by default; you may turn it off to increase performance if your database setup permits you to."

Note that if you see the error "ORA–01418: specified index does not exist" when running the script, follow the instructions in MetaLink Doc. ID 329738.1, *OWF.G Workflow Partitioning Fails At index Wf_item_activity_statuses_n4*.

Additional Languages

If additional languages are installed on the server, individual users can set their preferred language from their 'Workflow Home' page (see FIGURE 2.36). They must also set the NLS_LANG environment variable on their desktop (see FIGURE 2.37). Changing this preference only translates the prompts.

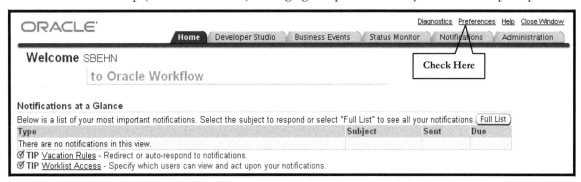

FIGURE 2. 36

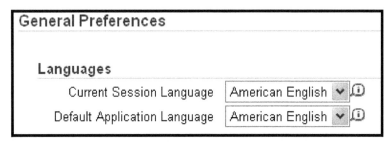

FIGURE 2. 37

Set Up the Notification Mailer

Prerequisites

Inbound processing requires setting up an IMAP compliant email account. It is strongly recommended that you do not use a user's email. It is an option, but additional setup is required. (See Help in OAM for additional details.) Create three folders for this email account named INBOX, PROCESSED and DISCARD. These folders must be in uppercase. It is preferred that you treat this email account as if you have an employee named WF mail. Make sure you can send email to and from this account and that email is not redirected. Ping the email server from the Oracle server to confirm communication is working.

Mailer Setup in Oracle Applications Manager (OAM)

To set up the Notification Mailer in OAM:

• Click on the icon next to Notification Mailers in OAM (see FIGURE 2.38).

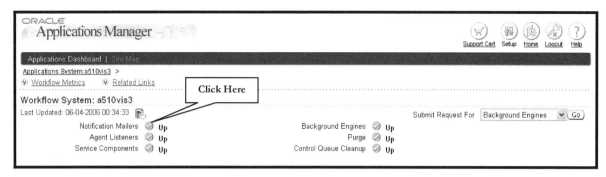

FIGURE 2. 38

- Click the 'Edit' button (see FIGURE 2.39).

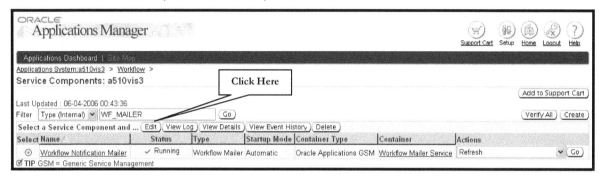

FIGURE 2. 39

Step 1 – Edit Workflow Mailer: Define:

- Make sure the 'Startup Mode' is 'Automatic'. Accept the other default values on this page and click Next (see FIGURE 2.40).

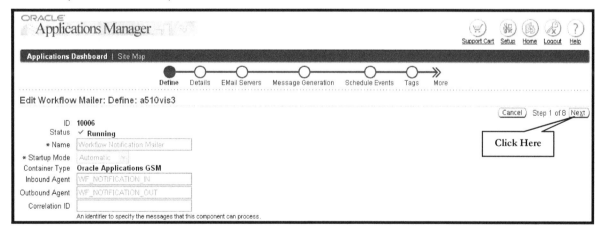

FIGURE 2. 40

Step 2 – Edit Workflow Mailer: Details:

To edit the Workflow Mailer Details (see FIGURE 2.41):

- Set the Max Error Count to 100 as recommended in MetaLink Doc. ID: 300141.1, *11.5.9/11.5.10 Java mailer: Can't send command to SMTP host;java.net.SocketException: Broken Pipe.*

- The 'Inbound Thread Count' and 'Outbound Thread Count' default to 1 to allow both Inbound and Outbound Processing. If you choose to block responses (some companies block responses for security reasons) to this email account, set the Inbound Thread Count to 0.

- Make sure the 'Processor Close on Read Timeout' box is checked so that it is enabled. You will experience contention or locking if multiple Java Mailers use the same SMTP Server (Outbound Server Name). When 'Processor Close on Read Timeout' is not checked, the Java Mailer does not close its connection to the SMTP Server after connecting to it.

- Until the Notification Mailer is tested and working properly, set the Log Level to Statement. This will provide detailed information in the log. After the Notification has been set up and verified, change the Log Level to Error to reduce space required by the logs. Accept the default values for the remaining parameters and click Next.

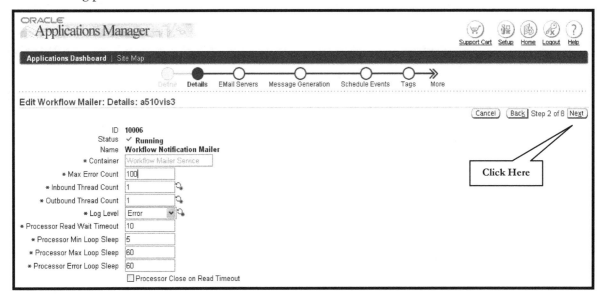

FIGURE 2. 41

Step 3 – Edit Workflow Mailer: Email Servers:

To edit the Workflow Mailer's Email Servers (see FIGURE 2.42):

- Enter the 'Mailer Node Name'. This name must be in uppercase, contain no special character and be 8 characters or less. This is the name of this Notification Mailer. It is included in Outbound Notifications and is used in Inbound Notifications to determine which Mailer should process the Message.

- The 'Email Parser' is the Java class used to parse an incoming Notification response. The default 'Email Parser' is oracle.apps.fnd.wf.mailer.TemplatedEmailParser. Do not change this value.

- The 'Alternate email parser' is used if you set the DIRECT_RESPONSE parameter to Y. The default value is oracle.apps.fnd.wf.mailer.DirectEmailParser. Do not change this value.

- Check the 'Expunge Inbox on Close' check box if you want processed or discarded Messages to be deleted when the email for the Notification Mailer is closed. MetaLink Doc. ID: 340402.1,

JMAILER java.lang.StackOverflowError – keeps crashing, states that if this box is not checked (and someone isn't manually purging), then the Mailer will crash when the mailbox is full.

- If responses will be allowed for this Notification, enter the 'Inbound EMail Account' parameters.

- The 'Inbound Protocol' must be IMAP.

- The 'Inbound Server Name' is the host name for the server. You may optionally include the port number using the format <server_name>:<port_number>. Otherwise, the Notification Mailer uses port 143. Do not specify the value 'localhost'.

- Enter the Username and Password of the mail account that was set up specifically for the Workflow Mailer.

- Accept the default values for the remaining parameters in the 'Inbound EMail Account' section.

- The 'Outbound Protocol' is SMTP

- The 'Outbound Server Name' is the host name for the server. You may optionally include the port number using the format <server_name>:<port_number>. Otherwise, the Notification Mailer uses port 143. Do not specify the value 'localhost'.

- The 'Test Address', if assigned, is displayed here. In earlier versions, this is where you would assign a Test Address for redirection of all Outbound Notification emails. New features and setup for assigning a Test Address will be covered in "Setting an Override Notification Mailer Address" later in this chapter.

- Accept the default values for the remaining parameters in the 'Outbound EMail Account' section.

- Accept the default values for the Processed Folder and Discard Folder. (You should have already created these folders in your email account.)

- Uncheck the 'Allow Forwarded Response' check box if you prefer to force the responder to be the recipient of the Notification.

- Click Next. Note that if your parameters are valid, you can proceed to Step 4. Otherwise, you will not be able to proceed.

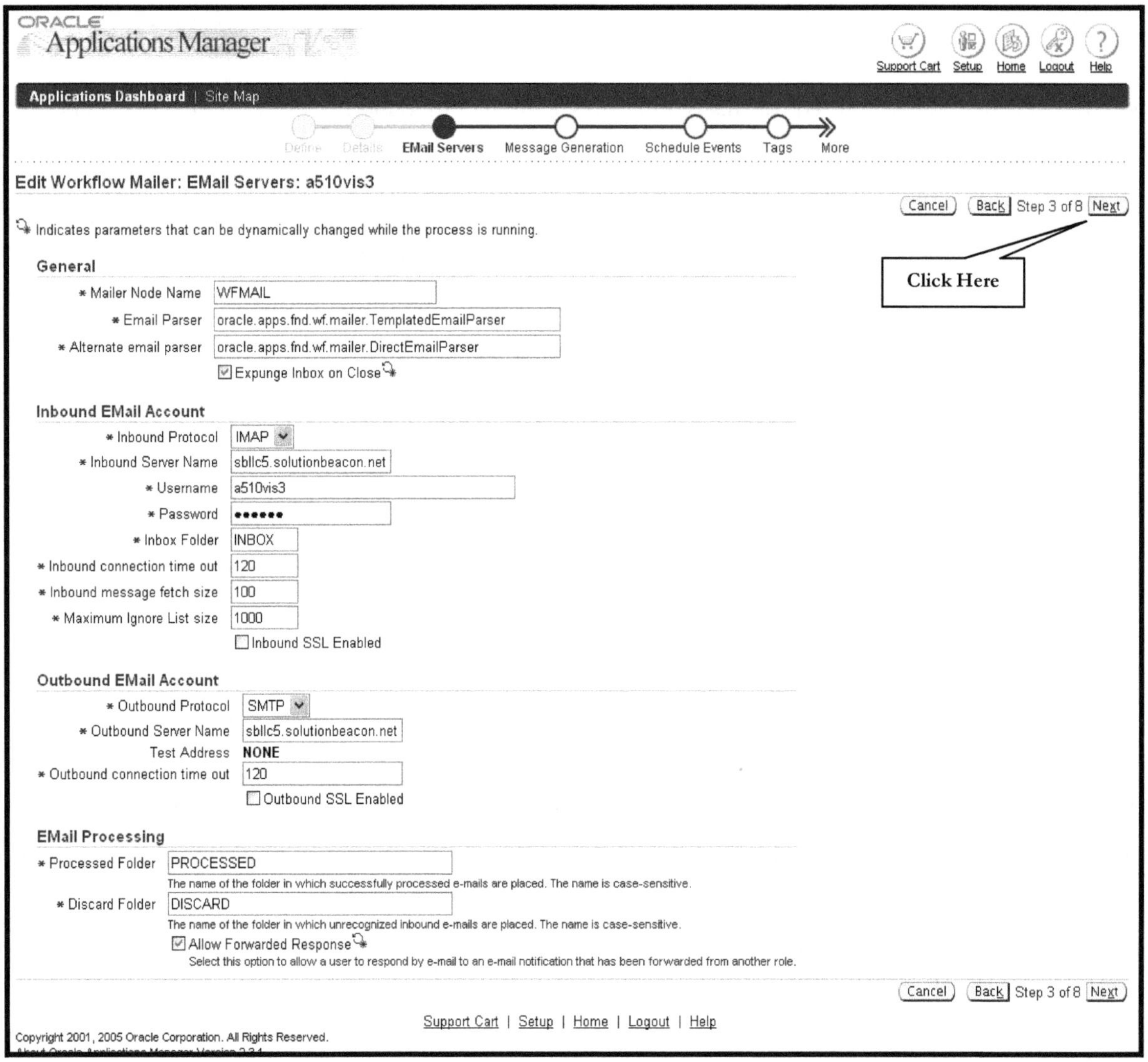

FIGURE 2. 42

Step 4 – Edit Workflow Mailer: Message Generation:

To set up Message Generation (see FIGURE 2.43):

- 'From' is the value that appears in the 'From' field of a Message Header.

- If 'Inbound Thread Count' is set to 1, specify the full email address of the mail account setup in the "Prerequisites" section of this chapter as the Reply-to Address. In 11i.ATG_PF.H.delta.3 (Rollup 3), this address is validated for the @ sign even if you are not allowing replies. If you are not allowing replies, enter noreply@noreply.com.

- 'HTML Agent' is the value of the 'Applications Web Agent' Profile Option. This is the 'HTML Agent' that handles Notification responses.

- Accept the default values for the Framework parameters.

- Check the 'Autoclose FYI' check box to automatically remove 'FYI' Notifications from the Worklist.

- Check the 'Reset NLS' check box to allow users to convert the NLS code set based on the user's preferences.

- Check the 'Inline Attachments' check box to display attachments in the body of the email.

- Choose to enable or disable the warning and cancellation emails by checking boxes or leaving them unchecked.

- Although not recommended, changing the Default Message Templates in the 'Templates' section of this screen is allowed.

- Click Next.

FIGURE 2. 43

Step 5 – Edit Workflow Mailer: Schedule Events:

To schedule Events to control running the Service Component at a specified time (see FIGURE 2.44):

- If anyone is using one of the Summary Email Notification Preferences, schedule the time and day to start sending summary emails and set the interval in minutes before restarting. 1440 minutes is 24 hours. You can tell if Summary Email Notification Preferences are being used by running the following query:

```
SELECT user_name FROM fnd_user_preferences
  WHERE module_name = 'WF' AND preference_name = 'MAILTYPE'
    AND preference_value IN ('SUMMARY', 'SUMHTML');
```

- Optionally, you can schedule Start, Refresh, Suspend, Resume or Stop Events for Service Components. Typically this would only be required for Custom Service Components. See *Chapter 13, New Features*, for an example of using scheduled Events to automatically stop and restart the Mailer.

- Click Next.

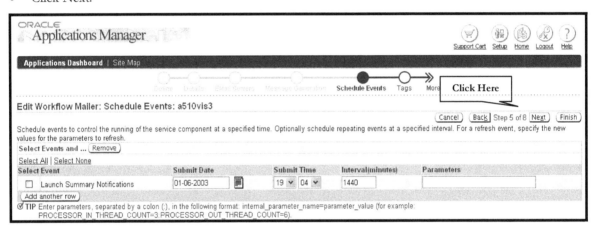

FIGURE 2. 44

Step 6 – Edit Workflow Mailer: Tags:

You can specify strings of text that identify unusual incoming Messages, such as returned or auto-reply Messages. Then you can specify the status to assign to Messages that contain those strings. The status determines how the Notification Mailer handles those Messages (see FIGURE 2.45).

- This step is a replacement for the wfmail.tag file required by the c-based Mailer. Tags allow the Notification Mailer to identify specific strings of text and respond appropriately. Consider adding a tag for out of office emails with an Action of Ignore.

- Click Next.

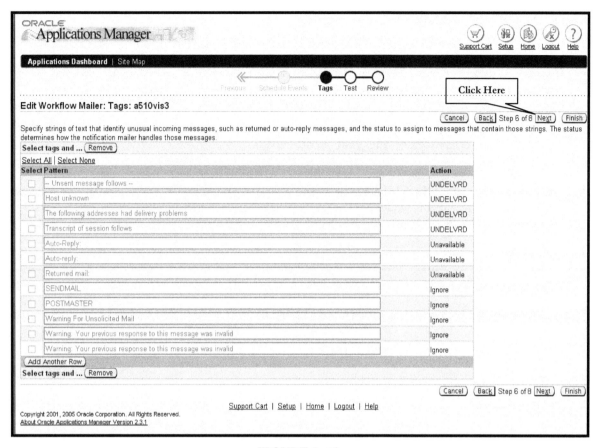

FIGURE 2. 45

Step 7 – Test the Notification Mailer

To test the Notification Mailer (see FIGURE 2.46):

• Click the flashlight to select a 'Recipient Role' with an email address to test the Notification Mailer.

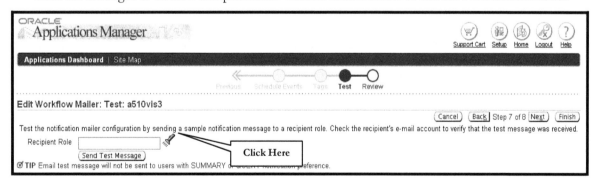

FIGURE 2. 46

• Click the 'Accept' button (See FIGURE 2.47).

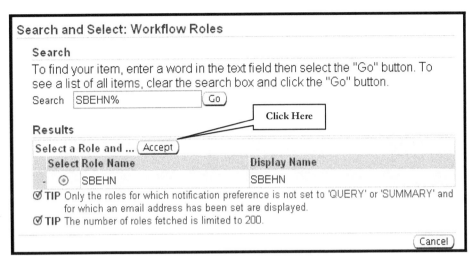

FIGURE 2. 47

- Click the 'Send Test Message' button (see FIGURE 2.48).

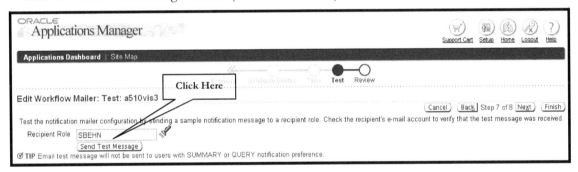

FIGURE 2. 48

- Verify that the email was received and that you can respond to the email (see FIGURE 2.49). Then click Next to review the 'Summary' page. If the settings are correct, click 'Finish' (see FIGURE 2.50).

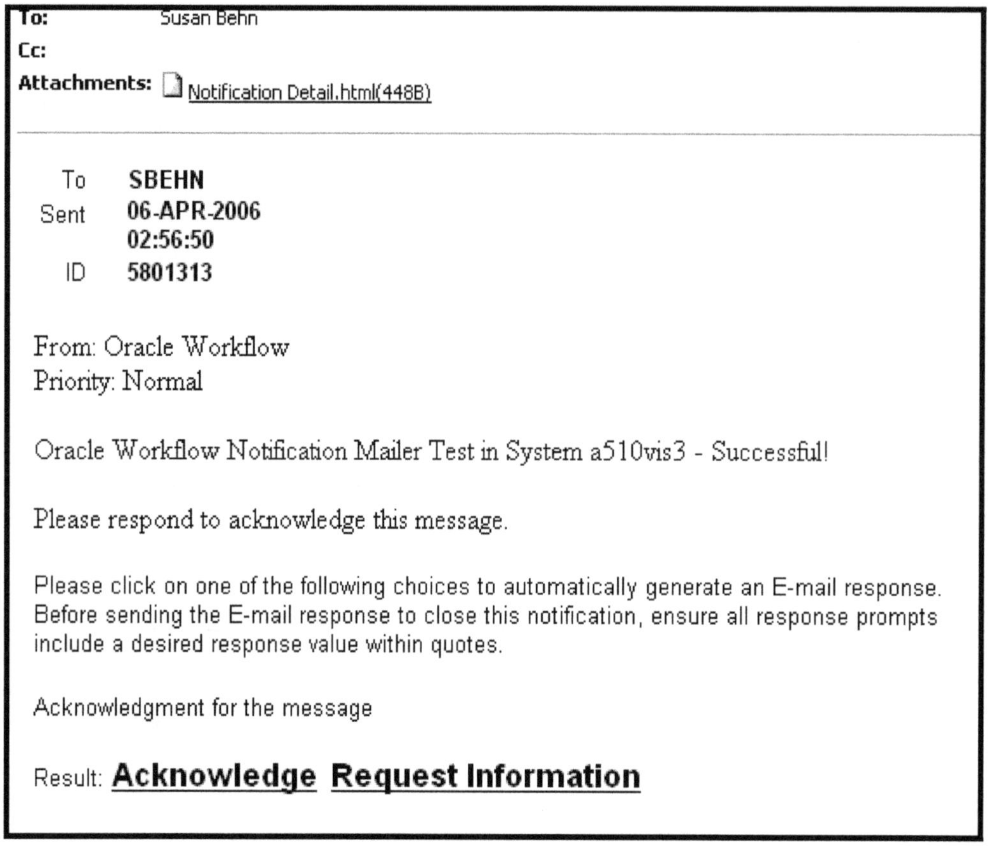

To: Susan Behn
Cc:
Attachments: ☐ Notification Detail.html(448B)

To   **SBEHN**
Sent   **06-APR-2006**
        02:56:50
ID   **5801313**

From: Oracle Workflow
Priority: Normal

Oracle Workflow Notification Mailer Test in System a510vis3 - Successful!

Please respond to acknowledge this message.

Please click on one of the following choices to automatically generate an E-mail response. Before sending the E-mail response to close this notification, ensure all response prompts include a desired response value within quotes.

Acknowledgment for the message

Result: **Acknowledge Request Information**

FIGURE 2. 49

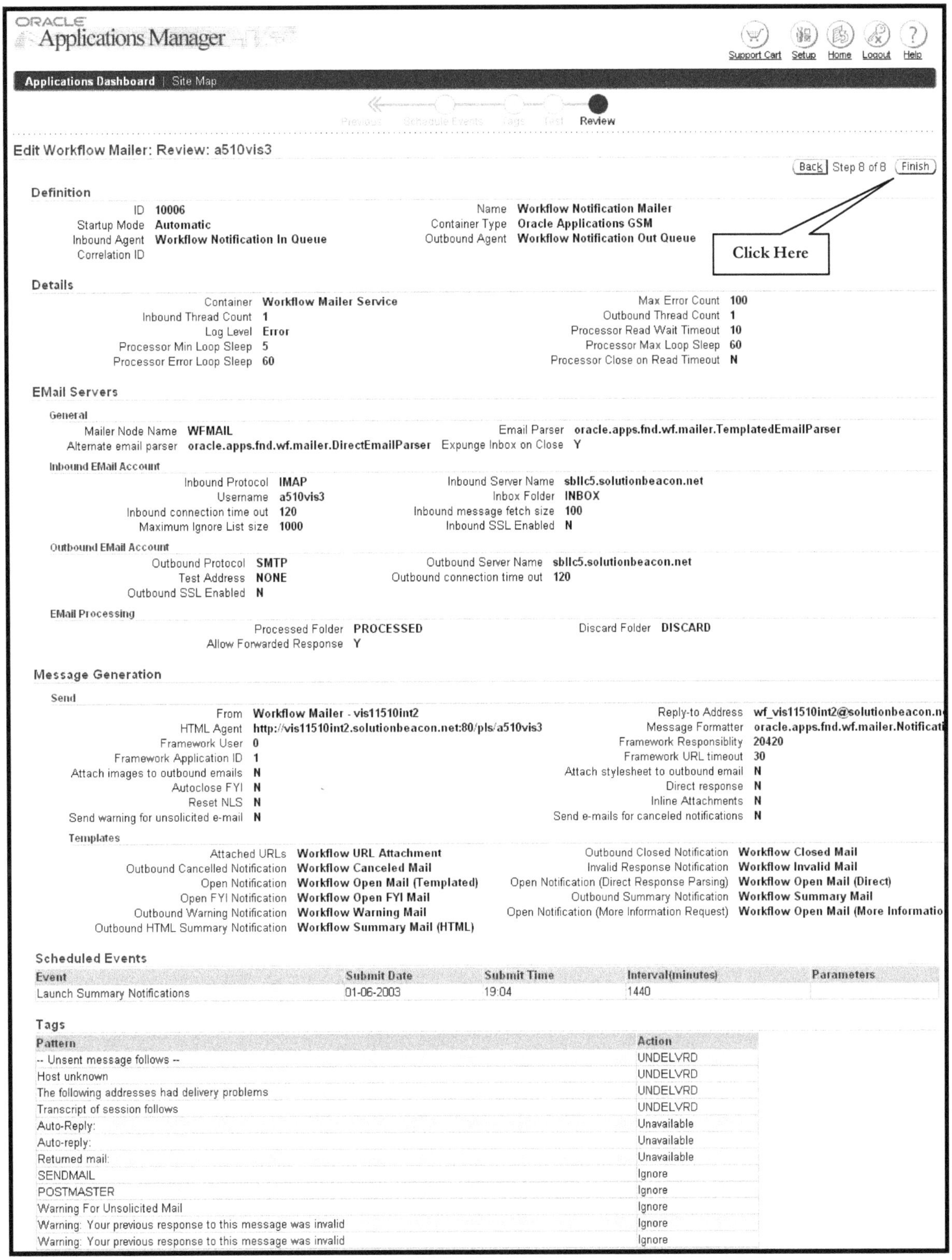

ORACLE
Applications Manager
Support Cart Setup Home Logout Help
Applications Dashboard | Site Map
Review
Edit Workflow Mailer: Review: a510vis3
Back Step 8 of 8 Finish
Click Here
Definition
ID 10006
Startup Mode Automatic
Inbound Agent Workflow Notification In Queue
Correlation ID
Name Workflow Notification Mailer
Container Type Oracle Applications GSM
Outbound Agent Workflow Notification Out Queue
Details
Container Workflow Mailer Service
Inbound Thread Count 1
Log Level Error
Processor Min Loop Sleep 5
Processor Error Loop Sleep 60
Max Error Count 100
Outbound Thread Count 1
Processor Read Wait Timeout 10
Processor Max Loop Sleep 60
Processor Close on Read Timeout N
EMail Servers
General
Mailer Node Name WFMAIL
Alternate email parser oracle.apps.fnd.wf.mailer.DirectEmailParser
Email Parser oracle.apps.fnd.wf.mailer.TemplatedEmailParser
Expunge Inbox on Close Y
Inbound EMail Account
Inbound Protocol IMAP
Username a510vis3
Inbound connection time out 120
Maximum Ignore List size 1000
Inbound Server Name sbllc5.solutionbeacon.net
Inbox Folder INBOX
Inbound message fetch size 100
Inbound SSL Enabled N
Outbound EMail Account
Outbound Protocol SMTP
Test Address NONE
Outbound SSL Enabled N
Outbound Server Name sbllc5.solutionbeacon.net
Outbound connection time out 120
EMail Processing
Processed Folder PROCESSED
Allow Forwarded Response Y
Discard Folder DISCARD
Message Generation
Send
From Workflow Mailer - vis11510int2
HTML Agent http://vis11510int2.solutionbeacon.net:80/pls/a510vis3
Framework User 0
Framework Application ID 1
Attach images to outbound emails N
Autoclose FYI N
Reset NLS N
Send warning for unsolicited e-mail N
Reply-to Address wf_vis11510int2@solutionbeacon.n
Message Formatter oracle.apps.fnd.wf.mailer.Notificati
Framework Responsiblity 20420
Framework URL timeout 30
Attach stylesheet to outbound email N
Direct response N
Inline Attachments N
Send e-mails for canceled notifications N
Templates
Attached URLs Workflow URL Attachment
Outbound Cancelled Notification Workflow Canceled Mail
Open Notification Workflow Open Mail (Templated)
Open FYI Notification Workflow Open FYI Mail
Outbound Warning Notification Workflow Warning Mail
Outbound HTML Summary Notification Workflow Summary Mail (HTML)
Outbound Closed Notification Workflow Closed Mail
Invalid Response Notification Workflow Invalid Mail
Open Notification (Direct Response Parsing) Workflow Open Mail (Direct)
Outbound Summary Notification Workflow Summary Mail
Open Notification (More Information Request) Workflow Open Mail (More Informatio
Scheduled Events
Event Submit Date Submit Time Interval(minutes) Parameters
Launch Summary Notifications 01-06-2003 19:04 1440
Tags
Pattern Action
-- Unsent message follows -- UNDELVRD
Host unknown UNDELVRD
The following addresses had delivery problems UNDELVRD
Transcript of session follows UNDELVRD
Auto-Reply: Unavailable
Auto-reply: Unavailable
Returned mail: Unavailable
SENDMAIL Ignore
POSTMASTER Ignore
Warning For Unsolicited Mail Ignore
Warning: Your previous response to this message was invalid Ignore
Warning: Your previous response to this message was invalid Ignore

FIGURE 2. 50

Setting an Override Notification Mailer Address

For non-production instances, you should set an override Mailer address to allow testing Notifications without sending Notifications to users who may confuse them with production Notifications.

Note that this functionality has moved in 11i.ATG_PF.H.delta.3 (Rollup 3) and now requires verification.

- From the OAM 'Notification Mailer' page, click the 'View Details' button (see FIGURE 2.51).

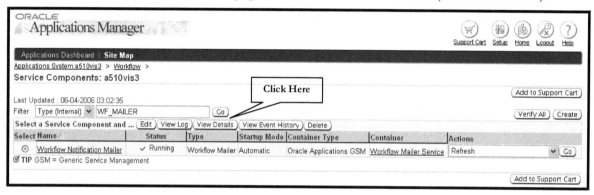

FIGURE 2. 51

- The 'Notification Mailer Details' page will appear. Click the 'Set Override Address' button (see FIGURE 2.52).

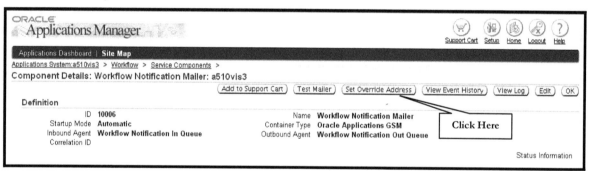

FIGURE 2. 52

- Enter the email address where you want to direct ALL Notifications and click 'Submit' (see FIGURE 2.53).

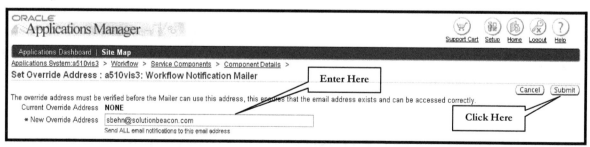

FIGURE 2. 53

- New ATG.PF_H.delta.3 (Rollup 3) functionality: You must wait until the email arrives for the override address (see FIGURE 2.54). This email will include a Verification Code that must be entered (see FIGURE 2.55). This prevents you from setting an override email address to an invalid or incorrect address which could result in sending an email with private information to an unintended recipient.

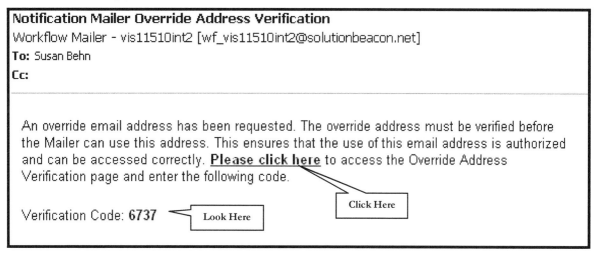

FIGURE 2. 54

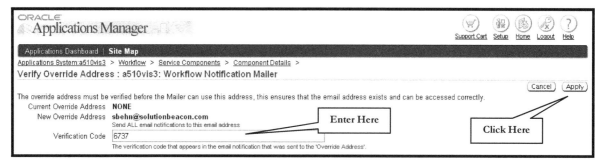

FIGURE 2. 55

- To clear the override address, go back to this page and click the 'Clear Override Address' button (see FIGURE 2.56).

FIGURE 2. 56

Responsibility Functions and Request Groups

Add Worklist Functions to other menus in System Administration → Application → Menu. The Function name is 'Advanced Workflow Worklist'. The sub-menu is 'Workflow User (New)'.

Vacation Rules

The default list of Item Types a user can select when creating Vacation Rules displays those Item Types for which the user has previously received at least one Notification. To allow users to create Vacation Rules for other Item Types, add the Item Type to the Lookup Code for the Lookup Type 'WF: Vacation Rule Item Types'. In earlier releases, this Lookup Type was called 'WF: Notification Rule Item Types'.

Note that the terminology has changed. 'Notification Rules' became 'Routing Rules', and are now called 'Vacation Rules'.

You can add items to the Lookup Code in the Application Developer Responsibility → Application → Lookups → Application Object Library

- Query for Meaning 'WF: Vacation Rule Item Types'. Add the Item Type and Meaning for Workflows you would like to include in the List of Values for Vacation Rules (see FIGURE 2.57).

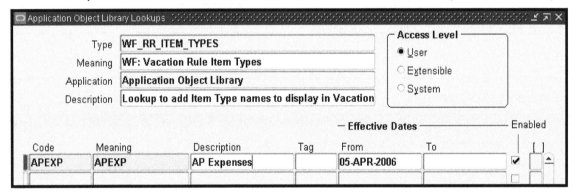

FIGURE 2. 57

- From the 'Home' page, the user can now set up Vacation Rules as shown in FIGURE 2.58 and FIGURE 2.59 for the Item Type that has been defined.

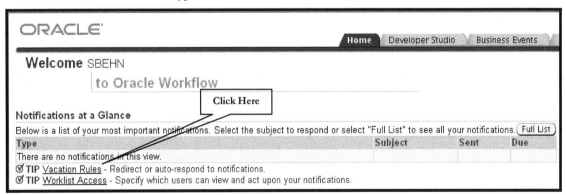

FIGURE 2. 58

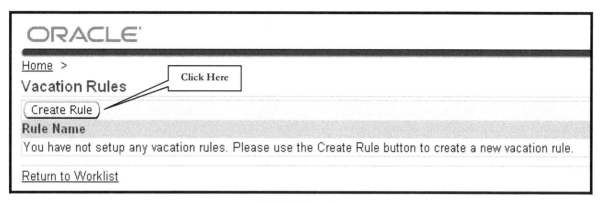

FIGURE 2. 59

- Click the 'Create Rule' button and then choose the 'Item Type' (see FIGURE 2.60).

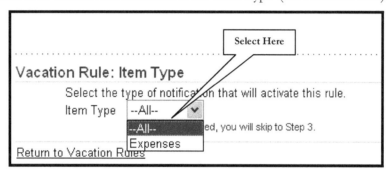

FIGURE 2. 60

Customize Logo

You can use your own logo that will appear on the Workflow pages. Create a logo file named FNDLOGOS.gif and store this file on the server in the virtual directory for OA_MEDIA.

Custom Icons

You can create custom icons to use in Workflow Builder that will subsequently appear in the Workflow Monitor. Store the .ico files on the desktop for Workflow Builder in <oracle home>/wf/icon. Convert the .ico files to .gif files and store on the server in the virtual directory for OA_MEDIA.

Verification Scripts

wfver.sql

The wfver.sql script is located in $FND_TOP/sql. As stated earlier in this chapter, the detailed information provided by this script can also be obtained using the Workflow Information Diagnostic (as of September 2007, this Diagnostic calls wfver.sql). Except for this Diagnostic, we cannot guarantee the details in the Diagnostic Reports exactly match the details in the sql scripts available in $FND_TOP/sql. As a general rule, the SQL scripts will be updated prior to the Diagnostic Reports, but the Diagnostic Reports are significantly more user friendly, provide information on how to correct errors, and include MetaLink Note references to support recommendations or to provide additional details. It is our recommendation that Diagnostic Reports be run on a monthly basis. If there are any problems that are not resolved by Diagnostic Reports, the next step should be to run the SQL scripts in $FND_TOP. Refer to *Chapter 9, Diagnostics*, for additional details on the Diagnostic Reports.

This script will provide details critical to determining whether or not the Workflow environment is configured correctly. If you open a Service Request (SR) on MetaLink regarding any issue with Workflow, Oracle Support will ask you to run this script and send the results. Therefore, prior to opening a Service Request, you should run this script and resolve any obvious problems first. For example, at a minimum, check the following items:

- Local system status must be enabled and active

- If you have any invalid objects, compile all objects and run this script again.

- Verify Agent Listeners are running

- Verify Queues are active

A partial sample output file is shown here. This script will typically return over 25 pages.

```
SQL> @wfver.sql
Server Version (last official install)
```

Workflow Version

```
Version
------------------------------
2.6.0


Local System Name
The Local System is ASSIGNED to A510VIS1.SOLUTIONBEACON.NET
PL/SQL procedure successfully completed.
```

Local System

```
Local System Status

Status
----------
ENABLED
```

Local System Status

```
Database Instance Details

Name                            Version              Status
------------------------------  -------------------  --------
a510vis1                        9.2.0.5.0            ACTIVE
```

init.ora parameters

Database Init.ora Parameter Values

```
Name                            Value
------------------------------  --------------------
aq_tm_processes                 1
job_queue_processes             10
nls_language                    american
nls_territory                   america
```

XML Parser
(1) Version
(2) Status

XML Parser version

```
Version
------------------------------------------------------
Oracle XML Parser      2.0.2.9.0      Production
```

XML Parser PL/SQL Package Installation Status

```
Status Details
------------------------------------------------------
INSTALLED and VALID in SYS Schema
INSTALLED and VALID in APPS Schema
```

XML Parser Schema Java Class Version

```
Status Details
------------------------------------------------------------------
/379229ed_javaxxmlparsersDocum INSTALLED and VALID in SYS Schema
/bc3b995a_javaxxmlparsersSAXPa INSTALLED and VALID in SYS Schema
README_xmlparser.txt INSTALLED and VALID in APPS Schema
xmlparser_2.0.2.1_production INSTALLED and VALID in APPS Schema
xmlparser_2.0.2.6_production INSTALLED and VALID in APPS Schema
xmlparser_2.0.2.7_production INSTALLED and VALID in APPS Schema
xmlparser_2.0.2.8_production INSTALLED and VALID in APPS Schema
xmlparser_2.0.2.9_production INSTALLED and VALID in APPS Schema
```

8 rows selected.

Queue Names/Status

Queue Information

```
Owner    Name                Status  Enqueue Dequeue Retries Retention  Delay
-------  ------------------  ------- ------- ------- ------- ---------- -------
APPLSYS  WF_CONTROL          VALID   YES     YES     5       0          0
APPLSYS  WF_DEFERRED         VALID   YES     YES     5       86400      3600
  .
  .
  .
24 rows selected.
```

```
Queue Subscriber Rule View Status
-------------------------------------------------------------
Queue_Name Name  Address  Protocol
-------------------------------------------------
AQ$_WF_DEFERRED_S Subscriber Information:
-------------------------------------------------
Queue Name : 0, Name : , Address : , Protocol :
Queue Name : WF_DEFERRED, Name : WF_DEFERRED, Address : , Protocol : 0
Queue Name : WF_DEFERRED, Name : , Address : APPLSYS.WF_DEFERRED, Protocol : 0
-------------------------------------------------
.
.
.
PL/SQL procedure successfully completed.

Queue Subscriber View Rules

AQ$WF_CONTROL_R Rules:
----------------------------------
(none)
.
AQ$WF_DEFERRED_R Rules:
----------------------------------
Name: WF_DEFERRED, Rule: 1=1
.
.
PL/SQL procedure successfully completed.

APPLSYS.AQ$_WF_CONTROL_S Subscriber Information:
SUBSCRIBER TYPE        COUNT
-------------------------------------------------
2                          67
4                           1
65                         10
1
-------------------------------------------------

PL/SQL procedure successfully completed.
```

Invalid Workflow PL/SQL Objects

```
Invalid PL/SQL Objects

no rows selected
```

PL/SQL Object Versions

```
PL/SQL Version Information

Name                          Type          Version
----------------------------  ------------  -----------------------------
WFJ_QUEUE                     PACKAGE       wfjques.pls 115.5 2002/12/03
WFJ_QUEUE                     PACKAGE BODY  wfjqueb.pls 115.5 2002/12/03
WF_ACTIVITIES_PKG             PACKAGE       wfacts.pls 115.15 2002/12/03
WF_ACTIVITIES_PKG             PACKAGE BODY  wfactb.pls 115.22 2003/03/27
WF_ACTIVITIES_VL_PUB          PACKAGE       wfdefs.pls 115.18 2002/12/03
```

```
WF_ACTIVITIES_VL_PUB              PACKAGE BODY wfdefb.pls 115.37 2004/06/29
WF_ACTIVITY                       PACKAGE      wfengs.pls 115.69 2004/06/24
 .
 .
 .
294 rows selected.
```

Workflow View Information

```
View Version Information

Name                            Status      View Text
------------------------------- ----------  -------------------------------
WF_ACTIVE_SUBSCRIPTIONS_V       VALID       SELECT evt.name EVENT_NAME, DECODE(
                                            evt.generate_function, NULL, DECODE
                                            (evt.JAVA_

WF_ACTIVITIES_VL                VALID       SELECT /* $Header: afwf.odf 115.140
                                             2004/08/24 12:29:41 ybreddy ship $
                                            */ B.ROWI
 .
 .
 .
79 rows selected.
```

WFT Versions

```
Workflow Definition (WFT) Version Information

Name     Display Name              Lang  Version
-------- ------------------------- ----- ----------------------------------
WFSNDPRT Workflow Send Protocol    US    wfsndprt.wft 115.7 2003/09/24
WFMAIL   System: Mailer            US    wfmail.wft 115.60 2004/06/23
WFDM     Document Management       US    fndwfstd.wft 115.42 2000/03/06
WFALERT  Periodic Alert            US    fndwfstd.wft 115.42 2000/03/06
```

WF Engine Status

```
Generated Static Engine Calls status
If package WF_FUNCTION_CALL is INVALID please recompile the file
$FND_TOP/patch/115/sql/wffncalb.pls and make sure there are no invalid
objects left

Name                            Type          Status
------------------------------- ------------- -------
WF_ENGINE                       PACKAGE       VALID
WF_ENGINE                       PACKAGE BODY  VALID
WF_ENGINE_UTIL                  PACKAGE       VALID
WF_ENGINE_UTIL                  PACKAGE BODY  VALID
WF_FUNCTION_CALL                PACKAGE       VALID
WF_FUNCTION_CALL                PACKAGE BODY  VALID

6 rows selected.
```

Agent Status

Service Component Agent Information

```
Agent Name                      System Name                       Status
------------------------------  ------------------------------  ---------
WF_CONTROL                      A510VIS1.SOLUTIONBEACON.NET       ENABLED
WF_DEFERRED                     A510VIS1.SOLUTIONBEACON.NET       ENABLED
WF_ERROR                        A510VIS1.SOLUTIONBEACON.NET       ENABLED
WF_NOTIFICATION_IN              A510VIS1.SOLUTIONBEACON.NET       ENABLED
WF_NOTIFICATION_OUT             A510VIS1.SOLUTIONBEACON.NET       ENABLED
```

Event Status

Service Component Control Events

```
Name                                               Type     Status      Licensed
-------------------------------------------------  -------  ----------  --------
oracle.apps.fnd.cp.gsc.SvcComponent.refresh        EVENT    ENABLED     Yes
oracle.apps.fnd.cp.gsc.SvcComponent.resume         EVENT    ENABLED     Yes
oracle.apps.fnd.cp.gsc.SvcComponent.start          EVENT    ENABLED     Yes
oracle.apps.fnd.cp.gsc.SvcComponent.stop           EVENT    ENABLED     Yes
oracle.apps.fnd.cp.gsc.SvcComponent.suspend        EVENT    ENABLED     Yes
oracle.apps.fnd.cp.gsc.bes.control.group           GROUP    ENABLED     Yes
oracle.apps.fnd.wf.mailer.Mailer.notification.summ EVENT    ENABLED     Yes
```

7 rows selected.

Notification System Status

Notification Subsystem Events

```
Name                                               Type     Status      Licensed
-------------------------------------------------  -------  ----------  --------
oracle.apps.wf.notification.cancel                 EVENT    ENABLED     Yes
oracle.apps.wf.notification.close                  EVENT    ENABLED     Yes
oracle.apps.wf.notification.denormalize            EVENT    ENABLED     Yes
oracle.apps.wf.notification.reassign               EVENT    ENABLED     Yes
oracle.apps.wf.notification.receive                GROUP    ENABLED     Yes
 .
 .
 .
```

17 rows selected.

Subscription Status

Service Component Control Event Subscriptions

```
Name
--------------------------------------------------
Subscription Rule Function      Subscription Out Agent          Status
------------------------------  ------------------------------  ----------
oracle.apps.fnd.cp.gsc.bes.control.group
WF_RULE.ERROR_RULE@A510VIS1.SO  WF_CONTROL@A510VIS1.SOLUTIONBE  ENABLED
LUTIONBEACON.NET                ACON.NET
```

```
oracle.apps.wf.notification.send.group
Not  Defined                    WF_NOTIFICATION_OUT@A510VIS1.S ENABLED
                                OLUTIONBEACON.NET

oracle.apps.wf.notification.send.group
wf_xml.SendNotification@A510VI Not Defined             DISABLED
S1.SOLUTIONBEACON.NET
```

Service Components

Service Component Types

```
Type                          Class
--------------------          ---------------------------------------
BASE                          oracle.apps.fnd.cp.gsc.SvcComponent
WF_AGENT_LISTENER             oracle.apps.fnd.wf.bes.AgentListener
WF_DOCUMENT_WEB_SERVICES
    oracle.apps.fnd.wf.ws.client.SOAPOutboundComponent
WF_JAVA_AGENT_LISTENER oracle.apps.fnd.wf.bes.AgentListenerNew
WF_MAILER                     oracle.apps.fnd.wf.mailer.Mailer
```

Service Components

```
Type                  Name                                Status
--------------------  ----------------------------------  --------------------
WF_AGENT_LISTENER     ECX Inbound Agent Listener          STOPPED
WF_AGENT_LISTENER     Workflow Deferred Agent Listener    RUNNING
WF_AGENT_LISTENER     Workflow Error Agent Listener       RUNNING
.
.
.
13 rows selected.
```

Queue Information

```
Notification Subsystem Queue Info
This requires package WF_QUEUE to be valid
----------------------------------------------------------------
WF_DEFERRED messages ready:0, waiting:19, expired:0, undeliverable:0,
processed:153
WF_NOTIFICATION_OUT messages ready:133564, waiting:0, expired:0,
undeliverable:0, processed:0
WF_NOTIFICATION_IN messages ready:0, waiting:0, expired:0, undeliverable:0,
processed:0
WF_ERROR messages ready:0, waiting:0, expired:16, undeliverable:0, processed:0

PL/SQL procedure successfully completed.

Other Invalid AOL PL/SQL Packages

no rows selected

GSM Profile Option Value

---------------------------------------------------
Enabled
```

```
ICM Status
--------------------------------------------------
ICM is running

PL/SQL procedure successfully completed.

Service Type Status
--------------------------------------------------
Generic Service Component Container is enabled

Service Instance Status
--------------------------------------------------
Workflow Document Web Services Service is enabled -> Actual: 1, Target: 1
Workflow Agent Listener Service is enabled -> Actual: 1, Target: 1
Workflow Mailer Service is enabled -> Actual: 1, Target: 1

PL/SQL procedure successfully completed.
```

┌────────────────────────────────────┐
│   Environment Variables   │
└────────────────────────────────────┘

```
Concurrent-tier Environment
------------------------------------------------------------
AFJVAPRG -
/oraappl/sb/a510vis1/a510vis1comn/util/java/1.4/j2sdk1.4.2_04/bin/java
AF_CLASSPATH -
/oraappl/sb/a510vis1/a510vis1comn/util/java/1.4/j2sdk1.4.2_04/lib/tools.jar:/or
aappl/sb/a510vis1/a510vis1comn/util/java/1.4/j2sdk1.4.2_04/lib/dt.jar:/oraappl/
sb/a510vis1/a510vis1comn/util/java/1.4/j2sdk1.4.2_04/jre/lib/charsets.jar:/oraa
ppl/sb/a510vis1/a510vis1comn/util/java/1.4/j2sdk1.4.2_04/jre/lib/rt.
   .
   .
   .
11 rows selected.

End of wfver.sql
```

WHAT'S NEXT

Generally, we find that Workflow setup actually occurs with relatively few problems if the steps in this chapter are followed closely. Additionally, we do not expect a significant amount of changes in the Workflow setup through the maturity of Release 12. Workflow is a very stable application that will be around throughout the Release 12 lifecycle. However, Oracle has announced that Workflow will be replaced by BPEL in the Fusion Applications. See *Chapter 15, What's on the Horizon* for more details. For this reason, we expect to see only critical bug fixes and very minor enhancements in Workflow functionality. We expect the same in the Workflow Builder product, which is discussed in the next chapter.

Builder Basics

The Workflow Builder is Oracle's PC-based graphical tool used to diagram Business Processes and define Attributes and Messages. The tool is most effective when used jointly by business users who own the process and the developers who will write PL/SQL, Java or Business Event Procedures. This tool can be used to modify existing Workflows or design new Workflows. The use of the word "designer" in this chapter refers to the person who actually uses the Builder to draw the Workflow. Regardless of whether your organization assigns this Role to the business users or someone in IT, it is critical that the business users determine the design and be involved in any subsequent changes.

This chapter will walk through designing a new Workflow that ensures employees are set up correctly. Obviously these Workflows will assume certain business rules. If your organization has different rules, then these Workflows will need to be modified.

The individual parts and fields will be explained as they are used. Readers are encouraged to use the Builder and follow along as the Workflow is designed.

A SAMPLE WORKFLOW – BUSINESS RULES

ABC Workflow Company hires several employees each month. When a new employee starts, at least two days are wasted ensuring the employee has the proper access to equipment and systems. ABC Workflow Company is running HR fully installed and tracks applicants. They want a process to reduce the time needed to setup access for a new employee. They have chosen Workflow as the solution. This Workflow will be started whenever a new employee is added or the applicant status changes to Employee.

Since the HR system allows the entry of employee records with a future start date, once an offer letter has been accepted, HR is supposed to record that the applicant has now become an employee and enter the employee's name, supervisor, position, start date, and cost center. Obviously, other information, such as salary and benefits choices, is also required, but this specific information is critical for the smooth operation of most of the 'Approval' Workflows. However, since the fields that store this information are not required fields, it is too easy to overlook entering this data. Therefore, we will use Workflow to validate the presence of this information and to remind HR if the information is missing.

The other critical piece of data is the employee's email address. Since HR typically does not manage the email system, a request to the email System Administrator must be generated, an email account set up, and the resulting address entered into the HR record.

It should be noted that Personalizations can be used to make any or all of these fields required. However, some of the information, such as the email address, is not usually assigned by the HR Department. If this field was made a required field, HR would not be able to enter any information until all the information, including the email address, was available.

In *Chapter 5, Business Events,* and *Chapter 11, Advanced Builder and PL/SQL,* the business rules for this Workflow will be expanded or modified to demonstrate other capabilities of the Builder tool. The abilities to easily modify a Workflow and to add additional business rules are a few of the many features that make the tool so powerful. Many people who read this will assert that they would have implemented the business rules in a different fashion with a different design. This again demonstrates the power of the tool. We encourage people to take the Workflow in these chapters, and use it to learn the tool, and then just experiment.

BUILDER TERMINOLOGY AND SYMBOLS

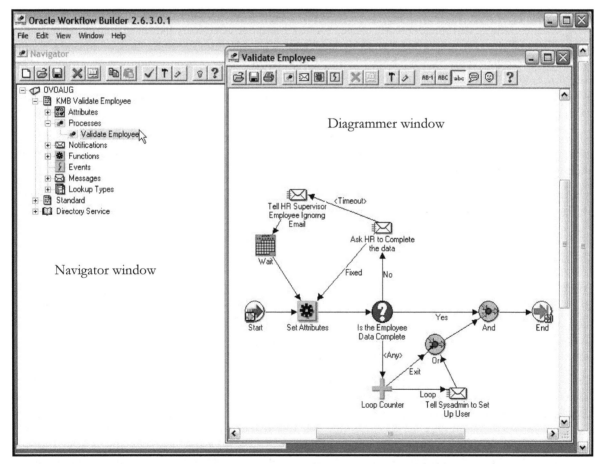

FIGURE 3. 1

FIGURE 3.1 shows that the Builder consists of two main parts, the Navigator window and the Diagrammer window. The Navigator contains the Workflow components grouped vertically in a structure similar to Windows directories. The Diagrammer window is the pictorial representation of a Process and the components in that Process. Many of the icons at the top of each window are standard:

Open ⬚, Save ⬚, Delete ✖, Copy ⬚, Paste ⬚, and Help ?. The other icons will be explained as they are used.

The top level in the Navigator window is the Datastore. The Datastore is represented by a yellow file folder ⬚ when not connected to a database and by a blue database icon ⬚ when connected to a database. This Datastore is the .wft file. Datastores can contain multiple Item Types or Workflows. Datastores are typically given the same name as the Internal Name of the main Workflow contained in that Datastore. POAPPRV.wft would therefore contain the POAPPRV Item Type. However, there is no rule that a Datastore can contain only one main Workflow or that the name of the Datastore must match the name of any of the contained Item Types. The point is, the Datastore or .wft file is not the Workflow; it contains the Workflow(s).

Underneath the Datastore are the Item Types. The Item Type is the Workflow and the terms 'Item Type' and 'Workflow' are used interchangeably. Each Workflow is represented by the ⬚ icon. Under each Item Type are the components used to define the Workflow: Attributes, Processes, Notifications, Functions, Events, Messages, and Lookup Types.

Included with every Datastore is the 'Standard' Item Type. This is a special Item Type that contains libraries of Functions and Lookup Types that can be used in the definition of other Item Types in the same Datastore. It is not a runnable Workflow.

Also included with every Datastore is the Directory Services node. This node allows the designer to load specific Roles from the database and use them as Performers.

GETTING STARTED

Determine the Item Key

Let's review some of the terms defined in *Chapter 1, Introduction*. The Workflow we will design is alternatively called an Item Type. This Item Type consists of all the Processes, Notifications, Functions, Events, Lookups and Attributes necessary to model the Process. To finish the definition, one must decide how to uniquely identify each running copy of the Workflow. This unique identifier is the Item Key.

A properly designed Item Key will allow the Workflow to derive all other data from the Item Key. Therefore, the Item Key is typically the key to the base table for the Business Process. If the table has multiple keys, the Item Key is comprised of all the keys concatenated together. Sometimes, even this is not enough to guarantee uniqueness. For example, if a requisition submitted for approval is rejected, the 'Requisition Approval' Workflow ends. However, the requisitioner can re-submit the requisition, which starts a new copy of the 'Approval' Workflow. If the Item Key is merely the key to the requisition table, it will error due to a non-unique Item Key when the requisition is re-submitted. Therefore, Oracle uses the key to the requisition table and concatenates a delimiter (usually a dash) and a number derived from a sequence. Since the sequence is incremented by 1 each time it is used, uniqueness is always guaranteed.

For our example, we will use the key to the employee table. The table PER_ALL_PEOPLE_F actually has three keys: EMPLOYEE_ID, EFFECTIVE_START_DATE and EFFECTIVE_END_DATE. But since there can only be one "active" record (active is defined as a record where the current date is between the EFFECTIVE_START_DATE and EFFECTIVE_END_DATE), the EMPLOYEE_ID and the date the Workflow started are sufficient to both uniquely identify the Workflow as well as find the appropriate record in the PER_ALL_PEOPLE_F table. Using the date the Workflow started replaces the need for creating and using a sequence as long as the representation of the date is fine-grained enough to guarantee that another Workflow for the same transaction cannot have that same date. This can usually be accomplished by using the following date representation: YYYYMMDDHH24MISS.

Oracle provides another field, 'User Key', which stores the user version of the Item Key. For example, the 'Requisition Approval' Workflow uses the REQUISITION_ID (plus the delimiter and sequence) as the Item Key, but sets the User Key to the requisition number. As most Item Keys are internal keys to tables that cannot be seen on the screen, Workflow designers should also set the User Key. This will be discussed further in *Chapter 4, Using PL/SQL in Workflow*.

For our example, the User Key will be set to the employee number.

 Define your Item Key as the key or keys to the transaction followed by a delimiter, and then by a sequence or the date the Workflow started. If multiple keys are used, separate the keys with the same delimiter. Define your User Key as the equivalent value as shown on the user's screen.

Open the Builder, Verify Access Level

- Click on the Workflow Builder icon on your desktop. The Builder will open showing a blank Navigator window and no Diagrammer window.

- At this point, stop and verify your 'Access Level'. The 'Access Level' assigned to new components is controlled through the 'Help' menu. Click Help → About Oracle Workflow Builder 2.6.3.0.1. It should be noted that this number can be modified at any time and changing this value does not change the 'Access Level' of current activities. See FIGURE 3.2:

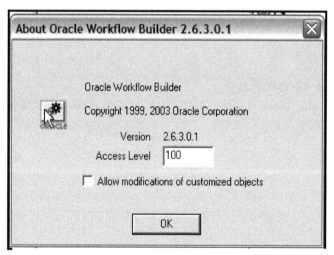

FIGURE 3. 2

- The 'Access Level' field works in conjunction with the 'Allow modifications of customized objects' and the 'Activity Access' tab fields 'Preserve Customizations' and 'Lock at this Access Level'. Together they control whether an Activity can be changed through the Builder and/or through the Workflow Loader program. Typically, the higher the number, the less access you have. Allowable values are 0-1000. Oracle reserves the numbers 0-99 for Oracle-defined activities and reserves the right to modify or delete any activity at these levels. Components delivered by the AOL group, such as the 'Standard' Item Type, are assigned the level 0. Components delivered by the individual applications, such as Purchasing, are assigned the level 20. Customer-designed Workflows and customizations to Workflows should be done at a level of 100 (or higher) unless you are customizing an Oracle- supplied Process that has been assigned a lower level.

- We also recommend un-checking 'Allow modifications of customized objects'. This will prevent Oracle from changing your customizations unless it matches your level exactly. See *Chapter 11, Advanced Builder and PL/SQL*, for further discussion of these features.

Define the Item Type and the Top Process – The Quick Start Wizard

Since our Workflow is a completely new Workflow, we will use the Quick Start Wizard.

- Using the menus at the top of the Builder, select File →Quick Start Wizard. A window pops open where the Item Type and first Process can be defined and a Datastore template is copied into the Navigator window (see FIGURE 3.3).

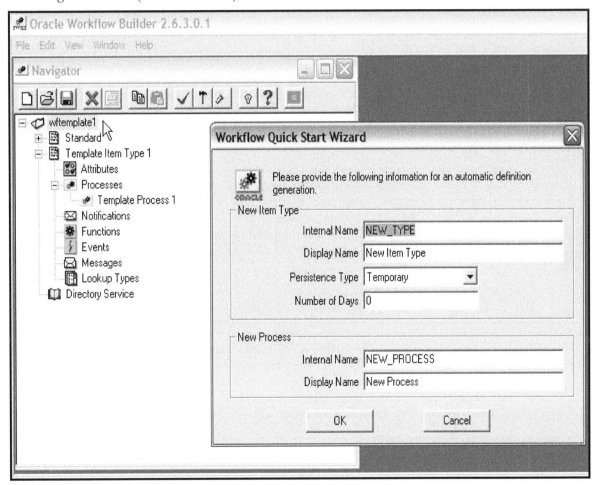

FIGURE 3.3

Note that in the Navigator window, the Datastore is called wftemplate1, the Item Type is called 'Template Item Type 1' and the Process is called 'Template Process 1'. Note also that our Datastore also contains the 'Standard' Item Type and a 'Directory Service' branch. Much more will be said about these two objects as we design our Workflow.

The New Item Type Internal Name is the Internal Name for the Workflow. It is limited to 8 characters. Oracle chose this limit for performance reasons, as this name is part of the primary key for nearly every Oracle table. This name must be unique across all Workflows.

Other component Internal Names allow 30 characters. All Internal Names prohibit leading or trailing spaces and colons (':'). Additionally, Oracle has reserved the characters '#' and '*' for special use. Oracle will force all Internal Names to be uppercase.

Avoid all special characters and limit the characters in all Internal Names to:
'ABCDEFGHIJKLIMNOPQRSTUVWXYZ0123456789_-'

- Once the OK button is pressed, Internal Names can only be changed using special Oracle scripts. See the *Oracle Workflow Administrator's Guide, Release 11.5.10 Part No. B15852-05, July 2006, or Release 12 Part No. B31431-01, December 2006,* for the scripts wfchita.sql, wfchact.sql, wfchacta.sql, wfchitt.sql, wfchluc.sql, wfchlut.sql, wfchmsg.sql, and wfchmsga.sql. These scripts and others are stored in the $FND_TOP/sql directory.

Normally custom objects are named XX<application short name><name>. For most applications this would use four or five of the available eight characters. However, this is still the only way to guarantee that Oracle will not suddenly deliver a Workflow with a name you've already chosen. So for our custom Workflow, we will use the Internal Name XXHRVEMP.

Display Names are used in most of the List of Values and are used as the labels in the 'Status Monitor'. The only rule or limitation is that the length cannot exceed 80 characters. The Display Name can be changed at any time. We will use 'XXHR Validate New Employee'.

For the Item Type Display Name, use XX<application short name> as the leading characters. This allows for easy loading into the Builder as well as ease of locating in the 'Status Monitor'.

It is not necessary to prefix Activity Internal Names (Process, Notification, Event, and Function) as they only need to be unique within the Item Type. Begin all Activity Internal and Display Names with a verb. The name of the activity should describe the purpose of the activity.

Identify the starting Process for the Workflow using words such as Top Process, Main, or Start. For Workflows with many Processes, this makes the identification of the first Process to open in the Builder much easier. We like to name the top Process the same name as the Workflow (minus the XX<app>), so our Process Internal Name will be 'VALIDATE_NEW_EMPLOYEE_TOP' with a Display Name of 'Validate New Employee Top Process'.

The last two fields, 'Persistence Type' and 'Number of Days', are used to determine how long to retain the Workflow runtime data once a Workflow is completed. As these values can be changed at any time, we will accept the defaults of Temporary and 0. Our screen now looks like FIGURE 3.4:

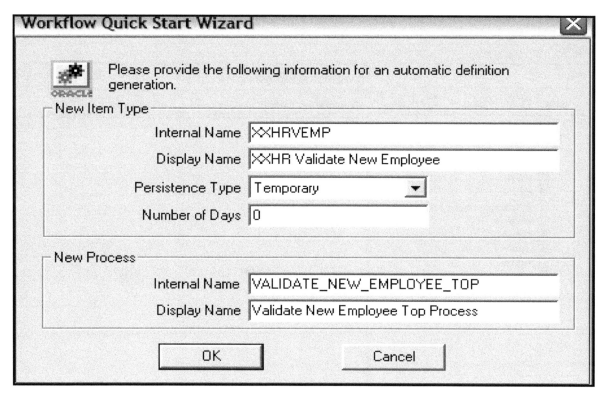

FIGURE 3. 4

- Click OK. The screen closes and is replaced by FIGURE 3.5. The Datastore name has been changed to Untitled-1, and the Item Type and Process now display our defined names. In addition, a Diagrammer window opens with a single Start and End Node.

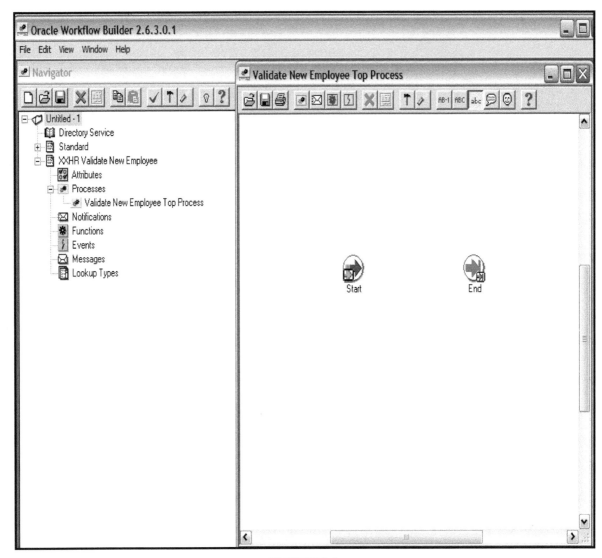

FIGURE 3.5

Finally, we are ready to model our Process.

Save Your Work FREQUENTLY

Workflow does not support autosave. If your PC crashes while you are working you will lose everything since your last save. Save frequently.

The first time you click the diskette icon or select File → Save, or File → Save As, the screen shown in FIGURE 3.6 appears. A subsequent selection of the diskette icon or File → Save will save the Datastore but will not display the screen.

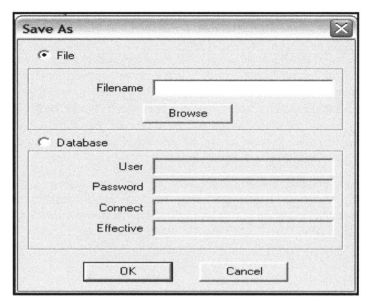

FIGURE 3.6

- Ignore the Database fields until you are finished or you need to access Directory Services. Click Browse, select a location on your PC or file server to save, give the file a name (you do not have to specify the .wft extension, Workflow will add that for you), and click OK. The name of the Datastore will now change from Untitled to the filename you just typed in. Remember that while the name of the Datastore is typically the same as the Item Type, it does not have to be. Also, data stores may contain multiple Item Types. See FIGURE 3.7:

FIGURE 3.7

PROCESS MODELING PHILOSOPHY

Business Processes are owned by the business, not IT. So when a designer can gather the appropriate business personnel into a room and have them describe a Process, the Process needs to be the focus. Questions like "Where does the Process start?", "What do you want to do next?", and "Does this require approval?" are questions that should be asked. Questions like "What should the Message say?", and "Can you define all the Rules in the approval hierarchy?" are better left for a subsequent session. Business owners don't care about PL/SQL Procedure naming standards. In other words, for the first session, cruise at the 100,000 foot level and leave the details for later.

Therefore, we suggest you define the bare minimum for each activity while focusing on the Process. Until the Process is complete, the only fields that will be specified are the Internal Name and Display Name (required fields for all activities) and, where needed, the Result Type. All the fields are discussed and defined either in this chapter or in *Chapter 6, Testing Workflows*.

 Focus initially on the Process, not the details.

ACTIVITIES

Workflow supports four kinds of Activities: Processes, Notifications, Functions, and Events. Events are discussed in *Chapter 5, Business Events*. Notifications send Messages to a user or a Role. The Notification can require a response or it can simply provide information (called an 'FYI' Notification). Functions represent a PL/SQL Stored Procedure. Thus, Functions are required when information needs to be retrieved from or supplied to the database. Processes are a collection of activities that determine the Action to be taken in the Workflow.

We can't think of a single Workflow that can operate with just the Item Key as the sole piece of information. Therefore, the first node of the Workflow should gather all the other information the Workflow will need. At this point, we don't need to know which particular additional pieces are needed; just that additional information will be needed. So the first activity will be a function.

It should be noted that if the Workflow is started from a screen or a program it is possible to set up all this additional information prior to transferring control to the Start Node. However, this approach is not possible for Workflows started from Events (see *Chapter 5, Business Events*); and as will be shown in *Chapter 4, Using PL/SQL in Workflow*, if the additional information is obtained before the execution of the Start Node, it severely complicates testing.

Function Without a Result

So our first activity in every Workflow is to have a Function that gathers any other required information. We always call this activity 'Set Attributes', as the additional information will be stored as Attributes.

Activities can be added by right-clicking the desired branch in the Navigator window and selecting 'New <activity type>', through the 'Edit' menu (Edit → New → <component>), by clicking the appropriate icon at the top of the Diagrammer window (in order, Process, Notification, Function, Event), or by right-clicking in the white space of the Diagrammer window and selecting 'New <activity type>'. If the activity is added by clicking 'New <activity type>' from the Navigator window, the resulting activity will have to be drag-and-dropped to the Diagrammer window, so we prefer to use either of the Diagrammer window methods.

FIGURE 3.8 shows the choices when right-clicking in the Diagrammer window.

FIGURE 3.8

Select 'New Function' to open the 'Function Properties' page (FIGURE 3.9).

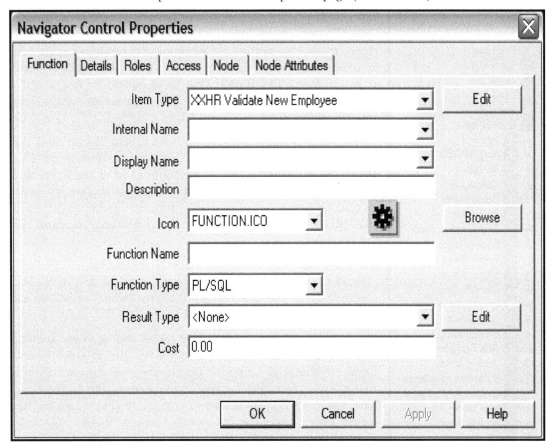

FIGURE 3. 9

The only required fields are Internal Name and Display Name. If the Display Name isn't enough to state the purpose of the node, then also add the Description. All other fields can be filled in later. Remember, focus on defining the Process, not the details of each activity. The purpose of this activity is to gather the rest of the information the Workflow needs and store this information in Attributes (we will discuss how to define these Attributes later). Therefore, the Internal Name will be SET_ATTRIBUTES and the Display Name will be 'Set Attributes'. Click OK. The definition box closes, and the diagram now displays a blue box with a gear inside (the default Function icon) labeled 'Set Attributes' (FIGURE 3.10).

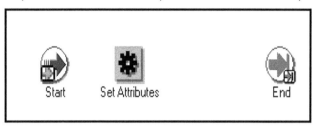

FIGURE 3.10

Function With a Result

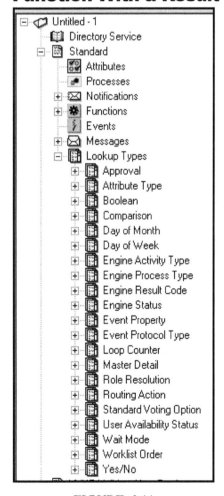

FIGURE 3.11

In our example, the next step in the process will be to check to see if all the required data for the employee was entered. Since this time we plan on having the Workflow behave differently depending on whether the data is complete or not, we must add a device to the Function so the Workflow can progress to different activities based on the result of the function. This device is called a Result Type. The Result Type is associated with a specific Lookup Type. The Lookup Type is a finite set of static values called Lookup Codes.

Remember when we invoked the Quick Start Wizard and the Builder added the 'Standard' Item Type to our Datastore? This Item Type contains a library of Functions and Lookup Types that can be used in any Workflow. In the Navigator window, click the + next to 'Standard', then the + next to Lookup Types. See FIGURE 3.11 for the seeded Result Types when 'Standard' has not been modified.

The most used Result Types are: Yes/No, Approval, and Boolean (True/False). If the value you need is not in the List of Values, you will have to define a new Lookup Type (which we will do for a later activity).

Using any of the methods described above, choose to add another new function. This time, in addition to the Internal Name, Display Name, and (optional) Description, we must specify the Result Type. Note that for display purposes in the Monitor, we have made the Display Name a question, so that values for the Result Type answer the question. Choose a 'Result Type' that matches the question (see FIGURE 3.12).

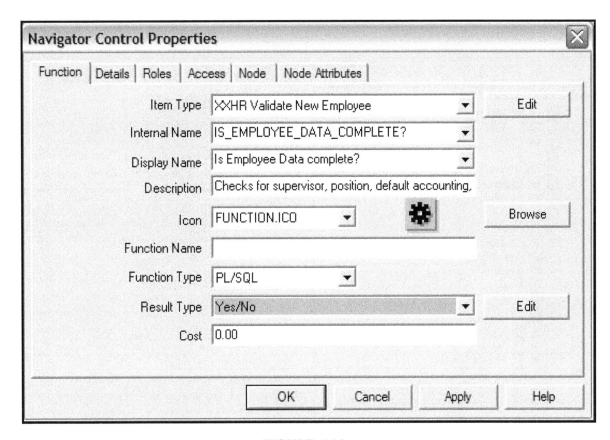

FIGURE 3.12

Our Workflow now looks like FIGURE 3.13.

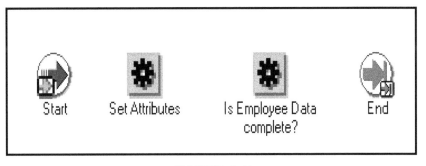

FIGURE 3.13

Our next task is to decide what to do if the answer is 'Yes' and what to do if the answer is 'No'.

Notifications – FYI vs. Response Required

For our example, if the answer is No, we will send a Notification to someone in HR and ask him/her to complete the data entry. This requires defining a Notification. From a design point, we have to decide whether a response to the Notification will be required. Our choices are to send an 'FYI' Notification and hope someone reads and acts on it, or to send a Notification and require a response. Note that when an 'FYI' Notification is sent, the Workflow moves immediately to the next node, while when a

'Response-Required' Notification is sent, the Workflow stops until the Notification is acted upon. Since we want to ensure the data is entered, we will require a response.

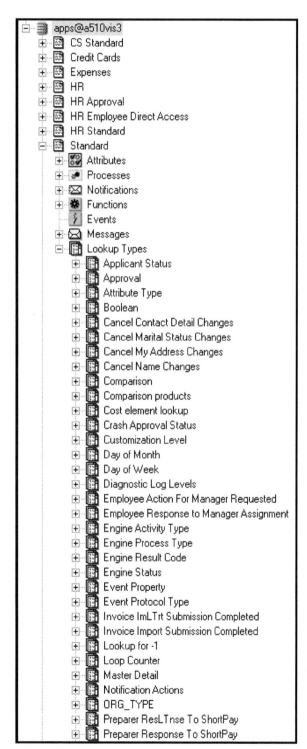

FIGURE 3.14

Custom Lookup Type and Lookup Code(s)

Although we haven't crafted what the Notification should say, all the Lookup Types in 'Standard' have at least two Lookup Codes. We don't want to give the user a choice of response ('Would you like to complete the missing setups? Please answer Yes or No'). We want to say something like 'The setups are missing. Fix them. Press the OK button when finished', so we will create a Lookup Type with a single Lookup Code.

Like Item Type, the Internal Name for the Result Type must be unique across the entire database. This might suggest that new Lookup Types should be added to 'Standard'. They shouldn't. 'Standard' is Oracle's library and is subject to being overridden by any patch. In addition, if you add your custom Lookup Type to 'Standard', you run the risk that anytime a Workflow is loaded that uses 'Standard', it will require your Workflow to be loaded also. We call this "Bringing along friends." It causes load times into the Builder to be horribly long. FIGURE 3.14 is the result of loading the Item Type 'Expenses' ('Expense Report Approval' in *i*Expenses) from Oracle's Release 11.5.10 Vision database. 'Expenses', 'HR' and 'HR Employee Direct Access' Item Types added custom Lookup Types to 'Standard'. Now they must all be loaded together.

If you think your Lookup Type is going to be used for several Workflows, then create an Item Type just to hold your custom Lookup Types (see 'PO Standard' Item Type for an example). For our example, we will just add it to our custom Workflow.

The only way to create a new Lookup Type is through the Navigator window. (Lookup Types are not activities, so they cannot be defined in the Diagrammer window). Using either the 'Edit' menu or right-clicking the Lookup Type branch and selecting 'New', open the 'Properties' page.

Oracle recommends using either the Item Type Internal Name or the application shortname as the prefix. Remember, the Lookup Type is not the code; it is the name for the group of codes. So if you were defining a Lookup Type for the codes Red, White, Blue, you might call the Lookup Type <prefix>_ COLORS. In our case, we just need to pause the Workflow so the person receiving the Notifications has enough time to correct the situation. So our Lookup Type definition looks like FIGURE 3.15.

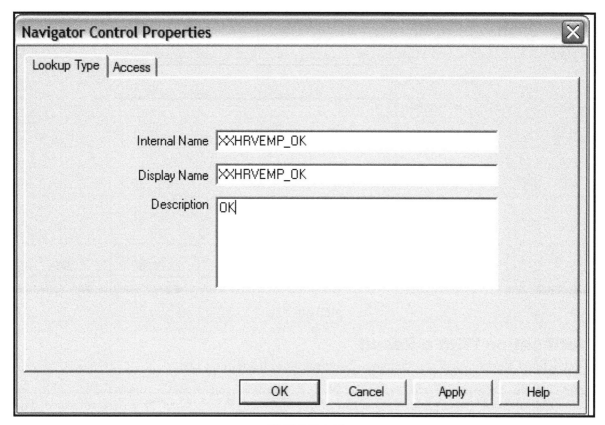

FIGURE 3.15

To create the actual codes for our new Lookup Type, right-click the Lookup Type and select New Lookup Code. While the Lookup Type must be unique across the database, the Lookup Code only has to be unique within the Lookup Type. The value entered for the Display Name determines what the buttons at the bottom of the Notification will say, so our Lookup Code will look like FIGURE 3.16.

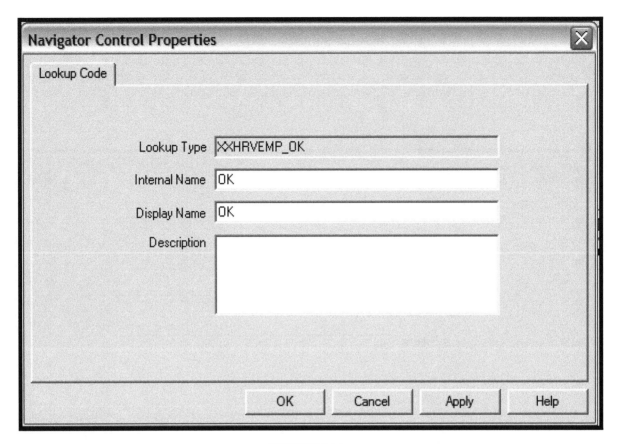

FIGURE 3.16

Notification With a Result

After defining the Lookup Type, defining a Notification with a result is easy.

Right-click the Diagrammer window, select 'New Notification' and enter the Internal Name, Display Name and (optional) Description. Use the List of Values to select the Lookup Type we just created. The values are listed alphabetically (see FIGURE 3.17).

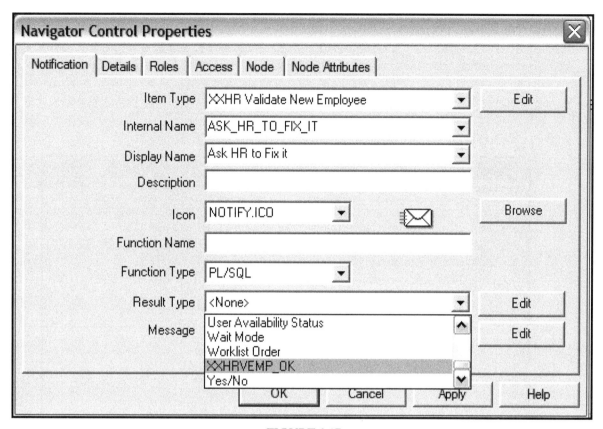

FIGURE 3.17

Our Workflow now looks like FIGURE 3.18.

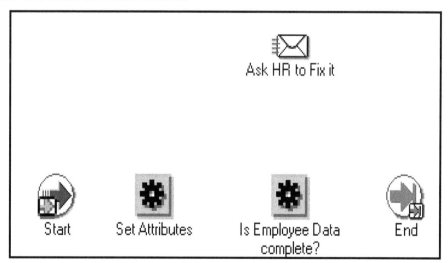

FIGURE 3.18

Time to Save Again

Each time you save the file, Workflow will validate your design and report on any errors found. Workflow performed this validation when we did our initial save after finishing the QuickStart Wizard, but since there weren't any activities, no errors were found. Meanwhile, we have been creating activities with just the minimal information needed to draw our Process. Our 'Save' Process will now display a page like FIGURE 3.19.

At this point, just ignore the errors, click the 'Save' button and keep designing.

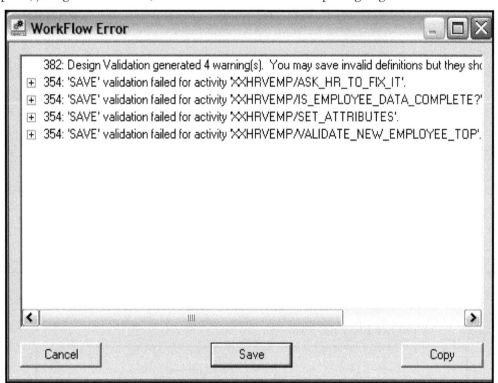

FIGURE 3.19

CONNECT THE DOTS – TRANSITIONS

Once you have defined any two activities, you can join them with a Transition Line.

Hold the cursor over the Start Node, click the right mouse button and while still clicking the right mouse button, drag the cursor over to the End Node. When the tiny black arrow appears under the cursor, you can release the mouse button. An arrow is drawn connecting the activities. If the End Node has no Result Type associated with it, that's the end of making the connection. See FIGURE 3.20

FIGURE 3. 20

If the start point has a Result Type, a window opens showing each of the values for the Lookup Type associated with the Result Type, plus the following – Default, Any, and (if a Timeout is defined), Timeout (see FIGURE 3.21). Results is the title for this box; it is not selectable.

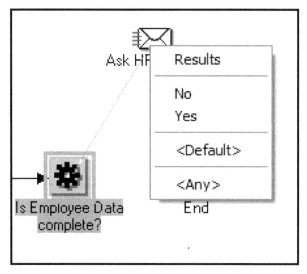

FIGURE 3.21

In this case we'll select the value 'No' as we only want to send the Message if the data is incomplete. The Builder will draw the arrow and label the arrow with the value we selected. If the label is not placed where it can be easily read, you can drag and drop the Label to any part of the arrow. The arrow also can be bent by right-clicking anywhere on the arrow and dragging to form a point. If you need to start over on drawing the line, you can right-click the line and select 'Delete Selection'. Notice that you can also change the value you selected if you picked the wrong one (see FIGURE 3.22).

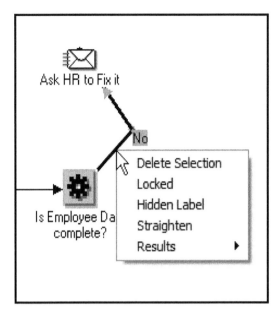

FIGURE 3.22

Finish drawing the lines by drawing a line from 'Is Employee Data complete?' to 'End' (choose the Result 'Yes') and from 'Ask HR to Fix it' to 'Is Employee Data complete?' (choose the Result OK. The Workflow now looks like FIGURE 3.23.

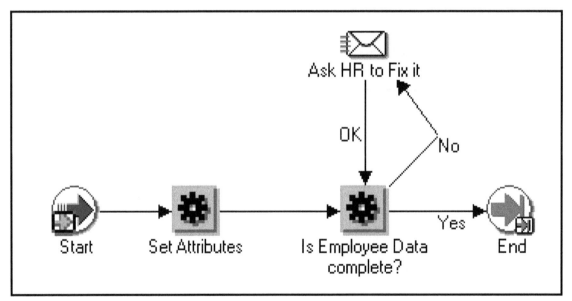

FIGURE 3.23

Note that this design chooses to have the line from 'Ask HR to Fix it' go back to 'Is Employee Data complete?' rather than to the End Node. By doing this the Workflow will verify that HR really did enter the missing data and that they entered ALL of the missing data.

Save the Workflow again. Ignore the errors.

THE DIAGRAM IS COMPLETE, BUT IS THE PROCESS?

Now is the time to look at the Process and see if there are any issues. We are sending a Notification to HR if the data is incomplete, but what if HR misses the Notification or just chooses not to answer it? The Workflow will stop at the Notification and never finish (and we still may not have complete data for the employee). One reason that HR may not have answered the Notification or finished the setup is that HR doesn't have all the information. Email addresses are set up by the email System Administrator. So if the only missing information is the email address, send the Notification to the email administrator, not HR. And since the email administrator will not have access to the HR screens, we ask the email administrator to enter the new email address in the Notification response and let the Workflow do the update. And we'll add a Timeout to the Notification to HR, re-verify the data, and if still bad, send another Notification. In order to avoid a permanent loop, we limit the reminders to 3 and then escalate the request to the HR manager. Remember, save your work frequently.

PROPERTY PAGE – NAVIGATOR VS DIAGRAMMER WINDOW

Except for Processes, double–clicking an activity in either the Navigator or Diagrammer window will open the 'Properties' page. The 'Properties' page for Messages, Lookup Types, and Lookup Codes is only available from the Navigator window. For Processes, the only way to open the 'Properties' page is to right–click the name of the Process in the Navigator window. The tabs available in the 'Properties' page vary based on whether the page was opened from the Navigator or Diagrammer window. The tabs for '<activity type>', 'Details', 'Roles', and 'Access' are always shown except for Lookup Types (missing 'Details' and 'Roles') and Lookup Codes (missing 'Details', 'Roles' and 'Access'). Messages have the tabs 'Body' and 'Result' and are missing 'Details'. The tabs 'Node', 'Node Attributes', and 'Event Details' are only shown when the Properties page is opened from the Diagrammer window. Keep this in mind when reading the rest of this chapter and *Chapter 5, Business Events*.

STANDARD ACTIVITIES – COMPARE

In addition to a library of Lookup Types, the 'Standard' Item Type provides a library of Functions. Three of these Functions are 'Compare Date', 'Compare Number', and 'Compare Text'. We can use the 'Compare Text' Function to validate whether there is an email address.

Open the 'Standard' Item Type (click the + next to 'Standard'). Open the Function tree. Drag-and-drop the 'Compare Text' icon to the Diagrammer window. Create the Notification to the email administrator, and then create the Function to update the database (see FIGURE 3.24 and FIGURE 3.25 for sample definitions).

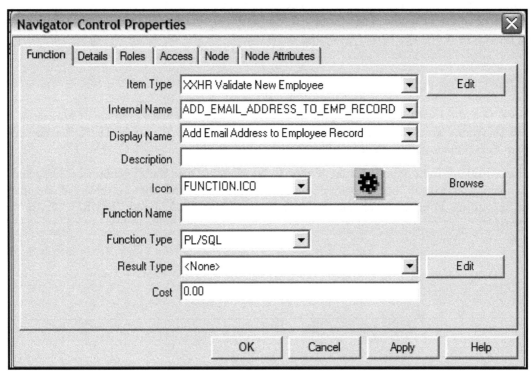

FIGURE 3.24

FIGURE 3.25

Be Careful Not to Add Activities to Standard

If you created the new Notification by clicking in the Diagrammer window, verify that the Item Type says 'XXHR Validate New Employee' and not 'Standard'. If you created the new Notifications using the Navigator window, the Item Type line does not display; instead, your last activity prior to the Notification was to drag a Function from 'Standard' and you just created the new Notification in the 'Standard' Item Type. (Delete it and recreate it in 'XXHR Validate New Employee'.)

Dragging-and-dropping is not the only Action that will cause the 'Standard' Item Type to open and become the Navigator default Item Type. Any time an activity copied from 'Standard' is touched in the Diagrammer window, the 'Standard' Item Type opens in the Navigator window and becomes the default Item Type. As you practice with Workflow, you will learn to see the motion of the 'Standard' Item Type opening. Designers can avoid most of the problems with accidentally placing activities in the 'Standard' Item Type by using the Diagrammer window to add the activities.

RESULTS <DEFAULT> AND <ANY>

Delete the line between 'Set Attributes' and 'Is Employee Data complete'. Now draw a line from 'Set Attributes' to 'Compare Text' and from 'Compare Text' to 'Is Employee Data Correct'. When the mouse is released, FIGURE 3.26 displays:

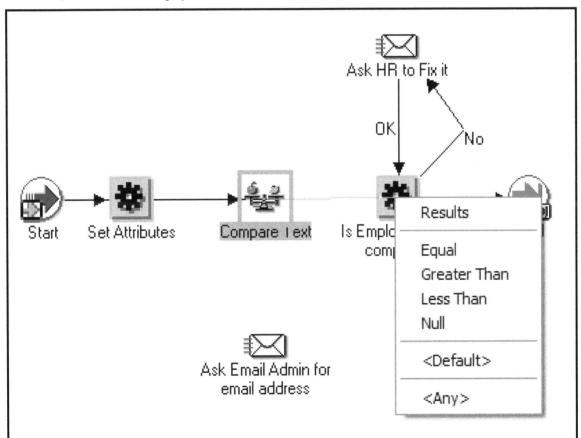

FIGURE 3.26

If the email address is missing (Null) we want to send a Notification to the email administrator. Otherwise, the email address exists (and is, therefore, Not Null), so the Workflow can move to the next node to check the rest of the data. When a Result Type only has two results (like 'Yes' or 'No'), modeling the "else" is easy ('Not Yes' = 'No'). But when the Result Type has more than two results, else becomes 'not answer A'. This is where <Default> is used. When a leg is labeled <Default> the Workflow Engine compares the answer from the Function to the label on each leg. If it doesn't find a matching leg, it takes <Default>. So for our Workflow, we label the leg from 'Compare Text' to 'Ask Email Admin for email address', Null, and from 'Compare Text' to 'Is Employee Data complete', <Default>.

<Any> is used to direct the Workflow Engine to travel a path regardless of the answer. This can be used to have the Workflow follow a second path in addition to the result, i.e., regardless of whether the email address is null, do a second task in parallel to the path taken based on the email address value. Or it can be used in place of <Default> to indicate that if the email address is null, start a secondary path that sends a Notification to the email administrator and then always (regardless of the value of the email address) proceed to node 'Is Employee Data complete'.

It should be noted that Builder requires all possible results to be modeled. Using <Any> or <Default> satisfies this requirement.

FIGURE 3.27 and FIGURE 3.28 show the difference between using <Default> or <Any>. Assume the email address is null. In FIGURE 3.27, the <Default> leg will not be taken, so the check for the rest of the employee data will not be processed until the email administrator answers the Notification.

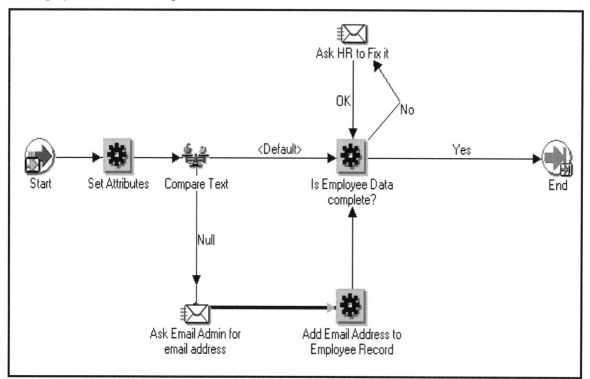

FIGURE 3.27

In FIGURE 3.28 the check for the employee data is done at the same time as the Notification to the email administrator.

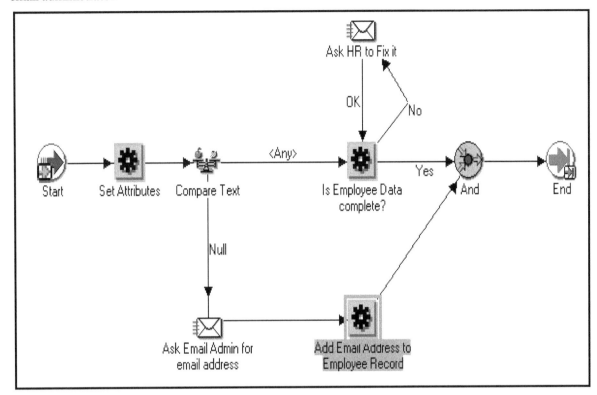

FIGURE 3.28

STANDARD ACTIVITIES – AND VS. OR

Choosing the second picture allows the work to be done in parallel, allowing both to be worked on at the same time. However, once a parallel track is introduced, the designer must plan for bringing the paths back together again (See FIGURE 3.28). Oracle provides the And and Or 'Standard' activities to accomplish this. The And Activity requires all incoming legs to be complete before proceeding down the Outbound leg. The Or Activity will activate the Outbound leg as soon as the first Inbound leg is completed.

In FIGURE 3.28, if an Or Activity had been used in place of an And Activity, and the email address was null, the Workflow will send the Notification to the email administrator (note: at this point in time the Notification is an 'FYI' Notification and therefore the Workflow will immediately proceed to the next node), then progress through the Package node, then progress through the Or node and immediately to the End Node. At this point the Workflow will stop.

If the other leg of the Workflow sent the Notification 'Ask HR to Fix it', this Notification will suddenly be invalidated, as the Workflow has now ended.

TIMEOUTS

If a Notification requires a response, the Workflow pauses until the response is received. If the Business Process is critical, waiting an unspecified amount of time is not acceptable. Therefore, the designer can set a limit on how long the Workflow should wait for an answer. This limit is called a 'Timeout'. 'Timeouts' can also be added to certain Functions, such as 'Block'. An example of where this is useful will be shown in *Chapter 12, Most Commonly Used Workflows*.

'Timeouts' are specified in the Node tab of the 'Properties' page of the Activity. Double-click the Activity to open the 'Properties' page, and then click the Node tab. The 'Timeout' can be set to a variable value (choose 'Item Attribute') or a fixed length of time (choose Relative Time). Unfortunately, Workflow does not recognize work calendars, so whether the value is fixed or variable, the expiration date is set by adding the 'Timeout' value to the date and time the Notification is sent. In our example (see FIGURE 3.29), the 'Timeout' is set for one day. If the original Notification is sent Friday at 4:30 PM, the Notification will time out Saturday at 4:30 PM. Thus, many organizations assign a variable value and write custom code to simulate the work calendar.

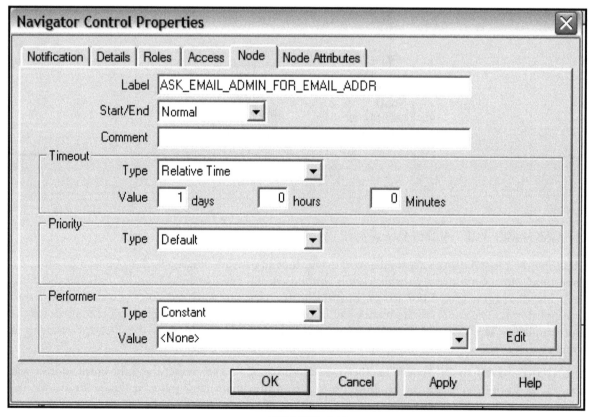

FIGURE 3.29

MetaLink Doc. ID: 50468.1, *WF 2.0.x: How to Create Dynamic Timeouts in Workflow Processes v 2.0.2 & Earlier* contains a simple algorithm that can be used to calculate Business Days.

One option when a Notification times out is to resend the Notification. This cancels the first Notification and re-starts the Timeout clock. To implement this option, right-click the node and drag the mouse away from the node then back to it. Release the mouse. A light blue line will be drawn (in FIGURE 3.30, it is the triangle) and the 'Results' page will display. Select the result <Timeout>. We will demonstrate later in this chapter using a Timeout to escalate a Notification.

Note that if a Timeout is defined, then <Timeout> is now another choice in the Results; therefore, there MUST be a leg emanating from the Notification assigned to the result <Timeout>. Unlike other results, Timeout is NOT included in <Default> or <Any>. As modeled in FIGURE 3.30, this loop will continue until the Notification is answered.

The Timeout loop back to itself will be a light blue triangle in FIGURE 3.30. It always draws on top of the object, so if the designer wishes to move the loop to the bottom of the object, use the mouse to grab each point and drag it. (Still remembering to save your work?)

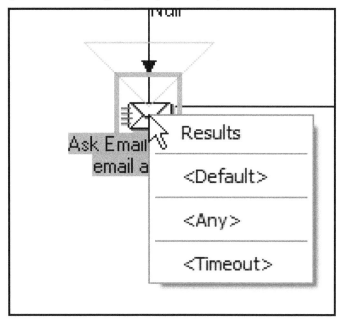

FIGURE 3.30

STANDARD ACTIVITY – LOOP COUNTER

Sometimes the designer needs to limit the number of times a Notification can Timeout (and loop back to itself or another Activity) before another Action is taken (such as escalating the Notification to another person). The Requisitions (REQAPPRV) Workflow accomplishes this by sending the Notification up to three times (see FIGURE 3.31).

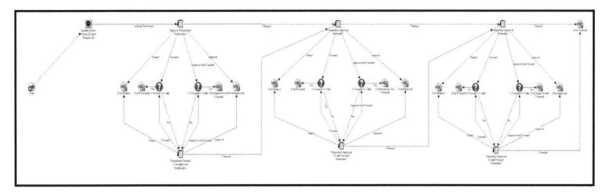

FIGURE 3.31

In our example Workflow, if 'Ask HR to Fix it' times out, we'd like to return to 'Is Employee Data complete?' since it is possible that HR fixed the data but didn't respond to the Notification. However, we don't want to get stuck in this loop. So we are going to use the 'Standard' Activity 'Loop Counter' to limit the number of times we repeat the Notification. If we exceed the limit (and exit the loop), we will escalate the Notification to the HR Manager. Delete the 'No' line between 'Is Employee Data complete?' and 'Ask Hr to Fix it' and drag the 'Ask HR to Fix it' up. Set the Timeout on 'Ask HR to Fix it' to a relative time of one day. Define the Notification that will serve as the escalation (see FIGURE 3.32).

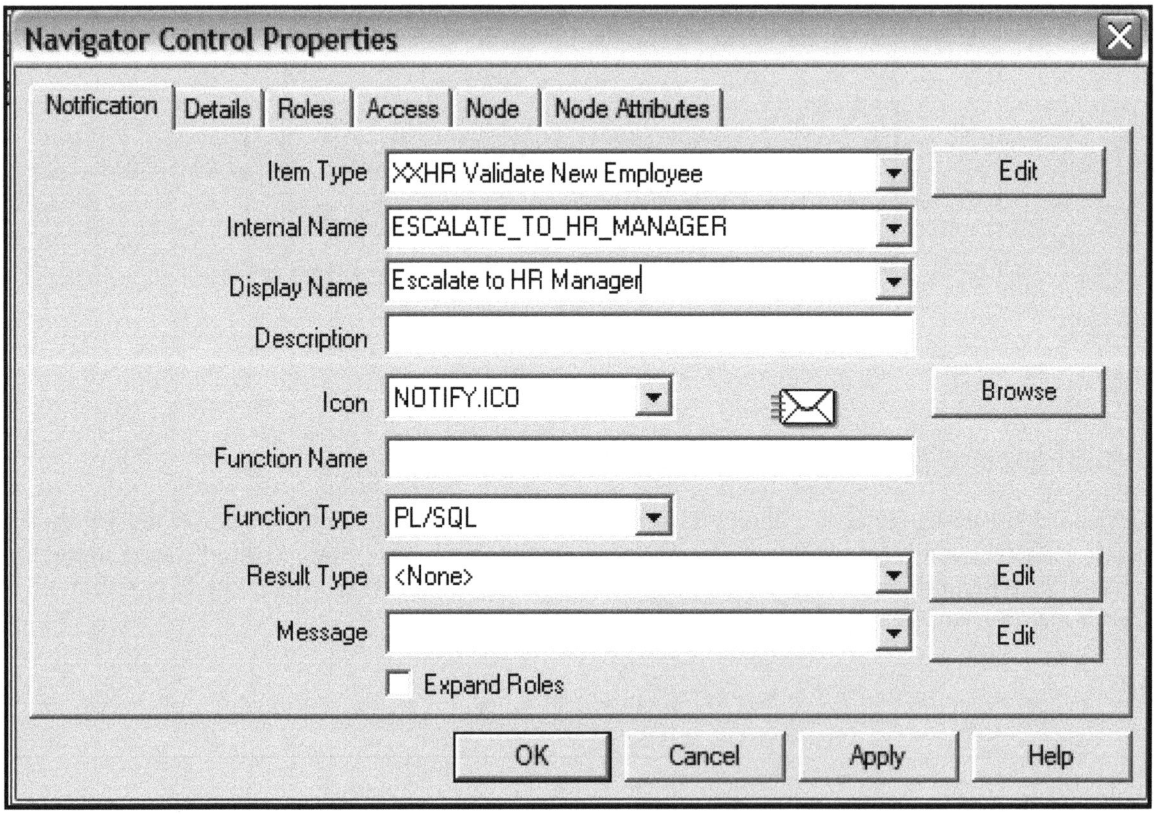

FIGURE 3.32

Then drag in a 'Loop Counter' node (   ) from 'Standard'. Draw a line from 'Is Employee Data complete?' to 'Loop Counter' and select the result 'No'. Draw a line from 'Loop Counter' to 'Ask HR to Fix it' and select 'Loop' as the result. Draw a line from 'Loop Counter' to 'Escalate to HR Manager' and select the result 'Exit'. Draw a second line from 'Ask HR to Fix it' to 'Is Employee Data complete' and select the result '<Timeout>'. (Note that when you draw this second line it will be on top of the first line with the result OK. Use the mouse to grab a line and bend it. If the wrong line is grabbed, then bend both lines, right-click the OK line and select 'Straighten'.)

Our Workflow should now look like FIGURE 3.33.

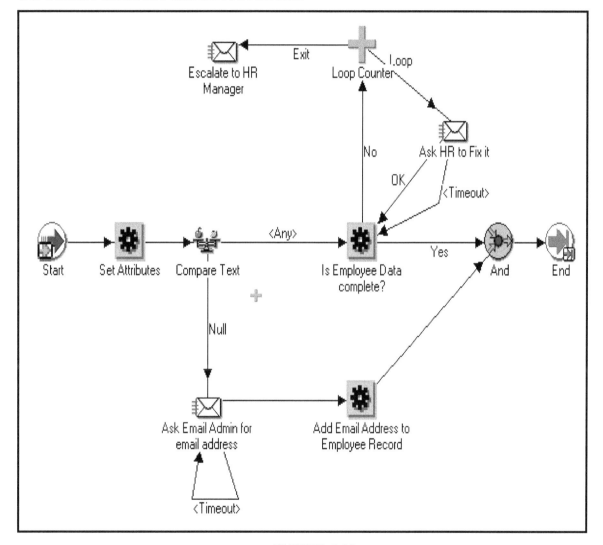

FIGURE 3.33

As drawn, the Workflow will behave as follows (assuming that 'Is Employee Data complete?' returns No): The 'Loop Counter' will start the count. The Notification 'Ask HR to Fix it' is sent. If the Notification is ignored, one day after being sent, the Notification will time out and transfer control back to 'Is Employee Data complete?' Assuming no updates were done, the Function will return 'No' and control will transfer again to 'Loop Counter'. The counter knows this will be the second time through the loop (we have not demonstrated how to set the limit for 'Loop Counter', just assume the limit is set to 3) and so passes control to 'Ask HR to Fix it'. This Process continues until 'Loop Counter' is hit the fourth time. Since we have already sent the 'Ask HR to Fix it' Notification three times, 'Loop Counter' takes the Exit leg and the Notification 'Escalate to HR Manager' is sent.

FIGURE 3.34 shows an alternative way to model this. The Notification 'Ask HR to Fix it' is sent. If the Notification is ignored, one day after being sent, the Notification will time out and transfer control to 'Loop Counter'. 'Loop Counter' will start the count and since the count is less than 3, traverse down the Loop leg back to 'Is Employee Data complete'. If no updates are done, the Workflow sends another 'Ask HR to Fix it' Notification. If another Timeout occurs, 'Loop Counter' checks that the count is less than 3, increases the count to 2 and travels back to 'Is Employee Data complete'. If the third Notification results in another Timeout, 'Loop Counter' checks that the count is less than 3 (and it is, because the Attribute that counts the number of times through the loop is not incremented until after the check is made) and returns to 'Is Employee Data complete'. So, if 'Loop Counter' is placed after the Notification, the Notification will be sent one extra time.

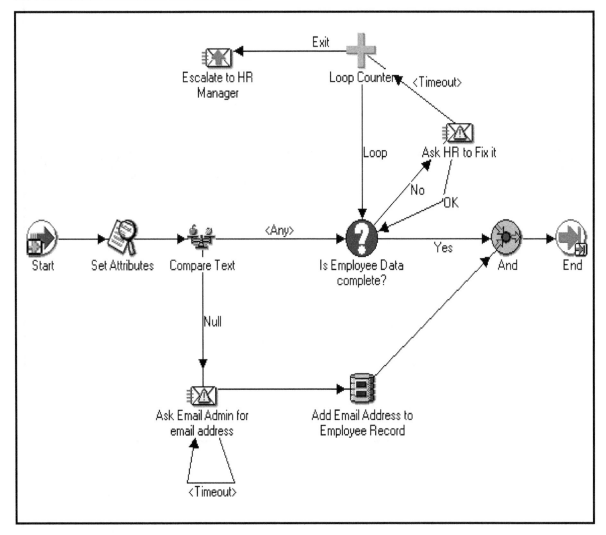

FIGURE 3.34

This Activity has another notable quirk that can cause unpredictable behavior. FIGURE 3.35 shows a Process where the desired behavior would allow the Notification to be repeated in case of a Timeout. Assuming the 'Loop Limit' is set to '1', each approver should have two chances to respond to the Notification before it is escalated to the next approver. Approver 1 receives the Notification and it times out. The 'Loop Counter' forces the Workflow to send a second Notification and sets the 'Count' to '1'. Approver 1 answers the Notification but his authority is insufficient. Approver 2 is sent the Notification and it times out. But this time LOOP_COUNT is already set to '1' and so Approver 2 is not given a second Notification. The 'Loop Counter' resets LOOP_COUNT to zero and transfers control to 'Does Next Approver Exist?' This anomaly can be managed by setting the Item Attribute 'LOOP_COUNT' to zero in the Procedure 'Does Next Approver Exist?' Remember, though, that when the Workflow is started, this Attribute does not exist. Special coding will be needed. See *Chapter 4, Using PL/SQL in Workflow*, for an example of this special code.

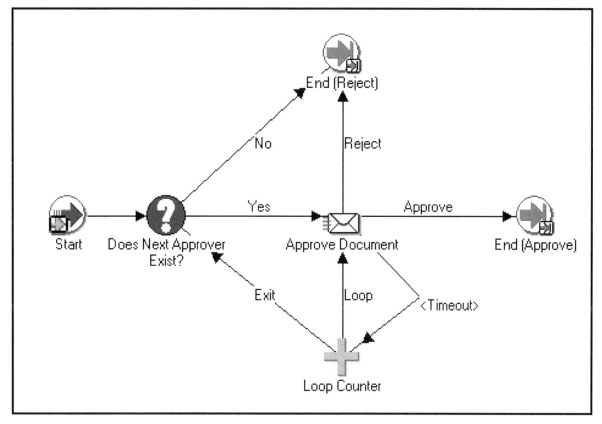

FIGURE 3.35

In the *Workflow Developers Guide, Release 11.5.10 Part No. B15853-04, July 2006, Release 12 Part No. B31433-01, December 2006*, Oracle provides an example of using 'Loop Counter' to ensure a branch is executed just once (See FIGURE 3.36). The 'Loop Limit' is set to '1'. When the first leg encounters 'Loop Counter', LOOP_COUNT is incremented to '1' and the Workflow proceeds down the Loop leg. When the second leg encounters 'Loop Counter', LOOP_COUNT is already '1' and so 'Loop Counter' resets LOOP_COUNT to 0 and the Workflow proceeds down the Exit leg. If the third leg encounters 'Loop Counter' before the Workflow ends (this scenario assumes the End Node does not end the Workflow but instead transfers control back to another Process), 'Loop Counter' will set LOOP_COUNT back to '1' and allow the Workflow to proceed down the Loop leg.

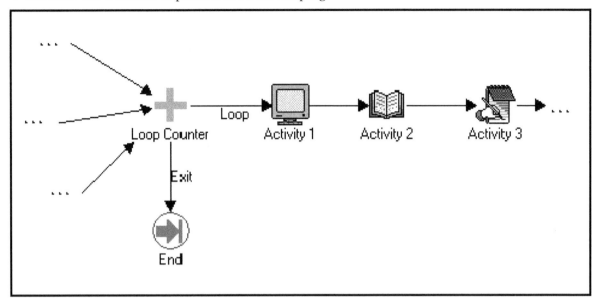

FIGURE 3.36

The point of all these examples is that the 'Loop Counter' Activity must be used with care.

STANDARD ACTIVITY – WAIT

We don't expect the HR Manager to enter the data so this will be just an 'FYI' Notification. In an ideal world, the HR Manager would order the data to be entered, the Workflow would return to 'Is Employee Data complete?' and the data would now be there. However, we need to delay the return to 'Is Employee Data complete?' so we are going to include a Wait Node. The Wait Node is a standard Function that can be configured to pause the Workflow until a specific date, a specific day of the week or month, a specific time of day, or just a set number of days (or fraction of a day) from the time the Wait Node is encountered.

Drag in the Wait Node (   ) and draw a line from 'Escalate to HR Manager' to the Wait Node, and then from the Wait Node to 'Is Employee Data complete?' Our Workflow (FIGURE 3.37) once again shows a complete loop. (Yes, save again.)

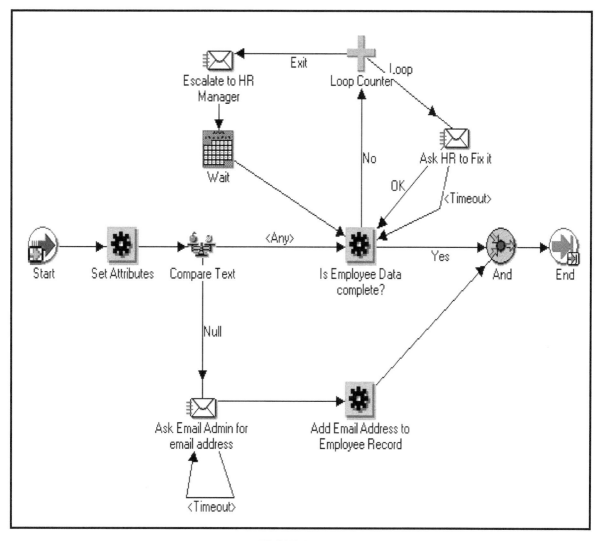

FIGURE 3.37

ITEM ATTRIBUTES

Although the diagram is complete, the Workflow is not finished. Notifications require Messages and Messages (usually) require Attributes. Attributes are variables whose value is dependent on the instance of the Workflow. For example, since this Workflow is started when a new employee is added, the employee's name will be necessary. Since this name will be different for each new employee, we will define a variable or Attribute to store this name. Based on our design, we'd also expect a variable to store the Employee Number, Email Address, Supervisor, Position, and Default Accounting.

Attributes can exist at the Item Type, Message, or Function level. There are several advantages to defining Attributes at the Item Type level and then copying them to the Message and/or Function level. Attributes defined at the Item Type level can be seen (and optionally updated) through the 'Status Monitor'. The APIs that Oracle provides to set Attribute values are easier to use at the Item Type level, as the only information needed at that level is the Item Type name, the Item Key, and the Attribute name.

Item Type Attributes are set up by right-clicking 'Attribute' on the Navigator tree and choosing 'New Attribute', or through the 'Edit' menu: Edit→New→Attribute. Enter the Internal Name (same rules), Display Name and Description. Pick a 'Type' that describes the type of data that will be stored in the Attribute. The choices are Text, Number, Date, Lookup, Form, URL, Document, Role, Attribute, or Event. This chapter will discuss four of the types – 'Text', 'Number', 'Date', and 'Role'. 'Event' is added in *Chapter 5, Business Events,* and the others will be discussed in *Chapter 11, Advanced Builder and PL/SQL.*

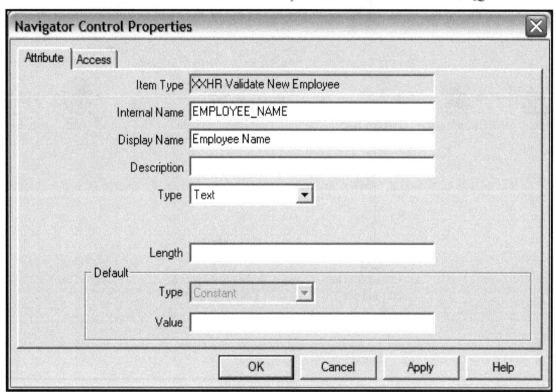

FIGURE 3.38

You can specify the length of a Text Attribute to limit the display size, but ensure you specify a size larger than the database Text Attribute or the Attribute won't be used in a comparison where a truncation would cause an erroneous comparison. (see FIGURE 3.38)

You can also specify a default value.

You can specify formatting for Number and Date Attributes. For Number Attributes, you are limited to typical formatting characters such as '$' and ','. You cannot, for example, format for a Social Security Number (999-99-9999).

It is helpful at this point to involve a developer who knows how the columns in the database are defined. For example, since Oracle allows companies to define their own employee numbering schema, 'Employee Number' is actually a text field in the database, not a number (see FIGURE 3.39).

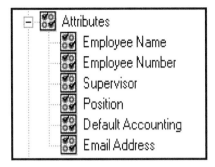

FIGURE 3. 39

Attributes are listed in the order in which they were entered. Where they are used in a List of Values, this can be confusing. If you have quite a few Attributes, it is a good idea to use drag-and-drop to order your Attributes alphabetically. One exception to this rule would be if you have more than 200 Attributes. In this case, make sure the first 200 Attributes are the ones you will need to see in the 'Status Monitor', as additional ones will not be displayed.

Do not worry about ensuring your initial list of Attributes is complete. Additional Attributes can always be added, and the order of appearance can always be changed.

One additional note: if you forgot to close the 'Standard' Item Type when you pulled in the Wait Node and accidentally defined all your Attributes in the 'Standard' Item Type, just drag each Attribute to your Item Type, then delete it from 'Standard'. (Still saving?)

COMPLETING NOTIFICATIONS – MESSAGES

At this point we've defined the Notification, but not the content. The content is the Message. Like Attributes, Messages are defined from the Navigator window by clicking the Message tree and selecting New Message or through the 'Edit' menu (Edit→New→Message).

Before opening a 'Message Properties' page, it is beneficial to toggle the 'Navigator' tree to display the Internal Names of all components instead of the Display Names. Since you must use the Internal Name when specifying Attributes in Messages, it will be easier to code them if you can see the Internal Names as you type. You toggle the names by clicking on the 'Hammer' icon in the Navigator window tool bar. Note that in FIGURE 3.40 the Internal Name displays with the Display Name in parentheses.

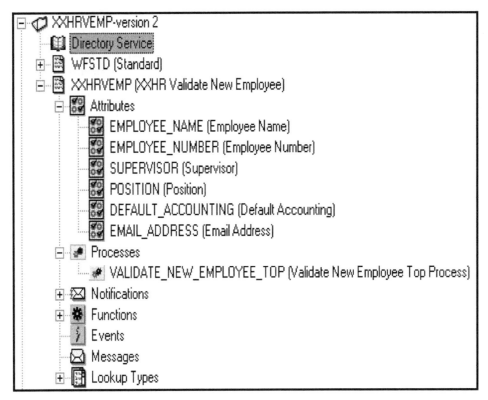

FIGURE 3.40

In addition to the Internal Name, Display Name, and Description, the Message tab allows the specification of the Notification 'Priority'. Valid values are 'High', 'Normal', and 'Low'. This field allows the designer to ensure that important Messages will sort at the top of the Notification list or be sent through email with the priority flag turned on. See FIGURE 3.41.

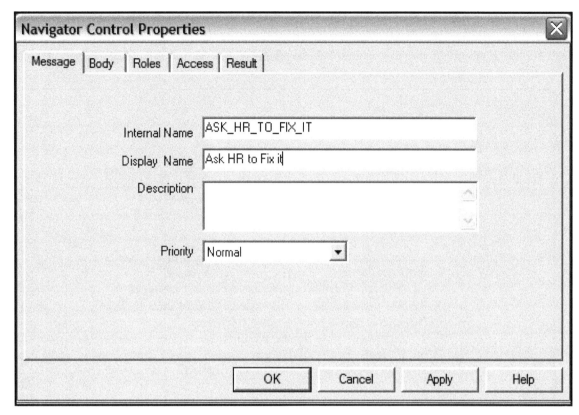

FIGURE 3.41

After entering the values on the Message tab, click the Body tab. This is where the actual Message that is sent out is defined. Drag the 'Properties' page icon so that the Internal Names of the Attributes can be seen. Notice in FIGURE 3.42 that the Message Display Name is defaulted as the Subject. This can be changed.

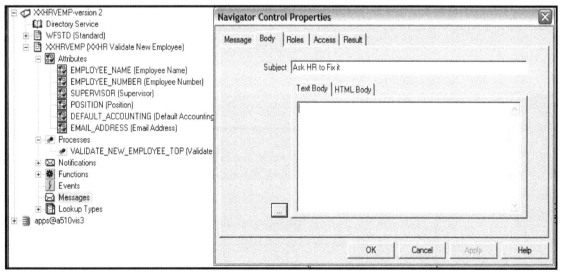

FIGURE 3.42

There are multiple ways to code the Message, especially if it contains a list of Attributes. One such method is shown in FIGURE 3.43. Note that all Attributes are listed by their Internal Name preceded by a '&'. The '&' is essential to indicate to the Workflow Engine that the following characters are the name of an Attribute and to substitute the current value.

Navigator Control Properties
Message
Body
Roles
Access
Result
Subject
Employee data for &EMPLOYEE_NAME is not complete
Text Body
HTML Body
Employee data for &EMPLOYEE_NAME, employee number &EMPLOYEE_NUMBER is not complete. Please look at the list below. If any of the fields are blank, please go to the 'Enter Employee' screen in Oracle and enter the appropriate values.
Supervisor: &SUPERVISOR
Position: &POSITION
Default Accounting: &DEFAULT_ACCOUNTING
After (and only after) entering the missing data, click the OK button at the bottom of this notification. Note that clicking the button before correcting the data will only result in receiving another copy of this
...
OK
Cancel
Apply
Help

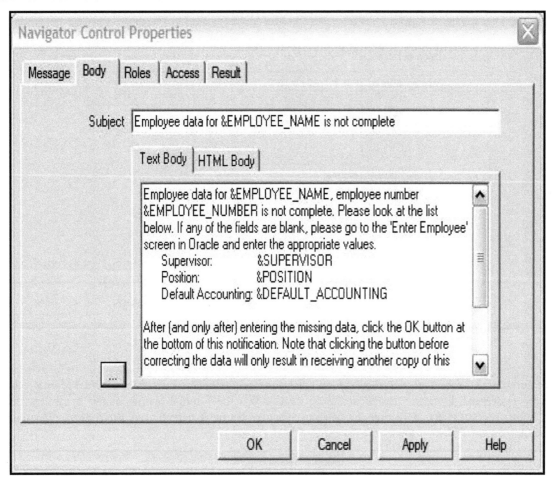

FIGURE 3.43

At the end of the Message there is text that describes when to respond to the Message and what will happen if these instructions are ignored. It is also good practice to include any time limits and what will happen when the time limit is ignored. The rest of our Message states (see FIGURE 3.44):

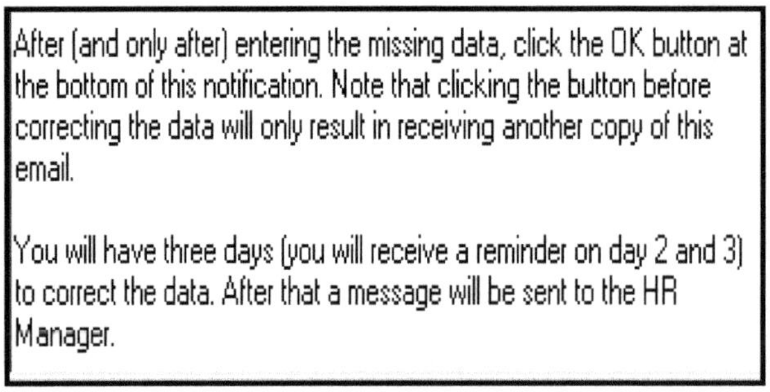

After (and only after) entering the missing data, click the OK button at the bottom of this notification. Note that clicking the button before correcting the data will only result in receiving another copy of this email.
You will have three days (you will receive a reminder on day 2 and 3) to correct the data. After that a message will be sent to the HR Manager.

FIGURE 3.44

Another method of displaying a list of Attributes is using the Message Function WF_NOTIFICATION(ATTRS,<attribute1>,<attribute2>,...<attribute>). Using this Function will produce a table of the Attributes listed showing the Display Name of the Attribute followed by the value. So our Message could have been coded as shown in FIGURE 3.45.

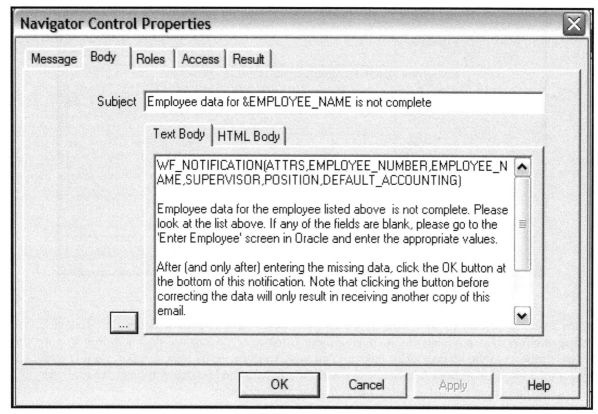

FIGURE 3.45

Note that there is no '&' in front of the Attributes in the list and that there are no spaces in the list. If spaces or the '&' are included, the list will not display correctly.

See *Chapter 11, Advanced Builder and PL/SQL,* for examples using HTML code in the HTML Body tab.

The 'Ask HR to Fix it' Notification specified the Result Type XXHRVEMP_OK. Therefore, the Message for this Notification must also reference this exact same Result Type. Unlike the Notification where the Result Type is specified on the main property tab, the Result Type for a Message is specified on the Result tab. See FIGURE 3.46. Note that there is no Internal Name field. The name of the tab, Result, is also the Internal Name. This tab is actually specifying a special Message Attribute.

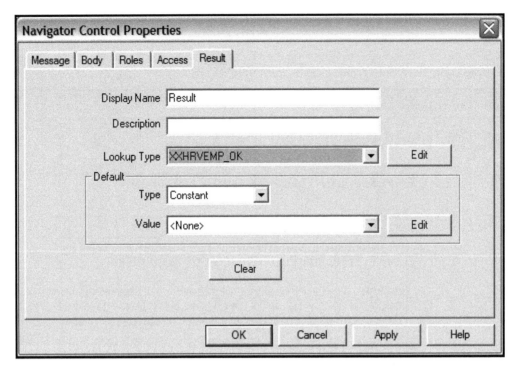

FIGURE 3.46

Each Attribute referenced by a Message (except the Result) must be listed under the Message in the Navigator tree. It is not necessary to re-type these Attributes; you can use drag-and-drop to copy the Item Attributes to the Message. This links the Message Attribute to the Item Attribute so that each time you set the value for an Item Attribute; it also sets the value for the Message Attribute. See FIGURE 3.47 to see the 'Properties' page of an Attribute created via drag-and-drop.

Note that the Message icon in FIGURE 3.47 has a red question mark. This indicates that a Result Type was specified on the Result tab.

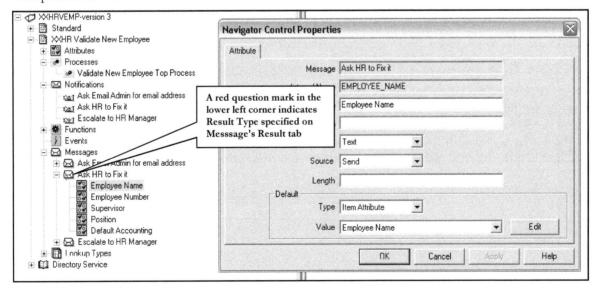

FIGURE 3. 47

FIGURES 3.48 and 3.49 show a possible definition of the 'Escalate to HR Manager' Message:

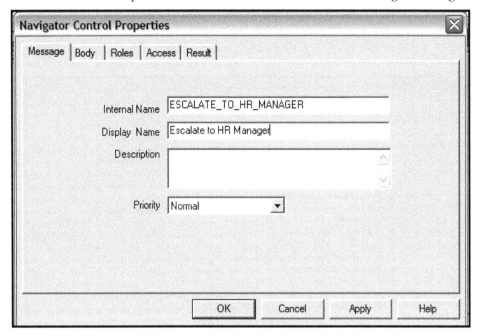

FIGURE 3.48

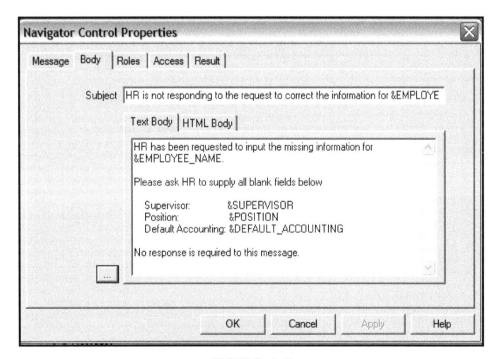

FIGURE 3.49

The 'Ask Email Admin for email address' Message in FIGURE 3.50 and FIGURE 3.51 demonstrates a method of coding a Notification and Message requesting a response when the response cannot be represented by a Result Type. Define the Message, but do not enter anything in the Result tab or include the Attribute &EMAIL_ADDRESS. Use drag-and-drop to create the Message Attributes 'Employee Name' and 'Email Address'.

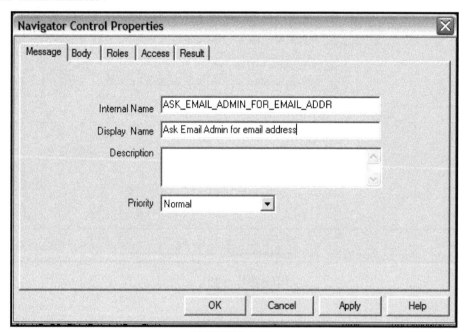

FIGURE 3.50

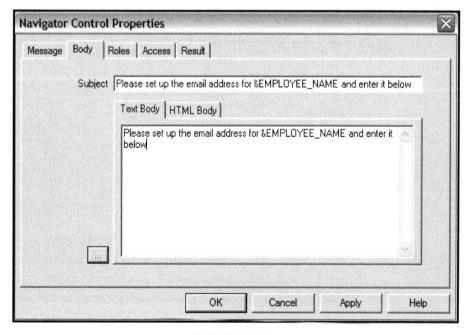

FIGURE 3.51

Open the 'Properties' page of the Message Attribute 'Email Address'. Change the Source from Send to Respond. In FIGURE 3.52, a red question mark on the Message Attribute indicates that the recipient is expected to enter a value for this Attribute. When this Message is sent, Oracle will create a labeled box for the recipient to enter the value. Although there is no Result Type, the Workflow will pause and wait for the result. Oracle will automatically add an OK button to the bottom of the Notification.

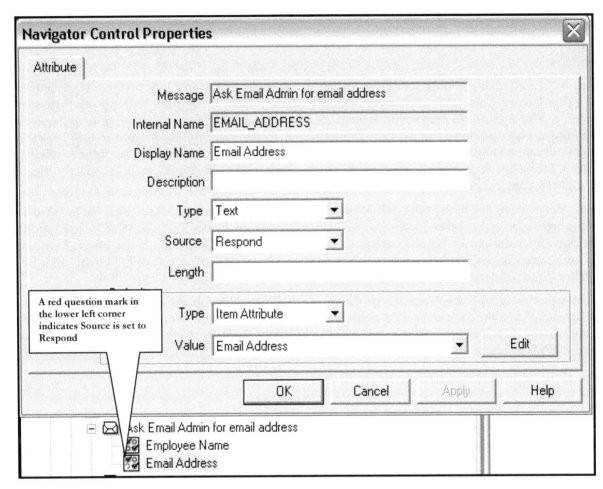

FIGURE 3. 52

Note that when the Developer mode (hammer) icon was clicked, the labels in the Diagrammer window also switched to the Internal Names. Clicking the Developer mode icon will switch the names back to Display Name in the Navigator window, but it doesn't affect the Diagrammer window. To change the labels back to Display Name in the Diagrammer window, click the abc icon. The AB-1 icon will display Instance Labels, while the ABC icon displays the Internal Names. Instance Labels are used to identify the specific node in a diagram. They will be the same as the Internal Name unless an Activity is used twice in a diagram. Then the Builder will add a dash and a number to distinguish the nodes.

Now that the Messages have been defined, they need to be associated with the Notifications. Double-click each Notification in either the Diagrammer or Navigator window to open the 'Properties' page. Select the Message that matches the Notification name. Repeat for all the Notifications.

COMPLETING NOTIFICATIONS – PERFORMERS

In addition to a Message, a Notification must also specify who will receive the Message, the 'Performer'. If the Notification is in a loop and the value of the Performer will change each time the loop is transgressed, then you want to set the Performer to be an Item Attribute and use a Function Activity prior to the Notification to set the value of the Item Attribute. If the value of the Performer is constant, as for a specific user, then you can use the Directory Services to load this value into the Workflow and use this constant value. Remember that you do not want to update your Workflow each time someone starts or quits work, so if using a constant value, it is better to use a Role such as a responsibility or position.

Release 11.5.10 changed how responsibility names are internally represented in Workflow. The length of this new Internal Name is usually greater than 30 characters. Since the Builder truncates any Performer value > 30 characters, the only way to assign a responsibility as a Performer is to use an Item Attribute and assign the responsibility to the Item Attribute. Due to this limitation, all Performers will be set to Item Attributes. However, we will use Directory Services to set a default value for two of the Attributes. This will have the same effect as assigning a constant Performer to the Notification but will not trigger the 30-character truncation error.

First, define three Attributes, 'HR', 'HR Manager', and 'Email Administrator'. Attributes that are used as Performers must either be assigned a type of Text or Role. If the type is Text, the value assigned to the Attribute must match the NAME column in the WF_LOCAL_ROLES table. If the type is Role, the value assigned to the Attribute must match the DISPLAY_NAME column in WF_LOCAL_ROLES. Define 'Email Administrator' with the type Text and the other Attributes with the type Role.

Performers are set on the Node tab of the 'Properties' page. Double-click the 'Notification' in the Diagrammer window to open the 'Properties' page, and then select the Node tab. For the Performer Type, choose 'Item Attribute', then for the 'Value', choose the Attribute that will contain the name of the person/Role to whom the Notification will be sent. See FIGURE 3.53, FIGURE 3.54 and FIGURE 3.55 for examples.

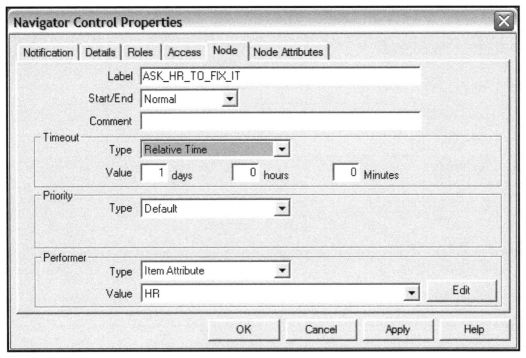

FIGURE 3.53

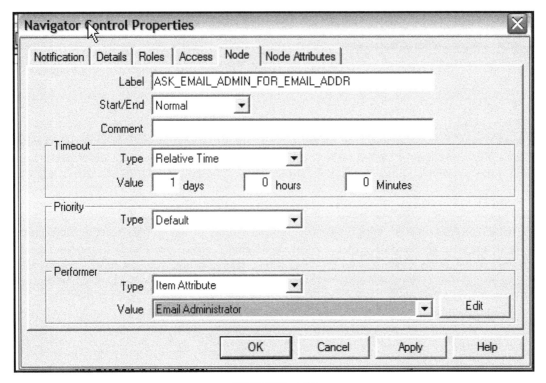

FIGURE 3.54

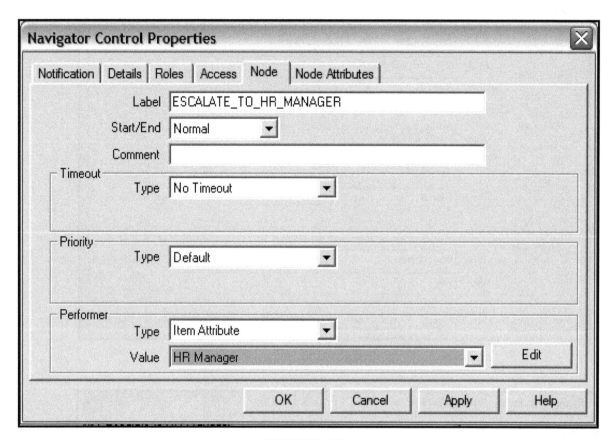

FIGURE 3.55

Setting the Performer using Directory Services requires that you connect to the database to load a Role or user. If you loaded your Item Type from the Database, you are already connected. If you loaded your Workflow from a PC file system or started a Workflow from scratch, you have to save the Workflow to the database in order to connect. Since saving to the database will require the APPS password, you will have to get your Applications DBA involved.

FIGURE 3.56 shows that from the File menu, you must select 'Save As' to open the 'Save Dialog' box. This time, click the Database button. Type APPS for the user name, the APPS password, and the name of the database (from your TNSNAMES.ORA file) for the Connect parameter. The Effective parameter allows you to enter the date on which this Workflow will be effective. Thus, you can save Workflows to become effective in the future. Note that once you type in an effective date for a save, subsequent saves where the 'Effective' field is left blank inherit the previous effective date.

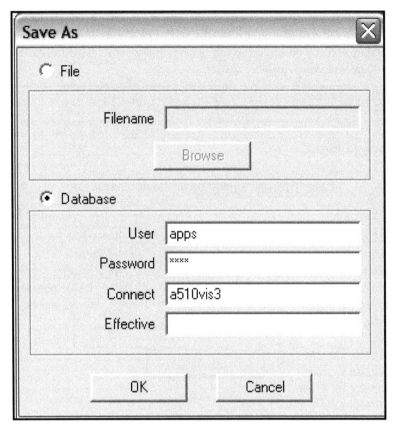

FIGURE 3.56

Since we have not finished defining all aspects of the Workflow, the 'Validation Error' screen will still appear. Click the 'Save' button. Although this Workflow will be saved to the database, it will not be marked runnable. An hourglass appears while the Builder connects to the database and saves the Workflow. When the hourglass has disappeared, note that the name of the Datastore has changed to apps@<database name>.

Now from the File menu, select 'Load Role' from Database. The 'Load Role' box opens. Fill in all or part of the Role/user you are trying to find and press the 'Find' button. Since you are connected to the database you can use the Oracle wildcard character ('%') to help in the search. The 'Query Results' screen shows the names of all records from the WF_LOCAL_ROLES table that meet the query criteria. You will have to know your data well enough to recognize whether you are selecting a responsibility, a position, a user name or Approval Group, or another object in these tables. If you pick an object from WF_LOCAL_ROLES (such as a responsibility or position), when the Notification is sent, it will be sent to all users of the responsibility or holders of the position. For our example, we will pick the position HR003.HR GENERALIST. You can select as many Roles as you wish. You can go back to the 'Find Roles' field and do additional queries. When you have all the Roles you need displayed in the 'Loaded Roles' window, press OK.

Although Oracle has changed how the responsibility names are stored, both the old and the new version of the responsibility are available as choices. Do not select any name with 'Any security group' at the end of the name. This is the old responsibility and Notifications sent to this value will simply error. As previously stated, it is important to know your data. Since this form only shows the Display Name and not the Internal Name, it may be necessary to query the data from WF_LOCAL_ROLES to discover the source. In the 'Loaded Roles' column in FIGURE 3.57, HR Clerk and HR Manager are positions. 'HRMS Management:Any security group' is the old responsibility name. 'HRMS Management and Global HR Professional V4.0' are valid responsibility names.

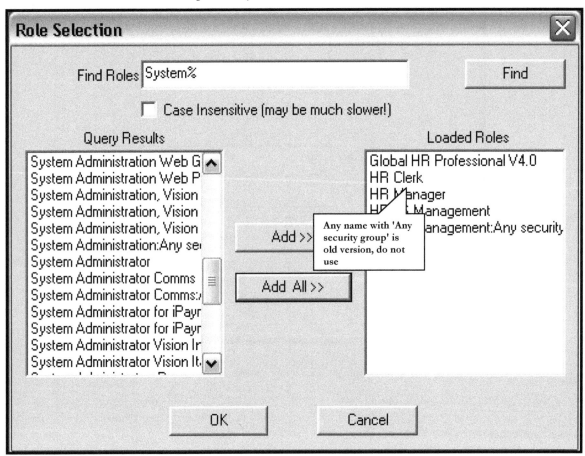

FIGURE 3. 57

If you press OK, then the names become available to be assigned as constant values to either the Notification or to an Item Attribute. To assign the value to an Attribute, double-click the 'Attribute' to open the 'Properties' page, and then use the List of Values to select a value. In FIGURE 3.58, we assigned 'HRMS Management' to the Attribute 'HR Manager' and 'Global Hr Professional V4.0' to the Attribute 'HR'.

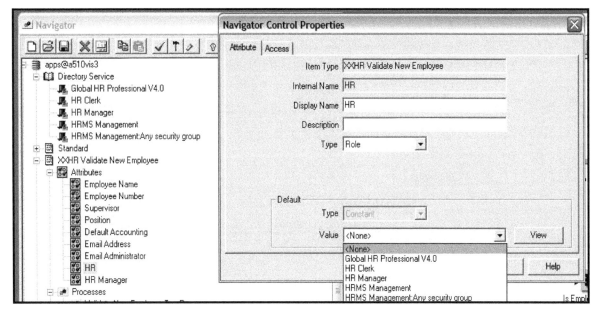

FIGURE 3.58

Note that at this point if you click the 'Save' icon, you are saving the Workflow back to the database. Since we have not finished our Workflow and we have gathered all the Directory Services values we need, choose 'Save As' from the File menu and save the Workflow back to your PC file system.

If you close your Workflow at this point and then open it from the file system you will notice that the Directory Services values you loaded but did not use have disappeared. This is normal.

COMPLETING FUNCTION ACTIVITIES – FUNCTION NAMES

In order to finish the Function Activity Definitions, you must specify the type and name of the Procedure the Function will execute. Typically this is information the developers will provide after they have written the Procedures. Through Release 11.5.10, External Java is a Function type limited to Standalone Workflow (not used with E-Business Suite). The *Workflow Developers Guide Release 12, Part No. B31433-01, December 2006*, states that External Java is not currently used. The External Function allows interaction with a Workflow in another database instance. We will limit our discussion to PL/SQL functions.

Open the 'Properties' page for each Function Activity. In the 'Function Name' field, fill in the name of the Package and Procedure. Although the Package name in this example is the Internal Name of the Item Type, you can specify any Package name.

Use XXHRVEMP.IS_EMPLOYEE_DATA_COMPLETE for the Function 'Is Employee Data complete?'

Use XXHRVEMP.ADD_EMAIL_ADDRESS_TO_EMP_REC for the Function 'Add Email Address to Employee Record'.

FIGURE 3.59 shows XXHRVEMP.SET_ATTRIBUTES for the Function 'Set Attributes'.

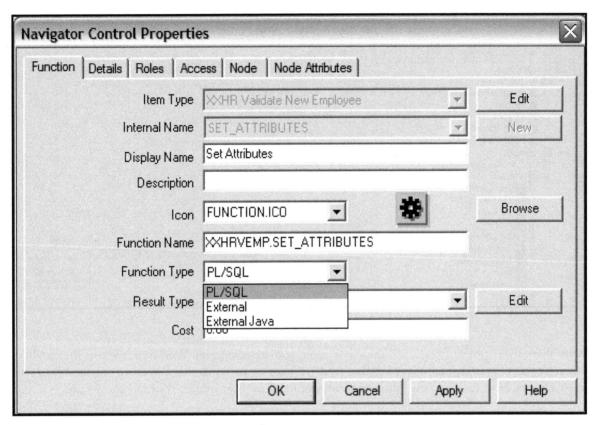

FIGURE 3.59

COMPLETING THE WAIT ACTIVITY – NODE ATTRIBUTES

Activities, like Messages, can have Attributes. These Attributes allow the designer to pass parameters to the Activity. Many of the standard activities have Attributes. This is indicated by the + next to the Attribute name. FIGURE 3.60 shows that all the 'Compare' Activities and the 'Assign' Activity have Attributes, but 'And' and 'Block' do not.

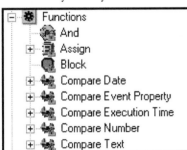

FIGURE 3. 60

When a 'Standard' Activity with Attributes is used in a design, these Attributes must be initialized. To initialize these Attributes, double-click the node in the Diagrammer window to open the 'Properties' page. Select the 'Node Attributes' tab. If the node has never been configured, the tab looks similar to FIGURE 3.61.

The information listed in the bottom window will be specific to the Activity. FIGURE 3.61 shows the Attributes for the Wait Function. The Attributes specific to each 'Standard' Activity are documented in the *Oracle Workflow Developer's Guide, Release 11.5.10 Part No. B15852-05, July 2006, Release 12 Part No. B31431-01, December 2006.*

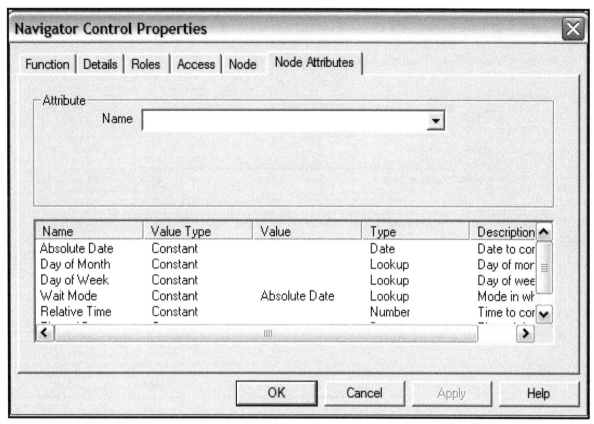

FIGURE 3. 61

For the Wait Activity, the designer must specify the Wait Mode. Use the LOV for the 'Name' field to select 'Wait Mode'. This opens up two new fields, 'Type' and 'Value'. The choices for 'Type' are 'Constant' and 'Item Attribute'. For the Attribute 'Wait Mode', the type should be 'Constant'. Then, for 'Value' choose the desired 'Wait Mode'. Our example Workflow will use Relative Time. See FIGURE 3.62.

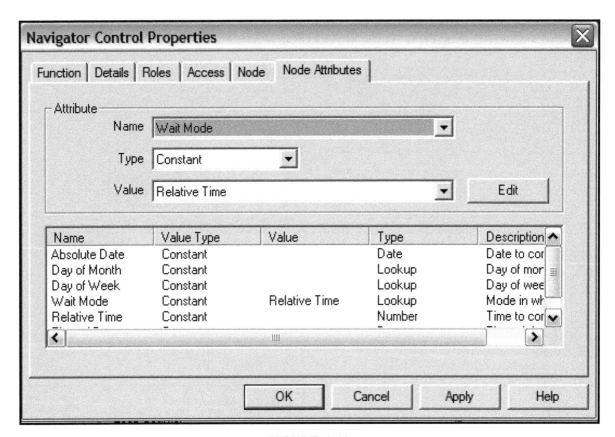

FIGURE 3.62

Now that the 'Wait Mode' is selected, move back to the 'Name' field and select Relative Time. Leave 'Type' set to 'Constant' and in the 'Value' field enter '1'. This tells the Workflow to wait 1 day. Relative Time can also be set to a fractional part of day. For example, to pause the Workflow for 1 hour, enter .04167. Experience has shown that 30 minutes or .021 is the minimum amount of time that can be entered. The configuration for our example Workflow should now look like FIGURE 3.63.

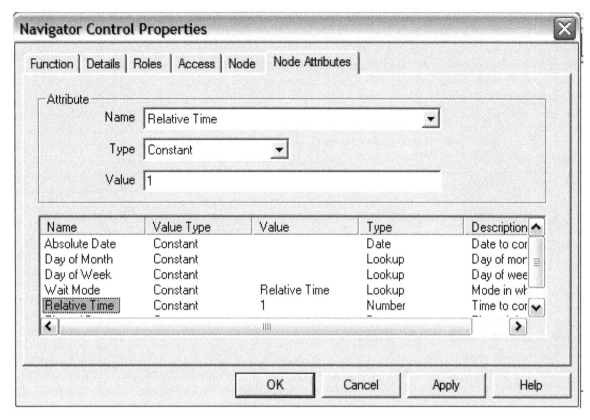

FIGURE 3.63

This Activity does not recognize work calendars, so if this Activity was executed Friday at 5 PM, then the Workflow will resume Saturday at 5 PM. Similarly, if the Relative Time is set to .333 (8 hours) and the Activity was executed Friday at 5 P.M. then the Workflow will resume Saturday at 1 A.M. To force this Activity to recognize non-working days and hours set the Type for Relative Time to Item Attribute and set the Value to the name of an Item Attribute. Then just prior to the Wait Node execute a Function Activity that sets the specified Item Attribute to the number of days that the Workflow should pause.

COMPLETING THE LOOP ACTIVITY – NODE ATTRIBUTES

The Loop Activity only has one Attribute – 'Loop Limit'. Since we placed the Loop Activity at the start of the loop, this Activity will allow activities down the leg labeled Loop to be executed the number of times specified in 'Loop Limit' (see FIGURE 3.64).

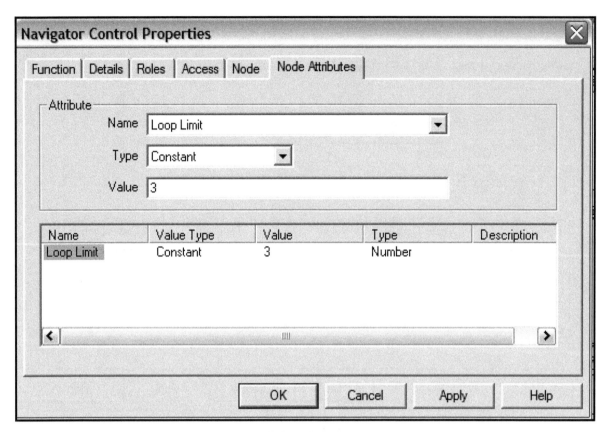

FIGURE 3.64

COMPLETE THE COMPARE TEXT ACTIVITY – NODE ATTRIBUTES

The 'Compare Text' / Number / Date activities are used to compare Item Attributes either to each other or to a constant. Use the Activity that matches the Attribute type. Since we are checking the value of a text type Attribute, we will use 'Compare Text'. This Activity has two 'Node Attributes', 'Test Value' and 'Reference Value'. 'Test Value' is typically set to the Item Attribute to be tested. Click the 'Name' field and select 'Test Value'. For 'Type', select 'Item Attribute'. For 'Value', use the List of Values to select the Item Attribute 'Email Address'. The result should look like FIGURE 3.65. Click the 'Name' field again and select 'Reference Value'. For 'Type', select 'Constant'. Our Workflow will check to see if the email address is null, so anything can be entered in the 'Value' field. Do not leave this value empty. See FIGURE 3.66.

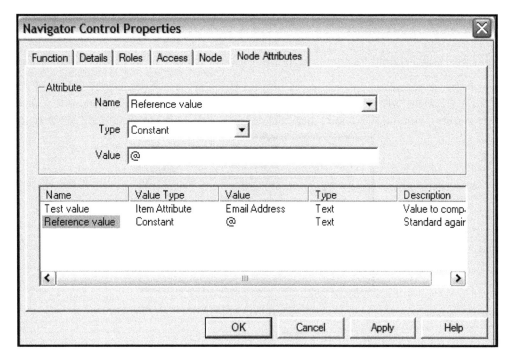

FIGURE 3.65

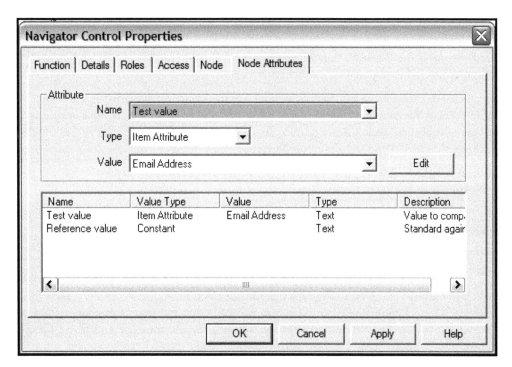

FIGURE 3.66

VALIDATE YOUR DESIGN

At this point the design should be complete, but in order to make sure, click the 'Validate Design' icon

. If the design is complete, you will see a pop-up box that says 'Successfully validated design' (see FIGURE 3.67). Click the OK box, and then save the Workflow to the PC file system. If you still receive the box listing errors with the Workflow, then click the + beside each error, note the problem, and fix it.

FIGURE 3.67

The following are the most common Error Messages and their causes:

345: Invalid activity message '<null>'. Messages are required by notification activities.
 201: Non-empty value required.

Cause: No message has been specified for the Notification indicated in the '354: 'SAVE' validation failed for activity '<Item Type name>/<notification name>' error message. Open the 'Properties' page, 'Notification' tab, for the specified Notification and select the appropriate message.

309: Invalid function name '<null>'. Function names have a maximum length of 240 bytes.
 201: Non-empty value required.

Cause: No Function Name has been specified for the Function specified in the '354: 'SAVE' validation failed for activity '<Item Type name>/<function activity name>' error message. Open the 'Properties' page, 'Activity' tab, for the specified Function Activity and select the appropriate Function Type and Function Name.

362: Validation failed for child activity '<Item Type name>/<notification name>'.
 383: Notification activity must be assigned a performer when used in a process.

Cause: No performer was specified for the Notification listed in the error message. Open the 'Properties' page, Node tab, and select the appropriate Performer Type and Value.

351: Notification activity's message must have a respond attribute named 'RESULT' with lookup type '<lookup type specified in the notification>.

Cause: The message assigned to the Notification specified in the '354: 'SAVE' validation failed for activity '<Item Type name>/<notification name>' error message is missing information in the Result tab. Open the 'Properties' page, Result tab, for the message and fill in the Display Name and Description. Select the Lookup Type specified in the 351 error message.

401: Could not find token <message attribute name> among message attributes.

Cause: You have used an attribute in the body of a message, but not copied the attribute from the item attribute list down to the message attributes. (Or you have mistyped the name of the attribute in the body of the message – remember to use the Internal name of the attribute). Either drag-and-drop the appropriate attribute to the appropriate message or open the 'Properties' page, Body tab, of the message and correct the typing.

362: Validation failed for child activity '<Item Type name>/<function activity name>'.
358: Activity result code <result code> has no transition defined for it.

Cause: All valid result codes must be modeled with specific transitions or a <Default> transition. If a function activity uses a Result, then there must be a transition leg for each possible value of the Lookup Type referenced, or one of the transitions must be labeled 'Default'. This can indicate that the design is incomplete (i.e., the Process for the missing branch hasn't been defined) or there are more than two values for the Result, and the unmodeled value follows a path already defined. If the latter, re-label that path 'Default'. If the former, add the missing Process to the design. Note that if the function activity referenced was copied from the Standard Item Type, the Item Type name will say 'WFSTD'.

Note that validation will catch most errors, but not all. For example, if the designer forgets to set the Node Attributes for the standard activities such as Wait and Loop Counter, the Workflow will validate with no errors. The Workflow will subsequently error when run. Thus, successful validation does not guarantee the Workflow will not error.

OPTIONAL (BUT FUN) – CHOOSE ICONS

Oracle defaults as the icon for a Function Activity and as the icon for a Notification and for a Process. Although you should not change the default Process icon, you can change the others so that the pictures on the diagram model the Activity they represent. You can do this either by using the library of icons Oracle provides, or by creating your own .ico files. Remember if you create your own .ico files, you'll need to get your Applications DBA to load them on the database server so that they will display in the 'Monitor' pages.

Although changing the icons was left to the last step for this Workflow, changing the icon can be used to indicate that the node is completely configured. In other words, once the Message and Performer is assigned to a Notification, change the icon to indicate all configuration is complete. For Functions, since the only missing piece is the PL/SQL 'Function Name', change the icon when you specify the PL/SQL function.

To change the icon for an Activity, open the 'Properties' page for that Activity. Click the Browse button on the icon line. The Builder will look in the directory <oracle home>\wf\icon and display all available choices. Normally the Builder will display what the icon looks like next to the icon name. However, you may have loaded software on your computer that has blocked showing the icon pictures. If this is the case, you should go to 'My Computer'. Pick the View menu, then 'Folder Options'. Click on the 'File Types' tab. Scroll down until you see ICON (it will have Extension ICO). Click 'Edit'. Click 'Enable Quick View'. Click OK twice. Close 'My Computer'. FIGURE 3.68 demonstrates that the diagram looks better once icons have been chosen that try to represent the purpose of each node in the diagram.

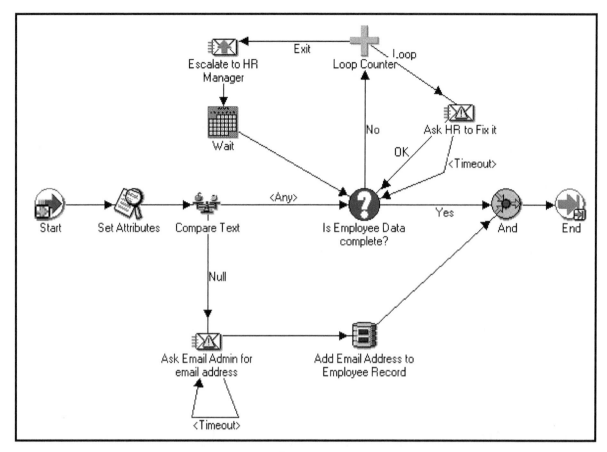

FIGURE 3.68

If you change the icons, save the file both to the PC directory and to the database.

SOME ADDITIONAL BUILDER FEATURES

Cost

Cost is specified on the 'Activity' tab of the 'Properties' page for Function Activities. It is meant to represent the number of seconds that it takes to execute the Procedure attached to the Activity. Most PL/SQL Procedures execute so quickly that they can be left with the default value of zero. However, if the Activity in question runs a long time, or you want to schedule the Activity for a specific time of day you can specify any cost from 0.00 to 1,000,000.00. When the Workflow Engine is asked to start the Activity in question, it will compare the cost of the Activity to the value stored in WF_ENGINE.Threshold. If the cost of the Activity is greater, then the Activity is deferred until a Background Engine starts that includes this cost in its parameters. See FIGURE 3.69.

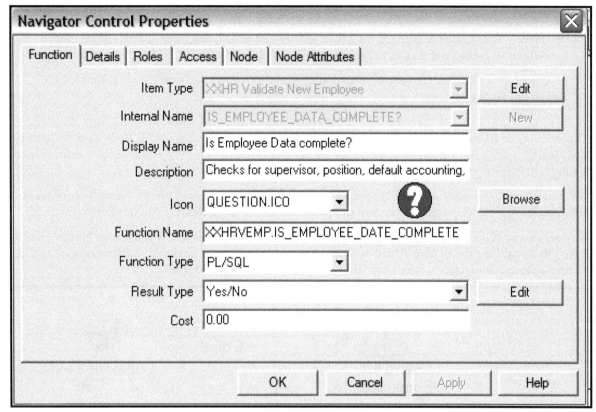

FIGURE 3.69

As delivered by Oracle, the WF_ENGINE.Threshold value is 50. However, any PL/SQL Procedure can set this value, so you will have to determine rules in your organization as to what the threshold should be.

 The Workflow Loader multiplies all values entered in the 'Cost' field by 100 when the Workflow definition is saved to the database. So assuming the engine default value remains 50, enter .51 or higher to defer an Activity to a Background Engine.

Notifications are delivered immediately. If a response is required, the Activity is automatically deferred, otherwise, the Activity behaves as if the cost is 0.00 and control passes immediately to the next Activity.

On Revisit

If you define a loop in your Workflow, you can instruct the Workflow Engine how to handle the loop on the second and following times it tries to execute the loop. 'On Revisit' is found on the 'Details' tab of the 'Properties' page of Notifications and Functions. This value is only meaningful on the first Activity of a loop and is ignored elsewhere. For our example, this value would be set for the 'Is Employee Data complete?' Activity. The possible values, according to the *Oracle Workflow Developer's Guide, Release 12, December 2006, page 3-89* are:

> Reset – (default value) – The Engine resets the completed activities in the loop by traversing through the loop in forward order from the pivot activity, executing each activity in CANCEL mode. You can include special logic in each function's CANCEL mode to undo prior operations. The Engine then traverses through the loop in forward order,

reexecuting each activity, starting with the pivot activity in RUN mode.

Loop – The Engine reexecutes the pivot activity and all activities that follow in the loop, without resetting, as if they have never been executed before..

Ignore – The Engine executes the activity only once and ignores the activity for all subsequent revisits.

The meaning of RUN and CANCEL mode are discussed in *Chapter 4, Using PL/SQL in Workflow*. Setting 'On Revisit' to Ignore will cause a Workflow to become stuck if the loop is executed a second time. Setting 'On Revisit' to Reset will cause all Notifications within the loop to be cancelled.

We actually need to ensure all open Notifications are cancelled and we will need to reset 'Loop Counter' before executing the loop again, so we will accept the default value of Reset for all our Functions.

However if our Workflow is sending a series of 'FYI' Notifications as in the Workflow in FIGURE 3.70, then 'On Revisit' for the Activity 'Build Message' must be set to 'Loop' or the 'FYI' Notification Send list of Employees to Supervisor will be cancelled before it can be emailed or read.

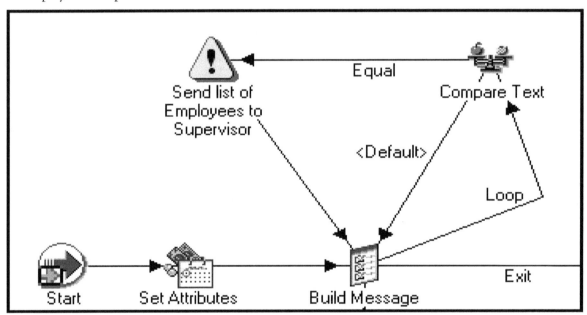

FIGURE 3.70

Error Handling

Workflow designers should try to anticipate problems and code for handling errors. But in the event of unexpected errors, the Builder allows the specification of an Item Type that will be called to handle the error. Oracle Applications provides an Item Type, WFERROR, containing three Procedures that can be used, DEFAULT_ERROR, DEFAULT_EVENT_ERROR, and RETRY_ONLY. You can also code your own error handling process. The error handling process is specified on the 'Details' tab of the 'Properties' page of Functions and Notifications. See FIGURE 3.71.

Workflow Builder will seed WFERROR, so unless you want to use your own Procedure, no further work is necessary. If you want a detailed explanation of the Processes in WFERROR, see *Chapter 11* in the *Oracle Workflow Developer's Guide, Release 12, Part No. B31433-01, December 2006.*

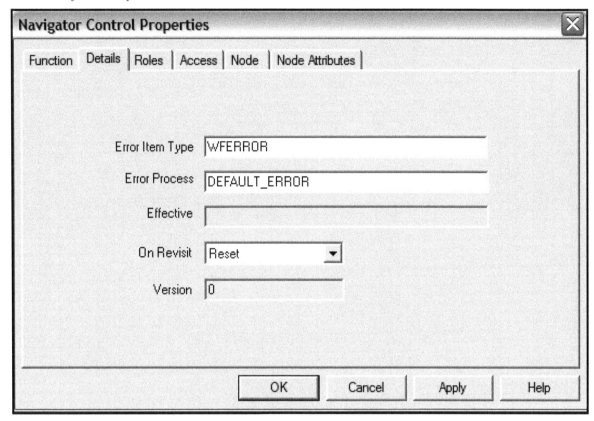

FIGURE 3.71

THERE'S ALWAYS MORE STUFF

This chapter was designed to show the more common design issues with Workflow and some of the common problems found with design. More material will be covered in *Chapter 11, Advanced Builder and PL/SQL.* However, now we need to look at both the code used inside the Workflow and the code used to start a Workflow.

Using PL/SQL in Workflow

Four types of PL/SQL Procedures will be written by developers; one to start the Workflow, one to maintain context (and optionally select the starting process), one Procedure used by the activities in the Workflow Processes, and one Procedure used by Document Attributes. This chapter will discuss the first three types of Procedures. The last type will be discussed in *Chapter 11, Advanced Builder and PL/SQL*.

Workflow allows each 'Function Name' to be a Procedure or a package.procedure. There is no requirement that Procedures should all be contained in the same Package. While Workflow allows all code to be individual Procedures (i.e., not contained in a Package), in order to facilitate the maintenance of custom Workflows, developers should place all Procedures related to a specific Workflow in a single Package. Thus, all our examples will be contained in the Package XXHRVEMP. This Package should also contain a comment indicating the name of the code that actually starts the Workflow.

As we'll discuss in *Chapter 15, What's on the Horizon*, Oracle is replacing Workflow with BPEL (Business Process Execution Language). The structure for using PL/SQL in BPEL will be different. For the Procedures called by Functions, developers can mitigate the changes this will require by carefully coding the PL/SQL routines used by the Functions. Our example routines in this chapter will demonstrate one of the recommended methods.

SPECIAL CONSIDERATIONS REQUIRED BY WORKFLOW

Starting Workflow

The code that starts a Workflow must be able to determine several key fields:

- **Item Type (Required)** – the Internal Name of the Workflow that should be started

- **Item Key (Required)** – the particular data that uniquely identifies an instance of a specific Workflow. Typically, the Item Key is the primary key(s) to a table concatenated with a sequence or other data structure that guarantees uniqueness. Examples are REQUISITION_HEADER_ID (requisitions), HEADER_ID (order headers), LINE_ID (order lines), EMPLOYEE_ID (employees), or REPORT_HEADER_ID (expense reports)

- **User Key (Optional, but highly recommended)** – the data that would allow an end user to identify a specific occurrence of a Workflow. Examples are the Requisition Number, Order Number, Order Line Number, Employee Number, or Expense Report Number

- **Owner (Optional, but highly recommended)** – the user responsible for tracking the progress of the transaction, usually the user that initiates a transaction. For applications (like Purchasing and *iExpenses*) that support surrogates entering data for others, the developer must decide whether the owner should be the surrogate or the user involved in the transaction

- **Top Process (Conditionally required)** – for Workflows with multiple runnable Processes, the Process that should be executed when the Workflow starts

Maintaining Context

When someone logs into the E-Business Suite, that person enters a username and password and then selects a responsibility. This starts a "session" and establishes the "context" for all activity performed by that user within that responsibility. If the user enters a transaction that starts a Workflow, this context information is available to the Workflow through FND_GLOBAL APIs. However if a Workflow is deferred to a Background Engine, the session is interrupted and the context information is lost. If this context information is required to enable viewing information via forms or to set UPDATED_BY columns, then the developer must provide code that re-establishes the correct context.

This code is contained in the Procedure specified in the Selector Function. The Selector Function is specified on the 'Properties' page of the Item Type (see FIGURE 4.1). Specifying the Selector Function is a piece of the Workflow definition that an end-user would not be concerned with. Thus, it was not mentioned in *Chapter 3, Builder Basics*. To specify a Selector Procedure, open the Workflow in the Builder tool, right-click the 'Item Type' and select 'Properties'. Enter a PL/SQL package.procedure.

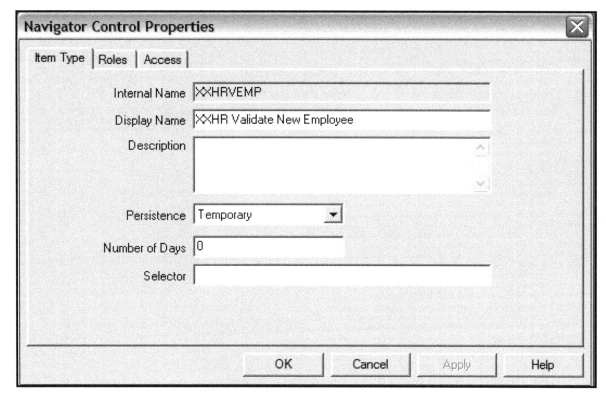

FIGURE 4.1

No Commits

MetaLink Doc. ID: 187735.1, *Workflow FAQ – All Versions*, has the following excellent discussion about commits in Workflows (authors' notes in [ ]):

> Can I commit in PL/SQL packages? Why not?
>
> You CANNOT commit inside a PL/SQL Procedure [assigned as the selector function or activity function], which is called by the Workflow Engine.
>
> If you issue a commit you, are committing the Workflow state as well as your application state. If you do commit and your PL/SQL function fails subsequently the Workflow Engine will not be able to rollback to a consistent state.
>
> Example:
>
> SP   SP   SP   SP   SP
>
> start ---> activity A -----> activity B ---> activity C ---> end
>
> The Workflow Engine issues a savepoint (SP) before executing each activity. It marks the activity as active and proceeds to execute the underlying PL/SQL.
>
> If you commit in the middle of an activity and the activity subsequently fails, the engine cannot rollback to its savepoint. Therefore, the work done in both the engine and the application before the commit cannot be rolled back.
>
> More over, even if the activity does not fail, another process (such as a background engine)

gains visibility to the status information just committed and may start processing prematurely leading to conflicts and unusual errors.

Similarly, you cannot ROLLBACK across PL/SQL Procedures. If you do, REALLY strange things happen when an error occurs. Either the activity status line won't exist (because it's rolled back) so WF can't write the error, or it may succeed in writing the error but then continues along the process rather than stopping because other status info has been rolled back. If you must undo something then rollback to a save point within your own package and not to one in a previous Function Activity.

What constitutes a single commit cycle in Workflow?

Here are some facts about the Workflow Engine activity execution and commits:

1. The Workflow Engine does not perform any internal commits. The caller of the Workflow API should always perform the actual commit.

2. Exceptions that occur in activity functions are not propagated back to the original Workflow API caller [thus it is recommended that a developer use a special API to make error information visible to the status monitor]. If an activity function raises an exception, the activity status is set to 'ERROR', and execution on that path is halted. If other activities are still eligible for execution, the engine will continue with those activities.

3. Exceptions that occur in activity functions do not invalidate the fact that earlier activities executed and completed successfully. In the engine, this is implemented by setting a savepoint just before each activity function is executed. If the function fails, the engine performs an internal rollback to the save point, marks the activity status as 'ERROR' and goes about its other business.

Therefore, Oracle Workflow never commits and it's up to your calling program to perform the commit that is necessary for other users to see the changes that have occurred. For example, notifications, deferred processes and any other data inserts will have taken place but will not be visible until the commit. [Yhe following is an example of a commit used in the Procedure that starts a Workflow:]

```
CreateProcess();
SetItemAttribute();
StartProcess();
commit;
```

Note: The background engine performs a commit after every piece of work (a piece of work is defined as a synchronous thread that starts from the activity that requires processing and ends when the engine can't proceed any further).

As MetaLink Doc. ID: 187735.1 states, the calling package (either the one starting the Workflow or the background engine) issues the commit. This restriction limits creating tables or other SQL DDL calls which do an automatic commit. Developers can use a pragma autonomous_transaction to code around this restriction. MetaLink Doc. ID: 196818.1, *How to execute simple DDL statements from a trigger*, shows an example of the use of this transaction in a Trigger.

You cannot execute a commit inside of a Trigger, this is a Trigger limitation.

All Data Definition Language (DDL) statements execute an implicit commit. Even if you create a separate Procedure, to execute the DDL statement, the execution of the separate Procedure within the Trigger is still in the same transaction, forcing a commit of any statement executed in the Trigger and hence causing an error.

A workaround is to use autonomous transactions to create the user:

1) Create a Procedure called ddl_proc that will execute as an autonomous transaction:

```
SQL> create or replace procedure ddl_proc
2  is
3    pragma AUTONOMOUS_TRANSACTION;
4  BEGIN
5    execute immediate 'CREATE USER shek IDENTIFIED BY shek';
6  END;
```

Procedure created.

2) Create the Trigger, that will call the autonomous Procedure to create the user:

```
SQL> create or replace trigger ddl_trig  after delete on emp
2  BEGIN
3    ddl_proc;
4  END;
```

Remember, if this Procedure is re-executed through a retry or rewind, the code in the pragma AUTONOMOUS_TRANSACTION has already been executed and committed. Therefore, the developer must include code in the pragma AUTONOMOUS_TRANSACTION either to test whether the transaction needs to be performed or to trap bogus errors. An example of testing whether a transaction needs to be performed would be to test the presence of the table in the ALL_OBJECTS table before issuing a CREATE TABLE command. An example of how to trap errors can be found in MetaLink Doc. ID: 168702.1 *Explanation of ORA-6502 When FETCHING Into a Cursor of %ROWTYPE*. Note that to use this technique you will have to know the error code that would be raised if the transaction fails. The following excerpt shows the code in the Procedure table_create:

```
PROCEDURE table_create
AS

  /*Create a table based on SCOTT.EMP.  If table already present
    ensure that  it is dropped before attempting to recreate.*/

SQL_t       varchr2(32767);
DROP_t      varchar2(100);

BEGIN

    SQL_t := 'CREATE TABLE test6502 as
                select * from SCOTT.EMP';

-- Drop any instance of test6502
```

```
DECLARE -- Sub Block declaration

drop_fail exception;
pragma exception_init(drop_fail, -942);

BEGIN -- Sub Block

        DROP_t := 'DROP TABLE test6502';
        EXECUTE IMMEDIATE DROP_t;

EXCEPTION
WHEN drop_fail THEN      -- Do nothing!
        dbms_output.put_line('An attempt was made to drop
                a table that did not exist');
END; -- Sub Block

    EXECUTE IMMEDIATE SQL_t;

END table_create;
```

Alternatively, if a SQL command that requires/implies a commit is required, try to execute it prior to executing the Procedure that starts the Workflow.

Error Handling

In a perfect world, data required by the Workflow always exists and code never errors. However, good programmers always assume the worst and provide for it. This section concerns errors that occur in the code called by activities. There are three basic types of errors:

1. The Workflow was started with an invalid Item Key. This is almost always attributable to an error in the code that starts the Workflow. Since any further Action would be done against the wrong data, if the Item Key is invalid, the Workflow should error immediately. This can be done by returning the result code ERROR.

2. There is a problem with the data, but the problem is detectable (such as a missing approver) and the error can be handled in a controlled manner through a Notification where the recipient can either adjust the data and indicate that it is okay to proceed or tell the Workflow to return the document as rejected. A good example of this is the Payables Expense Report Approval 'Workflow Expenses' (APEXP). In the 'Server Side Validation' Process, the code called by the Function 'AP Validate Expense Report' (FIGURE 4.2) returns a status of 'Fail' if the expense report cannot be processed due to data errors. A Message is sent to the Role 'Expense Report Workflow Administrator'. This person can either repair the data and reply 'Problem Fixed' or reply 'Return to Preparer'. Regardless of the reply, the situation is handled without the Workflow entering error status, which then would require action by the Workflow Administrator.

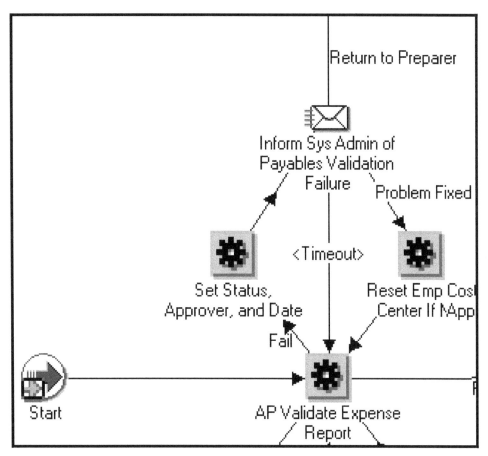

FIGURE 4.2

3. The code errors. These are the most frustrating errors as they require debugging the code. Debugging is difficult because the Oracle Error Message is rarely sufficient to detect which statement errored. Oracle's WF_CORE.Context API allows you to display coder-defined "breadcrumbs".

WF_CORE.Context

The first two parameters to this API are the Package name and the Procedure name. The coder can then list up to 10 additional parameters for the purpose of providing any information necessary to find the erroring code and help identify why it errored.

Oracle uses these additional parameters to display the Item Type, Item Key, and Function Mode. FuncMode is useful when a Procedure uses more than one mode. Since the Item Type and Item Key are displayed elsewhere in any Error Message, we prefer to display the information needed to find the exact statement that errored.

Although this Package accepts up to 10 parameters to display information necessary for troubleshooting, we prefer to use a single variable and concatenate all necessary information into this single variable. Regardless of the number of variables used, the length of each variable totaled together cannot exceed 32000 characters.

To effectively use this API, define three global variables: G_PKG, G_PROC, and G_TRACE. G_PKG and G_PROC should be VARCHAR2(30). We use VARCHAR2(2000) for G_TRACE, although any value up to the maximum allowed can be used. Set the value of G_PKG in the global declaration section. Set the value for G_PROC at the start of each Procedure. Then, throughout the Procedure, set the value for G_TRACE such that someone debugging the code could find where a particular value is set and use the information in G_TRACE to debug the following code.

Suppose our Workflow Package contained the following code:

```
BEGIN
FOR employee_rec IN employee_cur (l_supervisor_id, l_offset)
LOOP
        g_trace := 'Employee ID = ' || employee_rec.person_id;
        OPEN csr_gettimezone(employee_rec.person_id);
        FETCH csr_gettimezone INTO l_timezone;
        CLOSE csr_gettimezone;
        g_trace := 'Timezone = ' || l_timezone;
        SELECT DECODE(l_timezone, 'New_York',0,
                                  'Indianapolis',0,
                                  'Havana',0,
                                  'Chicago',1,
                                  'Regina',1,
                                  'Phoenix',2,
                                  'Denver',2,
                                  'Los_Angeles',3,
                                  'Pitcairn',3,
                                  'Anchorage',4,
                                  'Gambier',4,
                                  'Honolulu',5,
                                  'Adak',5,0)
     INTO    l_timezone_offset
   FROM DUAL;
EXCEPTION
    WHEN OTHERS
    THEN
        wf_core.context(g_pkg, l_proc, p_funcmode, g_trace);
        RAISE;
END;
```

If the Error Message shows 'Employee ID = <number>', then the Package errored either in opening, reading, or closing the cursor. If these statements execute correctly, G_TRACE is set to a new value. Thus, the erroring statements will always be between the setting of G_TRACE displayed in the Error Message and the next statement that sets a new value for G_TRACE.

In our example, PERSON_ID used in the cursor is appended as part of G_TRACE. Thus, not only will the Error Message show where the code errored but what value was passed into the cursor. This allows the person debugging the code to more accurately simulate what occurred at the time of the error.

While WF_CORE.Context is limited to Procedures called by Activities, the concept embodied in G_TRACE can be used in other Procedures as demonstrated in our example Trigger below.

STARTING OUR WORKFLOW

The Workflow designed in *Chapter 3, Builder Basics*, is depicted in FIGURE 4.3:

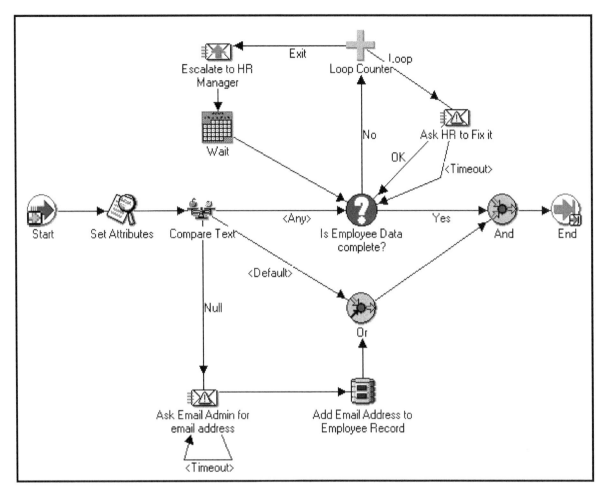

FIGURE 4.3

Oracle provides several APIs that will tell the Workflow Engine to start the Workflow. The name of the Procedure or form that contains the call to these APIs is not contained within the Workflow definition. This tends to hide how the Workflow is initiated.

The team designing the Workflow has to be aware of the base tables used to store the relevant data. Employees are stored in PER_ALL_PEOPLE_F. Remember that the keys to this table are EMPLOYEE_ID, EFFECTIVE_START_DATE and EFFECTIVE_END_DATE. There is also another field, PERSON_TYPE, which determines whether the record contains data about a contractor, employee or another defined PERSON_TYPE. For each PERSON_TYPE, the EFFECTIVE_START_DATE and EFFECTIVE_END_DATE cannot overlap. For the record with the most current EFFECTIVE_START_DATE, Oracle uses '31-DEC-4712' as the EFFECTIVE_END_DATE (currently the maximum date that can be stored in an Oracle date field). Employees have a PERSON_TYPE = 'E'. Usually the current record is the record where SYSDATE is between EFFECTIVE_START_DATE and EFFECTIVE_END_DATE, but since the purpose of our Workflow is to ensure critical functions are set up before the employee actually starts, the EFFECTIVE_START_DATE could be a date > SYSDATE.

Note, we are assuming that either core functionality or APIs have been utilized to enter employees. If this is not the case, as we sometimes see in installations that were implemented many years ago, don't count on the EFFECTIVE_END_DATE being '31-DEC-4712'. Check the quality of your data.

Thus, we will search for the record that has the maximum EFFECTIVE_END_DATE with the PERSON_TYPE = 'E'.

Except for the email address, the information we are validating is actually in the assignment record, PER_ALL_ASSIGNMENTS_F, attached to the employee. Since our Workflow will be invoked when a new employee record is created, we will only deal with the assignment records created at that time. The Process could be modified so that it is invoked each time an assignment record is created or updated. In *Chapter 11, Advanced Builder and PL/SQL*, we will modify the code to report on all current assignments using a Document Attribute. For the purposes of this initial PL/SQL chapter, we are going to validate the primary assignment.

The keys to this table are ASSIGNMENT_ID, EFFECTIVE_START_DATE and EFFECTIVE_END_DATE. As multiple assignments are permitted, the dates for assignment records can overlap. Like employee records, assignments can have start dates in the future. Our code will locate the assignment record with EFFECTIVE_END_DATE set to the maximum value of '31-DEC-4712' and PRIMARY_FLAG = 'Y'.

The team designing the Workflow has to decide what will initiate the need to start the Workflow. Typically this is a change in the data in the database through some data entry/update process such as a form or batch API process. If the change in the data is limited to a single source, you can modify that source to call a Procedure to start the Workflow. In Release 11.5.10 and higher, there are personalization options that can be used to start the Workflow. If there are multiple sources, the best approach may be to create a Trigger or a scheduled Concurrent Program that starts the Workflow. Each method has pros and cons regarding timing, patching and testing.

For the sake of our example, we are going to pick the creation of the employee record as the initiating Event. Having decided this, the designer must then be aware of the various methods to create an employee record, such as a form, API, or custom Procedure that inserts data directly into the tables. Since records can be created outside the form, customizing the form or using a form personalization is not a viable option. Therefore, we will utilize a Trigger.

It is important to note that the Workflow Engine issues a savepoint whenever a Workflow is initiated so that if an error occurs, it can issue a rollback. However, neither rollbacks nor savepoints are allowed in Triggers. Older versions of Workflow made the programmer responsible for ensuring that the Start Activity for the Workflow be deferred to the Background Engine either by adjusting the cost of the Start Activity to be > .5 or by temporarily adjusting the default background cost. Now the Workflow Engine automatically traps 'Savepoint not allowed' errors and defers the execution of the Activity to the Background Engine.

This chapter will show how to ensure that the Start Activity is deferred through the adjustment of the default background cost. This default background cost is an externalized constant called WF_ENGINE.Threshold. *Chapter 5, Business Events*, will demonstrate the preferred method of starting Workflows from a Trigger.

Regardless of the method used to start the Workflow, the designer must be able to ensure that all data required by the Workflow will be present when the Workflow starts.

The following code is a simple Trigger that starts our Workflow. The explanation of each of the statements follows.

```
CREATE OR REPLACE TRIGGER xxhr_start_xxhrvemp_workflow
1.► AFTER INSERT
    ON per_all_people_f
    FOR EACH ROW
    DECLARE
    l_save_threshold    NUMBER;
    l_item_key          applsys.wf_items.item_key%TYPE;
    l_owner             applsys.fnd_user.user_name%TYPE;
    l_user_person_type  hr.per_person_type.user_person_type%TYPE;
2.►g_trace             VARCHAR2(2000);
    BEGIN
    -- get the person_type
3.►g_trace := 'Getting the person type';
    SELECT user_person_type
      INTO l_user_person_type
      FROM hr.per_person_types ppt
     WHERE ppt.person_type_id = :NEW.person_type_id;
    -- If user_person_type <> 'Employee' do nothing
    IF l_user_person_type = 'Employee'
    THEN
        -- get the user name of the person who
        -- created the record
        g_trace := 'Getting created_by user name';
        SELECT user_name
          INTO l_owner
          FROM applsys.fnd_user
         WHERE :new.created_by = user_id;
        -- the following two statements save the current
        -- defer-to-background cost and reset it so that
        -- the start of the Workflow will be deferred
4.►     g_trace := 'Saving wf_engine threshold';
        save_threshold := wf_engine.threshold;
        wf_engine.threshold := -1;
        --the following statement creates the ItemKey
5.►     g_trace := 'Creating item_key';
        l_item_key := :new.person_id||'-'||
                TO_CHAR(SYSDATE,'YYYYMMDDHH24MISS');
        -- the following statement starts the Workflow
6.►     g_trace := 'Starting the Workflow';
        wf_engine.LaunchProcess    (ItemType => 'XXHRVEMP'
                ,ItemKey  => l_item_key
                ,process  => 'VALIDATE_NEW_EMPLOYEE_TOP'
                ,userkey  => :new.employee_number
                ,owner    => l_owner
                );
        -- the following statement restores the saved
        -- defer-to-background cost
7.►     g_trace := 'Restoring threshold';
            wf_engine.threshold := save_threshold;
    END IF:
8.► EXCEPTION
    WHEN OTHERS
    THEN
        ax_message_pkg.raise_message ('AX'
                    ,'AX_56010_COMM_MESG_TEXT'
                    ,'MESG_BUG'
                    ,'Error occurred while ' ||g_trace
                    );
            RAISE;
    END;
```

1. ▶ This Trigger fires whenever a record is inserted in PER_ALL_PEOPLE_F, which is the base table for employees.

2. ▶ G_TRACE will be used to help debug the Trigger if it fails. It will be set to the actions attempted throughout the Procedure. If the Trigger fails, the Message displayed will indicate that the Action following the setting of G_TRACE errored.

3. ▶ Check the PERSON_TYPE_ID against PER_PERSON_TYPES. If not 'Employee', then nothing else needs to be done.

4. ▶ Because we are starting a Workflow from a Trigger, we are saving off the Workflow Engine Threshold and re-setting it to −1. This way all activities, even those with a cost of zero, will be deferred until the Background Engine runs.

5. ▶ The Item Key must be unique for the Item Type specified. Since there can only be one EMPLOYEE_ID in PER_ALL_PEOPLE_F with the PERSON_TYPE of 'Employee' and EFFECTIVE_END_DATE = '31-DEC-4712', the EFFECTIVE_START_DATE and EFFECTIVE_END_DATE fields do not need to be included as the ITEM_KEY. However, using the recommendations outlined in *Chapter 3, Builder Basics*, we add a delimiter ('-') and SYSDATE to guarantee uniqueness.

6. ▶ WF_ENGINE.LaunchProcess is a seeded API which creates the Workflow in the run time tables and tells the Engine to start the Workflow. The parameters are:

   - **ItemType (required)** – the Internal Name of the Workflow you want to start

   - **ItemKey (required)** – a value that will make this iteration of the Item Type unique from any other iteration of this Item Type

   - **process (optional)** – the Internal Name of the top Process. If this value is left blank, either the Workflow can have only one Process with the Runnable Flag set to yes, or the Workflow must specify a Selector Function to determine the top Process (see "SET_CTX and TEST_CTX" section later in this chapter)

   - **userkey (optional)** – the user-seen equivalent of the ItemKey. For example, the EMPLOYEE_ID is never displayed in the 'Enter Employee' screen, but the employee number is

   - **owner (optional)** – a valid Role designated as the owner and thus enabled to see the progress of the Workflow. If no owner is specified, then only the administrator is allowed to see the progress of the Workflow (except for specific applications such as Order Management that provide special screens for viewing orders and lines)

7. ▶ Reset the Workflow Engine Threshold back to the value saved in Step 3.

8. ▶ If the Trigger errors, the exception routine calls ax_Message_pkg.raise_Message which will display the value set in G_TRACE.

Oracle provides an alternative set of APIs that can be used to start a Workflow: WF_ENGINE.CreateProcess and WF_ENGINE.StartProcess. The CreateProcess API sets up the Workflow in the runtime tables and utilizes the same parameters as LaunchProcess. The StartProcess API transfers execution to the Workflow and has only two parameters: ItemType and ItemKey. Once the call to WF_ENGINE.CreateProcess is executed, the developer can execute other statements, such as setting values for Attributes, prior to executing WF_ENGINE.StartProcess. Oracle uses this method to start the 'Expenses' (APEXP) Workflow. Between the call to WF_ENGINE.CreateProcess and

WF_ENGINE.StartProcess, Oracle sets values for approximately 30 Attributes. As will be shown in *Chapter 6, Testing Workflows*, this significantly complicates testing and is not considered a good practice. Additionally, if the Workflow is started from an Event (see next chapter), there is no ability to set Attribute values outside of the Workflow. Oracle has abandoned this practice and is selectively updating the Workflows to use Events and to set all Attribute values inside the Workflow.

One other situation exists where you might choose the Create and 'Start' APIs instead of the 'Launch' API. If you are designing an 'Approval' Workflow, the Workflow typically ends if an approver rejects the object being approved. In many Business Processes, this returns control of the object to the originator, who can make changes to the object and re-submit the object for approval. If the 'Purge Obsolete Run-time Data' Concurrent Program has not run since the conclusion of the Workflow rejecting the object, an instance of the Workflow with the object's key already exists. If you issue a Launch call using the same Item Key, it will error out due to violation of uniqueness constraints. Oracle avoids this problem by concatenating a new sequence number to the object key each time a Workflow is started. Thus, each submission of the object for approval is a separate Workflow with a unique Item Key.

For a custom Workflow, you can actually 'restart' the Workflow and append to the approval history (assuming that the 'Purge Obsolete Workflow Runtime Data' Concurrent Program has not run and removed the completed Workflow data).

Note that unless you can guarantee that the Trigger will not fire for the same object before the previous Workflow is finished, make sure you include the 'and end_date IS NOT NULL' clause in the check for an existing Item Key.

First, add to the DECLARE section:

```
l_count   NUMBER;
```

Then replace 5. ▶ and 6. ▶ with the following:

```
5.▶     -- Check if Workflow exists with person_id as part of key
        g_trace := 'Checking for existing completed Workflow';
        BEGIN
        SELECT item_key INTO l_item_key FROM wf_items
        WHERE item_key like TO_CHAR(:new.person_id)||'%'
         AND end_date is not null;
        l_count :=1;
        EXCEPTION
          WHEN OTHERS
          THEN
              g_trace := 'Finding no existing Workflow';
              l_count :=0;
              l_item_key := :new.person_id||'-'||
                    TO_CHAR(SYSDATE,'YYYYMMDDHH24MISS');
        END;
6.▶     -- if no Workflow found, create WF_ITEMS record
        g_trace := 'Creating WF_ITEMS record';
        IF l_count = 0
        THEN
            wf_engine.CreateProcess (ItemType => 'XXHRVEMP'
                    ,ItemKey   => l_item_key
                    ,process   => 'VALIDATE_NEW_EMPLOYEE_TOP'
                    ,userkey   => :new.employee_number
                    ,owner     => l_owner
                                    );
        END IF;
        g_trace := 'Starting Process';
```

```
wf_engine.StartProcess (itemypte => 'XXHRVEMP'
                       ,ItemKey  => l_item_key
                       );
```

This code checks the runtime tables to see if a completed Workflow with an ITEM_KEY beginning with the PERSON_ID already exists. If it doesn't (l_count=0), then it issues a CreateProcess. If it does (l_count>0), then it skips the CreateProcess and just re-starts the Workflow using StartProcess.

PROCEDURE CALLED WITHIN WORKFLOW – NO RESULT

PL/SQL Procedures that are called from within a Workflow must follow a certain standard. We will show a Procedure that doesn't require a Result Code and one that does. SET_ATTRIBUTES is the Procedure that doesn't require a Result Code.

As stated in *Chapter 3, Builder Basics*, SET_ATTRIBUTES should set all the static Item Attributes. This does not mean that Attribute values will not be set in other Procedures. In our example, the Workflow loops through 'Is Employee Data Complete' until the values for supervisor and position are set. Since this will require reading the assignment record each time this node is traversed, it is not necessary to duplicate the code in "Set Attributes".

The code for the SET_ATTRIBUTES procedure is:

```
1.▶ PROCEDURE set_attributes (
         ItemType        IN     VARCHAR2
        ,ItemKey         IN     VARCHAR2
        ,actid           IN     NUMBER
        ,funcmode        IN     VARCHAR2
        ,ResultOut       OUT    VARCHAR2
    )
    IS
2.▶   l_employee_name    per_all_people_f.full_name%TYPE
                            := NULL;
      l_employee_number per_all_people_f.employee_number%TYPE
                            := NULL;
      l_responsibility_name
          fnd_responsibility_tl.responsibility_name%TYPE
                            := NULL;
      l_email per_all_people_f.email_address%TYPE
                            := NULL;
      l_owner              wf_local_users.display_name%TYPE
                            := NULL;
      l_admin              wf_local_roles.name%TYPE
                            := NULL;
      l_email_admin        wf_local_roles.name%TYPE
                            := NULL;
      l_workflow_admin     wf_local_roles.name%TYPE;
      l_message            VARCHAR2(2000) := NULL;
      l_person_id          NUMBER := NULL;
      l_created_by         NUMBER := NULL;
      l_active             BOOLEAN:= FALSE;

3.▶   -- assumes value stored at site level
      CURSOR csr_get_administrator IS
          SELECT v.profile_option_value director
            FROM fnd_profile_option_values v, fnd_profile_options o, fnd_user u
           WHERE o.profile_option_id =v.profile_option_id
             AND o.profile_option_name =
```

```
                    'XXHR_EMAIL_ADMINISTRATOR'
              AND level_id = 10001
              AND v.profile_option_value = u.user_name
              AND nvl(u.end_date,sysdate+1)>sysdate;

     BEGIN
4.▶      -- Do nothing except in RUN mode
         g_proc := 'SET_ATTRIBUTES';
         g_trace := 'Checking funcmode';

5.▶      IF (funcmode <> wf_engine.eng_run)
         THEN
            ResultOut := wf_engine.eng_null;
            RETURN;
         END IF;
6.▶      g_trace := 'Retrieving employee_id from ItemKey';

         BEGIN
            -- parse out the key (assumes delimiter is '-'
            -- and that key is numeric
            SELECT TO_NUMBER(SUBSTR(ItemKey,1,
                          INSTR(ItemKey,'-')-1))
              INTO l_person_id
              FROM DUAL;
            --later set parsed value as attribute so other
            --routines don't have to re-parse the value
7.▶         IF l_person_id = 0
            THEN
                ResultOut := 'ERROR: Delimeter must be a ''-''';
            END IF;
         EXCEPTION
            WHEN OTHERS
            THEN
               ResultOut := 'ERROR:Cannot get employee_id
                              from ItemKey';
               RETURN;
         END;

8.▶      BEGIN
            g_trace := 'Get employee information';

            SELECT email_address,employee_number,full_name,created_by
              INTO l_email,l_employee_number,l_employee_name,l_created_by
              FROM per_all_people_f
              WHERE person_id = l_person_id AND SYSDATE < effective_end_date;

9. ▶     EXCEPTION
             WHEN NO_DATA_FOUND
             THEN
                ResultOut := 'ERROR:No Employee Record';
                RETURN;
          END;

10.▶     BEGIN
            g_trace := 'getting owner';

            SELECT wlr.display_name INTO l_owner
              FROM wf_local_roles wlr,fnd_user fu
              WHERE fu.user_name = wlr.name
```

143

```
                           AND fu.user_id = l_created_by;
11.▶       EXCEPTION
              WHEN NO_DATA_FOUND
              THEN
                 ResultOut := 'ERROR:Created_by not valid';
                 RETURN;
           END;
12.▶       BEGIN
              g_trace := 'getting workflow administrator';
              SELECT text INTO l_workflow_admin
                FROM wf_resources
               WHERE name = 'WF_ADMIN_ROLE';

              IF l_workflow_admin = '*'
              THEN
                 l_workflow_admin := 'SYSADMIN';
                    END IF;
           EXCEPTION
              WHEN NO_DATA_FOUND
              THEN
                 ResultOut := 'ERROR:No Workflow admin';
                 RETURN;
           END;
13.▶       -- get the Email Administrator from the profile option
           g_trace:= 'Check for email admin';
           OPEN csr_get_administrator;
           FETCH csr_get_administrator INTO l_email_admin;
           IF   csr_get_administrator%NOTFOUND
             OR l_email_admin IS NULL
           THEN
              l_email_admin := l_workflow_admin;
              l_message := 'Profile option ' ||
                          '''XXHR: Email Admin'' is not set';
           ELSIF l_email_admin <> l_workflow_admin
           THEN
              l_active:= wf_directory.UserActive(l_email_admin);
              IF NOT l_active
              THEN
                 L_email_admin := l_workflow_admin;
                 L_message := 'User in Profile Option '
                         ||'''XXHR: Email Admin'' is not active';
              END IF;
           END IF;
           CLOSE csr_get_administrator;
14.▶       g_trace := 'Get responsibility that created employee';
           SELECT frtl.responsibility_name INTO l_responsibility_name
             FROM fnd_login_responsibilities flr ,per_all_people_f pap
               ,fnd_responsibility_tl frtl
            WHERE SYSDATE BETWEEN pap.effective_start_date
                     AND pap.effective_end_date
              AND pap.person_type_id = 13
              AND pap.last_update_login = flr.login_id
              AND flr.responsibility_id = frtl.responsibility_id
              AND frtl.language = 'US'
              AND pap.last_update_date BETWEEN flr.start_time
                  AND nvl(flr.end_time,sysdate)
              AND pap.person_id = l_person_id;
15.▶          g_trace := 'Setting user key and owner';
           wf_engine.SetItemUserKey (ItemType
```

```
                                          ,ItemKey
                                          ,l_employee_name
                                          );
              wf_engine.SetItemOwner (ItemType
                                          ,ItemKey
                                          ,l_owner
                                          );
16.▶      g_trace := 'setting attributes';
          wf_engine.SetItemAttrText     (ItemType
                                          ,ItemKey
                                          ,'EMAIL_ADMINISTRATOR'
                                          ,l_email_admin
                                          );
          wf_engine.SetItemAttrText     (ItemType
                                          ,ItemKey
                                          ,'HR'
                                          ,l_responsibility_name
                                          );
          wf_engine.SetItemAttrText     (ItemType
                                                ,ItemKey
                                          ,'EMPLOYEE_NUMBER'
                                          ,l_employee_number
                                          );
          wf_engine.SetItemAttrText     (ItemType
                                                ,ItemKey
                                          ,'EMPLOYEE_NAME'
                                          ,l_employee_name
                                          );
          wf_engine.SetItemAttrNumber (ItemType
                                          ,ItemKey
                                          ,'EMPLOYEE_ID'
                                          ,l_person_id
                                          );
          wf_engine.SetItemAttrText     (ItemType
                                          ,ItemKey
                                          ,'EMAIL_ADDRESS'
                                          ,l_email
                                          );




          wf_engine.SetItemAttrText     (ItemType
                                          ,ItemKey
                                          ,'EMAIL_ADMIN_ERROR'
                                          ,l_message
                                          );

17.▶      ResultOut := 'COMPLETE:';
          RETURN;
18.▶ EXCEPTION
          WHEN OTHERS
          THEN
              wf_core.context (g_pkg
                                ,g_proc
                                ,funcmode
                                ,g_trace
                                );
          RAISE;
```

```
END set_attributes;
```

1. ▶ All Procedures called from within a Workflow have the same five parameters: ItemType, ItemKey, ActID, FuncMode and ResultOut. ItemType and ItemKey have already been defined. ActID is the identifier of the particular node in the Workflow and is used by the Engine. FuncMode indicates the execution mode of the Activity. Valid values and their use are:

- **RUN** – Normal mode for Function activities. All Function activities execute in RUN mode the first time the Activity is encountered. Post-Notification activities execute in RUN mode if they have first run in RESPOND mode. Setting ResultOut in this mode determines the next Action the Workflow will follow.

- **CANCEL** – Used to reset or undo actions taken in a loop. This mode is only used if the 'On Revisit' of the Pivot Activity in a Loop is set to Reset. CANCEL allows the developer to write special code to undo any database actions that were done when the loop was traversed the previous time. See the next Procedure for an example of this use. If any post-Notification functions are in the loop they are also executed in CANCEL mode.

- **SKIP, RETRY** – Used if the Activity is progressed through using the 'Status Monitor', answering an error Notification (WFERROR or other error routines), or using the WF_ENGINE.HandleError API. If the Activity should not be skipped, set ResultOut to WF_ENGINE.eng_noskip.

- **VALIDATE, TIMEOUT, RESPOND, TRANSFER, FORWARD, QUESTION, ANSWER** – If a Notification specifies a Function Name, this Procedure is executed just prior to transitioning to the next node. The Workflow Engine supplies the value for FuncMode based on the recipient's Action (see *Chapter 11, Advanced Builder and PL/SQL* for examples of these FuncModes). If the recipient's Action is a response, the Workflow Engine will run the Function first in VALIDATE mode, then RESPOND mode, then RUN mode.

ResultOut indicates to the Workflow Engine whether the Function completed normally and what the next Action should be. The possible results are:

- **COMPLETE:<result_code>** – This code indicates that the Activity completed successfully and that the Workflow should progress to the next Activity (no <result_code>) or down the leg that corresponds to the <result_code> label.

- **ERROR:<error_code>** – This code is used by the developer to stop the Workflow and pass control to the error Procedure. Unlike errors invoked through exception routines, this code is deliberately set by the developer to indicate that the Workflow should not progress but instead invoke the error Procedure and pass the <error_code> as part of the Message. <error_code> can be any of the Messages in FND_NEW_MESSAGES, or a SQL error code, or a developer-defined literal.

- **WAITING** – This code indicates that another Activity must also complete before the Workflow can progress. This is the status of the 'Standard' AND Activity until all legs into the AND complete.

- **DEFERRED:<date>** – This code indicates that the Activity is deferred to the Background Engine. It will remain deferred until <date> has passed. <date> must be of the format TO_CHAR (<date_string>, WF_ENGINE.date_format).

- **NOTIFIED:<notification_id>:<assigned_user>** – This code indicates that the Workflow is stopped and waiting for an external entity to indicate it is OK to proceed. This status is given to Notifications waiting for a response, and to activities such as 'Block', 'Wait for Flow', and Events in 'Receive' mode. The NOTIFICATION_ID and ASSIGNED_USER are optional and only used by Notifications.

2. ▶ Typical declare section. Because this routine sets Attributes, and the Attributes cannot be set in a SELECT statement, there are holding variables declared for the SELECT statements to use. All variables are initialized to NULL so that if any of the cursors or selects do not return data, the variable is NULL, not undefined.

3. ▶ Cursors are used to search for data where missing data is allowable and part of the Workflow design.

4. ▶ G_PROC is set to the name of the Procedure. This is required for the Generic Error Handling API WF_CORE.Context. G_TRACE will be periodically set to indicate key points in the code. If an unexpected error occurs, G_TRACE will be passed to the Error Stack and the designer will be able to isolate the area of code that malfunctioned. Note that G_TRACE is reset often and may include the value of selected variables used in subsequent statements.

5. ▶ In our Workflow, this routine can only be run once (not in a loop), therefore the only valid mode is RUN, so the Procedure will just exit if the FuncModes is not RUN. Since the Procedure has already exited unless the FuncMode is 'RUN', there is no need to test for this value. 'RUN' is the FuncMode that the Engine supplies when the Activity is transitioning through this node to perform the purpose intended by the designer.

6. ▶ Our Item Key is the PERSON_ID followed by a '-' followed by the date (to the hundredth of a second) that the Workflow started. We need to parse out the PERSON_ID so that it can be used to retrieve other information.

7. ▶ This shows two examples of checking a specific type of failure. This type of check is used when the failure to find a specific record would make continuation of the Workflow meaningless. If this type of error occurs, ResultOut is set to ERROR and the Procedure ends with the RETURN statement. When this result is received by the Workflow Engine, the Workflow Engine will mark the Workflow in error status and initiate the error Item Type that is specified on the 'Details' tab of the 'Properties' page of the function. The Builder will default WFERROR as the Error Item Type and DEFAULT_ERROR as the Error Process, but the designer can substitute another error Item Type and Process (See FIGURE 4.4). The Item Attribute RESULT_CODE in the WFERROR Item Type is set to the text after ERROR. See *Chapter 6, Testing Workflows*, for an example of returning this type of error.

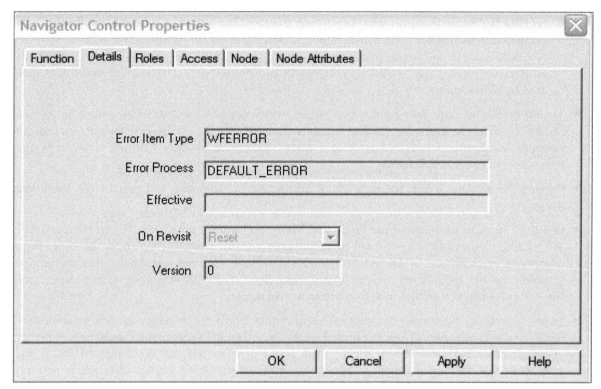

FIGURE 4. 4

See 17.► for an explanation of handling general un-expected errors.

8.► In our particular Workflow, the email address, employee name, and employee number (needed for the Messages) are stored in PER_ALL_PEOPLE_F. The other values, supervisor and position, are stored in PER_ALL_ASSIGNMENTS_F. Remember that we have programmed a loop to re-evaluate whether the employee data is complete. So in 'Set Attributes' we will retrieve only the data required to save an employee record (employee name and number) or for the next step (EMAIL_ADDRESS). We do not want to write code here to read data from PER_ALL_ASSIGNMENTS_F as that code belongs in the next function.

9.► If the SELECT into PER_ALL_PEOPLE_F fails, it means we do not have a valid PERSON_ID and thus cannot check any data about the employee. This is another case where a failure of the select means there are errors serious enough to warrant instructing the Workflow Engine to place the Workflow in error status.

10.► Since this Workflow is invoked when a new employee is created, we will use CREATED_BY to identify the Workflow owner. Setting the Owner allows this Role/person to view the progress of the Workflow. Owner must be set to NAME in WF_LOCAL_ROLES where PARTITION_ID = 1. 'Owner' is a field that could have been set when the Workflow was started if using LaunchProcess or CreateProcess. However, if using an Event to start a Workflow, it is easier to set the owner in the first Activity. Thus, the code is included in SET_ATTRIBUTES as we will re-use this code when we change this Workflow to start from an Event in *Chapter 5, Business Events*.

11.► Since CREATED_BY is a mandatory field in PER_ALL_PEOPLE_F and is populated with the USER_ID of the person who created the record, and since records in the FND_USER table cannot be deleted, this SELECT should never fail. Thus, if a failure does happen, it indicates serious data integrity issues. The Workflow Engine will be instructed to place the Workflow in error status.

12.▶The Workflow Administrator is retrieved as a "backup" for the email administrator. Since '*' is a valid value for the administrator, but not for a Performer, if the administrator is set to '*', SYSADMIN will be used as a substitute. A Workflow Administrator always exists. So again, if the SELECT fails, the Workflow should immediately error.

13.▶The Attribute 'Email Administrator', assigned as the Role in the Notification 'Ask Email Admin for email address', was not assigned a value in the Workflow design. Our design assumes that there is a custom Profile Option defined that will hold the user (not responsibility, although the design and code could be modified for this) who happens to be the Workflow Administrator. The cursor is used in case the Profile Option either doesn't exist or the value was never set.

For the purposes of this design, the Profile Option will be set to the field USER_NAME from the FND_USER table. This field corresponds to the field NAME in the WF_LOCAL_ROLES table. Thus, in the Builder the Attribute 'Email Administrator' must be set to a type of Text, not Role. To continue to use the type of Role, the selects in 12.▶ and the cursor referenced in 13.▶ would need to be modified to match to the DISPLAY_NAME in WF_LOCAL_ROLES.

Regardless of the design, the Workflow designer should ensure that the Notification has a valid Performer. The code first checks that the Profile Option exists and has a value. If so, the API WF_DIRECTORY.UserActive is used to ensure the value is an active user. If not, or if there is no value for the Profile Option, the Workflow Administrator is substituted as the user and an Attribute is set that will explain the recipient substitution.

There is no corresponding API to check whether any other type of Role, such as a responsibility, is still Active and able to be used as a Performer.

14.▶The Attribute 'HR', assigned as the Role in the Notification 'Ask HR to Fix it', was not assigned a value in the Workflow design. Since the Performer will be a responsibility the value must be assigned programmatically or the value will be truncated to 30 characters (per MetaLink Doc. ID: 304115.1, *Invalid performer Item attribute=Responsibility Role*). Even if this limitation didn't exist, our design requires that the Performer be set to the same responsibility that was used to create the employee. This choice was made to demonstrate that when the Item Attribute used as the Performer has the type of Role, the value for the Item Attribute should be set to the name of the responsibility. The name of the responsibility corresponds to the DISPLAY_NAME column in WF_LOCAL_ROLES.

15.▶This section sets two special Attributes, 'Owner' and 'UserKey', using the APIs WF_ENGINE.SetItemOwner and WF_ENGINE.SetItemUserKey. Both of these APIs use the following parameters:

- **ItemType** – the Internal Name of the Workflow. Use the parameter passed to the Procedure.

- **ItemKey** – Use the parameter passed to the Procedure.

- **Value** – Either the Owner or UserKey.

Setting the Owner allows this Role/person to view the progress of the Workflow. The value must match the field DISPLAY_NAME in the WF_LOCAL_ROLES table where PARTITION_ID = 1 (users). Setting the UserKey helps the Workflow Administer find Workflows when they are in trouble. UserKey can be set to whatever data makes sense to the Workflow. For our Workflow, since PERSON_ID is not a displayed field in the form (unless you are using automatic numbering and then the employee number is the PERSON_ID); the UserKey will be set to the employee's full name. The UserKey allows Workflow Administrators to find Workflows using data visible to the end-users. If the UserKey is not set, administrators typically have to resort to SQL to find the _ID field used as the Item Key.

16. ▶ This section sets the Item Attributes that store the email administrator, Employee Number, Employee Name, and Employee ID utilizing the API WF_ENGINE.SetItemAttr<type> where <type> is either Number, Text, Event, or Date. This API has four parameters:

- **ItemType** – the Internal Name of the Workflow. Use the parameter passed to the Procedure.

- **ItemKey** – Use the parameter passed to the Procedure.

- **Attribute Name** – Internal Name of the Item Attribute as defined in the Builder.

- **Attribute Value** – Value for the Item Attribute.

17. ▶ When the purpose of the Procedure is accomplished, ResultOut is set to COMPLETE: and the Procedure ends. The acceptable values for ResultOut were discussed earlier. The value should always be in all caps. Since the Activity to which this routine is attached does not have a Result Type, do not put anything after the colon. See next routine for how to code ResultOut when the Activity specifies a Result Type.

18. ▶ In the event of an unplanned error, WF_CORE.Context is used to display the information that will allow the code to be de-bugged.

Now that this Procedure is written, revisit the Workflow. Look for the following required changes and/or additions.

- Item Attributes referenced in the code, but not defined in the Workflow. Note: UserKey and Owner are reserved Attributes and should never be defined in the Builder.

- Item Attributes used as Performers in Notifications. Ensure that if the value is set to the corresponding WF_LOCAL_ROLES.NAME field then the Attribute type is set to Text. Alternatively, if the value is set to the corresponding WF_LOCAL_ROLES.DISPLAY_NAME field, then the Attribute type must be set to Role.

- New Message Attributes. If an Item Attribute was added so that it could be displayed in a Message, that Attribute has to be added to the appropriate Message and linked to the Item Attribute.

Our Workflow needs the Item Attributes 'Employee ID' (Internal Name must be EMPLOYEE_ID and the Type must be Number) and 'Email Admin Error Message' (Internal Name must be EMAIL_ADMIN_ERROR and the Type must be Text) added and the Type for the Item Attribute 'Email Administrator' changed to Text. Drag the Attribute 'Email Admin Error Message' to the Message 'Ask Email Admin for email address'. Open the 'Properties' page of the Message, click the Body tab and change the Text Body so that it looks like:

```
&EMAIL_ADMIN_ERROR

Please set up the email address for &EMPLOYEE_NAME and enter it below
```

Note that if the email administrator does exist, L_MESSAGE will remain at the default value of NULL, thus the Item Attribute EMAIL_ADMIN_ERROR will be null and the Message sent to the email administrator (as opposed to the Workflow Administrator) will not display anything for &EMAIL_ADMIN_ERROR.

Make the changes and re-save the Workflow to the database.

PROCEDURE CALLED WITHIN WORKFLOW – WITH RESULT

The Procedure XXHRVEMP.IS_EMPLOYEE_DATA_COMPLETE' does have a Result Type – Yes/No. It is also the first Procedure in a loop and may require a Pivot Activity code. As explained in *Chapter 3, Builder Basics*, the first Activity in a loop is called the Pivot Activity. This Activity must have a value set for 'On Revisit'. If this value is set to Reset, the Workflow Engine runs the assigned Procedure for each Activity in the loop with FuncMode = 'CANCEL', allowing the developer to "undo" or reset anything that happened in the previous iteration of the loop. Since the only other Functions in our loop are Oracle-supplied activities, this Activity will be responsible for any actions when FuncMode = 'CANCEL'. There is, however, nothing that needs to be "undone", so the code will simply return a completed status. The code for this Procedure is:

```
1. ►   PROCEDURE is_employee_data_complete (
               ItemType          IN   VARCHAR2
              ,ItemKey           IN   VARCHAR2
              ,actid             IN   NUMBER
              ,funcmode          IN   VARCHAR2
              ,ResultOut         OUT  VARCHAR2
        )
        IS
2. ►      l_position          per_all_positions.name%TYPE
                                    := NULL;

           l_supervisor        per_all_people_f.full_name%TYPE
                                    := NULL;

           l_default_accounting
             gl_code_combinations_kfv.concatenated_segments%TYPE
                                    := NULL;
           l_default_code_comb_id  NUMBER      := NULL;
           l_supervisor_id                 NUMBER      := NULL;
           l_position_id                   NUMBER      := NULL;
           l_employee_id                   NUMBER;



3. ►      CURSOR assignment_csr (
               X_person_id   NUMBER
           )
           IS
               SELECT position_id,supervisor_id,default_code_comb_id
                 FROM per_all_assignments_f paaf
                WHERE paaf.effective_end_date > SYSDATE
                  AND paaf.primary_flag = 'Y' AND paaf.assignment_type = 'E'
                  AND paaf.person_id = x_person_id;

           CURSOR position_csr (
               X_position_idNUMBER
           )
            IS
               SELECT name FROM per_all_positions pap
                 WHERE pap.position_id = x_position_id;

           CURSOR supervisor_csr (
               X_supervisor_id              NUMBER
           )
           IS
               SELECT full_name
                 FROM per_all_people_f papf
```

```
                        WHERE papf.effective_end_date > SYSDATE
                          AND papf.person_id = x_supervisor_id;

4. ▶    BEGIN
                g_proc := 'IS_EMPLOYEE_DATA_COMPLETE';

5. ▶            g_trace := 'Checking funcmode';

                IF funcmode <> wf_engine.eng_run
                AND funcmode <> wf_engine.eng_cancel
                THEN
                        ResultOut := wf_engine.eng_null;
                        RETURN;
                END IF;

6. ▶            IF funcmode = 'CANCEL'
                THEN
                        ResultOut := wf_engine.eng_completed;
                        RETURN;
                END IF;
7.▶             -- funcmode is now 'Run'
                g_trace := 'getting employee_id attribute';
                l_employee_id := wf_engine.GetItemAttrNumber
                                            (ItemType
                                            ,ItemKey
                                            ,'EMPLOYEE_ID'
                                            );

8.▶             g_trace := 'getting position and supervisor ids';

                OPEN assignment_csr (l_employee_id);
                FETCH assignment_csr
                 INTO l_position_id
                     ,l_supervisor_id
                      ,l_default_code_comb_id;


                IF     assignment_csr%FOUND AND l_position_id IS NOT NULL
                THEN
                        g_trace := 'getting position';

                        OPEN position_csr (l_position_id);
                        FETCH position_csr
                         INTO l_position;
                        CLOSE position_csr;
                END IF;

                IF     assignment_csr%FOUND AND l_supervisor_id IS NOT NULL
                THEN
                        g_trace := 'getting supervisor name';

                        OPEN supervisor_csr (l_supervisor_id);
                        FETCH supervisor_csr
                         INTO l_supervisor;
                        CLOSE supervisor_csr;
                END IF;

                g_trace := 'getting default accounting';

                IF     assignment_csr%FOUND AND l_default_code_comb_id IS NOT NULL
```

```
          THEN
                  SELECT concatenated_segments INTO l_default_accounting
                    FROM gl_code_combinations_kfv
                   WHERE code_combination_id = l_default_code_comb_id;
          END IF;

          CLOSE assignment_csr;
```

9.▶
```
          wf_engine.SetItemAttrText(ItemType
                                   ,ItemKey
                                   ,'SUPERVISOR'
                                   ,l_supervisor
                                   );
          wf_engine.SetItemAttrText(ItemType
                                   ,ItemKey
                                   ,'POSITION'
                                   ,l_position
                                          );
          wf_engine.SetItemAttrText(ItemType
                                   ,ItemKey
                                   ,'DEFAULT_ACCOUNTING'
                                   ,l_default_accounting
                                   );
          g_trace := 'checking for null values';
```
10.▶
```
          IF      l_position IS NULL
             OR l_supervisor IS NULL
             OR l_default_accounting IS NULL
          THEN
                  ResultOut := 'COMPLETE:N';
          ELSE
                  ResultOut := 'COMPLETE:Y';
          END IF;
```
11.▶
```
     EXCEPTION
          WHEN OTHERS
          THEN
                  wf_core.context (g_pkg
                                   ,g_proc
                                   ,funcmode
                                   ,g_trace
                                   );
                  RAISE;

   END is_employee_data_complete;
```

1.▶   Notice that the Procedure has the same parameters.

2.▶   This is a typical declare section. Because this routine sets Attributes, and the Attributes cannot be set in a SELECT statement, there are holding variables declared for the SELECT statements to use. All variables are initialized to NULL so that if any of the cursors or selects do not return data, the variable is NULL, not undefined.

3.▶   Cursors are used to search for data where missing data is allowable and part of the Workflow design. See previous Procedure discussion for further details.

4.▶   Every Procedure has to set the Procedure name into G_PROC as it is used in WF_CORE.Context.

5.▶ Since this Procedure is the Pivot Point (first Activity) in a loop, CANCEL is an expected FuncModes. RUN is always an expected FuncMode. The Workflow returns a result of null if any other (i.e., unexpected) FuncMode is encountered.

6.▶ If the FuncMode is 'CANCEL', then the loop has been traversed at least once. When the Pivot Activity is encountered the second and subsequent times, each Activity in the loop is run in CANCEL Mode. Then the Activity is re-run in RUN Mode. Since nothing needs to be "undone", ResultOut is set and the Procedure ends. After executing each Activity in the loop in CANCEL Mode, this Activity will be run again in RUN Mode.

7.▶ This is the 'RUN' mode code. First the EMPLOYEE_ID is retrieved from the Attribute set in the previous Procedure.

8.▶ The code then checks for the presence of an assignment record and valid values for POSITION_ID, SUPERVISOR_ID, and DEFAULT_CODE_COMB_ID. If the _ID fields exist, the resulting 'user' fields are returned for inclusion in the Notification.

9.▶ The fetched values are set as Item Attribute values so they will be available to the Notifications and other Procedures.

10.▶ Since this Activity has a Result Type, we must furnish the appropriate value for that Result Type as part of ResultOut. The COMPLETE indicates to the Engine that this Activity completed without error. The COMPLETE is followed by a colon (':'). Following the colon is the Internal Name of the Lookup Code that the designer wishes to return as the Result Value. Note that although the Diagrammer labels the results 'Yes' and 'No', these are the Display Names. The Internal Names are 'Y' and 'N'. Also note that there are no spaces between the colon and the result and no spaces between the result and the single quote. If the designer leaves spaces either before or after the result, these spaces become part of the result, the value returned to the Workflow will not match any of the labeled legs, and the Workflow will become "stuck".

11.▶ The general exception should always be WF_CORE.Context. Note that we include the Function mode as one of the parameters so that we will know which section of the code to search for the G_TRACE value.

ANOTHER "NO RESULT" PROCEDURE

The Workflow has a second Function Activity that requires a PL/SQL Package: 'Add Email Address to Employee Record'. Like 'Set Attributes', this Activity has no Result Code. The purpose of this Procedure is to update the database with the email address supplied in the response to the Notification 'Ask Email Admin for email address'. *Chapter 11, Advanced Builder and PL/SQL*, will describe the use of post-Notification Functions, which can be used to validate that an email address was actually entered.

```
1.▶    PROCEDURE add_email_address_to_emp (
           ItemType          IN     VARCHAR2
           ,ItemKey          IN     VARCHAR2
           ,actic            IN     VARCHAR2
           ,funcmode         IN     VARCHAR2
           ,ResultOut        OUT    VARCHAR2
       )
2.▶    IS
           l_employee_id NUMBER;
           l_email_address          per_all_people_t.email_address%TYPE;
3.▶    BEGIN
           g_proc := 'ADD_EMAIL_ADDRESS_TO_EMP_REC';
```

```
          -- Do nothing except in RUN mode
          g_trace := 'Checking funcmode';
          IF (funcmode <> wf_engine.eng_run)
          THEN
                  ResultOut := wf_engine.eng_null;
                  RETURN;
          END IF;

4.▶        g_trace := 'Retrieving Item Attributes';
          l_employee_id :=
                  wf_engine.GetItemAttrNumber (ItemType
                                              ,ItemKey
                                              ,'EMPLOYEE_ID'
                                              );
          l_email_address :=
                  wf_engine.GetItemAttrText (ItemType
                                            ,ItemKey
                                            ,'EMAIL_ADDRESS
                                            );
          g_trace := 'Updating Employee Record';

          UPDATE per_all_people_f
             SET email_address = l_email_address
           WHERE person_id = l_employee_id
             AND SYSDATE < effective_end_date;

5.▶        ResultOut := 'COMPLETE:';

6.▶   EXCEPTION
          WHEN OTHERS
          THEN
                  wf_core.context (g_pkg
                                  ,g_proc
                                  ,funcmode
                                  ,g_trace
                                  );
      END add_email_address_to_emp;
```

1.▶ Notice that the Procedure has the same parameters.

2.▶ Typical declare section.

3.▶ Every Procedure has to set the Procedure name into G_PROC as it is used in WF_CORE.Context.

   Since this Activity is not in a loop, all FuncModes except RUN will be ignored.

4.▶ The required Item Attributes are retrieved and used to update the employee record.

5.▶ When the purpose of the Procedure is accomplished, ResultOut is set to COMPLETE: and the Procedure ends. Since no Result Type is assigned to the Activity in the Builder, there should be nothing after the colon.

6.▶ In the event of an unplanned error, WF_CORE.Context is used to display the information that will allow the code to be de-bugged.

RESETTING THE LOOP COUNTER LOOP COUNT

Chapter 3, Builder Basics, detailed how 'Loop Counter' can behave erratically since the Activity Attribute 'Loop Count' is only initialized to zero when the Activity is first encountered or when 'Loop Count' exceeds the value in the Activity Attribute 'Loop Limit'.

In the design in FIGURE 4.5, if the 'Loop Limit' is set to '1' and the Notification times out once (therefore, setting 'Loop Counter' to 1), and then is subsequently answered Approve, but the authority isn't sufficient, the Workflow will select the next approver and start the Notification cycle again. If this Notification times out, 'Loop Counter' is already set to '1', so instead of sending another Notification, the Workflow will select the next approver. Therefore, the PL/SQL Package assigned to 'Does Next Approver Exist?' must reset 'Loop Counter' to zero.

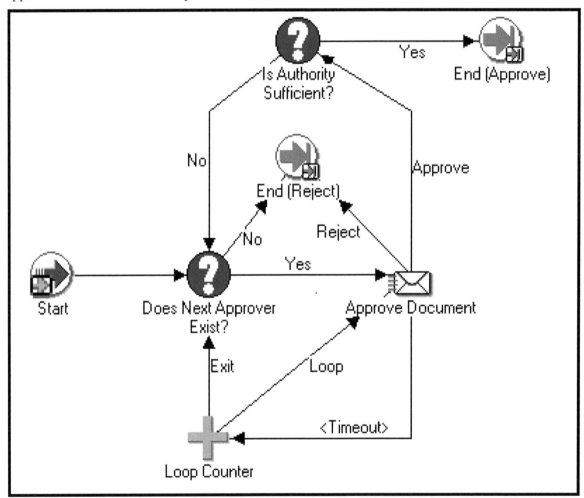

FIGURE 4.5

The code to reset 'Loop Counter' plus an explanation follows. The Declarative section is not shown. The variables L_INSTANCE_ID and L_LOOP_COUNT must be declared as NUMBER;

```
1. ▶   g_trace := 'getting instance id';

       SELECT instance_id INTO l_instance_id FROM wf_process_activities
```

```
        WHERE process_item_type = 'XXHRVEMP' AND activity_name = 'LOOPCOUNTER'
          AND process_version =
              (SELECT process_version FROM wf_process_activities
                WHERE instance_id = actid)
          AND process_name =
              (SELECT process_name FROM wf_process_activities
                WHERE instance_id = actid);

        g_trace := 'checking for item attribute';

        BEGIN
              L_loop_count :=
                    wf_engine.GetItemAttrNumber
                                (ItemType
                                ,ItemKey
                                ,'LOOP_COUNT:'||
                                l_instance_id
                                );
```

2. ►
```
        EXCEPTION
              WHEN OTHERS
              THEN
                    IF wf_core.error_name = 'WFENG_ITEM_ATTR'
                    THEN
                          l_loop_count :=0;
                    ELSE
                          wf_core.context (g_pkg
                                          ,g_proc
                                          ,funcmode
                                          ,g_trace
                                          );
                          RAISE;
                    END IF;
              END;
```

3. ►
```
        IF l_loop_count <> 0
        THEN
              wf_engine.SetItemAttrNumber (ItemType
                                          ,ItemKey
                                          ,'LOOP_COUNT:'|| l_instance_id
                                          ,0
                                          );
        END IF;
        RETURN;
        END IF;
```

1. ► This is one example where the ActID passed in as a parameter is useful. This ActID equates to INSTANCE_ID in a specific record in the WF_PROCESS_ACTIVITIES table. From this record we can get the Process name and the Process version. Then we can use this information to get the INSTANCE_ID for the 'Loop Counter' Activity. The Item Attribute we want is the concatenation of LOOP_COUNT and this INSTANCE_ID. This information was derived from the code in WF_STANDARD.LoopCounter.

It should be noted that every time a Workflow is saved to the database and any node in a Process changes, all activities in that Process receive a new INSTANCE_ID and new VERSION. Using the ActID passed in as a parameter allows us to connect to the version of the Process that existed when the Workflow was started. It is possible a more recent version of all the activities exist but our code must look at the activities based on when the Workflow was initiated. See the section "Versioning" later in this chapter for more details.

2. ▶ Since the 'Loop Counter' Activity creates the Item Attribute "on the fly", it is possible that the Item Attribute does not exist. If the GetItemAttrNumber fails, the exception routine checks whether the failure occurred because the Item Attribute has not yet been created (if the Notification doesn't time out, 'Loop Counter' never creates the Attribute). This is done by checking if WF_CORE.Error_Name = 'WFENG_ITEM_ATTR'. WF_CORE.Error_Name is set to this value by the GetItemAttr<type> APIs if the Attribute doesn't exist. If this is our error, then the variable is set to indicate that no updates are necessary.

If any other error is encountered, the standard WF_CORE.Context API is invoked.

3. ▶ If the variable tracking the counter is not zero, then the Attribute exists and needs to be reset to zero. The standard WF_ENGINE.SetItemAttr<type> API is used.

SET_CTX AND TEST_CTX

If your Workflow will use Form Attributes in Messages or will set 'row who' data (LAST_UPDATED_BY, CREATED_BY, etc.) or will need the Org Context set in order to use a particular view, then a Selector Function may be needed.

Workflows running in real time (not deferred to the Background Engine) inherit the database session information from the user's database session. However, once an Activity has been deferred to the Background Engine (and since our Workflow was started from a Trigger, it was deferred to the Background Engine), this session information is lost and may need to be re-established.

Oracle provides the ability to re-establish this information through the use of the Selector. This function is specified on the 'Properties' page of the Item Type Function (See FIGURE 4.6). While Oracle provides the ability to designate this function, it is the developer's responsibility to call the routine to validate whether the information is set and, if not, to re-establish either the org or 'row who' context, or both. It is also the developer's responsibility to ensure that the required information is either stored as Item Attributes or is obtainable from other sources available to PL/SQL (such as the ORG_ID or 'row who' information from a database record, for example, the expense report header).

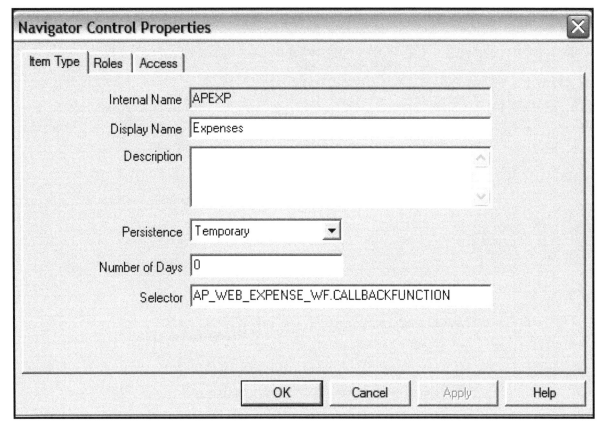

FIGURE 4.6

The Selector Function can also be used to pass the starting Process to the Workflow Engine. If the LaunchProcess or StartProcess API does not pass a Process name, this function is called in RUN Mode. ResultOut will then be coded as ResultOut := '<internal name of starting process>';.

This function also supports two other FuncModes, SET_CTX and TEST_CTX. Any time the Workflow Engine (this includes the Background Engine) detects a new or different Item Type or Item Key it calls this Package in TEST_CTX Mode. When called in TEST_CTX Mode, the Function can return three values:

- **ResultOut := 'TRUE'** – there is a current context and it is correct. The Procedure will not be run in SET_CTX Mode.

- **ResultOut:= 'NOTSET'** – the context is not set. The Workflow Engine will now run the Function in SET_CTX Mode.

- **ResultOut:= 'FALSE'** – the context is set, but it is incorrect for the current Workflow. If the Workflow Engine will permit context switching at this point, the Function will be run in SET_CTX Mode. If the Workflow Engine needs to maintain the current context, then the Activity will be deferred to the Background Engine. When the Background Engine starts to process this Activity, it will run the Function in TEST_CTX Mode. This time if ResultOut = 'FALSE', the Function will be run in SET_CTX Mode.

Since our Workflow does not use Form Attributes and the PER_ALL_PEOPLE_F table does not use ORG_ID, we will use the Selector Function from the Workflow used to approve expense reports in *i*Expenses. The name of this Workflow is 'Expenses' (the Internal Name of this Workflow is APEXP). As shown in FIGURE 4.6, the Selector Function is AP_WEB_EXPENSE_WF.CALLBACKFUNCTION.

Release 11*i* and Release 12 do not set context for ORG_ID with the same APIs. The code below is from Release 11*i*, Version 115.297 (dated 2005/01/12).

```
1.► PROCEDURE CallbackFunction   (p_s_item_type       IN VARCHAR2,
                                  p_s_item_key        IN VARCHAR2,
                                  p_n_actid           IN NUMBER,
                                  p_s_command         IN VARCHAR2,
                                  p_s_result          OUT NOCOPY VARCHAR2) IS
    --------------------------------------------------------------
2.►    l_n_org_id          Number;
       l_n_user_id         Number;
       l_n_resp_id         Number;
       l_n_resp_appl_id    Number;

BEGIN

3.►     AP_WEB_UTILITIES_PKG.logProcedure('AP_WEB_EXPENSE_WF',
                                  'start CallbackFunction');

       begin

4.►       l_n_org_id:=wf_engine.GetItemAttrNumber(p_s_item_type,
                                          p_s_item_key,
                                          'ORG_ID');
       exception
            when others then
          if (wf_core.error_name = 'WFENG_ITEM_ATTR') then
            -- ORG_ID item attribute doesn't exist,
            -- need to add it
            wf_engine.AddItemAttr(p_s_item_type,
            p_s_item_key, 'ORG_ID');
            -- get the org_id from header for old reports
        IF (AP_WEB_DB_EXPRPT_PKG.GetOrgIdByReportHeaderId (
                    to_number(p_s_item_key),
                    l_n_org_id) <> TRUE ) THEN
            l_n_org_id := NULL;
            END IF;             wf_engine.SetItemAttrNumber(p_s_item_type,
                                p_s_item_key,
                                'ORG_ID',
                                l_n_org_id);
          else
            raise;
          end if;
       end;

5.►IF (p_s_command = 'SET_CTX') THEN

    begin
6.►    l_n_user_id :=
            wf_engine.GetItemAttrNumber(p_s_item_type,
                                        p_s_item_key,
                                        'USER_ID');
        l_n_resp_id :=
```

```
                 wf_engine.GetItemAttrNumber(p_s_item_type,
                                             p_s_item_key,
                                             'RESPONSIBILITY_ID');
       l_n_resp_appl_id :=
                 wf_engine.GetItemAttrNumber(p_s_item_type,
                                             p_s_item_key,
                                             'APPLICATION_ID');
       -- Set the context
       FND_GLOBAL.APPS_INITIALIZE(  USER_ID => l_n_user_id,
                        RESP_ID => l_n_resp_id,
                        RESP_APPL_ID => l_n_resp_appl_id
                        );
    exception
      when others then
        if (wf_core.error_name = 'WFENG_ITEM_ATTR') then
          null;
        else
          raise;
        end if;
    end;

    -- Set Org context
    -- Needs to be after FND_GLOBAL.APPS_INITIALIZE because
    -- user_id, resp_id, and appl_id may be null because
    -- the attributes don't exist or because they are not set
7.▶if (l_n_org_id is not null) then
       fnd_client_info.set_org_context(l_n_org_id);
    end if;

8.▶ELSIF (p_s_command = 'TEST_CTX') THEN
     -- bug 2162684: USERENV('CLIENT_INFO') and l_n_org_id are null
     -- for single org environment
            IF (nvl(rtrim(substrb(USERENV('CLIENT_INFO'), 1, 10)),'NULL') =
            nvl(to_char(l_n_org_id),'NULL')) THEN
        p_s_result := 'TRUE';
     ELSE
        p_s_result := 'FALSE';
     END IF;
    END IF;

    AP_WEB_UTILITIES_PKG.logProcedure('AP_WEB_EXPENSE_WF',
      'end CallbackFunction');

  END CallbackFunction;
```

1.▶ The Attributes are the same for any Function Procedure. 'P_S_COMMAND' is equivalent to FuncMode.

2.▶ The variables that are used to set context are the ORG_ID, for applications that are multi-org enabled, and the USER_ID, RESPONSIBILITY_ID, and APPLICATION_ID, for providing accurate row who data.

3.▶ Oracle uses AP_WEB_UTILITIES_PKG.logProcedure to log information for testing and debugging. This is another way of tracking what happens in a Workflow. The Procedure called must be sure to perform all table inserts as autonomous transactions. Otherwise anything that happens in the called Package is part of the same session as the Workflow Procedure and would be rolled back in the event of failure in the Workflow Package resulting in the loss of all tracking information.

4.▶ This routine assumes that ORG_ID is an Item Attribute. If an error occurs retrieving the Attribute value, the exception routine checks if the error occurred because the Attribute didn't exist (WF_CORE.Error_Name = 'WFENG_ITEM_ATTR'). If this is the error, then the Attribute is added using the API WF_ENGINE.AddItemAttr. This API has three parameters: Item Type, Item Key, and Internal Name of the Attribute. This API inserts a record into the WF_ITEM_ATTRIBUTE_VALUES table for the specific occurrence of the Workflow. It does not add the Attribute to the Workflow design and thus unless the Attribute is added through the Builder, the next occurrence of this Workflow will encounter the same error. Additionally, since the record is added to the WF_ITEM_ATTRIBUTE_VALUES table rather than the WF_ITEM_ATTRIBUTES table, this Attribute will not be visible through the 'Status Monitor'.

The value for the ORG_ID is obtained from the ORG_ID in the export report header record.

5.▶ The Package checks for SET_CTX and then performs the logic in 6.▶ and 7.▶.

6.▶ The existence of the Attributes USER_ID, RESPONSIBILITY_ID, and APPLICATION_ID are checked. If they do not exist, the exception routine is invoked. This time the Attributes are not added, and the statement setting the 'row who' context is not executed.

If the Attributes do exist, FND_GLOBAL.APPS_INITIALIZE is called to set the 'row who' context.

7.▶ If the logic in 4.▶ found or set the ORG_ID, then FND_CLIENT_INFO.SET_ORG_CONTEXT is called to set the Org Context.

8.▶ If the Function mode is TEST_CTX, then the Org Context is checked. If that is set, then ResultOut is set to TRUE, otherwise, it is set to FALSE. Note that the 'row who' context is not checked. A check for the correct 'row who' context should be added. As this Procedure is written, it is possible that the next Function or Notification will have the wrong 'row who' information set. This can cause unusual errors such as the inability to open a form link or having the wrong user updated into the LAST_UPDATED_BY field.

The code below is the same Procedure. However it is from Release 12, Version 120.231.12000000.2 (dated 11-APR-2007).

```
1.▶ PROCEDURE CallbackFunction(
                p_s_item_type              IN VARCHAR2,
                p_s_item_key          IN VARCHAR2,
                p_n_actid             IN NUMBER,
                p_s_command           IN VARCHAR2,
                p_s_result            OUT NOCOPY VARCHAR2) IS
        -------------------------------------------------
2.▶    l_n_org_id              Number;
       l_n_user_id             Number;
       l_n_resp_id             Number;
       l_n_resp_appl_id        Number;
       l_current_org_id        Number;
       l_current_user_id       Number;
       l_current_resp_id       Number;
       l_current_resp_appl_id  Number;

    BEGIN

3.▶    AP_WEB_UTILITIES_PKG.logProcedure('AP_WEB_EXPENSE_WF',
                        'start CallbackFunction');
       begin
```

```
4. ▶      l_n_org_id :=
               wf_engine.GetItemAttrNumber(p_s_item_type,
                                         p_s_item_key,
                                         'ORG_ID');
       exception
             when others then
       if (wf_core.error_name = 'WFENG_ITEM_ATTR') then
       -- ORG_ID item attribute doesn't exist,
       -- need to add it
               wf_engine.AddItemAttr(p_s_item_type,
                   p_s_item_key, 'ORG_ID');
          -- get the org_id from header for old reports
          IF (AP_WEB_DB_EXPRPT_PKG.GetOrgIdByReportHeaderId(
                        to_number(p_s_item_key),
                        l_n_org_id) <> TRUE )
         THEN
            l_n_org_id := NULL;
         END IF;
         wf_engine.SetItemAttrNumber(p_s_item_type,
                                    p_s_item_key,
                                    'ORG_ID',
                                    l_n_org_id);
        else
           raise;
        end if;
      end;
5. ▶    begin
               l_n_user_id :=
                   wf_engine.GetItemAttrNumber(p_s_item_type,
                                      p_s_item_key,
                                      'USER_ID');

        l_n_resp_id :=
                   wf_engine.GetItemAttrNumber(p_s_item_type,
                                      p_s_item_key,
                                      'RESPONSIBILITY_ID');
         l_n_resp_appl_id :=
                   wf_engine.GetItemAttrNumber(p_s_item_type,
                                      p_s_item_key,
                                      'APPLICATION_ID');
      exception
          when others then
            if (wf_core.error_name = 'WFENG_ITEM_ATTR') then
              null;
            else
               raise;
            end if;
      end;

6. ▶    IF (p_s_command = 'SET_CTX') THEN

        -- Set the context
7. ▶    FND_GLOBAL.APPS_INITIALIZE(USER_ID => l_n_user_id,
                                  RESP_ID => l_n_resp_id,
                                  RESP_APPL_ID => l_n_resp_appl_id
                                  );

        -- Set Org context
        -- Needs to be after FND_GLOBAL.APPS_INITIALIZE because
```

```
            -- user_id, resp_id, and appl_id may be null because
            -- the attributes don't exist or because they aren't set
8.▶     if (l_n_org_id is not null) then
            mo_global.set_policy_context(p_access_mode => 'S',
                                         p_org_id => l_n_org_id);
        end if;

        -- Set Accounting Flexfield validation context
9.▶ AP_WEB_DB_GL_INT_PKG.set_aff_validation_org_context
            (l_n_org_id);

10.▶    ELSIF (p_s_command = 'TEST_CTX') THEN
            /* Bug 4319321 : Need to check the values of user_id,
             * resp_id and resp_appl_id as well.
             */
        l_current_user_id :=
                TO_NUMBER(FND_PROFILE.VALUE('USER_ID'));
        l_current_resp_id      :=
                TO_NUMBER(FND_PROFILE.VALUE('RESP_ID'));
        l_current_resp_appl_id  :=
                TO_NUMBER(FND_PROFILE.VALUE('RESP_APPL_ID'));
        l_current_org_id :=
                nvl(mo_global.get_current_org_id, -99);

        /* Bug 4711393: Should return NOTSET instead of FALSE in
         * test_ctx mode so that the actual context can get set
         * via call in set_ctx mode. This would avoid incorrect
         * deferred state
         */
        IF (nvl(mo_global.get_access_mode, 'NULL') <> 'S') THEN
                p_s_result := 'NOTSET';
        ELSIF l_n_user_id IS NULL
          OR l_n_resp_id IS NULL
          OR l_n_resp_appl_id IS NULL THEN
        /* This condition should not occur. But if it does,
         * do not reset the context*/
            p_s_result := 'TRUE';
        ELSIF l_current_user_id IS NULL
            OR l_current_resp_id IS NULL
            OR l_current_resp_appl_id IS NULL THEN
            /* Context is not set as yet. It will be set in
             * SET_CTX mode call */
            p_s_result := 'NOTSET';
        ELSIF l_n_user_id=l_current_user_id
          AND l_n_resp_id=l_current_resp_id
          AND l_n_resp_appl_id=l_current_resp_appl_id THEN
            IF l_n_org_id <> l_current_org_id THEN
        /* Context is incorrect. Need to set it correctly
         * in SET_CTX mode */
                p_s_result := 'NOTSET';
            ELSE
            /* will come here if either of l_org_id or
             * l_current_org_id is null or both are equal
             * l_org_id or l_current_org_id is NULL means
             * single org environment
             */
                p_s_result := 'TRUE';
            END IF;
            ELSE
          p_s_result := 'NOTSET';
```

```
    END IF;

    END IF;

    AP_WEB_UTILITIES_PKG.logProcedure('AP_WEB_EXPENSE_WF',
        'end CallbackFunction');

    END CallbackFunction;
```

1. ▶ No change from the Release 11*i* version.

2. ▶ The only change from the Release 11*i* version is the addition of a variable to store the current context information.

3. ▶ No change from the Release 11*i* version.

4. ▶ No change from the Release 11*i* version.

5. ▶ Same as 6. ▶ for the Release 11*i* version.

6. ▶ The Package checks for SET_CTX and then performs the logic in 7. ▶, 8. ▶, and 9. ▶.

7. ▶ FND_GLOBAL.APPS_INITIALIZE sets the context for the user, responsibility, and application.

8. ▶ If the logic in 4. ▶ found or set the ORG_ID, then MO_GLOBAL.SET_POLICY_CONTEXT (instead of FND_CLIENT_INFO.SET_ORG_CONTEXT) is called to set the Org Context.

9. ▶ New to Release 12 is the need to set the context for the Accounting Flexfield validation. The context is set based on ORG_ID.

10. ▶ If the Function mode is TEST_CTX, then the current user, responsibility, APPLICATION_ID, and ORG_ID are determined. Org Context is checked. If the Org Context is not set, then ResultOut is set to NOTSET. If the values for user, responsibility and APPLICATION_ID from the Profile Options are null (this shouldn't happen), then ResultOut is set to TRUE (which will cause the Workflow to fail due to missing Attributes in another Procedure). If the current context for user, responsibility or APPLICATION_ID is NULL, then ResultOut is set to NOTSET. If the user, responsibility, and APPLICATION_ID context matches the Profile Option values, but the current ORG_ID does not match the Profile Option values, then ResultOut is set to NOTSET. If the user, responsibility, and APPLICATION_ID context matches the Profile Option values, and the current ORG_ID equals the Profile Option value or is null, then either the context is correct or the environment is a single org and thus ResultOut is set to TRUE. If all of the above checks fail, then ResultOut is set to NOTSET. NOTSET will cause the Workflow Engine to immediately run the same Procedure in SET_CTX Mode.

For more information about setting context in a Release 12 environment, see MetaLink Doc. ID: 420787.1, *Oracle Applications Multiple Organizations Access Control for Custom Code*.

Some Additional Notes

What to Do if you Choose the Incorrect Attribute Type in the Builder

Suppose the Attribute EMPLOYEE_NUMBER had been defined with the type Number. When coding the Procedures, perhaps the developers noticed that employee_number in the database is actually a VARCHAR2 field. So they went into the Builder and changed the Attribute type to Text. Attempting to save the design, the validation fails, as changing the type breaks the link between the Message Attribute of the same name. To fix this, delete the Message Attribute and drag-and-drop the Item Attribute to the Message.

What if the Diagram Contains More than One Loop Counter?

The Procedure 'Is Employee Data Complete' will still find one of the activities and reset the 'Loop Count' Item Attribute. However, the second 'Loop Counter' does not have the ACTIVITY_NAME LOOPCOUNTER. See FIGURE 4.7. It will have the name LOOPCOUNTER-1.

When the Builder encounters a second Activity in a Process with the same Internal Name, it adds a dash and a number to that Activity's Label. It does not change the Internal Name. 'Label' is a field that is only found on the 'Properties' page of an Activity in a Process. The 'Label' field is found on the Node tab of the 'Properties' page. The designer can change this 'Label'. If the Process contained multiple 'Loop Counters', the code in section 6 of the Procedure 'Is_Employee_Date_Complete' would have to be modified to get both activities. Therefore, the designer should note that ACTIVITY_NAME in the table WF_PROCESS_ACTIVITIES maps to the 'Label' field, not to the Internal Name of the Activity. If you wish to quickly see all the Labels or Activity Names in a Process, click the [AB-1] icon at the top of the Diagrammer window. Holding the cursor over this icon will display Instance Labels.

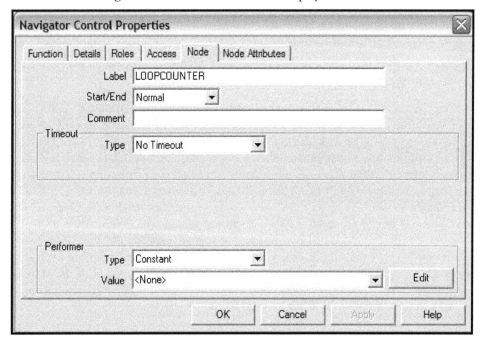

FIGURE 4.7

VERSIONING

Every time you save a Workflow definition to the database, it creates a new version. Unfortunately, not all aspects of the Workflow support Versioning. Specifically, there is no Versioning for Item Attributes, Messages, Lookup Types, and PL/SQL Procedures. This can lead to issues if you make changes to a Workflow that has been in production for some time. Suppose you add a new Attribute to an 'Approval' Workflow and include that Attribute in an existing PL/SQL Procedure. Workflows that were already in progress before the new version was saved do not have this Attribute defined, nor do they have a value for the Attribute, but they will execute the new PL/SQL Procedure that references this new Attribute and they will error out. There are two methods for overcoming this problem. One is a script that adds the Attribute definition (with a default value) to all active Workflows. This would be performed just prior to saving the new version of the Workflow and the new PL/SQL Procedures. The following code would be put in a script and run:

```
CURSOR get_active_work_items_cur IS
    SELECT item_type, item_key
      FROM wf_items
        WHERE end_date IS NULL AND item_type = '<item type internal name>';
gawi_rec get_active_work_items_cur%ROWTYPE
FOR get_active_work_items_rec IN get_active_work_tiems_cur
LOOP
 wf_engine.AddItemAttr(gawi_rec.item_type,
                        gawi_rec.item_key,
                        '<new_attribute_name>',
                        '<default value if text>',
                        '<default value if number>',
                        '<default value if date>);
END LOOP;
```

The other method makes the new Procedures referencing the Attribute do the work. The Workflow Engine raises the error WFENG_ITEM_ATTR whenever an Attribute is referenced that is not defined. So you can add an EXCEPTION routine to your Procedures that looks like:

```
ON EXCEPTION
    WHEN OTHERS
        IF wf_core.error_name = 'WFENG_ITEM_ATTR'
        THEN
            wf_engine.AddItemAttr(ItemType,
                ItemKey,
                '<new_attribute_name>',
                '<default value if text>',
                '<default value if number>',
                '<default value if date>);
        ELSE
            RAISE
        END IF;
```

Note that the partial Versioning of Workflow is the reason we recommend attempting to complete all Workflows in process prior to a major upgrade or significant patching effort. If active Workflows fail after an upgrade or patch, open a Service Request (SR) with Oracle Support to determine the best way to resolve the issue.

WHAT'S NEXT

At this point we have an Item Type saved to the database along with the appropriate PL/SQL Procedures. *Chapter 6, Testing Workflows*, will explain how to test this Workflow. It will also explain how to test the Event version of our Workflow. But first we'll take a look at Business Events in *Chapter 5, Business Events*, and use them to create a slightly different version of our Workflow.

Business Events

Oracle defines a Business Event as "an occurrence in an internet or intranet application or program that might be significant to other objects in a system or to external agents" (see definition in the 'Define Events' screen – FIGURE 5.2). Introduced (and optional) in Release 11.5.8, Business Events have become a vital (and required) part of the E-Business Suite in Release 11.5.9, Release 11.5.10, and Release 12.

This chapter will explain how Oracle has integrated Business Events into the Workflow technology, how Workflow developers can leverage this functionality, and what techniques Workflow Administrators can use to ensure that their Business Events are functioning properly. This chapter is not meant to replace the hundreds of pages on Business Events in the current Workflow guides or the Advanced Queuing guides.

This chapter presupposes that the reader is familiar with Workflow terminology and how to use the Builder tool. The Workflow created in *Chapter 3, Builder Basics* will be modified in this chapter to utilize Business Events.

BUSINESS EVENTS – TERMINOLOGY

If one asks the basic questions, "who?", "what?", "when?", "where?", "why?", "which?", and "how?", the Event is the "what". So a Business Event can be the creation of an invoice or a requisition, the receipt of an EDI transaction, and/or the need to notify someone about something. Most people will think at this point that Events sound much like Alerts or Triggers, but Events will allow for a greater choice of response, and provide abilities denied to Alerts and/or Triggers.

Events require an Event Key, the "which". This is a piece of data that uniquely identifies the specific occurrence of the Event, i.e., which invoice, which requisition. Event Keys are analogous to Item Keys. In fact, if the Event causes a Workflow to be executed, the Event Key becomes the Item Key.

"Where" the Event occurs or where the Action to be invoked by the Event occurs is called a System. A System is "a logically isolated piece of software on which either the Oracle Workflow Business Event System is installed, or with which the Oracle Workflow Business Event System communicates". Events may involve multiple Systems; for instance, the receipt or transmission of an EDI transaction. If you are logged into a database, this database is your Local System. When you log into a different database, this other database becomes your Local System. Therefore, the 'Local System' is the database to which you are currently connected and using. It then makes sense that the name of the Local System should match the name of the database or SID. In addition to a name, each System is given a GUID, or Globally Unique Identifier. The GUID is a 16-byte (128-bit) "number" (contains the characters 0-9 and A-F) that can be used across all computers and networks wherever a unique identifier is required. For a good explanation of this term, especially as it relates to Oracle databases, see *Going Global with GUIDs* by Steven Feuerstein. This article was originally published in *Oracle Professional*, but is also available at http://feuerthoughts.blogspot.com/2006/02/watch-out-for-sequential-oracle-guids.html.

Events happen at a specific point in time. This is one part of the "when". The other part of the "when" is the determination of the time at which the resulting Action should occur. You can write a Process to invoke or raise an Event at a set time (similar to Periodic Alerts), or instantly as a condition is detected (similar to Event Alerts).

This resulting Action is defined in a Subscription. Subscriptions define the "why" of an Event: Why is this Event important, and what should the System do when the Event occurs? Subscriptions can execute code, start Workflows, send Messages to an Agent or receive Messages from an Agent. One can define multiple Subscriptions for each Event. The execution of the Subscription can be immediate or delayed.

Events are stored in Queues. A Queue is a table with a data structure that is capable of handling the multi-dimensional aspects of the details that describe an Event. Except for the Control Queue, they come in pairs: one for Inbound traffic, one for Outbound traffic.

Agents are the "who". They place and remove Events on/from the Queues. They use Agent Listeners to let them know when an Event should be dequeued. Agent Listeners can be configured to listen for all Events for a given Queue or specific Events. Agent Listeners are assigned to a Container, a Java Concurrent Process that wakes up periodically to allow the Listeners to function.

The Process of placing a Message on an Outbound Queue is called Propagation.

The Oracle documentation may make reference to a 'Subscriber'. This is an Agent authorized by a Queue Administrator to retrieve Messages from a Queue. When Events are placed on a Queue (or enqueued), the enqueuer can specify the Agent or recipient allowed to retrieve the Event. If no recipient is specified, then the default list assigned to the Queue is used. The recipients or Agents in this default list are the Subscribers.

The rest of this chapter will address "how". How are Business Events and Subscriptions defined, how does one perform the necessary setups, and how can one manage the Events and Subscriptions when they don't perform as designed?

An Analogy

Most Workflow Administrators and users do not require an in-depth knowledge of the technology that comprises the whole of the Business Event System. They just need to know how to set it up, how to use it and how to administer it. For those individuals who need more, Oracle offers a 2-day class *Oracle 9i: Implement Advanced Queuing.*

For the rest of us, consider your email system. The majority of us don't have a clue how it really works, how a laptop connected to the internet can send/receive Messages through a server located in another city or building, or how the internet delivers Messages to the correct server. We just click 'New', type our Message, choose one or more recipients, click 'Send', and magically, our Message is delivered. Without doing anything other than connecting to the Internet, Inbound Messages appear in our mailbox. Additionally, we can define rules that sort our inbox into different folders.

In our analogy, the corporate email server is a System (our Local System), each user's mailbox is a Queue, the recipients of the email are the Agents, and we schedule or define how often our mail client listens to the corporate server for new mail or propagates (sends) Outbound emails. Our rules are special Listeners targeted for Messages by either source or topic. Messages can be text, HTML, or contain complicated data types such as attachments. Each time we choose to read or send an email, it is an Event. As a result of the Event, we take action (respond, delete, laugh, etc.). The decision as to what type of action to take is the Subscription.

THE QUEUES

So much of understanding Business Events lies in understanding the Queues they move through. Oracle provides Queues to process text, Java, and (in Release 11.5.10 and Release 12) Web Services Messages. As stated earlier, Oracle has defined special data types to store Event Messages (called the payload): WF_EVENT_T for text, and SYS.AQ$_JMS_TEXT_MESSAGE for Java and web services.

Each Queue has an underlying table with the same name to store the payloads. Just as programs run through the Concurrent Manager (and the resultant reports) are not kept indefinitely, the data in the Queue tables are periodically purged. Unlike the Concurrent Managers, the retention time can be (and by default is) different for each Queue. This retention time is managed through the PL/SQL Procedure DBMS_AQADM.Alter_Queue. To change the retention time, execute the following Procedure:

```
EXECUTE DBMS_AQADM.ALTER_QUEUE (
     queue_name          => '<name of queue>',
     retention_time      => <days>);
```

Following are the Queues that are delivered with the E-Business Suite, whether the Queue is text (payload type WF_EVENT_T) or Java (payload type SYS.AQ$_JMS_TEXT_MESSAGE), the default retention time, whether the Start-up mode is automatic or manual, the defined (if any or if applicable) Agent Listener, and a description of the Queue's purpose. The underlying table name has been omitted, as it is the same as the Queue name.

Queue (Agent) Name	Payload Type	Default Retention Time	Startup Mode	Default Agent Listener	Description
WF_CONTROL	Java	1 day	Automatic	N/A	Workflow internal Queue – do not use or change any parameter
WF_DEFERRED	Text	1 day	Automatic	Workflow Deferred Agent Listener	Deferred Subscription processing
			Automatic	Workflow Deferred Notification Agent Listener	Processes only oracle.apps.wf.notification % events
WF_ERROR	Text	0 days	Automatic	Workflow Error Agent Listener	Error handling – Event is placed here when Subscription fails on database tier
WF_JAVA_DEFERRED (added in R11.5.10)	Java	1 day	Automatic	Workflow Java Deferred Agent Listener	Deferred Subscription processing in the middle tier
WF_JAVA_ERROR (added in	Java	0 days	Automatic	Workflow Java Error Agent	Error handling – Event is placed here when

Queue (Agent) Name	Payload Type	Default Retention Time	Startup Mode	Default Agent Listener	Description
R11.5.10)				Listener	Subscription fails on middle tier
WF_NOTIFICATION_IN	Java	1 day	Automatic	Workflow Inbound Notifications Agent Listener	E-mail Notification responses
WF_NOTIFICATION_OUT	Java	1 day	Automatic	N/A	E-mail Notifications
WF_IN	Text	7 days	User defined	user defined	Inbound Text Messages
WF_OUT	Text	7 days	User defined	N/A	Outbound Text Messages
WF_JMS_IN	Java	7 days	Manual	Workflow Inbound JMS Agent Listener	Inbound Java Messages
WF_JMS_OUT	Java	7 days	Manual	N/A	Outbound Java Messages
WF_WS_JMS_IN (added in R11.5.10)	Java	7 days	Manual	Web Services IN Agent	Inbound web services Messages
WF_WS_JMS_OUT (added in Release 11.5.10)	Java	7 days	Manual	Web Services OUT Agent	Outbound web services Messages

TABLE 5. 1

Note that the Queues WF_JAVA_DEFERRED, WF_JAVA_ERROR, WF_WS_JMS_IN and WF_WS_JMS_OUT are currently used only in Oracle Applications and will not be seeded if using Standalone Workflow.

Agent Listeners are not defined for Outbound Queues (WF_JMS_OUT, WF_OUT, WF_NOTIFICATION_OUT, WF_WS_JMS_OUT). An Agent Listener would be required, but is not defined for WF_IN.

Oracle provides two Queues, WF_REPLAY_IN and WF_REPLAY_OUT, that are not currently used, and the Queue WF_SMTP_O_1_QUEUE that was used by the c-based Mailer and is no longer used. Listeners/Propagation should not be scheduled for these Queues.

Oracle also provides three Queues for the XML transactions: ECX_INBOUND, ECX_TRANSACTION, and ECX_OUTBOUND. Discussion and use of these Queues is outside the scope of this book as they are reserved for the XML Gateway application.

In addition there are three Queues used by the Background Engine, WF_DEFERRED_QUEUE_M (underlying table is WF_DEFERRED_TABLE_M), WF_OUTBOUND_QUEUE, and WF_INBOUND_QUEUE. These Queues, like WF_CONTROL, are for internal use by Oracle and the parameters for these Queues should not be adjusted unless directed by Oracle Support.

Later in the chapter, we will discuss methods for viewing the data in the Queues and the purpose of the fields in the Queue tables.

EVENT MENU STRUCTURE

The structures associated with Business Events (Systems, Agents, Events, and Subscriptions) are available from the Event Manager. This is the 'Business Events' tab on the 'Workflow' menu. You must have Workflow Administrator privileges to create or update Business Event components. If you do not have administrator privileges, then you will be able to query the components, but the Update, Delete, and Test icons will be missing. The navigation paths used in this chapter assume the developer has administrator privileges and is using the 'Workflow Administrator Web Applications' responsibility.

The navigation path to the Event Manager is Administrator Workflow → Business Events. The form will open to the 'Events' page (see FIGURE 5.1). To navigate to 'Systems' or 'Agents', click the link in the blue bar at the top of the page. To navigate to 'Subscriptions', you can use the 'Events' page to query the Event and then drill down to the Subscriptions, or you can click the 'Subscriptions' link and enter the Event name. We will use the 'Events' page.

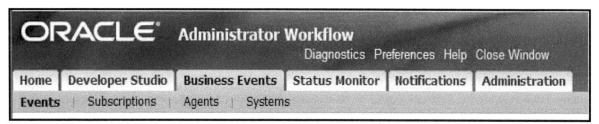

FIGURE 5.1

DEFINING BUSINESS EVENTS

Oracle has pre-defined over 1000 Events in Release 11.5.10 and Release 12. These Events start Workflows, execute Processes, and send/receive XML Messages. Unlike Workflows, where the Internal Name is limited to 8 characters and the Display Name doesn't always even identify the owning System, the standard for naming Business Events conveys a lot of information about the Event.

Naming Standard

Oracle recommends that Business Events be assigned a name that conforms to the following format (note that the name is case sensitive):

```
<company>.<family>.<product>.<component>.<object>.<action>
```

It should be no surprise then that all the seeded Events start with oracle.apps. and that the third node is the 2 or 3 character short name for the product. The following examples demonstrate how the remaining nodes can be utilized:

- oracle.apps.fnd.profile.value.update

- oracle.apps.ap.invoice.create

- oracle.apps.hz.customer.address.update

If an Event is appropriately named, you should be able to know whether the Event is seeded or custom, what application owns the Event, and when the Event will be raised, just by reading the name.

For custom Events, the first node would not be 'oracle', but the name of the company defining the Event. If the purpose of your custom Event is to synchronize employee tables between Oracle and Peoplesoft, the second node might be 'ps', so that the result would be similar to '<your company>.ps.per.employee.sync'. If you wish to perform different functions based on whether the employee is new or updated, you would define two Events '<your company>.ps.per.employee.new.sync' and '<your company>.ps.per.employee.update.sync'.

Query Existing Event

- To query an existing Event, enter all or part of the name (with '%') in the 'Name' field and click Go.

- To see or update the definition of the Event, click this icon.

- To see the definition of the Subscriptions for the Event, click this icon.

- To raise or test the Event, click this icon.

Note that you will not be able to delete Oracle seeded Events (you will not be able to click the box under 'Select'). See FIGURE 5.2.

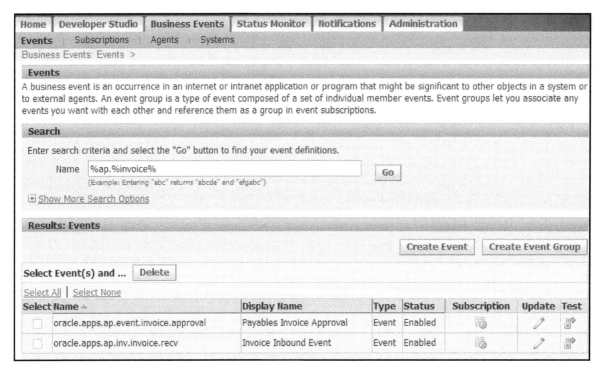

FIGURE 5.2

Create New Event

Create a new Event by clicking the 'Create Event' button. Remember that the name of the Event describes what happened. The Subscriptions will define the subsequent actions that should then be taken.

FIGURE 5.3 shows a sample Event definition.

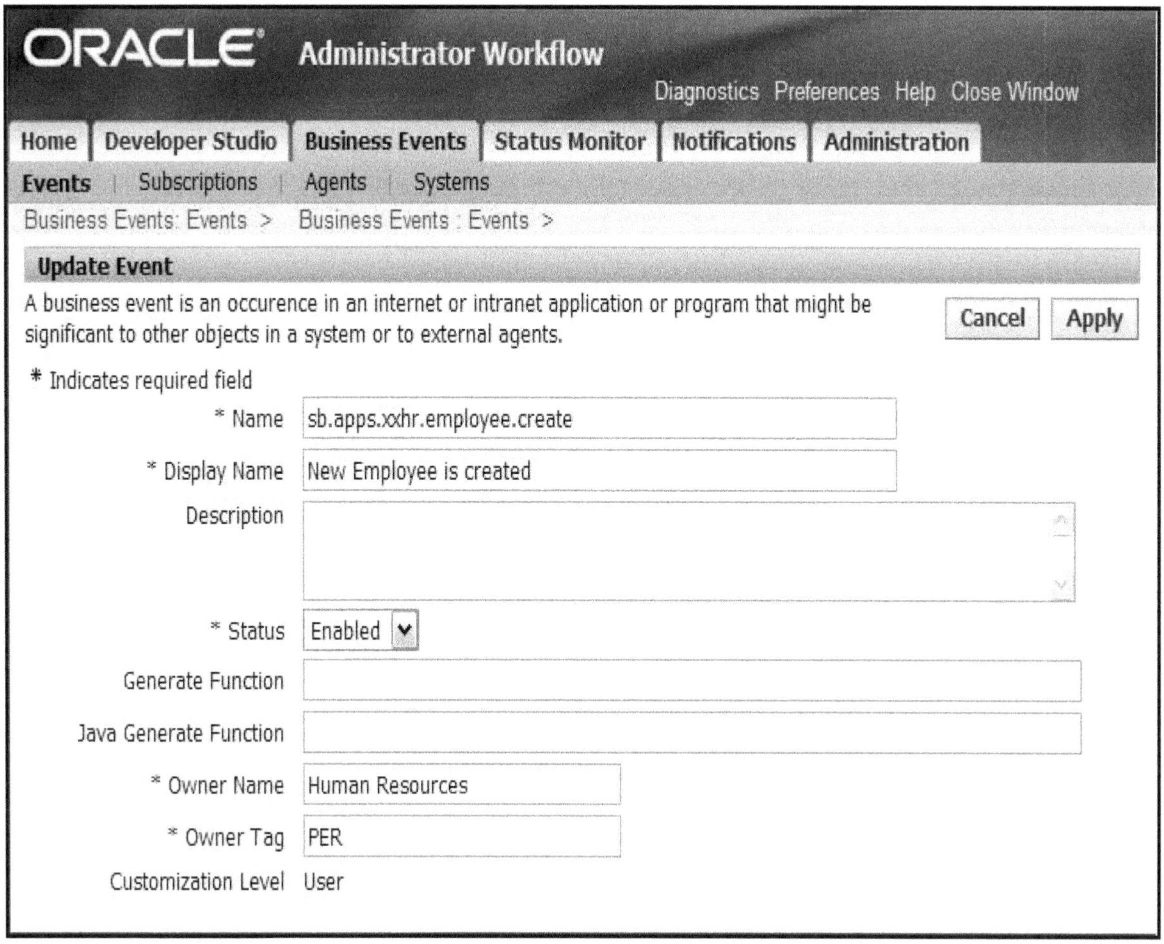

FIGURE 5.3

Enter the Name and Display Name. The Description is optional. The Status will default to Enabled but can be changed at any time. The 'Owner Name' and 'Owner Tag' were optional prior to Release 11.5.10 but are now required. There is no List of Values for either of these fields and Oracle is not currently verifying these fields against any database tables. However, 'Owner Tag' is used by the Concurrent Program 'Synchronize Product License and Workflow BES License'. This program will set the LICENSED_FLAG to 'N' for all Business Events and Subscriptions unless the product indicated by 'Owner Tag' is shared or installed. Therefore, it is required that 'Owner Tag' be set to an existing APPLICATION_SHORT_NAME in the FND_APPLICATION table that links (via APPLICATION_ID) to an installed or shared application in the FND_PRODUCT_INSTALLATIONS table. Although the 'Synchronize Product License and Workflow BES License' Concurrent Program will not update Events/Subscriptions registered to custom application short names, when an Event so registered is queried, you will receive the following warning: "The product specified for this Event is not licensed. This event will not be processed".

The Event we will create will be used to start the Workflow we created in *Chapter 3, Builder Basics* (after the Workflow is adjusted to be started from an Event later in this chapter). Therefore, we will name our Event sb.apps.xxhr.employee.create. 'sb' is an abbreviation for Solution Beacon.

If the Subscription to the Event requires more than the Event name and key, then you can specify either a PL/SQL Function (Generate Function) or a Java Function (Java Generate Function) to build the other aspects of the Event data structure. These Functions can also be specified at the Subscription level. Obviously if each Subscription requires the same Event data (assuming Event data is required), it would be easier to specify the Function at the Event level. If the Event data will be different depending on the Subscription, it is better to specify the Function at the Subscription level.

The 'Customization Level' governs the update actions that can be performed on the Event. If the level is 'Core', it is a seeded Event and no changes can be made. If the level is 'Limit', it is a seeded Event, but you can enable/disable the Event. If the level is 'User', your company created the Event and you can make any change, including deleting the Event. Note that only Oracle can create Events with a customization level of 'Limit' or 'Core'.

After filling in all the fields, click the Apply button to save the definition. To create the Subscriptions for the new Event, you must re-query the Event. This is accomplished by clicking either the blue 'Events' link or the 'Business Events: Events' hyperlink, and then re-querying the Event.

Note that since the customization level is 'User', you could click the box next to the Event and then click the 'Delete' button and delete the definition. This button will gray out once Subscriptions are defined.

FIGURE 5.4 shows two user–defined Events. sb.apps.fnd.user.group does not have Subscriptions and thus can be deleted. sb.apps.xxhr.employee.create has Subscriptions and thus the box in the 'Select' column is grayed out.

The symbol in the 'Subscription' column indicates whether or not Subscriptions exist. If the symbol contains a grid, Subscriptions exist.

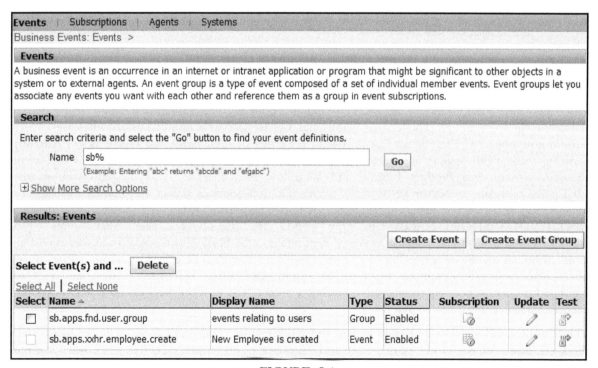

FIGURE 5.4

EVENT GROUPS

Occasionally you might want the same Action to occur for two or more Events. Since Subscriptions are the action, you would have to define the same Subscription multiple times. Oracle has resolved this duplication of effort through Event Groups. Click the 'Create Event Group' button instead of the 'Create Event' button.

Note that even though the Subscription exists at the group level, you raise the Event (not the Event Group) to execute the Subscription. Never raise an Event Group.

The resulting screen looks very similar to the 'Define Event' screen; same fields, same rules. The Event 'Name' should describe the group and have 'group' as the last node. This will alert anyone looking at the Event that this name should not be included as the parameter to the WF_EVENT.Raise API and that this Event has children. Enter all this information and click the Apply button. See FIGURE 5.5.

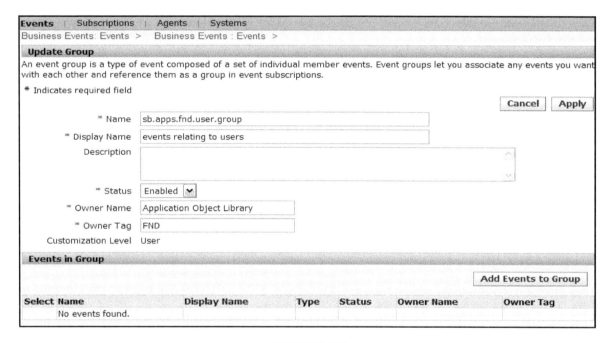

FIGURE 5.5

If an Event fails, the Message to SYSADMIN lists the Event, not the group where the Subscription resides. Therefore, it helps to be able to determine whether an Event belongs to a group. The following SQL will list any groups that include a specified Event as a member:

```
SELECT we.name FROM wf_events we
  WHERE we.guid =
    (SELECT group_guid FROM wf_event_groups
      WHERE member_guid =
        (SELECT we1.guid FROM wf_events we1 WHERE we1.name = '<event_name>'));
```

To add Events to a group, click the 'Add Event to Group' button. Remember, the Apply button must be clicked in order to illuminate the 'Add Event to Group' button.

When the resultant 'Search' page displays, enter your criteria and click Go. See FIGURE 5.6.

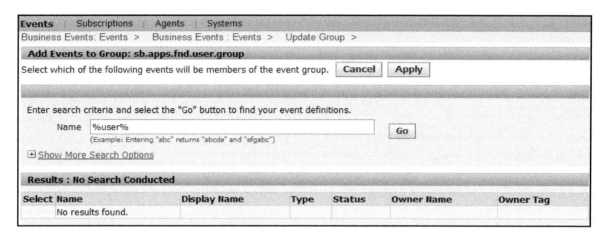

FIGURE 5. 6

Click the box next to the desired Event (or 'Select All' for all listed Events) and press the Apply button. See FIGURE 5.7.

Events	Subscriptions	Agents	Systems				

Business Events: Events > Business Events : Events > Update Group >

Add Events to Group: sb.apps.fnd.user.group

Select which of the following events will be members of the event group. [Cancel] [Apply]

Enter search criteria and select the "Go" button to find your event definitions.

Name %user%   [Go]
(Example: Entering "abc" returns "abcde" and "efgabc")

⊞ Show More Search Options

Add Events

Select Event(s) and ... [Add To Group]   ⊚ Previous 1-10 ▾ Next 10 ⊚

Select All | Select None

Select	Name	Display Name	Type	Status	Owner Name	Owner Tag
☐	oracle.apps.fnd.security.user.assignment.change	User Responsibility Assignment Change	Event	Enabled	Oracle Workflow	FND
☐	oracle.apps.fnd.umf.reg.user_approved	UMF User Registration Approved Event	Event	Enabled	User Management Framework	FND
☐	oracle.apps.fnd.umf.reg.user_invited	UMF User Invited Event	Event	Enabled	User Management Framework	FND
☐	oracle.apps.fnd.umf.reg.user_registered	UMF User Registration Event	Event	Enabled	User Management Framework	FND
☐	oracle.apps.fnd.umf.reg.user_rejected	UMF User Registration Rejected Event	Event	Enabled	User Management Framework	FND
☐	oracle.apps.fnd.umx.username.generate	User Management: Suggested User Name Generation	Event	Enabled	Oracle User Management	FND
☑	oracle.apps.fnd.user.delete	User Delete Event	Event	Enabled	Application Object Library	FND
☑	oracle.apps.fnd.user.insert	User Insert Event	Event	Enabled	Application Object Library	FND
☐	oracle.apps.fnd.user.name.validate	User Name Validation Event	Event	Enabled	Application Object Library	FND
☐	oracle.apps.fnd.user.password.reset_requested	User Password Reset Requested	Event	Enabled	FND	FND

Select Event(s) and ... [Add To Group]   ⊚ Previous 1-10 ▾ Next 10 ⊚

FIGURE 5. 7

Events may be deleted from a group at any time. Just query the group, click the 'Update' icon, select the desired 'Event' and click 'Delete from Group'. You will be asked if you are sure you want to delete the Event. Click 'Yes'. The Event is now deleted.

Edit/Create Subscription

Subscriptions can be created from the 'Events' or 'Subscriptions' page. If starting from the 'Events' page, query the Event. If an Event already has Subscriptions defined, the icon in the 'Subscription' column will look like [icon]. . If no Subscriptions exist, the icon will look like [icon] . Click the icon to navigate to the 'Edit/Define Subscription' page. Existing Subscriptions will be listed. To edit an existing Subscription, click the [icon] icon. To create a new Subscription, click the 'Create Subscription' button. See FIGURE 5.8.

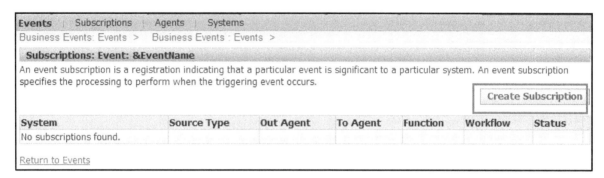

FIGURE 5.8

If you start from the 'Subscriptions' link, a 'Search' page appears. Existing Subscriptions can be queried by System or by using the More Search Options by Event, Source Type (Local, Error or External) or Status (Enabled or Disabled). To create a new Subscription, click 'Create Subscription'. See FIGURE 5.9.

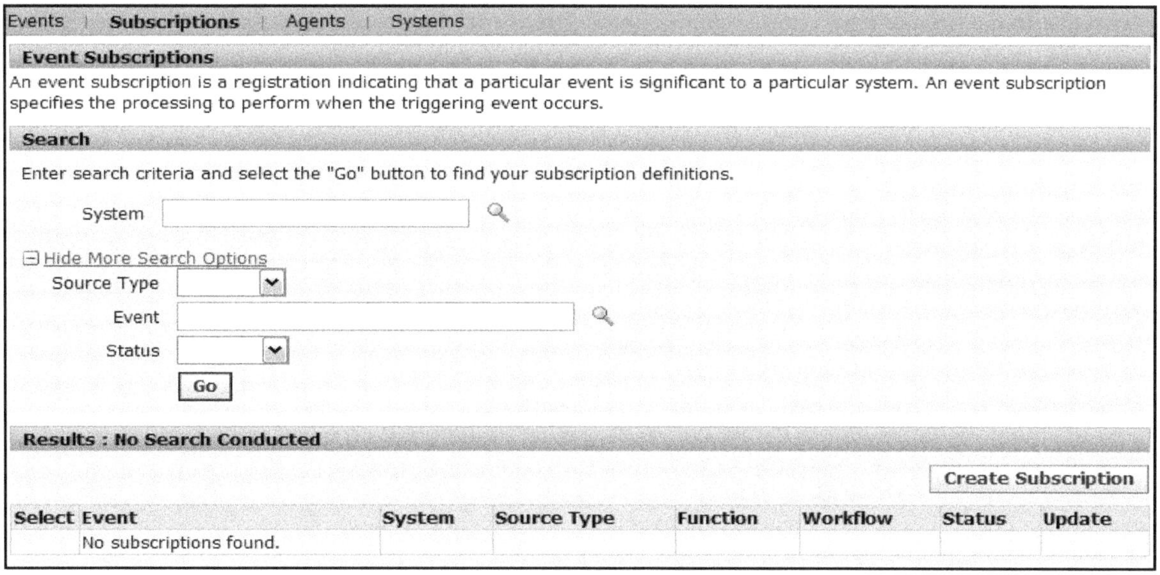

FIGURE 5. 9

Regardless of the starting point, the resulting screen has the same fields. The only difference is that starting from an Event autofills the Event name (see FIGURE 5.10).

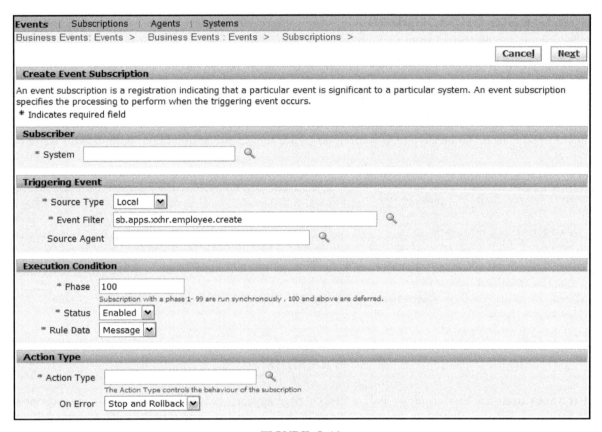

FIGURE 5. 10

If Oracle has seeded the Subscription, the 'Customization Level' will be 'Core' or 'Limit'. If 'Core', no changes can be made. If 'Limit', you can disable/enable the Subscription. Subscriptions defined by your company will be assigned the 'Customization Level' of 'User' and any can be changed. Note that there is currently no way to delete Subscriptions regardless of the 'Customization Level'.

Required fields for a new Subscription are marked with an asterisk. If the flashlight icon is next to the field, you can select the value by clicking the flashlight to open a 'Search' window. In the 'Search By' window, enter part of the value and click Go. You can use wildcard characters. When the results display, either click the desired row in the 'Select' column and click the Select button, or just click the icon in the 'Quick Select' column. See FIGURE 5.11 for an example of using search to select the System.

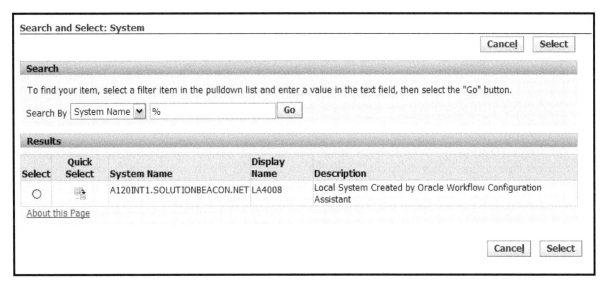

FIGURE 5.11

For each Subscription, the following fields can be entered.

- **System (Required)** – The System where the Subscription executes. This is usually the Local System

- **Source Type (Required)** – Defaults to 'Local' – Enter 'External' if the Event occurs on another System or 'Error' if this is a Subscription that should be executed if the Event was dequeued from the WF_ERROR Queue (which happens when the Event or Subscription errors out)

  If the Event is raised through a Message received by an Inbound Agent, the source should be External, even if the entire transaction is executed on the Local System

- **Event Filter (Required)** – The Event or group to which this Subscription belongs

- **Source Agent (Optional)** – If the Event is initiated by receiving a Message, this field will determine the Queue where the Message is placed (Agents are Subscribers to Queues). Note that if this field is specified, the source type should be External. This field is usually left blank

- **Phase (Required)** – The Phase defaults to 100. This field allows the sequencing of the execution of Subscriptions. If the value is less than 100, the Subscription is executed immediately; otherwise it is moved to the WF_DEFERRED Queue and executed based on the sleep parameters associated with this Queue. If creating multiple Subscriptions for the same Event, the combination of Event/Source Agent/Owner Name/Owner Tag/Phase must be unique. If this combination is not unique, when the Apply button is clicked to save the Subscription, the following Error Message is displayed: "ORA-20002: 3836: Could not create Subscription with the given information. Event '<event name>' already has a similar Subscription with Source Type '<source type>', Phase '<phase>', Owner Name '<owner name>' and Owner Tag '<owner tag>'. ORA-06512: at "APPS.WF_EVENT_SUBSCRIPTIONS_PKG", line <line number> ORA-06512: at line 1"

- **Status (Required)** – 'Status' defaults to 'Enabled'. Set status to 'Disabled' to prevent the Action defined in the Subscription

- **Rule Data (Required)** – 'Rule Data' defaults to Message. If the Subscription can execute with only the name of the Event and the Event Key, then specify 'Key'. If the Event requires any of the other fields in the Event data structure, specify Message

- **Action Type (Required)** – Select 'Launch Workflow' to define the Workflow the Subscription should start, 'Custom' to execute a PL/SQL or Java Procedure, 'Receive Trading Partner Message' to process the Message contained in the Event data (trading partner information will be contained in the parameters), 'Send Notification' to send a Notification to a Role, 'Send Trading Partner Message' to send a Message externally (trading partner information will be contained in the parameters), or 'Send to Agent' to send the Event data to another Agent. This chapter will explain 'Custom', 'Launch Workflow', and 'Send Notification'

- **On Error (Optional)** – Defaults to 'Stop and Rollback'. Enter the Action to be taken if the Subscription errors. Select 'Stop and Rollback' to have the Event stop, rollback changes, and (if defined) execute the error Subscription. Select 'Skip to Next' if there are multiple Subscriptions and they should be executed regardless of the outcome of the current Subscription

Action Type – Launch Workflow

If the Subscription should start or continue a Workflow, select 'Launch Workflow' as the Action Type and select Next to continue the definition. Specify the 'Workflow Type' and 'Top Process'. Note that the Internal Names are used, not the Display Names. Again, the 'Owner Name' and 'Owner Tag' are required and the 'Owner Tag' must match the short name for an Installed or Shared application. See FIGURE 5.12.

When the Subscription is executed, the Workflow Engine will look for any Workflow with a 'Receive' Activity that matches the Event. If the Activity is marked as a Start node (indicated by a green arrow in the lower–left corner of the Activity icon), then the Subscription will start the Workflow. If the Activity is not marked as a Start node, two conditions must be true: the node must have already been transitioned to (and thus in the status NOTIFIED) and the Item Key must match the Item Key the Subscription will furnish.

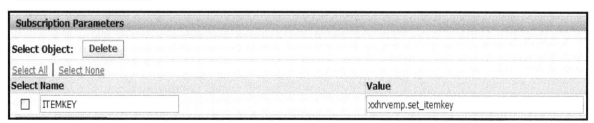

Business Events: Events > Business Events : Events > Subscriptions > Create Event Subscription >
Create Event Subscription - Launch Workflow

Cancel   Back   Apply

An event subscription can be routed to a Workflow process. Please specify the Workflow Type and Workflow Process to be launched.
* Indicates required field

Action

* Workflow Type   XXHRVEMP

* Workflow Process   VALIDATE_NEW_EMPLOYEE_TOP
Choose a Workflow Type, before choosing the Workflow Process for that Type

* Priority   Normal

Additional Options

Add Subscription Parameters
Launch when Business Key Matches
Send when Parameters Match

Subscription Parameter

Select Object: Delete

Select All | Select None

Select Name   **Value**

☐

Add Another Row

Enter parameters and their values with no spaces

Documentation

* Owner Name   Human Resources

* Owner Tag   PER

Customization Level   User

Description

FIGURE 5.12

The Subscription will furnish the Event Key as the Item Key unless you specify a Correlation ID in the Event Message. To specify a Correlation ID and have it become the Item Key, select 'Add Subscription Parameters' in the 'Additional Options'. Fill in 'ItemKey' as the name and '<package.procedure>' as the 'Value'. See FIGURE 5.13.

Subscription Parameters

Select Object: Delete

Select All | Select None

Select Name   **Value**

☐   ITEMKEY   xxhrvemp.set_itemkey

FIGURE 5.13

Since the code that issues the WF_EVENT.Raise can specify the Event Key, using a Subscription parameter to generate the Item Key is only necessary when a developer needs to find an Item Key for a

Workflow already started and then use this Item Key to start a Receive Event that is in the middle of this Workflow.

Values for other parameters can be passed in the same way. This is equivalent to using the WF_ENGINE.SetItemAttr<type> API between WF_ENGINE.CreateProcess and WF_ENGINE.StartProcess. See *Chapter 4, Using PL/SQL in Workflow*.

Choosing 'When Parameters Match' in the field 'Additional Options' allows you to specify parameters that, based on the value of the parameter, conditionally start the Workflow. When the Subscription is executed, the values specified in this section are compared to the values of the parameters in the Event Message. If they match, the Subscription is executed. Obviously this option requires an Event Message to be generated. Thus, either the Subscription or the Event must have a Generate Function. (In order to specify a Generate Function at the Subscription level, choose 'Custom' instead of 'Launch Workflow' when specifying the Action Type.) Make sure the Subscription has the 'Rule Data Attribute' set to 'Message' instead of 'Key'.

Choosing 'Launch when Business Key Matches' allows you to send the Event to multiple existing Workflows. Existing Workflows implies that this Subscription is not meant to start the Workflow. The Workflows have already started and are sitting at an Event Node where the Event Action is set to 'Receive'. The Activity has an Activity Attribute with an Internal Name of #BUSINESS_KEY. Every Workflow where the Event Key matches the value of #BUSINESS_KEY will receive the Event and move to the next node.

When an Event is sent to a Workflow Process, the Workflow Engine performs the following actions:

- Sets parameters from the Event Message as Item Attributes. If the Attribute does not exist, it creates it (only in WF_ITEM_ATTRIBUTE_VALUES, which means it cannot be viewed from the 'Status Monitor')

- Sets the Subscription's GUID (Globally Unique Identifier) as a Dynamic Item Attribute

- If the raise was issued by another Workflow, sets that Workflow as the new Workflow's parent and includes that Workflow and Item Key as parameters in the Message

- Searches for Receive Activities eligible to receive the Event. To be eligible the node must be a Start node with a matching Event name or the node must be a node with an Event Action of Receive and have a status of NOTIFIED. If 'Launch with Business Key Matches' was specified for the Subscription, then in addition to the aforementioned requirement, the Event Key must match the value in the Activity Attribute #BUSINESS_KEY

- If the Event is received by an Event Node marked as a Start Node, all other Event Start Nodes that do not match the Event filter are set to a status of NOTIFIED and are eligible to receive Events that match their Event filter. This means that Workflows can have multiple Event Start Nodes, each linked to a different Event and the path from each Start node will be initiated based on the receipt of that node's Event.

- Stores the Event name, Key, and Message in the Attributes specified in the 'Node Attributes' page of the Event node.

- Sets the status of the node that received the Event to 'COMPLETED' and then moves to the next node in the path.

Action Type – Custom

If the selected Action is Custom, then you can still specify a Workflow and Process, but you can also specify a PL/SQL or Java Function to execute. If the Function is to receive or send a Message, you can specify the 'Out Agent' and the 'To Agent'. If you specify both a Function and a Workflow, it becomes the responsibility of the Function to start the Workflow using the WF_EVENT.Send API. If you specify a Workflow but not a function, Oracle will insert the Function WF_RULE.DEFAULT_RULE (see FIGURE 5.14).

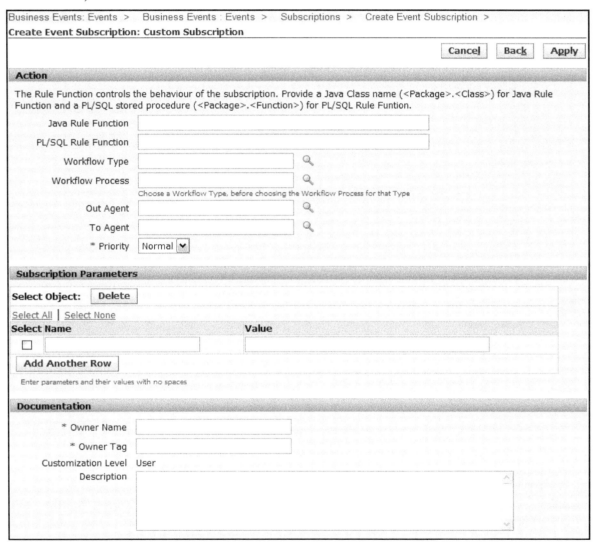

FIGURE 5.14

If you want to send the Event Message to an Agent (a Queue), then specify which Queue in the 'To Agent' field, and the Agent responsible for sending the Message in the 'Out Agent' field. Remember that 'To Agent' must have a Listener running and Propagation must be scheduled for the 'Out Agent'. If you omit the 'Out Agent', Oracle selects a defined Agent that matches the Message type (text, Java, web services). Oracle may pick an Agent that has no Propagation scheduled, so it is wise to specify the Agent. If you omit the 'To Agent', the 'Out Agent' must be linked to a Queue with at least one associated 'To Agent' or Subscriber.

Action Type – Send Notification

The Action Type 'Send Notification' will take a Message from a Workflow and send it to the Role specified. Enter the Workflow in Message Type and the Message Name in Message Name. Select a Recipient. Enter the Owner Name and Owner Tag. Optionally, enter a Priority and Comment.

If the Message has Message Attributes that are linked to Item Attributes, then the Subscription must provide the ability to set the context so that the values for the Item Attributes can be retrieved. A Function to set this may be specified in the 'Callback' field. If this field is left blank, the default Context Function supplied by Oracle, WF_ENGINE.CB, will be used. The default Context Function requires that the Item Type, Item Key and Activity ID be supplied in the 'Context' field in the format <ItemType>:<ItemKey>:<activityid> (see FIGURE 5.15).

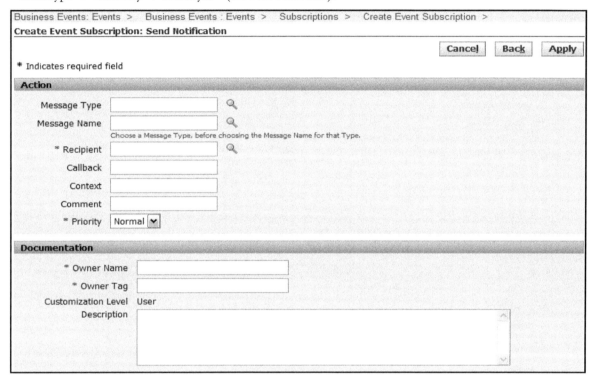

FIGURE 5. 15

When the Message is sent, the Event Manager sets the Notification ID into the Event parameter list with the name #NID. The Notification ID will be required if the Message requires a response or has respond variables not linked to Item Attributes. The Notification ID is a parameter to the API WF_NOTIFICATION.GetAttr<type>. To access the #NID parameter, use the API WF_EVENT.GetValueForParameter. Additionally, you must use the WF_EVENT.Raise3 API to start the Event instead of the usual WF_EVENT.Raise API.

PROGRAMMATICALLY START EVENTS

Events can be programmatically raised through the WF_EVENT.Raise API. We will take our Trigger from *Chapter 4, Using PL/SQL in Workflow*, and change it to start the Workflow using our Event. The explanation following the Trigger will denote if a section is the same as the Trigger or different.

```
CREATE OR REPLACE TRIGGER xxhr_start_xxhrvemp_workflow
1.▶AFTER INSERT
     ON per_all_people_f
  FOR EACH ROW
  DECLARE
        l_user_person_type hr.per_person_type.user_person_type%TYPE;
2.▶    g_trace            VARCHAR2(2000);
  BEGIN
        -- get the person_type
3.▶    g_trace := 'Getting the person type';
        SELECT user_person_type INTO l_user_person_type
          FROM hr.per_person_types ppt
         WHERE ppt.person_type_id = :NEW.person_type_id;
        -- If user_person_type <> 'Employee' do nothing
        IF l_user_person_type = 'Employee'
        THEN
           -- the following statement raises the event
4.▶       g_trace := 'Raising the event';
           wf_event.Raise
        (p_event_name => 'sb.apps.xxhr.employee.create'
        ,p_event_key => :new.person_id||':'||
                  TO_CHAR(SYSDATE,'YYYYMMDDHH24MISS');                );
        END IF:
5.▶EXCEPTION
        WHEN OTHERS
        THEN
           ax_message_pkg.raise_message ('AX'
                        ,'AX_56010_COMM_MESG_TEXT'
                        ,'MESG_BUG'
                        ,'Error occurred while ' ||g_trace
                        );
              RAISE;
  END;
```

1.▶ The above Trigger fires whenever a record is inserted in PER_ALL_PEOPLE_F, which is the base table for employees. The declaratives except L_USER_PERSON_TYPE and G_TRACE have been deleted, because owner and user_key are not parameters to the WF_EVENT.Raise API. Since our Subscription has a Phase that is greater than 99, the start of the Workflow will automatically be deferred and there is no longer any need to adjust the threshold of the Workflow Engine.

2.▶ Same. G_TRACE will be used to help debug the Trigger if it fails. It will be set to the Action that is attempted throughout the Procedure. If the Trigger fails, the Message displayed will indicate that the Action following the setting of G_TRACE errored.

3.▶ Same. Check the PERSON_TYPE_ID against PER_PERSON_TYPES. If PERSON_TYPE_ID is not Employee, then nothing else needs to be done.

4.▶ For our Workflow it is acceptable to use the Event Key as the Item Key. Remember that the Item Key must be unique for the Item Type specified in the Event Subscription. Since there can only be one EMPLOYEE_ID in PER_ALL_PEOPLE_F with the PERSON_TYPE of Employee and EFFECTIVE_END_DATE = '31-DEC-4712', the EFFECTIVE_START_DATE and EFFECTIVE_END_DATE fields do not need to be included as the ITEM_KEY. However, using the recommendations outlined in *Chapter 3, Builder Basics*, we add a delimiter ('-') and SYSDATE to guarantee uniqueness.

WF_EVENT.Raise is a seeded API that raises the Event. Raising an Event will cause the Subscriptions to be executed, which for this Event will start the Workflow. The parameters are:

- **p_event_name (required)** – the name of the Event to be raised

- **p_event_key (required)** – a value making this Event unique and that, based on the Subscription definition, will become the Item Key of the Workflow referenced in the Subscription

- **p_event_data (optional in the raise statement)** –This value can be passed to the Subscription (and subsequent Workflow or Message or Procedure) through the raise statement or through the Event or Subscription Generate Function. The EVENT_DATA has a data type of WF_EVENT_T (see *Chapter 10, Workflow Tables*). Since our Subscription has Rule Data set to Key, no EVENT_DATA is required.

- **p_parameters (optional)** – Event parameters are passed either as part of the EVENT_DATA or separately using a data type of WF_PARAMETER_T.

- **p_send_date (optional)** – If the Event should be delayed beyond the delay assigned to the WF_DEFERRED Queue, use this parameter to specify when the Event should be processed.

5. ► Same. If the Trigger errors, the exception routine calls ax_Message_pkg.raise_Message which will display the value set in G_TRACE.

USING EVENTS IN WORKFLOW

If the purpose of the Event Subscription is to start a Workflow, the Workflow must be configured to receive the Event. Use the Workflow Builder tool to define an Event Activity (double-click 'Events' ⚡ – see FIGURE 5.16, or in the Diagrammer window, right click the white space and select 'New Event').

FIGURE 5.16

Events require that three Attributes be defined (see FIGURE 5.17): one to store the Event name, one to store the Event Key, and one to store the Event Message. The first two must have a type of Text and the

Event Message must have a type of Event. If you have been alphabetizing the Attribute names, be sure to drag the new Attributes to their proper place.

FIGURE 5.17

Like all Workflow activities, enter the Internal Name and Display Name. In the Event Action, select 'Receive'. In the 'Event Filter', enter the name of the Event that will be raised when you wish the Workflow to start. This Event must either contain the Subscription that defines the Workflow to start or must belong to a group that contains the Subscription that defines the Workflow to start. If you leave the 'Event Filter' blank, or mistype the name (it is case sensitive), when the Event is raised, it will error, invoking the 'WFERROR' Workflow. The user SYSADMIN will then receive an Error Message stating "142: Process '<item type internal name>/<item key>' has no activities waiting to receive Event '<event name>'". FIGURE 5.18 shows an Event Node correctly configured (the 'Event Filter' contains an 'Event Name' and that 'Event Name' matches the 'Event Name' in FIGURE 5.3).

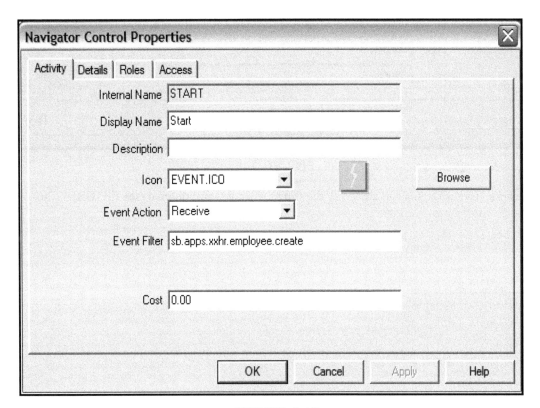

FIGURE 5.18

If you double-clicked the 'Event' tree in the Navigator window, drag the new Event to the Diagrammer window. This Event must be a Start node. Double-click the 'Event', select the Node tab, and change 'Start/End' to 'Start'. Note that since our original Start Node is still there, Oracle has appended '-1' to the Label to guarantee uniqueness (see FIGURE 5.19).

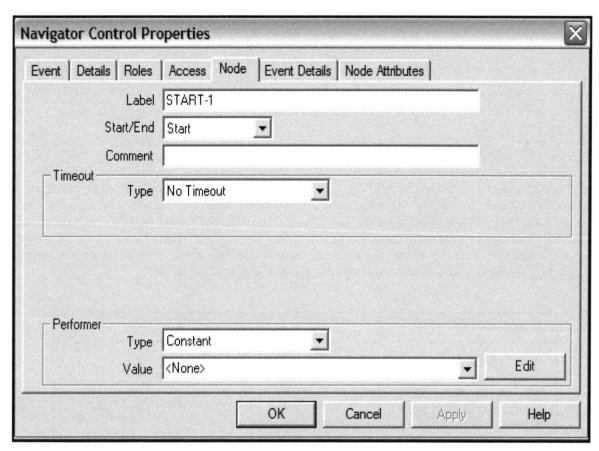

FIGURE 5.19

Now click the 'Event Details' tab and enter the three Attributes you defined (see FIGURE 5.20).

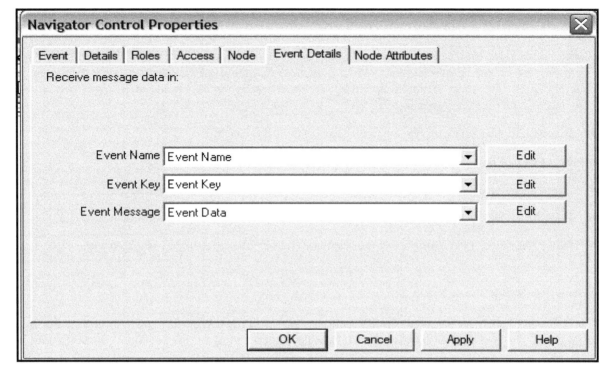

FIGURE 5.20

Delete the standard Start Node and draw a line from the Event Node to the first Activity. If this version is saved to the database, the Workflow will now be Event-enabled (see FIGURE 5.21).

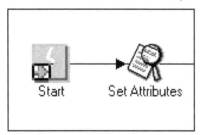

FIGURE 5. 21

OTHER USES OF THE RECEIVE ACTIVITY

It is possible for a Receive Event to be other than the first node, but in order to receive the Event, the Workflow must have transitioned to that node and be waiting (STATUS = 'NOTIFIED').

Workflows can also use the Event Activity to raise other Events. Set the Event Action to Raise and set the value of the Attribute specified in Event Name to the name of the Event to raise and set the value of the Attribute specified in Event Key to the Event Key to be passed to the Event. This type of node cannot be a Start Node.

Workflows can create Messages and send them. In this case, the Event Action is set to 'Send'. The Attribute specified in Event Message must contain a Message and a 'To Agent'. The Event Name is the Event that will process the Message. Event Key is also required.

EVENT STANDARD ACTIVITIES

Workflow provides the standard activities 'Compare Event Property', 'Get Event Property', and 'Set Event Property'. There are also several 'XML....' activities that the *Workflow Developers Guide* states are not currently used. Like most standard activities, you must configure the 'Node Attributes' tab or the Function won't work. The Attributes are:

- **Event** – An Attribute with type of Event that contains the Event data

- **Property** – Which part of the Event data – uses a LOV

- **Event Parameter** – If Property is set to Event Parameter, which parameter – no LOV

- **Item Attribute** – Either the source of the data (for 'Set'), or where the data will be placed (for 'Get')

- **Date, Numeric, Text Value** – For the Compare Activity, the value to be compared with.

WHAT'S NEXT

The Workflow has been designed, the PL/SQL is written, but the Workflow (either version) has not been tested. The next chapter will demonstrate how developers can test either version of the Workflow.

Testing Workflows

N ow that the Workflow design is finished and the code written, the Workflow can be tested. Although *Chapter 4, Using PL/SQL in Workflow*, and *Chapter 5, Business Events*, included Triggers to start the Workflow, developers should remember that others may be using the 'Enter Employees' screen in the development database. Therefore, compiling the Trigger or any Procedure that automatically starts a Workflow should be delayed until the developer is reasonably sure the Workflow will function as designed. Oracle has screens to test starting and running Workflows. The Developer Studio will start Workflows where the first node is the traditional Start Node and the 'Define Event' screen provides a Test icon that will start Workflows where the first node is an Event.

As pointed out in the preface, the majority of the screen shots in this book are from Release 12. Therefore, Release 12 screen shots will be used to simulate testing in the development environment. Release 11.5.10.2 screen shots will be used to simulate testing in UAT (User Acceptance Testing) to demonstrate some of the errors that can occur when Workflows are not carefully migrated.

The errors demonstrated in this chapter were caused by introducing errors into the code listed in *Chapter 4, Using PL/SQL in Workflow*.

TEST CASES

Testing workflows is the same as testing any screen or procedure. You must have a series of test cases that, when successful, will demonstrate that the workflow and associated code are production-ready. When testing workflows, test cases should be designed that will test all legs of the workflow. For the workflow XXHRVEMP, the following tests should be performed:

1. Set Attributes – Activity does not have a Result Type, so there is only one path to follow. Valid result would be that Item Attributes are correctly set

2. Compare Text – Possible results are Null and <Default> (Not Null). The <Any> leg should be followed in all cases

    2.1. <Any> leg was initiated regardless of value of email address

    2.2. Email Address was entered in the new employee record, the workflow progresses through the 'Or' node and waits at the 'And' node for 'Is Employee Data complete?' to return 'Yes'

2.3. Email Address was not entered in the new employee record, Notification is correctly delivered to the Email Administrator

   2.3.1. Ask Email Admin for email address – Possible results are the Notification is responded to or the Notification times out (even though there is no Result Type, there is a Respond attribute so the Notification should wait for a response)

      2.3.1.1. Notification to Email Administrator times out, Notification is correctly resent to the Email Administrator. Answer the Notification this time

      2.3.1.2. Email Administrator answers the Notification with a valid email address (Note: answering without an email address or with an invalid email address will be addressed as part of Chapter 11, "Advanced Builder and PL/SQL"), workflow updates the employee record with the email address, and proceeds through the 'Or' node and waits at the 'And' node for 'Is Employee Data complete? to return 'Yes'

3. 'Is Employee Data complete?' - Valid results are 'Yes' or 'No'

   3.1. Result is 'Yes' - Workflow proceeds to the 'And' node, and once both legs have reached the 'And' node, workflow proceeds to the 'End' node and stops

   3.2. Result is 'No' - Notification is sent to HR responsibility and correctly received

      3.2.1. 'Ask HR to Fix it' – Valid results are OK or <Timeout> and regardless of result, data can now be incomplete or complete

         3.2.1.1. Notification is answered OK, workflow returns to 'Is Employee Data complete?' and the Result is 'No'

            3.2.1.1.1. 'Ask HR to Fix it' Notification is sent and Result is OK, workflow returns to 'Is Employee Data complete?' and the Result is 'Yes', workflow proceeds to the 'And' node, and once both legs have reached the 'And' node, workflow proceeds to the 'End' node and stops

            3.2.1.1.2. 'Ask HR to Fix it' Notification is sent and Result is OK, workflow returns to 'Is Employee Data complete?' and the Result is 'No', and Notification is resent.

               3.2.1.1.2.1. Repeat twice either responding to the Notification without correcting the data or letting the Notification timeout without correcting the data to trigger the Loop Counter Exit branch

                  3.2.1.1.2.1.1. Loop Counter returns 'Exit', 'Escalate to HR Manager' Notification correctly received, workflow proceeds to 'Wait' node and after specified time expires, returns to 'Is Employee Data complete?'. At this time, complete loop is tested. The workflow will continue to follow the loop until the employee data is updated so the 'Is Employee Data complete?' can return 'Yes'

         3.2.1.2. Notification times out, workflow returns to 'Is Employee Data complete?'. Once both results are tested to ensure 'Is Employee Data complete?', the tests outlined in

3.2.1.1.2 and 3.2.1.1.2 are sufficient to complete the testing of Loop Counter returning the 'Loop' result

The above tests show that even a simple workflow requires significant testing. The rest of this chapter will discuss the screens available to the developer to perform these tests without the necessity of creating a new employee each time the test is to be repeated. In fact, SQL can be used to identify some employee records with the following characteristics (if the records cannot be found, they will need to be created)

- Employee with an email address

- Employee without an email address

- Employee with all data required by 'Is Employee Data complete?'

- Employee missing at least one field required by 'Is Employee Data complete?'

Since the Workflow processes the email check separately from the other data, the testing can be completed with as few as two employees.

ADJUST TIMEOUTS AND WAITS AND LOOP COUNTS

Timeouts and Waits are usually set to increments of days. When testing Workflows, these Timeouts and waits need to be tested. However, waiting days for a Timeout or for the Wait Activity to finish does not promote efficient testing. Timeouts are set by right-clicking on the 'Activity' in a Process diagram, selecting 'Properties', then clicking on the Node tab. Timeouts are easy to set in minutes.

Changing the time for the 'Wait Activity' is also done by clicking on the 'Activity' in a Process diagram and selecting 'Properties'. However, instead of clicking the Node tab, click the 'Node Attributes' tab and ensure 'Wait Mode' is set to Relative Time, and then set Relative Time to a number that represents days or fractions of days. For example, .02 equates to 28.8 minutes.

A Loop that allows for more than 2 cycles will also prolong testing. Reducing the count to 1 will not test for the "counter reset" issue discussed in *Chapter 3, Builder Basics*. Therefore, our recommendation is to set the number of cycles to 2. The number of cycles is controlled through setting 'Loop Limit' on the 'Node Attributes' tab of the 'Loop Properties' page.

Obviously, once all testing is done in the development instance, these values should be set to the original designed values before migrating the Workflow to other instances.

DEVELOPER STUDIO

When the first node of a Workflow is the standard Start Node (green circle with an arrow), developers should perform all initial testing using the 'Developer Studio' screen (see FIGURE 6.1). This screen can be accessed from any 'Workflow Administration' responsibility. The menu paths provided in this chapter will be from the 'Workflow Administration Web Applications' responsibility. Although anyone with any of the Workflow Administration responsibilities can open the screen, the icons to actually start the Workflow will be missing unless you belong to the Role assigned as the Workflow Administrator.

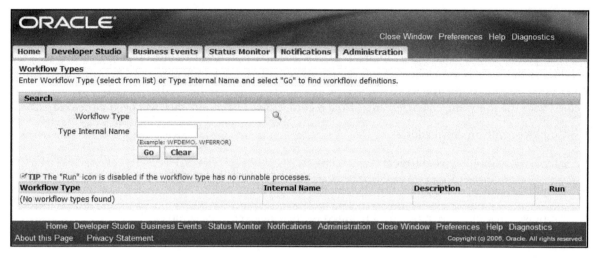

FIGURE 6.1

If opening the Developer Studio yields a screen like FIGURE 6.2 (the 'Run' column is missing), click the 'Administration' tab, note the Workflow Administration Role and ask the System Administrator to add you to this Role. Obviously if the Workflow Administrator is a user such as SYSADMIN, the System Administrator should change the Role to a responsibility (see *Chapter 2, Setup*, for the discussion on setting the Workflow Administrator and ensuring this Role is not changed during patching).

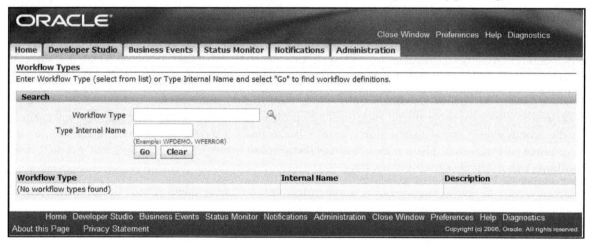

FIGURE 6.2

The navigation path to the Developer Studio is Administrator Workflow → Developer Studio. This screen can also be accessed by clicking the 'Developer Studio' tab from any of the Workflow Administration screens. Enter either the Internal Name of the Workflow in the 'Type Internal Name' field, or the Workflow Display Name in the 'Workflow Type' field and click Go. The screen will return the selected Workflow as shown in FIGURE 6.3.

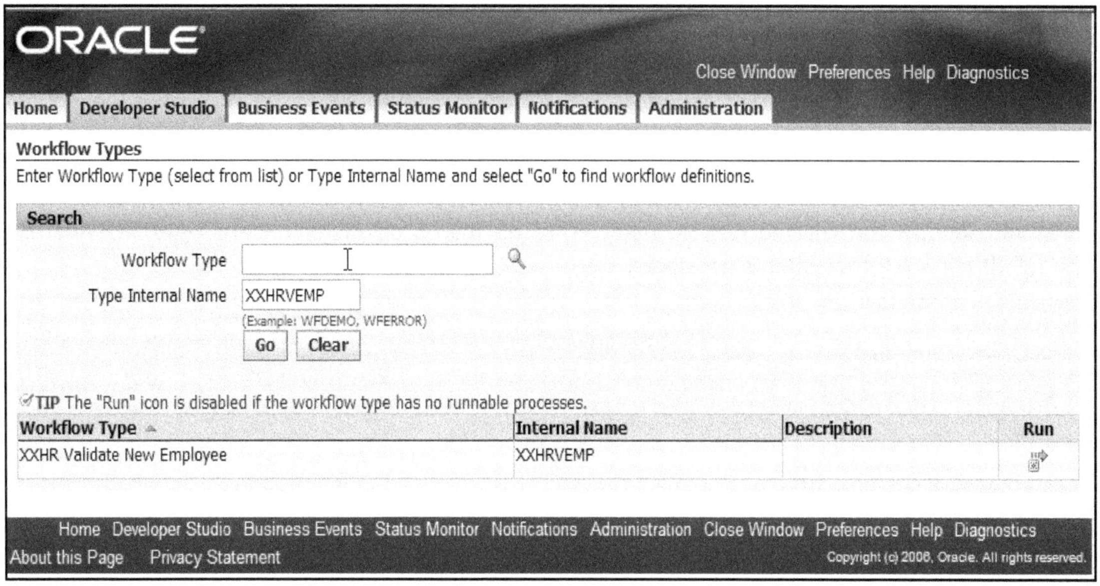

FIGURE 6.3

Click the Run icon to display the 'Run Workflow' page (see FIGURE 6.4).

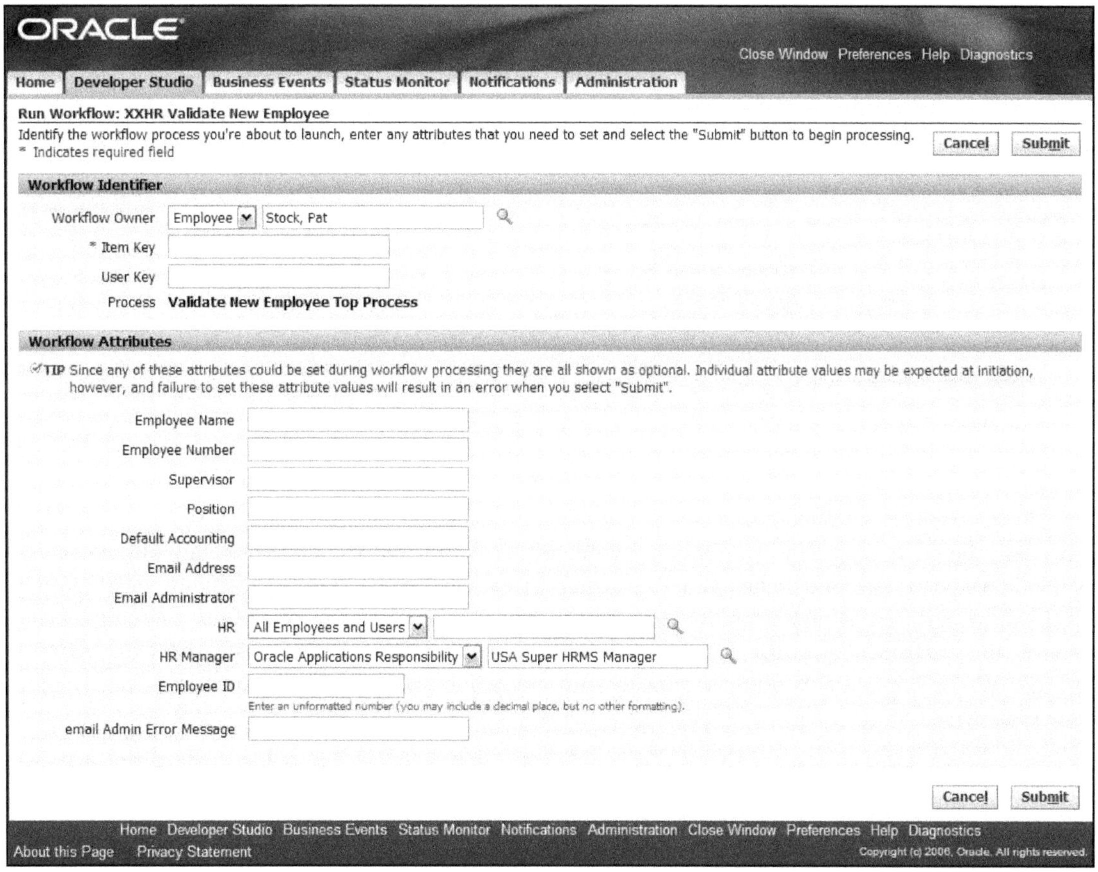

FIGURE 6.4

197

Errors Detected Before the Workflow is Initiated

Before entering any data, look at the top of the screen. Any invalid Performers will be noted (see FIGURE 6.5). An invalid Performer is defined as an Item Attribute used as a Performer, or a constant value assigned as a Performer, where the value is not null and either the value matches neither the NAME nor the DISPLAY_NAME column in the table WF_LOCAL_ROLES, or the Role is not active. Usually this error is caused by using Directory Services to assign a responsibility as a Performer and the responsibility key for the selected responsibility is greater than 8 characters. See *Chapter 3, Builder Basics*, for the full discussion of selecting Performers.

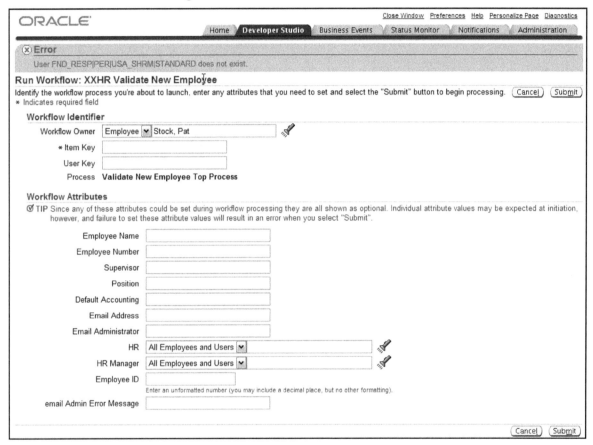

FIGURE 6.5

In this case the error is caused by an inconsistency in the definition of a responsibility. Directory Services was used to assign a responsibility as a Performer. However, when the responsibility was set up in the next database, a different responsibility key was selected. Thus, when the Workflow was migrated to this database, the Internal Name for that responsibility was different and the "user does not exist" error occurred. When migrating Workflows, make sure any other required setups are well-documented and accurately entered.

Since a responsibility key cannot be updated, correcting this error requires loading the Workflow from this database into the Builder, re-loading the Role from Directory Services, re-assigning the Role to the Attribute and re-saving the Workflow, or creating another responsibility with the correct name and key. Using the Builder to effect the change is usually prohibited outside of the development database. Therefore, despite the ease of using the Directory Services, it is better to use PL/SQL to find and assign

Performers. For responsibilities, the developer can match the responsibility name (which if typed incorrectly can be corrected without the need to change any code). However, if the Builder is used to make the change, remember to re-save the Workflow to the database.

Required and Optional Fields

When using the Developer Studio to start a Workflow, the only required field is the 'Item Key'. 'Process' is required if the definition of the Item Type did not specify a Selector Function that determines the starting Process (see *Chapter 4, Using PL/SQL in Workflow*, for a discussion of Selector Functions used to start a Workflow). Choices for this field are limited to 'Runnable Processes'. A Runnable Process is simply any Process defined in the Item Type that can be the "top" or starting Process for the Workflow. These Processes are designated runnable by clicking the 'Runnable' button on the 'Item Type Property' page in the Workflow Builder (see FIGURE 6.6). Since our Workflow only has one Runnable Process, the name of this Process is defaulted into the screen.

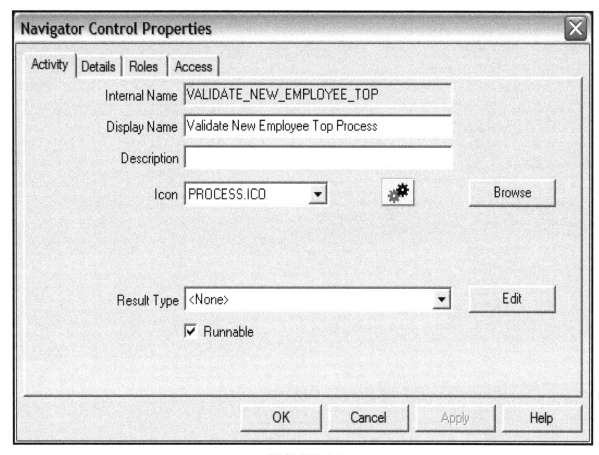

FIGURE 6.6

Our Workflow is designed to start when a new employee is entered. The code will return an error if the value specified as the Item Key does not link to a record in the PER_ALL_PEOPLE_F table.

The 'Workflow Owner' and 'User Key' fields are optional. Your user name will default into the 'Workflow Owner' field. Review the Workflow design and code. If another name should be substituted, then use the List of Values to select the appropriate value. If the code used to start the Workflow sets any

Attributes between the WF_ENGINE.CreateItem( ) API and the WF_ENGINE.StartProcess( ) API, then values for these Attributes must be entered. Our code (see *Chapter 4, Using PL/SQL in Workflow*) will set both the Owner and User Key and all other Attribute values, so only the Item Key is required.

For the first test, we will select an employee with an email address and all other required data – Pat Stock (user name OPERATIONS). The PERSON_ID for Pat Stock is 25. Our code requires that the ITEM_KEY be the PERSON_ID followed by a '-' then a date. Since our code only looks for what precedes the '-', what follows the '-' using the Developer Studio can actually be anything. If testing an Oracle-delivered Workflow, make sure the specified Item Key matches the format required by the first Function. We recommend using the date of the test in YYYYMMDDHH24MI format. So as shown in FIGURE 6.7, this test was submitted on August 24, 2007 at 3:00 PM. After entering the Item Key, click the 'Submit' button. The Workflow will start and continue to run until it reaches an End Node, reaches a Deferred Activity (such as a Notification that requires a response), or errors.

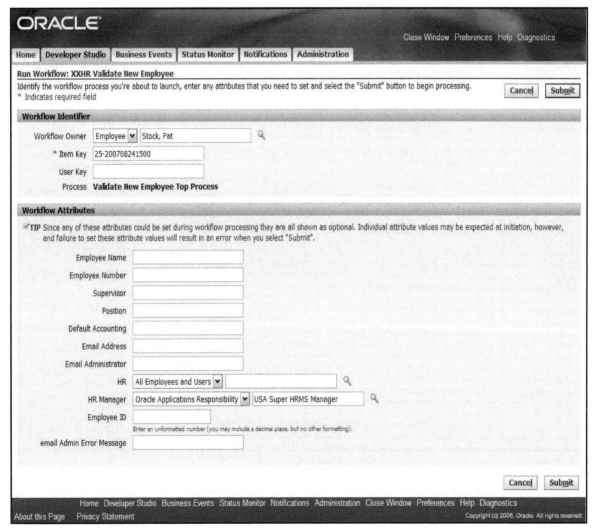

FIGURE 6.7

At this point, control is transferred back to the form and FIGURE 6.8 will appear.

FIGURE 6. 8

The form functions as the "calling program". This means that the form issues the API to start the Workflow and waits until control is transferred back to the form. As the calling program, the form also issues the Commit (see *Chapter 4, Using PL/SQL in Workflow*, for a discussion of commits in Workflow). If the form seems slow in responding, it is the result of what is happening in the Workflow. If the Workflow contains a Process that requires significant time to execute, it may be wise to increase the cost of that Function to a number > 0.5 so that it will be deferred to a Background Engine. The execution time of each Activity can be seen from the 'Status Monitor' (click the 'Activity History' button).

STARTING WORKFLOWS USING THE RAISE EVENT PAGE

If the first node in the Workflow is an Event Node, the 'Business Event' page should be used to raise the Event, which will start the Workflow. Click the 'Business Events' tab and query the Event (see FIGURE 6.9).

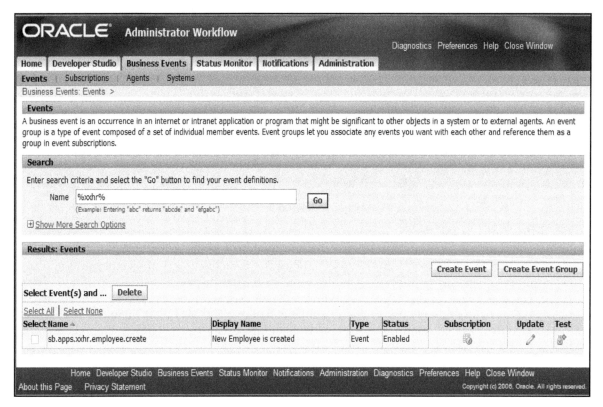

FIGURE 6.9

Click the 'Test' link located at the far right of the Business Event name. Notice that you cannot set values for the Item Attributes, only parameters. Code in the Workflow or the 'Standard' Activity Get Event Property can be used to retrieve the passed values.

Unless you have specified ItemKey as one of the parameters and specified code to set this value, the value entered for the Event Key will become the Item Key, so the same rules used for the Developer Studio will apply. Enter the Event Key and press the 'Submit' button (see FIGURE 6.10). A confirmation page (see FIGURE 6.11) displays stating "The Event '<event name>' has been raised". The developer can close the form or use the tabs or links under the tabs to navigate to another form. Note that unlike the Developer Studio, the 'Test Business Event' screen did not warn of invalid Performers.

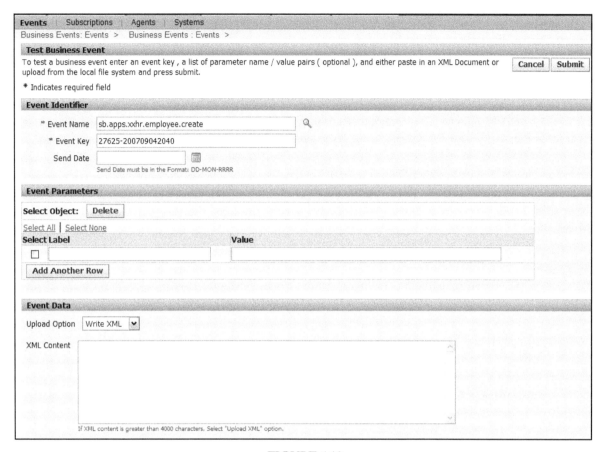

FIGURE 6.10

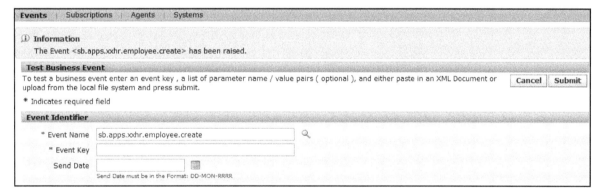

FIGURE 6.11

Why Workflow Didn't Start

When using the Developer Studio, the Workflow starts immediately and can be viewed instantly from the 'Status Monitor'. The 'Test Business Event' page works differently. As explained in *Chapter 5, Business Events*, when a Business Event is raised, the Subscription(s) is(are) executed. If the Phase number of the Subscription is greater than 99, the execution of the Subscription is moved to the WF_DEFERRED Queue. The Subscription will stay there until the next time the Agent Listener Container wakes up and allows the Listeners to process their Events.

You can check the status of the Subscription using the following query (assuming the query is executed the same day as the Event is raised):

```
SELECT corrid,state,enq_time,deq_time FROM wf_deferred
  WHERE corrd = 'APPS:<event name>' AND
SUBSTR(TO_CHAR(enq_time),1,9)=TO_CHAR(SYSDATE,'DD-MON-YY');
```

Fill in the Event Name exactly as defined. The query is case sensitive, APPS is all caps and there is no space between the ':' and the Event name. You should be able to find the Event you just raised by looking at the ENQ_TIME. If the STATE = 0, the Subscription has not been executed yet. Once the STATE = 2, the Subscription has been executed and the Workflow should have started.

If the 'Status Monitor' still shows no evidence of the Workflow, the Event has errored. When Events error, they invoke the System: Error (WFERROR) Workflow using the Process 'Default Event Error Process'. The Notification detailing the error will be sent to SYSADMIN.

The most common reason for the error is that the Event Filter was left blank or the Event Name was mistyped when defining the Event in the Workflow Builder. This results in the following error Notification (see FIGURE 6.12).

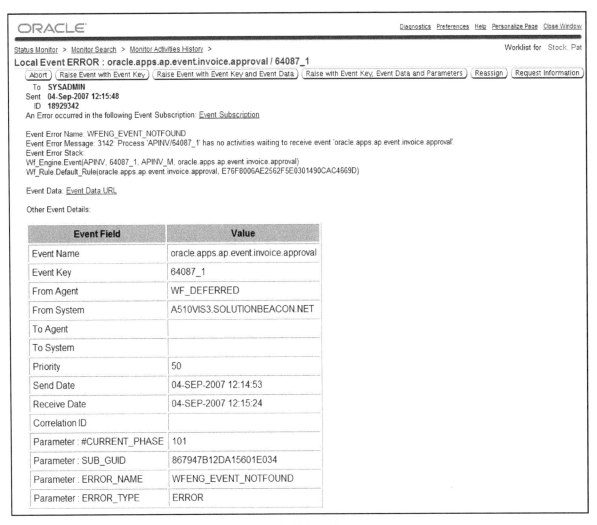

FIGURE 6.12

Load the Workflow into the Builder, open the 'Properties' page of the Event, correct the name in the Event Filter, and save the Workflow to the database. Then either answer the Notification with Abort (and use the 'Business Event' page to retry raising the Event) or Raise Event with Event Key (which will also retry raising the Event).

VIEWING THE RESULTS

Regardless of whether the Workflow is started using the Test Event or the Developer Studio, or whether a Trigger or Procedure invokes the API to start the Workflow, the 'Status Monitor' page will be used to view the results. *Chapter 8, Administration,* explains how to use the 'Status Monitor', so this chapter will assume the developer is familiar with this screen.

Notification with a Result Type

The Notification Ask HR to Fix it has the Result Type XXHR_OK assigned to it. This causes the Workflow to pause and wait for a response, even when the Lookup Type only has one Lookup Code.

Notifications with Result Types can be assigned Timeouts. FIGURE 6.13 shows this Notification. When the OK button is pressed, the Workflow Engine marks the Notification closed, stores the result, and moves down the leg labeled with the response given.

FIGURE 6.13

Timeouts can be assigned to these Notifications. If the Notification is not answered before the designated Timeout parameter, the Workflow Engine marks the Notification closed, sets the Result to TIMEOUT, and proceeds down the leg labeled '<Timeout>'

Notification Without a Result Type but With a Response Attribute

The Notification 'Ask Email Admin for email address' does not have a Result Type, but the Message Attribute EMAIL_ADDRESS has a source of Respond. This also causes the Workflow to pause waiting for a result and adds a 'Submit' button so that the person responding can indicate to the Workflow Engine that a response has been provided (see FIGURE 6.14).

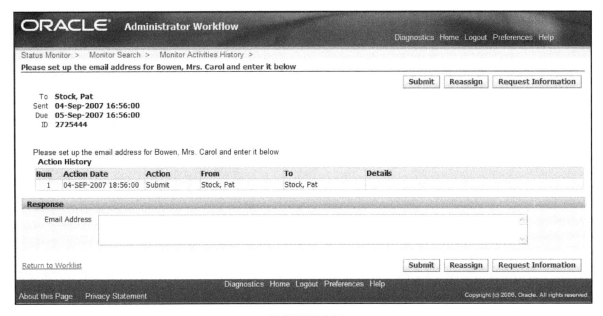

FIGURE 6.14

When the OK button is pressed, the Workflow Engine stores the value entered in all Message Attributes with a source of Respond, marks the Notification closed, and moves to the next Activity. There are no labels on the legs because there is no Result Type.

Because this Notification is also waiting for a response, a Timeout can be assigned. If the Notification times out, the behavior is the same as the Notification requiring a response.

'FYI' Notification – no Result Type nor Response Attribute

The Notification 'Escalate to HR Manager' does not have a Result Type or any Message Attributes with a source of Respond. The Workflow does not wait for a response, but moves immediately to the next Activity. The Workflow Engine does add an OK button, but that is to close the Notification when viewing it through the Notification Worklist (see FIGURE 6.15).

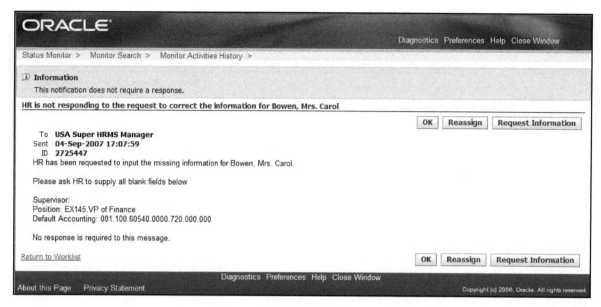

FIGURE 6.15

Since the Workflow does not pause when 'FYI' Notifications are sent, assigned Timeouts are ignored. The Notification will remain open until either the OK button is pressed from the Notification Worklist or the Notification is successfully emailed (and the 'Close FYI Notification' option on the Notification Mailer is checked).

TEST RESULTS – EXAMPLES OF ERRORS

This chapter also assumes knowledge of SQL and PL/SQL errors, so the focus will be on remediation particular to Workflow.

PL/SQL Procedure is Missing or Mistyped

Using the 'Status Monitor' page, query the Workflow that just started. Since we selected an employee with an email address and all the required data, the expected result would be that the Workflow is already complete. However FIGURE 6.16 shows that there is an error (the 'Status' column says <u>Error</u> preceded by a red X).

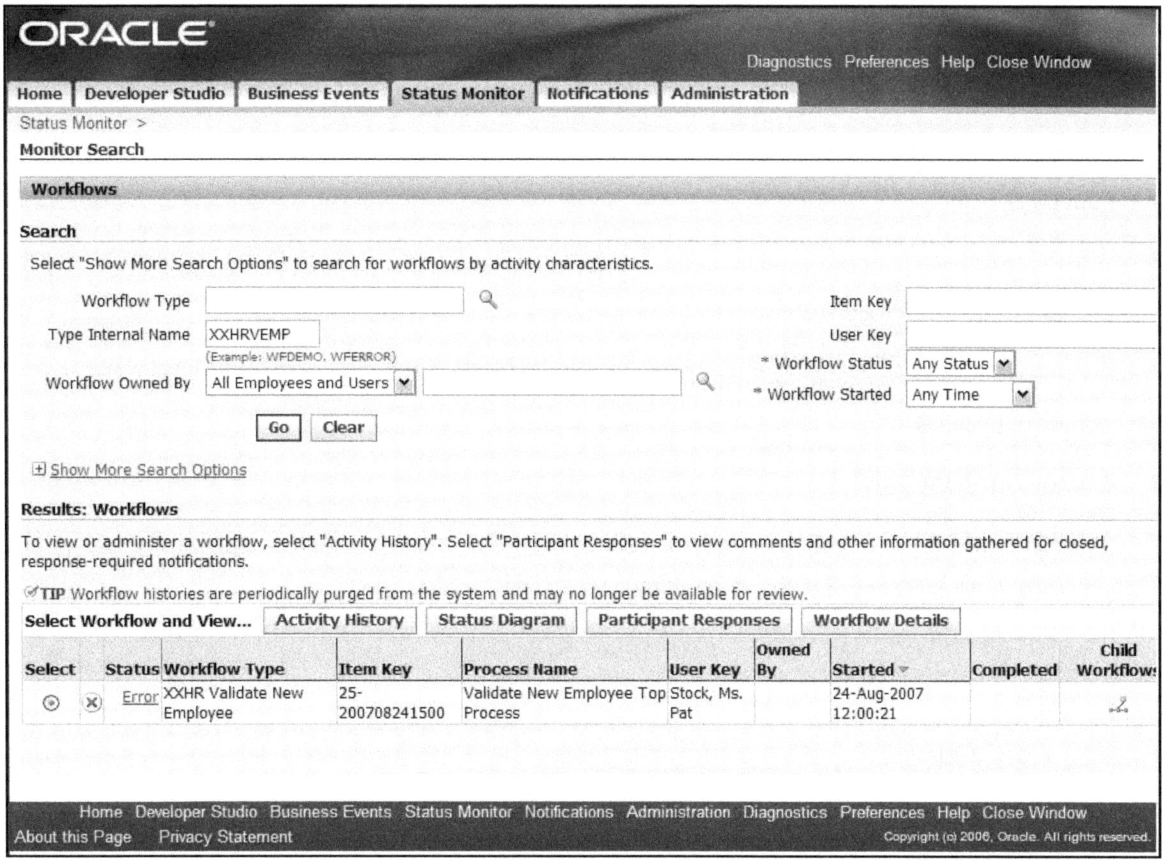

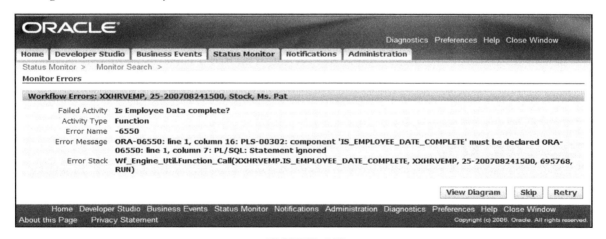

FIGURE 6.16

Clicking on the 'Error' link yields FIGURE 6.17.

FIGURE 6.17

This error was caused by incorrectly coding the name of the Procedure when assigning the Procedure to the Function Activity (the correct name is IS_EMPLOYEE_DATA_COMPLETE). At this point the developer has limited choices. If the name of the Function is corrected in the Workflow and the

Workflow re-saved, the change will cause a new version of that Activity to be created (see *Chapter 3, Builder Basics*, for a discussion of Versioning). Workflows that have already started will not use the new version. Future Workflows will not encounter this error. The following objects are versioned:

- Notifications

- Functions

- Events

- Processes and Sub Processes

- Process activities (i.e., changing anything on the Node, Node Attributes, or Event Details tabs)

- Activity Attributes

- Activity Attribute values

- Activity transitions

Certain objects can be changed without invoking a new version. These are:

- PL/SQL Procedures

- Messages

- Item Type Attributes

- Lookup Types

Therefore, the developer's choices are:

1. Abort this Workflow, correct the name of the Function using the Workflow Builder, re-save the Workflow to the database, and start another test. The same employee can be used; just append the current date and time to the PERSON_ID.

2. Recompile the PL/SQL Package, changing the name of the Procedure to match the Workflow definition, then click the 'Retry' button to have the Workflow Engine re-attempt to execute the Procedure.

Since this is development, choice 1 is the best. If this type of error were to occur with a Workflow provided by Oracle, ask Oracle Support to provide a script to correct all Workflows already started.

"Expected" Error

The code associated with this Workflow (see *Chapter 4, Using PL/SQL in Workflow*) sets ResultOut to ERROR if certain conditions are encountered. Since this is not an error exposed through a RAISE statement, when the 'Error' link is clicked, no 'Error Message' is displayed. The screen looks like FIGURE 6.18. Note, however, the name of the Procedure (shown as the value for 'Failed Activity').

FIGURE 6.18

To see the 'Error Message', return to the 'Monitor Search' screen and either click the icon in the 'Child Workflows' column (to open the associated WFERROR), click the 'Activity History' button, then click the icon in the 'Notification' column, or click the 'Activity History' button, click the 'Expand All' link, click the 'Default Error Process' link, and then click the icon in the 'Notification' column. FIGURE 6.19 will be displayed. Notice the value for 'Result Code'. This is the text assigned to ResultOut after the ':' as in the statement: ResultOut := 'ERROR:Delimiter must be a "-"';. Now look at the Procedure as identified in FIGURE 6.19 and look for a statement setting ResultOut. In this particular case, a previous version of the code had been migrated and that version was searching for the delimiter ':'. Since we had used '-', the code detected an error and deliberately ended in error status. See FIGURE 6.19.

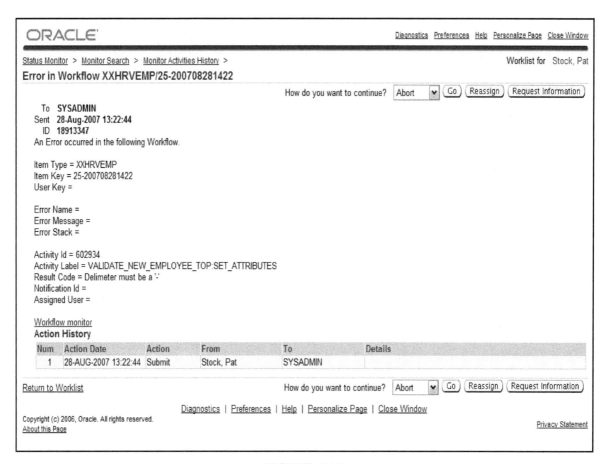

FIGURE 6.19

Since PL/SQL is not versioned, the code can be corrected and re-migrated, and this Notification can be answered Retry. This will execute the new version of the code and the Workflow will proceed.

This error again emphasizes the need to migrate not only the Workflow, but the PL/SQL associated with the Workflow as well as any setups such as responsibilities or Profile Options or any setup that the code is referencing.

Unexpected Error

Despite the best efforts of a developer, code sometimes isn't perfect and subsequently errors. These are the errors caught by 'ON EXCEPTION WHEN OTHERS'. Opening a Workflow that errors unexpectedly looks exactly the same as the previous error (see FIGURE 6.16), i.e., the 'Status' column says Error preceded by a red X. However, clicking on the 'Error' link yields a screen similar to FIGURE 6.20.

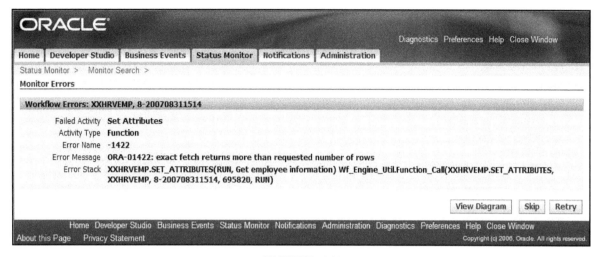

FIGURE 6.20

The Error Message is one all programmers have seen. But how to find which SQL statement caused the offense? *Chapter 4, Using PL/SQL in Workflow*, showed how to use WF_CORE.Context( ) to raise the error. Part of using this API requires periodically setting a variable to indicate the statement to be executed and including this variable as a parameter to this API. The parameters passed to this API were the Package, Procedure, Function Mode, and the Trace Variable. The first part of the Error Stack shows the parameters passed to this API. XXHRVEMP is the name of the Package, SET_ATTRIBUTES is the name of the Procedure, RUN is the Function Mode, and 'Get employee information' is the value of the Trace Variable. If SET_ATTRIBUTES had called a Function or Procedure, the called Function or Procedure would have been listed first in the Error Stack, so the developer may have to look through the Error Stack to find the Procedure actually called by the Workflow.

Now the developer can look at the code to find the phrase 'Get employee information'. The actual statement that errored is between setting the Trace Variable to this phrase and the next occurrence of setting the Trace Variable. Fix and recompile the code, then click the 'Retry' button shown in FIGURE 6.20 to have the Workflow execute the corrected code.

"Existing state of has been invalidated ORA-04601"

This Error Message occasionally occurs when the PL/SQL associated with a Workflow is re-compiled. It happens because the application server caches the version of the PL/SQL when a Workflow is viewed through the 'Status Monitor'. When the PL/SQL is re-compiled on the database, the cache is not always refreshed. Prior to Version 9.2.0.7 of the database, this was an Error Message that required the Applications DBA to bounce the Apache server. Now this error can usually be cleared by pressing the 'Retry' button. FIGURE 6.21 shows a Workflow with this error.

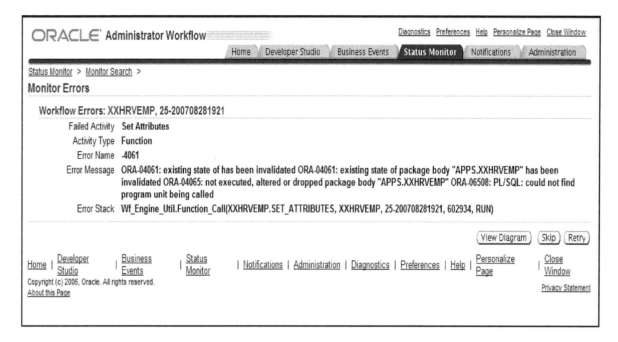

FIGURE 6. 21

If 'Retry' returns the same Error Message, have the Applications DBA bounce the Apache Server, then click 'Retry' again. If this error displays when viewing a Notification, the Notification Mailer must be stopped and restarted.

"Attribute <attribute name> does not exist"

One of the common Error Messages that occurs is "Attribute <attribute name> does not exist". An example of this error is shown in FIGURE 6.22.

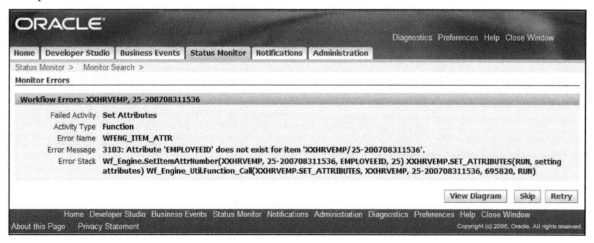

FIGURE 6.22

First check the code to ensure the name of the Attribute is typed correctly. If not, correct the code, recompile it, and click the 'Retry' button. If the code is correct, then the designer neglected to define the Attribute using the Workflow Builder. The Workflow should be corrected using the Workflow Builder and re-saved. At this point, the developer has the choice of aborting the Workflow and re-starting it, or the developer can add the optional Attribute ignore_notfound to the call to WF_ENGINE.GetItemAttr<type>'. This Attribute is BOOLEAN and should be added after the Attribute name. To avoid the error, set the Attribute to TRUE. So the new call would be

```
WF_ENGINE.GetItemAttrNumber (ItemType,ItemKey,'EMPLOYEEID',TRUE);
```

The above statement seems to conflict with an earlier statement that Item Attributes are not versioned. The earlier statement is true. However, when a Workflow is started, a record is inserted in WF_ITEM_ATTRIBUTE_VALUES for each defined Attribute. Re-saving the Workflow with the new Attribute does not create the associated record in this table for each instance of the Workflow that has already started. All the WF_ENGINE.GetItemAttr<type> APIs require not only a record in the WF_ITEM_ATTRIBUTES table, but also the WF_ITEM_ATTRIBUTE_VALUES table. Adding the Attribute ignore_notfound causes these APIs to ignore the NO_DATA_FOUND error and return the default value from the Item Attribute definition.

Another way of dealing with the error is used when a Workflow has been in production and changes introduce a new Attribute. Since PL/SQL is not versioned, all running copies of the Workflow would error trying to access the new Attribute. Oracle has provided an API and error check to catch this error and remediate it without causing the Workflow to end in error. The following example is from AP_WEB_EXPENSES_WF.StartExpenseReportProcess used in the 'Expenses' (APEXP) Workflow.

```
1.▶   BEGIN
          WF_ENGINE.SetItemAttrNumber(l_item_type,
                                      l_item_key,
                                      'ORG_ID',
                                      l_n_Org_ID);
2.▶   EXCEPTION
        WHEN OTHERS
      THEN
3.▶   IF (wf_core.error_name = 'WFENG_ITEM_ATTR') then
 --   item attribute doesn't exist, need to add it
4.▶        WF_ENGINE.AddItemAttr(l_item_type,
                                 l_item_key,
                                 'ORG_ID');
           WF_ENGINE.SetItemAttrNumber(l_item_type,
                                       l_item_key,
                                       'ORG_ID',
                                       l_n_Org_ID);
5.▶   ELSE
        RAISE;
        END IF;

      END;
```

1.▶ Each call to SetItemAttr<type> must be in its own BEGIN/END as the exception clause that adds the Attribute must specify the Attribute name.

2.▶ Standard EXCEPTION WHEN OTHER THEN

3.▶ When the Workflow APIs detect certain errors, WF_CORE.Error_Name is set to the appropriate error value using WF_CORE.Raise ('<error_name>'). WF_CORE.Raise also raises an exception so control is transferred to the EXCEPTION WHEN OTHERS. Now the developer can test WF_CORE.Error_Name. The error code for inability to find an Item Attribute is WFENG_ITEM_ATTR.

4. ▶ AddItemAttr adds the Attribute specified in the third parameter to the specific Workflow. This API actually adds to the table WF_ITEM_ATTRIBUTE_VALUES. Thus, you will not be able to see this Attribute using the 'Status Monitor' since there is still no record in WF_ITEM_ATTRIBUTES. This also means that the next time this Workflow is started, there is still no Attribute ORG_ID. The only way to permanently fix this error is to add the Attribute using the Workflow Builder and re-save the Workflow to the database.

5. ▶ If the SetItemAttrNumber returns any other error code, this is an unexpected error and so the RAISE is issued.

Completes Successfully, but Data is Incomplete

Our first test used an employee with a valid email address and valid assignment fields. So after correcting the errors above, the Workflow completes successfully. FIGURE 6.23 shows that the Workflow correctly determined that the email address exists and that the assignment record has all the desired fields. However, successful completion doesn't prove that all the routines functioned as designed. 'Is Employee Data Complete' and 'Set Attributes' are supposed to set values for the various Item Attributes so that if a Notification is required, the Notification will have the appropriate data. The developer must verify that these Attributes contain the correct values.

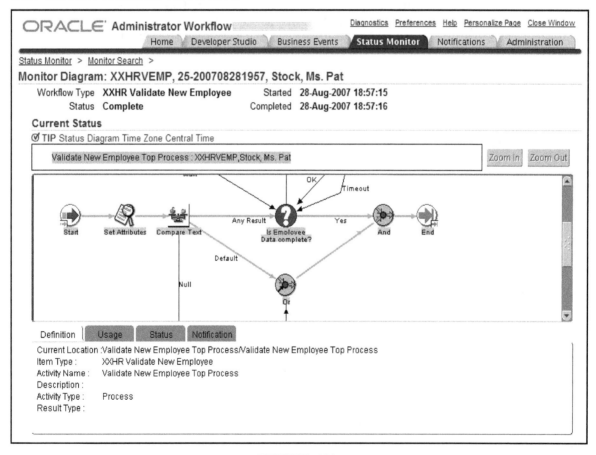

FIGURE 6.23

Return to the 'Monitor Search' page by clicking the 'Monitor Search' link at the top of the page. Click the 'Workflow Details' button to show the Item Attributes and their current value. The result is shown in

FIGURE 6.24. There is no value for the Attributes 'Supervisor', 'Position', or 'Default Accounting'. Additionally, although the Email Administrator is not a user (the List of Values for the Profile Option 'Email Administrator' limits the choices to a user), 'email Admin Error Message' does not indicate that an error occurred when retrieving this Profile Option value. Add the appropriate WF_ENGINE.SetItemAttrText() to the code and retest.

FIGURE 6.24

STARTING WORKFLOWS USING A TRIGGER OR OTHER PROCEDURE

Once the developer is confident that the Workflow and code is working as designed, testing needs to be expanded to include the code that will be used to start the Workflow.

Chapter 4, Using PL/SQL in Workflow, lists two versions of a Trigger used to start this Workflow. One starts the Workflow where the first node is the standard Start Node, and the other where the first node is an Event Node. Obviously after compiling either of these Triggers, the developer will need someone to enter data in the 'Enter Employees' screen to ensure that the Workflow starts and finishes successfully. The code provided in this book only fires when the employee record is first saved.

This final round of testing may surface some additional design errors. For example, you cannot navigate to the assignment screen where the position, supervisor, and default accounting are stored until you save the header record. This save fires the Trigger that starts the Workflow. Since the Workflow Engine will execute the code faster than someone can enter the assignment record, the Workflow as designed will always send an email stating the setup is incomplete. The designer can either modify the Workflow to place a Wait Node immediately after the Start Node so that the Workflow pauses for whatever time is specified as the wait time parameter, or the designer can replace the Trigger with a scheduled program that finds all employees created during a given time frame and starts a Workflow for each new employee. The designer could also use a scheduled program to start the Workflow for all employees or assignments updated during a specified time frame. These variations illustrate how even a simple design can be implemented in multiple ways.

ONCE TESTING IS COMPLETE

Although development environments exist to allow developers to test code and discover errors before a process is moved into productions, once testing is complete, some effort should be made to "clean up your mess". This effort involves ensuring all Workflows are complete, history is removed, and that the design tables are not cluttered with old versions of the Workflow.

Kill the Associated WFERROR

The number one reason Workflows cannot be purged is that they have an associated child Workflow that is still open. When a Workflow errors, it starts the WFERROR Workflow, which notifies SYSADMIN about the error. Most Workflows are remediated without responding to this Notification, which leaves the WFERROR Workflow open and prevents the parent Workflow from purging. So when killing a Workflow in development (or restarting it), ensure the attached WFERROR Workflow is also closed.

All developers should have access to SYSADMIN's Notifications in the development environment. See *Chapter 8, Administration*, for instructions on setting up Worklist access. This Notification can be used to abort or retry the Workflow (skip is only allowed when the error happens at a Notification or compare Activity). Answering the Notification Abort will abort the errored Workflow and end the associated WFERROR.

The other method of killing both Workflows is through the 'Activity History' button. When this button is first clicked, FIGURE 6.25 appears. This shows the Activity for the Workflow based on the Search filter criteria (Activity Type and Activity Status). To abort this Workflow, click the 'Cancel Workflow' button at the bottom.

FIGURE 6.25

Before canceling this Workflow, the developer can drill down to any children Workflows. Click either the 'Expand All' link at the top, or click on the + next to the 'Process Name'. This causes the top of the screen to look like FIGURE 6.26.

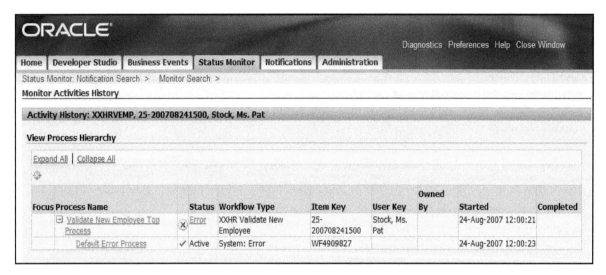

FIGURE 6.26

Clicking on 'Default Error Process' will cause the screen to display the Activity for WFERROR. Now when the 'Cancel Workflow' button is clicked, it cancels the WFERROR Workflow. Unfortunately, this Action returns the screen to a blank 'Monitor Search' screen, instead of to the 'Monitor Activities History' screen above, so the Workflow will have to be re-queried to cancel the main Workflow.

The Release 11.5.10 (with ATG_PF.H Rollup 5) version of 'Monitor Activities History' has one extra column in the 'Result:Activities' zone that is very useful for deleting the associated WFERROR – Notification (see FIGURE 6.27).

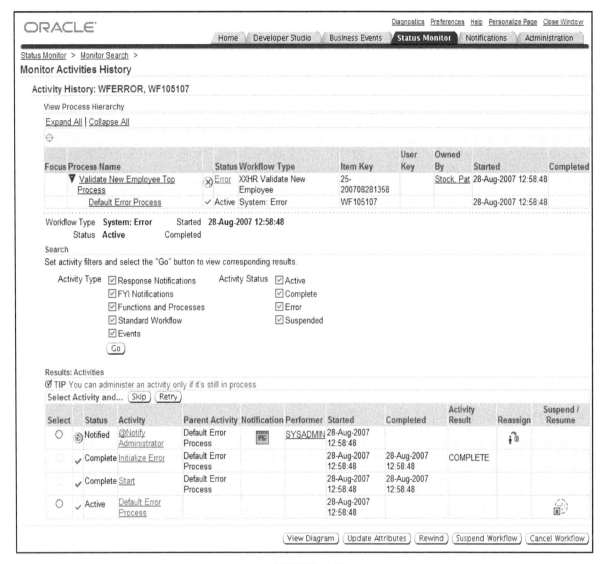

FIGURE 6.27

Clicking this icon opens the Notification sent to SYSADMIN. From this Notification the developer can answer Abort to both kill the XXHRVEMP Workflow and close the WFERROR Workflow. The best part is that after the Notification is answered, control is transferred back to the 'Monitor Activities History' form with the data still displayed. You don't have to re-query anything like you have to do when you click 'Cancel Workflow'.

Remove Runtime Data and Old Designs

Testing a new Workflow usually requires several attempts. Workflows that don't work may be abandoned. The Workflow definition may have been saved several times. At some point the developer may even wish to remove both the runtime history and the Workflow definition and just start over.

The standard 'Purge Obsolete Workflow Runtime Data' Concurrent Program will purge Workflow history as long as the Workflow is complete. This program will also remove all versions of the design data that are no longer current and not currently in use. To have the purge program delete the obsolete design data, set the parameter 'Core Workflow Only' to N.

If running the purge program does not sufficiently clean up this Item Type, or the developer wants to wipe the slate clean and start over using the Workflow Builder or WFLOAD to create a clean copy of the Workflow, the developer can choose to run one of the following Oracle-provided scripts. These scripts can be found in the $FND_TOP/sql directory.

- **WFRMTYPE.SQL** – this script removes runtime data. First, it lists all Workflows in the runtime tables and asks you to enter either an ITEM_TYPE or % for all. Then, the script asks if you want to remove all runtime data (enter ALL) or just remove the run time data for completed Workflows. (leave the parameter blank). If you answer 'ALL', even Workflows that are still open are removed.

- **WFRMITT.SQL** – this script removes all design and runtime data as well as any Vacation Rules. The script asks for the Internal Name of an Item Type as a parameter. This script removes runtime data regardless of the status and removes all the design data, even the current copy. Do no run this script unless you have first saved your Workflow as a .wft file.

Migration

Migrating Workflows requires moving the Workflow, all associated code, and all associated setups. The developer should provide a document detailing the Workflow, all required setups, and the steps necessary to perform the migration. See Appendix A for a document using a modified AIM format that documents the design, the auxiliary setups, and how to create the Workflow from the beginning (the cover page, document control, and table of contents are omitted). The order of creating the Workflow in this document is different than that described in *Chapter 3, Builder Basics*. This order assumes you've lost the Workflow and need to quickly re-create it.

All Workflows should be saved to a .wft file and stored on the Unix system. If you have created a $CUSTOM_TOP, the .wft file can be stored in the patch directory (Oracle Workflows are stored in $<product>_TOP/patch), or create a Workflow directory. Do not depend on the database as the sole source for the Workflow.

The Workflow can be moved from instance to instance either by using the Builder to save the Workflow in another instance or by using WFLOAD. Using the Builder to save the Workflow has already been discussed. WFLOAD can be run using the Concurrent Manager or from the UNIX command prompt.

The Concurrent Program 'Workflow Definitions Loader' may have to be added to the responsibility's Report Group. The program has the following parameters:

- **Mode** – specify 'Download' to move the Workflow from the database to a .wft file, 'Upload' to load a .wft file to the database, 'Upgrade' to apply changes from a .wft file to the Workflow already in the database (as long as the 'Access Level' and protection flags allow an overwrite), and 'Force' to apply changes from a .wft file to the Workflow already in the database regardless of the object's protection level

- **File** – specify the full path and name of the .wft file, whether you are uploading or downloading

- **Item Type** – if selecting 'Download' as the Mode, the name of the Workflow to download

The program can only process one Workflow per iteration of the program.

The Workflow definitions loader can also be run from the UNIX command prompt. To move a .wft file to the database use the syntax:

```
WFLOAD apps/<pwd> 0 Y <mode> <file.wft>
```

'<mode>' is either 'UPGRADE', 'UPLOAD' or 'FORCE'. See 'Mode' above for the guidelines on which mode to use.

To download a Workflow, use the syntax:

```
WFLOAD apps/<pwd> 0 Y DOWNLOAD <file.wft>ItemType1 [ItemType2….ItemTypen]
```

<file.wft> must be in the format:

```
@<application_short_name>:[<dir>/<file>.wft
```

You can download all the Item Types from the database by replacing ItemType1 with '*' (the single quotes are part of the required syntax).

WHAT'S NEXT

The past four chapters have all been about a Workflow that progressed a Business Process through a combination of Functions, Events, and Notifications. The E-Business Suite also uses Workflow to define the Account Combinations. These Workflows are known as Account Generators. The next chapter will discuss these special Workflows.

Account Generators

Account Generators are Workflows that provide the E-Business Suite modules the ability to automatically construct Accounting Flexfield combinations using Oracle-defined or your own business rules. Although automatic construction of Account Combinations improves the accuracy and ease of data entry, when new business situations arise that are not modeled by the Oracle seeded Account Generators companies will need to modify these Workflows.

This chapter will explain the Procedures that Oracle provides to build Account Generators, how Oracle initiates the seeded Account Generators, and the rules that companies must follow to customize the Account Generators. As part of this explanation, this chapter will discuss the Attributes that are present for all Account Generators, even though you will never see these Attributes in the Workflow Builder, and how to use these Attributes to send a Notification when the Account Generator fails. This chapter presupposes that the reader is familiar with Workflow terminology and how to use the Builder tool.

SEEDED ACCOUNT GENERATORS

Both Release 11.5.10 and Release 12 provide the ability to register custom Processes for the following Account Generators:

- **OM: Generate Cost of Goods Sold Account (OECOGS)** – generates the cost of goods sold account for each inventory transaction line when invoices are imported into AR. These lines are inserted into Oracle Inventory via the Inventory Interface Program

- **PSB Account Generator for OLD Integration (PSBLDMAG)** – used in Public Sector Budgeting to derive accounts for positions with POETA charging instructions that are then used to import salary distribution information from LD

- **ITR Account Generator (ITRWKFAG)** – Account Generator for self-service ITR. This Workflow will build creation and receiving accounts for ITR service lines

- **IAC Account Generator (IGIIACWF)** – used in Public Sector Assets for Inflation Accounting

- **MHCA Account Generator (IGIAMAWF)** – used in Public Sector Assets

- **IGC Charge Account Generator (IGCACGNC)** – used to generate a charge account for contract commitment for Public Sector Contracts

- **IGC Budget Account Generator (IGCACGNB)** – used in Public Sector Contracts, this Workflow is used to generate a budget account for contract commitment

- **Project Budget Account Generation (PABDACWF)** – used by Projects to generate Accounting Combinations for all budget items in an integrated project budget

- **AR: Substitute Balancing Segment (ARSBALSG)** – updates the balancing segment during various accounting activities against transactions and receipts

- **FA Account Generator (FAFLEXWF)** – used by Assets to generate the Accounting Combinations for each Asset Transaction

- **Project Supplier Invoice Account Generation (PAAPINVW)** – used by Payables to derive the Invoice Distribution Accounting Combination if the distribution is Project related. This Account Generator MUST be customized if using Projects. If not using Projects this Account Generator is not invoked

- **Generate Cost of Goods Sold Account (SHPFLXWF)** – Pre-Release 11*i* Cost of Goods Sold Account Generator – see MetaLink Doc. ID: 260697.1, *Account Generator Processes-Difference Between Generate Cogs and Om Generate Cogs*

- **Project Web Employees Account Generator (PAAPWEBX)** – used by *i*Expense to derive Accounting Combinations for expense report lines that reference a project. This Account Generator MUST be customized if using Projects. If not using Projects this Account Generator is not invoked

- **PO Account Generator (POWFPOAG)** – used by Purchasing to derive the charge, budget, variance, and accrual accounting distributions for each PO line. This Account Generator MUST be customized if using Oracle Projects. If not using Projects this Account Generator is still invoked but customization is not mandatory

- **PO Requisition Account Generator (POWFRQAG)** – used by Purchasing to derive the charge, budget, variance, and accrual accounting distributions for each requisition line. This Account Generator MUST be customized if using Oracle Projects. If not using Projects this Account Generator is still invoked but customization is not mandatory

- **Inventory Cost of Goods Sold Account (INVFLXWF)** – called while processing Intercompany Transactions

There are additional Account Generators that are not registered in this form. For unregistered Account Generators, the designer must ensure any changes are called by the default top Process.

- **OZF: Account Generator (OZFACCTG)** – this Account Generator replaced the AMS: Account Generator (AMSACCTG) used in Release 11.5.9. This Workflow is called from the 'Offer Approval' Workflow used in Trade Management for Public Sector to generate the funds budget account

- **FTE: Generate Distribution Account (FTEDIST)** – generates a distribution Accounting Flexfield for each Freight Payment Line interfaced to receivables from Transportation Execution

- **OKL Account Generator (OKLFLXWF)** – can be used in Lease Management to generate accounting instead of using the seeded sources

CUSTOMIZATION RULES

To customize an Account Generator, you must have the Workflow Builder on your desktop. *Chapter 2, Setup*, describes Workflow setup and provides instructions on downloading and installing Workflow Builder. You may also need a PL/SQL developer tool. You will either need the APPS user password, or your Applications DBA can extract the .wft file that contains the Item Type(s) that you wish to customize. If someone is creating the .wft file for you, make sure it contains the Account Generator(s) requested, the 'Standard' Item Type, and the 'Standard Flexfield' Workflow Item Type. The 'Standard' and 'Standard Flexfield' Workflow should load automatically when loading any Account Generator into the Builder.

The following is the seeded 'Generate Default Account' Process for 'Project Supplier Invoice Account Generation'. It contains the minimum required nodes for any Account Generator, plus the node 'Dummy default account generator', which must be replaced by your company's custom Procedure(s).

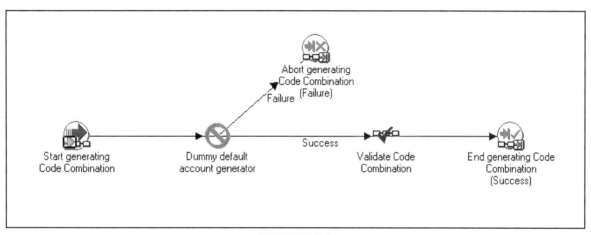

FIGURE 7.1

Notice that instead of the standard Start or Receive Event Activity, Account Generators begin with the node 'Start generating Code Combination'. This is required. Additionally, instead of End Nodes with result types, Account Generators must contain at least one 'Abort generating Code Combination' marked as an End Node on the Node tab with a result of Failure. Account Generators must also include at least one 'End generating Code Combination' marked as an End Node on the Node tab with a result of 'Success'. Processes that will be the top Process must specify a RESULT_TYPE of 'Flexfield Result'.

Prior to navigating to 'End generating Code Combination', you must include the node 'Validate Code Combination'. Note that this node does not have an associated RESULT_TYPE, so you cannot branch from this node to different nodes based on whether or not the code combination is valid. What this node does and how to get around the inability to branch will be explained later.

Since Account Generators are designed to be called from a form or batch process (hereafter referred to as 'the calling process') and return the combination to be used in the form or batch process, there are restrictions on the type of activities that can be included in the Account Generator:

- No Notifications

- No deferring activities to the Background Engine (see comment on cost later)

- No Parallel flows

- No Any transition

- No Master/Detail

- On Revisit behaves as if set to Loop

In addition, the following standard activities are not allowed (because they defer processing):

- And

- Block (unless the release of the block can be done from the calling program in the same thread, i.e., the block returns control to the calling program, the calling program must not issue any commits before issuing the command to release the block and continue the Workflow)

- Defer Thread

- Wait

- Continue Flow / Wait for Flow

- Role Resolution

- Voting

- Compare Execution Time

- Notify

The use of WF_ENGINE APIs is restricted to:

- CreateProcess

- StartProcess

- SetItemAttribute

- GetItemAttribute

- GetActivityAttribute

- CompleteActivity

- AddItemAttribute

- LaunchProcess

HOW ACCOUNT GENERATORS WORK

The calling process initiates the Account Generator by first calling the Function FND_FLEX_WORKFLOW.INITIALIZE. The parameters passed to this routine are:

- **Application Short Name** – for the Accounting Flexfield, this will be SQLGL. This value is used to find APPLICATION_ID from FND_APPLICATION (= 101)

- **Code** – use GL# for the Accounting Flexfield and GLAT for the Reporting Attributes Accounting Flexfield

- **Num** – ID_FLEX_NUM – along with the APPLICATION_ID and ID_FLEX_CODE, these fields form the primary key to FND_ID_FLEX_STRUCTURES, which stores the definitions of your Accounting Flexfield

- **ItemType** – the name of the Workflow that is your Account Generator

The Function returns a VARCHAR variable, which is the ItemKey. This Function performs the following tasks:

- Fetches the number of segments in your chart of accounts

- Determines, based on the Profile Option 'Account Generator:Run in Debug Mode', whether to set the Item Key to #SYNC or to FND_FLEX_WORKFLOW_ITEMKEY_S.nextval.

- Calls the API WF_ENGINE.CreateProcess

- Creates the following Attributes

    - **FND_FLEX_APPSNAME** – Flexfield Application Short Name (i.e., SQLGL)

    - **FND_FLEX_CODE** – GL# or GLAT

    - **FND_FLEX_NUM** – ID_FLEX_NUM

    - **FND_FLEX_APPLID** – 101

    - **FND_FLEX_NSEGMENTS** – the number of enabled segments in your Flexfield

    - **FND_FLEX_CCID** – the 'Code Combination ID' built by the Account Generator

    - **FND_FLEX_SEGMENTS** – the concatenated segments

    - **FND_FLEX_DATA** – the concatenated IDs

    - **FND_FLEX_DESCRIPTIONS** – the concatenated descriptions of each segment

    - **FND_FLEX_MESSAGE** – the Error Message if the generator fails

    - **FND_FLEX_STATUS** – the validation status

    - **FND_FLEX_INSERT** – denotes whether new combinations can be inserted

    - **FND_FLEX_NEW** – indicates whether the resulting combination is new or existing. This Attribute is initially set to <NULL> and set to 'Y' or 'N' by the Procedure called from the required Activity 'Validate Code Combination'

♦ **FND_FLEX_SEGMENTn** – there will be one Attribute for each segment of the Accounting Combination – this field will store the value of each segment

- Sets the values for FND_FLEX_APPSNAME, FND_FLEX_CODE, FND_FLEX_NUM, FND_FLEX_APPLID, and FND_FLEX_NSEGMENTS.

The Attributes created are added to the table WF_ITEM_ATTRIBUTE_VALUES, but not WF_ITEM_ATTRIBUTES. This is why even when the Profile Option 'Account Generator: Run in Debug' is set to Yes, these Attributes cannot be viewed in the Workflow Monitor.

The calling program then calls one of two versions of FND_FLEX_WORKFLOW.GENERATE. The first version is used when the Account Generator Workflow is to be started from a form. This Procedure calls the second FND_FLEX_WORKFLOW.GENERATE (yes, there are two Procedures with the same name, they have different parameters) and passes back to the form (via IN OUT variables) the code_combination_id, the concatenated segments, the concatenated descriptions, concatenated ids, an Error Message and (via a RETURN BOOLEAN) True/False as to the success of the generation. It is the responsibility of the form to check the Boolean variable to validate whether the generation was successful. The form is also responsible for calling the appropriate routines to validate whether the combination exists, whether a new combination can be added and whether the combination violates any security or cross–validation rules. The form is responsible for displaying any Error Messages and displaying the resulting Accounting Flexfield in the appropriate fields in the form.

The second version of FND_FLEX_WORKFLOW.GENERATE can be called directly from batch programs. The batch program passes to FND_FLEX_WORKFLOW.GENERATE whether insertion of new accounts is allowed. FND_FLEX_WORKFLOW.GENERATE returns (via IN OUT variables) the code_combination_id, the concatenated segments, the concatenated descriptions, and concatenated ids, an Error Message, whether the returned combination is a new combination (Boolean variable) and (via a RETURN BOOLEAN) True/False as to the success of the generation. If the batch program executes FND_FLEX_WORKFLOW.GENERATE with 'new combination allowed=TRUE', and this Function passes back 'new combination generated = TRUE', then the batch program must handle the insertion of the new combination and issue a commit. Failure to issue the commit places a lock on the Code Combination table.

FND_FLEX_WORKFLOW.GENERATE sets the Engine Threshold to 999999 so that none of the Functions will ever be run in the background, then issues a call to WF_ENGINE.StartProcess. Due to the value of the threshold, the Generate Function will not continue until the Account Generator finishes. If the generation is successful, the Generate Function returns TRUE as the result, and, via IN OUT variables, the ccid, the concatenated segments, concatenated ids, concatenated descriptions, Error Message and whether or not the code combination is new.

If the generation is not successful, the Procedure returns as much information as can be generated along with the Error Message.

STANDARD FLEXFIELD ACTIVITIES

When customizing an Account Generator, the developer can use any of the Functions contained in 'Standard Flexfield' Workflow, any of the Functions contained in the 'Standard' Workflow except those in the prohibited list, and/or develop custom Functions (as long as the custom Function obeys the rules already described). Any Function in the 'Standard Flexfield' Workflow ItemType that is copied into the Process diagram must have values set for its Activity Attributes. This is done by double-clicking the node in the Diagrammer window (which opens the 'Properties' page) and then setting the values in the 'Node Attributes' tab. See FIGURE 7.2.

There are several Activity Attributes that are common to many of the Functions including:

- **Segment Identifier** – from the List of Values, select 'Qualifier' if you can identify the Chart of Accounts segment by type (Balancing Segment, Cost Center, Natural Account, Intercompany, Secondary Tracking); otherwise select 'Name'

- **Segment** – enter the Qualifier or the name of the Chart of Accounts segment (there is no List of Values). If you specified name, and select the type 'Constant', you must match exactly the value in the 'Name' field of the 'Key Flexfield Segments' form. If you select the type 'Item Attribute', choose the Item Attribute that holds the name of the Chart of Accounts segment.

- **Value** – the value to be assigned to the segment

- **Structure Number** – the Accounting Flexfield structure number, if you are building a combination for a different set-of-books (Ledger in Release 12)

- **Replace existing value** – from the List of Values, select 'True' to override and replace any value that already is assigned to the segment; select 'False' to copy a value into a segment only if that segment is null

FIGURE 7.2 shows the 'Node Attributes' page for 'Assign Value to Segment'. It uses four of the five Attributes above. While you can choose to assign a constant value or an Item Attribute for each Attribute, the use of Item Attribute is rarely used for any of the above Attributes except 'Value' (and maybe 'Structure Number').

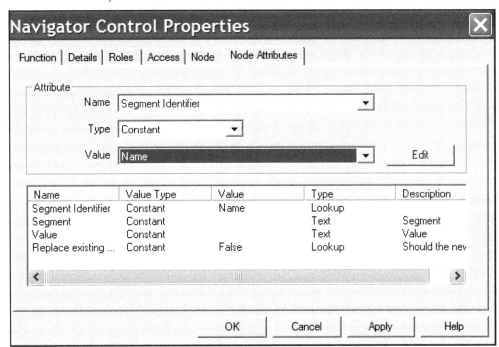

FIGURE 7.2

The activities contained in the 'Standard Flexfield' Workflow are:

- **Assign Value to Segment** – assigns a value to a specific segment. It uses the Activity Attributes 'Segment Identifier', 'Segment', 'Value', and 'Replace existing value'. The value contained in the Attribute Value is stored in the Item Attribute FND_FLEX_SEGMENTn (if 'Replace existing value' is TRUE or 'Replace existing value' is FALSE and FND_FLEX_SEGMENTn is null)

- **Copy Segment Value from Code Combination** – copies a specified segment value from one combination into the combination being built, using the Activity Attributes 'Code Combination ID', 'Segment Qualifier', 'Segment', and 'Replace existing value'. 'Code Combination ID' is usually set to an Item Attribute, which then must be populated prior to executing this Function Activity. The Function finds the 'Code Combination ID', extracts the segment specified and stores the result in the Item Attribute FND_FLEX_SEGMENTn provided that 'Replace existing value' is TRUE or 'Replace existing value' is FALSE and FND_FLEX_SEGMENTn is null

- **Copy Segment Value from Other Structure Code Combination** – copies a specified segment value from a combination in an Accounting Flexfield other than the set-of-books Accounting Flexfield into the combination being built. It uses the Activity Attributes 'Structure Number', 'Code Combination ID', 'Segment Identifier', 'Segment', and 'Replace existing value'. 'Code Combination ID' is usually set to an Item Attribute, which must be populated prior to executing this Function Activity. The PL/SQL Procedure assigned to this Activity uses the specified 'Code Combination ID' and 'Structure Number' (as the keys CODE_COMBINATION_ID and CHART_OF_ACCOUNTS_ID to GL_CODE_COMBINATIONS) to extract the value for the segment specified, and stores the result in the Item Attribute FND_FLEX_SEGMENTn (if 'Replace existing value' is TRUE or 'Replace existing value' is FALSE and FND_FLEX_SEGMENTn is null)

  Because the above routine is working with two different Accounting Flexfields, some additional rules must be followed. If 'Segment Identifier' is set to Name, both Flexfields must contain a segment with the name specified in Segment. If 'Segment Identifier' is set to Qualifier, both Flexfields must contain a segment assigned to that Qualifier. The rules for the specified segment must be the same (length of field, numeric allowed, etc.).

- **Copy Values from Code Combination** copies all values from a specified 'Code Combination ID' into the combination being built. It uses the Activity Attributes 'Code Combination ID' and 'Replace existing value'. 'Code Combination ID' is usually set to an Item Attribute, which must be populated prior to executing this Function Activity. The Function finds the 'Code Combination ID', extracts all the segments and stores each segment in the Item Attributes FND_FLEX_SEGMENTn (if 'Replace existing value' is TRUE or 'Replace existing value' is FALSE and FND_FLEX_SEGMENTn is null). 'Replace existing value' is evaluated for each segment

- **Get Value from Code Combination** – retrieves a value from a specific segment and stores the result in an Item Attribute. It uses the Activity Attributes 'Code Combination ID', 'Segment Identifier', 'Segment', and 'Attribute to assign value'. 'Code Combination ID' is usually set to an Item Attribute, which must be populated prior to executing this Function Activity. 'Attribute to assign value' must be set to an Item Attribute. The Function finds the specified segment in the specified code combination and copies the value to the specified Item Attribute

- **Copy Value from Other Structure Code Combination** – retrieves a value from a specific segment in a combination in another Accounting Flexfield and stores the result in an Item Attribute. It uses the Activity Attributes 'Structure Number', 'Code Combination ID', 'Segment Identifier', 'Segment', and 'Attribute' to assign a value. 'Code Combination ID' is usually set to an Item Attribute, which must be populated in a Function Activity prior to executing this Function Activity. The Function finds the 'Code Combination ID', extracts the segment specified and stores the result in the Item Attribute specified in 'Attribute to assign value'

The routine stores the retrieved value in an Item Attribute. The additional Rules detailed for 'Copy Segment Value from Other Structure Code Combination' do not apply.

- **Is Code Combination Complete** – checks to see if the combination being built has values in each segment. It uses the Activity Attribute 'Check only for required segments'. If the Attribute is set to False all segments are checked. If the Attribute is set to True only the required segments are checked. Note that the Reporting Attributes Flexfield does not have to have values in every segment

- **Validate Code Combination** – validates the generated code combination according to the values assigned to the Activity Attributes 'New code combinations are allowed' and 'Validation Type'. If 'New code combinations are allowed' is set to True and the Accounting Flexfield has Dynamic Insertion turned on, the fact that the generated combination does not already exist does not constitute an error. Conversely, if 'New code combinations are allowed' is set to False and/or the Accounting Flexfield has Dynamic Insertion turned off, the fact that the generated combination does not already exist is logged as an error

If Validation Type is set to 'Generate Code Combination ID', all segments must have a valid value and the resulting combination must be valid, subject to the checking dictated by 'New code combinations are allowed'. If Validation Type is set to 'Validate Segments with Values only', the only check done is whether the value assigned to each segment is enabled for that segment.

If the combination is new and allowed, this Procedure does not perform the insert nor does it generate a CCID. It merely sets the CCID to –1. It is up to the calling process to insert the combination and generate the CCID.

This routine becomes a Pivot Point in the Account Generator as it sets many of the added Item Attributes. Each value of the FND_FLEX_SEGMENTn is retrieved and the values are concatenated together and stored in FND_FLEX_SEGMENTS. If the validation fails, FND_FLEX_STATUS is set to INVALID, the reason is stored in FND_FLEX_MESSAGE, FND_FLEX_CCID is set to 0, FND_FLEX_DATA and FND_FLEX_DESCRIPTIONS are set to NULL, and FND_FLEX_NEW is set to N. If the validation is successful, FND_FLEX_STATUS is set to VALID, FND_FLEX_CCID contains either –1 (new combination) or the found combination_id, FND_FLEX_DATA contains the concatenated id of each segment, and FND_FLEX_DESCRIPTIONS contains the concatenated description of each segment. If the combination is a new one, then FND_FLEX_NEW = Y, otherwise it is set to N.

As stated earlier, 'Validate Code Combination' does not return a result code, so you cannot branch based on whether FND_FLEX_STATUS is VALID or INVALID. But as FIGURE 7.3 shows, you can insert a custom node and do your own checking.

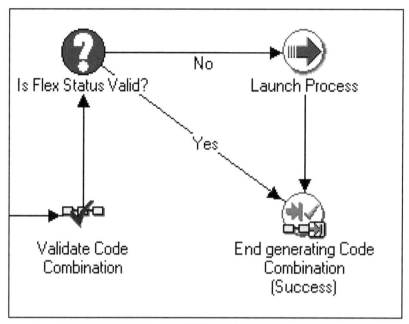

FIGURE 7.3

Most forms and programs that call Account Generators display the Error Message and other pertinent information returned from the Account Generator if the generation fails. However, the 'AR Invoice Interface' Concurrent Program, which calls the OECOGS Generator, does not. The 'AR Invoice Interface' Concurrent Program merely records in the log file that the OECOGS Generator failed. This program does not even identify the order or line that failed, making it very difficult to debug. Modifying the 'AR Invoice Import' Concurrent Program has all the problems of modifying any Oracle program: patches, maintenance, etc. Account Generators can be modified, but not to include Notifications. The solution to this dilemma is explained in the section "How to Send a Notification When Notifications are Prohibited".

REGISTER YOUR CUSTOMIZATION

To customize the Account Generator, open the ItemType seeded by Oracle. Note that the 'Standard' and 'Standard Flexfield Workflow' ItemTypes are copied in as well. Ensure your customization level is set to 100 or higher. Copy the default Process and rename it to your custom name by right-clicking the default Process and selecting 'Copy'. Then right-click 'Processes' and select 'Paste'. The 'Properties' page will open. Type in the new Internal Name, Display Name and (optionally) 'Description'. Now you can add any customization you choose, as long as you follow the rules described earlier. Once the customization is finished, save the Workflow back to the database, sign into the applications, and select a responsibility that has the Setup → Flexfields → Key menu. Select 'Accounts'. Query the records for the Accounting Flexfield and arrow down until the Key Flexfield for your set-of-books is displayed. Select the appropriate 'Account Generator' and change the default Process to your custom Process. See FIGURE 7.4.

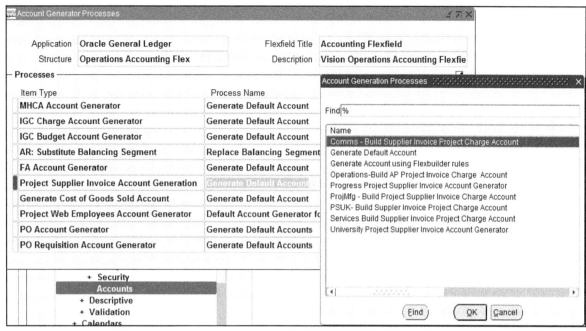

FIGURE 7.4

HOW TO SEND A NOTIFICATION WHEN NOTIFICATIONS ARE PROHIBITED?

Referring back to the customization shown in FIGURE 7.3 (Function Activity 'Is Flex Status Valid'), if FND_FLEX_STATUS is 'VALID', then the routine returns 'Y' and the Account Generator branches to the end. If FND_FLEX_STATUS is 'INVALID', the routine retrieves the HEADER_ID, LINE_ID, ORG_ID, and INVENTORY_ITEM_ID of the order (Item Attributes for the Workflow), and FND_FLEX_SEGMENTS (the concatenated segments). Then an Attribute is set to hold the Role of the person who will be responsible for clearing any Flexfield errors. Another Attribute is set to the concatenated segments and a third Attribute is set to the concatenation of the LINE_ID, HEADER_ID, INVENTORY_ITEM_ID, ORG_ID and SYSDATE. Each field is separated by a colon. SYSDATE is used to provide uniqueness. The result is set to 'N'. The next node launches a custom Workflow. The Item Key is the concatenated field formed by the LINE_ID, HEADER_ID, INVENTORY_ITEM_ID, ORG_ID and SYSDATE. The User Key is the concatenated segments. The Owner is the Role that will resolve the error.

The custom Workflow shown in FIGURE 7.5 calls a PL/SQL routine to break out the ItemKey, userkey and owner to Item Attributes. The owner becomes the Performer. Then a Notification is sent that includes the information extracted from the Account Generator. The fields 'Item Key' and 'User Key' are limited to 240 characters, so you can even modify 'Is Flex Status Valid' to pass part or all of FND_FLEX_MESSAGE.

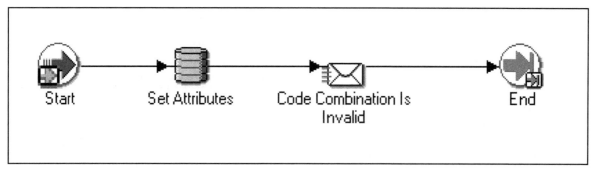

FIGURE 7. 5

The same logic could be used to launch the same custom Workflow before traversing to the 'Abort Generating Code Combination' node. However, many of the hidden Attributes are not set at this point (except for FND_SEGMENTn), so the logic to build the ItemKey and UserKey may be a bit more complex.

PROJECTS ACCOUNT GENERATORS

The picture shown at the beginning of this chapter (see FIGURE 7.1) shows the Account Generator used by AP invoices that reference projects. FIGURE 7.6 is the 'Build Expense Charge Account' from POWFPOAG, the PO Account Generator. Note that if the PO references a project, it branches to the 'Build Expense Project Charge Account' Process, which is shown below the 'Build Expense Charge Account' Process. This Process only has a Start and End Node. Thus, if you are using Projects, every Account Generator must be customized.

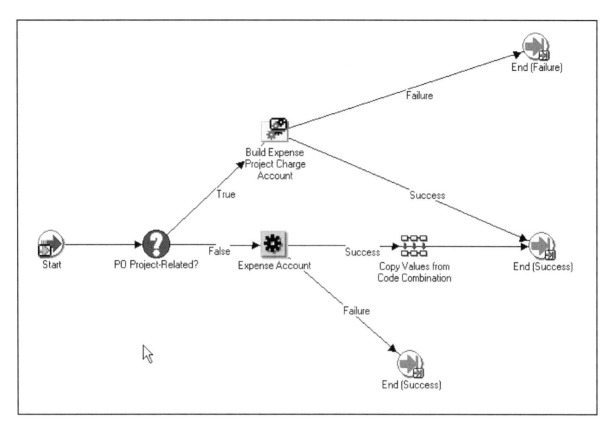

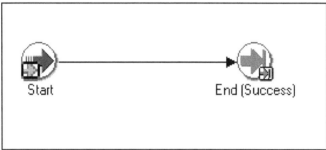

FIGURE 7.6

PA Account Generators do provide one more standard Function that can be used: 'Segment Lookup Set value'. If this Function is not already seeded in the Account Generator you start with, open PAAPINVW, Project Supplier Invoice Account Generator, and copy it from there. 'Segment Lookup Set value' has two Activity Attributes, 'Lookup Set Name', and 'Intermediate Value'. To use this Function, you must also define an Item Attribute with the Internal Name LOOKUP_SET_VALUE. After dragging this Function into a diagram, open the 'Properties' page and click the 'Node Attributes' tab. See FIGURE 7.7.

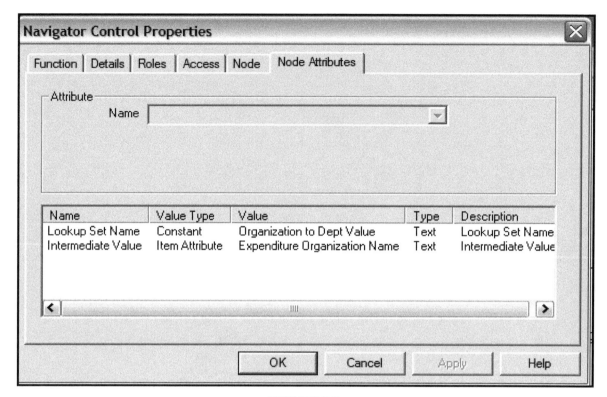

FIGURE 7.7

Set the Activity Attribute 'Lookup Set Name' to the name of a Projects Lookup Set and set 'Intermediate Value' to either an Item Attribute or a constant containing the value to transform. The Procedure called by this node will set the Item Attribute LOOKUP_SET_VALUE with the value from the Lookup Set. The Account Generator can then use this Item Attribute as a parameter to any of the standard Functions such as 'Assign Value to Segment' and thus be used to build the Account Combination.

DEBUGGING

Account Generators do not log records in the Workflow runtime tables, so you cannot view the results through the monitor. However, if you set the value for the Profile Option 'Account Generator:Run in Debug Mode' to Yes, a history will be generated and monitored. This is the best way to debug Account Generators that consist only of the standard Flexfield activities. Even with the Profile Option set to Yes, you will not see the hidden Attributes.

For some Workflows, Oracle provides scripts to help you with the debug Process. For example, MetaLink Doc. ID: 159998.1, *Debugging Cost of Goods Sold Account (cogs_11i.sql)*, has a script to help with debugging OECOGS. This script is also available in Oracle Diagnostics. Refer to *Chapter 9, Diagnostics*, for more information. The best place to look for these scripts is Top Tech Docs. Find your product and search for Account Generator.

Others, like 'SHPFLXWF Generate Cost of Goods Sold Account', have the ability to log "breadcrumbs" about every step that is taken. Generally, you'll have to recompile the Package used to set a global variable to True and you'll have to have UNIX access to see the DBMS_OUTPUT that the Package generates.

Information on the OKL Account Generator (OKLFLXWF) can be found in MetaLink Doc. ID:286675.1, *OKL Seeded Workflow Documents*.

RELEASE 12 CHANGES

With the introduction of Subledger Accounting (SLA), several applications have provided Profile Options that govern whether Account Generators or SLA will be utilized. The applications and the Profile Options include:

- Fixed Assets, 'FA: Use Workflow Account Generator' – upgrades set the value of this Profile Option to Yes, indicating to continue to use the Account Generator. Fresh installs set the value to No, indicating to use SLA. Upgrade customers can change the value of this option and configure SLA

- Public Sector Budgeting, 'PSB:Use Account Generator for Data Extract'

- Lease Management, 'OKL: Use Account Generator Workflow'

CONCLUSION

For certain E–Business Suite applications, Account Generators are required Workflows. However, you are allowed to modify Account Generators. Customizing these Workflows allows you to design Rules that fit your company's unique requirements. Additionally, you now know how to notify someone when errors occur in an Account Generator and the program that calls the Account Generator fails to display the Error Message. Remember, Project-related generators MUST be customized. Start by making simple customizations or using just the standard activities. Once you see expected results, then you can add to your Workflow until the accounting generated is exactly what is required.

WHAT'S NEXT

This chapter concludes a five chapter section on designing, developing and testing Workflows. *Chapter 11, Advanced Builder and PL/SQL*, includes some advanced topics, although there are additional APIs and uses of Workflow that could not be covered in one book. Be encouraged to experiment with your own designs.

These five chapters should familiarize the reader enough with the technology that they can also use the administration screens to ensure that both the Oracle-supplied Workflows and any custom Workflows continue to work as designed. The next chapter will show the standard administration screens, which have significantly improved since Workflow was introduced, and the additional improvements available through the Oracle Applications Manager (OAM).

Administration

A administering Workflow is really not that mysterious, though it may appear overwhelming at times because there are so many options. Oracle has worked hard to provide tools to make Workflow Administration less complex. Oracle Applications Manager (OAM), for example, can be used to look at many of the same details as the 'Status Monitor' in Workflow Administration. Diagnostic reports (covered in detail in *Chapter 9, Diagnostics*) are also available to obtain the same information. Successful administration often boils down to either using the tool that you prefer because of its features, or the tool that is available to you.

This chapter takes some of the mystery out of troubleshooting and administering Workflows. The chapter is broken out into three major areas:

1. Using Oracle Applications Manager (OAM) to administer Workflow

2. Using the Workflow Administration menu structure to administer Workflow

3. When all else fails, using SQL Queries to administer Workflow

Topics included in the Oracle Applications Manager (OAM) section include how to use and interpret the OAM Dashboard screens; the Background Engines, Purge and Control Queue Cleanup tools; and using the Administration page's Workflow Configuration to set up Workflow. Setup changes required after your Applications DBA clones an instance are also discussed in this section.

For those intrepid Workflow Administrators that really like to troubleshoot by running SQL queries, we have included some samples at the end of this chapter with the caveat that you use these scripts at your own risk.

The chapter concludes by explaining, step by step, how to solve one of the most common Workflow issues: how to resend Notifications when unexplainable things, such has hardware blips or sunspots, happen despite the fact that there are no obvious reasons for Notifications to have failed.

WHEN TO USE OAM VERSUS THE WORKFLOW ADMINISTRATION MENUS

Oracle Applications Manager (OAM) has always had a 'Workflow Manager' page. That page is now available from the Workflow Administrator responsibilities. The purpose of this page is to set up Workflow components and monitor the overall health of the Workflow system. For example, if *no one* is getting Notifications, use this OAM page to troubleshoot the problem. For troubleshooting *specific* Workflow items, use the Workflow Administrator menus that are described later in this chapter. For example, if a Notification was not received for a specific Workflow, you would use the 'Workflow Administration Home' page to research the issue rather than OAM's 'Workflow Manager' page.

USING ORACLE APPLICATIONS MANAGER (OAM) TO ADMINISTER WORKFLOW

Workflow Manager Page Overview

OAM's Applications Dashboard gives a bird's eye view of the overall health of Workflow (see FIGURE 8.1). Green icons are good, red icons mean something is wrong. The icons are hot links to view or update details for the specific components. If the Notification Mailer is configured, all lights (except Purge) MUST be green. Some companies prefer to exclusively utilize the Notification Worklist from within Oracle Applications and choose not to send Notifications via email for security reasons. If this is the case, then Notification Mailer is not configured or is unavailable ( ) is a legitimate status. Unavailable is not a legitimate status for Service Components, as these need to be up and running whether you use the Notification Mailer or not. Click the 'Refresh' button ( ) located next to the Last Updated time to update indicators.

Beginning with ATG_PF.H.delta.4 (Rollup 4), you must click the 'Refresh' button to refresh the details on this page as well as other pages within OAM.

As an alternative to using the 'Refresh' button, you can schedule the following Concurrent Programs from the Workflow Administration menus to keep these statistics updated. We prefer to use the 'Refresh' button since there is no reason to waste performance cycles on these Concurrent Programs when not utilizing OAM.

- 'Workflow Agent Activity Statistics' Concurrent Program

- 'Workflow Mailer Statistics' Concurrent Program

- 'Workflow Work Items Statistics' Concurrent Program

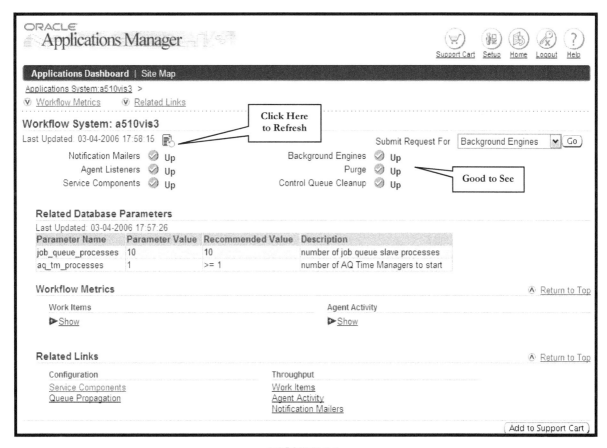

FIGURE 8.1

FIGURES 8.2 and 8.3 show valid Dashboard settings for two different environments. The first is using the Notification Mailer, and the second is not.

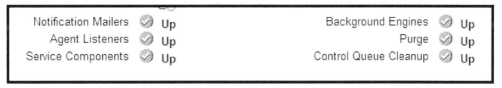

FIGURE 8.2

FIGURE 8.3

FIGURE 8.4 shows an example of an environment that is having problems. Both the Notification Mailers and the Service Components are down, which means that some services are not started and Notifications will not be emailed (however, they will show in the Notification Worklist).

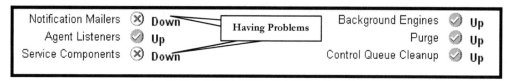

FIGURE 8.4

With these examples of good and bad Dashboard settings in mind, let's look at some definitions of the components of those Dashboards.

Notification Mailer

The Notification Mailer is the component for email Notifications. This is where you set up, test and change the Notification Mailers, view logs and Events, or set an override address for cloned instances. If the Notification Mailer is down, the icon with a red X will appear.

Agent Listeners

Using the Advanced Queuing (AQ) System, Agent Listeners wake up and process (dequeue) events/messages placed in queues based on the STATE of the event/message (STATE=0 indicates 'Ready to Process', 1 indicates 'Wait until has SEND_DATE has passed.') Agents (acting as a point of communication) receive/send messages from external Systems and translate the message to/from the format required by the Queue (XML, Text, SQL, Java). Since Agents typically have the same name as the queue they are assigned to, it is difficult to distinguish when the forms reference Agents or Queues. Agents and Agent Listeners are assigned to a Queue. Queues are database tables. Dequeuing an event causes all subscriptions associated with that event to be processed. See *Chapter 5, Business Events*. You can click on the icon next to Agent Listeners to access the detail page to edit Agents, view logs and other details, start/stop/refresh/resume Agent Listeners and view the status of Agent Listeners.

Service Components

Service Components show the same information as Agent Listeners with the addition of the Workflow Notification Mailer listener (with a link to the Workflow Mailer Service Container) and the Web Services OUT Agent Listener (with a link to the Workflow Document Web Services Service Container). Do not use these pages to change the configuration of Listeners or Containers seeded by Oracle:

- **WF_CONTROL** – Oracle Workflow Internal Agent, not for customer use

- **WF_DEFERRED** – Standard Agent for deferred Subscription processing in the database

- **WF_ERROR** – Standard Agent for error handling in the database

- **WF_JAVA_DEFERRED** – Standard Agent for deferred Subscription processing in the middle tier

- **WF_JAVA_ERROR** – Standard Agent for error handling in the middle tier

- **WF_IN** – Default Inbound Agent

- **WF_JMS_IN** – Default Inbound Agent for JMS Text Messages

- **WF_JMS_OUT** – Default Outbound Agent for JMS Text Messages

- **WF_NOTIFICATION_IN** – Standard Inbound Agent for email Notification responses

- **WF_NOTIFICATION_OUT** – Standard Outbound Agent for email Notifications

- **WF_OUT** – Default Outbound Agent

- **WF_WS_JMS_IN** – Default Inbound Agent for Web Service Messages

- **WF_WS_JMS_OUT** – Default Outbound Agent for Web Service Messages

Containers

Clicking the name of the Container from either the Agent Listeners or Service Components page opens the page to start/stop the Containers. Containers are Java Concurrent Managers. Oracle recommends not to stop/start the containers individually but to use the Start All / Stop All links in the upper right corner. Do not use these pages to change the configuration of these Services. See FIGURE 8.5:

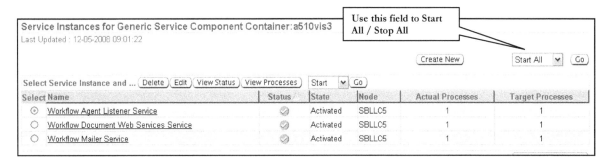

FIGURE 8.5

Background Engines

The 'Workflow Manager' page can also be used to schedule Concurrent Requests for Background Engines, Control Queue Cleanup, or to purge Workflow history. If the specified Concurrent Request is scheduled, a green icon will appear. Select the icon to see the details for the last execution of the Concurrent Program (see FIGURE 8.6).

FIGURE 8.6

Background Engines can be started from the OAM Dashboard or from the Concurrent Manager. When they are started from OAM, they are assigned a user-defined name that appears as the Concurrent Program name in View Concurrent Programs. For example, if a Background Engine named 'Stuck Processes' is started via OAM, it will appear as 'Stuck Processes (Workflow Background Process)'. *Chapter 2, Setup*, contains additional details on setting up Background Engines.

Purge

Execute, schedule and monitor Purge Concurrent Programs to purge details related to completed Workflows. If a Purge Concurrent Program is scheduled, a green icon will appear. Select the icon to see the details for the last execution of the Concurrent Program.

Clicking on the Purge ⊘ or ⊗ also reveals a link where you can see the Workflows that are eligible to be purged (see FIGURE 8.7).

Note that this is also another link to see the same charts shown as those displayed in Work Items.

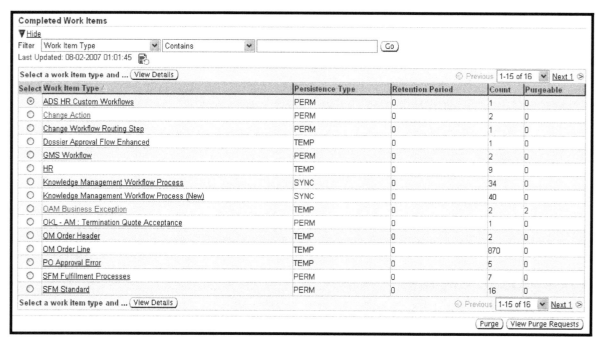

FIGURE 8.7

From FIGURE 8.7 you can select a 'Workflow Item Type' and (if purgeable) start a Concurrent Request to purge just that Workflow (or all of them), or choose 'View Details'. You may have to specify 'End Date within last ____ days' to see the completed Workflow items (the default that will be automatically queried is 30 days), or you can change the view to 'Active', 'Suspended', 'Errored', or 'Deferred'. See FIGURE 8.8.

Note that you should click the 'Refresh' button if you don't have the Concurrent Programs that refresh statistics scheduled.

FIGURE 8.8

After specifying the dates, the 'Completed Work Items' screen (see FIGURE 8.9) appears. You now see the Process name and the final result (if any). Click 'View Details' to drill down to the individual Workflows.

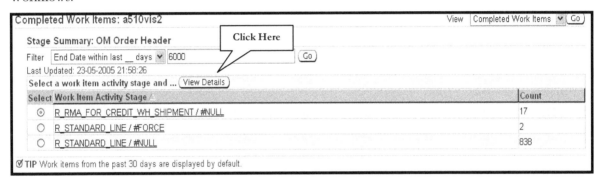

FIGURE 8. 9

Sometimes Workflows are not purgeable. If the retention period, which is set in the Workflow Builder client tool, has not expired, or the associated parent or child Workflow is still open, the Workflow will not purge. Note that WFERROR is a child Workflow that will prevent purging if still open. The bde_wf_clean_worklist.sql script will close WFERROR Workflows where the parent Workflow is complete. See MetaLink Doc. ID: 255048.1, *bde_wf_clean_worklist.sql – Cleans Out The Worklist of Obsolete Notifications*, and 270765.1, *Obsolete Workflow Runtime Data Is Not Purging All Data*, for additional information. Orphaned Notifications are Notifications where the rest of the Workflow runtime data was purged. Generally, these are Notifications to SYSADMIN. MetaLink Doc. ID: 253129.1, *How Do You Delete A Notification If The Item Key No Longer Exists?*, explains how to use the WFNTFPRG.sql script to remove these Notifications.

Starting a purge process executes the Concurrent Program 'Purge Obsolete Workflow Runtime Data'. The following tables are purged:

- WF_ITEMS

- WF_NOTIFICATIONS

- WF_NOTIFICATION_ATTRIBUTES

- WF_ITEM_ATTRIBUTE_VALUES

- WF_ITEM_ACTIVITY_STATUSES

- WF_ITEM_ACTIVITY_STATUSES_H

- WF_COMMENTS

Control Queue Cleanup

When a middle tier Process for Oracle Applications starts up, it creates a JMS Subscriber to the Queue. When an Event Message is placed on the Queue, a copy of the Event Message is created for each Subscriber to the Queue. If a middle tier Process dies, the corresponding Subscriber remains in the database. Schedule the 'Control Queue Cleanup' Concurrent Program to run every 12 hours to remove these inactive Subscriptions that occur when a middle tier Process dies. Failure to schedule this job will impact performance. If a 'Control Queue Cleanup' is scheduled, a green icon will appear in OAM. Select the icon to see the details for the last execution of the Concurrent Program.

Related Database Parameters

Certain parameters affect Workflow performance. You can see the current value as well as the recommended value for 'Related Database Parameters' from the 'Applications Dashboard' screen in FIGURE 8.10. If the values don't match the recommended values, you'll need to work with your Applications DBA to determine the appropriate parameters. Your Applications DBA will need to make those changes to the database's init.ora file. Your Applications DBA should check the following parameters:

- **job_queue_processes** - is the maximum number of Processes instantiated for the execution of user jobs, queue propagation, replication and jobs scheduled via DBMS_JOBS. Change the default value, which is 2, to at least 10. If there are delays in the amount of time required for a Notification to be received, try increasing this parameter

- **aq_tm_processes** - is the number of Advanced Queueing Monitor Processes to support delayed Events such as expiration, Wait Activities and Message Retention. This must be set to a value greater than 1 in database versions prior to RDBMS Version 10.1. Otherwise, the Workflow Background Process will error. When set to a value greater than 0, this parameter sets time monitoring for Queue Messages. The value specifies the number of Processes used for the monitoring

Workflow Metrics

Workflow metrics includes the graphical views for Work Items and Agent Activity. Click the + sign next to the 'Show' link shown in FIGURE 8.10 to display the graphs that are further described in the next section.

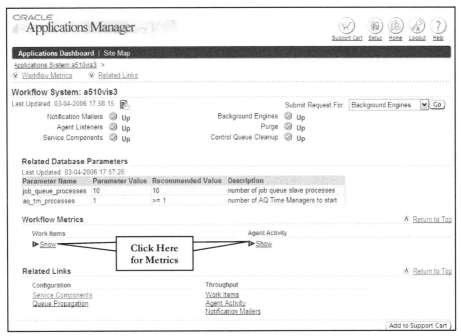

FIGURE 8.10

Work Items

Work Items provide a graphical view of Work Items by status (Active, Deferred, Suspended, Error). Click on the graph components to drill down. See FIGURE 8.11.

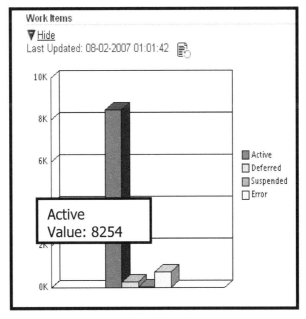

FIGURE 8.11

OAM provides charts of non-completed Work Items. If you move the cursor over the bar, you can see the exact number and if you click on the bar, you are taken to the screen shown in FIGURE 8.12 that lists all Item Types in that status. This is the OAM equivalent to the 'Workflow Administration Status Monitor' screen. Note that the count for Expenses is 23.

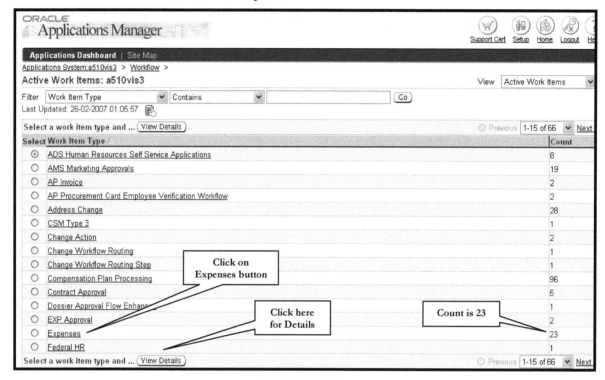

FIGURE 8.12

The count in FIGURE 8.12 is of *all* Workflows that are not complete. Thus, it includes Workflows that are working normally as well as those in error status. Additionally, the count here does not restrict responses based on when the Workflow started.

In FIGURE 8.13, we selected 'Expenses' and clicked on 'View Details'. The initial drilldown pulls only non-errored Workflows that started in the last 30 days, so the counts may not match (count = 0).

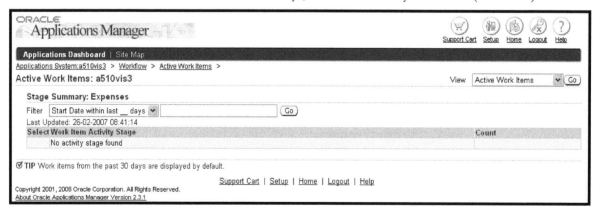

FIGURE 8. 13

If you increase the 'Start Date within last ___ days' parameter, the count now equals 1 in FIGURE 8.14.

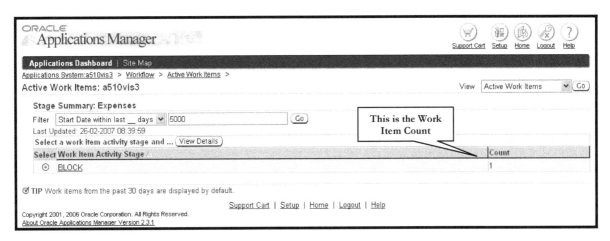

FIGURE 8. 14

To verify that the "missing" Workflows are in error status, change the View to 'Errored Work Items' and click Go. FIGURE 8.15 shows that the "missing" 22 expenses Workflows are active, but in error status.

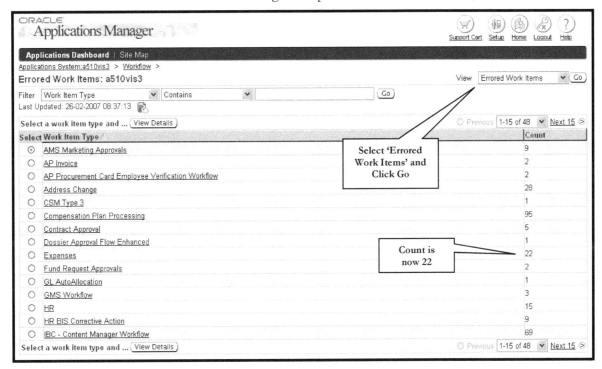

FIGURE 8. 15

Click the browser 'Back' button to return to the previous screen or change the view to 'Active Work Items' and drill down again.

Using OAM to research errored Workflows is very useful (although this doesn't help with errored Events). Immediately, in FIGURE 8.14, you can see there are 48 different Item Types that are in error status. Do not assume all Workflows for a given Item Type are in error status for the same reason. Drill down.

After clicking on 'Expenses', FIGURE 8.16 shows the drill down where we see the different types of errored Work Items. The 'Expenses' Workflow is in error in four different places. Click on INFORM_NO_APPROVER to drill down to the individual Workflow.

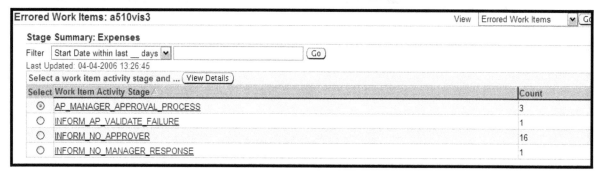

FIGURE 8. 16

Note that the 'Launch Workflow Monitor' button, shown in FIGURE 8.17, works in Release 11.5.9 (opens the old grayscale version) and in Release 11.5.10 with ATG_PF.H delta.3 (Rollup 3), which opens the Framework version. However, in Release 11.5.10, without ATG_PF.H.delta.3 (Rollup 3), you cannot open the monitor.

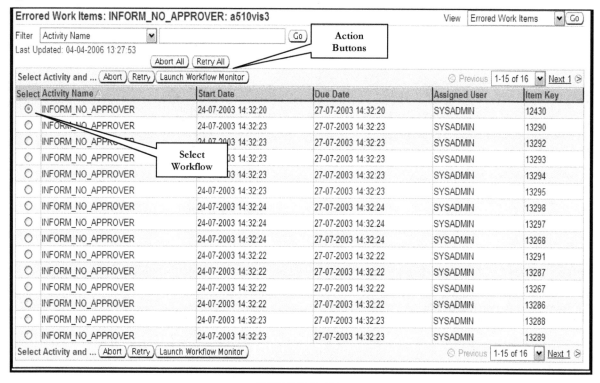

FIGURE 8. 17

For the sake of argument, suppose you saw this in your production environment. Before taking time to research the issue, ask the following questions:

- What E-Business Suite release was my company running in July 2003 (notice in FIGURE 8.17 that the Start Date for all the items is July 24 2003)?

- Since the newest error occurred in July 2003, wouldn't it be safe to assume that whatever caused the issue was obviously fixed in a later patch set?

- Is the data moving through the Workflow still valid?

  ◆ For expense reports, requisitions, purchase orders – probably not

  ◆ For order lines/headers – further research should be done

You can Abort, Retry, and Launch Workflow Monitor for any individual Activity Name. Collectively, you can Abort All or Retry All (these buttons are not repeated at the bottom of the page). Note that the collective retry or abort Action isn't just for the 15 Workflows displayed on the current page; it applies to all 16 Workflows selected.

For more details on the specific error, launch the 'Workflow Monitor'. From that point, choose 'Activity History'. Find the Activity in error and click on the 'Error' link. Often, you can find a direct hit on MetaLink for the listed error. You can see what the 'Activity History' screen looks like by going to the "Workflow Administration Menus to Administer Workflow" section later in this chapter.

Agent Activity

Agent Activity is a graphical view of all Events moving through the System by status ('Ready', 'Waiting', 'Expired', 'Undeliverable', 'Error'). Moving the cursor over the graph will show the amount in each column and clicking on the column will open a chart of the contents. See FIGURE 8.18.

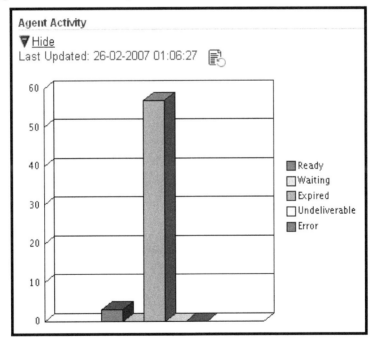

FIGURE 8. 18

Expired and Processed will self-purge based on the retention parameter associated with the Queue. Events are stored in Waiting when they have a future start date. If there are any Undeliverable, then you need to click on the 'Agent', and see which Events are firing and look at the Subscriptions to see why the Message is in the undeliverable column. In this case, FIGURE 8.19 shows that there is a large number in

WF_NOTIFICATION_OUT. However, since the number is in the Processed column, this just indicates the number of Notifications that were emailed in the last 24 hours (retention for this queue is 1 day). If this number was in the Ready column it would indicate that either the Global Preference is set to use the Notification Mailer and the Notification Mailer isn't turned on, or that there are individuals who have set their preference to use the Notification Mailer, which isn't set up. FIGURE 8.19 also shows that there is a large number in WF_DEFERRED. Again, the number is in the 'Processed' column, indicating the system is functioning normally. This queue displays the number of non–Mailer events with subscription phases greater than 99 that have been raised in the last 24 hours (retention for this queue is 1 day). If this number was in the 'Ready' column it could indicate the Agent Listeners are down. If this number was in the 'Waiting' column, then there are events with a SEND_DATE in the future.

Note that WF_DEFERRED is the queue for deferred events, not for activities waiting for the Background Engine. The queue that stores these activities is WF_DEFERRED_TABLE_M and is not shown in OAM.

Applications System:a510vis3 > Workflow >
Agent Activity: a510vis3
Review the numbers of event messages with different statuses on different Business Event System agents.
Last Updated: 26-02-2007 01:06:28

Select an Agent and ... (Search Agent Entry Details)

Select Agent	Ready	Waiting	Processed	Expired	Undeliverable
ECX_INBOUND	3	0	0	0	0
ECX_IN_OAG_Q	0	0	0	0	0
ECX_OUTBOUND	0	0	0	0	0
WF_CONTROL	0	0	0	0	0
WF_DEFERRED	0	0	316	0	0
WF_ERROR	0	0	0	16	0
WF_IN	0	0	0	0	0
WF_JAVA_DEFERRED	0	0	34	0	0
WF_JAVA_ERROR	0	0	0	0	0
WF_JMS_IN	0	0	0	0	0
WF_JMS_JMS_OUT	0	0	0	0	0
WF_JMS_OUT	0	0	0	0	0
WF_NOTIFICATION_IN	0	0	0	0	0
WF_NOTIFICATION_OUT	0	0	305	41	0
WF_OUT	0	0	0	0	0
WF_REPLAY_IN	0	0	0	0	0
WF_REPLAY_OUT	0	0	0	0	0
WF_WS_JMS_IN	0	0	0	0	0
WF_WS_JMS_OUT	0	0	0	0	0
WF_WS_SAMPLE	0	0	0	0	0

Select an Agent and ... (Search Agent Entry Details)

FIGURE 8. 19

Clicking on the 'Agent Name' displays information about the Agent. Selecting the 'Agent' and clicking 'Search Agent Entry Details' opens a window that lets you search for a specific Event, or search by age of the Message. This information lists the queue to which the Agent is assigned. Only ECX_INBOUND and ECX_OUTBOUND are assigned to queues with a different name than that of the Agent.

Related Links

FIGURE 8.20 shows the 'Related Links' at the bottom of the 'Applications Dashboard' screen. 'Configuration' links to the Service Components, which is the same as the link at the top of the page. 'Queue Propagation' shows database parameters and propagation Schedules for Outbound Queues.

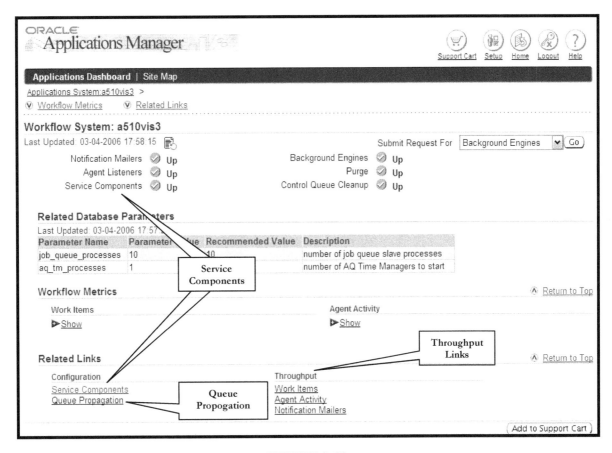

FIGURE 8. 20

Throughput

FIGURE 8.20 includes links under 'Throughput' at the bottom of the 'Applications Dashboard' screen. 'Throughput' includes:

- **Work Items** – shows the same detail retrieved from the graph in the Workflow Metrics section

- **Agent Activity** – shows the same detail retrieved from the graph in the Workflow Metrics section

- **Notification Mailers** – is a graph of Mailer throughput without drilldown showing Notifications Processed and waiting. If a large number of items are waiting, there is a problem with the Notification Mailer. Clicking on the bars of this graph doesn't link to other screens

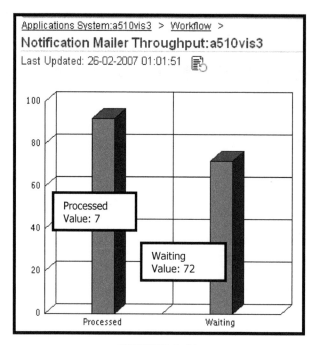

FIGURE 8. 21

The graph in FIGURE 8.21 corresponds to records in the WF_NOTIFICATIONS table. The Processed bar counts records with a status of OPEN and a MAIL_STATUS of SENT. The Waiting bar counts records with a MAIL_STATUS of MAIL. A complete query on the WF_NOTIFICATION table yields the following counts:

```
COUNT(*)   STATUS       MAIL STATUS
34         CANCELED     ERROR
1          CLOSED       ERROR
149        CANCELED     FAILED
8          OPEN         FAILED
5          CANCELED     MAIL
67         CLOSED       MAIL
111        CANCELED     SENT
300        CLOSED       SENT
7          OPEN         SENT
178        CANCELED
```

The STATUS column indicates the status of the Notification. The MAIL_STATUS column indicates the status of emailing the Notification. 'ERROR' and 'FAILED' indicate that the attempt to email the Notification failed. 'SENT' indicates the Notification was successfully emailed. 'MAIL' indicates that the Notification has yet to be mailed. 'CANCELED' Notifications are Notifications that no longer apply or have already been answered. For example, if a Notification is sent to a Role, the first person to reply will cause the Notifications to other recipients to be cancelled.

USING THE WORKFLOW ADMINISTRATION MENU STRUCTURE TO ADMINISTER WORKFLOW

Oracle converted the Oracle Workflow web pages to the Oracle Applications Framework user interface format utilizing Browser Look and Feel (BLAF) starting with 11.5.9. Instead of a series of gray-screen forms that were accessed individually and were singular in function, there is now a 'Home' page that from a single page allows access to multiple Functions. Be careful. Some older releases are missing menu items.

There are two versions of the menu structure: one that has all the Functions mentioned above (ATG_PF.H Rollup 3 included these fixes) and one that is missing the tabs on the 'Business Events and Administration' page. In the Release 11.5.10 Vision instance prior to ATG_PF.H.delta.3, the responsibility that shows all the tabs is 'Workflow Administrator Web (New)'. The missing functionality can be restored to the responsibility 'Workflow Administrator Web Applications' by adding the submenu 'Workflow Administrator Application' to the menu. This entry into the menu should have nothing specified in the 'Menu' or 'Function' columns and this entry should precede any other 'Workflow' menu rows.

If you are using a pre-ATG_PF.H Rollup 3 environment and you decide to fix the 'Workflow Administration' menu, you may wish to add the menu 'Requests', with the submenu 'Standard Report Submission'. If you do this, add the 'Workflow Administrator' Report Group to the responsibility, and then add the Concurrent Program 'Workflow Control Queue Cleanup' to the Report Group.

Refer to the *Oracle Applications Developer Guide* for additional information on the modification of menus and Report Groups.

The Home Page Tab

FIGURE 8.22 shows that the 'Home' page includes your "top 5" Personal Notifications based on due date, the 'Vacation Rules' link, and 'Worklist Access' link.

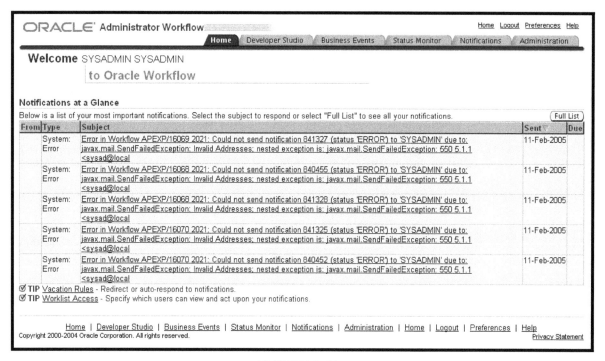

FIGURE 8. 22

The Developer Studio Tab

Use the Developer Studio to launch Workflows. This is a replacement for the Launch Processes window and is typically used to test custom Workflows. When launching a Workflow, all the parameters that are typically defined either in a form or programmatically must be manually entered. *Chapter 6, Testing Workflows,* gives detailed examples on launching Workflows using the Developer Studio.

The Business Events Tab

The 'Business Events' tab is used to update or view all Business Event details. This includes Events and Event Groups, Subscriptions, Agents and Systems. See *Chapter 5, Business Events and Chapter 6, Testing Workflows,* for details on all Business Events topics.

The Status Monitor Tab

Visit the 'Status Monitor' page to view all Workflow details for a specific Item Type or Workflow. In FIGURE 8.23, if a specific requisition appears to be stuck in the approval Process, use this page for troubleshooting.

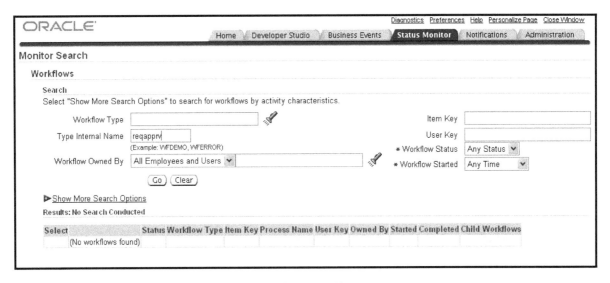

FIGURE 8. 23

FIGURE 8.24 shows that if you click on 'Show More Search Options' you can see Activity characteristics:

FIGURE 8. 24

You must specify either 'Workflow Type', 'Type Internal Name', 'Workflow Owned By', or 'Workflow Started' in the search page shown in FIGURE 8.23 before you will be allowed to search by the Activity characteristics in the 'Search Options' section. Activity characteristics include 'Days Without Progress' and 'Workflow Status'.

Note that placing "%" in Internal Name in FIGURE 8.23 satisfies this requirement.

Results

Click Go to search for Workflows matching the criteria entered. FIGURE 8.25 shows the Results: Workflows page after entering 'reqapprv' in the 'Type Internal Name' field of our Vision instance:

Results: Workflows

To view or administer a workflow, select "Activity History". Select "Participant Responses" to view comments and other information gathered for closed, response-required notifications.

☑ TIP Workflow histories are periodically purged from the system and may no longer be available for review.

Select Workflow and View... (Activity History) (Status Diagram) (Participant Responses) (Workflow Details)   ⊙ Previous 1-25 ⌄ Next 25 ⊚

Select	Status	Workflow Type	Item Key	Process Name	User Key	Owned By	Started ▽	Completed	Child Workflows
○	✓ Active	PO Requisition Approval	56815-149426	Main Requisition Approval		Behn, Susan	21-Oct-2007 22:43:21		
○	✓ Active	PO Requisition Approval	56814-149425	Main Requisition Approval		Behn, Susan	21-Oct-2007 22:42:07		
○	✓ Active	PO Requisition Approval	56813-149424	Main Requisition Approval		Behn, Susan	21-Oct-2007 22:41:16		
○	✓ Active	PO Requisition Approval	56689-149362	Main Requisition Approval		Jones, Gerald	29-May-2007 12:50:27		
○	⊗ Error	PO Requisition Approval	44727-120561	Main Requisition Approval			06-Aug-2003 13:02:35		
○	⊗ Error	PO Requisition Approval	43512118087	Main Requisition Approval		Boursin, Elisabeth	24-Jul-2003 09:07:34		▯ ▯▯▯
○	⊗ Error	PO Requisition Approval	31993-88499	Main Requisition Approval		Mikus, Michael	19-Feb-2003 13:39:49		▯ ▯▯▯
○	⊗ Error	PO Requisition Approval	31992-88484	Main Requisition Approval		Mikus, Michael	19-Feb-2003 12:38:16		▯ ▯▯▯

FIGURE 8. 25

From the 'Results' page, the Workflow Administrator can obtain all the information about the progress of the Workflow. To view the Activity History, Status Diagram, Participant Responses, or Workflow Details, click the Select radio button for the desired Workflow, then click one of the buttons at the top of the screen for the type of information desired. Click on the red X icon or the 'Error' hotlink to see the 'Error Message' for errored Workflows. The name in the 'Owned By' column is a hot link to send an email to the owner if an email address is available for the owner. The 'Child Workflows' column is a direct link to the child Workflow for the selected Workflow item.

Error Details

Clicking on the radio button next to the first 'Error Message' in FIGURE 8.25 will display the error details for the Item Key 44727-120561 as shown in FIGURE 8.26:

Monitor Errors

Workflow Errors: REQAPPRV, 44727-120561

Failed Activity	**Notify Requestor of No Approver Available**
Activity Type	**Notice**
Error Name	**WFENG_NOTIFICATION_PERFORMER**
Error Message	3120: Activity 'REQAPPRV/495357' has no performer.
Error Stack	Wf_Engine_Util.Notification_Send(REQAPPRV, 44727-120561, 495357, REQAPPRV:PO_REQ_NO_APPROVER)
	Wf_Engine_Util.Notification(REQAPPRV, 44727-120561, 495357, RUN)

(View Diagram) (Reassign) (Skip) (Retry)

FIGURE 8. 26

If the error is not immediately obvious, cut and paste the Error Message and search for the error on MetaLink. Often there is a direct reference that will provide information to correct the error. From the 'Error Message' page, there are buttons for additional options depending on the type of errored activities. Since this example is an errored Notification, skipping this Activity is allowed. In recent releases, you are no longer allowed to skip Functions (except the Compare Function), since skipping Functions can result in data corruption. Retrying Functions is allowed. The Activity Type shown in FIGURE 8.26 identifies the type of Activity.

The Activity History Button

The 'Activity History' page shown in FIGURE 8.27 displays each Activity Node in the Workflow and the result. Clicking on the 'Activity' link drills down to more detail.

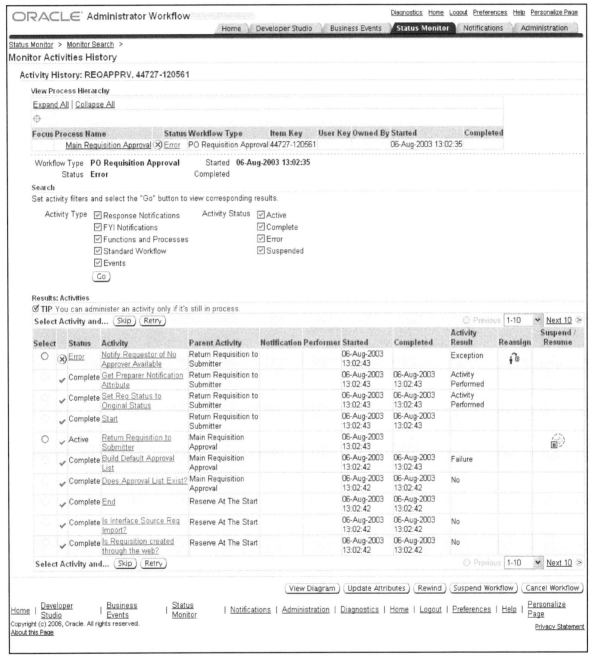

FIGURE 8. 27

FIGURE 8.28 shows the PL/SQL Function that is called. This helps developers performing advanced troubleshooting. If the Activity is active, Action buttons are available depending on the type of Activity, such as Retry, Skip or Reassign, to administer the Activity.

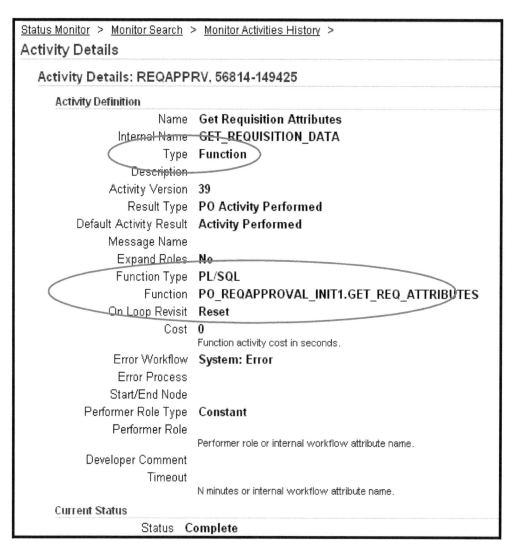

Status Monitor > Monitor Search > Monitor Activities History >

Activity Details

Activity Details: REQAPPRV, 56814-149425

Activity Definition

Name	**Get Requisition Attributes**
Internal Name	**GET_REQUISITION_DATA**
Type	**Function**
Description	
Activity Version	**39**
Result Type	**PO Activity Performed**
Default Activity Result	**Activity Performed**
Message Name	
Expand Roles	**No**
Function Type	**PL/SQL**
Function	**PO_REQAPPROVAL_INIT1.GET_REQ_ATTRIBUTES**
On Loop Revisit	**Reset**
Cost	**0**
	Function activity cost in seconds.
Error Workflow	**System: Error**
Error Process	
Start/End Node	
Performer Role Type	**Constant**
Performer Role	
	Performer role or internal workflow attribute name.
Developer Comment	
Timeout	
	N minutes or internal workflow attribute name.

Current Status

Status	**Complete**

FIGURE 8. 28

The Status Monitor Button

The Status Diagram is a graphical representation of the Activity History. Follow the green highlighted line to follow the path of a Workflow. If the Workflow errors, the Activity that resulted in error will be outlined in red. Note in FIGURE 8.29 that 'Skip' and 'Retry' buttons have been removed from the 'Status Monitor' page. As mentioned earlier, 'Skip' and 'Retry' are limited to certain Activity Types. Therefore, you must drill down to the Activity details for access to these administration buttons.

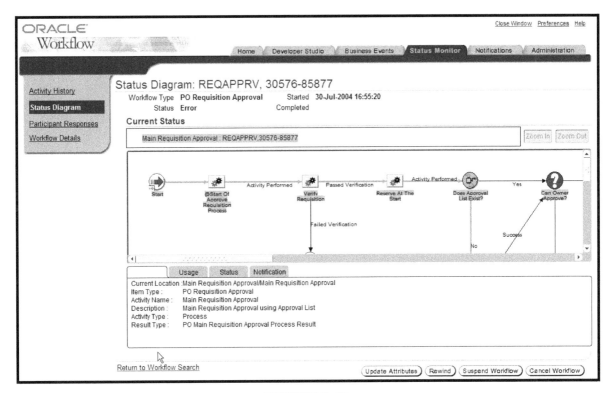

FIGURE 8. 29

The Participant Responses Button

Clicking on the Participant Responses button (from FIGURE 8.25) displays FIGURE 8.30. This page displays all the Notifications where a response is required for the Workflow item selected.

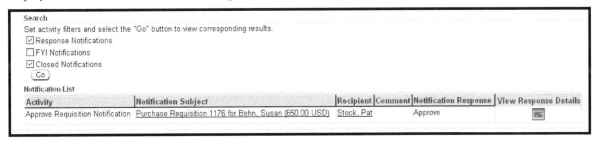

FIGURE 8. 30

FIGURE 8.31 shows what happens if you click on the icon in the 'View Response Details' column. You can see when the Notification was sent and responded to, who responded, and the original recipient:

```
┌────────────────────────────────────────────────────────────────────────────────┐
│ Notification Response Details                                                    │
│                                                                                  │
│   Notification Response Details                                                  │
│        Notification Subject  Purchase Requisition 1176 for Behn, Susan (650.00 USD) │
│             Respondent                                                           │
│        Original Recipient    Stock, Pat                                          │
│                              If different from "Respondent", the original recipient delegated responsibility for replying to the respondent. │
│        Notification Sent     21-Oct-2007 22:42:08                                │
│        Response Received                                                         │
│             Response                                                             │
│   Additional Response Information                                                │
│     This notification asked the respondent to provide the following information. Some or all fields may be blank. │
│         Forward To                                                               │
│             Note                                                                 │
└────────────────────────────────────────────────────────────────────────────────┘
```

FIGURE 8. 31

The Workflow Details Button

This page shows the value of all the Attributes in the Workflow item selected. Included in the Attribute values are the key references such as the specific PL/SQL package for Document Attributes, the recipient of Notifications (when the Performer is set to an Item Attribute), the function used to display framework pages, and other key information about the object that is the focus of the workflow. Becoming familiar with the detail available on this page will help the Workflow Administrator debug error conditions and keep Workflow running smoothly. Note that this page only displays the first 200 Attributes. If there are more than 200 Attributes, the page will display a message indicating that there are additional Attributes. Unfortunately the only way to see values for these Attributes is to query for them using SQL. Since these Attributes display in the order they are listed in the Workflow Builder, you can use the Builder to re-order the Item Attributes so that all key Attributes will be displayed in this window. See *Chapter 3, Builder Basics*.

FIGURE 8.32 shows that you can scroll all the way to the bottom of the Workflow Details page to locate additional buttons to view the diagram, update Attributes, rewind, suspend the Workflow or cancel the Workflow.

Status Monitor > Monitor Search >

Monitor Workflow Details: REQAPPRV, 44727-120561

View Process Hierarchy

Expand All | Collapse All

Focus Process Name	Status	Workflow Type	Item Key	User Key	Owned By	Started	Completed
Main Requisition Approval	⊗ Error	PO Requisition Approval	44727-120561			06-Aug-2003 13:02:35	

Workflow Type	PO Requisition Approval		Started	06-Aug-2003 13:02:35
Status	Error		Completed	

Workflow Definition

Internal Name	REQAPPRV
Description	Requisition Approval Process
Persistence Type	Temporary
Persistence Days	0
Selector	

Workflow Attributes

Approval Path ID	
Authorization Status	INCOMPLETE
Authorization Status Display	In Process
Closed Code	
Closed Code Display	
Document Id	44727
Requisition Number	1
Document Subtype	PURCHASE
Document Type	REQUISITION
Document Type Display	
Emergency PO Number	
Forward From Display Name	
Forward From Id	
Forward From User Name	
Forward To Display Name	
Forward To Id	
Forward-To ID Old Value	
Forward To User Name	
Response Forward-To	
Functional Currency	COP
Interface source	PO_FORM
Note	
Online Report Id For Doc Complete Check	
Online Report Text For Doc Complete Check	
Open Form Command	PO_POXRQERQ:P_REQUISITION_HEADER_ID="&DOCUMENT_ID" P_MODE="POXRQERQ_CALLING_FORM= "POXSTNOT"
Context ORG_ID	4044
Original Authorization Status	INCOMPLETE
Preparer Display Name	
Preparer ID	12191
Preparer User name	
Requisition Amount Display	500.00
Requisition Description	Paper
Update requisition	http://lm0023.us.oracle.com:80/pls/lm0023/por_redirect.reqserver?x_object=Order&x_doc_id=44727&x_org_id=4044
Resubmit Requisition	http://lm0023.us.oracle.com:80/pls/lm0023/por_redirect.reqserver?x_object=Order&x_doc_id=44727&x_org_id=4044
Requisition Detail	http://lm0023.us.oracle.com:80/pls/lm0023/por_redirect.reqserver?x_object=ReqsQueryOrder&x_doc_id=44727&x_org_id=4044
Document Manager Error Number	
System Administrator Error Message	
Approver Employee ID	12191
Approver Display Name	
Approver User Name	
Print Document	N
Concurrent Request ID	
"Invalid Forward To" Translated Message	
"Requires Approval" Translated Message	requires your approval.
User ID	1006790
Application ID	201
Responsibility ID	57831
Send PO Autocreation to Background	N
Approval List ID	
Responder ID	12191
Responder User Name	
Responder Display Name	
Tax Amount Display	80.00
Total Amount Display	580.00
PL/SQL Error Location	
PL/SQL Error Message	
PL/SQL Error Document	
Approve Requisition Message	PLSQL:PO_WF_REQ_NOTIFICATION.GET_PO_REQ_APPROVE_MSG/REQAPP
Requisition Approved Message	PLSQL:PO_WF_REQ_NOTIFICATION.GET_PO_REQ_APPROVED_MSG/REQAP 120561:&#NID

No Approver Found Message	PLSQL:PO_WF_REQ_NOTIFICATION.GET_PO_REQ_NO_APPROVER_MSG/RE 120561:&#NID
Requisition Rejected Message	PLSQL:PO_WF_REQ_NOTIFICATION.GET_PO_REQ_REJECT_MSG/REQAPPR
Requisition lines details	PLSQL:PO_WF_REQ_NOTIFICATION.GET_REQ_LINES_DETAILS/REQAPPRV:
Action history of the document	PLSQL:PO_WF_REQ_NOTIFICATION.GET_ACTION_HISTORY/REQAPPRV:447
RCS version	$Revision: 115.50 $
Advisory Warning	
Relative Time of Auto Retry for Document Manager	0
Auto Loop Limit for Document Manger	0
Responder User ID	
Responder Application ID	
Responder Responsibility ID	
Justification	
Attachment	
Requisition Amount Display with Currency	500.00 COP
Tax Amount Display with Currency	80.00 COP
Document Subtype Display	
Deliver-To Location Line 1	
Deliver-To Location Line 2	
Deliver-To Location Line 3	
Deliver-To Location Line 4	
Deliver-To Location Line 5	
Interface source line ID	
Item description line1	
Item description line 2	
Item description line 3	
Item description line 4	
Item description line 5	
Item price line 1	
Item price line 2	
Item price line 3	
Item price line 4	
Item price line 5	
Line 1	
Line 2	
Line 3	
Line 4	
Line 5	
Quantity line 1	
Quantity line 2	
Quantity line 3	
Quantity line 4	
Quantity line 5	
Need-By Date Line 1	
Need-By Date Line 2	
Need-By Date Line 3	
Need-By Date Line 4	
Need-By Date Line 5	
Requestor name Line1	
Requestor name Line 2	
Requestor name Line 3	
Requestor name Line 4	
Requestor name Line 5	
Requisition Amount	
Requisition Status	
Requisition Type	
Unit of measure line 1	
Unit of measure line 2	
Unit of measure line 3	
Unit of measure line 4	
Unit of measure line 5	
Line Number Translated	

(View Diagram) (Update Attributes) (Rewind) (Suspend Wor

Home | Developer Studio | Business Events | Status Monitor | Notifications | Administration | Diagnostics | Home | Logout | Preferences
Copyright (c) 2006, Oracle. All rights reserved.
About this Page

FIGURE 8. 32

The Notifications Tab

This page has no added functionality – it is the same as the 'Workflow User Home' page after choosing the 'Full List' button. The 'Home' link at the top of the page returns you to the Personal Home Page, not to the Home tab.

The Administration Tab

Workflow Configuration

The 'Administration' page shown in FIGURE 8.33 allows you to set Global Preferences, view and reassign other users' Notifications, and set Vacation Rules for other users. This 'Workflow Configuration' screen replaces the 'Global Preferences' page in earlier E-Business Suite releases. Boxes around the fields indicate you are logged in as the administrator and can update fields. Otherwise, this page is available for view only. Visit this page after patching to verify the Workflow System Administrator is set to a responsibility and assign this responsibility to the user SYSADMIN.

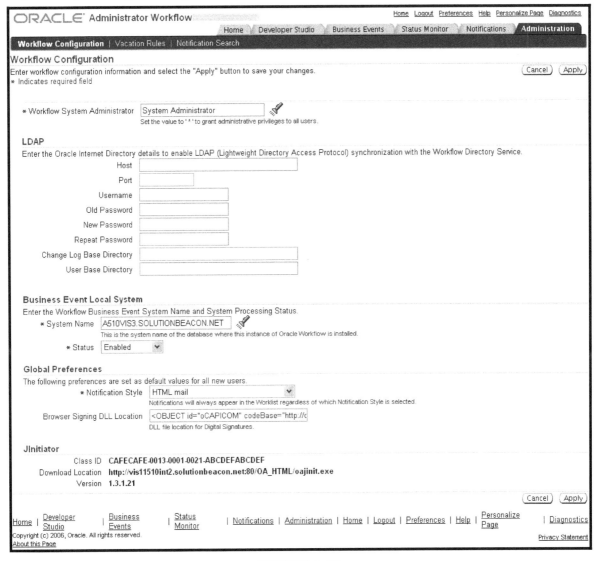

FIGURE 8. 33

Note that Oracle will restore the System Administrator value to SYSADMIN each time you run AutoConfig. AutoConfig is run after each patch. MetaLink Doc. ID: 274842.1, *How To Set The Workflow*

System Administration Role To Be Performed By A Specific Responsibility Instead Of The User SYSADMIN And Not Letting Autoconfig Overwrite It, states that you can set the Workflow Administrator in the AutoConfig context file to reset the System Administrator to the value of your choice. Look for the following line in $APPL_TOP/admin/SID.xml:

```
<username oa_var="s_wf_admin_role">SYSADMIN</username>
```

When AutoConfig runs it invokes afadmprf.sh, which in turn invokes afadmprf.sql. Open your version of afadmprf.sql (located at $FND_TOP/admin/template). If the script contains the following SQL statement then upgrade to version 115.26 or higher of afadmprf.sh (you'll have to download this patch from MetaLink).

```
UPDATE WF_RESOURCES set text = 'SYSADMIN'
  WHERE name = 'WF_ADMIN_ROLE' AND type = 'WFTKN';
```

Now afadmprf.sql will contain the statement:

```
UPDATE WF_RESOURCES set text = '%s_wf_admin_role%'
  WHERE name = 'WF_ADMIN_ROLE' AND type = 'WFTKN';
```

To find the value to use in the SID.xml file, use the form to set the Workflow Administrator to your desired Role. Then perform the following query:

```
SELECT text from wf_resources
  WHERE name = 'WF_ADMIN_ROLE' AND type = 'WFTKN'
```

For example, if the administrator Role in Release 11.5.10 is set to Workflow Administrator Web Applications, the query will return FND_RESP|FND|FNDWF_ADMIN_WEB|STANDARD. Using this value the line in the context file becomes:

```
<username oa_var="_wf_admin_role">FND_RESP|FND|FNDWF_ADMIN_WEB|STANDARD</username>
```

Workflow Configuration for Cloned Database Instances

Cloning an Applications environment is a vital task in maintaining the overall health and welfare of your Oracle Applications System. Without the ability to effectively copy your production environment to a downstream environment you would have infinite problems testing patches, working through bugs, developing required code and then testing that code. While it is true that you could still do this in your production environment, doing so directly to your production environment is simply not recommended. Cloning, therefore, is one of the more vital skill sets your Applications DBA must have, as testing and developing on cloned instances is a primary key to a predictable and stable production system.

While the actual cloning steps themselves are out of scope for this book, we do want to make sure you have the necessary tools to ensure your Workflow environment is baggage free when you bring it over from production (or any other Applications environment you may be working with). To this end we will discuss several tables that may require updates after you have run your AutoConfig scripts but before you release the system for general use. We've also included sample code. In many cases, the sample code includes Solution Beacon-specific values – SBLLC12, a120int2, a120int4, etc. Be careful, therefore, to substitute your own values!

Throughout these scripts you will note that some of the values are uppercase and some are lowercase. All systems are very specific about the case of the values and so will yours. However, yours may be a different case so ensure that you take a few minutes to learn what these values look like in your system so you can combine these scripts into a single script that runs just after AutoConfig completes.

Oracle strives to improve the cloning process with each new release of the AutoConfig code, but it is always best to make sure the following tables have the correct information in them.

After completing AutoConfig of both tiers complete the following steps:

1. Stop all services on the Applications tier including the Concurrent Managers, no matter which tier they are on

2. Set the global Notification preference to 'Do not send me mail'

3. Change the email address in the employee and user tables (optional)

4. Update the FND_USER_PREFERENCES table

5. Update the WF_NOTIFICATIONS table

6. Update the FND_CONCURRENT_REQUESTS table

7. Update the FND_FORM_FUNCTIONS table

8. Update the FND_SVC_COMP_PARAM_VALS table

9. Update the ICX_PARAMETERS table

10. Update the WF_AGENTS table

11. Update the WF_ITEM_ATTRIBUTE_VALUES table

12. Update the WF_NOTIFICATION_ATTRIBUTES table

13. Update the WF_SYSTEMS table

14. Run the script to re-populate the WF_NOTIFICATION_OUT Queue

15. Set an override Notification Mailer address (optional)

Set the Global Notification Preference to 'Do not send me mail'

To prevent email Notification at the global level, set the Global Preference to 'Do not send me mail'. Instruct any individual that would like to receive their Notifications via email to click on the 'Preferences' link at the top of the Personal Home Page, and set the option 'Email Style' to 'HTML mail' or 'HTML mail with Attachments'.

Change the email Address in the Employee and User Tables (optional)

Do not remove the email addresses from the employee records. This causes the attempt to email the Notifications to error and adds records to the SYSADMIN's Notification Queue. Execute the following SQL statement if you would like to update the email addresses in the PER_ALL_PEOPLE_F table to a group email so Notifications for all employees will go to the same email address.

```
UPDATE per_all_people_f
SET email_address = '<group email>'
WHERE email_address is not null;
```

The corresponding SQL for FND_USER is:

```
UPDATE fnd_user
SET email_address = '<group email>'
WHERE email_address is not null;
```

Note that these updates do not update the email address in WF_LOCAL_ROLES. This update is:

```
UPDATE wf_local_roles
SET email_address = '<group email>'
```

```
WHERE email_address is not null AND partition_id = 1;
```

These updates will ensure most Notifications will now use the <group email>. However, other partitions exist in WF_LOCAL_ROLES with email addresses and over 500 tables with the column EMAIL_ADDRESS. Workflows may use the data in these tables to obtain an email address. For example, the PO Approval workflow uses the email_address in the supplier files to email POs.

Setting a test address is the only fail–safe method of preventing emails going to "real" email addresses You can set up a group email and assign this value to the test address. This causes all emails to be sent to this address instead of the email addresses in the employee, user or other tables records. This is preferable, since changing everyone's email in the cloned instance also means you lose the "production" look. Technicians will not be able to troubleshoot email related problems outside of the Workflow scope in the cloned instances. Instructions for this option are in the next section.

The test address may be set using OAM or the following SQL:

```
UPDATE fnd_svc_comp_param_vals a
   SET a.parameter_value = '<group email>'
 WHERE a.parameter_id =
       (SELECT c.parameter_id FROM fnd_svc_comp_params_vl c
          WHERE c.component_type = 'WF_MAILER'
            AND c.parameter_name = 'TEST_ADDRESS');
```

Update the FND_USER_PREFERENCES Table

Even if the Notification Mailer is not turned on, if individuals have set their preference to something other than 'Do not send me mail', then records will start accumulating in the table WF_NOTIFICATION_OUT with a STATE=0. Therefore, if the Notification Mailer is turned off, execute the following SQL statement to reset the individual preferences to QUERY:

```
UPDATE fnd_user_preferences
SET preference_value = 'QUERY'
WHERE preference_name = 'MAILTYPE' AND preference_name != 'QUERY';
```

Although NOTIFICATION_PREFERENCE is a column in WF_LOCAL_ROLES, the Notification Mailer does not use this field or this table to determine mailer preferences. Only the table FND_USER_PREFERENCES is used.

Notifications sent via Workflow are stored in the table WF_NOTIFICATIONS. This table has two columns, STATUS and MAIL_STATUS. STATUS is the status of the Notification in the Workflow. MAIL_STATUS is the status of the Notification as regards the Notification Mailer. Records with a MAIL_STATUS of NULL will not be mailed. While the Notification Mailer is not turned on, execute the following SQL statement to 'unmark' the Notifications that are marked for mailing:

```
UPDATE wf_notifications SET mail_status = NULL;
```

Per MetaLink Doc. ID 453137.1, *Oracle Workflow Best Practices Release 12 and Release 11i*, the Notification System raises the event oracle.apps.wf.notification.send for each Notification and enqueues it on the queue WF_NOTIFICATION_OUT, even if the Notification Mailer is down or the recipient has a Notification preference of QUERY. To avoid a buildup of records in this queue, disable the Subscription referencing an 'Out Agent' for the Group Subscription oracle.apps.wf.notification.send.group using the following SQL:

```
UPDATE wf_event_subscriptions
   SET status = 'DISABLED'
 WHERE out_agent_guid IS NOT NULL
```

```
AND event filter guid =
    (SELECT guid FROM wf events
       WHERE NAME = 'oracle.apps.wf.notification.send.group');
```

Note that since Oracle Alert uses the Notification Mailer, this will also disable emailing Alerts.

Update the FND_CONCURRENT_REQUESTS Table

The FND_CONCURRENT_REQUESTS table stores pathing information as part of the absolute name for the logfiles and outfiles. The following SELECT query shows you the information stored in the table containing the SID and HOST names from a Solution Beacon cloned source system. You may choose not to update this information since these files should have been removed as part of the overall cloning, but we'll provide you the update statements anyway.

```
SELECT * FROM applsys.fnd_concurrent_requests
 WHERE logfile_name LIKE '%a120int2%'
    OR    logfile_name LIKE '%sbllc12%'
    OR    logfile_node_name LIKE '%SBLLC12%'
    OR    outfile_name LIKE '%a120int2%'
    OR    outfile_name LIKE '%sbllc12%'
    OR    outfile_node_name LIKE '%SBLLC12%'
 ORDER BY logfile_node_name;

UPDATE applsys.fnd_concurrent_requests
   SET logfile_name = replace(logfile_name,'a120int2','a120int4')
 WHERE instr(logfile_name,'a120int2') != 0;

UPDATE applsys.fnd_concurrent_requests
   SET logfile_name = replace(logfile_name,'sbllc12','sbllc14')
 WHERE instr(logfile_name,'sbllc12') != 0;

UPDATE applsys.fnd_concurrent_requests
   SET outfile_name = replace(outfile_name,'a120int2','a120int4')
 WHERE instr(outfile_name,'a120int2') != 0;

UPDATE applsys.fnd_concurrent_requests
   SET outfile_name = replace(outfile_name,'sbllc12','sbllc14')
 WHERE instr(outfile_name,'sbllc12') != 0;

UPDATE applsys.fnd_concurrent_requests
   SET logfile_node_name = replace(logfile_node_name,'SBLLC12','SBLLC14')
 WHERE instr(logfile_node_name,'SBLLC12') != 0;

UPDATE applsys.fnd_concurrent_requests
   SET outfile_node_name = replace(outfile_node_name,'SBLLC12','SBLLC14')
 WHERE instr(outfile_node_name,'SBLLC12') != 0;
```

Update the FND_FORM_FUNCTIONS Table

This table stores the WEB_HOST_NAME and/or PL/SQL Listener name associated with a Form Function. Obviously, not all Form Functions are going to have associations so make sure to only change the rows that do. In this example, we provided a structure for doing the update; however, in our tests we haven't come across either a web host name or web Agent name that needed to be changed for cloning purposes.

```
SELECT web_host_name, web_agent_name FROM applsys.fnd_form_functions
 WHERE web_host_name IS NOT NULL OR web_agent_name IS NOT NULL;

UPDATE applsys.fnd_form_functions
```

```
      SET web_agent_name = replace(web_agent_name,' ',' ')
   WHERE instr(web_agent_name,' ') != 0;

   UPDATE applsys.fnd_form_functions
      SET web_host_name = replace(web_host_name,' ',' ')
   WHERE instr(web_host_name,' ') != 0;
```

Update the FND_SVC_COMP_PARAM_VALS Table

This table stores the URL for your system in at least one row. There may be additional URLs stored in this table but we are only concerned with this one value.

```
   select * from fnd_svc_comp_param_vals where parameter_value like 'http://%';

   update fnd_svc_comp_param_vals
      set parameter_value = replace(parameter_value,'sbllc12','sbllc14'),
      set parameter_value = replace(parameter_value,'8002','8003'),
      set parameter_value = replace(parameter_value,'a120int2','a120int3')
   where instr(parameter_value,'a120int2') != 0;
```

Update the ICX_PARAMETERS Table

This table stores the AppsLogin URL for your system in at least one row. Run the SELECT statement after cloning to insure that it has been correctly changed by AutoConfig. We have never seen AutoConfig miss this change but we do believe in being thorough.

```
   SELECT home_url FROM icx.icx_parameters;

   UPDATE icx.icx_parameters
      SET home_url = replace(home_url,'a120int1','a120int2')
   WHERE instr(home_url,'a120int1') != 0;
```

Update the WF_AGENTS Table

This table stores the address of the global database name for use with the Workflow Queues and links. Use the SELECT statement below to insure that the values are correct. If changes are needed, use an UPDATE statement like the one provided below.

```
   SELECT address FROM applsys.wf_agents;

   UPDATE applsys.wf_agents
      SET address = replace(address,'A120INT2','A120INT3')
   WHERE instr(address,'A120INT2') != 0;
```

The SYSTEM_GUID in this table must match GUID in WF_SYSTEMS. So after ensuring the system name in WF_SYSTEMS is correct (see "Update the WF_SYSTEMS Table" below), run the following SQL:

```
   UPDATE wf agents
      SET system guid = (SELECT guid FROM wf systems
                           WHERE NAME LIKE 'A510VIS3%')
   WHERE system guid <> (SELECT guid FROM wf systems
                           WHERE NAME LIKE 'A510VIS3%');
```

Update the WF_ITEM_ATTRIBUTE_VALUES Table

This table stores the text values that utilize the system's SID, HOST and PORT number. Our instances have lower case values but the SELECT statement below will find lower and upper case values to make sure we catch everything.

```
SELECT * FROM applsys.wf_item_attribute_values
 WHERE (text_value like '%a120int%'
    OR    text_value like '%sbllc%'
    OR    text_value like 'A120INT%'
    OR    text_value like '%SBLLC%')
 ORDER BY text_value;

UPDATE applsys.wf_item_attribute_values
    SET text_value = replace(text_value,'sbllc12','sbllc14')
 WHERE instr(text_value, 'sbllc') != 0;

UPDATE applsys.wf_item_attribute_values
    SET text_value = replace(text_value,'a120int2','a120int3')
 WHERE instr(text_value, 'a120int') != 0;

UPDATE applsys.wf_item_attribute_values
    SET text_value = replace(text_value,'8010','8016')
 WHERE instr(text_value, ':8010/') != 0;
```

Update the WF_NOTIFICATION_ATTRIBUTES Table

This table stores the web host information for your system.

```
SELECT * FROM applsys.wf_notification_attributes
 WHERE (text_value like '%a120int%'
    OR    text_value like '%sbllc%'
    OR    text_value like '%solutionbeacon%'
    OR    text_value like 'A120INT%'
    OR    text_value like '%SBLLC%')
 ORDER BY text_value;

UPDATE applsys.wf_notification_attributes
    SET text_value = replace(text_value,'sbllc12','sbllc14')
 WHERE instr(text_value, 'sbllc') != 0;

UPDATE applsys.wf_notification_attributes
    SET text_value = replace(text_value,'a120int2','a120int3')
 WHERE instr(text_value, 'a120int') != 0;

UPDATE applsys.wf_notification_attributes
    SET text_value = replace(text_value,'8010','8011')
 WHERE instr(text_value, ':8010/') != 0;
```

Update the WF_SYSTEMS Table

This table stores the fully qualified database global name in the NAME field. Assuming your clone remains in the same domain you will only need to insure that the database name is correct. The values in our system were uppercase but you should confirm what they are in your system. This is another table that we have not seen AutoConfig miss so you will probably not have to make a change here. But, as we have said previously, the efficiency of AutoConfig is dependent upon the patch level, so it is better to be safe than have strange problems.

```
SELECT * FROM applsys.wf_systems;

UPDATE applsys.wf_systems
    SET name = replace(name,'A120INT2','A120INT3')
 WHERE instr(name,'A120INT2') != 0;
```

Run the Script to Rebuild the WF_NOTIFICATION_OUT Queue

Oracle provides a script to rebuild the WF_NOTIFICATION_OUT Queue based on the MAIL_STATUS of records in WF_NOTIFICATIONS. Since the MAIL_STATUS is now null, running this script will dequeue all the existing records. This script is located in $FND_TOP/patch/115/sql. Run this script: (apw is the password to the APPS account):

```
sqlplus apps/<apw>@<database name> @wfntfqup apps <apw> applsys
```

Setting an Override Notification Mailer Address

For non-production instances, you should set an override Mailer address to allow for testing of Notifications without sending Notifications to users who may confuse them with production Notifications. See *Chapter 2, Setup*, for details on setting the override Notification Mailer address.

The Vacation Rules Tab

FIGURE 8.34 shows the 'Vacation Rules' screen. Visit this page when employees quit (or are suddenly incapacitated and can't set the Rules for themselves) to set Vacation Rules. Choose the employee or user and click the 'Create Rule' button.

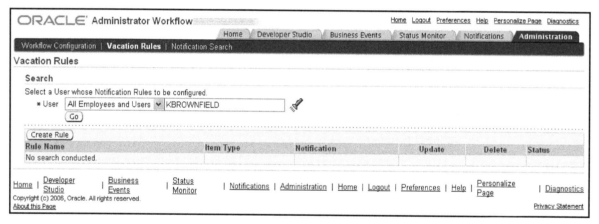

FIGURE 8.34

FIGURE 8.35 shows that Rules can be created by Item Type and by Notification to delegate or transfer ownership of Notifications. However, transfer may be limited in some cases such as for Payables Invoices when Approvals Management is implemented.

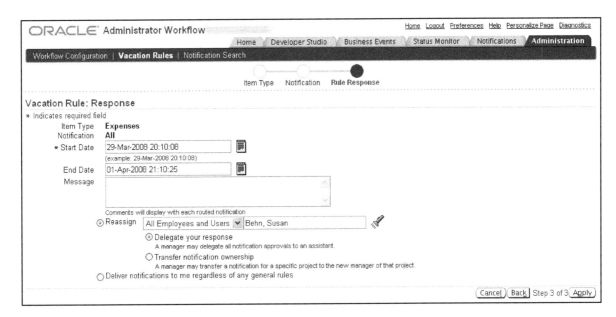

FIGURE 8. 35

Notification Search

To search for a Notification, you must specify either the 'Notification ID', 'Owner', 'To' or 'From'. Other selection criteria are optional. Once the list of Notifications is returned, click on the Subject to open the Notification. At that point, act upon the Notification or reassign it to another employee or user (see FIGURE 8.36).

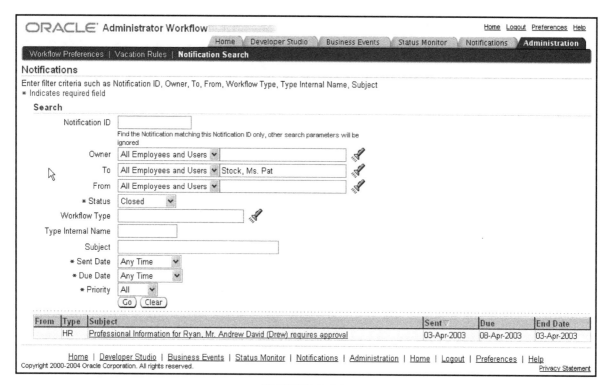

FIGURE 8. 36

Visit this page to transfer or delegate existing Notifications to another employee or user once the Vacation Rule is set to transfer or delegate future Notifications. This page can also be used to act upon any Notification as a delegate. This is useful for testing.

WHEN ALL ELSE FAILS – SOME SQL QUERIES

There may be times when you conclude that having all these tools at your disposal just can't beat reaching into the database and querying the tables yourself. This section includes some of our favorite code for doing so. We caution you again not to run update statements against your production database.

To Count Errors by Error Message

```
SELECT COUNT(*),message_type,SUBSTR(subject,1,25) FROM wf_notifications
WHERE recipient_role = 'SYSADMIN'
GROUP BY message_type, SUBSTR(subject,1,25);
```

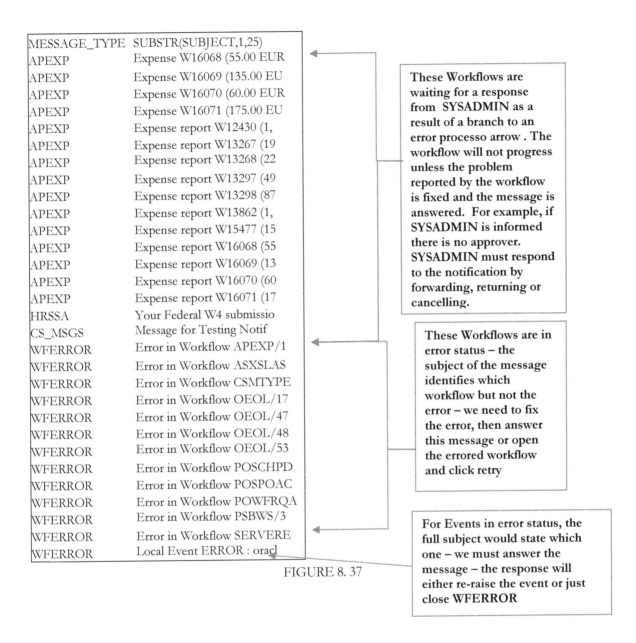

FIGURE 8. 37

To Determine Which Workflow/Event Invoked WFERROR

Use the following query to find which Workflow invoked WFERROR:

```
SELECT parent_item_type,COUNT(*) FROM wf_items
  WHERE item_type = 'WFERROR' GROUP BY parent_item_type;
```

If there is a row where PARENT_ITEM_TYPE is null, this indicates the number of events that have errored. To identify which events, use the following query:

```
SELECT   COUNT (*)
        ,v.text_value
```

```
       FROM wf_item_attribute_values v
      WHERE v.item_type = 'WFERROR'
        AND v.NAME = 'EVENT_NAME'
        AND v.text_value IS NOT NULL
        AND EXISTS
              (SELECT 'X'
                  FROM wf_item_activity_statuses s
                WHERE s.item_key = v.item_key
                  AND s.item_type = 'WFERROR'
                  AND s.activity_status = 'ERROR'
                  AND s.end_date IS NULL)
   GROUP BY text_value
   ORDER BY text_value;
```

The two queries at the end of *Chapter 13, New Features* can be used to display the detailed error messages from Workflows and events that error. Use MetaLink to research by either Event name or error message. Keep in mind the Messages may be old, and may have occurred in an earlier E-Business release. Follow the instructions in the MetaLink note or file a service request for additional assistance.

WFERRORs Still Not Closed

It is likely that the above counts include WFERRORs that reference closed or nonexistent Workflows. Remember to use the bde_wf_clean_worklist.sql program to close these Workflows. This script still may not close those Workflows linked to OEOL or OEOH. See MetaLink Doc. ID: 398822.1, *Order Management Suite – Data Fix Script Patch,* for two patches that provide scripts to help close any unnecessary OEOH, OEOL, and associated OMERROR and WFERROR Workflows. MetaLink Doc. ID 405275.1, *How to Detect Data Corruption and Purge More Eligible OEOH/OEOL Workflow Items for Order Management Workflow* contains a wealth of information for troubleshooting the OEOH and OEOL and ensuring history for these Workflows can be purged.

This script identifies WFERRORs still not closed:

```
prompt WFERRORS where parent Workflow doesn't exist
SELECT i1.parent_item_type,COUNT(*) FROM wf_items i1
 WHERE i1.item_type = 'WFERROR' AND i1.parent_item_type IS NOT NULL
   AND i1.parent_item_key NOT IN
     (SELECT i2.item_key FROM wf_items i2
       WHERE i2.item_type = i1.parent_item_type
         AND i2.item_key = i1.parent_item_key)
GROUP BY i1.parent_item_type;

prompt WFERRORS where parent Workflow is closed
SELECT i1.parent_item_type,COUNT(*) FROM wf_items i1
 WHERE i1.item_type = 'WFERROR' AND i1.parent_item_type IS NOT NULL
   AND i1.parent_item_key IN
     (SELECT i2.item_key FROM wf_items i2
       WHERE i2.item_type = i1.parent_item_type
         AND i2.item_key = i1.parent_item_key
         AND i2.end_date IS NOT NULL)
GROUP BY i1.parent_item_type;
```

WFERROR is not the only error–invoked Workflow

The above queries assume that when a Workflow errors, it calls WFERROR. However, any Workflow can be assigned as the Error Item Type. A query of the field ERROR_ITEM_TYPE in WF_ACTIVITIES yields that the following Workflows are assigned: CUNNLWF, DOSFLOW, DOSFLOWE, ECXERROR, HRSSA, HRSTAND, HXCEMP, IBUHPSUB, OKLAMERR, OMERROR, PARMAAP, PARMATRX, POERROR,

WFSTD, XDPWFSTD, and ZPBWFERR. The following query shows all the Workflows that have errored but that called another workflow other than WFERROR. This query also shows the earliest and latest occurrence of the error and whether the Error Item Type is open or closed.

```
SELECT   item_type
        ,parent_item_type
        ,DECODE (end_date, NULL, 'OPEN', 'CLOSED')
                  error_type_status
        ,COUNT (*)
  FROM wf_items
 WHERE parent_item_type is not null
   AND item_type in ('CUNNLWF','DOSFLOW','DOSFLOWE','ECXERROR','HRSSA',
       'HRSTAND','HXCEMP','IBUHPSUB','OKLAMERR','OMERROR','PARMAAP',
       'PARMATRX','POERROR','WFSTD','XDPWFSTD','ZPBWFERR')
GROUP BY item_type
        ,parent_item_type
        ,DECODE (end_date, NULL, 'OPEN', 'CLOSED')
ORDER BY item_type,parent_item_type;
```

HOW TO RESEND NOTIFICATIONS

Occasionally you may notice that users are no longer getting their Notifications via email. You've checked the obvious: the Notification Mailer is running, the global Notification preference has not been set to 'Do not send me mail'. Now what?

This section is based partly on MetaLink Doc. ID: 332152.1, *OWF H Diagnostics and Solutions*. This note is excellent for determining some of the common issues with the Java Notification Mailer in Release 11.5.10. This article assumes you are on Release 11.5.10. If this is not true, then you should check with Oracle Support or look at MetaLink Doc. ID: 260393.1, *Java Mailer and Other 11.5.9/OWF G Current Issues in Applications 11i*, or use Oracle Diagnostics to run the Java Mailer setup.

First we'll address the fact that no one is getting emails. Use the Test Mailer functionality in OAM to verify that the Notification Mailer is indeed working. If not, ask your Applications DBA to try bouncing the apache server. If this doesn't fix it, then bounce the whole database. If this doesn't work, regenerate the JAR files with FORCE. Run the Notification Mailer Diagnostic and fix any issues. Of course the final step is to file a Service Request (SR). However, usually one of the above steps will get the Notification Mailer running again. If you have applied 11i.ATG_PF.H.delta 5 (Rollup 5), see *Chapter 13, New Features* for the patches and parameter adjustments this RUP requires. Unfortunately, Notifications created before fixing the Notification Mailer may still show as not mailed.

Identify which Notifications weren't mailed. This can be verified by the following query:

```
SELECT status,mail_status,count(*) FROM wf_notifications
GROUP BY status, mail_status;
```

You may get results such as:

```
STATUS      MAIL STATUS    COUNT(*)
CANCELED    ERROR               79
CLOSED      ERROR              101
OPEN        ERROR              201
CLOSED      MAIL                 1
CANCELED    SENT               465
CLOSED      SENT             27183
OPEN        SENT             11642
```

```
CANCELED              669
CLOSED               5500
OPEN                 5971
```

OPEN is either an 'FYI' Notification that hasn't been closed or a 'Response Required' Notification that hasn't been responded to yet. CLOSED means the Notification can no longer be acted upon (i.e., 'FYI' was closed, or 'Response Required' replied to). CANCELED means either the Notification timed out or the Workflow was aborted.

MAIL_STATUS indicates the status of the email copy of the Notification. NULL indicates no email will be sent. SENT indicates the email was sent. MAIL indicates the Notification Mailer has not acted on this transaction. ERROR indicates that the Notification Mailer tried to email the Notification but couldn't.

Option to Resend Notifications with mail_status = 'ERROR'

With 11i.ATG_PF.H Rollup 3 (see MetaLink Doc. ID: 337274.1, *About Oracle Applications Technology 11i.ATG_PF.H Rollup 3*) there is a new program that will requeue Notifications with a mail status of ERROR (See FIGURE 8.38). You can choose to resend all, or only those for a particular Item Type, or only those to a specific recipient. You can also specify a date range based on the date of the original Notification attempt. However, before running this program, you should look for Messages in SYSADMIN's Queue, find out why the Notifications are erroring and fix the problem. If the underlying issue is still present, the Notifications will just error again. Note that running this program does not rewind the Workflow; it just resends the Notification. Also, for Notifications that have been canceled or closed, there is really no need to mail these Notifications. Thus, you may want to run the following update first:

```
UPDATE wf_notifications
   SET mail_status = NULL
 WHERE mail_status = 'ERROR'
   AND status in ('CLOSED','CANCELLED');
```

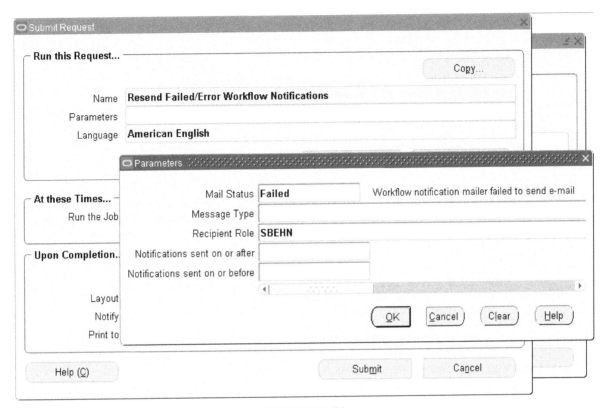

FIGURE 8. 38

Don't Email Closed Notifications

In our example, there is one email with a status of CLOSED and a Mail Status of MAIL. Again, there is no reason to mail a closed Notification. Use SQL to change the Mail Status to NULL.

```
UPDATE wf_notifications
SET mail_status = NULL
WHERE mail_status = 'MAIL'
AND status in ('CLOSED','CANCELLED');
```

Know Your Data – FYI Notifications vs. Response Notifications

Suppose that our query had returned the following:

STATUS	MAIL STATUS	COUNT(*)
CANCELED	ERROR	79
CLOSED	ERROR	101
OPEN	MAIL	201
CLOSED	MAIL	1
CANCELED	SENT	465
CLOSED	SENT	27183
OPEN	SENT	11642
CANCELED		669
CLOSED		5500
OPEN		5971

You should still do the above updates to avoid resending closed Notifications. However, now there are 201 Notifications that should have been mailed, but have not been. We assume that regardless of age, any

Notification that is open and still is waiting for a response should be emailed. However, some of the 201 Notifications may be 'FYI' Notifications (which don't require a response) and may be so old that they shouldn't be emailed. Do the following query to identify the 'FYI' Notifications:

```
SELECT n.notification_id, n.message_type, n.message_name,
       n.recipient_role,n.begin_date
  FROM wf_notifications n,wf_activities a
 WHERE n.message_name = a.message
         AND n.status = 'OPEN'
   AND n.mail_status = 'MAIL'
   AND a.result_type IS NULL;
```

For the identified 'FYI' Notifications, you must decide whether to resend all, none, or only those that have a recent begin date (for example, less than a week old). To resend all, proceed to the next paragraph. To resend none, execute the following update:

```
UPDATE wf_notifications
   SET mail_status = NULL WHERE notification_id in
        (SELECT n.notification_id FROM wf_notificaitons n, wf_activities a
          WHERE n.message_name = a.message
            AND n.status = 'OPEN'
            AND n.mail_status = 'MAIL'
            AND a.result_type IS NULL);
```

To resend only those less than a week old, execute the following update:

```
UPDATE wf_notifications
   SET mail_status = NULL
        WHERE notification_id in
        (SELECT n.notification_id FROM wf_notificaitons n, wf_activities a
            WHERE n.message_name = a.message
              AND n.status = 'OPEN'
              AND n.mail_status = 'MAIL'
              AND a.result_type IS NULL
              AND n.begin_date < (SYSDATE-7));
```

Rebuild WF_NOTIFICATION_OUT

Emails are sent using the oracle.apps.wf.notification.% Events. Sometimes invalid data is cached in these Events and they get stuck in the Queues. Initially the Event is stored in the WF_DEFERRED Queue and then moved to WF_NOTIFICATION_OUT. So do the following steps (these steps are taken directly from MetaLink Doc. ID: 332152.1):

1. Determine your patch level. The following steps assume that OWF.H has been applied (Workflow patch level in Release 11.5.10). Some of the steps are dependant on whether ATG CU2 has been applied (included in Release 11.5.10 CU2). The following script will list installed patches, so if Release 11.5.10 CU2 and ATG CU2 aren't listed, they aren't installed.

2. Shut down the Workflow Mailer Service and 'Workflow Agent Listener Service' (ideally this should be done when users are out of the database).

3. Run the following to remove oracle.apps.wf.notification.% Events from the WF_DEFERRED Queue.

    a. If you have not applied Release 11.5.10 CU2 and ATG CU2

        ```
        sqlplus apps/<pswd> @FND_TOP/sql/wfevqcln.sql WF_DEFERRED oracle.apps.wf.notification.%
        ```

b. If you have applied Release 11.5.10 CU2 (or higher) or ATG CU2 (or higher)

```
sqlplus apps/<pswd> @FND_TOP/sql/wfevqcln.sql WF_DEFERRED oracle.apps.wf.notification.% 0
```

4. Run the following statement to verify that all the oracle.apps.wf.notification.% Events either do not exist in the WF_DEFERRED Queue or are in a Retained State (STATE = 2).

```
set linesize 155;
set pagesize 200;
set verify off;
select substr(wfd.corrid,1,45) corrid,
        substr(wfd.user_data.event_name,1,45) EVENT_NAME,
        decode(wfd.state,
                    0,'0=Ready',
                    1,'1=Delayed',
                    2,'2=Processed/Retained',
                    3,'3=Exception',
                    to_char(substr(wfd.state,1,12))) STATE,
            count(*) COUNT
from applsys.wf_deferred wfd
group by wfd.corrid, wfd.user_data.event_name,wfd.state;
```

Sample Results are shown in FIGURE 8.39:

CORRID	EVENT_NAME	STATE	COUNT
APPS:oracle.apps.wf.notification.send	oracle.apps.wf.notification.send	2=Processed/Retained	288

FIGURE 8. 39

5. Recreate the Workflow histograms. Note that <fndusr> is, by default, APPLSYS

```
sqlplus apps/<pswd> @$FND_TOP/patch/115/sql/wfhistc <fndusr>
```

6. Create indexes on the WF Queue tables.

a. First, find the name of the INDEX tablespace. The original script has 'where index_name like 'WF_%_N1', but this yields the tablespaces for Workflow Activity tables and seed data tables as well. You can run the original script to ensure that there are not multiple tablespaces, but the only two Queues that were impacted by the above scripts are WF_DEFERRED and WF_NOTIFICATION_OUT.

```
SELECT tablespace_name, index_name FROM dba_indexes
WHERE index_name in ('WF_DEFERRED_N1','WF_NOTIFICATION_OUT_N1');
```

b. Run the script based on your patch level. Note that <fndusr> is, by default, APPLSYS.
  i. If you have not applied Release 11.5.10 CU2 and ATG CU2:

```
sqlplus apps/<pswd> @FND_TOP/patch/115/sql/wfquidxc <fnduser> <fnduser pswd> <tablespace name>
```

  ii. If you have applied Release 11.5.10 CU2 (or higher) or ATG CU2 (or higher):

```
sqlplus apps/<pswd> @FND_TOP/patch/115/sql/wfquidxc2 <fnduser> <fnduser pswd> <tablespace name>
```

7. Restart the Workflow Mailer Service and the 'Workflow Agent Listener Service'. Repeat the script from Step 4. You may have to repeat it several times. The key to a successful rebuild is that the STATE will change from 0 to 2. Note that once the STATE changes to 2, Oracle will purge the record from the Queue after 24 hours. If the STATE does not change, then file a Service Request (SR) with Oracle Support.

RECOMMENDATIONS

This section summarizes our recommendations for administering your Workflow environment:

- Verify the user SYSADMIN has no Notifications

- Use Worklist Access to read SYSADMIN's Notifications or use Vacation Rules to transfer them

- Visit Knowledge → Knowledge Browser → Workflow at least once a month

    ◆ The 'All Articles' tab is sorted by note date – review all notes since your last review

    ◆ Be careful of scripts older than 2004 – these may only be applicable to Release 11.5.7 and lower

- Visit Oracle Applications Manager (OAM) daily

    ◆ Review the Dashboard

    ◆ Review and clean up Work Items in error

    ◆ For Agent Activity, if Ready Count is increasing and Processed Count is zero, Notifications are undeliverable. Check the Notification Mailer

WHAT'S NEXT

As if you haven't already seen enough tools to examine your Workflow environment, Oracle has kindly provided a set of Diagnostic Reports. You should run the Diagnostic Reports periodically as described in the next chapter, *Chapter 9, Diagnostics*.

Diagnostics

Diagnostic Reports for Workflow are provided as SQL scripts to be executed at the database level and as XML reports to be executed at the application level. This chapter describes both the SQL and XML Diagnostic Reports identifying differences and similarities. A brief introduction on the new application level Diagnostics tool is also included. Refer to MetaLink Doc. ID: 167000.1, *Oracle E-Business Suite Diagnostics for Release 11i and 12 Installation Instructions*, for detailed documentation about Oracle Diagnostics. Oracle creates new Diagnostic Tests frequently. It is your Applications DBA's responsibility to track new Diagnostic patches and apply them to your environment. See *Chapter 8, Administration*, and *Chapter 1, Introduction*, for more details about Applications DBA Workflow-related administrative tasks.

THE BASICS

What is Oracle Diagnostics?

The Oracle Diagnostics framework provides a test repository, execution engine, and user interface for customers, support analysts, and developers to plug-in Diagnostic Test tools/scripts. Users can run these tests either for troubleshooting or for periodic sanity checks of Oracle Workflow setup, status, and execution details. Each execution of a test tool/script generates an output report that provides detailed information, remediation, and additional references.

The Diagnostic Reports available at the application level are intended to provide all the details that have been traditionally available through the Workflow SQL scripts located in $FND_TOP/sql at the database level. However, the SQL scripts and the Diagnostic Reports might not always be in sync. They are also not a one for one replacement, as will be detailed later in this chapter. The Workflow Administrator should be familiar with both the traditional SQL scripts and Diagnostic Reports and understand the benefits and drawbacks of each troubleshooting tool. FIGURE 9.1 outlines some of the differences in the two types of troubleshooting reports.

Oracle Diagnostics	$FND_TOP/sql scripts
Available at application level with built-in security	Requires UNIX access to get to scripts. Requires SQL access to run scripts.
Can be run by non-technical users	Requires technical expertise in UNIX and SQL
User friendly html format with links	Text output.
Includes references to MetaLink Doc. IDs	No references
Includes details to remediate error conditions	Limited information on remediation
Sometimes not as up to date as SQL scripts	Generally updated before Diagnostics
Stores historical output until purged	No history
Can be scheduled to run periodically	Scheduling would be manual through UNIX tools such as cron, or by creating a custom Concurrent Program to run the program and scheduling through the Concurrent Manager
Batch reporting available	No batch reporting

TABLE 9.1

Access to Diagnostics and Security

Diagnostics are accessed via the following Navigation Paths

- Oracle Applications Manager (OAM) → Diagnostics

- Oracle Diagnostics Tool Responsibility

- CRM HTML Administration Responsibility → Setup → Diagnostics

- http://<domain_name>/OA_HTML/jtflogin.jsp

- The Diagnostics link shows in the upper right hand corner of the 'Home' page if the Profile Option 'FND: Diagnostics', is set to Yes (See FIGURE 9.1):

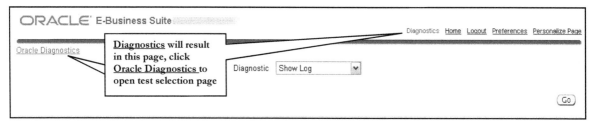

FIGURE 9. 1

Some standalone tests still exist in older versions of the Diagnostics tool that must be run from UNIX or SQL*Plus. These are denoted by an * in the Diagnostic Report library.

Users can only run tests for which they are assigned an applicable responsibility. For example, most Workflow tests will require the 'Workflow Administrator' or 'System Administrator' responsibility. However, the 'PO Requisition Test' that reports details about the 'Requisition Approval' Workflow requires a purchasing responsibility. It is safe to assign the 'Oracle Diagnostics Tool' responsibility to many users due to these built-in security features.

Grouping of Diagnostic Tests

Diagnostic Tests are grouped by application, then grouped by type of test. For most applications, tests are grouped as:

- **Setup** – required setups, validity of existing setups, mutual exclusion issues

- **Activity** – details related to a specific Activity (e.g., 'Period Closing Tests')

- **Data Collection** – application and system data. Use to validate conversions and upgrades. (e.g., Invoices, Workflow Item Errors, Active Users)

Other groupings are created as appropriate for applications such as Application Object Library (FND). For example, Workflow Tests can be found in the following groups:

- **Workflow Tests** – includes setup and status tests

- **Mailer Tests** – Diagnostic Test for specific Notification

Since Workflow Tests are available in multiple applications, the best way to find all the Workflow Diagnostic Tests is to utilize the search functionality on the 'Diagnostic Home' page. Most Workflow Reports can be found by using the key words workflow, generator, approval and notification.

Running Diagnostic Tests

- To run a Diagnostic Report, first click on the 'Advanced' tab at the top of the screen. Advanced reports require that users input parameters. Next, choose the 'Application' and click the + sign on the left-hand side of the screen to expand a group and choose a report. In FIGURE 9.2, notice that the Application at the top of the screen for Workflow Diagnostics is Application Object Library, rather than Workflow. Oracle bundles a number of products under Application Object Library because they affect the entire E-Business Suite.

In FIGURE 9.2, the 'Application Object Library' has been selected for the Application, and 'Workflow Tests' has been selected to list the available Diagnostic Tests. 'Workflow Status Monitor' is the identified report. The description at the top of the page defines the purpose of the report. Following the description, the parameter section will describe parameters and indicate which parameters are required. Enter the parameters required and click the 'Run Test' button.

ORACLE
Diagnostics

Home   Logout   Help

Home | Basic | **Advanced** | Configuration

Application [Application Object Library ▼]

Workflow Tests - Workflow Status Monitor

⊞ Logging Tests

⊞ EBusinessSecurity

⊞ Database Tests

⊟ Workflow Tests
Duplicate User Test
Notification Preference
Validation Test
Rule Function Validation
Test
GSM Setup Test
BES Clone Test
GSC Control Queue Test
Workflow Advanced
Queue Rule Validation
Test
Workflow Agents/AQ
Status Test
Workflow Objects Validity
Test
XML Parser Installation
Test
Mailer Component Test
Mailer Component
Parameter Test
Workflow Advance Queue
Check
Event Diagnostic Test
Workflow Status Monitor
Worklist User Interface

⊞ TechStack_Tests

⊞ SSO Setup Tests

⊞ Mailer Tests

⊞ Web Services
Tests

⊞ XML Gateway
Tests

⊞ OID Setup

⊞ Oracle Applications
Manager

⊞ Setup

⊞ Setup (continued)

Description: The Workflow Status Monitor is an user interface to monitor and intervene in workflow items. Execute this test to get information about the Workflow Status Monitor. If there is a service request logged for an issue occuring in Workflow Status Monitor pages, please upload the test output to support.

Parameters:
Apps Password is required in order to run and spool the output of the seeded script "$FND_TOP/sql/wfver.sql".

To resolve any issues with the execution of this test, please refer to the Diagnostics FAQ

Responsibility ID [20420]

Apps Password [●●●●]

[Run Test]

FIGURE 9. 2

Viewing Test Results

When the test is completed, the results will be returned to this page (see FIGURE 9.3). Click on the Report icon 🗗 on the right to view the report.

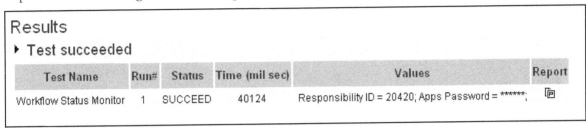

FIGURE 9. 3

The Results page may say 'Test failed' or 'Test succeeded with Warnings' or 'Severe Error occurred in test'. Except for the last, this doesn't indicate that the Diagnostic isn't working, it indicates that it found issues that need to be addressed. Open the report and look at the Summary. It will have links to all the sections in the report. If there is a red x next to the section, there are problems that should be addressed immediately. If there is a yellow caution marker, then the Diagnostic found issues that need to be addressed, but they aren't usually critical. If there is no caution flag, then search the report for the word Warning.

Finding the Diagnostic Version and Date

If you are reporting an SR on the Diagnostic, Support will ask for the version and date of your Diagnostics tools. Right–click on the title of the Diagnostic and select 'View Source'. Copy what displays and include it in your Service Request (SR). See FIGURE 9.4:

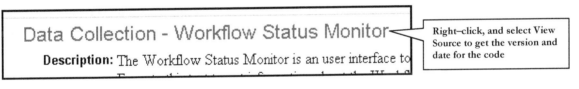

FIGURE 9. 4

Administration Workflow Tests

Workflow Diagnostic Tests are located in many applications and groups within the Oracle Diagnostics tool. FIGURE 9.5 shows the groups located in the Application Object Library. The tests located in the Application Object Library module are traditionally used by the technical team. However, many of these tests, such as 'Workflow Item Detail', would be beneficial for the functional team. Tests can be moved or added to other applications and groups if preferred. Refer to the Diagnostics documentation provided by Oracle for instructions on adding tests to test groups.

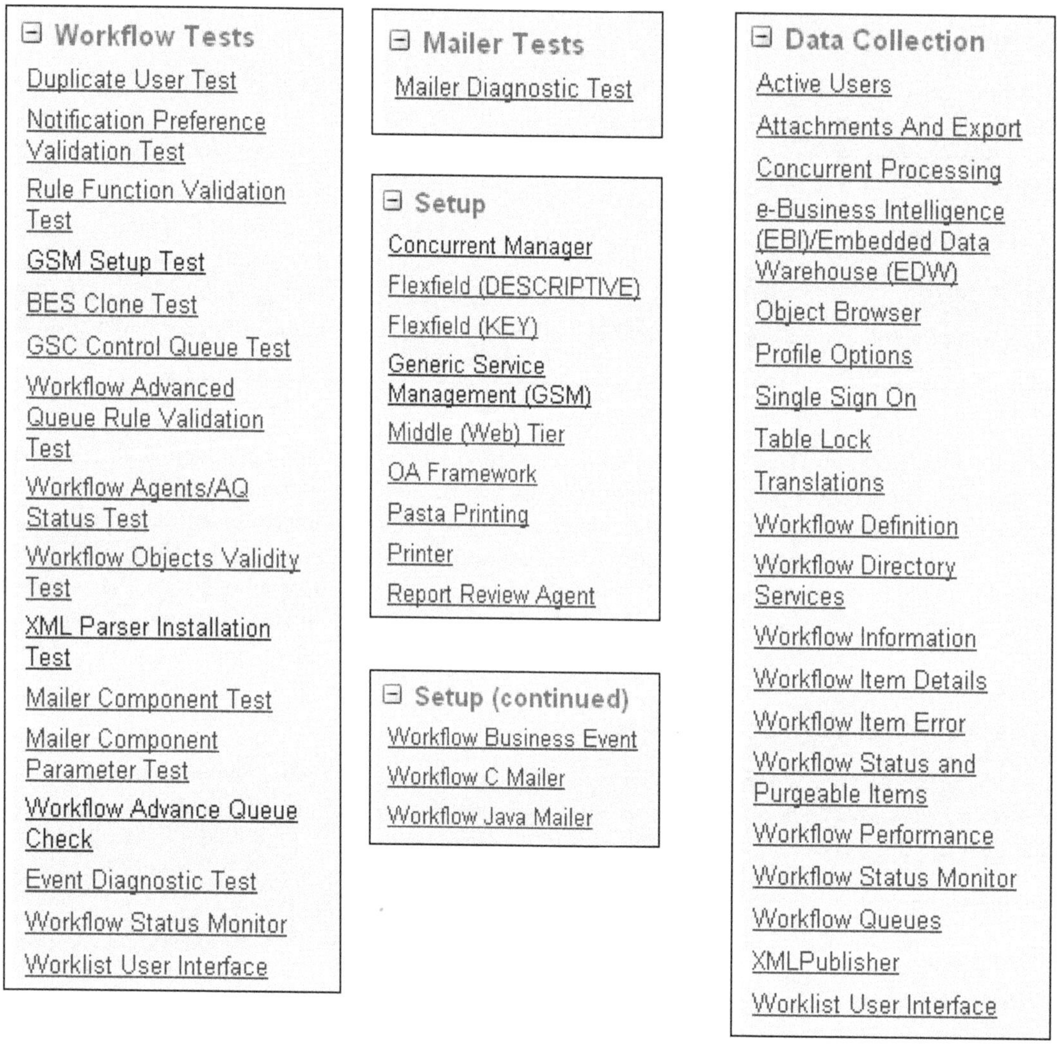

⊟ **Workflow Tests**

Duplicate User Test

Notification Preference
Validation Test

Rule Function Validation
Test

GSM Setup Test

BES Clone Test

GSC Control Queue Test

Workflow Advanced
Queue Rule Validation
Test

Workflow Agents/AQ
Status Test

Workflow Objects Validity
Test

XML Parser Installation
Test

Mailer Component Test

Mailer Component
Parameter Test

Workflow Advance Queue
Check

Event Diagnostic Test

Workflow Status Monitor

Worklist User Interface

⊟ **Mailer Tests**

Mailer Diagnostic Test

⊟ **Setup**

Concurrent Manager

Flexfield (DESCRIPTIVE)

Flexfield (KEY)

Generic Service
Management (GSM)

Middle (Web) Tier

OA Framework

Pasta Printing

Printer

Report Review Agent

⊟ **Setup (continued)**

Workflow Business Event

Workflow C Mailer

Workflow Java Mailer

⊟ **Data Collection**

Active Users

Attachments And Export

Concurrent Processing

e-Business Intelligence
(EBI)/Embedded Data
Warehouse (EDW)

Object Browser

Profile Options

Single Sign On

Table Lock

Translations

Workflow Definition

Workflow Directory
Services

Workflow Information

Workflow Item Details

Workflow Item Error

Workflow Status and
Purgeable Items

Workflow Performance

Workflow Status Monitor

Workflow Queues

XMLPublisher

Worklist User Interface

FIGURE 9. 5

The best way to become familiar with the Workflow Diagnostic reports is to start with the Diagnostic Library on MetaLink. These reports are very well documented. FIGURE 9.6 shows an example of the documentation for the 'Workflow Item Error Data Collection Test' Diagnostic Report. Required inputs and outputs are clearly identified.

Oracle Workflow Cartridge (WF): Workflow Item Error Data Collection Test

Updated: 31-Jan-2007

Usage Quick Reference

Diagnostics Tab	Application Name	Test Group	Test Name
Advanced	Application Object Library	Data Collection	Workflow Item Error

Description

This data collection test will gather item errors based on the item type provided.

No validation will be done on the data collected, therefore no error or warning messages will be provided.

Details

Input (* required)

- Responsibility Id *
- Item Type * (LOV)

Output

- Errored Item Summary
- Summary of Errant Items By Item Type, Result And Activity
- Summary of Errant Items By Item Type, Item Key

FIGURE 9. 6

It is also helpful to run the Diagnostic Reports to become familiar with the data provided. FIGURE 9.7 shows a portion of the output for the 'Summary of Errant Items' report for the 'AP Invoice Approval' (APINV) Item Type.

Summary of Errant Items by Item Type, Result and Activity   [Top]

Item Type	Result	Process Activity Label	Instance Id	Error Count
APINV	#EXCEPTION	APINV_M:APINV_IA	436703	2

1 row retrieved

Summary of Errant Items by Item Type, Item Key   [Top]

Item Type	Result	Process Activity Label	Instance Id	Item Key	Item Type	Error Key
APINV	#EXCEPTION	APINV_M:APINV_IA	436703	50161_1		
APINV	#EXCEPTION	APINV_M:APINV_IA	436703	50166_1	WFERROR	WF105184

2 rows retrieved

FIGURE 9. 7

We recommend running key Diagnostic Reports after upgrades or patching. For example, the 'Duplicate User Test' is critical in Release 11.5.10 and above. In earlier releases, it was common practice to link multiple users to a single employee for a variety of reasons. This is no longer acceptable. The Duplicate User Test will identify where this has occurred. Failure to correct this problem causes problems in Directory Services and may result in the delivery failure of a Notification.

Another critical test is the 'Notification Preference Validation Test'. This test will identify users who have a Notification preference to receive email, but do not have an email address. This is also a common source of Workflow errors.

Other tests to run after patching and upgrades include:

- **Rule Function Validation Test** – checks the Rule Functions defined for Subscriptions and the generate Functions defined for Events in the Business Event System. For PL/SQL Functions, the test verifies that the Package and Function exist in the database and are valid. For Java Functions, the test verifies that the Java class exists in the classpath

- **GSM Setup Test** – checks the Generic Service Management (GSM) setup required for Workflow in OAM and verifies that GSM and Workflow Service instances are enabled

- **BES Clone Test** – checks certain standard Agents and Subscriptions required for the internal Business Event System and Notification Mailer Processing to verify they are enabled and their definitions include the correct Local System

- **GSC Control Queue Test** – verifies that the Workflow Control Queue, WF_CONTROL, is properly accessible. The Generic Service Component Framework uses this Queue to handle control Events for Containers and Service Components

- **Workflow Advanced Queue Rule Validation Test** – checks the standard WF_ERROR and WF_DEFERRED Queues to verify that only one Subscriber Rule is defined for each Queue. These Queues are reserved for internal Workflow Processing; do not add any custom Subscribers to these Queues

- **Workflow Agents/AQ Status Test** – checks the Business Event System Agents for Workflow and XML Gateway, as well as the Queues associated with these Agents. The test verifies that the Agents are enabled within the Business Event System. It also verifies that the QUEUES and the QUEUE tables in which they reside are valid database objects, and that the Queues are enabled for enqueuing and dequeuing within Oracle Streams Advanced Queuing

- **Workflow Objects Validity Test** – checks the Workflow and XML Gateway database objects to verify that all the objects are valid

- **XML Parser Installation Test** – checks your applications installation to verify that the Oracle XML parser is installed and valid

- **Mailer Component Test** – checks the Notification Mailer Service Components to verify that at least one Notification Mailer has been configured with all the parameters needed to run it

- **Mailer Component Parameter Test** – checks your Notification Mailer Service Components to validate their configuration parameters. The test checks only those Notification Mailers for which all mandatory configuration parameters have been defined

In addition to running Diagnostic Reports after upgrades and patching, the following Workflow Diagnostic Tests should be run monthly to validate the health of the Workflow system.

- **Event Diagnostic Test** – MetaLink Doc. ID: 229404.1, *Oracle Workflow Cartridge Workflow Business Event Setup Test*

- **Workflow Java Mailer** – MetaLink Doc. ID: 274764.1, *Oracle Workflow Cartridge Workflow Java Mailer Setup Test*

- **Workflow Queues** – MetaLink Doc. ID: 248395.1, *Oracle Workflow Cartridge Workflow Queues Setup Test*

- **Workflow Information** – MetaLink Doc. ID: 279166.1, *Oracle Workflow cartridge Workflow Information Data Collection Test*

- **Workflow Performance** – MetaLink Doc. ID: 286672.1, *Oracle Workflow Cartridge Performance Data Collection Test*

- **Workflow Directory Services** – MetaLink Doc. ID: 388458.1, *Oracle Workflow Cartridge Directory Services Data Collection Test*

- **Workflow Status and Purgeable Items** – MetaLink Doc. ID: 388459.1, *Oracle Workflow Cartridge Workflow Status and Purgeable Items Data Collection Test*

Table 9.2 provides a map of the most frequently used scripts available in the database in $FND_TOP/sql to the reports available in the Oracle Diagnostics tool with a brief description and guidelines for report usage.

FND_TOP/sql Test	Oracle Diagnostics Test	Description
wfbesdbg.sql	Application Object Library --> Workflow Tests --> Event Diagnostic Test	Check the setup for an Event – Status, Subscriptions and Listener status. Use this report as a starting point to debug Event errors.
wfbkgchk.sql	Application Object Library --> Data Collection --> Workflow Queues	Status report on background work waiting to be processed. Use this report to resolve problems when activities get stuck in a wait state in Queues.
wfdirchk.sql	Application Object Library --> Data Collection --> Workflow Directory Services	Check Directory Services data model for all known problems. This output is requested for open Service Requests related to Directory Services. When emails or Notifications from Workflow are not received, start with this report.
wfmlrdbg.sql	Application Object Library --> Mailer Tests --> Mailer Diagnostic Test	This script gives all the required information for a Notification – Recipient, Status, Mail Status etc. Start with this report to debug a specific Notification that is not received.
wfver.sql	Application Object Library --> Data Collection --> Workflow Information	Displays diagnostic information for all components, product installation status and versions, Role errors and more. Executes `wfver.sql`. This report is requested when a Workflow related Service Request is opened.
wfverchk.sql	None	When Workflows are modified, Versioning keeps track of the current version for new Workflows that are starting, but Workflows in process continue in the version started. This script checks all Workflow activities for potentially invalid version histories (more than one version of an activity active at any given time). Invalid versions are corrected.
wfsmrdbg.sql	None	This script gives all the required information for summary Notifications. This includes who is set up to receive summary Notifications, templates, schedule, etc.
wfstatus.sql	Application Object Library --> Data Collection --> Workflow Item Details and Workflow Item Error	Workflow item Status report with error details. This report will provide information that appears in Oracle Applications Manager or through Workflow Administration. For users without access to those Functions, this report will provide all the information needed to troubleshoot errors.

Table 9.2

Other Workflow Tests

Use the search functionality shown in FIGURE 9.8 in the Oracle Diagnostic Tool to search for other Workflow-related tests related to specific modules. Search all applications for key words such as Workflow, generator (for Account Generators) and approval. Also search test names for specific names such as 'Account Generator.' Finding all the Workflow tests through the search functionality will require a little experimentation.

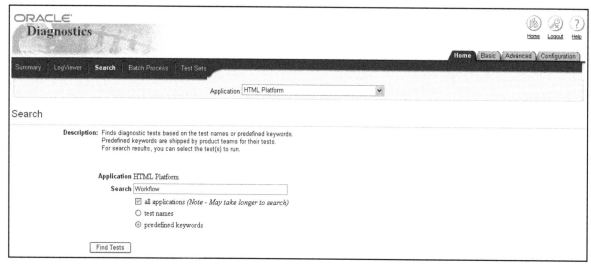

FIGURE 9. 8

Some application-related Workflow tests include the 'Requisition Approval' Workflow Status report to check the approval status of an *i*Procurement purchase requisition and the COGS Debug report for troubleshooting issues related to the cost of goods sold Account Generator in Order Management. Account Generator reports also exist for Assets, Projects and Purchasing.

SUMMARY

Many of the details available in the reports located in the Oracle Diagnostic Tool are generally available to Applications DBAs and Workflow Administrators through Oracle Applications Manager (OAM) and/or Workflow Administration. However, most functional users do not have access to OAM or Workflow Administration. With the security built in to the Oracle Diagnostic Tool, most users can be given access to these error reports to allow SuperUsers to troubleshoot issues that are often more easily resolved by the functional experts. Since Diagnostic Tool reports do not contain sensitive data, do not update data and as a general rule do not return more than the first 100 rows for any query, experimenting in this module is safe with minimal concern for performance impact.

WHAT'S NEXT

This book has discussed Workflow and Business Event System setup, developing and testing custom Workflows, administering Workflows, customizing Account Generator Workflows and how to use Oracle Diagnostics to enhance administration of Workflow. The next chapter will explain the major tables that store all the Workflow data and provide some simple SQL queries to review this data for both reporting and additional troubleshooting.

Workflow Tables

There are five types of Workflow tables: Run-time, Design, Event, Directory Services, and Miscellaneous. This chapter will discuss the major tables in each group and provide some simple queries to extract data from these tables.

WORKFLOW IS LANGUAGE ENABLED

Like most of the E-Business Suite tables, the Workflow tables support multiple languages. Thus, for many of the tables there is a corresponding _TL table. These tables allow the storage and display of the Display Names and descriptions in multiple languages. Like all _TL tables, the translations of the user-defined data are not automatic. The data must be entered in the correct language and the language must be enabled in the database. To use the Builder to load the Workflows requires additional setups on the PC. These setups and the Procedure for loading and using the Workflow in other languages are detailed in the *Oracle Workflow Administrator's Guide* (either *Release 12 Part No. B31431-01 December 2006* or *Release 2.6.4 Part No. B 15853-04 July 2006*).

As each group of tables is discussed, the tables that also have a _TL counterpart will be identified. The _TL counterpart stores the same primary key, Display Name, Description, and Language.

DESIGN VS. RUN-TIME

The tables used to store the design of the Workflow are very similar to those used to store the run-time information. The names and the columns are similar. The corresponding tables are:

```
Design                   Run-time
WF_ITEM_TYPES            WF_ITEMS
WF_ITEM_ATTRIBUTES      WF_ITEM_ATTRIBUTE_VALUES
WF_ACTIVITIES           WF_ACTIVITY_STATUSES
                        WF_ACTIVITY_STATUSES_H
WF_MESSAGES             WF_NOTIFICATIONS
WF_MESSAGE_ATTRIBUTES   WF_NOTIFICATION_ATTRIBUTES
                        WF_COMMENTS
```

There are several design tables without an equivalent run-time equivalent. These tables are:

- WF_LOOKUPS_TL

- WF_LOOKUP_TYPES_TL

- WF_PROCESS_ACTIVITIES

- WF_ACTIVITY_TRANSITIONS

- WF_ACTIVITY_ATTRIBUTES

- WF_ACTIVITY_ATTR_VALUES

Note that WF_LOOKUPS_TL and WF_LOOKUP_TYPES_TL only exist as translation tables. There is neither WF_LOOKUPS nor WF_LOOKUP_TYPES. The following tables, however, have a corresponding translation (_TL) table:

- WF_ITEM_TYPES

- WF_ITEM_ATTRIBUTES

- WF_ACTIVITIES

- WF_ACTIVITY_ATTRIBUTES

- WF_MESSAGES

- WF_MESSAGE_ATTRIBUTES

There are several sources for obtaining an entity relationship diagram (ERD) of these tables. None of them show the complete picture, but together they provide much information.

1. MetaLink Doc. ID: 444446.1, *Diagram Relationship between Core Workflow Tables,* is the clearest source.

2. The link in MetaLink Doc. ID: 150230.1, *ETRM DIRECT ACCESS DOCUMENT,* leads to the *eTRM Technical Reference* page. Regardless of whether you choose Release 11.5.10 or Release 12.0, the links are the same for the ERDs. Click either 11.5.10 or 12.0. Click 'Diagrams and PDF Files'. Workflow is part of the FND family. Click the 'FND – Application Object Library' link. Click the 'AF11WORKFLOW.pdf' link. Click the 'R1159 AOL Workflow ERD.pdf' link (this is still the table model for Release 11.5.10)

The eTRMs also will give you links to all the table and view layouts. This is release specific. To access the table and view layouts in the eTRMs, pick your release. Click the 'HTML Files' link. Click the 'FND – Application Object Library' link. Click the 'FND_Tables.html' link. At this point you can view all the tables or download a copy.

The following diagram is our attempt to show all the links between the run-time and design tables (see FIGURE 10.1).

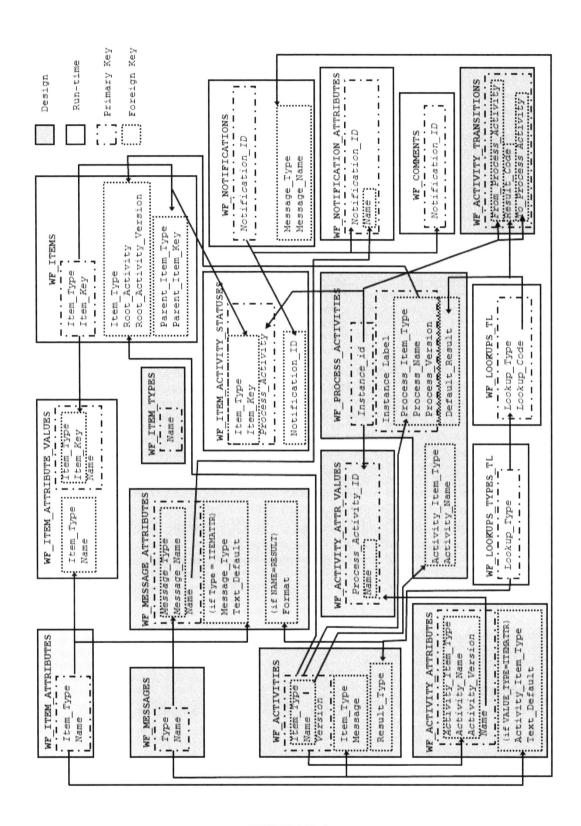

FIGURE 10. 1

The tables in gray are the design tables. These tables are populated when the Workflow definition is saved to the database. The tables in white are the run-time tables. These tables are populated when the Workflow starts and as the Workflow progresses. The primary key(s) to each table are denoted by a dashed box. Fields that are used to link to other tables are enclosed by a dotted box. The arrows run from primary key to foreign key.

There are no arrows from WF_ITEM_TYPES to the various foreign keys. This would have made the diagram unreadable. Instead the references from Name are listed as:

```
Table                            Foreign Key
WF_ITEMS                         ITEM_TYPE
WF_ITEM_ATTRIBUTES               ITEM_TYPE
WF_ITEM_ATTRIBUTE_VALUES         ITEM_TYPE
WF_MESSAGES                      TYPE
WF_MESSAGE_ATTRIBUTES            MESSAGE_TYPE
WF_ACTIVITIES                    ITEM_TYPE
WF_ACTIVITY_ATTRIBUTES           ACTIVITY_ITEM_TYPE
WF_PROCESS_ACTIVITIES            PROCESS_ITEM_TYPE
WF_ITEM_ACTIVITY_STATUSES        ITEM_TYPE
WF_ITEM_ACTIVITY_STATUSES_H      ITEM_TYPE
WF_LOOKUP_TYPES_TL               ITEM_TYPE
WF_NOTIFICATIONS                 MESSAGE_TYPE
```

The diagram does not list the table WF_ITEM_ACTIVITY_STATUSES_H. This table is identical to WF_ITEM_ACTIVITY_STATUSES. MetaLink Doc. ID: 444446.1, *Diagram of Relationship between Core Workflow Tables*, states: "When the same Activity is executed multiple times within a Workflow (i.e., looping Activity), WF_ITEM_ACTIVITY_STATUSES will only contain information on the last execution of the Activity, whereas the information on all the previous executions will be stored in WF_ITEM_ACTIVITY_STATUSES_H. When an Activity is executed only once within a Workflow, only WF_ITEM_ACTIVITY_STATUSES will be populated."

The design tables can be mapped to the 'Properties' page of each Activity in the Workflow Builder. Remember that when the 'Properties' page is opened from the Activity as listed in the Navigator window, the tabs 'Activity', 'Details', 'Roles', and 'Access' are shown. Only from the Diagrammer window can you see how the Process is diagrammed and access the information shown in the Node, Event Details, and Node Attributes tabs. The diagram and the information stored in these last three tabs correlate to the tables:

- WF_PROCESS_ACTIVITIES

- WF_ACTIVITY_ATTR_VALUES

- WF_ACTIVITY_TRANSITIONS.

_TL Tables

With the exception of WF_MESSAGES_TL, the _TL tables contain the following columns:

- LANGUAGE

- DISPLAY_NAME

- DESCRIPTION

- SOURCE_LANG

- SECURITY_GROUP_ID

* The table WF_LOOKUPS has the column 'MEANING' instead of 'DISPLAY_NAME'.

WF_MESSAGES_TL also contains the fields

- SUBJECT

- BODY

- HTML_BODY

When viewing Workflows from the Oracle Applications screens, LANGUAGE maps to the user's language preference (or if none is specified, the default language). When viewing Workflows using Workflow Builder, the language is mapped to the language specified in the NLS_LANG parameter found at HKEY_LOCAL_MACHINE/SOFTWARE/ORACLE. If the language of the PC does not match the 'LANGUAGE' column, the database default language is used. Translating the Workflow definitions to the various languages is part of the Workflow setup. The values in both 'LANGUAGE' and 'SOURCE_LANG' match to the 'CODE' column in WF_LANGUAGES. You cannot use any language that isn't installed in the database ('INSTALLED_FLAG' in WF_LANGUAGES must be 'Y'). See the *Oracle Workflow Administrator's Guide* (either *Release 12 Part No. B31431-01 December 2006* or *Release 2.6.4 Part No. B15852-05 July 2006*), *Setting Up Additional Languages* for more details.

According to the eTRM, 'SOURCE_LANG' is "The Language the text will mirror. If text is not yet translated into 'LANGUAGE' then any changes to the text in the source language will be reflected here as well".

'SECURITY_GROUP_ID' is null in all the tables.

'DISPLAY_NAME' and 'DESCRIPTION' are found on the 'Activities' tab of the Item Type, and all components under the Item Type (see FIGURE 10.2). The mapping of the names is obvious.

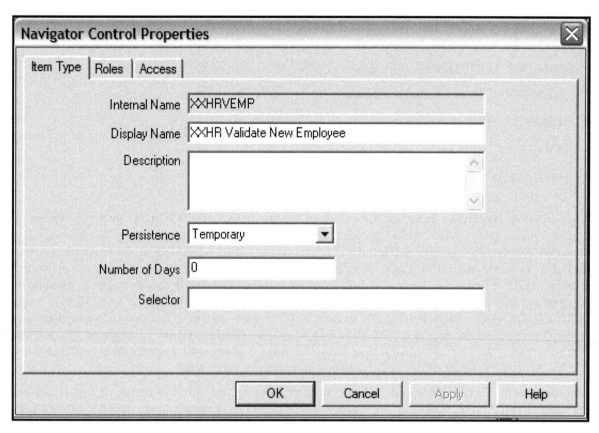

FIGURE 10.2

Obviously since the _TL tables store fields visible to the user in the user's selected language, the 'Subject' and 'Body' of Notifications are also language-enabled fields. These fields are stored in the WF_MESSAGES table and defined on the Body tab of Messages (see FIGURE 10.3)

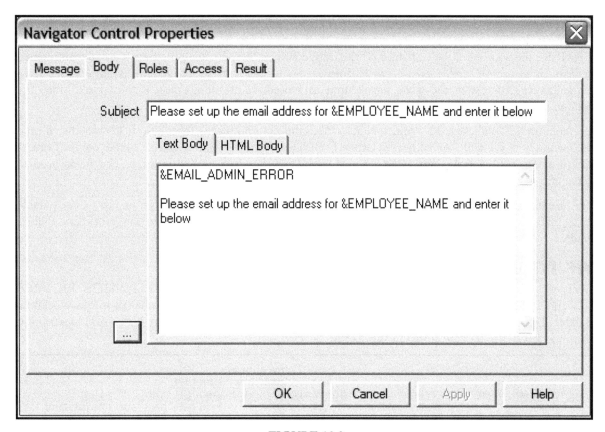

FIGURE 10.3

PROTECT_LEVEL and CUSTOM_LEVEL

PROTECT_LEVEL and CUSTOM_LEVEL, found in all the design tables, relate to the fields found on the 'Access' tab and on the Help → About Oracle Workflow Builder <version number> screen. As stored in the database, CUSTOM_LEVEL is the value of the 'Access Level' from the About Oracle Workflow Builder <version number> screen at the time the component was defined. 'PROTECT_LEVEL' is normally equal to CUSTOM_LEVEL, unless one of the Oracle APIs such as WFPROT.sql is used to change this value. These fields, in conjunction with 'Allow modifications of customized objects' from the 'About Oracle Workflow Builder <version>' screen and 'Preserve Customizations and Lock at this Access Level' from the 'Access' tab of any object, control whether this Activity can be modified using the Workflow Builder. See *Chapter 11, Advanced Builder and PL/SQL*, for further discussion of these fields.

READ_ROLE, WRITE_ROLE and EXECUTE_ROLE

These fields appear in all the design tables and correlate to the 'Roles' tab that appears in the Workflow Builder for all objects. This tab and these fields exist to specify the Roles that have access to the object. Oracle has not implemented any functionality to support this tab or these fields. They can therefore be ignored.

Characteristics Common to All Design/Runtime Tables

The following discussion will take each of the design tables and show the corresponding fields from the Workflow Builder or other data sources. The following comments apply to all tables.

The column 'NAV/DIAG WINDOW or OTHER' indicates whether the 'Properties' page in the Workflow Builder should be opened from the Navigator or Diagrammer window. If the designation is 'OTHER', the source will be explained. If the designation is 'Not Visible', the data is usually an internal key similar to the _ID fields used by all E-Business Suite tables. If the designation is 'N/A', then for a particular type of row in the table, the column isn't used. If the designation is 'Not Used', then the column is not currently in use.

The column 'PK' indicates the Primary Key. A '*' in this column means that these fields together form a unique index to the table. As with most of the E-Business Suite tables, the database table option Primary Key is not set. One table, WF_PROCESS_ACTIVITIES, has two unique indexes. The fields used to create the second unique index are indicated by '**'.

The columns COLUMN NAME, TYPE, and NULLABLE were furnished from the Oracle table ALL_TAB_COLUMNS. The other columns were added to map these fields to the Workflow Builder fields.

WF_ITEM_TYPES – design

Every Workflow or Item Type saved to the database exists as a record in WF_ITEM_TYPES. FIGURES 10.4 and 10.5 show the columns in this table and the corresponding window and tab in the Workflow Builder. This is one of the tables with a corresponding _TL table, so the Display Name and Description shown in FIGURE 10.5 are stored in WF_ITEM_TYPES_TL.

PK	COLUMN_NAME	TYPE	NULLABLE	NAV / DIAG WINDOW or OTHER	BUILDER OBJECT	TAB	FIELD
*	NAME	VARCHAR2(8)	N	NAV	Item Type	Item Type	Internal Name
	WF_SELECTOR	VARCHAR2(240)	Y	NAV	Item Type	Item Type	Selector
	PERSISTENCE_TYPE	VARCHAR2(8)	N	NAV	Item Type	Item Type	Persistence
	PERSISTENCE_DAYS	NUMBER	Y	NAV	Item Type	Item Type	Number of Days
	NUM_ACTIVE	NUMBER	Y	OTHER			
	NUM_ERROR	NUMBER	Y	OTHER			
	NUM_DEFER	NUMBER	Y	OTHER			
	NUM_SUSPEND	NUMBER	Y	OTHER			
	NUM_COMPLETE	NUMBER	Y	OTHER			
	NUM_PURGEABLE	NUMBER	Y	OTHER			

FIGURE 10.4

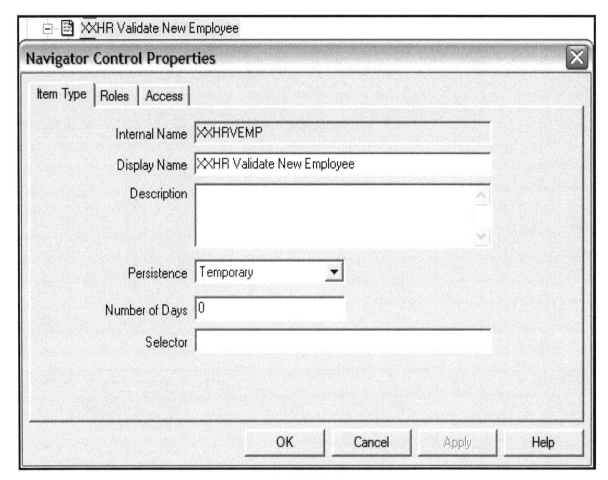

FIGURE 10.5

The columns designated 'OTHER' are used to count the number of records in WF_ITEMS where WF_ITEM_TYPES.NAME=WF_ITEMS.ITEM_TYPE. These fields were added to improve the performance in the administration screens in the Oracle Applications Manager, Workflow Manager section. FIGURE 10.6 shows the 'Completed Work Items' screen. The column 'Count' corresponds to NUM_COMPLETE and the column 'Purgeable' corresponds to NUM_PURGEABLE. FIGURE 10.7 shows 'Active Work Items'. The screen for Deferred Work Items, Suspended Work Items and Errored Work Items is similar. The column 'Count' corresponds to NUM_ACTIVE, NUM_DEFER, NUM_SUSPEND and NUM_ERROR respectively.

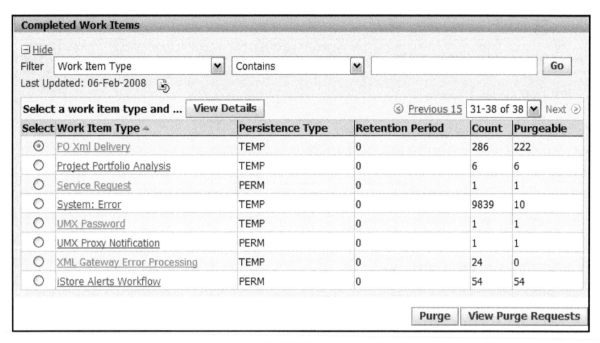

FIGURE 10.6

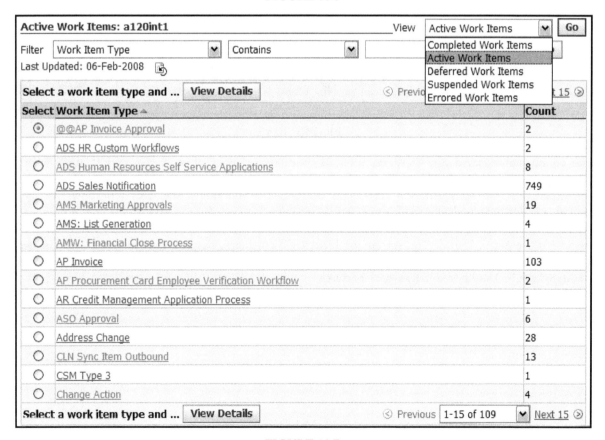

FIGURE 10.7

WF_ITEM_ATTRIBUTES – design

When a Workflow is saved to the database, a row is created in this table for each Item Attribute. FIGURES 10.8 and 10.9 show the columns in this table and the corresponding window and tab in the Workflow Builder. This is one of the tables with a corresponding _TL table, so the Display Name and Description shown in FIGURE 10.9 are stored in WF_ITEM_ATTRIBUTES_TL.

PK	COLUMN_NAME	TYPE	NULLABLE	NAV / DIAG WINDOW or OTHER	BUILDER OBJECT	TAB	FIELD
*	ITEM_TYPE	VARCHAR2(8)	N	NAV	Item Attribute	Attribute	Item Type
*	NAME	VARCHAR2(30)	N	NAV	Item Attribute	Attribute	Internal Name
	SEQUENCE	NUMBER	N	Not Visible			
	TYPE	VARCHAR2(8)	N	NAV	Item Attribute	Attribute	Type
	SUBTYPE	VARCHAR2(8)	Y	Not Used			
	FORMAT	VARCHAR2(240)	Y	NAV	Item Attribute	Attribute	If Type = Text, Length If Type = Number, Format If Type = Date, Format If Type = Lookup, Lookup Type If Type = URL, Frame Target If Type = Document, Frame Target not used if Type = Form, Role, Attribute, Event
	TEXT_DEFAULT	VARCHAR2(4000)	Y	NAV	Item Attribute	Attribute	Default Value
	NUMBER_DEFAULT	NUMBER	Y	NAV	Item Attribute	Attribute	Default Value
	DATE_DEFAULT	DATE	Y	NAV	Item Attribute	Attribute	Default Value

FIGURE 10.8

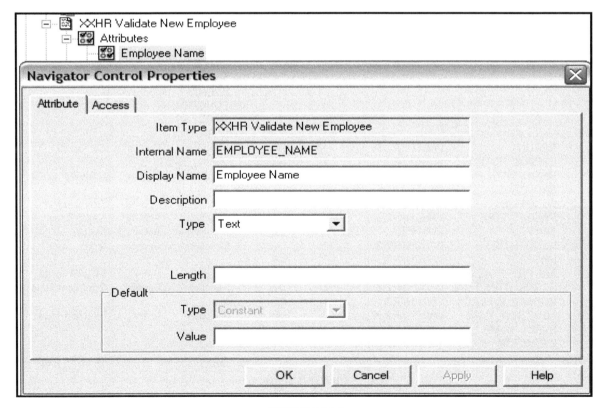

FIGURE 10.9

The Workflow Builder field 'Default Type' is always set to 'Constant' and cannot be changed. Therefore, the table has no column that reflects this field.

The table field SEQUENCE is the order listed in the Builder. If the Attributes are re-ordered in the Workflow Builder and the Workflow saved to the database, this number will change. Remember that Item Attributes are not versioned, so there is no column referencing a version.

The value for ITEM_TYPE in the table is actually the Internal Name for the field shown in FIGURE 10.9. Therefore, the value in the table would be 'XXHRVEMP', not 'XXHR Validate New Employee'.

WF_ACTIVITIES – design

WF_ACTIVITIES stores the definitions of Functions, Notifications, Events, and Processes. The columns used by each Activity Type are different. Four pictures will be used to show the different mappings. Regardless of the Activity Type, the Display Name and Description are stored in the WF_ACTIVITIES_TL table.

FIGURES 10.10 and 10.11 show the columns in this table and the corresponding window and tab in the Workflow Builder for a Function. FIGURES 10.12 and 10.13 show 'Notifications', FIGURES 10.14 and 10.15 show 'Events', and FIGURES 10.16 and 10.17 show 'Processes'. The fields referenced in the 'Details' tab are the same for all Activity Types; therefore this tab will not be shown until the end (see FIGURE 10.18).

when TYPE = FUNCTION

Functions

PK	COLUMN NAME	TYPE	NULLABLE	NAV / DIAG WINDOW or OTHER	BUILDER OBJECT	TAB	FIELD
*	ITEM_TYPE	VARCHAR2(8)	N	Not Visable			
*	NAME	VARCHAR2(30)	N	NAV	Function	Activity	Internal Name
*	VERSION	NUMBER	N	NAV	Function	Details	Version
	TYPE	VARCHAR2(8)	N	NAV	<this is the object type, EVENT, FUNCTION, PROCESS, NOTICE>		
	RERUN	VARCHAR2(8)	N	NAV	Function	Details	On Revisit
	EXPAND_ROLE	VARCHAR2(1)	N	N/A			
	BEGIN_DATE	DATE	N	NAV	Function	Details	Effective
	END_DATE	DATE	Y	Not Visable			
	FUNCTION	VARCHAR2(240)	Y	NAV	Function	Activity	Function Name
	RESULT_TYPE	VARCHAR2(30)	Y	NAV	Function	Activity	Result Type
	COST	NUMBER	Y	NAV	Function	Activity	Cost
	ICON_NAME	VARCHAR2(30)	Y	NAV	Function	Activity	Icon
	MESSAGE	VARCHAR2(30)	Y	N/A			
	ERROR_PROCESS	VARCHAR2(30)	Y	NAV	Function	Details	Error Process
	ERROR_ITEM_TYPE	VARCHAR2(8)	N	NAV	Function	Details	Error Item Type
	RUNNABLE_FLAG	VARCHAR2(1)	N	N/A			
	FUNCTION_TYPE	VARCHAR2(30)	Y	NAV	Function	Activity	Function Type
	EVENT_NAME	VARCHAR2(240)	Y	N/A			
	DIRECTION	VARCHAR2(30)	Y	N/A			

FIGURE 10.10

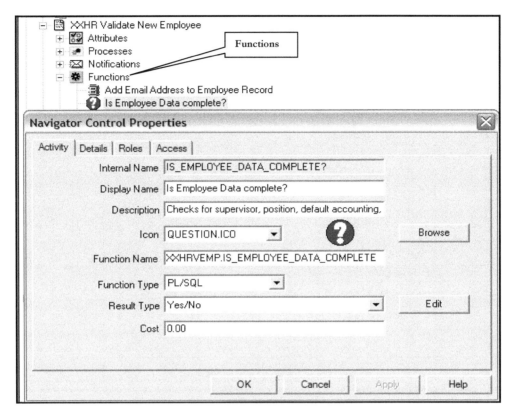

FIGURE 10.11

when TYPE = NOTICE

Notifications

PK	COLUMN_NAME	TYPE	NULLABLE	NAV / DIAG WINDOW or OTHER	BUILDER OBJECT	TAB	FIELD
*	ITEM_TYPE	VARCHAR2(8)	N	Not Visable			
*	NAME	VARCHAR2(30)	N	NAV	Notification	Activity	Internal Name
*	VERSION	NUMBER	N	NAV	Notification	Details	Version
	TYPE	VARCHAR2(8)	N	NAV	<this is the object type, EVENT, FUNCTION, PROCESS, NOTICE>		
	RERUN	VARCHAR2(8)	N	NAV	Notification	Details	On Revisit
	EXPAND_ROLE	VARCHAR2(1)	N	NAV	Notification	Activity	Expand Roles
	BEGIN_DATE	DATE	N	NAV	Notification	Details	Effective
	END_DATE	DATE	Y	Not Visable			
	FUNCTION	VARCHAR2(240)	Y	NAV	Notification	Activity	Function Name
	RESULT_TYPE	VARCHAR2(30)	Y	NAV	Notification	Activity	Result Type
	COST	NUMBER	Y	N/A			
	ICON_NAME	VARCHAR2(30)	Y	NAV	Notification	Activity	Icon
	MESSAGE	VARCHAR2(30)	Y	NAV	Notification	Activity	Message
	ERROR_PROCESS	VARCHAR2(30)	Y	NAV	Notification	Details	Error Process
	ERROR_ITEM_TYPE	VARCHAR2(8)	N	NAV	Notification	Details	Error Item Type
	RUNNABLE_FLAG	VARCHAR2(1)	N	N/A			
	FUNCTION_TYPE	VARCHAR2(30)	Y	NAV	Notification	Activity	Function Type
	EVENT_NAME	VARCHAR2(240)	Y	N/A			
	DIRECTION	VARCHAR2(30)	Y	N/A			

FIGURE 10.12

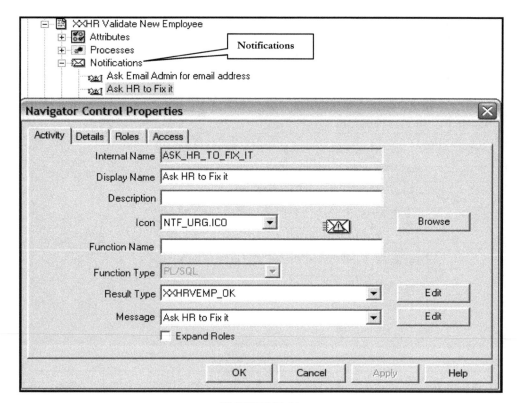

FIGURE 10.13

when TYPE = EVENT

Events

PK	COLUMN_NAME	TYPE	NULLABLE	NAV/DIAG WINDOW or OTHER	BUILDER OBJECT	TAB	FIELD
*	ITEM_TYPE	VARCHAR2(8)	N	Not Visable			
*	NAME	VARCHAR2(30)	N	NAV	Event	Activity	Internal Name
*	VERSION	NUMBER	N	NAV	Event	Details	Version
	TYPE	VARCHAR2(8)	N	NAV	<this is the object type, EVENT, FUNCTION, PROCESS, NOTICE>		
	RERUN	VARCHAR2(8)	N	NAV	Event	Details	On Revisit
	EXPAND_ROLE	VARCHAR2(1)	N	N/A			
	BEGIN_DATE	DATE	N	NAV	Event	Details	Effective
	END_DATE	DATE	Y	Not Visable			
	FUNCTION	VARCHAR2(240)	Y	N/A			
	RESULT_TYPE	VARCHAR2(30)	Y	N/A			
	COST	NUMBER	Y	NAV	Event	Activity	Cost
	ICON_NAME	VARCHAR2(30)	Y	NAV	Event	Activity	Icon
	MESSAGE	VARCHAR2(30)	Y	N/A			
	ERROR_PROCESS	VARCHAR2(30)	Y	NAV	Event	Details	Error Process
	ERROR_ITEM_TYPE	VARCHAR2(8)	N	NAV	Event	Details	Error Item Type
	RUNNABLE_FLAG	VARCHAR2(1)	N	N/A			
	FUNCTION_TYPE	VARCHAR2(30)	Y	N/A			
	EVENT_NAME	VARCHAR2(240)	Y	NAV	Event	Activity	Event Filter
	DIRECTION	VARCHAR2(30)	Y	NAV	Event	Activity	Event Action

FIGURE 10.14

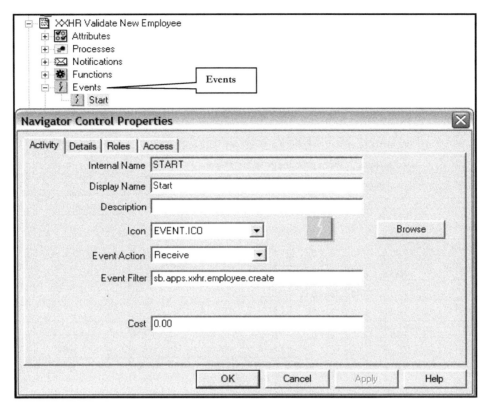

FIGURE 10.15

when TYPE = PROCESS → Processes

PK	COLUMN_NAME	TYPE	NULLABLE	NAV / DIAG WINDOW or OTHER	BUILDER OBJECT	TAB	FIELD
*	ITEM_TYPE	VARCHAR2(8)	N	Not Visable			
*	NAME	VARCHAR2(30)	N	NAV	Process	Activity	Internal Name
*	VERSION	NUMBER	N	NAV	Process	Details	Version
	TYPE	VARCHAR2(8)	N	NAV	<this is the object type, EVENT, FUNCTION, PROCESS, NOTICE>		
	RERUN	VARCHAR2(8)	N	NAV	Process	Details	On Revisit
	EXPAND_ROLE	VARCHAR2(1)	N	N/A			
	BEGIN_DATE	DATE	N	NAV	Process	Details	Effective
	END_DATE	DATE	Y	Not Visable			
	FUNCTION	VARCHAR2(240)	Y	N/A			
	RESULT_TYPE	VARCHAR2(30)	Y	NAV	Process	Activity	Result Type
	COST	NUMBER	Y	N/A			
	ICON_NAME	VARCHAR2(30)	Y	NAV	Process	Activity	Icon
	MESSAGE	VARCHAR2(30)	Y	N/A			
	ERROR_PROCESS	VARCHAR2(30)	Y	NAV	Process	Details	Error Process
	ERROR_ITEM_TYPE	VARCHAR2(8)	N	NAV	Process	Details	Error Item Type
	RUNNABLE_FLAG	VARCHAR2(1)	N	NAV	Process	Activity	Runnable
	FUNCTION_TYPE	VARCHAR2(30)	Y	N/A			
	EVENT_NAME	VARCHAR2(240)	Y	N/A			
	DIRECTION	VARCHAR2(30)	Y	N/A			

FIGURE 10.16

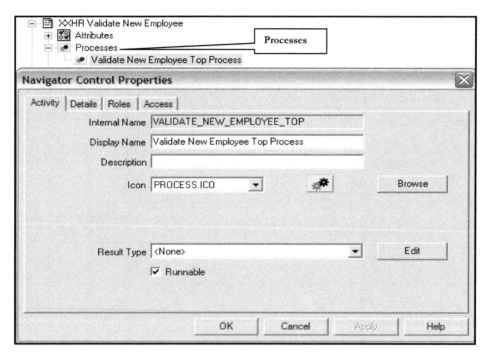

FIGURE 10.17

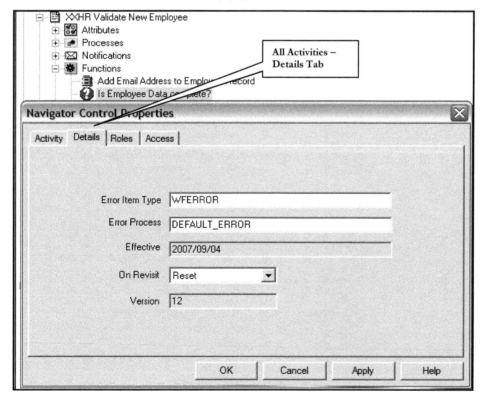

FIGURE 10.18

WF_ACTIVITY_ATTRIBUTES – design

WF_ACTIVITY_ATTRIBUTES stores the definitions of the Attributes that are configured in the 'Node Attributes' tab of the 'Properties' page (the values entered into this tab are stored in WF_ACTIVITY_ATTR_VALUES). FIGURES 10.19 and 10.20 show the columns in this table and the corresponding window and tab in the Workflow Builder.

The 'Activity Item Type' column stores the name of the Item Type where the activity is defined, not where it is used. So activities like Wait and 'Loop Counter' will have the value WFSTD (Internal Name for the 'Standard' Item Type).

This is one of the tables with a corresponding _TL table, so the Display Name and Description shown in FIGURE 10.20 are stored in WF_ITEM_TYPES_TL.

Attributes are typically defined for activities. However, they can also be defined for Notifications. Notification Attributes are only used (required) when the Expand Role box is checked and the required Notification is counting the responses (see *Chapter 11, Advanced Builder and PL/SQL*, for further explanation).

The value for the Activity Name is the Internal Name of the Activity displayed in the 'Function' field. The value for Activity Version can be found on the 'Properties' page ('Details' tab) of the Activity.

Like Item Attributes, SEQUENCE is the order listed in the Builder (and also the 'Node Attributes' tab).

PK	COLUMN_NAME	TYPE	NULLABL	NAV / DIAG WINDOW or OTHER	BUILDER OBJECT	TAB	FIELD
*	ACTIVITY_ITEM_TYPE	VARCHAR2(8)	N	Not Visiable			
*	ACTIVITY_NAME	VARCHAR2(30)	N	NAV	Attribute attached to Function or Notification	Attribute	Function
*	ACTIVITY_VERSION	NUMBER	N	Not Visiable			
*	NAME	VARCHAR2(30)	N	NAV	Attribute attached to Function or Notification	Attribute	Internal Name
	SEQUENCE	NUMBER	N	Not Visiable			
	TYPE	VARCHAR2(8)	N	NAV	Attribute attached to Function or Notification	Attribute	Type
	VALUE_TYPE	VARCHAR2(8)	N	NAV	Attribute attached to Function or Notification	Attribute	Default Type
	SUBTYPE	VARCHAR2(8)	Y	Not Visiable			
	FORMAT	VARCHAR2(240)	Y	NAV	Attribute attached to Function or Notification		If Type = Text, Length If Type = Number, Format If Type = Date, Format If Type = URL, Frame Target If Type = Lookup, Lookup Type If Type = Document, Frame Target not used if Type = Form, Role, Attribute, Event
	TEXT_DEFAULT	VARCHAR2(4000)	Y	NAV	Attribute attached to Function or Notification	Attribute	Default Value
	NUMBER_DEFAULT	NUMBER	Y	NAV	Attribute attached to Function or Notification	Attribute	Default Value
	DATE_DEFAULT	DATE	Y	NAV	Attribute attached to Function or Notification	Attribute	Default Value

FIGURE 10.19

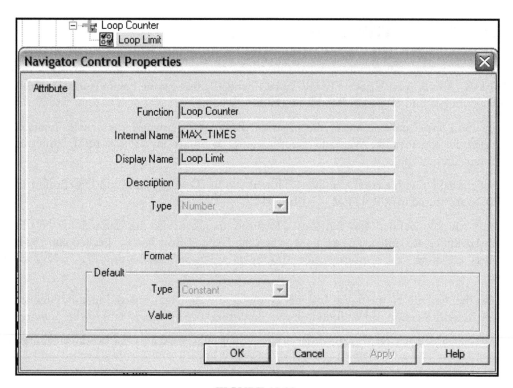

FIGURE 10.20

WF_ACTIVITY_ATTR_VALUES – predominately design

The WF_ACTIVITY_ATTR_VALUES table stores the values for activity Attributes defined for Functions or Notifications. This table also stores the value for all Timeouts and for the values entered into the 'Event Details' tab.

Activity Attributes are defined in the Navigator window, but they are assigned a value in the Diagrammer window. Note that Activity Attributes assigned to a Notification are given values in the post-Notification Function assigned to the Notification.

There is no WF_ACTIVITY_ATTR_VALUES_TL table.

The value shown in the 'Name' field of the 'Node Attributes' tab is the DISPLAY_NAME for the Attribute from WF_ACTIVITY_ATTRIBUTES_TL. The value stored in the 'NAME' column is the corresponding ACTIVITY_NAME from WF_ACTIVITY_ATTRIBUTES.

FIGURES 10.21 and 10.22 show the columns in this table and the corresponding window and tab in the Workflow Builder for Attribute values assigned through the 'Node Attributes' window.

PK	COLUMN NAME	TYPE	NULLABLE	NAV / DIAG WINDOW or OTHER	BUILDER OBJECT	TAB	FIELD
*	PROCESS_ACTIVITY_ID	NUMBER	N	Not Visable			
*	NAME	VARCHAR2(30)	N	DIAG	Attribute attached to Function or Notification	Node Attributes	Attribute Name
	VALUE_TYPE	VARCHAR2(8)	N	DIAG	Attribute attached to Function or Notification	Node Attributes	Attribute Type
	TEXT_VALUE	VARCHAR2(4000)	Y	DIAG	Attribute attached to Function or Notification	Node Attributes	Attribute Value
	NUMBER_VALUE	NUMBER	Y	DIAG	Attribute attached to Function or Notification	Node Attributes	Attribute Value
	DATE_VALUE	DATE	Y	DIAG	Attribute attached to Function or Notification	Node Attributes	Attribute Value

FIGURE 10.21

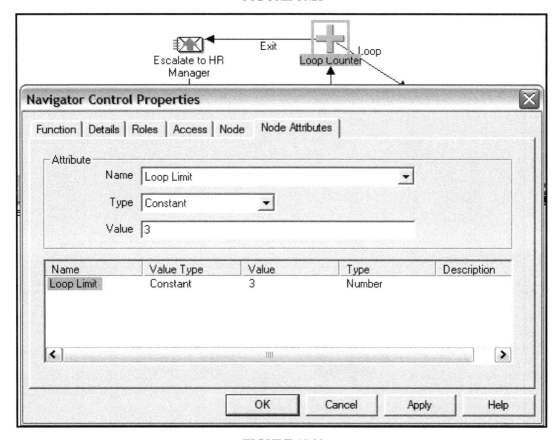

FIGURE 10.22

FIGURES 10.23 and 10.24 show the columns in this table and the corresponding window and tab in the Workflow Builder for Timeouts. An Activity only has a corresponding row in this table when a Timeout is defined.

Although Timeouts are usually assigned to Notifications, they can be assigned to Functions that are placed into a wait state for an indeterminate amount of time. See the section "A Common Modification of 'PA Timecard Approval (PATCARD)'" in *Chapter 12, Most Commonly Used Workflows*, for an example of using a Timeout with a Function Activity.

Timeouts

PK	COLUMN_NAME	TYPE	NULLABLE	NAV / DIAG WINDOW or OTHER	BUILDER OBJECT	TAB	FIELD	VALUE
*	PROCESS_ACTIVITY_ID	NUMBER	N	Not Visable				
*	NAME	VARCHAR2(30)	N	DIAG	Notification or Function	Node		#TIMEOUT
	VALUE_TYPE	VARCHAR2(8)	N	DIAG	Notification or Function	Node	Timeout Type	=CONSTANT or ITEMATTR
	TEXT_VALUE	VARCHAR2(4000)	Y	DIAG	Notification or Function	Node	Timeout Value	
	NUMBER_VALUE	NUMBER	Y	DIAG	Notification or Function	Node	Value days hours minutes - stored as minutes	
	DATE_VALUE	DATE	Y	N/A				

FIGURE 10.23

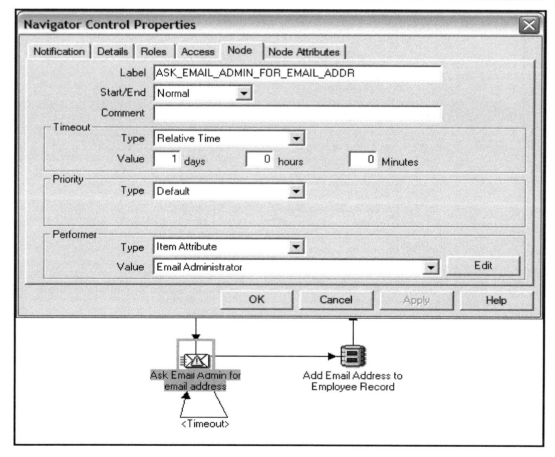

FIGURE 10.24

The data entered into the 'Event Details' page is also stored in the WF_ACTIVITY_ATTR_VALUES table. FIGURES 10.25, 10.26, 10.27, and 10.28 show the columns in this table and the corresponding window and tab in the Workflow Builder for the Event details. FIGURE 10.26 is the 'Event Details' tab when the Event Action on the 'Event' tab is set to 'Receive'. FIGURE 10.27 is the 'Event Details' tab when the Event Action on the 'Event' tab is set to 'Send', and FIGURE 10.28 is the 'Event Details' tab when the Event Action on the 'Event' tab is set to 'Raise'.

Each value entered is stored as a separate row in the table. For example, if the Event Action is set to 'Receive', there will be 3 records in this table: one with NAME = #EVENTNAME , VALUE_TYPE = ITEMATTR, and TEXT_VALUE = EVENT_NAME (the Internal Name for the Item Attribute 'Event Name'); one with NAME = #EVENTKEY, VALUE_TYPE = ITEMATTR, and TEXT_VALUE = EVENT_KEY (the Internal Name for the Item Attribute 'Event Key'); and one with NAME = #EVENTMESSAGE, VALUE_TYPE = ITEMATTR, and TEXT_VALUE = EVENT_DATA (the Internal Name for the Item Attribute 'Event Data').

Events

PK	COLUMN_NAME	TYPE	NULLABLE	NAV / DIAG WINDOW or OTHER	BUILDER OBJECT	TAB	FIELD	VALUE
*	PROCESS_ACTIVITY_ID	NUMBER	N	Not Visable				
*	NAME	VARCHAR2(30)	N	DIAG	Event	Event Details	Event Name or	#EVENTNAME or
							Event Key or	#EVENTKEY or
							Event Message or	#EVENTMESSAGE or
							Out Agent or	#EVENTOUTAGENT or
							To Agent	#EVENTTOAGENT
	VALUE_TYPE	VARCHAR2(8)	N	DIAG	Event	Event Details	Event Name Type or Out Agent Type or To Agent Type	=CONSTANT or ITEMATTR
	TEXT_VALUE	VARCHAR2(4000)	Y	DIAG	Event	Event Details	<field> Value	
	NUMBER_VALUE	NUMBER	Y	N/A				
	DATE_VALUE	DATE	Y	N/A				

FIGURE 10.25

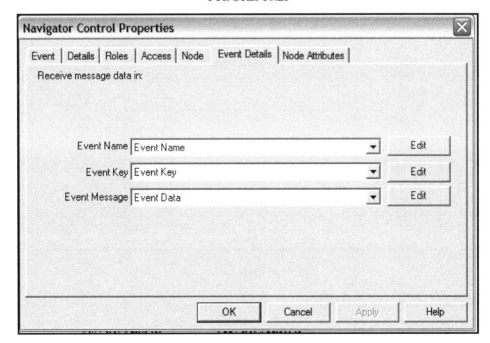

FIGURE 10.26

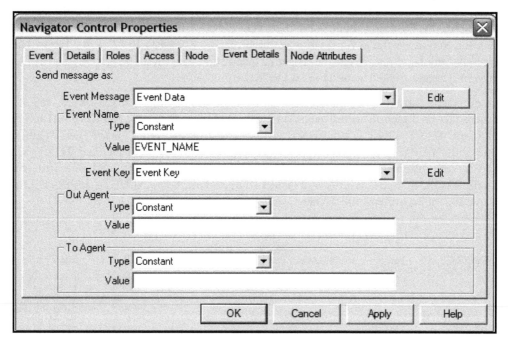

FIGURE 10.27

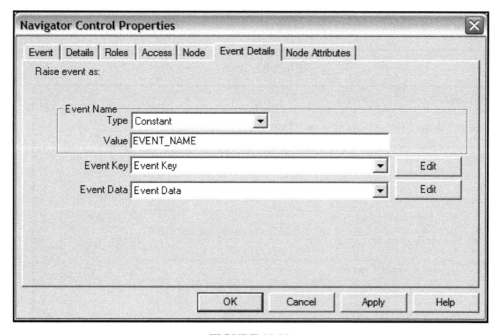

FIGURE 10.28

WF_MESSAGES – design

WF_MESSAGES stored the definition of the Message attached to a Notification. There is a corresponding WF_MESSAGES_TL table that, along with the Display Name and Description, stores the Subject, Text Body and HTML Body. This is one of the few tables where the _TL table stores more pertinent information that the non _TL table. The columns in WF_MESSAGES relate to the fields in the Message tab. The columns in WF_MESSAGES_TL relate to the columns in the Body tab. FIGURES 10.29 and 10.30 show the relationship to WF_MESSAGES and figures 10.31 and 10.32 the relationship to WF_MESSAGES_TL. NAME in WF_MESSAGES_TL is the same NAME as in WF_MESSAGES.

The Display Name and Description shown in FIGURE 10.30 are stored in WF_MESSAGES_TL.

PK	COLUMN_NAME	TYPE	NULLABLE	OTHER	NAV / DIAG WINDOW or BUILDER OBJECT	TAB	FIELD
*	TYPE	VARCHAR2(8)	N	Not Visable			
*	NAME	VARCHAR2(30)	N	NAV	Messages	Message	Internal Name
	DEFAULT_PRIORITY	NUMBER	Y	NAV	Messages	Message	Priority

FIGURE 10.29

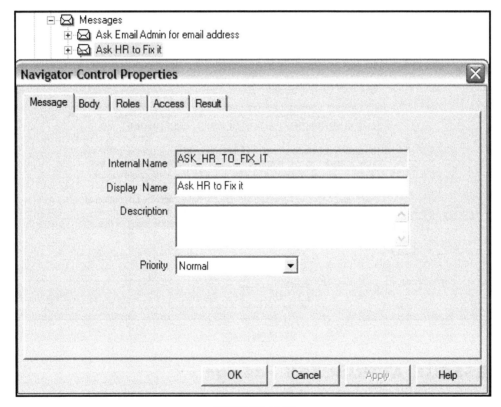

FIGURE 10.30

PK	COLUMN_NAME	TYPE	NULLABLE	NAV / DIAG WINDOW or OTHER	BUILDER OBJECT	TAB	FIELD
*	TYPE	VARCHAR2(8)	N	Not Visable			
*	NAME	VARCHAR2(30)	N	NAV	Messages	Message	Internal Name
*	LANGUAGE	VARCHAR2(30)	N	Not Visable			
	SUBJECT	VARCHAR2(240)	N	NAV	Messages	Body	Subject
	BODY	VARCHAR2(4000)	Y	NAV	Messages	Body	Text Body
	HTML_BODY	VARCHAR2(4000)	Y	NAV	Messages	Body	HTML Body

FIGURE 10.31

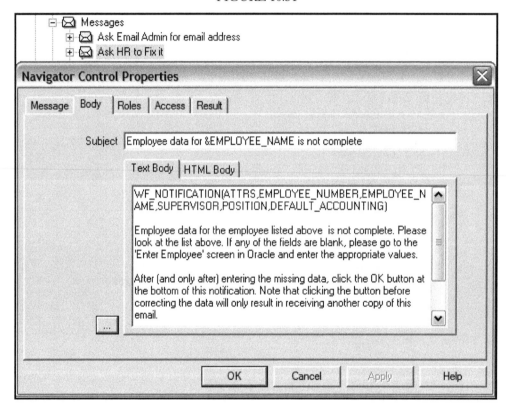

FIGURE 10.32

WF_MESSAGE_ATTRIBUTES – design

WF_MESSAGE_ATTRIBUTES stores the definitions of the Attributes assigned to the Message and used in the Subject and the Body. FIGURES 10.33 and 10.34 show the columns in this table and the corresponding window and tab in the Workflow Builder.

This table also stores the definition of the RESULT Attribute. RESULT is the Internal Name of the Attribute whose definition is stored on the Result tab of the Message. This Attribute is defined for Messages that require a response and contains the Lookup Code used to formulate the Result buttons. FIGURES 10.35 and 10.36 show the columns in this table and the corresponding window and tab in the Workflow Builder.

This is one of the tables with a corresponding _TL table, so the Display Name and Description shown in FIGURE 10.28 are stored in WF_ITEM_TYPES_TL.

PK	COLUMN_NAME	TYPE	NULLABL	NAV / DIAG WINDOW or OTHER	BUILDER OBJECT	TAB	FIELD
*	MESSAGE_TYPE	VARCHAR2(8)	N	Not Visable			
	MESSAGE_NAME	VARCHAR2(30)	N	NAV	Attribute attached to Message	Attribute	Message
*	NAME	VARCHAR2(30)	N	NAV	Attribute attached to Message	Attribute	Internal Name
*	SEQUENCE	NUMBER	N	Not Visable			
	TYPE	VARCHAR2(8)	N	NAV	Attribute attached to Message	Attribute	Type
	SUBTYPE	VARCHAR2(8)	N	NAV	Attribute attached to Message	Attribute	Source
	VALUE_TYPE	VARCHAR2(8)	N	NAV	Attribute attached to Message	Attribute	Default Type
	FORMAT	VARCHAR2(240)	Y	NAV	Attribute attached to Message	Attribute	If Type = Text, Length If Type = Number, Format If Type = Date, Format If Type = URL, Frame Target If Type = Lookup, Lookup Type If Type = Document, Frame Target not used if Type = Form, Role, Attribute, Event
	TEXT_DEFAULT	VARCHAR2(4000)	Y	NAV	Attribute attached to Message	Attribute	Default Value
	NUMBER_DEFAULT	NUMBER	Y	NAV	Attribute attached to Message	Attribute	Default Value
	DATE_DEFAULT	DATE	Y	NAV	Attribute attached to Message	Attribute	Default Value
	ATTACH	VARCHAR2(1)	Y	NAV	Attribute attached to Message	Attribute	If Type = URL or Document, Attach Content

FIGURE 10.33

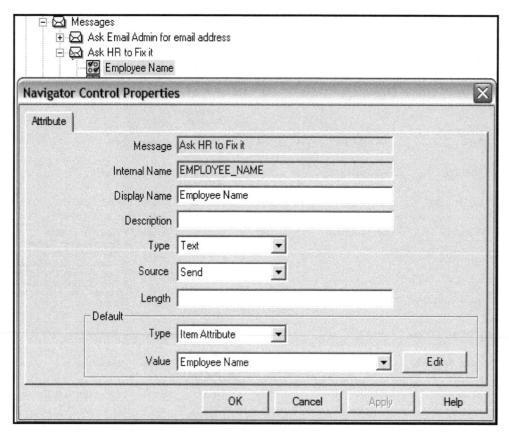

FIGURE 10.34

NAME=RESULT

PK	COLUMN NAME	TYPE	NULLABL	NAV / DIAG WINDOW or OTHER	BUILDER OBJECT	TAB	FIELD
*	MESSAGE_TYPE	VARCHAR2(8)	N	Not Visable			
*	MESSAGE_NAME	VARCHAR2(30)	N	NAV	Message	Message	Internal Name
*	NAME	VARCHAR2(30)	N	NAV	Message	Result	constant, = RESULT
	SEQUENCE	NUMBER	N	Not Visable			
	TYPE	VARCHAR2(8)	N	Not Visable	Message		constant, = LOOKUP
	SUBTYPE	VARCHAR2(8)	N	Not Visable	Message		constant, = RESPOND
	VALUE_TYPE	VARCHAR2(8)	N	NAV	Message	Result	Default Type
	FORMAT	VARCHAR2(240)	Y	NAV	Message	Result	Lookup Type
	TEXT_DEFAULT	VARCHAR2(4000)	Y	NAV	Message	Result	Default Value
	NUMBER_DEFAULT	NUMBER	Y	N/A			
	DATE_DEFAULT	DATE	Y	N/A			
	ATTACH	VARCHAR2(1)	Y	N/A			

FIGURE 10.35

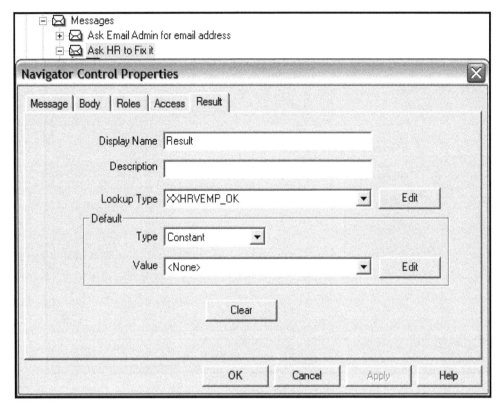

FIGURE 10.36

WF_LOOKUP_TYPES_TL – design

WF_LOOKUP_TYPES_TL stores the name of the list-of-values used as results for activities (Functions, Notifications and Processes). Although a Lookup Type must be unique across the entire database, the table does store the Item Type where the Lookup Type was defined so that the Workflow Builder knows which Lookup Types to load or save when loading or saving an Item Type. FIGURES 10.37 and 10.38 show the columns in this table and the corresponding window and tab in the Workflow Builder.

This table only exists as an _TL table.

PK	COLUMN_NAME	TYPE	NULLABLE	OTHER	NAV / DIAG WINDOW or OBJECT	BUILDER TAB	FIELD
*	LOOKUP_TYPE	VARCHAR2(30)	N	NAV	Lookup Type	Lookup Type	Internal Name
	DISPLAY_NAME	VARCHAR2(80)	N	NAV	Lookup Type	Lookup Type	Display Name
*	LANGUAGE	VARCHAR2(30)	N	Not Visable			
	ITEM_TYPE	VARCHAR2(8)	N	Not Visable			

FIGURE 10.37

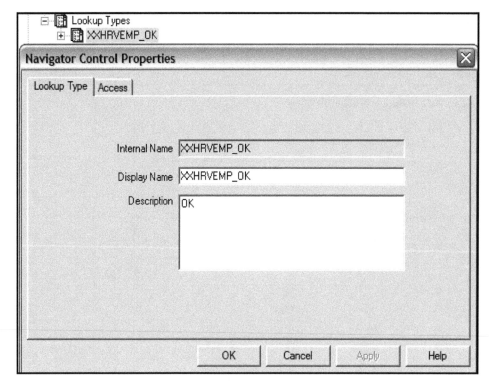

FIGURE 10.38

WF_LOOKUPS_TL – design

WF_LOOKUPS_TL stores the definition of each value for a Lookup Type. FIGURES 10.39 and 10.40 show the columns in this table and the corresponding window and tab in the Workflow Builder.

This table only exists as an _TL table.

PK	COLUMN NAME	TYPE	NULLABLE	NAV / DIAG WINDOW or OTHER	BUILDER OBJECT	TAB	FIELD
*	LOOKUP_TYPE	VARCHAR2(30)	N	NAV	Lookup Code attached to Lookup Type	Lookup Code	Lookup Type
*	LOOKUP_CODE	VARCHAR2(30)	N	NAV	Lookup Code attached to Lookup Type	Lookup Code	Internal Name
	MEANING	VARCHAR2(80)	N	NAV	Lookup Code attached to Lookup Type	Lookup Code	Display Name
*	LANGUAGE	VARCHAR2(30)	N	Not Visable			

FIGURE 10.39

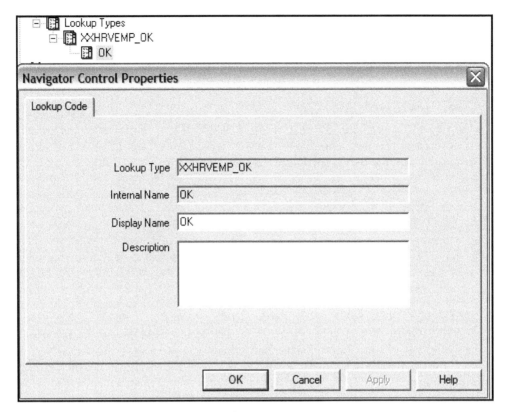

FIGURE 10.40

WF_PROCESS_ACTIVITIES – design

All the tables we have looked at so far (except WF_ITEM_ATTRIBUTE_VALUES) show the definitions from the Navigator window. WF_PROCESS_ACTIVITIES stores the information about the Process flow, or what happens in the Diagrammer window. The table stores the information particular to a specific node, such as the Performer, the node label, the node comment, and whether the node is a Start or End Node. Along with WF_TRANSITIONS, this table stores the information necessary to re-draw the diagram.

Note that this table has two sets of primary keys. INSTANCE_ID by itself will identify a unique row and is the key used as a foreign key to all tables except WF_ACTIVITIES. This number represents the Activity as drawn in a specific place in the diagram. Thus, if there were two 'Compare Text' activities in the diagram, each Activity would have a different INSTANCE_ID. Furthermore, if a change is made to the diagram and the change saved to the database, each Activity in that Process will receive a new INSTANCE_ID, even if there was no change to that Activity.

The other set of columns that form a unique instance to this table are identified by '**' in FIGURE 10.41. PROCESS_ITEM_TYPE is the Internal Name of the Item Type. PROCESS_NAME is the name of the Process where an Activity resides. PROCESS_VERSION is the version of the Process, not of any Activity in the Process. INSTANCE_LABEL corresponds to the 'Label' field on the Node tab of the Activity in the diagram. If there is only one copy of the Activity in the Process, this will default to the Internal Name of the Activity. If there are multiple copies of the Activity, this field defaults to the Internal Name of the Activity followed by a dash and a number.

The links to/from this table are somewhat difficult to follow. Using the diagram in FIGURE 10.1 they are:

- WF_PROCESS_ACTIVITIES to WF_ACTIVITY_TRANSITIONS – See explanation of WF_ACTIVITY_TRANSITIONS

- WF_PROCESS_ACTIVITIES.INSTANCE_ID to WF_ACTIVITY_ATTR_VALUES.PROCESS_ACTIVITY_ID – Note that the name of the Attribute is not part of this link. This allows using WF_ACTIVITY_ATTR_VALUES to store data that isn't associated with the 'Node Attributes' page, such as Timeouts and the data from the 'Event Details' page

- WF_PROCESS_ACTIVITIES.INSTANCE_ID to WF_ITEM_ACTIVITY_STATUSES.PROCESS_ACTIVITY – this links the definition of the Activity in a diagram to a specific occurrence of that Activity in a specific Workflow. The link is identical to WF_ITEM_ACTIVITY_STATUSES_H. Remember that if an Activity occurs in a loop, the most recent execution of that Activity is found in WF_ITEM_ACTIVITY_STATUSES. Older occurrences are stored in the _H table

- WF_PROCESS_ACTIVITIES.PROCESS_ITEM_TYPE and .PROCESS_NAME and PROCESS_VERSION to WF_ACTIVITIES.ITEM_TYPE and .NAME and .VERSION – this will link to the definition of the Process. This link allows you to access the BEGIN_DATE and END_DATE for the Process which can be used in the next link to identify all the activities in that version of the Process

- WF_PROCESS_ACTIVITIES.ACTIVITY_ITEM_TYPE and .ACTIVITY_NAME to WF_ACTIVITIES.ITEM_TYPE and .NAME – this links the occurrence of an Activity in a diagram to the definition of the Activity. This link will yield all versions of the Activity. Use the dates from the above link and match the dates to the Activity dates to get the activities for a specific version of the Process

- WF_PROCESS_ACTIVITIES.PROCESS_ITEM_TYPE and .PROCESS_NAME and PROCESS_VERSION to WF_ITEMS.ITEM_TYPE and .ROOT_ACTIVITY and .ROOT_ACTIVITY_VERSION – this links the instance of a Workflow to the top (starting) Process

FIGURES 10.41 and 10.40 show the columns in this table and the corresponding window and tab in the Workflow Builder.

PK	COLUMN_NAME	TYPE	NULLABLE	NAV / DIAG WINDOW or OTHER	TAB	FIELD
**	PROCESS_ITEM_TYPE	VARCHAR2(8)	N	Not Visable		
**	PROCESS_NAME	VARCHAR2(30)	N	Not Visable		
**	PROCESS_VERSION	NUMBER	N	Not Visable		
	ACTIVITY_ITEM_TYPE	VARCHAR2(8)	N	DIAG	<Activity Type>	Item Type
	ACTIVITY_NAME	VARCHAR2(30)	N	DIAG	<Activity Type>	Internal Name
*	INSTANCE_ID	NUMBER	N	Not Visable		
**	INSTANCE_LABEL	VARCHAR2(30)	N	DIAG	Node	Label
	PERFORM_ROLE_TYPE	VARCHAR2(8)	N	DIAG	Node	Performer Type
	START_END	VARCHAR2(8)	Y	DIAG	Node	Start/End
	DEFAULT_RESULT	VARCHAR2(30)	Y		Node (if Start/End = End)	Result
	ICON_GEOMETRY	VARCHAR2(2000)	Y	Not Visable		
	PERFORM_ROLE	VARCHAR2(320)	Y	DIAG	Node	Performer Value
	USER_COMMENT	VARCHAR2(240)	Y	DIAG	Node	Comment

**   This table has a second set of columns that function as a primary key

FIGURE 10.41

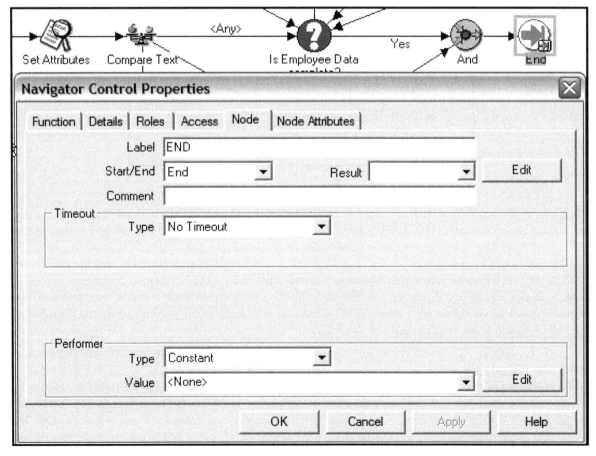

FIGURE 10.42

WF_ACTIVITY_TRANSITIONS – design

This table stores the arrows (legs) in the diagram. The table stores the starting and ending Activity and the geometry necessary to redraw the arrow. If the starting Activity has a result and/or Timeout, this table stores the value assigned to the leg. FIGURE 10.43 shows the columns in this table.

PK	COLUMN_NAME	TYPE	NULLABLE
*	FROM_PROCESS_ACTIVITY	NUMBER	N
*	RESULT_CODE	VARCHAR2(30)	N
*	TO_PROCESS_ACTIVITY	NUMBER	N
	ARROW_GEOMETRY	VARCHAR2(2000)	Y

FIGURE 10.43

WF_ITEMS – runtime

FIGURE 10.44 shows the columns in this table.

PK	COLUMN_NAME	TYPE	NULLABLE
*	ITEM_TYPE	VARCHAR2(8)	N
*	ITEM_KEY	VARCHAR2(240)	N
	ROOT_ACTIVITY	VARCHAR2(30)	N
	ROOT_ACTIVITY_VERSION	NUMBER	N
	OWNER_ROLE	VARCHAR2(320)	Y
	PARENT_ITEM_TYPE	VARCHAR2(8)	Y
	PARENT_ITEM_KEY	VARCHAR2(240)	Y
	PARENT_CONTEXT	VARCHAR2(2000)	Y
	BEGIN_DATE	DATE	N
	END_DATE	DATE	Y
	USER_KEY	VARCHAR2(240)	Y

FIGURE 10.44

Whenever a Workflow is started, a record is inserted in this table. ITEM_TYPE and ITEM_KEY form the unique key to this table. USER_KEY and OWNER_ROLE may be set as the Workflow is initiated or set in the Workflow using special APIs. OWNER_ROLE maps to NAME in WF_LOCAL_ROLES. ROOT_ACTIVITY and ROOT_ACTIVITY_VERSION store the starting Process for the Workflow. BEGIN_DATE indicates when the Workflow started and END_DATE when it completed. There is nothing in this record to indicate whether the Workflow is operating normally or is in error status. Thus, counting Workflows in this table where END_DATE is NULL gives the number of active Workflows, but will also include the count of errored Workflows.

If the Workflow is initiated from another Workflow then PARENT_ITEM_TYPE and PARENT_ITEM_KEY will contain the name of the original Workflow. Thus, whenever a Workflow errors and invokes the System Error (WFERROR) Workflow, these fields in the WFERROR Workflow identify which Workflow errored. Another example of parent/child is the Order Header (OEOH) and Order Line (OEOL) Workflows. Each of the OEOL Workflows refer back to a specific OEOH Workflow. Remember that you will not be able to purge a child or parent Workflow until the parent and all the children are complete.

PARENT_CONTEXT links to the Activity that either called the child Workflow or where the parent Workflow should resume. WFERROR uses this field to store the INSTANCE_ID (key to WF_PROCESS_ACTIVITIES) of the node that errored causing WFERROR to start. The CONTINUE_FLOW Activity uses this field to identify which CONTINUE_FLOW in the parent to link to.

WF_ITEM_ATTRIBUTE_VALUES – runtime

FIGURE 10.45 shows the columns in this table.

PK	COLUMN_NAME	TYPE	NULLABLE
*	ITEM_TYPE	VARCHAR2(8)	N
*	ITEM_KEY	VARCHAR2(240)	N
*	NAME	VARCHAR2(30)	N
	TEXT_VALUE	VARCHAR2(4000)	Y
	NUMBER_VALUE	NUMBER	Y
	DATE_VALUE	DATE	Y
	EVENT_VALUE	WF_EVENT_T	Y

FIGURE 10.45

This table stores the values of the Item Attributes for a particular Workflow. ITEM_TYPE and ITEM_KEY are the foreign keys to WF_ITEMS. ITEM_KEY identifies the specific Workflow. If the WF_ITEM_ATTRIBUTE.TYPE is NUMBER, the value is stored in NUMBER_VALUE; otherwise, if it is DATE, the value is stored in DATE_VALUE; otherwise, if it is EVENT, the value is stored in EVENT_VALUE; otherwise, for all other types, the value is stored in TEXT_VALUE.

This is the table populated by the APIs WF_ENGINE.SetItemAttr<type>.

WF_NOTIFICATIONS – runtime

FIGURE 10.46 shows the columns in this table.

PK	COLUMN_NAME	TYPE	NULLABLE
*	NOTIFICATION_ID	NUMBER	N
	GROUP_ID	NUMBER	N
	MESSAGE_TYPE	VARCHAR2(8)	N
	MESSAGE_NAME	VARCHAR2(30)	N
	RECIPIENT_ROLE	VARCHAR2(320)	N
	STATUS	VARCHAR2(8)	N
	ACCESS_KEY	VARCHAR2(80)	N
	MAIL_STATUS	VARCHAR2(8)	Y
	PRIORITY	NUMBER	Y
	BEGIN_DATE	DATE	Y
	END_DATE	DATE	Y
	DUE_DATE	DATE	Y
	RESPONDER	VARCHAR2(320)	Y
	USER_COMMENT	VARCHAR2(4000)	Y
	CALLBACK	VARCHAR2(240)	Y
	CONTEXT	VARCHAR2(2000)	Y
	ORIGINAL_RECIPIENT	VARCHAR2(320)	N
	FROM_USER	VARCHAR2(320)	Y
	TO_USER	VARCHAR2(320)	Y
	SUBJECT	VARCHAR2(2000)	Y
	LANGUAGE	VARCHAR2(4)	Y
	MORE_INFO_ROLE	VARCHAR2(320)	Y
	FROM_ROLE	VARCHAR2(320)	Y
	USER_KEY	VARCHAR2(240)	Y
	ITEM_KEY	VARCHAR2(240)	Y
	PROTECTED_TEXT_ATTRIBUTE1	VARCHAR2(4000)	Y
	.....		
	PROTECTED_TEXT_ATTRIBUTE10	VARCHAR2(4000)	Y
	PROTECTED_FORM_ATTRIBUTE1	VARCHAR2(4000)	Y
	.....		
	PROTECTED_FORM_ATTRIBUTE5	VARCHAR2(4000)	Y
	PROTECTED_URL_ATTRIBUTE1	VARCHAR2(4000)	Y
	.....		
	PROTECTED_URL_ATTRIBUTE5	VARCHAR2(4000)	Y
	PROTECTED_DATE_ATTRIBUTE1	DATE	Y
	.....		
	PROTECTED_DATE_ATTRIBUTE5	DATE	Y
	PROTECTED_NUMBER_ATTRIBUTE1	NUMBER	Y
	.....		
	PROTECTED_NUMBER_ATTRIBUTE5	NUMBER	Y
	TEXT_ATTRIBUTE1	VARCHAR2(4000)	Y
	.....		
	TEXT_ATTRIBUTE10	VARCHAR2(4000)	Y
	FORM_ATTRIBUTE1	VARCHAR2(4000)	Y
	.....		
	FORM_ATTRIBUTE5	VARCHAR2(4000)	Y
	URL_ATTRIBUTE1	VARCHAR2(4000)	Y
	.....		
	URL_ATTRIBUTE5	VARCHAR2(4000)	Y
	DATE_ATTRIBUTE1	DATE	Y
	.....		
	DATE_ATTRIBUTE5	DATE	Y
	NUMBER_ATTRIBUTE1	NUMBER	Y

FIGURE 10.46

This table not only stores the Notifications sent by Workflows, but also those sent by the Concurrent Manager when one asks to be notified that a program completes. If the 'Expand Roles' box is checked for a Notification, this table stores a separate copy of the Notification for each member of the Role assigned to the Notification Activity. As of ATG_PF.H.delta.4 (Rollup 4), Oracle Alert uses the Notification Mailer to send Notifications. However, these Notifications are not stored in

WF_NOTIFICATIONS. Oracle Alert places the Notification directly in the WF_NOTIFICATION_OUT queue..

The key to this table is NOTIFICATION_ID. However GROUP_ID is the link to WF_ITEM_ACTIVITY_STATUSES.NOTIFICATION_ID. If the 'Expand Roles' box is checked, all copies of the Notification will have the same GROUP_ID but a different NOTIFICATION_ID. Additionally, if the 'Request More Information' button is checked, the Notification resulting from this will have the same GROUP_ID, but a different NOTIFICATION_ID.

MESSAGE_TYPE and MESSAGE_NAME are the foreign keys to WF_MESSAGES. MESSAGE_TYPE is also the foreign key to WF_ITEMS and WF_ITEM_TYPES. Thus, you can use this table to determine which Item Type is generating the most Notifications.

PRIORITY originates from the Node tab of the Notification. SUBJECT will be the Message subject with the run-time values of all Message Attributes.

BEGIN_DATE indicates when the Notification was first generated. END_DATE indicates when the Notification was closed. DUE_DATE is set if a Timeout is assigned to the Notification Activity.

ORIGINAL_RECIPIENT indicates the Role assigned to the Notification Activity in the Workflow. RECIPIENT_ROLE indicates the actual Role that is to receive the Notification. These values will be different if there are Vacation Rules or if the 'Expand Roles' box is checked. RESPONDER indicates the Role that answered the Notification. FROM_USER, TO_USER, MORE_INFO_ROLE, and FROM_ROLE are used to track forwarding and the Request More Information Notifications.

11*i*.ATG_PF.H RUP 3 and Release 12 added columns to this table to support Worklist Flexfields. Worklist Flexfields allow the mapping of Message Attributes not included in the subject to special columns that can be seen in the 'Notification Worklist' page along with the subject. For an explanation of how to set up this feature, see *Chapter 13, New Features*.

The following columns are reserved for Oracle–defined Worklist Flexfields:

- PROTECTED_TEXT_ATTRIBUTE1...10

- PROTECTED_NUMBER_ATTRIBUTE1...5

- PROTECTED_DATE_ATTRIBUTE1...5

- PROTECTED_URL_ATTRIBUTE1...5

- PROTECTED_FORM_ATTRIBUTE1....5

The following columns are available for customer–defined Worklist Flexfields:

- USER_KEY

- ITEM_KEY

- TEXT_ATTRIBUTE1...10

- NUMBER_ATTRIBUTE1...5

- DATE_ATTRIBUTE1...5

- URL_ATTRIBUTE1...5

• FORM_ATTRIBUTE1….5

STATUS indicates the status of the Notification and MAIL_STATUS the status of the email copy of the Notification. Table 10.1 shows the possible values for these columns and what each value represents.

STATUS

Value	Meaning
OPEN	Either an 'FYI' Notification that hasn't been closed or a 'Response Required' Notification that hasn't been responded to
CLOSED	The Notification can no longer be acted on (i.e., the 'FYI' was closed or the 'Response Required' was replied to)
CANCELED	The Notification timed out or the Workflow was aborted

MAIL_STATUS

Value	Meaning
<NULL>	No email will be sent
SENT	The Notification was emailed successfully
MAIL	The Mailer has not acted on this transaction
ERROR	Either the recipient is invalid or the Notification Mailer received a response to a Notification and the subject of the email matches a pattern in the Notification Mailer tag file and the Action for that tag is ERROR. The Notification remains open, but the status of the Notification is marked in ERROR status and the appropriate error Workflow is invoked
FAILED	Status introduced in Release 12 and 11i.ATG_PF.H.delta.5 (RUP 5) to indicate the Notification Mailer has marked the recipient's Notification preference to DISABLED due to a missing or invalid email address
UNAVAIL	The Mailer received a response to a Notification and the subject of the email matches a pattern in the Notification Mailer tag file and the Action for that tag is UNAVAIL. The Notification remains open and waiting for a reply. This would be a typical reaction to receiving an 'Out of Office' reply
INVALID	The Mailer received a response to a Notification but the response is not in the Lookup Type. The Notification remains open and waiting for a reply. The responder is sent an email indicating the response was invalid. This usually happens when the Notification preference is set to 'Plain Text' and the responder types in a response either spelled incorrectly or not matching the case of valid response values

TABLE 10. 1

Chapter 13, New Features, details how to correct invalid email addresses and how to use the program 'Resend Failed/Error Workflow Notifications' to resend Notifications with a status of ERROR or FAILED.

USER_COMMENT is obsolete with Release 11.5.10 and is replaced with the table WF_COMMENTS.

Prior to Release 11.5.10, ACCESS_KEY was used to determine whether users were required to log into the applications to reply to emails. Now it only has significance for stand-alone Workflow.

CALLBACK is set to WF_ENGINE.CB. CONTEXT is set to <item type (internal name)>:<item key>:<WF_PROCESS_ACTIVITIES.INSTANCE_ID for the Notification Activity>. CONTEXT is passed to WF_ENGINE.CB which checks for and calls the post-Notification Function if one exists.

WF_NOTIFICATION_ATTRIBUTES – runtime

FIGURE 10.47 shows the columns in this table

PK	COLUMN_NAME	TYPE	NULLABLE
*	NOTIFICATION_ID	NUMBER	N
*	NAME	VARCHAR2(30)	N
	TEXT_VALUE	VARCHAR2(4000)	Y
	NUMBER_VALUE	NUMBER	Y
	DATE_VALUE	DATE	Y
	EVENT_VALUE	WF_EVENT_T	Y

FIGURE 10.47

This table contains the run-time values of all the Message Attributes for a specific Notification. The key to this table is NOTIFICATION_ID and NAME. NOTIFICATION_ID links to NOTIFICATION_ID in WF_NOTIFICATIONS and NAME links to NAME in WF_MESSAGE_ATTRIBUTES. The value of the Attribute is stored in TEXT_VALUE, NUMBER_VALUE, DATE_VALUE, or EVENT_VALUE based on WF_MESSAGE_ATTRIBUTE.TYPE.

WF_COMMENTS – runtime

FIGURE 10.48 shows the columns in this table.

PK	COLUMN_NAME	TYPE	NULLABLE
	NOTIFICATION_ID	NUMBER	N
	FROM_ROLE	VARCHAR2(320)	N
	FROM_USER	VARCHAR2(360)	N
	COMMENT_DATE	DATE	N
	ACTION	VARCHAR2(30)	N
	USER_COMMENT	VARCHAR2(4000)	Y
	LANGUAGE	VARCHAR2(4)	Y
	TO_ROLE	VARCHAR2(320)	Y
	TO_USER	VARCHAR2(360)	Y
	PROXY_ROLE	VARCHAR2(320)	Y
	ACTION_TYPE	VARCHAR2(30)	Y
	SEQUENCE	NUMBER	Y

FIGURE 10.48

This table was introduced in Release 11.5.10 and replaces the WF_NOTIFICATIONS.USER_COMMENT column. This table is used to construct the Notification History table.

'FROM_ROLE' is the Role that made the comment, 'FROM_USER' is the Display Name of 'FROM_ROLE', 'TO_ROLE' and 'TO_USER' are the Role and Role Display Name of the person to whom a Notification is transferred or forwarded. 'PROXY_ROLE' will be utilized as the Workflow recognizes the difference between 'TRANSFER' and 'FORWARD'.

ACTION can be QUESTION ('Request More Information' button), ANSWER (response to 'Request More Information' button), TRANSFER, TRANSER_WA, FORWARD or FORWARD_WA ('Reassign' button), CANCEL (Notification was in a loop and 'On Revisit' was set to 'Reset' or Notification was one of 'Expand Roles' and answer was received by someone else), TIMEOUT' (Notification times out) or RESPOND (Notification was answered).

ACTION_TYPE is very similar to ACTION and is used to refine ACTION_TYPE (for example if ACTION = 'REASSIGN', ACTION_TYPE may be 'TRANSFER' or 'FORWARD').

Sequence orders the Notifications for a specific Notification Activity so that the Notification history is correctly displayed.

WF_ITEM_ACTIVITY_STATUSES – runtime

FIGURE 10.49 shows the columns in this table.

PK	COLUMN_NAME	TYPE	NULLABLE
*	ITEM_TYPE	VARCHAR2(8)	N
*	ITEM_KEY	VARCHAR2(240)	N
*	PROCESS_ACTIVITY	NUMBER	N
	ACTIVITY_STATUS	VARCHAR2(8)	Y
	ACTIVITY_RESULT_CODE	VARCHAR2(30)	Y
	ASSIGNED_USER	VARCHAR2(320)	Y
	NOTIFICATION_ID	NUMBER	Y
	BEGIN_DATE	DATE	Y
	END_DATE	DATE	Y
	EXECUTION_TIME	NUMBER	Y
	ERROR_NAME	VARCHAR2(30)	Y
	ERROR_MESSAGE	VARCHAR2(2000)	Y
	ERROR_STACK	VARCHAR2(4000)	Y
	OUTBOUND_QUEUE_ID	RAW	Y
	DUE_DATE	DATE	Y
	ACTION	VARCHAR2(30)	Y

FIGURE 10.49

This table has a companion table, WF_ITEM_ACTIVITY_STATUSES_H. Together these tables contain all the activities executed by a specific occurrence of a Workflow. The unique key to this table is ITEM_TYPE combined with ITEM_KEY and PROCESS_ACTIVITY. PROCESS_ACTIVITY links to INSTANCE_ID in WF_PROCESS_ACTIVITIES.

BEGIN_DATE and END_DATE give the start and completion dates for the Activity. EXECUTION_TIME is used to sequence the Events. If the Activity has been assigned a Timeout, DUE_DATE indicates when the Timeout will expire.

If the Activity is a Notification, ASSIGNED_USER holds the Role that should receive the Notification according to the Notification Activity definition. NOTIFICATION_ID links to GROUP_ID in WF_NOTIFICATIONS. Remember, WF_NOTIFICATIONS will hold the Role name of the actual recipient of the Notification. The actual recipient is the assigned Role with the application of any Vacation Rules, forwarding, etc.

OUTBOUND_QUEUE_ID is used to store the Outbound Queue ID if the Activity is an Event with an Action of SEND.

ERROR_NAME, ERROR_MESSAGE, and ERROR_STACK are set when the Workflow errors. These columns can be used for all Workflows of a particular type that have the same error. However, many times the ERROR_MESSAGE contains a piece of data (such as the item_key) that makes the Message unique for each Workflow. This unique value is usually preceded by a '/' so it is possible to craft SQL that masks these unique values.

ACTIVITY_STATUS may be any of the Workflow Engine statuses. The statuses are:

- **COMPLETE** – the Activity is finished, either the Event was processed, the code assigned to the Activity completed normally, the Notification has been sent (and if a response is required, the response was received), or the Process has completed

- **NOTIFIED** – this is the status assigned to Notifications waiting for a response or activities, such as BLOCK, that require an external program to indicate it is OK for the Workflow to proceed, or Event activities that are not Start activities, but are waiting to receive an Event

- **ERROR** – the Activity did not complete as designed

- **DEFERRED** – the Activity has a cost that exceeds the Background Engine cost and is waiting for the appropriate Background Engine to run

- **ACTIVE** – the Activity is running – this is the status assigned to the first node of a Process when the Process is started and indicates that the Process is running

- **WAITING** – a Notification has 'Expand Roles' checked and all the responses have not been received

- **SUSPEND** – this status is assigned if the Workflow Administrator suspends the Process or Process Activity

ACTIVITY_RESULT_CODE indicates the result returned for a Notification or Function Activity. Oracle uses this column to indicate:

- **#EXCEPTION** – when an Activity has errored

- **#FORCE** – when the 'Status Monitor' has been used to abort a Workflow or skip a Notification

- **#MAIL** – when a Notification cannot be emailed or when the Workflow Engine is trying to cancel a Notification and there is no Notification waiting to be cancelled

- **#TIMEOUT** – when a Notification has timed out

- **#STUCK** – when an Activity returns a result not modeled by the diagram or when a Loop Activity transitions back to the starting node and 'On Revisit' is set to Ignore, or when a Activity reaches an End Node not properly configured as an End Node

WF_ITEM_ACTIVITY_STATUSES_V – runtime View

The joins for these tables can get complex. Oracle has created a view that mirrors the information shown in the 'Status Monitor' when the 'Activities History' button is clicked. FIGURE 10.50 shows the columns in this view and the source table or view for each column. FIGURE 10.51 shows the joins for the various tables and views.

COLUMN NAME	TYPE	SOURCE TABLE	SOURCE COLUMN
ROW_ID	ROWID	ITEM_ACTIVITY_STATUSES	ITEM_TYPE
SOURCE	CHAR	'R'	
ITEM_TYPE	VARCHAR2(8)	ITEM_ACTIVITY_STATUSES	ITEM_TYPE
ITEM_TYPE_DISPLAY_NAME	VARCHAR2(80)	WF_ITEM_TYPES_VL	DISPLAY_NAME
ITEM_TYPE_DESCRIPTION	VARCHAR2(240)	WF_ITEM_TYPES_VL	DESCRIPTION
ITEM_KEY	VARCHAR2(240)	ITEM_ACTIVITY_STATUSES	ITEM_KEY
USER_KEY	VARCHAR2(240)	WF_ITEMS	USER_KEY
ITEM_BEGIN_DATE	DATE	WF_ITEMS	BEGIN_DATE
ITEM_END_DATE	DATE	WF_ITEMS	END_DATE
ACTIVITY_ID	NUMBER	ITEM_ACTIVITY_STATUSES	PROCESS_ACTIVITY
ACTIVITY_LABEL	VARCHAR2(30)	WF_PROCESS_ACTIVITIES	INSTANCE_LABEL
ACTIVITY_NAME	VARCHAR2(30)	WF_ACTIVITIES_VL	NAME
ACTIVITY_DISPLAY_NAME	VARCHAR2(80)	WF_ACTIVITIES_VL	DISPLAY_NAME
ACTIVITY_DESCRIPTION	VARCHAR2(240)	WF_ACTIVITIES_VL	DESCRIPTION
ACTIVITY_TYPE_CODE	VARCHAR2(8)	WF_ACTIVITIES_VL	TYPE
ACTIVITY_TYPE_DISPLAY_NAME	VARCHAR2(80)	WF_LOOKUPS*	
EXECUTION_TIME	NUMBER	ITEM_ACTIVITY_STATUSES	EXECUTION_TIME
ACTIVITY_BEGIN_DATE	DATE	ITEM_ACTIVITY_STATUSES	BEGIN_DATE
ACTIVITY_END_DATE	DATE	ITEM_ACTIVITY_STATUSES	END_DATE
ACTIVITY_STATUS_CODE	VARCHAR2(8)	ITEM_ACTIVITY_STATUSES	ACTIVITY_STATUS
ACTIVITY_STATUS_DISPLAY_NAME	VARCHAR2(80)	WF_LOOKUPS**	
ACTIVITY_RESULT_CODE	VARCHAR2(30)	ITEM_ACTIVITY_STATUSES	ACTIVITY_RESULT_CODE
ACTIVITY_RESULT_DISPLAY_NAME	VARCHAR2(4000)	***	
ASSIGNED_USER	VARCHAR2(320)	ITEM_ACTIVITY_STATUSES	ASSIGNED_USER
ASSIGNED_USER_DISPLAY_NAME	VARCHAR2(4000)	****	
NOTIFICATION_ID	NUMBER	ITEM_ACTIVITY_STATUSES	NOTIFICATION_ID
OUTBOUND_QUEUE_ID	RAW	ITEM_ACTIVITY_STATUSES	OUTBOUND_QUEUE_ID
ERROR_NAME	VARCHAR2(30)	ITEM_ACTIVITY_STATUSES	ERROR_NAME
ERROR_MESSAGE	VARCHAR2(2000)	ITEM_ACTIVITY_STATUSES	ERROR_MESSAGE
ERROR_STACK	VARCHAR2(4000)	ITEM_ACTIVITY_STATUSES	ERROR_STACK

* LOOKUP_TYPE = 'WFENG_ACTIVITY_TYPE' and LOOKUP_CODE = WF_ACTIVITIES_VL.TYPE
**LOOKUP_TYPE='WFENG_STATUS' and LOOKUP_CODE = WF_ITEM_ACTIVITY_STATUSES.ACTIVITY_STATUS
***WF_CORE.ACTIVITY_RESULT(WF_ACTIVITIES_VL.RESULT_TYPE, WF_ITEM_ACTIVITY_STATUSES.ACTIVITY_RESULT_CODE)
****WF_DIRECTORY.GetRoleDisplayName(WF_ITEM_ACTIVITY_STATUSES.ASSIGNED_USER)

FIGURE 10.50

This view is excellent for simple queries; however, it is a view. Performance will degrade if this view is used in complex joins to other tables or views.

	JOINS		
	WF_ITEM_ACTIVITY_STATUSES.ITEM_TYPE	=	WF_ITEMS.ITEM_TYPE
AND	WF_ITEM_ACTIVITY_STATUSES.ITEM_KEY	=	WF_ITEMS.ITEM_KEY
AND	WF_ITEM.BEGIN_DATE	between	WF_ACTIVITIES_VL.BEGIN_DATE
		and	nvl(WF_ACTIVITIES_VL.END_DATE, WF_ITEMS.BEGIN_DATE)
AND	WF_ITEMS.ITEM_TYPE	=	WF_ITEM_TYPES_TL.NAME
AND	WF_ITEM_ACTIVITY_STATUSES.PROCESS_ACTIVITY	=	WF_PROCESS_ACTIVITIES.INSTANCE_ID
AND	WF_PROCESS_ACTIVITIES.ACTIVITY_NAME	=	WF_ACTIVITIES_VL.NAME
AND	WF_PROCESS_ACTIVITIES.ITEM_TYPE	=	WF_ACTIVITIES_VL.ITEM_TYPE

FIGURE 10.51

SAMPLE QUERIES – RUNTIME AND DESIGN

The runtime and design tables contain a lot of data. The following queries show some examples we have found useful in managing large Workflow environments. These are just samples; there are many more queries that can be constructed.

Open and Closed Workflow Counts

It is useful to know which Workflows an organization is running and how many are active, closed, or in error status. This information is also available from the charts in the 'Workflow Manager' page of the Oracle Applications Manager.

The following query returns the total number of Workflows, active and inactive.

```
SELECT COUNT(*), item_type FROM wf_items
GROUP BY item_type
ORDER BY item_type;
```

Closed Workflows should eventually be purged. The following query will indicate the oldest Workflows by type. If the age pre-dates your purge criteria, then the Workflow may have a child or parent that is still open.

```
SELECT  MIN (begin_date),item_type FROM wf_items WHERE end_date IS NOT NULL
GROUP BY item_type
ORDER BY item_type;
```

Errored Workflow Counts

Errored Workflows are always of concern. The following query shows the oldest Workflow in error status by Item Type. Replacing MAX with MIN shows the newest error status by Item Type. These queries help identify Workflows whose errors are either still occurring or haven't occurred recently. If the latter, the assumption can be made that recent patches have fixed the error, but not dealt with the errors.

```
SELECT  COUNT (*),item_type,MAX (item_begin_date)
  FROM  wf_item_activity_statuses_v
 WHERE  activity_status_code = 'ERROR' AND item_end_date IS NULL
GROUP BY item_type
ORDER BY item_type;
```

When troubleshooting Workflows, it is dangerous to assume that Workflows are erroring at the same Activity each time. The following query identifies the Activity in the Workflow that is erroring.

```
SELECT  COUNT (*),item_type,activity_name
  FROM  wf_item_activity_statuses_v
 WHERE  activity_status_code = 'ERROR' AND item_end_date IS NULL
GROUP BY item_type,activity_name
ORDER BY item_type,activity_name;
```

The following query identifies the WFERRORs that need to be closed because the Workflow that errored is already closed. Until WFERROR is closed, the associated completed Workflow cannot be purged.

```
SELECT  i1.parent_item_type,COUNT (*) FROM wf_items i1
 WHERE i1.item_type = 'WFERROR'
   AND end_date IS NULL
   AND i1.parent_item_type IS NOT NULL
   AND i1.parent_item_key IN (
       SELECT i2.item_key FROM wf_items i2
        WHERE i2.item_type = i1.parent_item_type
          AND i2.item_key = i1.parent_item_key
          AND i2.end_date IS NOT NULL)
GROUP BY i1.parent_item_type
ORDER BY i1.parent_item_type;
```

WFERROR is not the only Workflow that sends a Message to SYSADMIN. If these Messages are ignored, Workflows do not progress. The following query identifies open Notifications to SYSADMIN that do not originate from WFERROR.

```
SELECT  COUNT (*),n.MESSAGE_TYPE,SUBSTR (n.recipient_role, 1, 20),
        SUBSTR (n.subject, 1, 22)
  FROM  wf_notifications n
```

```
   WHERE    n.status = 'OPEN' AND n.MESSAGE_TYPE <> 'WFERROR'
      AND    n.notification_id IN
             (SELECT notification_id FROM wf_notification_attributes
               WHERE NAME = 'ERROR_MESSAGE')
   GROUP BY n.MESSAGE_TYPE,n.recipient_role,SUBSTR (n.subject, 1, 22)
   ORDER BY n.message_type,n.recipient_role,SUBSTR (n.subject, 1, 22);
```

Notification Counts

The following query returns counts of Notification by status and mail status. This is useful for managing Notifications that are not being emailed correctly.

```
SELECT   COUNT (*),status,mail_status FROM wf_notifications
GROUP BY status,mail_status;
```

The result of this query is shown in FIGURE 10.52.

COUNT(*)	STATUS	MAIL STATUS
34	CANCELED	ERROR
1	CLOSED	ERROR
156	CANCELED	FAILED
13	OPEN	FAILED
5	CANCELED	MAIL
67	CLOSED	MAIL
3	OPEN	MAIL
111	CANCELED	SENT
299	CLOSED	SENT
41	OPEN	SENT
6074	CANCELED	
1091	CLOSED	
165825	OPEN	

FIGURE 10.52

Remember, the STATUS field indicates the status of the Notification. OPEN is either an 'FYI' Notification that hasn't been closed or a 'Response Required' Notification that hasn't been responded to yet. CLOSED means the Notification can no longer be acted upon (i.e., 'FYI' was closed, or 'Response Required' replied to). CANCELED means either the Notification timed out or the Workflow was aborted.

The MAIL_STATUS field indicates the status of the email copy of the Notification. NULL indicates no email will be sent. SENT indicates the email was sent. MAIL indicates the Notification Mailer has not acted on this transaction. ERROR indicates that the Notification Mailer tried to email the Notification but couldn't.

Although there are 35 Notifications in ERROR status and 169 in FAILED status, only 13 of these Notifications are open and should be of any concern. MAIL_STATUS = MAIL indicates either that the Notification Mailer is down, or the Event to actually email the Notification is no longer in WF_NOTIFICATION_OUT. MetaLink Doc. ID: 332152.1, *OWF.H Diagnostics and Solutions* contains a section on troubleshooting the Notification Mailer.

Oracle provides the Concurrent Program 'Resend Failed/Error Workflow Notifications' to re-attempt Notifications with MAIL_STATUS in ('ERROR', 'FAILED'). However, of the 204 Notifications in these statuses, only 13 should be re-attempted. Before running this program, execute the following update:

```
UPDATE wf_notifications
   SET mail_status = NULL
 WHERE mail_status = 'ERROR'
   AND status in ('CLOSED','CANCELLED');
```

The MetaLink note mentioned above also includes instructions for re-building WF_NOTIFICAITON_OUT (which is the only way to resend Notifications where MAIL_STATUS = 'MAIL'). Again look at the 'STATUS' column. Use the above update, substituting 'MAIL' for 'ERROR' to ensure closed and canceled emails are not resent.

EVENT TABLES

The Event tables consist of the definition of Systems, Agents, Events, Subscriptions and the Queue tables. Rather than focus on every column in every table, this section will focus on key columns and their impact on troubleshooting Workflows.

WF_SYSTEMS

This table contains the Local System and the identification of all systems to which Event Messages are sent or from which Event Messages are received. The GUID is a 34-character string of hexadecimal characters that uniquely identifies a system. This ID is especially important when sending/receiving Messages to/from External Systems. The NAME and DISPLAY_NAME identify the database instance. When the database is installed, it is automatically defined as a system in the Event Manager and set as the Local System in the 'Workflow Configuration' page (see FIGURE 10.53).

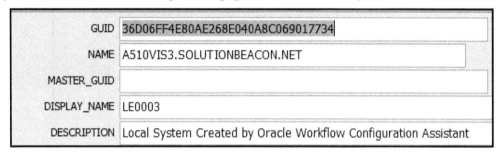

FIGURE 10.53

Make sure all clones have a different GUID, NAME, and DISPLAY_NAME, especially if they reside on the same server.

WF_AGENTS

This table contains the Agents on the Local System. GUID in this table is the unique identification of the Agent. SYSTEM_GUID should be the same as the WF_SYSTEMS.GUID for the row in WF_SYSTEMS that identifies the Local System.

The 'NUM_<>' columns are used to provide the information in the Agent Activity Histogram and chart. These numbers are updated by clicking the 'Refresh' button or by running the Concurrent Program 'Workflow Agent Activity Statistics' Concurrent Program (see FIGURE 10.54).

When cloning, make sure the SYSTEM_GUID and the address are updated to match the new instance. See *Chapter 8, Administration*, for further details on cloning.

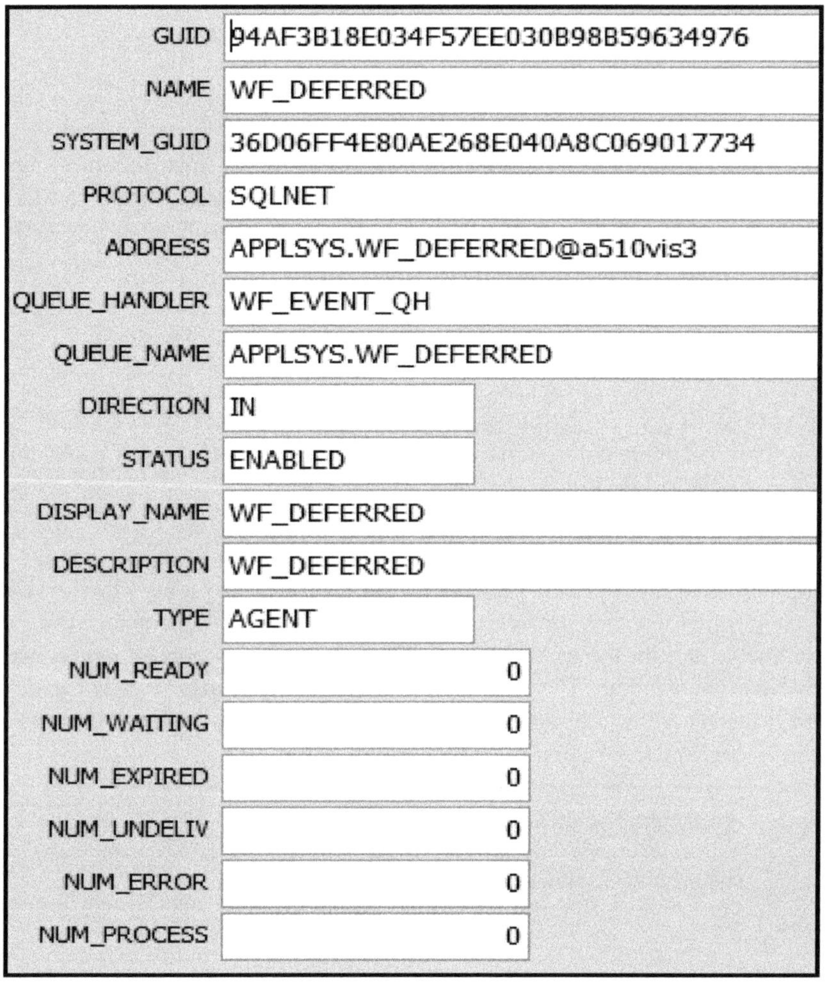

GUID	94AF3B18E034F57EE030B98B59634976
NAME	WF_DEFERRED
SYSTEM_GUID	36D06FF4E80AE268E040A8C069017734
PROTOCOL	SQLNET
ADDRESS	APPLSYS.WF_DEFERRED@a510vis3
QUEUE_HANDLER	WF_EVENT_QH
QUEUE_NAME	APPLSYS.WF_DEFERRED
DIRECTION	IN
STATUS	ENABLED
DISPLAY_NAME	WF_DEFERRED
DESCRIPTION	WF_DEFERRED
TYPE	AGENT
NUM_READY	0
NUM_WAITING	0
NUM_EXPIRED	0
NUM_UNDELIV	0
NUM_ERROR	0
NUM_PROCESS	0

FIGURE 10.54

WF_EVENTS

This table stores the definition of all the Events and Event Groups (see FIGURE 10.55).

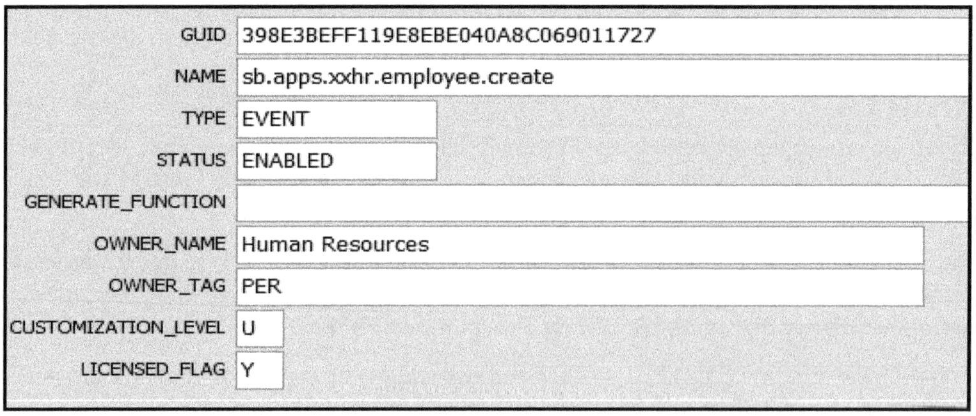

GUID	398E3BEFF119E8EBE040A8C069011727
NAME	sb.apps.xxhr.employee.create
TYPE	EVENT
STATUS	ENABLED
GENERATE_FUNCTION	
OWNER_NAME	Human Resources
OWNER_TAG	PER
CUSTOMIZATION_LEVEL	U
LICENSED_FLAG	Y

FIGURE 10.55

'GUID' is the unique identifier of the Event. Remember that the 'OWNER_TAG' must match FND_APPLICATION.APPLICATION_SHORT_NAME. 'LICENSED_FLAG' is set to 'Y' if the application referenced by 'OWNER_TAG' is Installed or Shared; otherwise, it is set to 'N'. The customization level is 'U' if user-defined, 'C' if Oracle-defined and Oracle will not allow the Event to be disabled, and 'L' if Oracle-defined and Oracle will allow the Event to be disabled.

WF_EVENT_GROUPS

This table stores the link between the Event Group and the members of the group. Both 'GROUP_GUID' and 'MEMBER_GUID' link to 'WF_EVENT.GUID'. The former is the group definition and the latter the member of the group.

WF_SUBSCRIPTIONS

This table stores the definition of all the Subscriptions. See FIGURE 10.56.

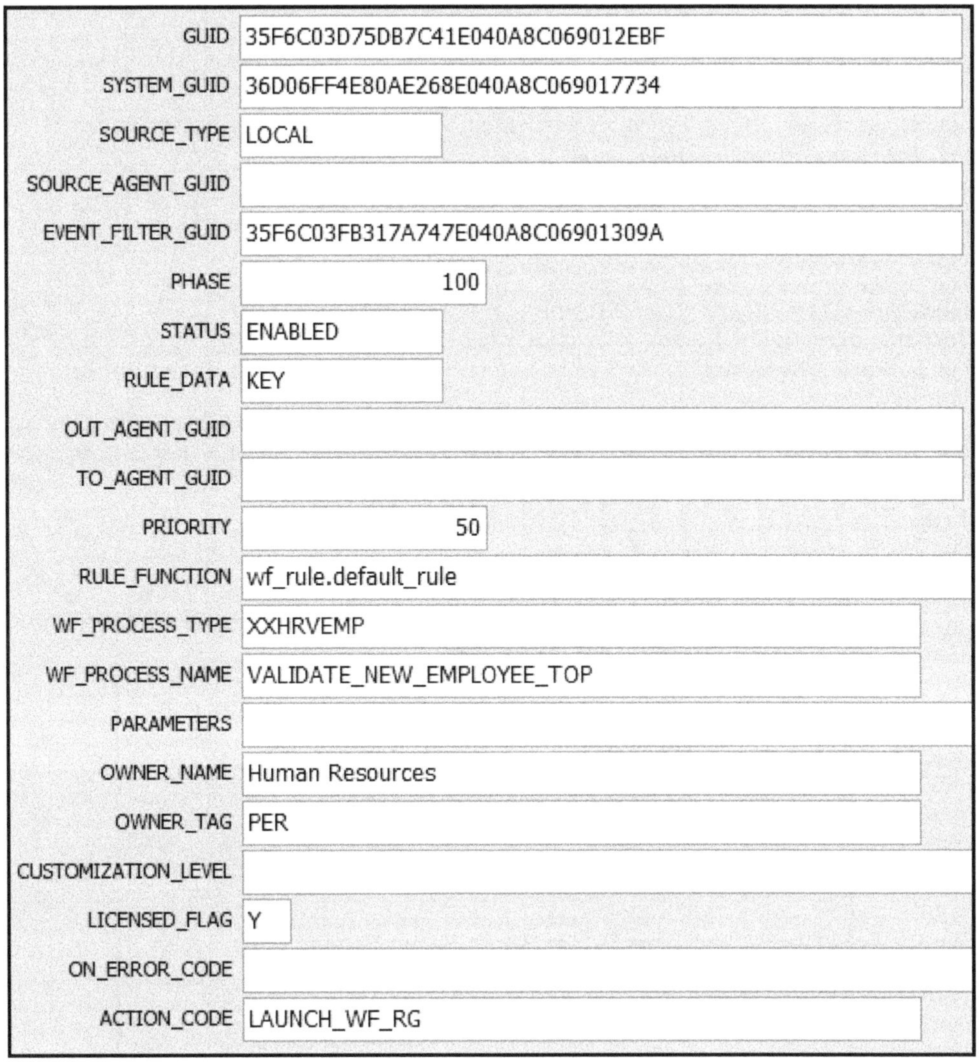

GUID	35F6C03D75DB7C41E040A8C069012EBF
SYSTEM_GUID	36D06FF4E80AE268E040A8C069017734
SOURCE_TYPE	LOCAL
SOURCE_AGENT_GUID	
EVENT_FILTER_GUID	35F6C03FB317A747E040A8C06901309A
PHASE	100
STATUS	ENABLED
RULE_DATA	KEY
OUT_AGENT_GUID	
TO_AGENT_GUID	
PRIORITY	50
RULE_FUNCTION	wf_rule.default_rule
WF_PROCESS_TYPE	XXHRVEMP
WF_PROCESS_NAME	VALIDATE_NEW_EMPLOYEE_TOP
PARAMETERS	
OWNER_NAME	Human Resources
OWNER_TAG	PER
CUSTOMIZATION_LEVEL	
LICENSED_FLAG	Y
ON_ERROR_CODE	
ACTION_CODE	LAUNCH_WF_RG

FIGURE 10.56

'GUID' identifies the Subscriptions. 'EVENT_FILTER_GUID' links to 'GUID' in WF_EVENTS. 'SYSTEM_GUID' links to 'GUID' in WF_SYSTEMS. Like Events, 'OWNER_TAG' must match FND_APPLICATION.APPLICATION_SHORT_NAME and 'LICENSED_FLAG' is set to 'Y' if the application referenced by 'OWNER_TAG' is Installed or Shared, otherwise, it is set to 'N'.

'ACTION_CODE' relates to the Action Type field on the 'Define Event Subscriptions' screen. 'LAUNCH_WF_RG' equates to 'Launch Workflow', 'CUSTOM_RG' to 'Custom', 'RECEIVE_TP_MSG_RG' to 'Receive Trading Partner Message', 'SEND_TP_MSG_RG' to 'Send Trading Partner Message', 'SEND_NTF_RG' to 'Send Notification', and 'SEND_AGENT_RG' to 'Send to Agent'.

'ON_ERROR_CODE' relates to the 'On Error' field on the 'Define Event Subscriptions' screen. 'ABORT' or '<NULL>' equates to 'Stop and Rollback' and 'Skip' equates to 'Skip to Next'. The other fields are explained in *Chapter 5, Business Events*.

QUEUE TABLES

The Queues are described in *Chapter 5, Business Events*. Each Queue has a table with the same name as the Queue as well as a set of tables whose name begins with AQ$. All of the AQ$ tables are beyond the scope of this book. To learn more about these tables, read MetaLink Doc. ID: 224027.1, *Objects Created When Creating a Queue Table*. This chapter will focus on the columns in the table that impact the administration of Workflow.

Another table closely resembles the Queue tables, WF_DEFERRED_TABLE_M. This table holds the activities that the Background Engine Processes when Deferred = 'Y'. The discussion of the Queue tables will include this table as well.

FIGURE 10.57 shows some of the key fields in the Queue tables. 'Q_NAME' contains the name of the Queue. 'MSGID' is the unique key to this table. 'CORRID' is 'APPS:' concatenated with the name of the Event (Event Queues) or 'APPS:' concatenated with the Internal Name of the Workflow (WF_DEFERRED_TABLE_M). 'ENQ_TIME' is the time the record was placed in the Queue. 'DEQ_TIME' is the time the Event was processed. 'TIME_MANAGER_INFO' is the time when the record will be purged from the Queue (STATE = 2) or the record will be marked ready (STATE = 1).

Q_NAME	WF_DEFERRED
MSGID	3A725CE1B5198003E040A8C069016FD4
CORRID	APPS:oracle.apps.wf.notification.send
STATE	2
TIME_MANAGER_INFO	9/19/2007 6:36:50.468085 PM
ENQ_TIME	9/18/2007 6:34:37.867973 PM
DEQ_TIME	9/18/2007 6:36:50.468085 PM

FIGURE 10.57

'STATE' indicates the status of the record in the Queue. The following table shows the possible values for this field and what each value represents.

Value	Meaning
0	The Event or activity is ready to process. Usually the Event or activity is processed the next time the Listener wakes up or Background Engine runs.
1	The Event or activity is delayed until the time in TIME_MANAGER_INFO passes.
2	The Event or activity has been processed and will be purged from the table when the retention period has expired.
3	The Event or activity did not process successfully.

TABLE 10. 2

All of these tables contain the field 'USER_DATA'. The data type for this Queue depends on whether the Queue is designed to contain Deferred Activities, SOAP, JAVA, or Text Messages. The following discussion will talk about the data contained in this field for Queues that carry Deferred Activities (WF_PAYLOAD_T), Text Messages (WF_EVENT_T) and Java Messages (SYS.AQ$_JMS_TEXT_MESSAGE).

The Event Data Structure – WF_EVENT_T

Oracle has created several Abstract Datatypes (ADTs) to contain the 'Event Data'. The two basic structures are WF_EVENT_T for text Events and SYS.AQ$_JMS_TEXT_MESSAGE. These structures include other ADTs: WF_AGENT_T, WF_PARAMETER_T, and WF_PARAMETER_LIST_T. ADTs are fully described in the *User Defined Datatypes* chapter of the *Oracle Concepts* manual.

Oracle refers to the WF_EVENT_T and SYS.AQ$_JMS_TEXT_MESSAGE structures as the Event Message. As we drill down into the components of these structures, there will be a piece Oracle calls the 'Event Data', or "a set of additional details describing what occurred in the Event". Other parts of the Oracle Documentation refer to the contents of the field 'Event Data' as the Message, as this field contains the information that needs to be communicated when the Event occurs (such as a XML document or PDF containing an invoice or PO). Usually, the word 'Message' refers to the entire WF_EVENT_T structure.

Workflow API Reference, Release 2.6.4, Part No. B15855-05, June 2006, shows the WF_EVENT_T structure (our comments are in italics):

1. PRIORITY (datatype NUMBER) – the priority with which the Message recipient should dequeue the Message. *50 is normal but the smaller the number, the higher the priority.*

2. SEND_DATE (datatype DATE) – the date and time the Message is available for dequeuing. *The default value is SYSDATE, indicating the Event should be dequeued immediately. If the date is > SYSDATE, the Event is placed on the WF_DEFERRED Queue and waits there until SYSDATE >= SEND_DATE.*

3. RECEIVE_DATE (datatype DATE) – the date and time when the Message is dequeued by an Agent Listener.

4. PARAMETER_LIST (datatype WF_PARAMETER_LIST_T) – A list of additional parameter name and value pairs. *Up to 100 parameters (NAME – VARCHAR2(30) /*

VALUE – VARCHAR2(2000)) can be specified.

5. EVENT_NAME (datatype VARCHAR2(240)) – The Internal Name of the Event.

6. EVENT_KEY (datatype VARCHAR2(240)) – The string that uniquely identifies the instance of the Event.

7. EVENT_DATA (datatype CLOB) – A set of additional details describing what occurred in the Event.

8. FROM_AGENT (datatype WF_AGENT_T) – The Agent from which the Event is sent. For locally raised Events, this Attribute is initially null. *This field contains both the NAME – VARCHAR2(30) and the SYSTEM – VARCHAR2(30).*

9. TO_AGENT (datatype WF_AGENT_T) – The Agent to which the Event should be sent (the Message recipient). *This field contains both the Agent name and the system name.*

10. ERROR_SUBSCRIPTION (datatype RAW(16)) – If an error occurs while processing this Event, this is the Subscription that was being executed when the error was encountered.

11. ERROR_MESSAGE (datatype VARCHAR2(4000)) – An Error Message that the Event Manager generates if an error occurs while processing this Event.

12. ERROR_STACK (datatype VARCHAR2(4000)) – An Error Stack of arguments that the Event Manager generates if an error occurs while processing this Event.

The pictures in FIGURE 10.3 show an example of this data.

```
(Q_CORRELATION_ID, CNCOMPPR:ACCEPT_COMP_PLAN), (#CURRENT_PHASE, 100)
((NOTIFICATION_ID, 18948345), (ROLE, ASMITH), (GROUP_ID, 18948345),
,,,,,,,,,,,,,,,,,,,,,,,,,,,,,,,,,,,,,,,,,,,,,,,,,,,,,,,,,,,,,,,,,,,,,,,,,,,,,,,,),
(WF_DEFERRED, A510VIS3.SOLUTIONBEACON.NET), , ¾ò¤€}ŽdÑà0¹‹Yc□Ø, , )
oracle.apps.wf.notification.send, 18948345, ,
```

TABLE 10. 3

Oracle provides APIs (all in the Package WF_EVENT) for the retrieval or setting of each item in the structure. The whole of the Event Message, or WF_EVENT_T field is stored in the 'USER_DATA' column of the Queue tables.

If you are using the Business Event System to transmit data, and must build the WF_EVENT_T structure, you must call the WF_EVENT. Initialize the (new_wf_event_t) API. This API initializes the WF_EVENT_T specified in the new_wf_event_t parameter by setting the PRIORITY to 0, the EVENT_DATA to empty, and all other Attributes to NULL.

The Event Data Structure – SYS.AQ$_JMS_TEXT_MESSAGE

JMS Messages follow the standard defined by Sun Microsystems, Oracle, IBM and other vendors. According to *Oracle Workflow API Reference, Release 2.6.4, Part No. B15855–05, June 2006:*

The SYS.AQ$_JMS_TEXT_MESSAGE datatype contains the following attributes:

HEADER – Header properties

TEXT_LEN – The size of the Message payload, set automatically

TEXT_VC – The Message payload in VARCHAR2 format, if the payload is equal to or less than 4000 bytes

TEXT_LOB – The Message payload in CLOB format, if the payload is greater than 4000 bytes

The SYS.AQ$_JMS_HEADER datatype contains the following attributes:

REPLYTO – A destination supplied by a client when a Message is sent

TYPE – The type of the Message

USERID – The identity of the user sending the Message

APPID – The identity of the application sending the Message

GROUPID – The identity of the Message group of which this Message is a part; set by the client

GROUPSEQ – The sequence number of the Message within the group

PROPERTIES – Additional Message properties in the datatype SYS.AQ$_JMS_USERPROPARRAY

This same reference contains a chart that maps the two structures. Retrieving data from this structure is described in *Using Oracle Java Message Service to Access AQ*, *Oracle Applications Developer's Guide – Advanced Queuing* , *Using Oracle Java Message Service (OJMS) to Access Oracle Streams AQ*, *Oracle Streams Advanced Queuing User's Guide and Reference*, and *Package oracle.jms*, *Oracle Supplied Java Packages Reference*.

The WF_DEFERRED_TABLE_M Structure – WF_PAYLOAD_T

This abstract data type contains information needed by the Background Engine to process Deferred Activities. MetaLink Doc. ID: 186361.1, *WF2.x: Workflow Background Process Performance Troubleshooting Guide* describes this data type. The following figure shows an example of this data.

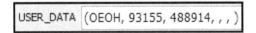

USER_DATA (OEOH, 93155, 488914, , ,)

TABLE 10. 4

- **ItemType** – the Internal Name of the Workflow

- **ItemKey** – identifies the specific instance of the Workflow

- **ACTID** – matches WF_PROCESS_ACTIVITIES.INSTANCE_ID and identifies the Activity that caused the Workflow to be deferred

- **FUNCTION_NAME**

- **PARAM_LIST**

- **RESULT**

USING SQL TO ACCESS THE DATA IN THE QUEUES

There are several fields in the Queue table that are used to administer the Queues. The first is the field CORRID. This field will contain the Event name prefaced by 'APPS:'. The field STATE is a numeric code indicating whether the Event has been processed or not. The following query can be used to see what Events are passing through the Queue and the current STATE. Substitute any Queue name for WF_ERROR:

```
SELECT corrid,
       decode(state,
              0, '0 = Ready',
              1, '1 = Delayed',
              2, '2 = Retained',
              3, '3 = Exception',
              to_char(state))  State,
       count(*) COUNT
  FROM wf_error
GROUP BY corrid, state;
```

Note that this query decodes the value in the STATE field.

The field USER_DATA contains the WF_EVENT_T structure. A simple SELECT of this field yields part of the data, but you can't see all of it, so you have to break the WF_EVENT_T structure into its subparts.

```
SELECT a.user_data.priority,a.user_data.send_date,a.user_data.receive_date,
       a.user_data.correlation_id,a.user_data.event_name,
       a.user_data.event_key,a.user_data.from_agent,a.user_data.to_agent,
       a.user_data.error_subscription,a.user_data.error_message,
       a.user_data.error_stack,a.user_data.event_data,
       a.user_data.parameter_list
  FROM wf_error a;
```

The fields that are most useful for troubleshooting are the SEND_DATE (when the Subscriptions to the Event should execute), the EVENT_KEY, the ERROR_MESSAGE, and the PARAMETER_LIST.

If the field starts with a '(', such as FROM_AGENT, TO_AGENT, and PARAMETER_LIST, then the field is an abstract data type and may need an additional breakout. Following is the result of selecting just a.user_data.parameter_list:

```
((NOTIFICATION_ID, 659436), (ROLE, DGRAY), (SUB_GUID,
AAE4B3CC9583DA5EE030B98B59632591), (SUB_GUID,
C31D7C623B541465E030B98B6C637B2B), (ERROR_NAME, WFENG_EVENT_NOTFOUND),
(ERROR_TYPE, ERROR), , , , , , , , , , , , , , , , , , , , , , , , , , , , , ,
 , , , , , , , , , , , , , , , , , , , , , , , , , , , , , , , , , , , , , , ,
 , , , , , , , , , , , , , , , , , , , , , , , , , )
```

At this point, it may be easier to revert to the APIs that Oracle has written. For example, to retrieve the value of the first parameter in the list, you can use:

```
SELECT wf_event.GetValueForParameterPos
(1,a.user_data.parameter_list)
```

```
FROM wf_error a
```

Or to get the value for the parameter ROLE, you can use:

```
SELECT wf_event.GetValueForParamter
('ROLE',a.user_data.parameter_list)
FROM wf_error a;
```

Because Oracle uses abstract datatypes, you may have to upgrade your SQL tool. If you get the Error Message 'Data type is not supported', then you need an upgrade. Patch 4334965, *11i.ATG_PF.H RUP 3*, added a field, USER_PROP, with a type of ANYDATA, to all the Queues. This will prohibit the use of 'SELECT * FROM <queue name>'.

Queues contain Events. When an Event errors, it invokes WFERROR. However, these WFERRORs will not have any value in PARENT_ITEM_TYPE or PARENT_ITEM_KEY. The following query will identify the Events that have errored.

```
SELECT COUNT (*),text_value FROM wf_item_attribute_values
  WHERE item_type = 'WFERROR' AND NAME = 'EVENT_NAME'
    AND text_value IS NOT NULL
GROUP BY text_value
ORDER BY text_value;
```

To retrieve each individual error message, see the two queries at the end of *Chapter 13, New Features.*

DIRECTORY SERVICES TABLES

The last set of tables control the valid Roles in Workflow. The main tables in this group are WF_LOCAL_ROLES and WF_LOCAL_USER_ROLES. Supporting these tables are WF_DIRECTORY_PARTITIONS and WF_DIRECTORY_PARTITIONS_TL. The tables WF_USER_ROLE_ASSIGNMENTS and WF_ROLE HIERARCHIES support Oracle User Management (UMX). To understand how the data in these tables is kept current, see *Step 3: Setting Up an Oracle Workflow Directory Service, Oracle Workflow Administrator's Guide Release 12, Part No. B31431-01 December 2006.*

Other tables in this group are FND_USER_PREFERENCES, which contains the data related to individual user preferences for the Notification Mailer and Language, and WF_ROUTING_RULES and WF_ROUTING_RULE_ATTRIBUTES, which contain the definition of Vacation Rules.

WF_LOCAL_ROLES

This table contains all the Roles that can be used as Performers in Workflow. The table is divided into 14 partitions. Each partition represents a different source of data. The definitions of the partitions are contained in WF_DIRECTORY_PARTITIONS and WF_DIRECTORY_PARTITIONS_TL. The following query can be used to get the relevant information from these tables:

```
SELECT    wdp.partition_id,wdp.orig_system, wdptl.display_name,wdp.role_view,
          wdp.user_role_view
   FROM   wf_directory_partitions wdp,wf_directory_partitions_tl wdptl
  WHERE   wdp.orig_system = wdptl.orig_system
ORDER BY partition_id;
```

The result of this query is shown in FIGURE 10.58. If ROLE_VIEW or USER_ROLE_VIEW says NOBS, then there is no view for this table, either because it is hierarchy enabled (FND_RESP) or because the partition is a mixture of users and Roles (WF_LOCAL_ROLES). If there is no Role view listed, the Workflow Engine still expects that a Role view exists with the name 'WF_'||<orig_system>||'_ROLES' and that a USER_ROLE_VIEW exists with the name 'WF_||<orig_system>||'_UR'. The row with the ORIG_SYSTEM = 'PER' has no PARTITION_ID because this is the secondary original system for PARTITION_ID 1.

PARTITION_ID	ORIG_SYSTEM	DISPLAY_NAME	ROLE_VIEW	USER_ROLE_VIEW
0	WF_LOCAL_ROLES	Ad Hoc Roles	NOBS	
1	FND_USR	Oracle Applications User	FND_USR_ROLES	FND_USR_UR
2	FND_RESP	Oracle Applications Responsibility	NOBS	NOBS
3	PER_ROLE	Internal Employee	PER_ROLE_ROLES_V	
4	POS	Employee Position	PQH_POS_ROLES	PQH_POS_UR
5	AMV_APPR	Marketing Approvals		
6	AMV_CHN	Marketing Channels		
7	ENG_LIST	Engineering List		
8	HZ_GROUP	Trading Community Architecture Groups		
9	HZ_PARTY	Trading Community Architecture Parties		
10	GBX	Government Group Box	GHR_GBX_ROLES	GHR_GBX_UR
11	HTB_SEC	Healthcare Security Group	NOBS	
12	PQH_ROLE	Public Sector Employee	PQH_ROLE_ROLES	PQH_ROLE_UR
13	UMX	User Management	NOBS	NOBS
	PER	Employee		

FIGURE 10.58

In addition to the Ad Hoc Roles, PARTITION_ID 0 contains AP_BANK_BRANCHES, AP_BANK_BRANCHES_SITES, JRES_GRP, JRES_IND and IGS.

This book will only discuss partitions 0 (where ORIG_SYSTEM = WF_LOCAL_ROLES or WF_LOCAL_USERS), 1, and 2, as these are the partitions that have the most significant impact on the Workflow Performers.

PARTITION ID = 1 – FND_USR or PER

FIGURE 10.59 shows a record from this table for a user not linked to an employee and FIGURE 10.60 shows a record from this table for a user linked to an employee. FIGURE 10.61 shows the corresponding user definition record for OPERATIONS.

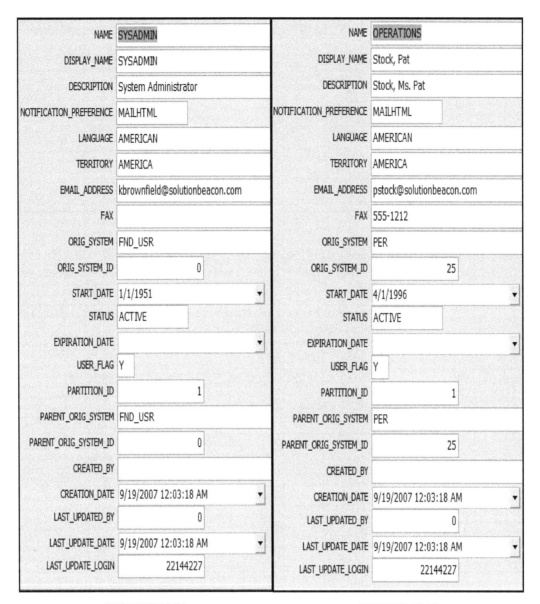

NAME	SYSADMIN	NAME	OPERATIONS
DISPLAY_NAME	SYSADMIN	DISPLAY_NAME	Stock, Pat
DESCRIPTION	System Administrator	DESCRIPTION	Stock, Ms. Pat
NOTIFICATION_PREFERENCE	MAILHTML	NOTIFICATION_PREFERENCE	MAILHTML
LANGUAGE	AMERICAN	LANGUAGE	AMERICAN
TERRITORY	AMERICA	TERRITORY	AMERICA
EMAIL_ADDRESS	kbrownfield@solutionbeacon.com	EMAIL_ADDRESS	pstock@solutionbeacon.com
FAX		FAX	555-1212
ORIG_SYSTEM	FND_USR	ORIG_SYSTEM	PER
ORIG_SYSTEM_ID	0	ORIG_SYSTEM_ID	25
START_DATE	1/1/1951	START_DATE	4/1/1996
STATUS	ACTIVE	STATUS	ACTIVE
EXPIRATION_DATE		EXPIRATION_DATE	
USER_FLAG	Y	USER_FLAG	Y
PARTITION_ID	1	PARTITION_ID	1
PARENT_ORIG_SYSTEM	FND_USR	PARENT_ORIG_SYSTEM	PER
PARENT_ORIG_SYSTEM_ID	0	PARENT_ORIG_SYSTEM_ID	25
CREATED_BY		CREATED_BY	
CREATION_DATE	9/19/2007 12:03:18 AM	CREATION_DATE	9/19/2007 12:03:18 AM
LAST_UPDATED_BY	0	LAST_UPDATED_BY	0
LAST_UPDATE_DATE	9/19/2007 12:03:18 AM	LAST_UPDATE_DATE	9/19/2007 12:03:18 AM
LAST_UPDATE_LOGIN	22144227	LAST_UPDATE_LOGIN	22144227

FIGURE 10.59   FIGURE 10.60

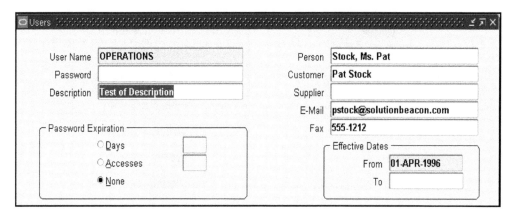

FIGURE 10.61

The following table shows the source of the data for key fields based on whether the user is or is not linked to an employee. If EXPIRATION_DATE is null, then the STATUS field will be set to ACTIVE, otherwise, it will be set to INACTIVE.

Field	Source of Value When User Not Linked to an Employee	Source of Value When User Linked to an Employee
NAME	FND_USER.USER_NAME	FND_USER.USER_NAME
DISPLAY_NAME	FND_USER.USER_NAME	PER_ALL_PEOPLE_F. GLOBAL_NAME
DESCRIPTION	FND_USER.DESCRIPTION	PER_ALL_PEOPLE_F. FULL_NAME
EMAIL_ADDRESS	FND_USER.EMAIL_ADDRESS	PER_ALL_PEOPLE_F. EMAIL_ADDRESS
FAX	FND_USER.FAX	FND_USER.FAX
ORIG_SYSTEM	'FND_USR'	'PER'
ORIG_SYSTEM_ID	FND_USER.USER_ID	PER_ALL_PEOPLE_F. PERSON_ID
START_DATE	FND_USER.START_DATE	FND_USER.START_DATE
EXPIRATION_DATE	FND_USER.END_DATE	FND_USER.END_DATE
USER_FLAG	'Y'	'Y'
PARTITION_ID	1	1
PARENT_ORIG_SYSTEM	'FND_USR'	'PER'
PARENT_ORIG_SYSTEM_ID	FND_USER.USER_ID	PER_ALL_PEOPLE_F. PERSON_ID

TABLE 10. 5

For users (PARTITION_ID = 1), this table is not the source for information normally stored in the fields NOTIFICATION_PREFERENCE, LANGUAGE, and TERRITORY. Instead, Workflow uses the view WF_FND_USR_ROLES. This view uses the Function WF_PREF. GET_PREF('<user_name>', '<preference_name>').

This Function checks to see if there is a record in FND_USER_PREFERENCES where USER_NAME matches <user_name>, MODULE_NAME = 'WF', and PREFERENCE_NAME matches

<preference_name>. <preference_name> is 'MAILTYPE' for NOTIFICATION_PREFERENCE, 'LANGUAGE' for LANGUAGE and 'TERRITORY' for TERRITORY.

If this query does not yield a value (if value is NULL, this is not considered a match), a search is made with USER_NAME ='-WF_DEFAULT-'. For NOTIFICATION_PREFERENCE there is always a record where the USER_NAME = '-WF_DEFAULT-'. This is the value entered in the 'Global Administration' page. For 'LANGUAGE' and 'TERRITORY', if there is no '-WF_DEFAULT-' record, the values 'AMERICAN' and 'AMERICA' respectively are used.

HRMS Family Pack K added the columns 'GLOBAL_NAME' and 'LOCAL_NAME' to PER_ALL_PEOPLE_F. MetaLink Doc. ID: 359995.1, *How to Access Global Name Format Functionality* explains these new columns and how to ensure they are set correctly.

If the user is linked to an employee, the email address must be entered in the employee record, not the user record. However, this email address will not appear in the user record unless the employee is re-linked.

If the email address is entered via the 'Enter Employees' form, the new email will be synched with WF_LOCAL_ROLES; but the change will not be reflected in FND_USER, not even after running either the 'Workflow Directory Services User/Role Validation' Concurrent Program or 'Synchronize WF LOCAL Tables' Concurrent Program. The only way to effect a change in the email address in FND_USER is to re-link the employee or use SQL. If the email address is updated in PER_ALL_PEOPLE_F via SQL, the change will only be populated to WF_LOCAL_ROLES by running the 'Synchronize WF LOCAL Tables' Concurrent Program. This anomaly is explained in MetaLink Doc. ID: 473471.1, *Change of Employee E–Mail in HR Is Not Reflected in FND User Definition* and MetaLink Doc. ID: 364647.1, *How are FND_USERS, HR, and WF_LOCAL_ROLES Kept In Synchronization?*.

If you are running the 'WF Bulk Synchronize Local Tables' Concurrent Program, the 'row who' fields (CREATED_BY, CREATION_DATE, LAST_UPDATED_BY, LAST_UPDATE_DATE, and LAST_UPDATE_LOGIN) will reflect the date and time and session information from the last run of the program.

PARTITION_ID = 2 – FND_RESP

Prior to Release 11.5.10, the 'NAME' column for responsibilities was FND_RESP<application_id>:<responsibility_id>. Release 11.5.10 changed this to FND_RESP|<application short name>|<responsibility key>|<security group>. Thus, the responsibility System Administrator, which used to have NAME = 'FND_RESP1:20420', now has NAME = 'FND_RESP|SYSADMIN|SYSTEM_ADMINISTRATOR|STANDARD'. For the old responsibility records (which are still in the table), DISPLAY_NAME had ':Any security group' added to the responsibility name. Using these old records as Performers will cause a Workflow to fail. Do not select any Role for any purpose that ends in ':Any security group'.

Responsibilities cannot receive emails; therefore, regardless of the value in NOTIFICATION_PREFERENCE, the WF_NOTIFICATIONS.MAIL_STATUS will be NULL. However, since each user assigned to the responsibility gets a copy of the email, whether each copy is emailed is determined by the Notification preference of that user.

If you have unchecked the Notification Mailer parameter Allow Forwarded Responses, you may have problems responding to these Notifications by email. See MetaLink Doc. ID: 432966.1, *Role Members Can't Approve Notifications By Email When Forwarded Responses are Not Allowed.*

- USER_FLAG will always be N

- ORIG_SYSTEM will always be FND_RESP

- ORIG_SYSTEM_ID will be the corresponding FND_RESPONSIBILITY.RESPONSIBILITY_ID

- OWNER_TAG will be FND_APPLICATION.APPLICATION_SHORT_NAME where FND_RESPONSIBILITY.APPLICATION_ID = FND_APPLICATION.APPLICATION_ID

Responsibilities are hierarchy-enabled and cannot be bulk synched. Therefore, the 'row who' data will reflect the last time a change was made to FND_RESPONSIBILITY.

PARTITION_ID = 0 – ad-hoc roles

Although select applications (such as AP) use this partition, this partition was created to store ad-hoc Roles. Data is added to this Role using the AdHoc APIs. A description of how to use these APIs can be found in the Directory Service APIs chapter of the *Oracle Workflow API Reference (Release 12 Part No. B31434-01, December 2006* or *Release 2.6.4 Part No. B15855-05, June 2006)*.

WF_LOCAL_USER_ROLES

This table joins the Role to each member of the Role. For example, a responsibility would be joined to all users assigned to that responsibility. Even if the Role is an individual user, it will exist in this table joined to itself. FIGURE 10.62 shows the key columns where the user OPERATIONS is a member of the Role System Administrator.

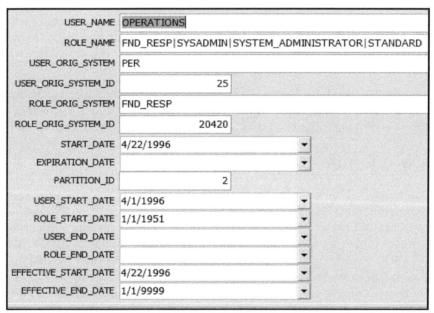

FIGURE 10.62

USER_NAME and ROLE_NAME link to WF_LOCAL_ROLES.NAME. PARTITION_ID is the PARTITION_ID of the Role, not the user. START_DATE, EXPIRATION_DATE, EFFECTIVE_START_DATE and EFFECTIVE_END_DATE are for the assignment to the Role.

WF_ROLES and WF_USER_ROLES

In earlier versions of Workflow, these used to be the tables that are now WF_LOCAL_ROLES and WF_LOCAL_USER_ROLES. These two objects are now views across the tables and contain active Roles and active users assigned to each Role.

WF_ROLE_HIERARCHY and WF_USER_ROLE_ASSIGNMENTS

WF_ROLE_HIERARCHY and WF_USER_ROLE_ASSIGNMENTS were added in Release 11.5.10 to support Role Hierarchy functionality in Oracle User Management (UMX). FIGURE 10.63 contains the relevant columns from WF_ROLE_HIERARCHY.

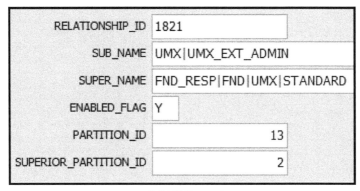

FIGURE 10.63

RELATIONSHIP_ID is the primary key and assigned by a sequence when a UMX Role relationship is created. SUB_NAME is the name of the Role stored in WF_LOCAL_ROLES in the partition references by PARTITION_ID. SUPER_NAME is the name of the Role stored in WF_LOCAL_ROLES referenced by SUPERIOR_PARTITION_ID.

WF_USER_ROLE_ASSIGNMENTS is very similar to WF_LOCAL_USER_ROLES. In fact, a row must exist in both tables for the Role to be valid for Workflow. For users assigned to a responsibility, either directly or indirectly, a row must exist in both these tables for the assignment to be recognized. FIGURE 10.64 shows corresponding rows from WF_USER_ROLE_ASSIGNMENTS (left) and WF_LOCAL_USER_ROLES (right). See explanation of columns for WF_LOCAL_USER_ROLES for the explanation of the corresponding columns.

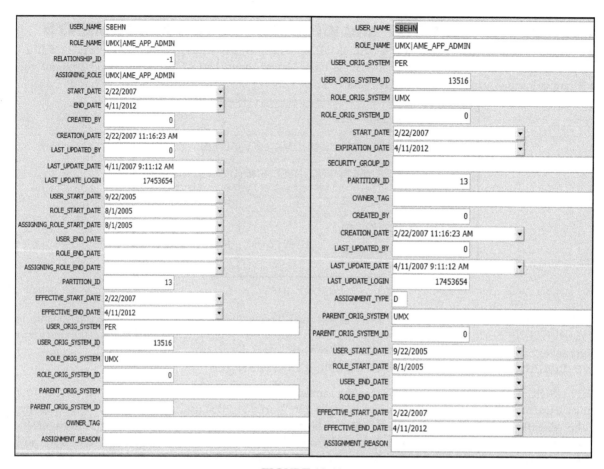

FIGURE 10.64

WF_ROUTING_RULES and WF_ROUTING_RULE_ATTRIBUTES

This table stores the definitions of the Vacation Rules. FIGURE 10.65 shows the definition of a forwarding Rule that applies to all Messages.

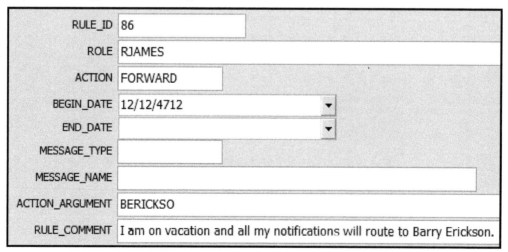

FIGURE 10.65

ROLE is the person who created the Rule, ACTION_ARGUMENT is the person to whom the Notifications will be forwarded. If forwarding is restricted to a specific Item Type, MESSAGE**Error! Bookmark not defined.**_TYPE will contain the Internal Name of the Item Type. If forwarding is further restricted to a specific Message, MESSAGE_NAME will contain the Internal Name of the Message.

If the Vacation Rule has 'Deliver Notifications to me regardless of any general rules' clicked, ACTION_ARGUMENT will be NOOP.

If the Vacation Rule is auto-answering a Notification with a result, ACTION will be RESPOND and there will be two records in WF_ROUTING_RULE_ATTRIBUTES: one to store the result, one to store the Action (result code). FIGURE 10.66 shows a Rule where there is no comment and the answer is always Approve.

RULE_ID	NAME	TYPE	TEXT_VALUE	NUMBER_VALUE	DATE_VALUE
3	AMS_NOTE	RESPOND			
3	RESULT	RESPOND	APPROVE		

FIGURE 10.66

Vacation Rules need to be monitored. They do not automatically expire if the recipient becomes inactive. Earlier releases of the applications allowed one to pick invalid recipients for the forwarding Rule. Either case will cause the Workflow to error. The following two SQL statements will identify Rules that will cause the Workflow to error. The first lists Rules where the person creating the Rule picked an invalid recipient because it is from the HZ_PARTY partition of WF_LOCAL_ROLES. The second lists Rules where the recipient is not an active user.

```
SELECT  r.ROLE,r.action,r.begin_date, r.end_date,r.action_argument,
        r.MESSAGE_TYPE wkflow,r.message_name
  FROM wf_routing_rules r
 WHERE action_argument LIKE 'HZ%' AND r.end_date IS NULL
ORDER BY ROLE;

SELECT  r.ROLE,lr2.status role_status, lr2.expiration_date role_expiration,
        r.begin_date rule_begin,r.end_date rule_end, r.action_argument,
        lr.display_name action_display_name, lr.status action_status,
        lr.expiration_date action_expiration
  FROM wf_routing_rules r,wf_local_roles lr,wf_local_roles lr2
 WHERE r.action_argument = lr.NAME
   AND r.ROLE = lr2.NAME AND r.end_date IS NULL
   AND nvl(lr.expiration_date,SYSDATE+1) < SYSDATE
ORDER BY ROLE;
```

Worklist Access

Worklist Access is used to grant the ability to read and respond to one's Notifications to another user. The table that stores these grants is FND_GRANTS. Explaining the tables in UMX is outside the scope of this book, but the following query can be used to list all grants:

```
SELECT   parameter1 from user,grantee key to user
        ,DECODE (parameter2, NULL, 'ALL', parameter2) for_item_types
        ,start date,end_date
    FROM fnd grants
   WHERE instance_type = 'SET'
```

```
            AND grantee type = 'USER'
            AND program_name = 'WORKFLOW_UI'
    ORDER BY 1,2;
```

FND_USER_PREFERENCES

The FND_USER_PREFERENCES table contains records to store defaults used by Workflow and information used to draw the charts in Oracle Applications Manager (OAM). FIGURE 10.67 shows the defaults. For the defaults, USER_NAME will always be '-WF_DEFAULT-'.

USER_NAME	MODULE_NAME	PREFERENCE_NAME	PREFERENCE_VALUE
-WF_DEFAULT-	WF	DATEFORMAT	
-WF_DEFAULT-	WF	DMHOME	
-WF_DEFAULT-	WF	MAILTYPE	MAILHTM2
-WF_DEFAULT-	WF	WF_SIG_IE_DLL	<OBJECT id="oCAPICOM
-WF_DEFAULT-	WF	WF_SIG_TEXT_ONLY	
-WF_DEFAULT-	WFManagerActiv	LAST_UPDATE_TIME	07/09/2007 13:58:28
-WF_DEFAULT-	WFManagerCom	LAST_UPDATE_TIME	07/09/2007 13:49:44
-WF_DEFAULT-	WFManagerDefe	LAST_UPDATE_TIME	03/09/2007 23:35:47
-WF_DEFAULT-	WFManagerError	LAST_UPDATE_TIME	03/09/2007 23:36:00
-WF_DEFAULT-	WFManagerSusp	LAST_UPDATE_TIME	18/08/2007 01:59:06
-WF_DEFAULT-	WFManagerWFA	LAST_UPDATE_TIME	18/08/2007 01:59:42
-WF_DEFAULT-	WFManagerWFA	LAST_UPDATE_TIME	18/08/2007 01:59:42
-WF_DEFAULT-	WFManagerWFA	NUM_ERROR	0
-WF_DEFAULT-	WFManagerWFA	NUM_EXPIRED	57
-WF_DEFAULT-	WFManagerWFA	NUM_PROCESSED	0
-WF_DEFAULT-	WFManagerWFA	NUM_READY	7
-WF_DEFAULT-	WFManagerWFA	NUM_UNDELIV	0
-WF_DEFAULT-	WFManagerWFA	NUM_WAITING	0
-WF_DEFAULT-	WFManagerWFIt	LAST_UPDATE_TIME	18/08/2007 01:59:06
-WF_DEFAULT-	WFManagerWFIt	NUM_ACTIVE	3063
-WF_DEFAULT-	WFManagerWFIt	NUM_DEFER	258
-WF_DEFAULT-	WFManagerWFIt	NUM_ERROR	754
-WF_DEFAULT-	WFManagerWFIt	NUM_SUSPEND	26
-WF_DEFAULT-	WFManagerWFN	LAST_UPDATE_TIME	18/08/2007 01:57:01
-WF_DEFAULT-	WFManagerWFN	NUM_PROCESSED	19
-WF_DEFAULT-	WFManagerWFN	NUM_WAITING	72

FIGURE 10.67

The most common record for an individual user is a record for MAILTYPE. This record is inserted when a user overrides the default Mailer preference. MODULE_NAME will be WF, USER_NAME will be

WF_LOCAL_ROLES.USER_NAME, and PREFERENCE_NAME will be MAILHTML, MAILTHTM2, QUERY, DISABLED MAILATTH, SUMMARY, or SUMHTML.

MISCELLANEOUS

There are other tables and views, tables for digital signatures, views to support all the tables already discussed, old tables and views not used any more. This chapter discussed the main ones necessary to develop and administer Workflows. The only remaining table of interest is WF_RESOURCES. This is a table that stores the Workflow Administrator (TEXT where TYPE = 'WFTKN' and NAME = 'WF_ADMIN_ROLE'). But the main purpose of this table is to store the column headers and Error Messages for all the forms. The table has the column 'LANGUAGE', so if multiple languages are supported, there will be multiple rows for each combination of TYPE and NAME. See *Chapter 11, Advanced Builder and PL/SQL*, for an example of using this table to raise Error Messages when validating Notification responses.

WHAT'S NEXT

The next chapter will focus on some additional features of the Builder and PL/SQL to support constructs such as Document Attributes and response Notifications.

Chapter

Advanced Builder and PL/SQL

This chapter will describe some of the functionality that can be used in Workflow Builder and PL/SQL to enhance your ability to model Business Processes. Where appropriate, we will continue to use the Workflow developed in *Chapter 3, Builder Basics*, as our example Workflow.

COMMENTS AND LABELS

Up to this point, the Functions have been defined with an Internal Name, Display Name and optional Description. Workflow provides two other fields, 'Label' and 'Comment', which allow a developer to enter information about the node. Both fields are only available in the Node tab, and thus only enterable in the Diagrammer window.

The 'Label' field is one of the primary keys to the table WF_PROCESS_ACTIVITIES. It is defaulted to the Internal Name of the Function. If more than one copy of the Activity exists in a Process, uniqueness is preserved by adding a dash ("-") and a number. For example, if a Process contains multiple End Nodes, the first one will have the label END, the second one will have the label END-1, the third one will have the label END-2, and so forth.

The 'Comment' field provides a secondary description field. This field allows the developer to explain the use of each Activity in the diagram. This is very helpful when the diagram contains standard activities such as 'Compare Text' or any of the Account Generator Functions.

The Diagrammer window normally shows the Display Name under each Function. However, it can be set to show the Internal Name, the 'Label', the Display Name, the 'Comment', or the 'Performer' for each Activity.

DIAGRAMMER DISPLAY BUTTONS

At the top of the Diagrammer window are a series of buttons (see FIGURE 11.1). Starting from the left, the buttons are:

FIGURE 11.1

- **Open File (<Ctrl>O)** – Opens a new Datastore

- **Save File (<Ctrl>S)** – Saves the current Datastore

- **Print Diagram** – Prints the current 'Diagrammer' page

- **New Process** – Adds a new Process to the current 'Diagrammer' page (this will be a sub-process)

- **New Notification** – Adds a new Notification to the current 'Diagrammer' page

- **New Function** – Adds a new Function to the current 'Diagrammer' page

- **New Event** – Adds a new Event to the current 'Diagrammer' page

- **Delete Selection (<Del>)** – Deletes the highlighted Activity and any lines leading in or out

- **Properties (<Enter>)** – Opens the 'Properties' page of the highlighted Activity

- **Developer Mode (<Ctrl>D)** – Toggle switch that in the Navigator window shows both the Internal Name and Display Names and in the Diagrammer window, shows the Internal Name; when toggled off, the Diagrammer window continues to show the Internal Name

- **Overview** – Opens a miniature Diagrammer window with a list of all the activities listed alphabetically using the names currently in the Diagrammer window (i.e., 'Label', 'Internal', 'Display', 'Comments', 'Performer')

- **Show Instance Labels** – In the Diagrammer window, displays the 'Label' of each Activity

- **Show Internal Name** – In the Diagrammer window, displays the Internal Name of each Activity

- **Show Display Name** – In the Diagrammer window, displays the Display Name of each Activity

- **Show Comments** – In the Diagrammer window, displays any Comments assigned to each Activity

- **Show Performers** – In the Diagrammer window, shows the Performers assigned to each Notification Activity

- **Help (<F1>)** – opens Workflow Builder Help

START AND END NODES

The QuickStart Wizard creates the initial Process with a Start and End Node. However, if you wish to start your Workflow with an Event, or wish to have multiple End Nodes, or you create a sub-process and drag in the Start and End Nodes, these nodes must be configured to Function as a Start or End Node.

FIGURE 11.2 shows Event, Start, and End Nodes used as Start and End Nodes. The top row shows these nodes properly configured. The bottom row shows the nodes as they are created or dragged in from the 'Standard' Item Type. They are not properly configured. If a Start or Event Node is not properly configured, the Workflow will not start. If an End Node is not configured, when the Workflow reaches that node, it will become stuck and unable to complete.

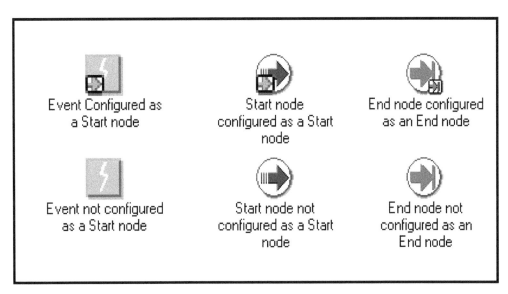

FIGURE 11.2

When a node is properly configured to start a Workflow, it will have a green arrow in the lower left corner. Properly configured End Nodes have a red arrow in the lower right corner. To configure a node as a Start or End Node, open the 'Properties' page of the Activity and click on the Node tab.

Click the LOV in the 'Start/End' field and select the appropriate value. If the node is an End Node and a Result Type has been assigned to the Process, then select the Result to be assigned to that End Node. The Result field only displays if Start/End is set to End. The field will be grayed out if the Process has no Result Type (see FIGURE 11.3).

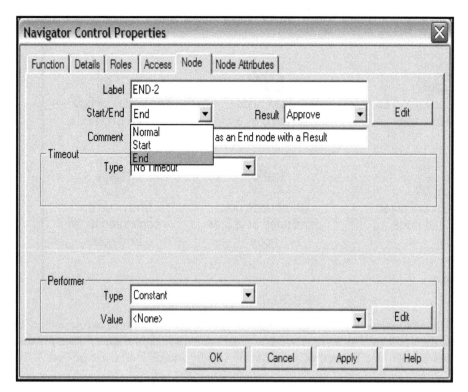

FIGURE 11.3

ACCESS LEVEL

Oracle's documentation mentions three preferences that determine whether an object can be modified: 'Preserve Customizations', 'Lock at this Access Level', and 'Access Level' (both for the object and for the person using the Workflow Builder). There is a fourth preference, 'Allow modifications of customized objects', which also impacts this ability. And if you are trying to modify an object in the Diagrammer window, then the 'Access Level' of the Process also becomes important.

The 'Access Level' of an object is found on the 'Access' tab of the object's 'Properties' page. When an object is created, the 'Access Level' is set to the current Workflow Builder Access Level (found in Help → About Oracle Workflow Builder 2.6.3.<x>). 'Preserve Customizations' and 'Lock at this Access Level' are checked. If the 'Access' tab reads 'Customized objects can be modified', then the 'Allow modifications of customized objects' in Help → About Oracle Workflow Builder 2.6.3.<x> is also checked. If this box is not checked, then the text will read 'Customized objects cannot be modified'. FIGURE 11.4 shows the 'Access' tab of an object created with 'Access Level' set to 20 and 'Allow modifications of customized objects' checked. FIGURE 11.5 shows the screen from Help → About Oracle Workflow Builder 2.6.3.<x>.

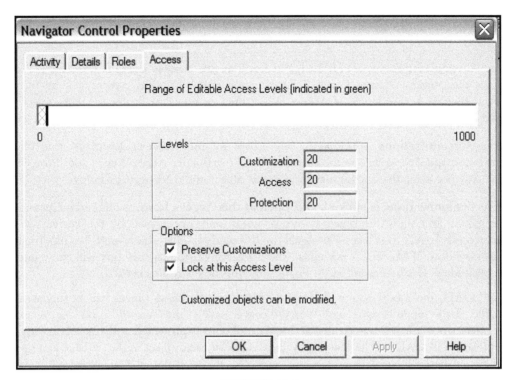

FIGURE 11.4

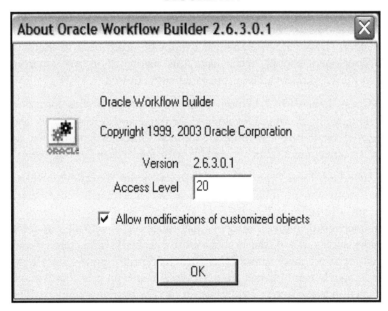

FIGURE 11.5

In the simplest situations, such as changing an object in the Navigator window, these preferences function as:

- **Neither Preserve Customizations nor Lock at this Access Level is clicked** – anybody at any level can update the object in the Navigator window. The value for Customization will be 0, the value for Protection will be 1000 and the value for Access will be the current Workflow Builder Access Level.

- **Preserve Customizations is not clicked, but Lock at this Access Level is checked** – Protection will show the object's 'Access Level', Customization will be 0, and Access will be the current Workflow Builder Access Level. If Access is less than or equal to Protection, the object may be modified in the Navigator window.

- **Preserve Customizations is clicked, but Lock at this Access Level is not clicked** – Customization and Access will be the current 'Workflow Builder Access Level' and 'Protection' will be 1000. Any one using the Builder may modify this object in the Navigator window.

- **Preserve Customizations is clicked, and Lock at this Access Level is clicked** – Customizations and Protection will show the object's 'Access Level' and Access will be the current 'Workflow Builder Access Level'. If 'Access' is equal to 'Protection', the object may be modified in the Navigator window. If 'Access' is not equal, the 'Preserve Customization' box will show unchecked. This is misleading. If 'Customization' = 'Protection', this box is really checked.

If using WFLOAD, the mode option determines whether a database object will be updated by the WFLOAD file. If the mode is 'Upgrade', WFLOAD will look at the 'Workflow Builder Access Level' that was in effect when the .wft was created and update all objects protected at that level or above. If the mode is 'Upload', WFLOAD will look at the 'Access Level' of each object in the .wft file and update the corresponding database object if that object is protected at the same level or above. If the mode is 'Force', WFLOAD will update the object regardless of any protection level.

It is notoriously easy to change the 'Access Level' for the Workflow Builder and to check the 'Allow modifications of customized objects'. So nothing you do can stop someone from changing an object using the Workflow Builder. However, since changes cannot be saved back to the database without the APPS password, and developers should never have this password in any environment outside of development, changes to the Workflow can be propagated with control.

Oracle has declared 'Access Levels' 0-19 belong to the Application Technology development group, Access Levels 20-99 belong to the Product Development groups, and Access Levels greater than 99 (100 and above) are to be used by E-Business Suite customers. Oracle will not assist in troubleshooting customizations made to an object unless they were made with the Access Level greater than 99.

Thus, activities in the 'Standard' Item Type (which is owned by the Workflow development group) will have an access tab that looks like FIGURE 11.6. The access will match the access of the Workflow Builder. Customization and Protection will be 0, 'Lock at this Access Level' will be checked and 'Preserve Customization' will be unchecked (Note: 'Preserve Customization' is actually checked, but because the current Workflow Builder access is > 0, the box shows unchecked). Changing 'Allow modifications of customized objects' will not affect these values. This combination of options will allow you to set values in the 'Node Attributes' page, but not change anything else. And even this ability may be blocked if the Process in which the Function is used says (Read Only) in the Diagrammer window title bar.

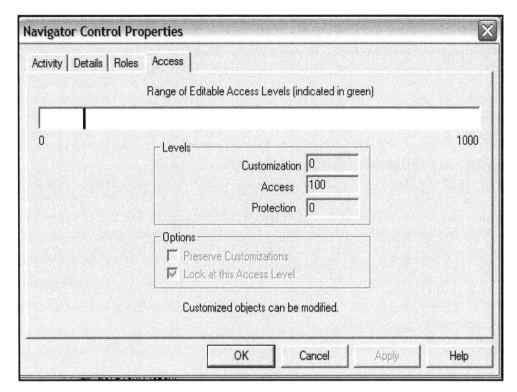

FIGURE 11.6

The Product Development group will usually define their activities at the level 20. If customization of this Activity is permitted, 'Lock at this Access Level' will not be clicked. An example of an Activity that Oracle expects you to customize are the Account Generator Processes for Purchasing and Payables when Projects is installed. However, if the setup guides, or MetaLink or Oracle Support indicate that an object must be modified to ensure the proper working of the Workflow, and Lock at this Access Level is checked and shows a value less than 100, then use the 'Help' menu to match this number and make your changes. Make sure you change your level back to 100 after making your changes.

Making Changes in the Diagrammer Window

Certain changes can only be made in the Diagrammer window: Timeouts, Performers, Node Attribute values, and changes to the Process flow. When these types of changes are required, the Process' preferences also affect the ability to make changes. To test whether the Process will restrict the ability to make changes, open the Process in the Diagrammer window. If the title bar has '(Read only)' after the name of the Process, you will not be able to make any changes to any object on this page regardless of the object's access preferences.

How to Customize Objects Oracle has Locked

The easiest way to customize a Workflow object delivered by Oracle is to change the Builder Access Level (using Help → About Oracle Workflow Builder 2.6.3.x) so that it matches the level of the Activity you are changing. Be aware that this violates Oracle's instructions to not change your Access Level. But if you must change an Activity or Item Attribute and it has a little red lock in the lower right corner, you don't have any choice.

Using the Builder to Save to the Database

If you make changes or additions to the Workflow in the Workflow Builder, check these objects for the presence of the red lock before saving the Workflow back to the database. The Builder will compare these objects to the version in the database and if different or the object is new, the changes will not be saved. You can get around this limitation by changing your Access Level to match the locked object, open the 'Properties' page of the object, click the 'Access' tab, and unclick 'Lock at this Access Level'. Or you can save the Workflow to a .wft file and use WFLOAD in 'Force' mode to load the Workflow.

Changing an Object's Access Level

Any objects added to a Workflow should be added at a level 100 or higher. However, if you are working on a Workflow with mixed Access Levels, you may accidentally create an object at level 20 or level 0. If this happens, change the Workflow Builder access to match the object's Access Level. Open the object's Property Page and unclick 'Lock at this Access Level' and 'Preserve Customizations'. Change the 'Workflow Builder Access Level' to the correct value. Open the object's 'Properties' page and click 'Lock at the Access Level' and 'Preserve Customizations'.

Another method of changing Access Levels is to run the script wfprot.sql. This script will change the Access Level of every component of the Item Type. It will also set 'Lock at this Access Level and Preserve Customization'. Run this script:

```
sqlplus <user/pwd> @wfprot <item_type> <new_protection_level>
```

For <item_type> substitute the Internal Name of the Workflow. <new_protection_level> is any number between 0 and 1000.

AND OTHER MESSAGE ATTRIBUTES

Oracle provides a series of special Attributes that can be added to Messages to enhance security or the look of the Message. This section will list a few of the key Attributes available. Others Attributes are described in various places in the *Oracle Workflow Developer's Guide*. The Release 12 version is Release 12, Part No. B31433-02, June 2007 and the Release 11.5.10 version is Release 2.6.4, Part No. B15853-04 July 2006. The Attributes listed are available in either version unless otherwise noted. This section will list a few of the key Attributes available.

The name of the Attribute must appear as the Internal Name exactly as typed. The Display Name can be any name unless otherwise specified. The majority of these Attributes have a type of Text. The allowable values are defined per Attribute and must match exactly. Therefore, many developers assign the type Lookup to the Attribute and use a Lookup Type to ensure that the value assigned will be an allowable value. When using a Lookup Type, make sure the internal value of each Lookup Code matches an allowed value for the Attribute. For example, if the Attribute allows the values 'Y' or N, you can use the Lookup Type Yes/No. The developer will pick the value 'Yes' or 'No', but the Workflow Builder will store the Internal Name for 'Yes' or 'No', which is the required 'Y' or 'N'. Obviously if an Attribute allows more values than those defined for a standard Lookup Type, you can define a custom Lookup Type to contain all the values. Thus, for an Attribute that allows the values 'Y', 'N', or 'B' (for Both), you will not be able to use the standard 'Yes/No' (as it only has the values 'Y' and 'N'), but you can define a custom Lookup Type with all three values. Remember that your Lookup Type must be unique across your database, but the Lookup Codes only have to be unique within the Lookup Type.

WF_NOTE

This Attribute allows responders to include comments, in addition to selecting the 'Response' button. These comments are then automatically added as a comment in the Notification History table. The Display Name and Description for this Attribute should be 'Note' and the 'Source' should be set to 'Respond'.

#HIDE_REASSIGN

All Notifications include a 'Reassign' button. This allows the Notification recipient to redirect the Notification to another Role. This button may alternately be labeled 'Delegate' or 'Transfer' depending on the setting of the Profile Option 'WF: Notification Reassign Mode'. You can use this to block reassigning Notifications either through the 'Worklist' pages or through 'Vacation Rules' or both. This Attribute must be either the type Text or the type Lookup. The body of the Message will only be translated if the body has been saved in WF_MESSAGES_TL in that language. The following values are recognized:

- **N** – allow reassignment from both Notifications and Vacation Rules

- **Y** – allow reassignment using Vacation Rules, but not through viewing a Notification

- **B** – prohibit reassignment using both Vacation Rules and viewing a Notification

Note that this Attribute only removes the button from the 'Notification Web' page. The button will still show on the 'Advanced Worklist', 'Personal Worklist', or self-service 'Home' page. However, users will receive an error message if the button is pressed.

#WF_REASSIGN_LOV

Many times companies want to continue to allow users to reassign a Notification; they just want to restrict the choice of alternate recipients. This Attribute provides that functionality, but only for the Notification to which it is assigned, not for Vacation Rules. This Notification must have the type of Role and have a source of Send. You can specify a specific Role or specify an Item Attribute and use custom code to set the value of the Attribute at runtime. If none of the pre-seeded Roles satisfy your requirements, then you can use the Directory Services APIs to create an AdHoc Role and populate the users.

If the members of the Role will be dependent on whom the original Message recipient is, then you will have to create a different AdHoc Role for each iteration of the Workflow and ensure the Role contains the correct members. This is because the members of the Role are resolved when the List of Values is invoked (i.e., when someone looking at their Notification selects the 'Reassign' button and uses the List of Values to pick an alternate). You do not want someone receiving a list of alternates that was generated based on criteria for a person in a different iteration of the Workflow.

#HIDE_MOREINFO

This Attribute Function controls the display of the 'Request Information' button. This Attribute must be either the type Text or the type Lookup. The following values are recognized:

- **N** – show the 'Request Information' button

- **Y** – do not show the 'Request Information' button

If this Attribute is defined, the behavior is governed by the value. If the Attribute is not defined, the button will display for the 'Notification Details' page, but will not be displayed for HTML-formatted email Notifications.

#FROM_ROLE

Use this Attribute to add a 'From' line to the header of the Notification. This Attribute must be the type Role and have a source of 'Send'. The Display Name and description of the Attribute must be 'From Role'. You can assign an Item Attribute to this Role to control the value during runtime. For example, the Notification to a requisitioner that the requisition was approved can set this Attribute to 'Approver Display Name' to have the Notification seem to come from the final approver. FIGURES 11.7 shows the header where this Attribute is not specified. FIGURE 11.8 shows the header where this Attribute was added to the Message.

```
   To   SYSADMIN
 Sent   22-Oct-2007 21:43:14
   ID   18969350
```

FIGURE 11.7

```
 From   Stock, Pat
   To   SYSADMIN
 Sent   26-Oct-2007 20:18:02
   ID   18972345
```

FIGURE 11.8

#WF_SECURITY_POLICY

This Attribute is used to prohibit sending sensitive information via email. The Attribute must be the type Text. The following values are recognized:

- **NO_EMAIL** – the email will simply inform the recipient that they have a Notification but that to see the content, the user must access the Notification from the 'Notifications Details Web' page.

- **EMAIL_OK or DEFAULT** – the email will have the full content of the Notification.

If this Attribute is omitted, the Notification behaves as if the value is EMAIL_OK or DEFAULT.

#RELATED_HISTORY

This Attribute allows you to attach the Action History from a Notification, such as the approval Notification, to an 'FYI' Notification, such as the Notification to the requestor that the document is approved/rejected. The Attributes must be the type Text and have a source of Send. Set the value to the label name (see the 'Properties' page, Node tab, to find this information) whose Action History is to be included. To guarantee uniqueness (i.e., the Activity is used in more than one Process), preface the Internal Name with the Internal Name of the Process followed by a ':' so that the value looks like:

```
<process internal name>:<notification label_name>
```

#WFM_FROM, #WFM_REPLYTO, #WFM_NODENAME

Use these Attributes to direct the response of a Notification to a different Mailer than the Notification Mailer that sent the Notification. The value for these Attributes must match the corresponding values in the Notification Mailer definition. These Attributes must be the type Text and have a source of Send. You can assign an Item Attribute to this Role to control the value during runtime.

#WFM_LANGUAGE

Use this Attribute to specify the language for the email Notification. This Attribute must be the type Text and have a source of Send. It must be set to a language supported by and installed in the Oracle Database. This value will override the language preference of the recipient Role.

#WFM_RESET_NLS

Use this Attribute to have the email Notification translated to the Notification recipient's preference. If the Role has multiple members, the email Notification is translated for every member of the Role based on that member's preference. This Attribute must be the type Text and have a source of Send. The body of the message will only be translated in the Notification, if the body has been saved in WF_MESSAGES_TL in that language. The following values are recognized:

- **Y** – translate the Notification

- **N** – do not translate the Notification

#WFM_HTML_DELIMITER

Use this Attribute to specify the character used to delimit response values for HTML-formatted email Notifications (this Attribute is ignored for plain text Notifications). This Attribute must be the type Text and have a source of Send. The following values are recognized:

- **DEFAULT** – The Mailer uses the default delimiters (currently a single quote)

- **APOS** – The Mailer uses the single quote or apostrophe (')

- **QUOTE** – The Mailer uses the double quote(")

- **BRACKET** – The Mailer used the left bracket ([) as the opening delimiter and the right bracket (]) as the closing delimiter.

Using this Attribute accommodates email applications, such as Microsoft Outlook Express, that do not support double quotes.

#WFM_CC and #WFM_BCC

These Attributes allow the specification of one or more secondary recipients for an email Notification and function like the CC and BCC fields of your email application. These Attributes must be of the type Text and have a source of Send. Specify the value as a list of email addresses or Role names separated by semicolons (;). If you specify an email address, it must be the full address including the @ and domain name. If you specify a Role name, this Role name must have a valid email address. The Mailer will send the email even to CC and BCC recipients with a preference of 'QUERY' (i.e., Do not send me mail). However, it will recognize the preference of DISABLED and ignore those Roles. You can specify an Item Attribute to set the values at runtime.

The recipients listed in these Attributes are not recorded in WF_NOTIFICATIONS. To receive a copy of the Message, the primary recipient must have a Notification preference of MAILTEXT (Plain text mail), MAILHTML (HTML mail with attachments), MAILHTM2 (HTML Mail) or MAILATTH (Plain text mail with HTML attachments). The format, including language, is determined by the primary recipient. If the primary recipient is a Role containing multiple members, the recipients listed in these Attributes will receive a copy for each member Role.

The CC and BCC recipients can reply to these Notifications unless:

- Allow Forwarded Response is set to No

- A post-Notification Function checks the recipient against this list and prohibits accepting the response

- Electronic signature is required

- CC and BCC recipients are not users of the application and guest access is disabled (i.e., Notification responses require one to be logged into the applications)

ITEM ATTRIBUTE TYPES – URL, FORM, DOCUMENT

URL

Item or Message Attributes with the type URL are used to store either a web page link or a link to a self-service (OA Framework) form. When a Message Attribute with the type URL is used in a Message, instead of displaying the value of the Attribute, the Attribute Display Name is shown and is underlined. The URL Attribute in FIGURE 11.9 is the word here.

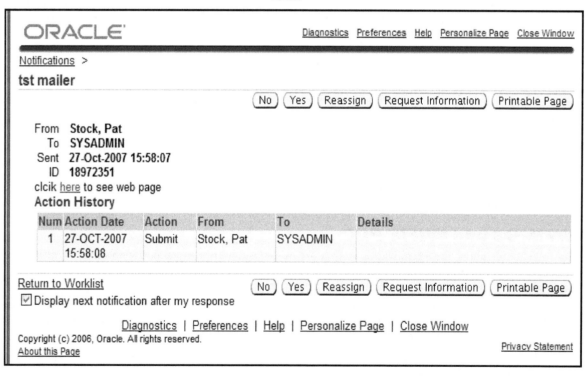

FIGURE 11.9

To reference a web page with no parameters, simply set the default value to the web page (see FIGURE 11.10). The full address should be used.

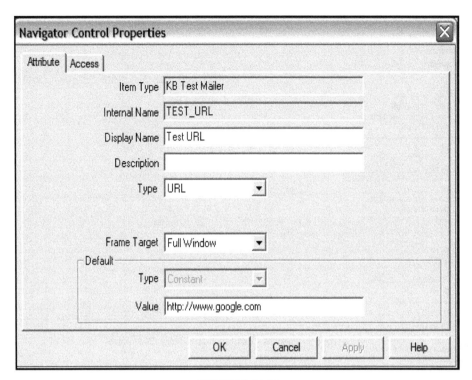

FIGURE 11.10

Frame Target governs how the URL opens. If 'New Window' is selected, the URL loads in a new unnamed browser window. If 'Full Window' is selected, the URL loads into the full, original window. All other values ('Same Frame' or 'Parent Frameset') are no longer supported and will behave as though 'Full Window' was selected.

If the web page you are trying to reference requires parameters, you can use token substitution with other Message Attributes. The format for specifying a Message Attribute in a URL Attribute is: '-&<internal name of Message Attribute>-'. So if the Internal Name of a Message Attribute is ATTR1, and that Attribute is to be a token substitute in a URL Attribute, the value of the URL Attribute would be

   http://www.my_site.com?arg1=-&ATTR1-

The Message Attributes functioning as tokens in the URL definition can be linked to Item Attributes. This allows the value for the token to be set at runtime. Workflow does not support double substitution. If the value for ATTR1 is set to &ATTR2, &ATTR2 will be evaluated as a literal. Workflow will not look for an Attribute with the name &ATTR2 and perform further substitution.

If a URL requires the Notification ID as an argument, then use -&#NID- as the argument. Do not define a Message Attribute with the Internal Name #NID. #NID is a special Attribute that instructs the Workflow Engine to use the current Notification ID.

Any date Attribute used as an argument to a URL must be expressed in the format 'YYYY/MM/DD+HH24:MI:SS'.

A URL Attribute can also be used to display images with an extension of .gif, .jpg, .png, .tif, .bmp, or .jpeg. The value for the URL can be a web address or any file location, as long as that location is available to the Notification Mailer. These Attributes are resolved to the image instead of using the Message Attribute's Internal Name as a link to the address. See FIGURE 11.11 and observe the Solution Beacon logo.

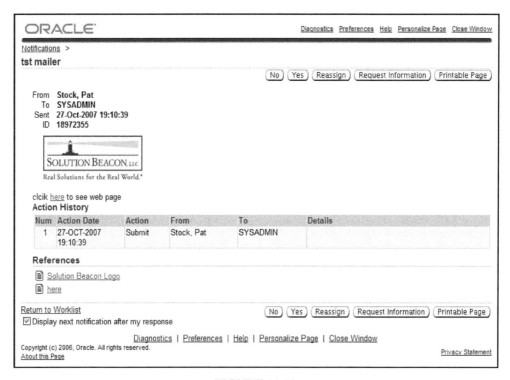

FIGURE 11.11

If you would rather have the image displayed as a link using the Message Attribute's Internal Name, preface the value with LNK:. For example:

```
LNK:http://www.my_site.com/logo.gif
```

If you choose this format, the link in the 'References' section will not resolve to the image. The image will only display from the link in the Message Body. The same holds true for the email version of the Notification. The link found in 'Notification References.html' will not resolve to the image.

To list a URL Attribute in the 'References' or 'Notification References.html' section as well as in the Message Body, click 'Attach Content' in the 'Message Attribute Properties' page. If this field is not checked, the URL Attribute will not be included in this section.

URL Attributes are also used to reference OA Framework pages. For example, the 'iExpense Expense Report Header' page is accessed by:

```
JSP:/OA_HTML/OA.jsp?OAFunc=OIEMAINPAGE&retainAM=Y&startFrom=WF&ReportHeaderId=-
&EXPENSE_REPORT_ID-&NtfId=-&#NID-
```

Note that this example uses token substitution to furnish the Expense Report Header ID (-&EXPENSE_REPORT_ID-) and the Notification ID (-&#NID-).

FORM

Form Attributes are used to specify links to the "Professional" forms. "Professional" forms are those forms developed with Oracle Developer. The following is the call to open the 'Requisition Header' form:

```
PO_POXRQERQ:P_REQUISITION_HEADER_ID="&DOCUMENT_ID"  P_MODE="MODIFY"
POXRQERQ_CALLING_FORM= "POXSTNOT"
```

Form arguments are included in quotes (" "). Item Attributes are used for token substitution, not Message Attributes. The token substitution is the Internal Name of the Item Attribute prefaced by '&'. Do not use hyphens to include the token substitution as is done for URL Attributes. In the above example, "&DOCUMENT_ID" is a token substitution using the Item Attribute with the Internal Name DOCUMENT_ID.

Item Attributes with a type of Document may not be used as token substitutes. Token substitutions in an Item Attribute used as a token substitute will not be resolved.

This Attribute displays as the underlined Internal Name of the Message Attribute. Clicking this Attribute will navigate to the designated form. If the form's arguments are configured in the value of the Message Attribute, the form will perform the required query.

When a 'Form' link is clicked, Oracle will display a list of responsibilities assigned to the user that include the form. If the user only has one responsibility with the form, the form will open. If the user has no responsibilities with the form, the link will display an error. If clicking the link from an email Notification, the user will have to log into the applications unless Guest User is configured.

To specify the responsibility to be used, include the arguments '#RESP_KEY' and '#APP_SHORT_NAME'. So, to call the 'Requisition Header' form from the responsibility 'Purchasing Requestor' (responsibility key = PURCHASING_REQUESTION, application short name = PO), change the example above to:

```
PO_POXRQERQ:#RESP_KEY="PURCHASING_REQUESTOR"#APP_SHORT_NAME="PO"P_REQUISITION_H
EADER_ID="&DOCUMENT_ID"P_MODE="MODIFY" POXRQERQ_CALLING_FORM= "POXSTNOT"
```

DOCUMENT

Document Attributes are used for Oracle Application Framework regions and for PL/SQL, PL/SQL CLOB, and PL/SQL BLOB documents. A PL/SQL, PL/SQL CLOB or PL/SQL BLOB document represents data from the database using a PL/SQL Procedure, which returns a character string, character large object (CLOB), or binary large object (BLOB), respectively. Document Attributes are ideal for representing rows of data, such as requisition lines or expense report header lines, or any object where the number of rows is variable.

The format for specifying PL/SQL, PL/SQL CLOB and PL/SQL BLOB values is:

- plsql:<package.procedure>/<document_identifier>

- plsqlclob:<package.procedure>/<document_identifier>

- plsqlblob:<package.procedure>/<document_identifier>

PL/SQL documents have a maximum length of 32 kilobytes. PL/SQL CLOB documents containing text or HTML may be displayed in the Message body or included as an attachment. PL/SQL BLOB documents can contain an image or application file stored as binary data, such as a PDF or RTF document. PL/SQL BLOBs cannot be displayed in the Message body of a Notification. They appear as attachments only.

If the document identifier requires more than one value, string the values together separated by a colon (:). For example:

```
plsqlclob::my_package.my_procedure/value1:value2
```

You can use Message Attributes in the document identifier as tokens. Use the Internal Name of the Message Attribute in uppercase prefaced by '&'. If multiple Message Attributes are used, separate the value with a colon. For example: plsqlclob:my_package.my_procedure/&VALUE1:&VALUE2. The Message Attribute cannot be the type Document; however, these Message Attributes can be linked to Item Attributes so that the values can be set at runtime. If the value of the Message Attribute contains tokens, these tokens will not be resolved.

It should be noted that the PL/SQL Package is executed as the Notification is processed either by the Notification Mailer when sending an email, or when the Notification is opened in the Notification Worklist. Be careful that the code used to generate this Attribute is not time–sensitive. Also be aware that if this code fails, the Notification will be marked in error even though the Workflow has continued past this point. Make sure the Attributes used as the Document Identifier are declared as Message Attributes. Otherwise the Message will show the definition of the Attribute instead of executing the code.

The rules for specifying an OA Framework page are very similar to those for specifying a URL, except that Item Attributes are used as tokens instead of other Message Attributes. The following example is used in the approval Notification for the Expense Report Header Workflow. Notice the required hyphen before and after the Attribute Name.

```
JSP:/OA_HTML/OA.jsp?akRegionCode=NotifBodyRN&akRegionApplicationId=200&ReportHe
aderId=-&EXPENSE_REPORT_ID-&NtfId=-&#NID-
```

MetaLink Doc. ID: 377010.1, *How to modify Workflow Message bodies due to functionality change in 11.5.10.2*, explains how to change the contents of these Attributes.

PL/SQL Used to Generate a Document Attribute

The PL/SQL used to generate a Document Attribute must follow the required guidelines. To provide an example, let's return to the Workflow built in *Chapter 3, Builder Basics*. The Message to HR shows only the primary assignment. Since Oracle Human Resources allows multiple active assignments, it is important that all of these assignments have the proper data. We will use a plsqlclob to display the table.

First we must add an Item Attribute with the type Document. See FIGURE 11.12. The text in the 'Value' field is plsqlclob:xxhrvemp.assignment_table/&EMPLOYEE_ID.

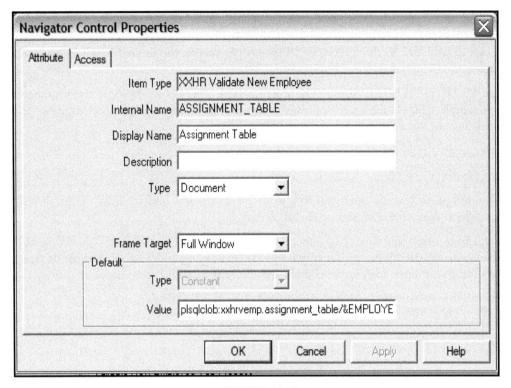

FIGURE 11.12

Next we either modify the 'Ask HR to Fix it' Message or create a new Message. The header will still contain the values for the primary assignment, but the text is modified to reference a table for any other assignments. The resulting Text Body becomes:

```
WF_NOTIFICATION
(ATTRS,EMPLOYEE_NUMBER,EMPLOYEE_NAME,POSITION,SUPERVISOR,DEFAULT_ACCOUNTING)
```

Employee data for the employee listed above is not complete. The information above is for the primary assignment. Additional assignments (if any) are listed in the table below. If any of the fields are blank, please go to the 'Enter Employee' screen in Oracle and enter the appropriate values.

After (and only after) entering the missing data, click the OK button at the bottom of this Notification. Note that clicking the button before correcting the data will only result in receiving another copy of this email.

You will have three days (you will receive a reminder on day 2 and 3) to correct the data. After that a Message will be sent to the HR Manager.

&ASSIGNMENT_TABLE

Remember to either create a Message Attribute with the Internal Name 'ASSIGNMENT_TABLE' and link it to the Item Attribute with the same name, or drag the Item Attribute down to the Message, which will do the creation and linkage automatically. Repeat this Process for the Message Attribute 'Employee ID' (Internal Name EMPLOYEE_ID) so that it is linked to the Item Attribute by the same name.

Now we add the Procedure ASSIGNMENT_TABLE to our XXHRVEMP Package.

Document Attributes are ideal for representing data in a table format. The table can be a text or HTML table. The disadvantage to using a text table is that the data doesn't line up properly in columns due to the use of proportional fonts in the Notifications. HTML tables resolve the 'doesn't line up properly' problem, but the HTML formatting adds significantly to the size of the Message. Additionally, these tables may not display well in the screens of PDA devices due to the limited width of the screen. Our code will create an HTML table.

To create an HTML table, HTML formatting must be used. This book will show the code necessary to generate our sample table. Much more sophisticated coding is possible. Two good sources for learning HTML formatting are the web sites:

http://www.html-html.com/

http://www.w3schools.com/html/

The latter site has pages you can open and type in your HTML code and see how the result will display. This is an excellent source for testing your HTML syntax.

Our table will have three columns: 'Assignment ID', 'Position' and 'Supervisor'. Our code will assume that the table is the standard Western horizontal left-to-right orientation. For an example of how to build a vertical or right-to-left table, look at the code in WF_NOTIFICATIONS.

```
1.▶ PROCEDURE assignment_table (document_id IN VARCHAR2
    ,display_type       IN  VARCHAR2
    ,document           IN OUT NOCOPY   CLOB
    ,document_type      IN OUT NOCOPY   VARCHAR2
   )
   IS

2.▶   l_position      per_all_positions.NAME%TYPE        := NULL;
      l_supervisor    per_all_people_f.full_name%TYPE    := NULL;
      l_length_rs     NUMBER                             := 0;
      l_person_id     NUMBER;
      l_exists        NUMBER                             := 0;
      rs              LONG;

3.▶ -- characteristics to be applied to entire table
    table_border varchar2(2) := '0';
    table_cellpadding varchar2(2) := '1';
    table_cellspacing varchar2(2) := '0';
    -- characteristics to be applied to the header row
    th_bgcolor varchar2(7) := '#cccc99';
    th_fontcolor varchar2(7) := '#336699';
    th_fontface varchar2(80) :=
    'Arial, Helvetica, Geneva, sans-serif';
    th_fontsize varchar2(2) := '2';
    -- characteristics to be applied to the detail row(s)
    td_bgcolor varchar2(7) := '#f7f7e7';
    td_fontcolor varchar2(7) := 'black';
    td_fontface varchar2(80) :=
    'Arial, Helvetica, Geneva, sans-serif';
    td_fontsize varchar2(2) := '2';

4.▶ CURSOR assignment_cur (
        x_person_id   NUMBER
    )
    IS
        SELECT assignment_number,position_id,supervisor_id
          FROM per_all_assignments_f paaf
         WHERE paaf.effective_end_date > SYSDATE
           AND paaf.primary_flag <> 'Y'
```

```
                    AND paaf.assignment_type = 'E'
                    AND (position_id IS NULL OR supervisor_id IS NULL)
                    AND paaf.person_id = x_person_id;

          CURSOR position_csr (
            x_position_id    NUMBER
          )
          IS
             SELECT NAME FROM per_all_positions pap
              WHERE pap.position_id = x_position_id;

          CURSOR supervisor_csr (x_supervisor_id NUMBER)
          IS
             SELECT full_name FROM per_all_people_f papf
              WHERE papf.effective_end_date > SYSDATE
                AND papf.person_id = x_supervisor_id;
       BEGIN
5.▶      g_proc := 'PROC_TIMECARDTABLE';
         g_trace := 'getting person_id from '|| document_id;

6.▶      l_person_id := TO_NUMBER (document_id);
         g_trace := 'setting headers';

7.▶      rs := '<table width=100% ><tr><td>';
         rs := rs
               || '<table width="100%"'
               || ' cellpadding="'
               || table_cellpadding
               || '"'
               || ' cellspacing="'
               || table_cellspacing
               || '"'
               || ' border="'
               || table_border
               || '" >';
8.▶      rs := rs || '<tr bgcolor="' || th_bgcolor || '">';
         rs := rs
               || '<th align="left"><font color='
               || th_fontcolor
               || ' face="'
               || th_fontface
               || '"'
               || ' size='
               || th_fontsize
               || '>';
         rs := rs || 'Assignment #' || '</font></th>';
         rs := rs
               || '<th><font color='
               || th_fontcolor
               || ' face="'
               || th_fontface
               || '"'
               || ' size='
               || th_fontsize
               || '>';
         rs := rs || 'Position' || '</font></th>';
         rs := rs
               || '<th><font color='
               || th_fontcolor
               || ' face="'
```

```
            || th_fontface
            || '"'
            || ' size='
            || th_fontsize
            || '>';
      rs := rs || 'Supervisor' || '</font></th></tr>';
```

```
 9.► FOR assignment_rec IN assignment_cur (l_person_id)
     LOOP
            l_exists := 1;
```

```
10.►        IF LENGTHB (rs) >= 25000
            THEN
                g_trace := 'Writing to Clob for ' ||
                assignment_rec.assignment_number;
                wf_notification.writetoclob (document, rs);
                l_length_rs := l_length_rs + LENGTHB (rs);
                rs := '';
            END IF;
```

```
            l_position := '';
            l_supervisor := '';
```

```
11.►            IF assignment_rec.position_id IS NOT NULL
            THEN
                g_trace := 'getting position';
                OPEN position_csr (assignment_rec.position_id);
                FETCH position_csr
                 INTO l_position;
                CLOSE position_csr;
            END IF;
```

```
            IF assignment_rec.supervisor_id IS NOT NULL
            THEN
                g_trace := 'getting supervisor name';
                OPEN supervisor_csr (assignment_rec.supervisor_id);
                FETCH supervisor_csr
                 INTO l_supervisor;
                CLOSE supervisor_csr;
            END IF;
```

```
12.►        g_trace := 'adding to rs for assignment' ||
                        assignment_rec.assignment_number;
            rs := rs || '<tr bgcolor="' || td_bgcolor || '">';
            rs := rs
                || '<td><font color='
                || td_fontcolor
                || ' face="'
                || td_fontface
                || '"'
                || ' size='
                || td_fontsize
                || '>';
            rs := rs || assignment_rec.assignment_number
                || '</font></td>';
            rs := rs
                || '<td><font color='
                || td_fontcolor
                || ' face="'
                || td_fontface
```

```
                  || '"'
                  || ' size='
                  || td_fontsize
                  || '>';
          rs := rs || l_position || '</font></td>';
          rs := rs
                  || '<td><font color='
                  || td_fontcolor
                  || ' face="'
                  || td_fontface
                  || '"'
                  || ' size='
                  || td_fontsize
                  || '>';
          rs := rs || l_supervisor || '</font></td></tr>';
      END LOOP;

13.▶  g_trace := 'finishing rs';
      rs := rs || '</table></td></tr></table>';

14.▶  IF l_exists = 0
      THEN
          rs := '';
      END IF;


15.▶  g_trace := 'writing to CLOB';
      l_length_rs := l_length_rs + LENGTHB (rs);
      wf_notification.writetoclob (document, rs);
   EXCEPTION
      WHEN OTHERS
      THEN
16.▶      wf_core.CONTEXT (g_pkg
                          ,g_proc
                          ,g_trace
                          , 'length=' || TO_CHAR (l_length_rs)
                          );
          RAISE;
   END assignment_table;
```

1.▶ All Procedures referenced by a plsql, plsqlclob, or plsqlblob document type Item or Message Attribute have the same four parameters, DOCUMENT_ID, DISPLAY_TYPE, DOCUMENT, and DOCUMENT_TYPE. DOCUMENT_ID is VARCHAR2 and will be what is coded after the '/' when defining the Attribute. DISPLAY_TYPE is VARCHAR2 and represents how the resulting variable will display. The Workflow Engine will pass in a value based on the type of DOCUMENT and the recipient's Notification preference. DOCUMENT has a type of VARCHAR2 for PL/SQL CLOB for plsqlclob and BLOB for plsqlblob. This variable will contain the contents of the table that is built. DOCUMENT_TYPE can be used in plsqlclob documents to display .pdf or .rtf documents and the file name. In plsqlblob documents it can reference any file type and the file name. See the *Oracle Workflow Developer's Guide (Release 12 Part No. B31433-02, June 2007* or *Release 2.6.4, Part No. B15853-04, July 2006)* for further details.

The definition of the Attribute will contain the value for DOCUMENT_ID. The Procedure will create document, and if appropriate, will set the value for DOCUMENT_TYPE.

2.▶ Typical declare section. Note that the variable RS has a type of LONG.

3. ▶ These variables can be defined as global or local variables, or you can simply hardcode the values in the statements that generate the table. You do not have to use the values specified. For example, the link http://www.theodora.com/gif4/html_colors.gif displays a chart of sample color codes. Any code may be used for the background and/or font colors.

4. ▶ Cursors are used to search for data where missing data is allowable and part of the Workflow design.

5. ▶ G_PROC is set to the name of the Procedure. This is required for the Generic Error Handling API WF_CORE.Context. G_TRACE will be periodically set to indicate key points in the code. If an unexpected error occurs, G_TRACE will be passed to the Error Stack and the designer will be able to isolate the area of code that malfunctioned. Note that G_TRACE is reset often and may include the value of selected variables used in subsequent statements.

6. ▶ DOCUMENT_ID is passed in as a VARCHAR2. In this case, DOCUMENT_ID is set to the Attribute EMPLOYEE_ID, so a conversion to numeric is required. Notice that G_TRACE is set to the value passed in as DOCUMENT_ID. See the following section on Document Procedure error troubleshooting

7. ▶ RS is used to build the document. RS can hold up to 32,000 bytes of data. See code in section 10.▶ to see how to add RS to the document. Building the document starts with loading the defaults for the table.

8. ▶ This section loads the defaults for the header row and the header values for each column

9. ▶ The cursor will return the data for each row.

10. ▶ Although RS can be up to 32,000 characters, once it has passed 25,000 characters, it is added to document and reset to null. The length is tracked to help identify any errors due to amount of data to be processed.

11. ▶ This is a standard fetch from a cursor.

12. ▶ This section loads the detail row into RS.

13. ▶ This section adds the ending character for the table.

14. ▶ If there were no additional assignments, RS is set to null so that the table will be null and not display.

15. ▶ This section does the final add of RS to the document. Note that there is no result for this type of Procedure.

16. ▶ This is the standard use of WF_CORE.Context to display the value of G_TRACE if any errors occur.

FIGURE 11.13 shows a Notification containing a Document Attribute.

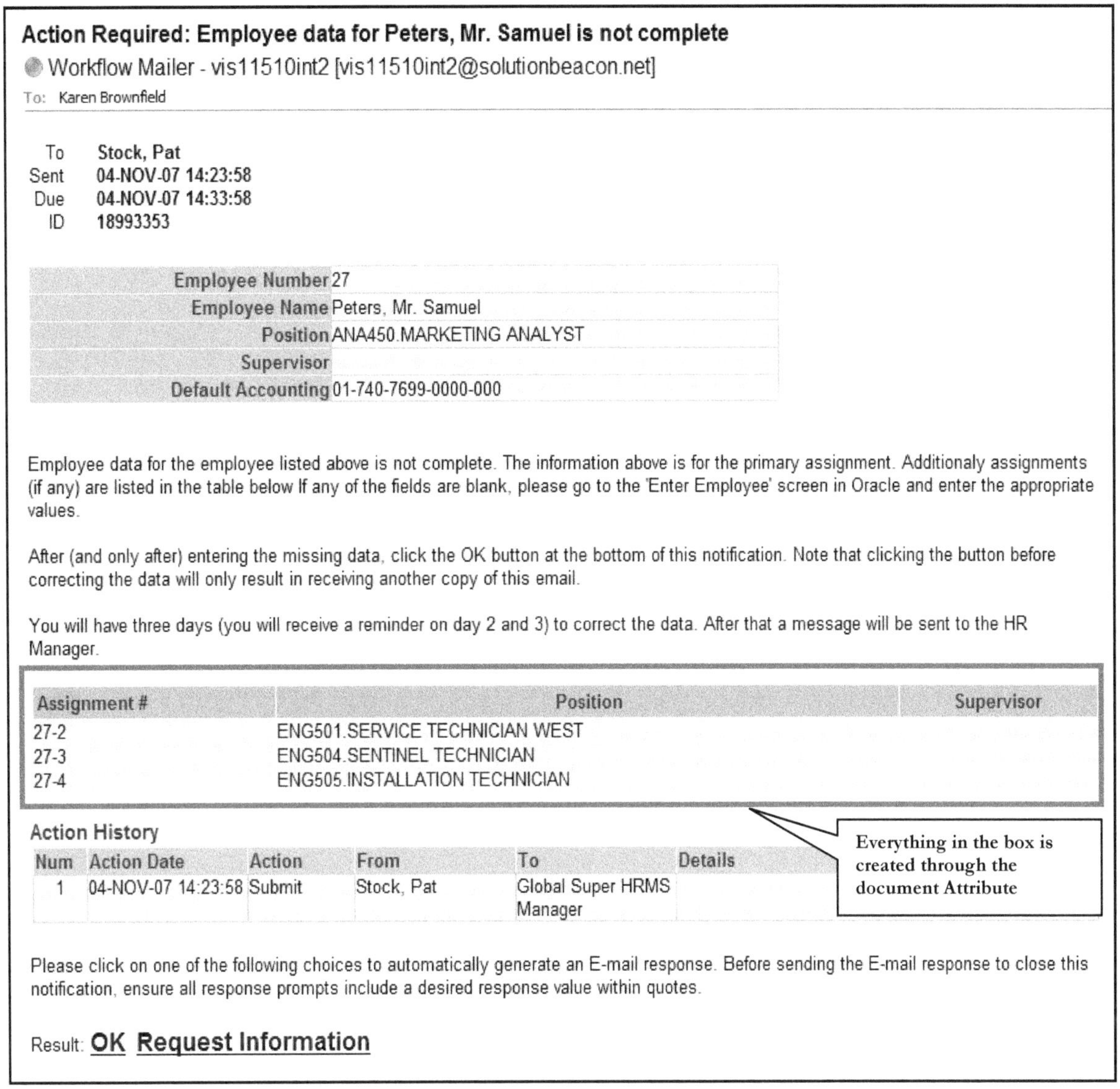

Action Required: Employee data for Peters, Mr. Samuel is not complete

Workflow Mailer - vis11510int2 [vis11510int2@solutionbeacon.net]

To: Karen Brownfield

To	Stock, Pat
Sent	04-NOV-07 14:23:58
Due	04-NOV-07 14:33:58
ID	18993353

Employee Number	27
Employee Name	Peters, Mr. Samuel
Position	ANA450.MARKETING ANALYST
Supervisor	
Default Accounting	01-740-7699-0000-000

Employee data for the employee listed above is not complete. The information above is for the primary assignment. Additionaly assignments (if any) are listed in the table below If any of the fields are blank, please go to the 'Enter Employee' screen in Oracle and enter the appropriate values.

After (and only after) entering the missing data, click the OK button at the bottom of this notification. Note that clicking the button before correcting the data will only result in receiving another copy of this email.

You will have three days (you will receive a reminder on day 2 and 3) to correct the data. After that a message will be sent to the HR Manager.

Assignment #	Position	Supervisor
27-2	ENG501.SERVICE TECHNICIAN WEST	
27-3	ENG504.SENTINEL TECHNICIAN	
27-4	ENG505.INSTALLATION TECHNICIAN	

Action History

Num	Action Date	Action	From	To	Details
1	04-NOV-07 14:23:58	Submit	Stock, Pat	Global Super HRMS Manager	

Everything in the box is created through the document Attribute

Please click on one of the following choices to automatically generate an E-mail response. Before sending the E-mail response to close this notification, ensure all response prompts include a desired response value within quotes.

Result: **OK Request Information**

FIGURE 11.13

Anomalies and PL/SQL Document Procedure Errors

If using the Worklist to review Notifications, it is important to know that the Procedure that builds the Document Attribute is not executed until the Notification is opened. This can cause the Notification to display data that is different than what existed at the time the Notification was sent.

Since the Procedure doesn't execute until the Notification opens, if the Procedure errors, the error is not detected until the Notification is opened. This type of error will not cause the Workflow to error, but the resulting Notification will not display the body or the result code and thus cannot be answered. And while the Error Message displays the error, the information provided in WF_CORE.Context is not shown (see FIGURE 11.14).

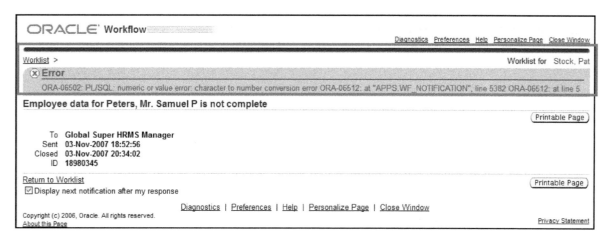

FIGURE 11.14

But this error does cause an iteration of System Error (WFERROR) to be initiated. The Message sent by this Workflow will contain the full Error Stack (see FIGURE 11.15). Read through the Error Stack in the Message until you see the name of the Procedure used to build the Document Attribute. This line will show whatever values are passed via WF_CORE.Context. In this case, the Workflow Engine could not resolve the document id &EMPLOYEE_ID to the Attribute value because there was no Message Attribute by that name. The good news is that since Messages are not versioned, the EMPLOYEE_ID Item Attribute can be copied to the Message (thereby creating a Message Attribute by the same name). The Workflow can be saved to the database and the Notification re-opened.

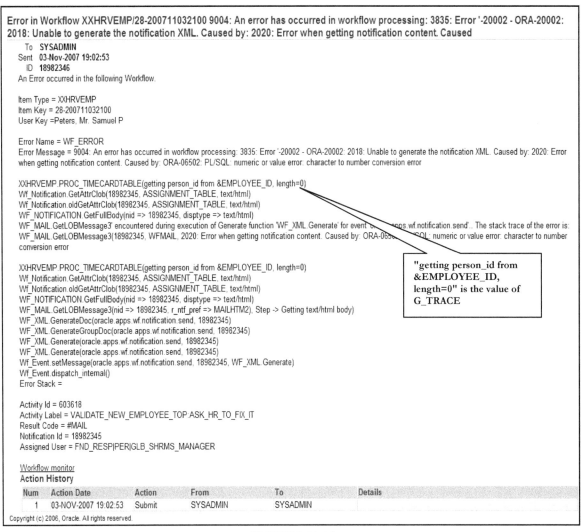

FIGURE 11.15

POST NOTIFICATION FUNCTIONS

A PL/SQL Procedure can be assigned to a Notification to perform logic specific to that Notification. This logic can validate the accuracy of a response or whether the responder is valid. *Chapter 3, Builder Basics*, explained the format for a Procedure attached to a Function Activity and the allowable FuncModes. Procedures attached to a Notification Activity follow the same format and accept the FuncModes RUN and CANCEL, but there are several additional FuncModes:

- **VALIDATE** – Used to test whether a response is valid before that response is recorded. After running the Function in VALIDATE mode it will run it in RESPOND mode

- **RESPOND** – Also used to validate a response value, but the response will be recorded. After running the Function in RESPOND mode, it will run it in RUN mode

- **FORWARD** – Used to validate a Role when a Notification is being forwarded

- **TRANSFER** – Used to validate a Role when a Notification is being transferred. Also used to reset any Attributes so that the approval chain and authority limits will be based on the new recipient rather than the original recipient

- **QUESTION** – Used to validate a Role when the 'Request More Information' button is selected

- **ANSWER** – Used to validate the answer to any questions or to validate the Role that responded

- **TIMEOUT** – Used to check whether another Action other than Timeout should be set. For example, if 'Expand Roles' is checked for a Notification, then this Procedure can check if enough people have responded to answer the Notification and if so, can set ResultOut to the value based on the responses to date. If the Timeout leg should be followed, set ResultOut to WF_ENGINE.eng_timedout

When the STATE of a Notification changes, because it timed out or is answered, or a responder clicked the 'Transfer' or 'Request More Information' button, or someone responded to the request for more information, then the Workflow Engine calls the post-Notification Procedure using the FuncMode appropriate to the action.

The Workflow Engine takes additional action when someone responds to a Notification. Before running the Procedure with FuncMode = 'RESPOND', it runs the Procedure with FuncMode = 'VALIDATE'. This allows you to validate the response before accepting it. After running the Procedure in 'RESPOND' mode, the Workflow Engine runs the Procedure in 'RUN' mode. This allows the developer to code special logic when 'Expand Roles' is checked to tally the responses.

When the FuncMode is set to 'VALIDATE', 'RESPOND', 'FORWARD', 'TRANSFER', 'QUESTION', or 'ANSWER', the ResultOut parameter is ignored unless it is set to 'ERROR'. So if the code detects some reason why the Workflow should not proceed, then either set the ResultOut to ERROR:<errorcode> or raise an exception directly in the Procedure.

A SAMPLE PROCEDURE TO VALIDATE DATA RETURNED IN A NOTIFICATION

In the Workflow in *Chapter 3, Builder Basics*, the Notification to the email administrator asks that the email address be entered. This is a free-form field. The Workflow developer can assign a post-Notification Procedure to the Notification to check whether the response to the Notification is valid. This Function could also be used to include any code needed if the Notification is forwarded, if the 'Request More Information' button is clicked, if someone responds to the request for more information, or if the Notification times out.

The following Procedure is used in our Workflow to ensure that the email address contains a '@' and that the text following the '@' contains a period. Code could be added to ensure the domain matched a specific value.

```
1.▶ PROCEDURE is_response_valid (
     p_item_type    IN      VARCHAR2
    ,p_item_key     IN      VARCHAR2
    ,p_actid        IN      NUMBER
    ,p_funcmode     IN      VARCHAR2
    ,p_result       OUT     VARCHAR2
   )
   IS
```

```
2.▶  l_notificationid    NUMBER;
     l_email             VARCHAR2 (30);
   BEGIN
3.▶  g_proc := 'IS_RESPONSE_VALID';

4.▶  IF p_funcmode = 'RESPOND' THEN
         g_trace := 'Get the Notification ID';

5.▶       l_notificationid := wf_engine.context_nid;
          g_trace := 'Get email';

6.▶       l_email :=
             wf_Notification.getattrtext (l_notificationid,'EMAIL_ADDRESS');
          g_trace := 'Test email';

7.▶       IF    l_email IS NULL
             OR INSTR (l_email, '@') = 0
             OR INSTR (LTRIM (l_email, '@'), '.') = 0
          THEN
             wf_core.token
                ('CUSTOM', 'The following was entered as the email'
                || 'address: ' || l_email
                || '. This value is invalid. '
                || 'Either you failed to enter the '
                || 'email address or the email address '
                || 'does not contain the domain.  Please '
                || 'reply again to this notification with '
                || 'a valid email address. '
                );
             wf_core.RAISE ('WFLDRS_CUSTOM');
          END IF;
       END IF;

8.▶  EXCEPTION
        WHEN OTHERS
        THEN
           wf_core.CONTEXT (g_pkg, g_proc, g_trace);
           RAISE;
     END is_response_valid;
```

1.▶   The parameters to this Procedure are identical to those for a Function Activity Procedure

2.▶   Typical declare section.

3.▶   G_PROC is set to the name of the Procedure. This is required for the Generic Error Handling API WF_CORE.Context. G_TRACE will be periodically set to indicate key points in the code. If an unexpected error occurs, G_TRACE will be passed to the Error Stack and the designer will be able to isolate the area of code that malfunctioned. Note that G_TRACE is reset often and may include the value of selected variables used in subsequent statements.

4.▶   In this case, the FuncMode can be either VALIDATE or RESPOND.

5.▶   Responses to Notifications are stored in the Message Attribute. Even when that Attribute is linked to a Notification Attribute, the Notification Attribute is not updated until the Notification is marked complete. Since our Function is part of executing the Notification, the only way to retrieve these values is through the use of the Function WF_NOTIFICATION.GetAttr<type>. This Function requires the Notification ID as a parameter. The Function WF_ENGINE.context_nid returns this value.

6. ▶ Now that we have the Notification ID, the Function WF_NOTIFICATION.GetAttrText is used to retrieve the value returned for the email address. The Internal Name of the Message Attribute (note: not the Internal Name of the linked Item Attribute) is EMAIL_ADDRESS. The NOTIFICATION_ID and Message Attribute Internal Name are the only two parameters to this Function.

7. ▶ The value entered as a response is parsed and checked for a '@' and a period ('.') after the '@'. If either does not exist then WF_CORE.Token is used to set the value of our desired Error Message into the token CUSTOM. This token is part of the Error Message WFLDRS_CUSTOM. WF_CORE.Raise is then called with the name of the Error Message as the parameter. A list of available Error Messages can be found in WF_RESOURCES where TYPE = 'WFERR'. The column 'NAME' will contain the name of the 'Error Message' and the column 'TEXT' will show the error. Any text in the 'Error Message' beginning with '&' is a token that can be substituted at run-time with the appropriate value.

8. ▶ This is the standard use of WF_CORE.Context to display the value of G_TRACE if any errors occur.

If the Notification is answered through the Worklist and the entered email address is invalid, the returned Error Message looks like FIGURE 11.16.

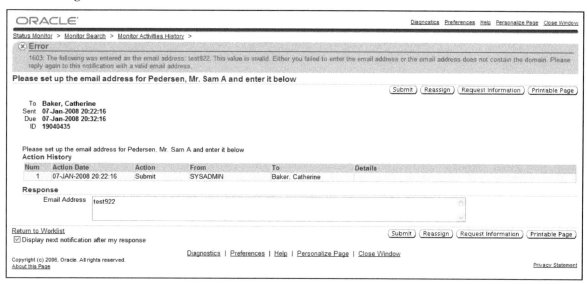

FIGURE 11.16

The email address can be re-entered and the 'Submit' button pressed to record a different answer.

The response to a Notification answered through the Worklist is instantaneous. If the Notification is answered through email, the Notification Mailer must record that the Notification has been answered. When a Background Engine runs for Deferred Activities, the Workflow can act on the answer. This will cause the resulting response to take a few minutes.

The response sent back through email looks like FIGURE 11.17. Note that the Error Message is not in red. The value tested is not in the Email Address box (as there is no Email Address box). Other than in the Error Message, the erroneously entered email address does not display. Even when using RESPOND the value will not be recorded unless ResultOut is set to COMPLETE. Thus, when coding an Error Message, make sure the value that caused the error is included in the Error Message.

Invalid: Please set up the email address for Pedersen, Mr. Sam A and enter it below

Workflow Mailer - vis11510int2 [vis11510int2@solutionbeacon.net]

To: Karen Brownfield

Attachments: Notification Detail.html (661 B)

Warning: Your previous response to this message was invalid (see error message below). Please resubmit your response.

Error Message: 1603: The following was entered as the email address: test939A. This value is invalid. Either you failed to enter the email address or the email address does not contain the domain. Please reply again to this notification with a valid email address.

Value Found: None

Remarks: None

To	Baker, Catherine
Sent	07-JAN-08 20:38:44
Due	07-JAN-08 20:48:44
ID	19040440

Please set up the email address for Pedersen, Mr. Sam A and enter it below
Action History

Num	Action Date	Action	From	To	Details
1	07-JAN-08 20:38:44	Submit	SYSADMIN	Baker, Catherine	

Please click on one of the following choices to automatically generate an E-mail response. Before sending the E-mail response to close this notification, ensure all response prompts include a desired response value within quotes.

Important: Some mail clients, notably early releases of Microsoft Outlook Express, may not copy the 'NID' line properly in your response. Please verify that the 'NID' line is included in full and contains the prefix 'NID' and all the details between the square brackets when responding.

Click for response values

FIGURE 11.17

EXPAND ROLES – VOTING

When the 'Expand Roles' button is not checked on a Notification and a Role such as a responsibility is specified as the recipient of a Notification, each member of the Role receives a copy of the Notification. However, the Notification is only available from the Worklist. The copies are not emailed. If the Notification requires a response, the response from the first reply is used. Once the first response is received, the other copies of the Notification are removed from all inboxes. If by chance two people had opened the Notification at the same time and both responded, the first response received is processed and the second response is discarded. The person sending the second response will receive a Notification indicating that the response was discarded.

If the 'Expand Roles' button is checked on a Notification and a Role such as a responsibility is specified as the recipient of a Notification, each member of the Role receives a separate Notification that has a unique Notification ID. This allows all members of the Role to respond to the Notification. Because each response can be different, the developer must specify a post Notification Function that "counts" the responses and determines the final result. In addition to allowing all members to respond, clicking the 'Expand Roles' button allows each individual in the Role to receive the Notification based on the individual's Notification preference.

Oracle provides a sample Function, WF_STANDARD.VoteForResultType that counts 'Yes' or 'No' votes. The result of the vote is based on the method and percentages specified in the 'Node Attributes' tab for the possible results. The Attribute 'Voting Option' determines how the votes will be counted. This Procedure is assigned to the 'Standard' Notification Vote Yes/No. This Notification is assigned the Result Type 'Yes/No'.

Thus, assuming you assigned WF_STANDARD.VoteForResultType as the post_Notification Function to the Message, additional Attributes must be defined for your Notification. One MUST have the Internal Name VOTING_OPTION. This Attribute must be assigned 'Lookup' as the Attribute Type and 'Standard Voting Option' as the Attribute Lookup Type. Then for every possible value for your result type, you must have an Attribute with the Internal Name as the result. For example, if using the result type Approval, you would create two Attributes, one with the Internal Name of APPROVED and one with the Internal Name of REJECTED.

Make sure you check the 'Expand Roles' box.

Then in the Diagrammer window, open the 'Node Attributes' page. Set the Attribute VOTING_OPTION to one of the values determined by the Lookup Code. Set a value for the other two Attributes to equate to a percentage of votes required to determine the answer. You can read more about this Function in the *Oracle Workflow Developer's Guide*.

The Function WF_STANDARD.VoteForResultType provides a good model for coding custom Procedures to count votes. This Function provides code for the following options:

- **Tally on Every Vote** – the required % to "win" is entered for 'Percent No' and 'Percent Yes'. As each Notification is received, the percentages are recalculated. Once either percentage is met or exceeded, that answer is set for the Notification

- **Wait for All Votes** – the numbers entered for 'Percent No' and 'Percent Yes' must equal 100. The result of the Notification is not set until all votes are cast. If the Notification times out, the number of allowable responses is reset to the number that have already responded, the percentages are calculated and the result set accordingly. A branch labeled 'Timeout' would never be used.

- **Require All Votes** – the numbers entered for 'Percent No' and 'Percent Yes' must equal 100. The result of the Notification is not set until all votes are cast. If the Notification times out, the Workflow proceeds along the 'Timeout' branch. If no 'Timeout' branch is specified, the Workflow errors.

- **Simple Majority** – set values for 'Percent Yes' and 'Percent No' to 50. After all votes are cast, if no response gets more than 50%, #NOMATCH is the result. If used to model a result with 3 or more values, set all values to 50. Again, if none of the responses gets more than 50%, #NOMATCH is the result

- **Simple Majority with Default** – set the value for all but one of the responses to 50 and leave one blank. If any response gets more than 50%, that response is the winner, otherwise, the response with the blank value is the winner

- **Simple Majority with Multiple Defaults** – leave more than one percentage blank. If there is no single response with more than 50%, then the winner is the blank response with the highest percentage

- **Popularity** – leave all percentages blank. The one with the highest percent, even if it is less than 50, wins

- **Black Ball** – set one response to 100, everything else to 0. All votes must agree or the zero wins. This is only applicable when there are two choices

- **Jury** – set all responses to 100. If the responses are not unanimous, then '#NOMATCH' is returned.

A SAMPLE PROCEDURE TO COUNT VOTES

Many people want the Notification to behave as if 'Expand Roles' was not checked, but want the copies to be sent based on the global or individual Mailer preference. This can be accomplished by checking 'Expand Roles' and providing a post Notification Function that uses the Rule 'first response wins', i.e., the post-Notification Procedure will use the choice from the first responder and all other responders will get a Message stating that their response was rejected as the Notification is closed. This behavior is identical to sending the Notification to a group and not checking the 'Expand Roles' button, except that using 'Expand Roles' allows each copy of the Notification to be delivered based on that individual's preference. Remember that when 'Expend Roles' is not clicked, each member of the Role gets a copy of the Notification, but only in their Worklist. The Notification will not be emailed.

Following is a sample Procedure for 'first response wins':

```
1.▶ PROCEDURE tally_vote (
        p_item_type    IN        VARCHAR2
       ,p_item_key     IN        VARCHAR2
       ,p_actid        IN        NUMBER
       ,p_funcmode     IN        VARCHAR2
       ,p_result       OUT       VARCHAR2
    )
    IS
2.▶   l_group_id         NUMBER;
      l_user                       VARCHAR2 (320);
      l_rejected_count             PLS_INTEGER;
      l_approved_count             PLS_INTEGER;
      l_per_of_total               NUMBER;
      l_per_of_vote                NUMBER;
    BEGIN
3.▶   g_proc := 'TALLY_VOTE';
      g_trace := 'Check funcmode';

4.▶   IF    (p_funcmode <> wf_engine.eng_run)
         AND (p_funcmode <> wf_engine.eng_timeout)
      THEN
          p_result := wf_engine.eng_null;
          RETURN;
      END IF;

      IF p_funcmode = wf_engine.eng_timeout
      THEN
          p_result := wf_engine.eng_timedout;
          RETURN;
      END IF;

      -- Get Notifications group_id for activity

      -- in case multiple responses,
      -- count number of rejects,number of approves

      g_trace := 'Get the Notification group ID';
5.▶   wf_item_activity_status.notification_status
                        (p_itemtype
                        ,p_itemkey
                        ,p_actid
                        ,l_group_id
                        ,l_user );
```

```
            g_trace := 'count number of rejects, approves';
   6.►     wf_notification.votecount (l_group_id
                                ,'REJECTED'
                                ,l_rejected_count
                                ,l_per_of_total
                                ,l_per_of_vote
                                );
            wf_notification.votecount (l_group_id
                                ,'APPROVED'
                                ,l_approved_count
                                ,l_per_of_total
                                ,l_per_of_vote
                                );

   7.►     -- if anyone rejects, answer is reject
            g_trace:= 'Count rejections and approvals';
            IF l_rejected_count > 0 THEN
                p_result := 'COMPLETE:REJECTED';

            --  if no rejections and an approval exists, approve
            ELSIF l_approved_count > 0 THEN
                p_result := 'COMPLETE:APPROVED';

            -- shouldn't ever get here, but need a default
            ELSE
                p_result := wf_engine.eng_waiting;
            END IF;

            RETURN;

   8.►  EXCEPTION
            WHEN OTHERS
            THEN
                wf_core.CONTEXT (g_pkg, g_proc, g_trace);
                RAISE;
         END tally_vote;
```

1.► The parameters to this Procedure are identical to those for a Function Activity Procedure

2.► Typical declare section.

3.► G_PROC is set to the name of the Procedure. This is required for the Generic Error Handling API WF_CORE.Context. G_TRACE will be periodically set to indicate key points in the code. If an unexpected error occurs, G_TRACE will be passed to the Error Stack and the designer will be able to isolate the area of code that malfunctioned. Note that G_TRACE is reset often and may include the value of selected variables used in subsequent statements.

4.► If FuncMode is anything other than 'RUN' or 'TIMEOUT', set ResultOut to 'NULL' and exit. If FuncMode is 'TIMEOUT', set ResultOut to WF_ENGINE.eng_timedout and return.

5.► Use WF_ITEM_ACTIVITY_STATUS.notification_status to return the GROUP_ID of the Notification. The inputs to this API are item_type, item_key, and activity_id. The outputs are the GROUP_ID and the assigned user. Remember that WF_NOTIFICATIONS.GROUP_ID links to WF_ITEM_ACTIVITY_STATUSES.NOTIFICATION_ID. Each copy of the Notification shares the same GROUP_ID, but has a different NOTIFICATION_ID.

6. ► Use the GROUP_ID as the input to WF_NOTIFICATION.vote_count. The other input is a possible result code for the Notification. The Procedure counts the possible responses, the total number of responses and the number of responses that returned the result code input as a parameter. The Procedure returns the count of responses with the input result code, what percentage that count is of total possible votes and what percentage that count is of the responses returned.

7. ► If even a single REJECTED response is returned, P_RESULT is set to COMPLETE:REJECTED which will cause the Workflow to proceed down the Rejected leg. If no REJECTED responses have been received but even a single APPROVED response is returned, ResultOut is set to COMPLETE:ACCEPTED with will cause the Workflow to proceed down the Accepted leg. If there are no responses that match this value, P_RESULT is set to WF_ENGINE.eng_waiting. As this routine was designed to be assigned to a Notification that uses the Lookup Type Approval, there should not be any responses except REJECTED or APPROVED.

8. ► This is the standard use of WF_CORE.Context to display the value of G_TRACE if any errors occur.

OTHER NOTIFICATION APIS

If the purpose of the Notification Function is to validate the person responding, then use one or more of the following APIs:

- **WF_ENGINE.context_user** – returns the user who is responsible for taking the Action that updated the Notification state.

  - ♦ If FuncMode = 'RESPOND', 'FORWARD', 'TRANSFER', 'QUESTION', or 'ANSWER' and you are using the 'Worklist' page and have clicked 'Switch User' to answer someone else's Notification then this Function returns the name of the user whose Worklist you are accessing

  - ♦ If FuncMode = 'RUN' or 'TIMEOUT', this will be the Performer assigned to the Notification

  - ♦ If FuncMode = 'RESPOND', 'FORWARD', 'TRANSFER', 'QUESTION', or 'ANSWER' and you are acting on your own behalf, then this Function returns a value based on whether you answer the Notification through email or through the Notification Worklist

    - o From email – the first six characters will be email: followed by the email address used to respond. You will have to match this email address to WF_LOCAL_ROLES.EMAIL_ADDRESS where PARTITION_ID = 1 to retrieve NAME (the user name)

    - o From the Notification Worklist – the user name of the logged in user

- **WF_ENGINE.context_user_comment** – comments entered by the responder. The source of the comments depends on the Function Mode

  - ♦ If FuncMode = 'RESPOND', this will be value of the WF_NOTE Attribute, if this Attribute exists for the Notification

  - ♦ If the FuncMode = 'FORWARD' or 'TRANSFER', this will be the comments entered when the Notification is forwarded or transferred

- ◆ If the FuncMode = 'QUESTION', this will be the question or comment entered when the 'Request More Information' button is selected

- ◆ If the FuncMode = 'ANSWER', this is the response to 'Request More Information'

- **WF_ENGINE.recipient_role** – the Role currently designated as the recipient of the Notification. This Function will return the same value as WF_ENGINE.context_user if the recipient is a single person. If the recipient is a Group Role, then this Function returns the Group Name, whereas, WF_ENGINE.context_user returns the individual who belongs to the role

- **WF_ENGINE.context_original_recipient** – the Role to whom the Notification was originally addressed. If this value is different than WF_ENGINE.context_recipient_role, then the Notification has been re-assigned and WF_ENGINE.context_original_recipient returns the original recipient and WF_ENGINE.context_recipient_role returns the current recipient

- **WF_ENGINE.context_from_role** – the Role currently specified as the From Role for the Notification. If there is no #FROM_ROLE Message Attribute, this Function will return null

  - ◆ If the FuncMode = 'RESPOND', this will be null. #FROM_ROLE is linked to an Item Attribute and a Function prior to the Notification has set the value of the Item Attribute

  - ◆ If the FuncMode = 'FORWARD' or 'TRANSFER', this will be the Role that reassigned the Notification, overriding any value set by a previous function

  - ◆ If the FuncMode = 'QUESTION', this will be the Role that sent the request for more information, overriding any value set by a previous function

  - ◆ If the FuncMode = 'ANSWER', this will be the Role that responded to the request for more information, overriding any value set by a previous function

- **WF_ENGINE.context_new_role** – the Role to which a Notification is forwarded or transferred or to whom the 'Request More Information' is addressed, otherwise, null

- **WF_ENGINE.context_more_info_role** – the Role to which the most recent Request More Information is addressed, otherwise, null. Thus, if the current FuncMode = 'ANSWER', WF_ENGINE.context_from_role will contain the Role of the person who answered the Request for More Information and this Function will still return the Role who asked the question

- **WF_ENGINE.context_user_key** – the User Key of the Workflow to which the Notification belongs (if the Notification was sent as part of a Workflow). This is usually the person who initiated the transaction that started the Workflow

- **WF_ENGINE.context_proxy** – for RESPOND, FORWARD, TRANSFER, QUESTION or ANSWER mode, if the user who answered the Notification is acting on behalf of another user through the use of Switch User functionality in the 'Worklist' page, then this Function returns the user who actually answered the Notification, otherwise, null

These are Functions. There are no parameters to these Functions and a VARCHAR2 value is returned.

Previous versions of Workflow had a Function: WF_ENGINE.context_user. This has been replaced by the Functions WF_ENGINE.context_new_role and WF_ENGINE.context_user. Code referencing the old Function will still succeed, but should be updated to reference the new Functions.

It should be noted that if FuncMode = 'RUN' or 'TIMEOUT', values are only available for WF_ENGINE.context_nid and WF_ENGINE.context_user.

If 'Allow Forwarded Response' is set to 'No' (unchecked), the Mailer will not process responses from anyone except the Role to whom the Notification is addressed.

Thus, Custom code to validate the responder is only needed to perform additional checks such as enforcing a Rule that the responder cannot be a subordinate of the original recipient or to reset the approval chain to the responder.

CONCURRENT MANAGER FUNCTIONS

Oracle provides standard Workflow activities that can be used to execute a Concurrent Program (and wait for the result), submit a Concurrent Program (and not wait for a result), or wait for the completion of a Concurrent Program submitted by another Activity. To use these activities, you must load the Item Type 'Concurrent Manager Functions' (FNDCMSTD) and drag-and-drop the activities into your Process. This Item Type is also found in the file fndwfaol.wft in the $FND_TOP/admin/import directory.

Each of these activities has assigned Attributes that must be set in the 'Node Attributes' tab once the Activity is dragged into a Process.

It is important that the context for the Item Type (USER_ID, RESP_ID, RESP_APPL_ID, ORG_ID) be set properly before this Activity is executed. If the Item Type is executed from a form or another Concurrent Program, it will inherit the context. However, any Deferred Activities may cause the context to be missing or incorrect. As two of these activities are themselves Deferred Activities, it is very important that Item Types that use these Functions have a Selector Function that appropriately sets the context. See *Chapter 4, Using PL/SQL in Workflow*, for a discussion of the Selector Function.

Execute Concurrent Program Activity

This Activity submits a Concurrent Request and then waits for the request to finish and passes back the status of the Concurrent Request to the Workflow. Although the assigned Lookup Type contains the values Cancelled, Error, Normal, Terminated, and Warning, MetaLink Doc. ID: 431219.1, *Oracle Workflow Documentation Updates for 11i.ATG_PF.H.delta.6 (RUP6)* states that only the values Normal, Error, and Warning can be returned by the Procedure assigned to this Activity. Workflow Builder will force you to model all the available Lookup Types, so you can model the Process as if these values would be returned or you can have these results follow the same leg as one of the valid results.

The Attributes that must be configured on the 'Node Attributes' page are:

- **Application Short Name** – the two or three letter acronym for the application to which the Concurrent Program is registered

- **Program Short Name** – the short name of the Concurrent Program

- **Number of Arguments** – the number of arguments defined for the program including hidden Attributes

- **Item Attribute Name** – optional name of the Item Attribute to store the resulting Concurrent Request ID

- **Argument1….Argument100** – Value of each Concurrent Program argument. The order of the arguments must match the argument list in the definition of the Concurrent Program. Although there are 100 Attributes, do not define more Attributes than the number specified in Number of Arguments

Submit Concurrent Program Activity

This Activity submits a Concurrent Request and then moves to the next Activity. It has no result type. It has the same Activity Attributes that must be configured on the 'Node Attributes' tab as the 'Execute Concurrent Program Activity'.

Wait for Concurrent Program Activity

This Activity will pause a Workflow and wait for a specific Concurrent Process to complete. It uses the same Result Type and follows the same Rules for this Result Type as the Execute Concurrent Activity.

This Activity has only one Attribute that must be configured on the 'Node Attributes' page:

- **Request ID** – the Concurrent Request ID

MASTER / DETAIL PROCESSES

Master/Detail Processes allow a Workflow to initiate another Workflow and then wait for the child Workflow to finish before continuing. The Workflow that initiates the secondary or child Workflow is called the master and each initiated Workflow is the detail or child. FIGURE 11.18 shows a simple Master Process and FIGURE 11.19 shows a simple Detail Process.

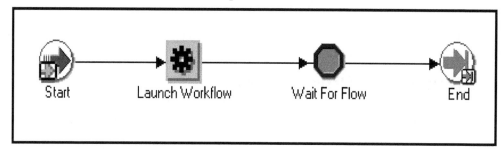

FIGURE 11.18

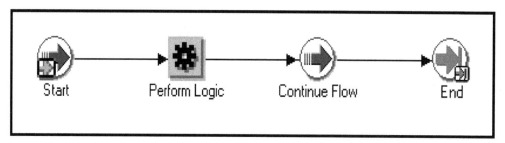

FIGURE 11.19

The Procedure assigned to Launch Workflow must contain code that issues a call to WF_ENGINE.SetItemParent between calls to WF_ENGINE.CreateProcess and WF_ENGINE.StartProcess. Sample code follows:

```
wf_engine.createProcess(child_item_type
                        ,child_item_key
                        ,child_wf_process_name);
```

```
wf_engine.SetItemParent
          (ItemType           => child_wf_item_type,
           ItemKey            => child_item_key,
           parent_itemtype    => p_itemtype,
           parent_itemkey     => p_itemkey,
           parent_context     => NULL);

wf_engine.startProcess(l_wf_item_type, l_item_key);
```

P_ITEMTYPE and P_ITEM_KEY reference the Item Type and Item Key of the Parent Process and would have been passed into this Procedure as part of the Procedure's parameters. If the Master Process initiated several child Workflows and contained several Wait for Flow statements, then PARENT_CONTEXT in WF_ENGINE.SetItemParent would be set to the Activity label name of the Wait for Flow node associated with the child Workflow being initiated. Since our child Workflow only has one Continue Flow node, parent_context is left null.

The 'Node Attributes' for 'Wait for Flow' are seeded as in FIGURE 11.20 and for 'Continue Flow' as in FIGURE 11.21. Normally the parent Workflow contains the 'Wait for Flow' node and the child Workflow contains the 'Continue Flow' node. However, it can be reversed. If the parent Workflow contains the 'Continue Flow' node and the child Workflow contains the 'Wait for Flow' node, then the 'Continuation Flow' parameter would be set to Master in FIGURE 11.20 and to Detail in FIGURE 11.21.

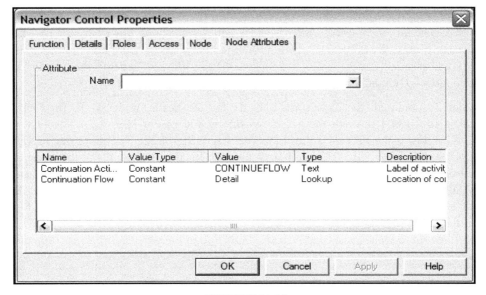

FIGURE 11.20

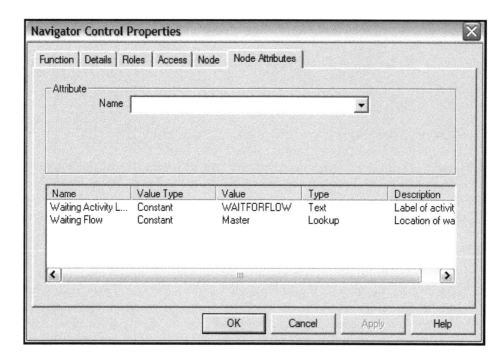

FIGURE 11.21

The Order Management Workflows, Order Header and Order Line, are examples of Master/Detail Workflows. Each of these Workflows has both a 'Wait for Flow' and a 'Continue Flow' Activity. For our illustration we will assume that the order is using the 'Order Flow – Generic' Process and each line is using the 'Line Flow – Generic' Process.

When an order is submitted, the code starts OEOH for the header and OEOL for each line. Each OEOL is linked to OEOH through the parent Workflow and parent Item Key. The first Activity for each OEOL Workflow is the Process 'Enter Line' (see FIGURE 11.22). The first node in this Process is 'Wait for Booking' (see FIGURE 11.23). Although the icon for this Activity is not the standard 'Wait for Flow', the Procedure called by this Activity, WF_STANDARD.WaitForFlow, is the same Activity assigned to Wait for Flow. Continuation Activity for this node is set to BOOK_CONT_L and Continuation Flow is set to Master. The label for this Activity is BOOK_WAIT_FOR_H. Thus, the OEOL Workflows will wait until the Activity with Continuation Activity set to BOOK_WAIT_FOR_H, Continuation Flow set to Detail, and label BOOK_CONT_L in the parent OEOH is completed.

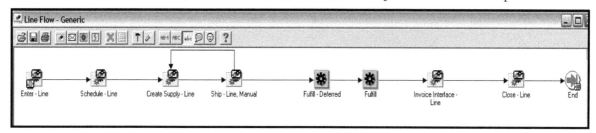

FIGURE 11.22

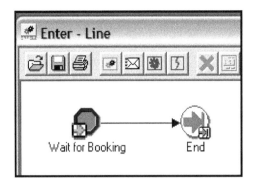

FIGURE 11.23

Meanwhile OEOH is executing the activities in 'Order Flow – Generic' (see FIGURE 11.24).

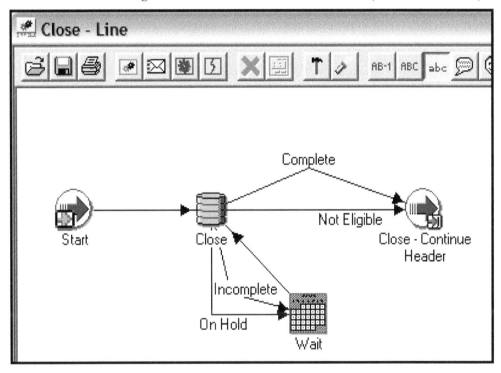

FIGURE 11.24

This Process executes the sub-process 'Book – Order, Manual' (see FIGURE 11.25).

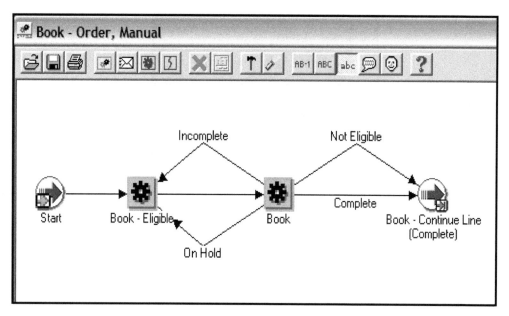

FIGURE 11.25

When the order is booked, the Process executes the Book – Continue Line (Complete) Activity. This Activity uses the Continue Flow icon and calls the Procedure WF_STANDARD.ContinueFlow, which is assigned to the Continue Flow Activity. This Activity has Waiting Activity set to BOOK_WAIT_FOR_H and Waiting Flow set to Detail. The Label for this Activity is BOOK_CONT_L. This Activity completes the Book – Order, Manual sub-process so OEOH now executes the sub-process Close – Order (see FIGURE 11.26).

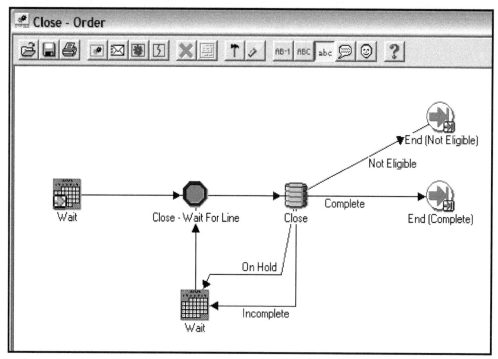

FIGURE 11.26

Close – Order executes a Wait Activity and then moves to Close – Wait for Line. This Activity executes WF_STANDARD.WaitForFlow and has Continuation Activity set to CLOSE_CONT_H and Continuation Flow set to Detail. The label of this Activity is CLOSE_WAIT_FOR_L.

The completion of Book – Continue Line (Complete) also causes all the OEOL Workflows to continue. The Enter – Line Process is now complete. The OEOL Workflows continue through shipping and invoicing and eventually execute the sub-process Close – Line (see FIGURE 11.24). Once the line can be closed, the Process proceeds to Close – Continue Header. This Activity executes WF_STANDARD.ContinueFlow and has Waiting Activity set to CLOSE_WAIT_FOR_L and Waiting Flow set to Master. The label of this Activity is CLOSE_CONT_H. Completing this Activity signals OEOH to continue. Because there can be multiple lines, OEOH checks if all lines are closed. If so, the Workflow completes, otherwise, it returns to the Close – Wait for Line Activity and waits for the next line to close.

Thus, these Workflows use the Master/Detail twice, once to have the lines wait for the header, then again to have the header wait for the lines.

MISCELLANEOUS APIs

WF_ENGINE.CompleteActivity or
WF_ENGINE.CompleteActivityInternalName

Either of these APIs can be used by activities outside the Workflow (such as a form) to cause an Activity within a Workflow to be marked complete so that the Workflow will proceed. The most common use of this Activity is to continue Workflows that are stopped at the standard Block Activity (or any Activity calling the WF_STANDARD.Block Procedure). After the block Activity has executed, the status of the Activity is NOTIFIED (Display Name is Notified). This API can even set a result code for the Activity and thus determine a specific transition to take.

In addition to completing Block activities, the CompleteActivity API (but not the CompleteActivityInternalName API) can be used to start Workflows instead of the APIs LaunchProcess or CreateProcess/StartProcess. Unlike CreateProcess/StartProcess and LaunchProcess, CompleteActivity can be used to start a Workflow "in the middle", i.e., at an Activity with incoming transitions. Whereas CreateProcess/StartProcess and LaunchProcess cause every Activity (marked as a Start Node with no Inbound transitions) in a Process to start, CompleteActivity only completes the specified Activity. CreateProcess/StartProcess and LaunchProcess actually execute the code specified in the start activities. CompleteActivity does not execute the code, it just marks the Activity with a status of COMPLETE.

If CompleteActivity is used to start a Workflow, there must either be a Selector Function assigned to the Item Type or there must be only one runnable Process. This API has no parameter where the starting Process can be specified. Additionally the node specified as the parameter to this API must be specified as a Start Node on the Node tab, even if the node is in the middle of a Process. This last requirement (must be specified as a Start Node) does not apply when using CompleteActivity to continue existing Workflows.

Both CompleteActivity and CompleteActivityInternalName have the same four Attributes:

- **ItemType** – the Internal Name of the Workflow

- **ItemKey** – the Item Key of an existing Workflow or the Item Key to be used to start a new Workflow

- **Activity** – if using CompleteActivity, this is the Activity node label name (found on the Node tab); if using CompleteActivityInternalName, this is the Internal Name of the Activity. If this name does not uniquely identify the node, preface the name with the Internal Name of the Process followed by a colon. For example:

  ```
  <internal name of process>:<activity node label or activity internal name>
  ```

- **Result** – (optional) the result code; the Internal Name of one of the Lookup Codes associated with the Lookup Type specified as the result type. If no result type is specified for this Activity, leave this Attribute null

When CompleteActivityInternalName is invoked, only one activity matching the activity Attribute can have the status NOTIFIED. If there are more than one activity with this status or there are no activities with this status, the Workflow will be placed in error status.

CompleteActivityInternalName cannot be used with Synchronous Processes, CompleteActivity can.

WF_ENGINE.CreateForkProcess and WF_ENGINE.StartForkProcess

These APIs create and start a Workflow that is a copy of the Workflow specified as a parameter. CreateForkProcess inserts the appropriate records in the runtime tables. Therefore, once this API is invoked, you can use other APIs to set the owner or Item Attribute values. StartForkProcess causes the new copy to start executing. These APIs are used in Order Management when items are backordered and in *i*Expenses when an expense report is short paid.

Do not use these APIs from within a parallel branch in a Process, as the APIs will not copy the activity happening in the parallel branch.

The parameters to the CreateForkProcess API are:

- **Copy_ItemType** – the Internal Name of the Item Type to be copied

- **Copy_ItemKey** – the Item Key of the Item Type to be copied

- **New_ItemKey** – the Item Key to be assigned to the copy

- **Same_version** – Boolean variable (set it to TRUE or FALSE) that indicates whether the copy should use the same version of the Item Type as the original (including statuses of activities in the copied Workflow) or should use the latest version of the Item Type (and start from the beginning); defaults to TRUE

  When StartForkProcess is called, if same_version was set to TRUE, the status and history of each activity is copied to the new Workflow. The status of any activity that had a status of ACTIVE is set to NOTIFIED in the new Workflow. Therefore, in order to continue the new copy, CompleteActivity must be called. Any open Notifications in the copied Workflow with a status of OPEN are copied, refreshed with the new Item Key, and sent again. Closed Notifications are copied, but not resent.

  If the copied Workflow contains a Wait activity that is already active, the new Workflow will inherit the status of this activity, including the remaining wait time, i.e., if the Wait activity had an initial wait time of 24 hours and only 2 hours are left, the Wait activity in the new Workflow will also only have 2 hours left.

StartForkProcess has two parameters:

- **ItemType** – the Internal Name of the ItemType

- **ItemKey** – the Item Key of the new Workflow

WF_DIRECTORY.GetUserName

This API returns the name and Display Name for a user based on inputting the original system and original system id. This API is very useful in Workflows where columns reference PERSON_ID instead of USER_ID and you need to set the Performer to the correct name or DISPLAY_NAME from WF_LOCAL_ROLES. The parameters are:

- **p_orig_system** – the original repository table; use PER to retrieve users linked to employees, FND_USR to retrieve users not linked to employees

- **p_orig_sytem_id** – the id to the original repository table:

  use PERSON_ID if: `p_orig_system = 'PER'`,

  use USER_ID if: `p_orig_system_it = 'FND_USR'`

- **p_name** – returned value matching:

  `WF_LOCAL_ROLES.NAME where WF_LOCAL_ROLES.ORIG_SYSTEM = p_orig_system and`
  `WF_LOCAL_ROLES.ORIG_SYSTEM_ID = p_orig_system_id`

- **p_display_name** – returned value matching WF_LOCAL_ROLES.DISPLAY_NAME where:

  WF_LOCAL_ROLES.ORIG_SYSTEM = p_orig_system and
  WF_LOCAL_ROLES.ORIG_SYSTEM_ID = p_orig_system_id

WF_DIRECTORY.CreateAdHocUser

This API adds a Role to the Directory Services tables with the USER_FLAG set to 'Y' and PARTITION_ID set to 0. This API is useful when you need to send a Notification to someone that is not a user or employee or customer contact. The parameters are:

- **Name** – Internal Name of the user. This name should be all uppercase and no longer than 320 characters. The name cannot already exist in WF_LOCAL_ROLES. If no name is specified, an Internal Name in the format '~WF_ADHOC-'<sequence number>

- **Display_name** – Display Name of the user. This name cannot already exist in WF_LOCAL_ROLES. If no name is specified, an Internal Name in the format '~WF_ADHOC-'<sequence number>

- **Language** – using a name recognized as a NLS_LANGUAGE parameter, set to the user's language preference. If left null, resolves to the language of the current session

- **Territory** – using a name recognized as a NLS_TERRITORY parameter, set to the user's territory preference. If left null, resolves to the territory of the current session

- **Description** – (optional) description of the user

- **Notification_preference** – user's Notification preference. Valid values are MAILTEXT, MAILHTML, MAILATTH, MAILHTM2, QUERY, SUMMARY, or SUMHTML. If null, set to MAILHTML

- **Email_address** – (optional) email_address of the user. Although this parameter is optional, since this API is used to define Roles that are not users of the applications and thus cannot access the Notification Worklist, an email address should be specified

- **Fax** – (optional) fax number for the new Role

- **Status** – availability of the user to participate in a Workflow. Possible values are ACTIVE, INACTIVE, EXTLEAVE, and TEMPLEAVE. If left blank, set to ACTIVE

- **Expiration_date** – (optional) the date at which the user is no longer valid

- **Parent_orig_system** – (optional) code indicating the source table of the user

- **Parent_orig_system_id** – (optional) code indicating the key to the source table of the user

This API sets ORIG_SYSTEM to WF_LOCAL_ROLES and ORIG_SYSTEM_ID to 0.

WF_DIRECTORY.CreateAdHocRole

This API adds a Role to the Directory Services tables with the USER_FLAG set to 'N' and PARTITION_ID set to 0. This API is useful when you need to send a Notification to a Role or group that is not already included in WF_LOCAL_ROLES. The parameters are:

- **Role_name** – Internal Name of the Role. This name should be all uppercase and no longer than 320 characters. The name cannot already exist in WF_LOCAL_ROLES. If no name is specified, an Internal Name in the format '~WF_ADHOC-'<sequence number>

- **Role_display_name** – Display Name of the Role. This name cannot already exist in WF_LOCAL_ROLES. If no name is specified, an Internal Name in the format '~WF_ADHOC-'<sequence number>

- **Language** – using a name recognized as a NLS_LANGUAGE parameter, set to the Role's language preference. If left null, resolves to the language of the current session

- **Territory** – using a name recognized as a NLS_TERRITORY parameter, set to the Role's territory preference. If left null, resolves to the territory of the current session

- **Description** – (optional) description of the Role

- **Notification_preference** – Role's Notification preference. Valid values are MAILTEXT, MAILHTML, MAILATTH, MAILHTM2, QUERY, SUMMARY, or SUMHTML. If null, set to MAILHTML

- **Role_users** – the names of the users assigned to this Role. Use commas or spaces to delimit the list

- **Email_address** – (optional) email_address of the Role. This can be an email address that is a group or distribution email address

- **Fax** – (optional) fax number for the new Role

- **Status** – availability of the user to participate in a Workflow. Possible values are ACTIVE, INACTIVE, EXTLEAVE, and TEMPLEAVE. If left blank, set to ACTIVE

- **Expiration_date** – (optional)) the date at which the user is no longer valid

- **Parent_orig_system** – (optional) code indicating the source table of the user

- **Parent**_orig_system_id – (optional) code indicating the key to the source table of the user

- **Owner_tag** – A code to identify the program or application that owns the information for this Role

This API sets ORIG_SYSTEM to WF_LOCAL_ROLES and ORIG_SYSTEM_ID to 0.

WF_DIRECTORY.CreateAdHocRole2

This API is identical to CreateAdHocRole except that the role_users parameter is set to a single value in the format WF_DIRECTORY.UserTable.

WF_DIRECTORY.AddUsersToAdHocRole

This API adds users to an existing Ad-Hoc Role. The Role specified must have the user_flag set to N. Note that you cannot add a Role to a Role. Do not use this API to add users to Roles maintained by Oracle (WF_LOCAL_ROLES.PARTITION_ID <> 0). The parameters are:

- **Role_name** – the Internal Name (WF_LOCAL_ROLES.NAME) of the Ad-Hoc Role

- **Role_user** – the list of users delimited by a comma or space that are to be added to the Ad-Hoc Role. These users must already exist in WF_LOCAL_ROLES

WF_DIRECTORY.AddUsersToAdHocRole

This API adds users to an existing Ad-Hoc Role. The Role specified must have the user_flag set to N. Note that you cannot add a Role to a Role. Do not use this API to add users to Roles maintained by Oracle (WF_LOCAL_ROLES.PARTITION_ID <> 0) The parameters are:

- **Role_name** – the Internal Name (WF_LOCAL_ROLES.NAME) of the Ad-Hoc Role

- **Role_user** – the list of users delimited by a comma or space that are to be added to the Ad-Hoc Role. This users must already exist in WF_LOCAL_ROLES

WF_DIRECTORY.RemoveUsersFromAdHocRole

This API removes users from an existing Ad-Hoc Role. The Role specified must have the user_flag set to N. The parameters are:

- **Role_name** – the Internal Name (WF_LOCAL_ROLES.NAME) of the Ad-Hoc Role

- **Role_user** – the list of users delimited by a comma or space that are to be deleted from the ad-hoc role

SQL SCRIPTS

Oracle provides a series of scripts that can be used to facilitate the development of Workflows. These scripts are found in the $FND_TOP/sql directory.

Change Internal Name of a component

When using the Builder to define a component, once the OK button is pressed, the Internal Name grays out and cannot be changed. Oracle provides a series of scripts to change these Internal Names. These scripts should be used with extreme care and only in a development environment. Changing the Internal Name of a design component will cause any running copies of that Workflow to error.

- **WFCHITT.sql** – This script changes the Internal Name of the Item Type and updates the new Internal Name into all associated design components (Attributes, activities, Lookup Types, and Messages). This script should be run:

```
sqlplus <user/pwd> @wfchitt <old_item_type> <new_item_type>
```

- **WFCHITA.sql** – This script changes the Internal Name of an Item Attribute and updates the new Internal Name into all associated design components. This script should be run:

```
sqlplus <user/pwd> @wfchitta <item_type> <old_attr> <new_attr>
```

- **WFCHACT.sql** – This script changes the Internal Name of an activity and updates the new Internal Name into all associated design components. This script should be run:

```
sqlplus <user/pwd> @wfchact <item_type> <old_activity> <new_activity>
```

- **WFCHACTA.sql** – This script changes the Internal Name of an activity Attribute and updates the new Internal Name into all associated design components. This script should be run:

```
sqlplus <user/pwd> @wfchacta <item_type> <old_actv_attr> <new_actv_attr>
```

- **WFCHMSG.sql** – This script changes the Internal Name of a Message and updates the new Internal Name into all associated design components. This script should be run:

```
sqlplus <user/pwd> @wfchmsg <item_type> <old_msg> <new_msg>
```

- **WFCHMSGA.sql** – This script changes the Internal Name of a Message Attribute and updates the new Internal Name into all associated design components. This script should be run:

```
sqlplus <user/pwd> @wfchmsga <item_type> <old_msg_attr> <new_msg_attr>
```

- **WFCHLUT.sql** – This script changes the Internal Name of a Lookup Type and updates the new Internal Name into all associated design components. This script should be run:

```
sqlplus <user/pwd> @wfchlut <old_lookup_type> <new_lookup_type>
```

- **WFCHLUC.sql** – This script changes the Internal Name of a Lookup Code and updates the new Internal Name into all associated design components. This script should be run:

```
sqlplus <user/pwd> @wfchluc <lookup_type> <old_luc> <new_luc>
```

Forcibly Delete Design or Run-time data

There are times when it is useful to be able to delete all design, all run-time, or all design and run-time data for a particular Item Type. For example, after working on developing a new Workflow, the final definition can be saved to a .wft file. Then wfrmitt.sql can be run to remove all design and run-time data. Finally, the .wft file can be saved to the database and a final test run.

While these scripts are useful, they are dangerous and should be used with great care and usually only in a development database. One of the scripts, wfrmall.sql, is so dangerous that Solution Beacon recommends renaming this script so that it is not accidentally run in place of one of the other removal scripts.

- **WFRMALL.sql** – This script removes all design and run-time data for all Workflows. If this script is run, the developer must, at a minimum, reload wfwst.wft, wfmail.wft, and wferror.wft for any Workflow to function. The script should be run as:

  ```
  sqlplus <user/pwd> @wfrmall
  ```

- **WFRMITT.sql** – This script removes all design and run-time data for a specific Workflow. If this script is run, the Item Type can only be replaced through loading the .wft file. The script has no parameters. However, the script will immediately produce a list of Workflows (lists the Internal Name) in the database and ask which Workflow should be removed (input the Internal Name). The script should be run as:

  ```
  sqlplus <user/pwd> @wfrmitt
  ```

- **WFRMTYPE.sql** – This script removes either all run-time data for a specific Workflow or all run-time data for completed Workflows. The script has no parameters. However, the script will immediately produce a list of Workflows (lists the Internal Name) in the database and ask which Workflow should be removed (input the Internal Name). Next the script asks that 'ALL' be entered to remove run-time data for all instances. Enter anything else to have only the completed items removed. The script should be run as:

  ```
  sqlplus <user/pwd> @wfrmtype
  ```

- **WFRMITMS.sql** – This script removes all run-time data for a specific instance of a specific Workflow. The script asks that 'ALL' be entered to remove run-time data regardless of whether the Workflow is complete. Enter anything else to have only a completed Workflow removed. The script should be run as:

  ```
  sqlplus <user/pwd> @wfrmitt <item_type_internal_name> <item_key>
  ```

- **WFRMITA.sql** – This script removes all design and run-time data for a specific Item Attribute for a specific Workflow. The script has no parameters. However, the script will immediately ask for the Internal Name of the Workflow and then the Internal Name of the Item Attribute. The script should be run as:

  ```
  sqlplus <user/pwd> @wfrmita
  ```

WHAT'S NEXT

There are many, many more APIs and Activities that can be used in Workflow Builder or PL/SQL. For further reading see *Oracle Workflow API Reference (*Release 2.6.4, Part No. B15855-05, June 2006 or Release 12 Part No. B31434-02, June 2007), *Oracle Workflow Developer's Guide* (Release 2.6.4, Part No. B15853-04, July 2006 or Release 12, Part No. B31433-02, June 2007), and *Oracle Workflow Administrator's Guide* (Release 2.6.4, Part No. B15852-05, July 2006 or Release 12, Part No. B31431-02, June 2007).

Chapter 3, Builder Basics, Chapter 4, Using PL/SQL in Workflow, Chapter 6, Testing Workflows, and *Chapter 11, Advanced Builder and PL/SQL* have been designed to illustrate how to use Workflow Builder and PL/SQL to design custom Workflows. Now we will look at a few of the hundreds of workflows provided by

Oracle to demonstrate how this Builder knowledge can be used to set up and configure these Oracle Workflows so they will function in your environment according to your business rules.

Some Commonly Used Workflow Setups

Just like any application that Oracle delivers, setups are required before most of the Workflows are ready to be used. Since the individual Workflows belong to a product, the setups for each Workflow are described in the users or install guide for that product. Some products, like Order Management, even have a separate guide just for the Workflows. Oracle has also provided white papers on MetaLink for many of these Workflows that describe how to set up the Workflow.

Many times the required setups require that the Workflow be loaded into the Workflow Builder, be configured, and then be re-saved to the database. These setups will include Timeouts, Performers, and values for Item Attributes that determine Process flows.

Many Workflows also require setups to be performed through the application screens. These setups include Profile Options, approval hierarchies, limits and System Options. Some Workflows have special screens that determine which Workflow or which Process to be used.

Some Workflows even include places to add your own custom code which Oracle promises not to overlay.

This chapter will discuss some of the most commonly used Workflows and the required setups. Required changes to Account Generators (such as customizing them if Projects is installed) were discussed in *Chapter 7, Account Generators,* and will not be discussed here. Additionally, setups required to use AME are discussed in *Chapter 14, Approvals Management Engine (AME),* and will not be repeated here.

After a general discussion on some of the setups that can only be done using the Workflow Builder, a discussion of several Workflows will follow demonstrating the various setups.

Just as application setups are documented in a setup document, changes to the Workflow or changes to application setups that impact the Workflow should be documented in the setup document. The charts used to document the setups for APEXP can be used to document changes to Item Attributes, Performers, and Timeouts. See *Appendix A – Sample BR110* for examples of documenting additions of any component or of modifying or creating a Process.

SETUPS THAT REQUIRE WORKFLOW BUILDER

Timeouts

Many Workflows are configured with a Process that includes paths labeled <Timeout>. However, many of these activities are either missing the Timeout specification or it has been set to zero, in effect nullifying the Timeout.

The following statements will find the Item Types, Processes, and activities that have a <Timeout> transition leg where the Timeout is either missing or set to zero, or set to an Item Attribute with no value. These statements return results for all Workflows. The only ones requiring attention are for those products used in your installation.

If after reviewing the diagram associated with these Processes, you decide not to utilize the Timeouts Oracle has diagrammed, then the default values can be left as null or zero. The Workflow will not error if this step is omitted.

```
PROMPT Timeout Transitions with no #Timeout attribute
SELECT MAX (process_version),wpa.process_item_type,
       wittl.display_name item_type_name,watl.display_name process_name,
       watl1.display_name activity_name, wpa.instance_label
  FROM wf_process_activities wpa,wf_activities_tl watl,
       wf_activities_tl watl1,wf_item_types_tl wittl
 WHERE watl.item_type = wpa.process_item_type
   AND watl.NAME = wpa.process_name
   AND watl1.item_type = wpa.activity_item_type
   AND watl1.NAME = wpa.activity_name
   AND wittl.NAME = wpa.process_item_type
   AND wpa.process_version =
       (SELECT MAX (wpa1.process_version) FROM wf_process_activities wpa1
          WHERE wpa1.process_item_type = wpa.process_item_type
            AND wpa1.process_name = wpa.process_name)
          AND wpa.instance_id IN (
            SELECT wat.from_process_activity
              FROM wf_activity_transitions wat
             WHERE wat.result_code = '#TIMEOUT' AND NOT EXISTS (
              SELECT 'X' FROM wf_activity_attr_values waav
                WHERE NAME = '#TIMEOUT'
                  AND waav.process_activity_id = wat.from_process_activity))
 GROUP BY wpa.process_item_type,wittl.display_name,watl.display_name,
          watl1.display_name,wpa.instance_label
 ORDER BY wpa.process_item_type,watl.display_name,watl1.display_name;

PROMPT Timeout Transitions with constant #Timeout
PROMPT attribute with NULL or 0 value

SELECT MAX (process_version),wpa.process_item_type,
       wittl.display_name item_type_name, watl.display_name process_name,
       watl1.display_name activity_name, wpa.instance_label
  FROM wf_process_activities wpa, wf_activities_tl watl,
       wf_activities_tl watl1, wf_item_types_tl wittl
 WHERE watl.item_type = wpa.process_item_type
   AND watl.NAME = wpa.process_name
   AND watl1.item_type = wpa.activity_item_type
   AND watl1.NAME = wpa.activity_name
   AND wittl.NAME = wpa.process_item_type
   AND wpa.process_version =
       (SELECT MAX (wpa1.process_version)
```

```
      FROM wf_process_activities wpa1
     WHERE wpa1.process_item_type = wpa.process_item_type
       AND wpa1.process_name = wpa.process_name)
       AND wpa.instance_id IN (
        SELECT wat.from_process_activity
          FROM wf_activity_transitions wat
         WHERE wat.result_code = '#TIMEOUT' AND EXISTS (
            SELECT 'X' FROM wf_activity_attr_values waav
             WHERE waav.process_activity_id =
                   wat.from_process_activity
               AND waav.NAME = '#TIMEOUT'
               AND waav.value_type = 'CONSTANT'
               AND (  waav.number_value = 0
                   OR waav.number_value IS NULL)))
GROUP BY wpa.process_item_type,wittl.display_name,watl.display_name,
       watl1.display_name,wpa.instance_label
ORDER BY wpa.process_item_type,watl.display_name,watl1.display_name;


PROMPT Timeout Transitions with #Timeout attribute set to item attribute
PROMPT and item attribute has NULL or 0 value. Just the item attribute is
PROMPT listed

SELECT DISTINCT (wia.item_type),wittl.display_name item_type_name,
       wia.NAME ATTRIBUTE, wiatl.display_name attribute_name,
       wia.TYPE, DECODE (wia.TYPE,'NUMBER', TO_CHAR (wia.number_default),
       'DATE', TO_CHAR (wia.date_default)) VALUE
  FROM wf_activity_attr_values waav, wf_item_attributes wia,
       wf_process_activities wpa, wf_item_types_tl wittl,
       wf_item_attributes_tl wiatl
 WHERE waav.text_value = wia.NAME AND wia.item_type = wittl.NAME
   AND wia.NAME = wiatl.NAME
   AND wia.item_type = wiatl.item_type
   AND waav.process_activity_id = wpa.instance_id
   AND wpa.process_item_type = wia.item_type
   AND waav.NAME = '#TIMEOUT'
   AND waav.value_type = 'ITEMATTR'
   AND (DECODE (wia.TYPE,'NUMBER',
                TO_CHAR (wia.number_default),'DATE',
                TO_CHAR (wia.date_default)) IS NULL
     OR DECODE (wia.TYPE,'NUMBER',
                TO_CHAR (wia.number_default),'DATE',
                TO_CHAR (wia.date_default)) = '0')
   AND wpa.process_version =
       (SELECT MAX (wpa1.process_version) FROM wf_process_activities wpa1
         WHERE wpa1.process_item_type = wpa.process_item_type
           AND wpa1.process_name = wpa.process_name)
 ORDER BY wia.item_type,wia.NAME;


PROMPT Timeout Transitions with #Timeout attribute set to item attribute
PROMPT and item attribute has NULL or 0 value. The attribute and where
PROMPT used is listed
```

407

```
SELECT DISTINCT (wia.item_type),wittl.display_name item_type_name,
       wia.NAME ATTRIBUTE, wiatl.display_name attribute_name, wia.TYPE,
       DECODE (wia.TYPE,'NUMBER', TO_CHAR (wia.number_default),'DATE',
       TO_CHAR (wia.date_default)) VALUE, watl.display_name process_name,
       watl1.display_name activity_name, wpa.instance_label
   FROM wf_activity_attr_values waav,wf_item_attributes wia,
       wf_process_activities wpa, wf_item_types_tl wittl,
       wf_item_attributes_tl wiatl, wf_activities_tl watl,
       wf_activities_tl watl1
  WHERE watl.item_type = wpa.process_item_type
    AND watl.NAME = wpa.process_name
    AND watl1.item_type = wpa.activity_item_type
    AND watl1.NAME = wpa.activity_name
    AND waav.text_value = wia.NAME
    AND wia.item_type = wittl.NAME
    AND wia.NAME = wiatl.NAME
    AND wia.item_type = wiatl.item_type
    AND waav.process_activity_id = wpa.instance_id
    AND wpa.process_item_type = wia.item_type
    AND waav.NAME = '#TIMEOUT'
    AND waav.value_type = 'ITEMATTR'
    AND (   DECODE (wia.TYPE,'NUMBER',
            TO_CHAR (wia.number_default),'DATE',
            TO_CHAR (wia.date_default)) IS NULL
     OR     DECODE (wia.TYPE,'NUMBER',
            TO_CHAR (wia.number_default),'DATE',
            TO_CHAR (wia.date_default)) = '0')
    AND wpa.process_version =
        (SELECT MAX (wpa1.process_version)
          FROM wf_process_activities wpa1
         WHERE wpa1.process_item_type = wpa.process_item_type
           AND wpa1.process_name = wpa.process_name)
  ORDER BY wia.item_type,wia.NAME,watl.display_name,watl1.display_name;
```

Performers

Many Workflows have Performers set to "seed" values. This allows the Workflow to be saved without error, but when the Workflow is run, it will error with "invalid Performer". The following statements show where the Performers are set to values that do not exist as valid Roles (whether that value is assigned directly or is assigned to the Item Attribute used as the Performer), and where the Performers are set to Item Attributes that do not have a value.

Performers set to an invalid value, whether as a constant or as the value assigned to the Item Attribute, should be fixed if the Workflow will be used in your company.

You can see what Performers are assigned to each Notification by opening the Process in the Diagrammer window in the Workflow Builder and clicking the 'Show Performers' ☺ icon in the tool bar. See FIGURE 12.1.

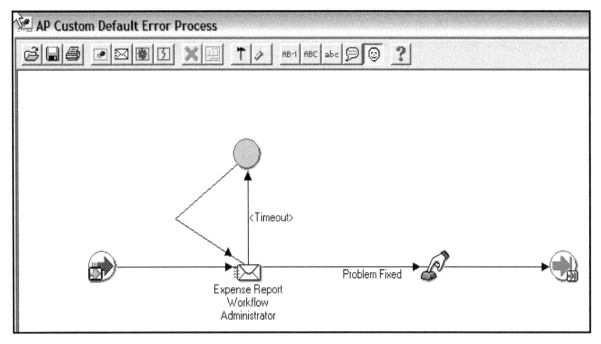

FIGURE 12.1

Item Attributes with no value that are used as Performers are usually set to a valid value in the code that started the Workflow or that belongs to an activity in the Workflow. Thus, Attributes such as Approver or Manager or Requestor are probably OK. Attributes such as AP or Administrator are the ones that bear further investigation. Each Workflow is unique and the setup documentation for that Workflow should be the final guide.

```
PROMPT Performers who are constants and either do not exist in
PROMPT WF_LOCAL_ROLES or are INACTIVE or are old responsibility name

SELECT wpa.perform_role,wpa.process_item_type,wpa.process_version,
       wpa.process_name, wpa.activity_item_type, wpa.activity_name,
       wpa.instance_label
  FROM wf_process_activities wpa
 WHERE wpa.perform_role IS NOT NULL
   AND EXISTS (
        SELECT 'X' FROM wf_activities wa
          WHERE wpa.activity_name = wa.NAME
            AND wpa.activity_item_type = wa.item_type
            AND wa.TYPE = 'NOTICE')
            AND wpa.process_version =
              (SELECT MAX (wpa1.process_version)
                 FROM wf_process_activities wpa1
                WHERE wpa1.process_item_type = wpa.process_item_type
                  AND wpa1.process_name = wpa.process_name)
                  AND perform_role_type = 'CONSTANT'
                  AND (perform_role LIKE 'FND_RESP%:%'
                   OR NOT EXISTS
                      (SELECT 'X' FROM wf_local_roles wlr
                         WHERE wpa.perform_role = wlr.NAME)
                    OR EXISTS
                      (SELECT 'X' FROM wf_local_roles wlr
                         WHERE wpa.perform_role = wlr.NAME
```

```
                            AND wlr.status = 'INACTIVE')
                )
    ORDER BY wpa.perform_role,wpa.process_item_type,wpa.process_name,
             wpa.activity_name;


PROMPT Performers with Performer set to item attribute and item attribute has a
PROMPT value and that value either does not exist in WF_LOCAL_ROLES or is
PROMPT INACTIVE or is old responsibility name. Just the item attribute is
PROMPT listed

SELECT DISTINCT (wia.item_type),wittl.display_name item_type_name,
                wia.NAME ATTRIBUTE, wiatl.display_name attribute_name,
                wia.TYPE, wia.text_default
           FROM wf_process_activities wpa, wf_item_types_tl wittl,
                wf_item_attributes wia, wf_item_attributes_tl wiatl
          WHERE wpa.perform_role_type = 'ITEMATTR'
            AND wpa.process_item_type = wittl.NAME
            AND wpa.perform_role = wia.NAME
            AND wia.item_type = wiatl.item_type
            AND wia.NAME = wiatl.NAME
            AND wpa.process_item_type = wia.item_type
            AND wia.text_default IS NOT NULL
            AND EXISTS (
                SELECT 'X' FROM wf_activities wa
                  WHERE wpa.activity_name = wa.NAME
                    AND wpa.activity_item_type = wa.item_type
                    AND wa.TYPE = 'NOTICE')
            AND wpa.process_version =
                (SELECT MAX (wpa1.process_version)
                   FROM wf_process_activities wpa1
                  WHERE wpa1.process_item_type = wpa.process_item_type
                    AND wpa1.process_name = wpa.process_name)
            AND (wia.text_default LIKE 'FND_RESP%:%'
                OR NOT EXISTS (
                    SELECT 'X' FROM wf_local_roles wlr
                      WHERE wia.text_default IS NOT NULL
                        AND wia.text_default = wlr.NAME)
                OR EXISTS (
                    SELECT 'X' FROM wf_local_roles wlr
                      WHERE wia.text_default = wlr.NAME
                        AND wlr.status = 'INACTIVE')
                )
        ORDER BY wia.item_type,wia.NAME;


PROMPT Performers with Performer set to item attribute and item attribute has a
PROMPT value and that value either does not exist in WF_LOCAL_ROLES or is
PROMPT INIACTIVE or is old responsibility name. The attribute and where used is
PROMPT listed

SELECT DISTINCT (wia.item_type), wittl.display_name item_type_name,
                wia.NAME ATTRIBUTE, wiatl.display_name attribute_name,
                wia.TYPE, wia.text_default, watl.display_name process_name,
                watl1.display_name activity_name, wpa.instance_label
           FROM wf_process_activities wpa, wf_item_types_tl wittl,
                wf_item_attributes wia, wf_item_attributes_tl wiatl,
                wf_activities_tl watl, wf_activities_tl watl1
          WHERE watl.item_type = wpa.process_item_type
            AND watl.name = wpa.process_name
            AND watl1.item_type = wpa.activity_item_type
```

```
           AND watl1.name = wpa.activity_name
           AND wpa.perform_role_type = 'ITEMATTR'
           AND wpa.process_item_type = wittl.NAME
           AND wpa.perform_role = wia.NAME
           AND wia.item_type = wiatl.item_type
           AND wia.NAME = wiatl.NAME
           AND wpa.process_item_type = wia.item_type
           AND wia.text_default IS NOT NULL
           AND EXISTS (
                 SELECT 'X' FROM wf_activities wa
                  WHERE wpa.activity_name = wa.NAME
                    AND wpa.activity_item_type = wa.item_type
                    AND wa.TYPE = 'NOTICE')
           AND wpa.process_version =
                 (SELECT MAX (wpa1.process_version)
                    FROM wf_process_activities wpa1
                   WHERE wpa1.process_item_type = wpa.process_item_type
                     AND wpa1.process_name = wpa.process_name)
           AND (   wia.text_default LIKE 'FND_RESP%:%'
               OR NOT EXISTS (
                   SELECT 'X' FROM wf_local_roles wlr
                    WHERE wia.text_default IS NOT NULL
                      AND wia.text_default = wlr.NAME)
               OR EXISTS (
                   SELECT 'X' FROM wf_local_roles wlr
                    WHERE wia.text_default = wlr.NAME
                      AND wlr.status = 'INACTIVE')
               )
      ORDER BY wia.item_type, wia.NAME, watl.display_name,
               watl1.display_name;

PROMPT Performers with Performer set to item attribute and item attribute
PROMPT has NULL value. Just the item attribute is listed

SELECT DISTINCT (wia.item_type), wittl.display_name item_type_name,
               wia.NAME ATTRIBUTE, wiatl.display_name attribute_name,
               wia.TYPE, wia.text_default
        FROM wf_process_activities wpa, wf_item_types_tl wittl,
             wf_item_attributes wia, wf_item_attributes_tl wiatl
       WHERE wpa.perform_role_type = 'ITEMATTR'
         AND wpa.process_item_type = wittl.NAME
         AND wpa.perform_role = wia.NAME
         AND wia.item_type = wiatl.item_type
         AND wia.NAME = wiatl.NAME
         AND wpa.process_item_type = wia.item_type
         AND wia.text_default IS NULL
         AND EXISTS (
               SELECT 'X' FROM wf_activities wa
                WHERE wpa.activity_name = wa.NAME
                  AND wpa.activity_item_type = wa.item_type
                  AND wa.TYPE = 'NOTICE')
         AND wpa.process_version =
               (SELECT MAX (wpa1.process_version)
                  FROM wf_process_activities wpa1
                 WHERE wpa1.process_item_type = wpa.process_item_type
                   AND wpa1.process_name = wpa.process_name)
      ORDER BY wia.item_type,wia.NAME;

PROMPT Performers with Performer set to item attribute and item attribute
PROMPT has NULL value. The attribute and where used is listed
```

```
SELECT DISTINCT (wia.item_type), wittl.display_name item_type_name,
                wia.NAME ATTRIBUTE, wiatl.display_name attribute_name,
                wia.TYPE, wia.text_default, watl.display_name process_name,
                watl1.display_name activity_name, wpa.instance_label
           FROM wf_process_activities wpa, wf_item_types_tl wittl,
                wf_item_attributes wia, wf_item_attributes_tl wiatl,
                wf_activities_tl watl, wf_activities_tl watl1
          WHERE watl.item_type = wpa.process_item_type
            AND watl.name = wpa.process_name
            AND watl1.item_type = wpa.activity_item_type
            AND watl1.name = wpa.activity_name
            AND wpa.perform_role_type = 'ITEMATTR'
            AND wpa.process_item_type = wittl.NAME
            AND wpa.perform_role = wia.NAME
            AND wia.item_type = wiatl.item_type
            AND wia.NAME = wiatl.NAME
            AND wpa.process_item_type = wia.item_type
            AND wia.text_default IS NULL
            AND EXISTS (
                    SELECT 'X' FROM wf_activities wa
                     WHERE wpa.activity_name = wa.NAME
                       AND wpa.activity_item_type = wa.item_type
                       AND wa.TYPE = 'NOTICE')
            AND wpa.process_version =
                    (SELECT MAX (wpa1.process_version)
                       FROM wf_process_activities wpa1
                      WHERE wpa1.process_item_type = wpa.process_item_type
                        AND wpa1.process_name = wpa.process_name)
          ORDER BY wia.item_type,wia.NAME,watl.display_name,watl1.display_name;
```

Activity Attributes

The behavior of many activities is determined by the value of activity Attributes. These values are set in the 'Node Attributes' tab of the 'Properties' page when this page is opened from the Diagrammer window.

The Builder clearly indicates Functions have activity Attributes, as there is a 'boxed +' (box with a + inside) next to that Function. Yet, just because the activity has activity Attributes, these Attributes may be leftover from previous Workflow versions, or customers should not set values for these Attributes. So if the Function activity belongs to the Item Type, only configure the activity Attributes if directed by the Oracle implementation guides (or a MetaLink note or Oracle Support).

Any time one of the activities from the 'Standard' Item Type is used and that activity has activity Attributes, these Attributes must be configured. Oracle usually has assigned the appropriate values to these Attributes. The implementation guide will list any Functions and Attributes that can be adjusted by the customer. See the discussion for the 'Expenses' (APEXP) Workflow for an example of such activities.

The following code is inefficient, but it will list the Attribute values for the activities copied from the 'Standard' Item Type. Note that the Internal Name of the Item Type using the 'Standard' activities must be substituted in two different places.

```
SELECT DISTINCT (watl.display_name) process_name,
                watl1.display_name activity_name,wpa.instance_label,
                waatl.display_name activity_attribute_name,waav.value_type,
                DECODE (waav.value_type,'ITEMATTR', waav.text_value,
                    DECODE (waa.TYPE,'NUMBER',
                            TO_CHAR (waav.number_value),'DATE',
                            TO_CHAR (waav.date_value),
                            text_value)) VALUE
        FROM wf_process_activities wpa,wf_activity_attributes waa,
             wf_activity_attr_values waav,wf_activities_tl watl,
             wf_activities_tl watl1,wf_activity_attributes_tl waatl
        WHERE watl.item_type = wpa.process_item_type
          AND watl.NAME = wpa.process_name
          AND watl1.item_type = wpa.activity_item_type
          AND watl1.NAME = wpa.activity_name
          AND waav.NAME = waatl.NAME
          AND waatl.activity_name = wpa.activity_name
          AND waatl.activity_item_type = 'WFSTD'
          AND waa.activity_item_type = 'WFSTD'
          AND waa.activity_name = wpa.activity_name
          AND waa.NAME = waav.NAME
          AND wpa.process_item_type = '<item type internal name>'
          AND wpa.activity_item_type = 'WFSTD'
          AND wpa.instance_id = waav.process_activity_id
          AND wpa.process_name = watl.NAME
          AND wpa.process_item_type = watl.item_type
          AND wpa.process_version =
              (SELECT MAX (wpa1.process_version)
                 FROM wf_process_activities wpa1
               WHERE wpa1.process_item_type = '<item type internal name>'
                 AND wpa.process_name =  wpa1.process_name);
```

Item Attributes (not used as Performers)

Many Workflows have Item Attributes that determine how the Workflow behaves. The more sophisticated Workflows use Profile Options to furnish the values for these Item Attributes. The code in an activity must still read the value of the Profile Option and set that value into the Item Attribute, but it avoids having to use the Workflow Builder, which requires the use of the APPS password.

To furnish code that lists all Attributes without a value would be pointless, as the Attributes are individual to each Workflow. Again, read the documentation for each Workflow.

JOURNAL BATCH – GLBATCH

This Workflow is optional and is used to approve manual journal batches. The Workflow is described under the Journal Entry heading in the Journal Approval sub-heading in the *General Ledger Users' Guide*. This chapter mentions some of the setups required, but you need to read the *Setting Up Journal Approval* section in the Setup section to get all the settings. For example, the description of the Workflow does not mention the setting that governs whether or not the Workflow is invoked. This is covered in *Chapter 2, Setup*.

The documentation listed above states there are three prerequisites to using this Workflow – setting up Workflow (covered in *Chapter 2, Setup*), setting two Profile Options, and using the Builder to make some optional changes to the Workflow itself. It is not necessary to do the last two steps prior to the other steps mentioned in the Journal Approval Setup. They are listed as prerequisites because they are performed by individuals other than the GL Functional SuperUser.

For Release 12, the applicable sections and manuals are *Using Accounting Setup Manager, Oracle Financials Implementation Guide, Release 12, Part No. B16386-02, April 2007; Setting Up Journal Approval, Oracle General Ledger Implementation Guide, Release 12, Part No. B31219-02, June 2007*. For Release 11.5.10, the applicable sections and manuals are *Defining Sets of Books, Setting Up Journal Approval* and *Journal Approval Overview*, in *Oracle General Ledger User Guide, Release 11i, Part No. B12270-03, April 2005*.

The Applications Part

The Journal Approval Setup lists enabling this Workflow as the first step in the setup. Since this Workflow can be turned on as part of the original installation, or anytime thereafter (including in a working GL environment), it is probably best to leave this step until last. Note: this is one of the few setups that can be done, undone, redone, etc. Because this setup step is associated with a Set of Books (Release 11.5.10) or Ledger (Release 12), the screens look very different.

Release 11.5.10

Whether or not the 'Journal Approval' Workflow is invoked is governed by a check box in the set-of-books setup window (From the 'General Ledger SuperUser' responsibility's main menu, choose Setup → Financials → Books → Define. Click the 'Journaling' tab). When 'Journal Approval' is clicked, a pop-up window asks if you want the Workflow to be active for journals with a source of Manual. Choose 'Yes' or 'No'. See FIGURE 12.2.

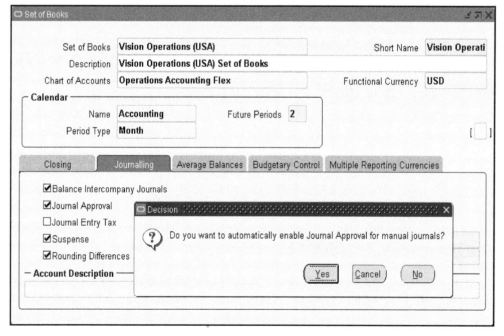

FIGURE 12.2

Once you've responded to the pop-up, you have to navigate to the Journal Source window (Setup → Journal → Sources). If there are any other sources for which the 'Journal Approval' Workflow should run, check the 'Require Journal Approval' flag. Remember that Budget and Encumbrance journals do not have a source of Manual, so if you want to run the 'Approval' Workflow for these JEs, find the appropriate source and check the box. See FIGURE 12.3. Obviously, if you do this step prior to checking the 'Journal Approval' box in the 'Set of Books' screen, and you check the box for the source Manual, the pop-up window shown in FIGURE 12.2 will not appear as the need to perform this setup was just eliminated.

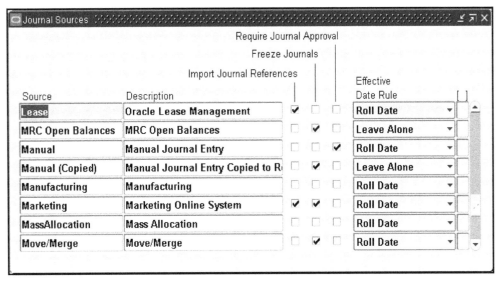

FIGURE 12.3

Release 12

Instead of the 'Set of Books' window, enabling the 'Journal Approval' Workflow is done in the Accounting Setups window (from General Ledger SuperUser, Setup → Financials → Accounting Setup Manager → Accounting Setups). When FIGURE 12.4 appears, query the desired Ledger. Click 'Update Accounting Options'. FIGURE 12.5 appears.

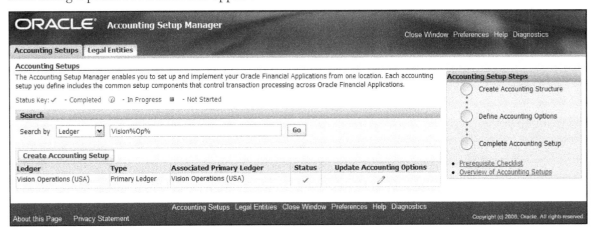

FIGURE 12.4

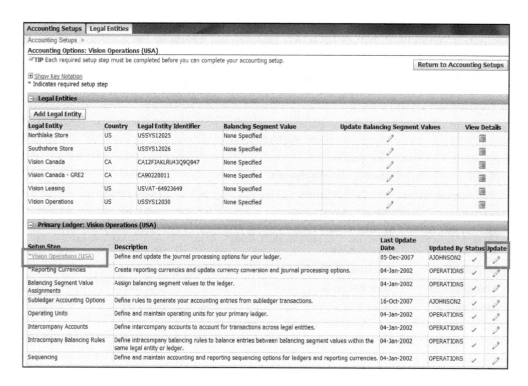

FIGURE 12.5

In the 'Primary Ledger: <ledger name>' section, find the row '*<ledger name>'. It will be a hyperlink (underlined and blue) and the Description will say 'Define and update the journal processing options for your ledger'. Click the yellow pencil icon in the 'Update' column for that row. FIGURE 12.6 will appear. Click Next so that Page 2 appears. See FIGURE 12.7.

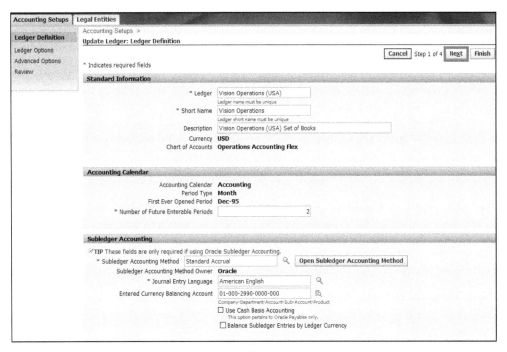

FIGURE 12.6

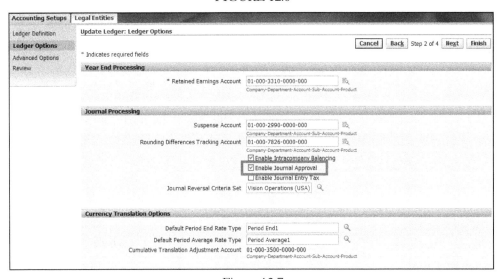

Figure 12.7

Click Finish to save your change. Unlike Release 11.5.10, no pop-up displays and the 'Journal Source Manual' is not automatically marked for 'Require Journal Approval'. See the Release 11.5.10 steps above for instructions on setting this flag.

Profile Options

The two Profile Options that need to be set are 'Journals: Allow Preparer Approval' and 'Journals: Find Approver Method'. These options must be set by someone with access to the 'System Administrator' responsibility.

'Journals: Allow Preparer Approval' determines whether the creator of a Journal Entry (JE) can approve it. Values are 'Yes' or 'No'. If you choose 'Yes', the preparer becomes the first approver in the chain and if the amount of the JE is within the preparer's approval limits, the batch is approved. If you choose 'No', then the Workflow looks at the next Profile Option to determine the approval path.

JE Approvals use the employee/supervisor method of approval. 'Journals: Find Approver Method' just determines whether any levels in the hierarchy can be skipped. The valid values are:

- **Go Up Management Chain** – starts with the preparer's immediate supervisor and requests approval from everyone in the chain until a supervisor with sufficient authority approves the JE.

- **Go Direct** – finds the first person in the chain with sufficient authority and requests approval from that person first. Preparer's immediate supervisor is sent a courtesy 'FYI' Notification.

- **One Stop Then Go Direct** – the preparer's supervisor is sent a request for approval. If he/she does not have sufficient authority, then the person with sufficient authority is identified. Any levels in-between are skipped.

Approval Hierarchy and Limits

All persons who will either create or be involved in the Approval Process must be set up as employees and they must have a supervisor specified in their assignment. This is done through the 'Enter Employees' screen.

Once employees are created, they must be assigned an approval limit (From the 'General Ledger SuperUser' responsibility, choose Setup → Employees → Limits). Make sure that the top person in the hierarchy has a limit large enough to cover any entry that might be made. FIGURE 12.8 shows the Release 11.5.10 version of the screen and FIGURE 12.9 shows the Release 12 version of the screen.

Employee	Employee ID	Authorization Limit [ ]
Brock, Mr. Kim	30	100,000.00
Brown, Ms. Casey	31	1,000,000,000.00
Hof, Mr. David	295	50,000.00
Langham, Ms. Kelly	297	10,000.00
Seller, Mr. James	296	20,000.00
Stock, Ms. Pat	25	20,000.00

FIGURE 12.8

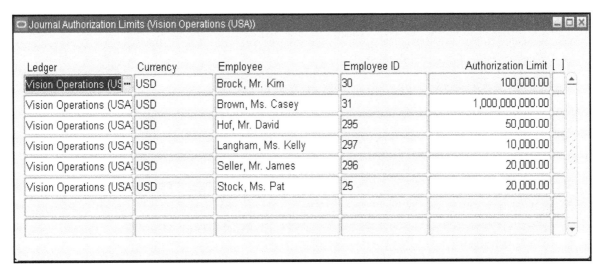

FIGURE 12.9

Restrict Assignee and Notification Reassignment Approval Lists

To restrict the assignee List of Values for journal approval requests and the Notification reassignment list to employees who are defined in the above form, run the Concurrent Request program 'Maintain Authorized Users for Journal Approval Reassignment'. There are no parameters. Rerun the program any time changes are made in the 'Journal Authorization Limits' screen.

The Builder Part

The remaining steps are optional, but must be performed from the Builder. The Internal Name of the 'Journal Approval' Workflow is GLBATCH. The Display Name is 'Journal Batch'. If your Applications DBA is sending you the file from the UNIX/LINUX file system, the file is $GL_TOP/patch/115/import/US/glwfjea.wft. If the Applications DBA has used the Builder to create the .wft file it may have more than the 'Journal Approval' Workflow. This is normal. This Workflow uses some definitions that cause it to become linked to other Workflows. When this happens, all the linked Workflows must be loaded along with the requested Workflow.

When you are finished with all your setups, the Applications DBA can load the Workflow back into the database. If any PL/SQL Procedures are modified that are attached to Function or Notification activities or to Document Attributes, then the modified Packages must be compiled. Make sure this code is migrated with the Workflow as testing is completed and the Workflow is moved to production. Once any changes to the definition of the Workflow have been made, in addition to saving the Workflow to the database, a .wft should be created and stored under your $CUSTOM_TOP directory. This copy of the file should be used when making any additional changes instead of the glwfjea.wft file. Note that the name of the .wft file is not limited to 8 characters.

Oracle states that the customizations allowed for this Workflow are:

- Change 'Timeout' value for 'Request Approval from Approver'

- Increase 'Limit' value for 'Reached Manager Notification Resend Limit'

- Customize the sub-process 'Customizable: Verify Authority' sub-process

- Create custom code in the PL/SQL Procedures attached to the following activities

   ♦ 'Customizable: Is Journal Batch Valid'

   ♦ 'Customizable: Does Journal Batch Need Approval'

   ♦ 'Customizable: Is Preparer Authorized to Approve'

   ♦ 'Customizable: Verify Authority (process)'

   ♦ 'Customizable: Verify Authority (activity)'

Load the Workflow, click the + next to Journal Batch, then the + next to Processes. The Navigator window will look like FIGURE 12.10

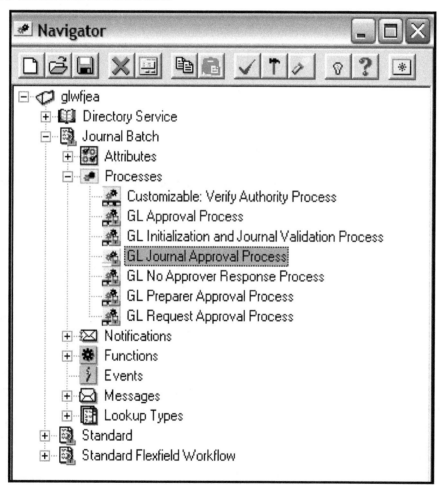

FIGURE 12.10

The seeded 'Timeout' for 'Request Approval From Approver' is set to 7 days. To change this value, open the 'GL Request Approval Process' Process (See FIGURE 12.11). If the top of the Diagrammer window says 'Read Only', you will have to change your Access Level to 20 (Remember this? – Help → About Oracle Workflow Builder <version>). Double-click the 'Request Approval' From Approver, click the Node tab, update the 'Timeout' to be the value you wish and click OK.

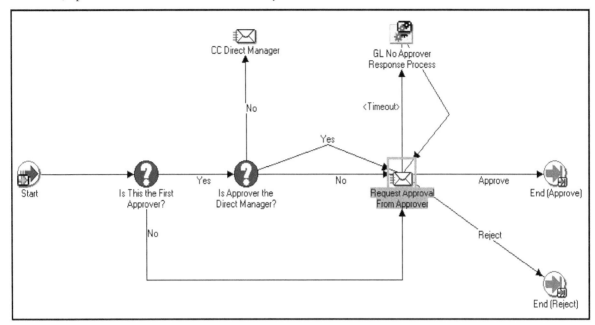

FIGURE 12.11

Now double-click the 'GL No Approver Response Process'. See FIGURE 12.12.

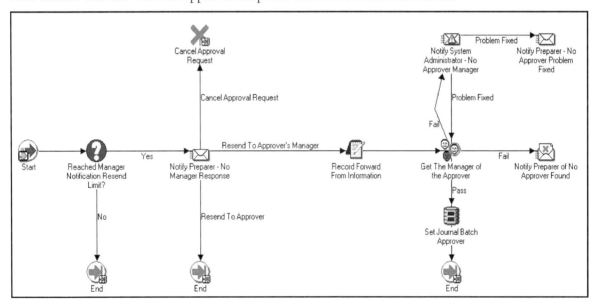

FIGURE 12.12

Open the 'Properties' page of the 'Reached Manager Notification Send Limit?' node and click the 'Node Attributes' tab. Choose 'Number of Times to Notify Manager' in the 'Attribute Name' field. Oracle seeds the Attribute value to be 1. For this Workflow, decreasing the value to zero has no effect. But note that increasing the value acts as a 'multiplier' of the Timeout value specified above. For example, if the 'Timeout' is set for 2 days and the 'Send Limit' is set to 2 and the manager does not respond within 2 days, the request for approval is resent and the Timeout counter set back to zero. Thus, the total amount of time that a manager has to respond before their manager is notified is a product of multiplying the 'Timeout' by the 'Send Limit'.

If your business rules for approval limits are more complex than just dollar amount per person, Oracle provides a sub-process you can customize to model your business rules called 'Customizable: Verify Authority Process'. This sub-process is part of the 'GL Approval' sub-process. When you open this Process you see FIGURE 12.13.

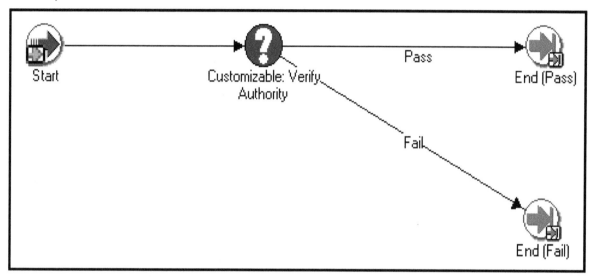

FIGURE 12.13

The purpose of this Process is to determine whether to by-pass the current approver and move up the chain to the next approver (goes to the End(Fail) node), or send the Approval Notification to the current approver (goes to the End(Pass) node). If you make any changes to this Process, make sure that you don't ever eliminate the top person in your hierarchy. If this happens, the Workflow branches to the 'Notify System Administrator – No Approver' node and you will have to add a new top person and then answer the Notification 'Problem Fixed'.

The majority of the PL/SQL used by this Workflow is stored in the Package GL_WF_JE_APPROVAL_PKG. Four PL/SQL Procedures that Oracle states can be customized are stored in GL_WF_CUSTOMIZATION_PKG. If you customize any of the Procedures in this Package, Oracle will not touch them in any patches or upgrades.

The 'Customizable: Verify Authority' activity uses the Procedure VERIFY_AUTH. As delivered, it doesn't do anything except set ResultOut to COMPLETE:PASS (Internal Name for the Lookup Type 'GL Pass or Fail Result Type'). You can add custom code to cause the current approver to be skipped. If you want to skip the current approver, make sure you include the statement ResultOut := 'COMPLETE:FAIL' just before the RETURN.

The 'Customizable: Is Journal Batch Valid' activity uses the Procedure IS_JE_VALID. As delivered, it doesn't do anything except set ResultOut to COMPLETE:Y. This activity is in the GL Initialization and Journal Validation Process. If you have company specific business logic that you want to check before sending the JE through the Approval Process, this is the routine to add that logic. If you wish to make the JE Invalid, include the statement ResultOut := 'COMPLETE:N' just before the RETURN.

The Customizable: Does Journal Batch Need Approval activity uses the Procedure DOES_JE_NEED_APPROVAL. As delivered, it doesn't do anything except set ResultOut to COMPLETE:Y. This activity is also in the GL Initialization and Journal Validation Process. If you have company specific business logic that you want to check before sending the JE through the Approval Process, this is the routine to add that logic. If you wish to bypass approvals and cause the JE to be approved, include the statement ResultOut := 'COMPLETE:N' just before the RETURN.

The Customizable: Is Preparer Authorized to Approve activity uses the Procedure CAN_PREPARER_APPROVE. As delivered, it doesn't do anything except set ResultOut to COMPLETE:Y. This activity is in the GL Preparer Approval Process. This routine is called after Oracle has verified that the preparer can approve the JE. This is your chance to block approval of the JE by the approver due to any special Rules. If you wish to bypass preparer approval and request approval by the next person in the chain, include the statement ResultOut:= 'COMPLETE:N' just before the RETURN.

Once you have made all your changes, the Workflow must be saved back to the database. This will replace Oracle's version of the Workflow.

Note that any patches you apply that contains a new version of this Workflow can overwrite the changes made to the Timeout value for 'Request Approval from Approver' and the limit for 'Reached Manager Notification Resend Limit', but it will not touch your customizations if you have restricted your changes to the areas described above. Still, anytime a patch is applied to GL (or Financials or Workflow), be sure to test this Workflow to ensure that it behaves as expected.

EXPENSES – APEXP

This Workflow is required if using *i*Expenses. It is the Workflow used to approve expense reports by the employee's manager and to coordinate the receipt approval by the Payables Department. The setups in this section assume that you are not using Approvals Management Engine (AME). The use of AME is discussed in *Chapter 14, Approvals Management Engine (AME).*

This Workflow requires that all the setup steps be completed for *i*Expenses. These steps are documented in the *Oracle Internet Expenses Implementation and Administration Guide.* This manual is over 400 pages. Thus, this book will not cover setting up employee/supervisor relationships, expense report templates, policies, audit automation, credit cards, exchange rates, and Profile Options that do not impact the Workflow.

The applicable sections and manuals are *Defining Workflow Processes, Expenses Workflow, Oracle Internet Expenses Implementation and Administration Guide.* The Release 12 manual is *Part No. B315501-03, April 2007* and the Release 11.5.10 manual is *Part No. B40083-01, December 2006.*

The Builder Part

This Workflow will require setups that can only be performed using the Workflow Builder. The Internal Name of the 'Expenses' Workflow is APEXP. If your Applications DBA is sending you the file from a UNIX/LINUX file system, the file is $AP_TOP/patch/115/import/US/apwxwkfl.wft. If the Applications DBA has used the Builder to create the .wft file it will have more than the 'Expenses' Workflow. This is normal. This Workflow uses some definitions that caused it to become linked to other Workflows. When this happens, all the linked Workflows must be loaded along with the requested Workflow.

When you are finished with all your setups, the Applications DBA can load the Workflow back into the database. If any PL/SQL Procedures are modified that are attached to Function or Notification activities or to Document Attributes, then the modified Packages must be compiled. Make sure this code is migrated with the Workflow as testing is completed and the Workflow is moved to production. Once any changes to the definition of the Workflow have been made, in addition to saving the Workflow to the database, a .wft should be created and stored under your $CUSTOM_TOP directory. This copy of the file should be used when making any additional changes instead of the apwxwkfl.wft file. Note that the name of the .wft file is not limited to 8 characters.

If you are unable to make any required changes to the Workflow, make sure your Access Level is set to 20 (Remember this? – Help → About Oracle Workflow Builder <version>).

Oracle states that the setups *required* for this Workflow are:

- Set Workflow Activity Attributes

- Set expense report Performers

Oracle states that the setups that are *optional* for this Workflow are:

- Set Workflow Timeouts

- Defer Workflow Process at run-time

- Create custom code in the PL/SQL Procedures attached to the following Process/Activity:

  ♦ Custom Validate Expense Report

  ♦ (Release 11.5.10) Manager (Spending) Approval Process / Find Approver

  ♦ (Release 12) Non AME Approval Process / Find Approver

  ♦ (Release 11.5.10) Manager (Spending) Approval Process / Level of Manager Involvement

  ♦ (Release 12) Non AME Approval Process / Level of Manager Involvement

  ♦ (Release 11.5.10) Manager (Spending Approval Process / Verify Authority

  ♦ (Release 12) Non AME Approval Process / Level of Manager Involvement

Activity Attributes

The following table lists Attributes in the Expense Report Workflow that impact how the Workflow behaves. To change the Attributes, perform the following steps in the Workflow Builder (after loading from the database the following Item Types (Expenses, Standard). Double click the Process indicated. The Process will be drawn in the Diagrammer window. Double-click the icon that matches the Function name. Select the 'Node Attributes' tab. In the 'Name' field, select the 'Activity Attribute'. Do not change the Type. Select or enter the desired value in the 'Value' field. Click Apply, and then click OK. After all changes are made, save the Workflow back to the database.

Process	Function Display Name	Activity Attribute	Purpose	Allowable Values	Seeded Value
Non AME Approval Process	Find Approver	Find Approver Method	Controls how Workflow routes expense reports Go Up Management Chain – starting with employee's supervisor, sends a request to each	Go Up Management Chain	Go Up Management Chain

Process	Function Display Name	Activity Attribute	Purpose	Allowable Values	Seeded Value
			manager in the hierarchy until one with sufficient authority is asked Go Directly to Person with Signing Authority – looks at employee's hierarchy until manager with sufficient authority is found and sends request only to that manager One Stop Then Go Directly – requests approval from employee's manager and if that isn't sufficient, then walks up hierarchy until manager with sufficient authority is found and notifies that manager, skipping any managers in-between	Go Directly to Person with Signing Authority One Stop Then Go Directly	
Manager (Shortpay) Approval Process	Missing Receipts Sum Exceed Limit	AP Limit of Sum of Missing Receipt Expense Lines	If expense reports are missing receipts and shortpay not created, then 2nd approval from manager is requested if the value of the expense report exceeds value specified here	Any positive value	1000
Manager (Spending) Approval	Req Proof of Payment Even if Mgr Apprvd Receipt Missing	Always Require Proof of Payment	If employee marks that a required receipt is missing, controls whether that receipt will still be required. Y – still required N – not still required	Y N	Y
No Manager Response Process	Notify Preparer When Resend Count Equals Limit	Number of times to notify manager	Controls the number of times Workflow sends an expense report to a manager for approval. If the number of times a manager does not respond equals the number defined here, then a note is sent to the preparer who can choose whether to try again, or send the request to the manager's manager	Any positive integer value > 0	2
No Manager Response Process 2	Notify Preparer When Resend Count Equals Limit	Number of times to notify manager	Controls the number of times Workflow sends an expense report to a manager for approval. If the number of times a manager does not respond equals the number defined here, then a note is sent to the preparer who can choose whether to try again, or send the request to the manager's manager	Any positive integer value > 0	2
Third Party Expense Report	Individual's Approval Required	Employee Approval Required	If an authorized delegate creates an expense report for an employee, controls whether the employee is required to approve the expense report before submitting it up the management chain Yes – employee approval required No – employee is sent Notification that expense report submitted, no approval by employee required	Yes No	Yes
Third Party Expense Report	Loop Counter	Loop Limit	Controls number of times employee asked to approve submission of expense report by authorized delegate (if employee ignores first Notification). If limit exceeded, expense report continues on for approval	Any positive integer value > 0	2

TABLE 12. 1

Timeouts

The Oracle manuals are not accurate in the list of Activities with a Timeout. This points out the need to use the SQL provided in this chapter to compare against the Oracle guides and reconcile any differences.

Table 12.2 lists the Release 12 Timeouts for various Functions and Notifications, the default value, and the Action taken if the Timeout occurs. Wherever the Process has modeled a transition labeled <Timeout>, the Timeout values can be adjusted. To change the default value, perform the following steps in the Workflow Builder (after loading from the database the 'Expenses' Item Types). Double click the Process indicated. The Process will be drawn in the Diagrammer window. Double-click the icon that matches the Function/Notification name. Select the Node tab. Leave the Timeout Type field set to Relative Time. Type in the Days, Hours, and Minutes. Click Apply, and then click OK. After all changes are made, save the Workflow back to the database.

Process	Function / Notification Display Name	Purpose and Action When Invoked	Default Value
Bothpay Process	Inform System Administrator – No Vendor	The credit card company to be paid was not specified on the expense report and a Message to the Expense Report Administrator is sent. If the Timeout is invoked, the conditions are re-checked. The Workflow remains in this loop until the problem is fixed.	3 days
Server Side Validation Process	Inform Individual of Expense Allocation Failure	Something is wrong with the expense report and the preparer is being asked to fix the problem. If the Timeout is invoked, the expense report is checked to see if errors still exist. The Workflow will remain in this loop until the problem is fixed or until the preparer answers the Message 'Return to Preparer'	3 days
Server Side Validation Process	Inform Sys Admin of Payables Validation Failure	Oracle has determined that something is wrong with the expense report and asked 'Expense Report Workflow Administrator' to fix the problem. If the Timeout is invoked, the Oracle logic is re-executed. The Workflow will remain in this loop until the problem is fixed or until the 'Expense Report Workflow Administrator' answers the Message 'Return to Preparer'	3 days
Server Side Validation Process	Inform Sys Admin of Custom Validation Failure	Customer has coded logic that determined something is wrong with the expense report and asked 'Expense Report Workflow Administrator' to fix the problem. If the Timeout is invoked, the custom logic is re-executed. The Workflow will remain in this loop until the problem is fixed or until the 'Expense Report Workflow Administrator' answers the Message 'Return to Preparer' Note: Only need to set this if you customize the Function Custom Validate Expense Report	3 days
AME Approval Process	Inform System Administrator – No Approver	An approver could not be found. The System Administrator must insure that an approver is set up. The Workflow will continue in the loop of trying to find an approver and notifying the System Administrator until an approver is set up.	3 days
AME Request Approval Process	AME Expense Report Approval Notification	This is the request for approval when AME is used. If the Notification times out the result is set to NO_RESPONSE.	5 days
Non AME Approval Process	Inform System Administrator – No Approver	An approver could not be found. The System Administrator must insure that an approver is set up. The Workflow will continue in the loop of trying to find an approver and notifying the System Administrator until an approver is set up.	3 days
Rejection Process	Wait for Resubmission	This is a Block Function not a Notification. The expense report is rejected and the Workflow is paused waiting for the preparer to resubmit the expense report. If the Timeout is invoked the expense report is deleted	32
Return Expense Report Process	Wait for Resubmission	The expense report had problems and the preparer told the Workflow to return the expense report back to the preparer. The Workflow is now waiting for the preparer to re-submit the corrected expense report. If the Timeout is invoked, the expense report is deleted.	32 days
Withdraw Expense Report Process	Wait for Resubmission	This is Block Function not a Notification. The expense report has been withdrawn by the preparer during the Approval Process. If the Timeout is invoked, the expense report is deleted.	32 days

Process	Function / Notification Display Name	Purpose and Action When Invoked	Default Value
AP Rejection Process	Wait for Resubmission	This is Block Function not a Notification. The expense report has been rejected by an approver and returned to the preparer for correction. If the Timeout is invoked, the expense report is deleted.	32 days
No Manager Response Process 2	Inform Preparer – No Manager Response	The manager did not respond to the request to approve an expense report, reminders have been sent until the limit was reached and the preparer is being asked whether to bump the approval up the chain or send another reminder to the manager. If Timeout is invoked, a reminder is sent to the preparer. The Workflow continues in this loop until the preparer answers the Notification.	7 days
No Manager Response Process	Inform Preparer – No Manager Response	The manager did not respond to the request to approve an expense report with violations or missing receipts, reminders have been sent until the limit was reached and the preparer is being asked whether to bump the approval up the chain or send another reminder to the manager. If Timeout is invoked, a reminder is sent to the preparer. The Workflow continues in this loop until the preparer answers the Notification.	7 days
Manager (Shortpay) Approval Subprocess	Verify With Mgr the Amt Approved With Policy Violations	When an expense report has receipts whose $ amount exceeds the amount in the Attribute 'AP Limit of Sum of Missing Receipt Expense Lines' then the manager receives another Notification informing them that the expense report they just approved has missing receipts. If the Notification times out, the No Manager Response Process is invoked.	5 days
Missing Receipt Policy Non-Compliance Process	Inform preparer of Policy Non-Compliance for Missing Receipts	When Payables marked required receipts as missing, this Process is started to inform the preparer. This Notification must be answered. Timeouts just send another copy of this Notification.	7 days
Policy Non-Compliance Process	Inform Preparer of Policy Non-Compliance Additional Info Required	Payables has noted an exception to a line on the expense report other than missing receipt and this Process is started and sent a Notification to the preparer. This Notification must be answered. Timeouts just send another copy of this Notification	7 days
Request Approval Process	Request Approval from APPROVER	One of the managers in the employee's hierarchy has been asked to approve the expense report. If the Timeout is invoked, the No Manager Response Process 2 in invoked.	5 days
Third Party Expense Report Process	Request Individual's Approval	A designated preparer has submitted an expense report and the employee is being asked to approve the submission. If Timeout is invoked a reminder is sent until the loop counter is exceeded and then the expense report is continued for approval minus a note that the employee approved the submission	5 days
AP Request More Info	Inform Preparer of Auditor Requesting More Information	Payables has requested more information. This Notification must be answered. If the Notification times out, it is resent.	7 days
AP Custom Default Error Process	AP Custom Default Error Notification	This Process is only used if assigned as the error process for an activity (on the 'Details' tab). This Notification Functions as the WFERROR Notification to SYSADMIN, except that the only response is Retry. The Notification will continue to be resent until Retry is selected.	1 day

TABLE 12. 2

Performers

The Release 11.5.10 version of this Workflow has three Performers that must be configured: AP, 'Expense Report Workflow Administrator' and Expense Allocation Administrator. The Release 12 documentation states shows all three of the Performers as required setups, but the version of this Workflow in the Vision database eliminated all Notifications to the Performer AP in January 2007. These Performers are actually Item Attributes, so when a value is assigned to the Attribute, it assigns that value to all places where the Attribute is used. Use Load Roles from Database to assign Roles to these Attributes. *Chapter 3, Builder Basics* describes how to use this feature.

The Performers are used in the following activities. The activities not in the Release 12 version have an asterisk (*) in front of the Process name.

Process	Notification Display Name	Action That Must be Taken by Performer	Attribute Used as Performer	Potential Substitutes
Server Side Validation Process	Inform SysAdmin of Payables Validation Failure	Something is wrong with the expense report, such as charged to invalid code combination. If the error must be fixed by editing the expense report, the response should be 'Return to Preparer' so the changes can be made and the expense report re-submitted. If the problem can be fixed without editing the expense report, then fix the problem and respond 'Problem Fixed'. If the preparer is not the person to fix the problem the preparer should click the Forward To button and select the person who can fix the error. That person should then respond to the Notification with 'Problem Fixed'	Expense Report Workflow Administrator	Preparer Name Note: sending this to the preparer allows the preparer to recall the expense report, fix it, and resubmit. Or it can then be forwarded to the Expense Report Workflow Administrator (who was the Oracle seeded Performer for this activity)
Server Side Validation Process	Inform Sys Admin of Custom Validation Failure	Fix the error, reply 'Problem Fixed', or if expense report must be edited to fix the problem reply 'Return to Preparer'. If no customization to the Process in 'Custom Validate Expense Report' this Notification will never be sent	Expense Report Workflow Administrator	
Server Side Validation Process	Inform Individual of Expense Allocations Failure	This Message is sent if there are errors when an expense line is split between multiple distributions. The errors must be fixed as the Workflow will continue in this loop until then. Answer 'Problem Fixed'.	Expense Allocation Administrator	Expense Report Workflow Administrator or Preparer
*Manager (Spending) Approval Process	Inform AP Mgr Approvd ShortPay with Missing Receipts	This is an 'FYI' Notification – expense report was shortpaid due to missing receipts, the resulting "new" expense report was approved by a manager (i.e., manager said lack of receipts was OK)	AP	
Manager (Spending) Approval Process	Inform System Administrator – No Approver	Either Preparer did not specify alternate approver or there is something wrong with hierarchy. The hierarchy must be repaired and the Workflow will continue to send this Notification until fixed.	SYSADMIN	Expense Report Workflow Administrator
*AP Approval Process	Request AP to Review for Spending Policy Compliance	This is an 'FYI' Notification – no response to Message required, however, AP needs to query up expense report, review and mark it as Payables Approved	AP	
*Mileage Process	Inform AP Mileage Rate Has Been Adjusted	This is an 'FYI' Notification – no response to Message required – AP can verify mileage rate meets IRS guidelines and mark mileage line with exception if needed	AP	
*Rejection Process	Inform AP Expense Report They Reviewed Is Mgr Rejected	This is an 'FYI' Notification – AP should ask employee what to do with any received receipts	AP	
Bothpay Process	Inform System Administrator – No Vendor	Credit Card company not set up as supplier – set up and reply to Message Note: If not using credit card functionality, this Process will never be used, nothing has to be changed	Expense Report Workflow Administrator	

Process	Notification Display Name	Action That Must be Taken by Performer	Attribute Used as Performer	Potential Substitutes
AP Custom Default Error Process	AP Custom Default Error Notification	Fix the error and reply 'Problem Fixed'	Expense Report Workflow Administrator	

TABLE 12. 3

Defer Workflow to Background Engine When Workflow Starts

This Workflow is started when the expense report is submitted for approval from the '*i*Expenses' form. Thus, the form becomes the "calling program" (see discussion on Background Engines and cost in *Chapter 3, Builder Basics*) and waits for the Workflow to reach a deferred activity. This can cause performance issues. This can be alleviated by ensuring that the first activity in the Workflow has a cost high enough to ensure the Workflow is immediately deferred to the Background Engine. The Workflow will then continue the next time the Background Engine runs for Deferred Processes. To defer the Workflow, perform the following steps:

1. From the Workflow Builder (assumes Workflow is loaded into the Builder), open the Process 'AP Standard Expense Report Process'.

2. Double-click the activity 'Determine Which Process to Start From'.

3. This causes the 'Properties' page to open to the 'Function' tab. Change the 'Cost' field to a value greater than 0.5. If you cannot change this field, set your Access Level to 20. See FIGURE 12.14.

4. Click OK.

5. Save the Workflow back to the database.

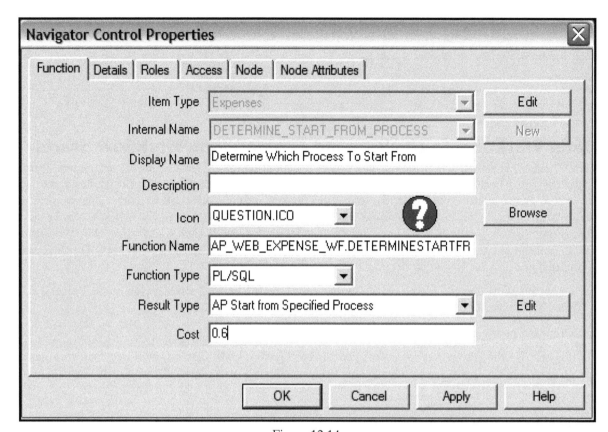

Figure 12.14

Saving the Workflow

When the Workflow is saved, it invokes validation. It validates not only APEXP, but all Item Types that were loaded with it. This validation has always shown errors. If APEXP is listed in any of the Error Messages, click the + next to the Error Message to see further details. Click Cancel. Correct the error and resave. If the validate errors look like FIGURE 12.15 (errors are for HRSSA and WFERROR), click 'Save'.

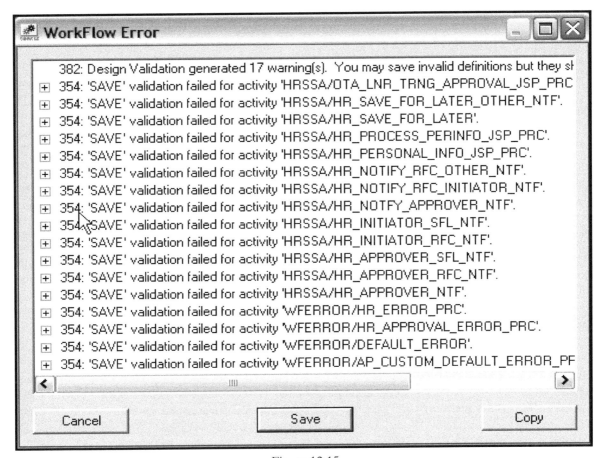

Figure 12.15

REQUISITION AND PURCHASE ORDER APPROVALS

The Workflows to approve POs and requisitions were two of the first Workflows delivered by Oracle. As Release 11*i* moved through the various Point Releases, additional Workflows were added. Now in order to have just the basic approval functionality, the following Workflows must be set up:

- PO Requisition Approval (REQAPPRV)

- PO Approval (POAPPRV)

- Requestor Change Order Approval (POREQCHA)

- PO Change Approval for Requestor (PORPOCHA)

- PO Change Request Tolerance Check (PORCOTOL)

- PO Create Documents (CREATEPO)

- PO Approval Error (POERROR)

The above also applies if using *i*Procurement. The other Procurement modules have additional Workflows, but this book will only discuss the Workflows above.

For Release 12, the applicable sections and manuals are *Choosing Workflow Options* and *Procurement Workflows, Oracle Purchasing Users Guide Release 12, Part No.B28669-01, December 2006.* For Release 11.5.10 the applicable sections and manuals are *Choosing Workflow Options* and *Procurement Workflows, Oracle Purchasing Users Guide Release 11i, Part No.A82913-06, September 2004.* Neither of these guides discusses the 'Requestor Changer Order Approval', the 'PO Change Approval for Requestor', or the 'PO Change Request Tolerance Check' Workflows. These Workflows are discussed in a white paper accessed from MetaLink Doc. ID: 296367.1, *Requester Change Order in Procurement – An Oracle White paper.*

Although this book will not discuss general Purchasing setups, including approval limits and hierarchies, these setups are critical to the smooth working of all the Workflows. This chapter will also not cover any changes to the setups if Approvals Management Engine (AME) is used. General AME setups are discussed in *Chapter 14, Approvals Management Engine (AME).*

The "Procurement Workflows" section contains sections on how to customize this Workflow. If your requirements for customization just require additional approvers, then the use of AME should be strongly considered. Otherwise read this section and follow the guidelines.

Background vs. Online Processing

The Profile Option 'PO: Workflow Processing Mode' governs whether the Approval Workflows try to finish while the user who clicked the 'Submit for Approval' button is waiting, or whether they are deferred to the next Background Engine. While seeing the status set to Approved has some immediate benefit, especially for Purchase Orders, running online can cause performance issues as the form becomes the "calling program" (see discussion on Background Engines and cost in *Chapter 3, Builder Basics*) and will wait until the Workflow completes or the Workflow reaches a deferred activity. The default for this Profile Option is Background, i.e., defer processing to the next Background Engine. To use online processing, change the value to Online.

Replacing Oracle Workflow or Process with Custom Workflow or Process

The Workflow and starting Process for each document type is defined in the Documents window. This window also contains the Workflow to use when the document is changed. It is strongly recommended that if the PO Requisition Approval or PO Approval is customized that one of the following methods is used

- Copy the Workflow to a new Workflow and make the changes to the copied version. Register this Workflow in the Document Types window.

- Make a copy of any Process that will be changed and apply the changes there. Find the Process that called the custom Process, make a copy, and in the copy change the Process to the custom Process. Continue finding the calling Process until the main Process is copied. Register this Process in the Document Types window

The advantage of this approach is that Oracle's patches will not erase your customization. The disadvantage is that your custom Workflow will not inherit any of the improvements made by a patch. NOTE: if the custom Workflow uses Oracle's PL/SQL Procedures, the custom Workflow will inherit any changes made in those Packages. If these changes require new objects, such as Item Attributes, the custom Workflow could error.

The alternative is to examine every Purchasing patch and note if a new version of the Workflow is delivered by the patch. Then after applying the patch, examine the Workflow to see if any of the customizations were overwritten.

None of these approaches is fool-proof. Each company will have to decide the best approach based on the amount of customization and where the customizations are applied.

Note that the code that starts the Requestor Change Order Approval (POREQCHA) Workflow does not read the Document Types definitions to pick the Workflow or the starting Process. You can still make copies of Sub-Processes and work up the chain making copies, but when the starting Process is reached, make changes directly to this.

Document Types Attributes

The Document Types window allows configuration of Attributes that control which Workflow is used and how the Workflow behaves. This window is accessed using the path Setup → Purchasing → Document Types. For Release 11.5.10, when the 'Find' window opens, select the desired document type. The resulting form looks like FIGURE 12.16

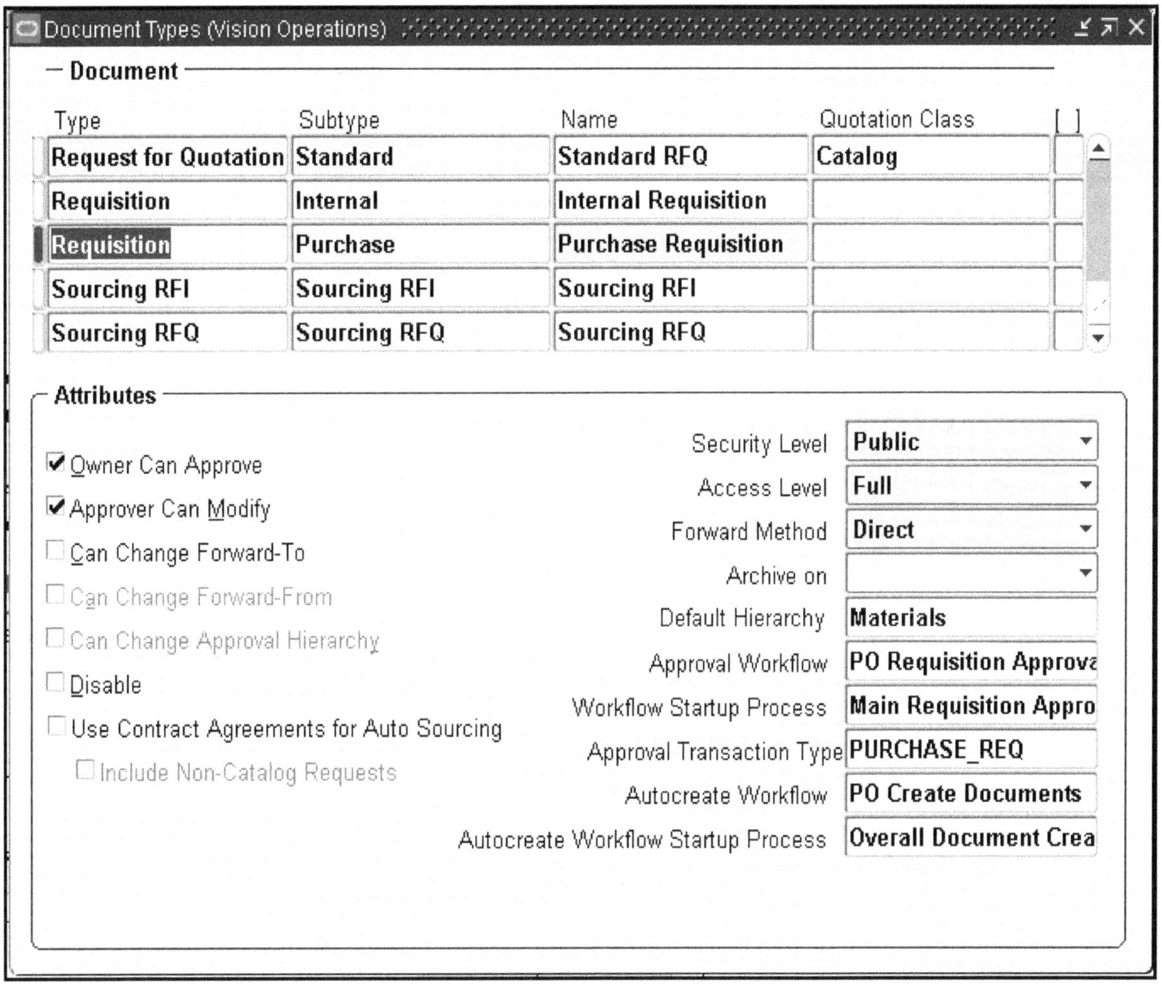

FIGURE 12.16

For Release 12, when the Document Types window opens, select the desired row and click the 'Update' icon (looks like a pencil). The resulting form looks like FIGURE 12.17.

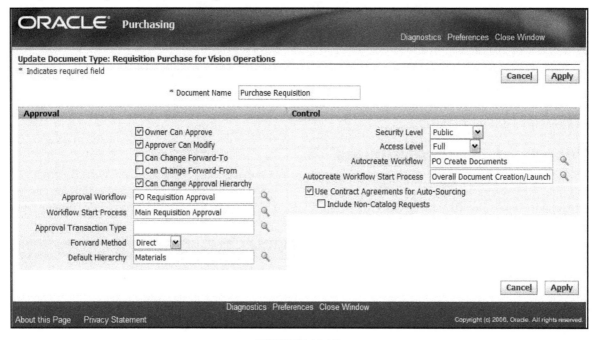

FIGURE 12.17

The fields that affect the behavior of the Workflow are:

- **Approval Workflow** – the Display Name of the Workflow to use. This field is not used for 'Change Order Request Requisition'

- **Workflow Start Process** – the starting Process for the Workflow. This field is not used for 'Change Order Request Requisition'

- **Autocreate Workflow** – for requisitions only, the Workflow to use to create the PO

- **Autocreate Workflow Startup Process** – for requisitions only, the starting Process for the Autocreate Workflow

- **Approval Transaction Type** – only for requisitions where Approvals Management (AME) is installed, the AME Transaction Type. If not using AME, leave this field blank

- **User Contract Agreements for Auto Sourcing** – for Purchase Requisitions only. The autosourcing logic will include contract purchase agreements. Set the Profile Option 'PO: Automatic Document Sourcing' to Yes

- **Include Non-Catalog Requests** – for iProcurement only, checking this box enables the use of contract purchase agreements when autosourcing non-catalog requisitions

- **Owner Can Approve** – whether the owner can be the final approver for a document. Even with this flag checked, the owner must have the appropriate approval authority or the document is forwarded to the next person in the hierarchy. If using budgetary control, use the Financial Options window to enable 'Reserve at Requisition Completion'

- **Approver Can Modify** – if checked the current approver can modify the document

- **Can Change Forward-To** – if checked the user can change the person the document will be forwarded to

- **Can Change Forward From** – if checked the preparer can change the name of the document creator if the Document Type is Requisition

- **Can Change Approval Hierarchy** – if checked the preparer and/or approvers can change the default approval hierarchy in the Approve Documents window

- **Forward Method** – choose one of the following values

  - **Direct** – the default approver is the first person in the preparer's approval path with sufficient authority

  - **Hierarchy** – the default approver is the next person in the preparer's approval path regardless of authority

- **Default Hierarchy** – if 'Use Approval Hierarchies' is enabled in the Financial Options window, then this is the name of the position hierarchy to use

- **Archive When** – if the Document Type is Purchase Agreement, Purchase Order, or Release, choose one of the following values

  - **Approve** – the document is archived upon approval (prior to printing, faxing, EDI, or email). The Change Order Workflow begins only if this option is chosen

  - **Communicate** – the document is archived upon transmission (printing, faxing, EDI, or email)

Start the Document Approval Manager

The Document Approval Manager is a Concurrent Manager that executes code needed by various 'Approval' Workflows. It must be active or the Workflows will fail. The default settings for this Concurrent Manager are correct. It just needs to be started each time all the other Concurrent Managers are started. No additional programs should be assigned to this manager. See the section on PO Approval Error (POERROR) for further information.

PO REQUISITION APPROVAL – REQAPPRV

This Workflow controls the approval of requisitions. It is initiated:

- When the 'Submit for Approval' is selected in the 'Approve Document' window in Purchasing or when a requisition is submitted for approval in *i*Procurement

- When you respond to a reminder about submitting a document for approval

- When a requisition is imported and AUTHORIZATION_STATUS <> 'APPROVED'.

This Workflow has optional setups that can only be performed using the Workflow Builder. The Internal Name of the 'PO Requisition Approval' Workflow is REQAPPRV. If your Applications DBA is sending you the file from the UNIX/LINUX file system, the file is $PO_TOP/patch/115/import/US/poxwfrqa.wft. If the Applications DBA has used the Builder to create the .wft file it may have more than the 'PO Requisition Approval' Workflow. This is normal. This

Workflow uses some definitions that caused it to become linked to other Workflows. When this happens, all the linked Workflows must be loaded along with the requested Workflow.

When you are finished with all your setups, the Applications DBA can load the Workflow back into the database. Developers may be required if the business chooses to customize the Workflow. Once any changes to the definition of the Workflow have been made, in addition to saving the Workflow to the database, a .wft should be created and stored under your $CUSTOM_TOP directory. This copy of the file should be used when making any additional changes instead of the poxwfrqa.wft file. Note that the name of the .wft file is not limited to 8 characters.

If you are unable to make any required changes to the Workflow, make sure your Access Level is set to 20 (Remember this? – Help → About Oracle Workflow Builder <version>).

Item Attributes

The following Attributes impact how the Workflow functions. To change the Attribute, perform the following steps in the Workflow Builder (after loading 'PO Requisition Approval' from the database). Double click the Item Attribute indicated. The 'Properties' page will open. Select or enter the desired value in the 'Value' field. Do not change anything else. Click Apply, and then click OK. After all changes are made, save the Workflow back to the database.

Attribute Display Name	Purpose	Allowable Values	Seeded Value
Send PO Autocreation to Background	Governs whether the Create PO Workflow is initiated and the Workflow will wait for it to finish before moving on, or whether to defer creation of the PO to a Background Engine. If = 'Y', the creation of the PO will be deferred. If = 'N', the Workflow will pause while the PO Create Documents Workflow runs	Y or N	Y
Is AME used for approval?	If = 'Y', AME is used to determine the approvers. Do not set this to 'Y' unless Oracle Approvals Management Engine (AME) is set up. See *Chapter 14, Approvals Management Engine (AME)*.	Y or N	N

TABLE 12. 4

Timeouts

The following table lists Timeouts for various Functions and Notifications and the Action taken if the Timeout occurs. Wherever the Process has modeled a transition labeled <Timeout>, the Timeout values can be adjusted. To change the default value, perform the following steps in the Workflow Builder (after loading from the database the 'Expenses' Item Types). Double click the Process indicated. The Process will be drawn in the Diagrammer window. Double-click the icon that matches the Function/Notification name. Select the Node tab. Leave the Timeout Type field set to Relative Time. Type in the Days, Hours, and Minutes. Click Apply, and then click OK. After all changes are made, save the Workflow back to the database.

If the Default Value is 0 (zero), then the Workflow will behave as if no Timeout is modeled and thus wait indefinitely (without any reminders) for the response to the Notification.

Process	Function / Notification Display Name	Purpose and Action when invoked	Default Value
Notify Approver	Approve Requisition Notification	This is the Notification requesting approval. If the Timeout is invoked, then Requisition Approval Reminder 1 is sent, else the Workflow waits here for a response	No Timeout
Notify Approver	Requisition Approval	This is the first reminder and now serves as the Approval Notifications. If the Timeout is invoked, then Requisition Approval Reminder 2 is sent, else	No Timeout

Process	Function / Notification Display Name	Purpose and Action when invoked	Default Value
	Reminder1	the Workflow waits here for a response	
Notify Approver	Requisition Approval Reminder 2	This is the first reminder and now serves as the Approval Notifications. If the Timeout is invoked, the Action History is updated that the approver timed out and the next approver is selected, else the Workflow waits here for a response	No Timeout

TABLE 12. 5

Special Note

One common error seen in this Workflow is that the Workflow is stuck at the activity 'Is Requisition Pre-Approved?' in the Process 'Approval List Routing'. The activity will show a status of COMPLETE, but the Workflow will not have moved past this activity. Investigation of the Requisition Processing through the Workflow will show that the AUTHORIZATION_STATUS field in PO_REQUISITION_HEADERS_ALL is set to APPROVED. Although it may be difficult to find anyone who will admit to it, someone has used SQL to update this record. The code for this Function is checking whether the authorization status of the requisition is IN PROCESS or PRE_APPROVED. Since neither status was found, the code returns a result of INVALID_AUTH_STATUS. This status is not part of the Yes/No Lookup Code and thus cannot be modeled as a transition. The Workflow Engine is unable to tell the Workflow where to go next and has set the status ACTIVITY_RESULT_CODE to #STUCK. The next time the Background Engine runs for Stuck Processes, the ACTIVITY_STATUS of the activity will be set to ERROR and the appropriate error routine started.

The only way to progress any Workflow in this status is to use SQL to set the status of the requisition to PRE_APPROVED or IN PROCESS and retry this activity. Set the status to PRE_APPROVED if the requisition should progress to an approved status. Set the status to IN PROCESS to have the requisition returned to the submitter.

Before doing this action, verify the age of the Workflow and associated requisition. Your business rules may dictate that the Workflow should just be aborted (this will prevent any further action on this requisition).

This behavior also can happen for Purchase Order approvals and is described in MetaLink Doc. ID: 352672.1, *Requisition Approval Workflow Can Complete With a #Stuck Status.*

PO APPROVAL – POAPPRV

This Workflow controls the approval of Purchase Orders. It is initiated:

- When the 'Submit for Approval' is selected in the 'Approve Document' window in Purchasing

- When you respond to a reminder about submitting a document for approval

Additionally this Workflow is called when changes are made to a Purchase Order that causes its Status to change to 'Requires Reapproval', the document revision number increases and the 'Submit for Approval' is selected.

This Workflow has optional setups that can only be performed using the Workflow Builder. The Internal Name of the 'PO Approval' Workflow is POAPPRV. If your Applications DBA is sending you the file from a UNIX/LINUX file system, the file is $PO_TOP/patch/115/import/US/poxwfpoa.wft. If the Applications DBA has used the Builder to create the .wft file it may have more than the PO Approval

Workflow. This is normal. This Workflow uses some definitions that caused it to become linked to other Workflows. When this happens, all the linked Workflows must be loaded along with the requested Workflow.

When you are finished with all your setups, the Applications DBA can load the Workflow back into the database. If any PL/SQL Procedures are modified which are attached to Function or Notification activities or to Document Attributes, then the modified Packages must be compiled. Make sure this code is migrated with the Workflow as testing is completed and the Workflow is moved to production. Once any changes to the definition of the Workflow have been made, in addition to saving the Workflow to the database, a .wft should be created and stored under your $CUSTOM_TOP directory. This copy of the file should be used when making any additional changes instead of the poxwfpoa.wft file. Note that the name of the .wft file is not limited to 8 characters.

If you are unable to make any required changes to the Workflow, make sure your Access Level is set to 20 (Remember this? – Help → About Oracle Workflow Builder <version>).

Timeouts

The following table lists Timeouts for various Functions and Notifications and the Action taken if the Timeout occurs. Wherever the Process has modeled a transition labeled <Timeout>, the Timeout values can be adjusted. To change the default value, perform the following steps in the Workflow Builder (after loading from the database the 'Expenses' Item Types). Double click the Process indicated. The Process will be drawn in the Diagrammer window. Double-click the icon that matches the Function/Notification name. Select the Node tab. Leave the Timeout Type field set to Relative Time. Type in the Days, Hours, and Minutes. Click Apply, and then click OK. After all changes are made, save the Workflow back to the database.

If the Default Value is 0 (zero), then the Workflow will behave as if no Timeout is modeled and thus wait indefinitely (without any reminders) for the response to the Notification.

Process	Function / Notification Display Name	Purpose and Action When Invoked	Default Value
Notify Approver Sub Processs	Approve PO Notification	This is the Notification requesting approval and includes a pdf of the PO. If the Timeout is invoked, then Requisition Approval Reminder 1 is sent, else the Workflow waits here for a response	No Timeout
Notify Approver Sub Process	Approve PO Notification with PDF	This is the Notification requesting approval but it doesn't include a pdf of the document. If the Timeout is invoked, then Requisition Approval Reminder 1 is sent, else the Workflow waits here for a response	No Timeout
Notify Approver	PO Approval Reminder1	This is the first reminder and now serves as the Approval Notifications. If the Timeout is invoked, then Requisition Approval Reminder 2 is sent, else the Workflow waits here for a response	No Timeout
Notify Approver	PO Approval Reminder 2	This is the first reminder and now serves as the Approval Notifications. If the Timeout is invoked, the Action History is updated that the approver timed out and the next approver is selected, else the Workflow waits here for a response	No Timeout

TABLE 12. 6

Item Attributes

These Item Attributes impact whether the changed Workflow will automatically reapprove or whether human approval is required. Note that the seeded values indicate that all changes require re-approval. To change the Attribute, perform the following steps in the Workflow Builder (after loading 'PO Requisition Approval' from the database). Double click the Item Attribute indicated. The 'Properties' page will open.

Select or enter the desired value in the 'Value' field. Do not change anything else. Click Apply, and then click OK. After all changes are made, save the Workflow back to the database.

Attribute Display Name	Purpose	Allowable Values	Seeded Value
Change Order Distribution Quantity Ordered Tolerance	If the change in the Distribution Quantity Ordered is less than this percentage, the document is reapproved automatically	0-100	0
Change Order Header Amount Limit Tolerance	If the change to the Amount Limit is less than this percentage, the document is reapproved automatically	0-100	0
Change Order Header Blanket Total Tolerance	If the change to the Blanket Total is less than this percentage, the document is reapproved automatically	0-100	0
Change Order Header Purchase Order Total Tolerance	If the change to the Purchase Order Total is less than this percentage, the document is reapproved automatically	0-100	0
Change Order Line Agreed Amount Tolerance	If the change in Amount Agreed is less than this percentage, the document is reapproved automatically	0-100	0
Change Order Line Price Limit Tolerance	If the change in Price Limit is less than this percentage, the document is reapproved automatically	0-100	0
Change Order Line Quantity Committed Tolerance	If the change in Quantity Agreed is less than this percentage, the document is reapproved automatically	0-100	0
Change Order Line Quantity Tolerance	If the change in Quantity Ordered is less than this percentage, the document is repapered automatically	0-100	0
Change Order Line Unit Price Tolerance	If the change in Unit Price is less than this percentage, the document is reapproved automatically	0-100	0
Change Order Shipment Price Override Tolerance	If the change in Price Override is less than this percentage the document is reapproved automatically	0-100	0
Change Order Shipment Quantity Tolerance	If the change in the Shipment Quantity Ordered is less than this percentage, the document is reapproved automatically	0-100	0
Change Order Hdr Auto Approve Retroactively Priced Releases	If the source of the change is a retroactive price change, does the document require full approval again	Y or N	N

TABLE 12. 7

Special Note

One common error seen in this Workflow is that the Workflow gets stuck at the activity Is PO Pre-Approved in the Process 'PO Approval Process'. The activity will show a status of COMPLETE, but the Workflow will not have moved past this activity. Investigation of the PO Processing through the Workflow will show that the AUTHORIZATION_STATUS field in PO_HEADERS_ALL is set to APPROVED. Although it may be difficult to find anyone who will admit to it, someone has used SQL to update this record. The code for this Function is checking whether the authorization status of the PO is IN PROCESS or PRE_APPROVED. Since neither status was found, the code returns a result of INVALID_AUTH_STATUS. This status is not part of the Yes/No Lookup Code and thus cannot be modeled as a transition. The Workflow Engine is unable to tell the Workflow where to go next and has set the status ACTIVITY_RESULT_CODE to #STUCK. The next time the Background Engine runs for stuck Processes, the ACTIVITY_STATUS of the activity will be set to ERROR and the appropriate error routine started.

The only way to progress any Workflow in this status is to use SQL to set the status of the PO to PRE_APPROVED or IN PROCESS and retry this activity. Set the status to PRE_APPROVED if the

PO should progress to an approved status. Set the status to IN PROCESS to have the Workflow find another approver.

Before doing this action, verify the age of the Workflow and associated PO. The Purchasing department may just want the Workflow aborted. This will prevent any further action on this PO.

This behavior also can happen for requisition approvals and is described in MetaLink Doc. ID: 352672.1, *Requisition Approval Workflow Can Complete With a #Stuck Status*.

REQUESTOR CHANGE ORDER APPROVALS

Oracle has provided the following three Workflows to control changes to approved requisitions:

- Requestor Change Order Approval (POREQCHA)

- PO Change Approval for Requestor (PORPOCHA)

- PO Change Request Tolerance Check (PORCOTOL)

The initiating Workflow is Requestor Change Order Approval. This Workflow calls the PO Change Request Tolerance Check to verify whether the change requires re-approval. For each change that is then approved, the PO Change Approval for Requestor is called so that the buyer can approve the changes. If the buyer approves the changes, the PO Approval Workflow is initiated if necessary.

Since these Workflows cannot run independently, the setups will be discussed together in this section.

This Workflow has optional setups that can only be performed using the Workflow Builder. If your Applications DBA is sending you the file from the UNIX/LINUX file system, the file for POREQCHA is $PO_TOP/patch/115/import/US/poreqcha.wft and for PORPOCHA is $PO_TOP/patch/115/import/US/porpocha.wft. PORCOTOL will have to be loaded from the database using the Workflow Builder. If the Applications DBA has used the Builder to create the .wft file it may have more than the PO Approval Workflow. This is normal. This Workflow uses some definitions that caused it to become linked to other Workflows. When this happens, all the linked Workflows must be loaded along with the requested Workflow.

When you are finished with all your setups, the Applications DBA can load the Workflow back into the database. If any PL/SQL Procedures are modified which are attached to Function or Notification activities or to Document Attributes, then the modified Packages must be compiled. Make sure this code is migrated with the Workflow as testing is completed and the Workflow is moved to production. Once any changes to the definition of the Workflow have been made, in addition to saving the Workflow to the database, a .wft should be created and stored under your $CUSTOM_TOP directory. This copy of the file should be used when making any additional changes instead of the original file. Note that the name of the .wft file is not limited to 8 characters.

If you are unable to make any required changes to the Workflow, make sure your Access Level is set to 20 (Remember this? – Help → About Oracle Workflow Builder <version>).

Function Security

Companies can block the ability to request a change to approved requisitions in *i*Procurement through excluding the Function 'View my Reqs Change Order'.

Companies can block the ability to access the 'View Change History' button by excluding the Function 'View Reqs Change Order History'.

These two changes do not require the Workflow Builder.

Item Attributes

Item Attributes impact how the Workflow functions. To change the Attribute, perform the following steps in the Workflow Builder (after loading the appropriate Workflow from the database). Double click the Item Attribute indicated. The 'Properties' page will open. Select or enter the desired value in the 'Value' field. Do not change anything else. Click Apply, and then click OK. After all changes are made, save the Workflow back to the database.

The Workflow 'Requestor Change Order Approval' contains the following Attribute that can be configured to determine whether Approvals Management Engine (AME) is to be used.

Attribute Display Name	Purpose	Allowable Values	Seeded Value
Is AME used for approval?	If = 'Y', AME is used to determine the approvers. Do not set this to 'Y' unless Oracle Approvals Management Engine (AME) is set up. See *Chapter 14, Approvals Management Engine (AME)*.	Y or N	N

TABLE 12. 8

The Workflow 'PO Change Request Tolerance Check' contains the following Item Attributes that can be configured to determine whether a change requires re-approval. The Attributes are evaluated in the order: Need by Date, Unit Price, Quantity Ordered, Start Date, End Date, Line Amount, and Requisition Total. Once a change requiring re-approval is detected, the other Attributes are not checked.

Attribute Display Name	Purpose	Allowable Values	Seeded Value
Need By Date Lower Tolerance	If the new date is earlier than the old date, then number of days it can be earlier before re-approval is required	Any Number	30
Need By Date Upper Tolerance	If the new date is later than the old date, then number of days it can be later before re-approval is required	Any Number	100
Unit Price Lower Tolerance	If the price has decreased, the % of decrease allowed before re-approval is required	0-100	100
Unit Price Upper Tolerance	If the price has increased, the % of increase allowed before re-approval is required	0-100	100
Line Quantity Ordered Lower Tolerance	If the quantity has decreased, the % of decrease allowed before re-approval is required	0-100	100
Line Quantity Ordered Upper Tolerance	If the quantity has increased, the % of increase allowed before re-approval is required	0-100	100
Requisition Total Upper Tolerance	If the requisition total has increased, the % of increase allowed before re-approval is required	0-100	100
Requisition Total Lower Tolerance	If the requisition total has decreased, the % of decrease allowed before re-approval is required	0-100	100
End Date Upper Tolerance	If the new date is later than the old date, then number of days it can be later before re-approval is required	Any Number	0
End Date Lower Tolerance	If the new date is earlier than the old date, then number of days it can be earlier before re-approval is required	Any Number	0
Budget Amount Upper Tolerance	If the Line Amount has increased and it is a service line, the % of increase allowed before re-approval is required	0-100	0
Budget Amount Lower Tolerance	If the Line Amount has decreased and it is a service line, the % of decrease allowed before re-approval is required	0-100	100
Start Date Upper Tolerance	If the new date is later than the old date, then number of days it can be later before re-approval is required	Any Number	0

Attribute Display Name	Purpose	Allowable Values	Seeded Value
Start Date Lower Tolerance	If the new date is earlier than the old date, then number of days it can be earlier before re-approval is required	Any Number	0

TABLE 12. 9

PO CREATE DOCUMENTS – CREATEPO

When a requisition is approved, this Workflow is invoked and checks to see if the PO can be automatically created or whether a buyer must manually create the PO.

This Workflow has optional setups that can only be performed using the Workflow Builder. The Internal Name of the 'PO Approval' Workflow is CREATEPO. If your Applications DBA is sending you the file from the UNIX/LINUX file system, the file is $PO_TOP/patch/115/import/US/poxwfatc.wft. If the Applications DBA has used the Builder to create the .wft file it may have more than the PO Approval Workflow. This is normal. This Workflow uses some definitions that caused it to become linked to other Workflows. When this happens, all the linked Workflows must be loaded along with the requested Workflow.

When you are finished with all your setups, the Applications DBA can load the Workflow back into the database. If any PL/SQL Procedures are modified which are attached to Function or Notification activities or to Document Attributes, then the modified Packages must be compiled. Make sure this code is migrated with the Workflow as testing is completed and the Workflow is moved to production. Once any changes to the definition of the Workflow have been made, in addition to saving the Workflow to the database, a .wft should be created and stored under your $CUSTOM_TOP directory. This copy of the file should be used when making any additional changes instead of the poxwfpoa.wft file. Note that the name of the .wft file is not limited to 8 characters.

If you are unable to make any required changes to the Workflow, make sure your Access Level is set to 20 (Remember this? – Help → About Oracle Workflow Builder <version>).

Item Attributes

The following Attributes impact how the Workflow functions. To change the Attribute, perform the following steps in the Workflow Builder (after loading PO Create Document from the database). Double click the Item Attribute indicated. The 'Properties' page will open. Select or enter the desired value in the 'Value' field. Do not change anything else. Click Apply, and then click OK. After all changes are made, save the Workflow back to the database.

Attribute Display Name	Purpose	Allowable Values	Seeded Value
Is Automatic Creation Allowed?	If set to N, the Workflow ends immediately and does not create the PO	Y or N	Y
Is Automatic Approval Allowed?	If set to N, the PO Approval Workflow is launched after the PO is created, else the PO is marked approved	Y or N	Y
Should Workflow Create The Release	If a Blanket PO, should the release be autocreated? (can't be one-time item and ASL Release Generation Method = AutoCreate)	Y or N	Y
Should Contract be used to autocreate Doc?	If set to N, blocks autocreation of non-blanket except for P-CARD	Y or N	N
Should non-catalog requests be	If non-blanket requisition references non-catalog lines, and this is N,	Y or N	N

Attribute Display Name	Purpose	Allowable Values	Seeded Value
autosourced from contract?	autocreation is disallowed (even if Y, contract must exist)		
Is Contract Required on Requisition Line?	If set to Y, contract must exist for non-blanket except for P-CARD. If no contract, PO is not autocreated	Y or N	N
Is Grouping of Requisition Line Allowed?	If set to N, the table used to create the PO has a flag set that indicates the PO can only contain the one requisition	Y or N	Y
Is Grouping of One Time Address Line Allowed?	If set to N, a line with a One Time Address must not be combined with other requisition lines	Y or N	Y
Should temp labor request be autosource from contracts?	If a non-blanket requisition for temp labor, should this be autosourced from Contracts – if Y, and a contract exists, allows autocreation of PO	Y or N	Y

TABLE 12. 10

PO APPROVAL ERROR – POERROR

In addition to the user guides, information about this Workflow can be found in the white paper *Oracle Purchasing POERROR Workflow Setup and Usage Guide*. This paper can be downloaded from MetaLink Doc. ID: 224028.1, *Oracle Purchasing POERROR Workflow Setup and Usage Guide White Paper*. The purpose of the Workflow is to retry activities that error due to errors in the Document Approval Manager Concurrent Manager. Because this Workflow replaces WFERROR, it also must perform the function of delivering Error Messages when the failure is not due to errors in the Document Approval Manager. As delivered, this Workflow will send a Notification for error types 1 and 2, but that Notification will cause the Workflow to error as the Performer has no value.

This Workflow is assigned as the error process (instead of System: Error – WFERROR) in the 'PO Requisition Approval (REQAPPRV)' Workflow for the activities:

- Approve the Requisition

- Build Default Approver List

- Rebuild Approval List After Document Updated

- Rebuild Approval List for Invalid Approver

- Reject the Requisition

- Update Approval List Response

- Update Approval List Response Using AME

- Does Approver Have Authority

It is assigned as the error process in the 'Requestor Change Order Approval (POREQCHA)' Workflow for the activities:

- Build Default Approver List

- Rebuild Approval List for Invalid Approver

- Update Approval List Response'

- Update Approval List Response Using AME

- Does Approver Have Authority

It is assigned as the error process in the 'PO Approval (POAPPRV)' Workflow for the activities:

- Approve and Forward the PO

- Approve the PO

- Forward PO With Status 'In-Process'

- Forward PO With Status 'Pre-Approved'

- Open Document Status

- Reject The PO

- Is the Document Complete?

- Does Approver Have Authority?

This Workflow has optional setups that can only be performed using the Workflow Builder. The Internal Name of the 'PO Approval Error' Workflow is POERROR. If your Applications DBA is sending you the file from the UNIX/LINUX file system, the file is $PO_TOP/patch/115/import/US/poxwfpoe.wft. If the Applications DBA has used the Builder to create the .wft file it may have more than the PO Approval Workflow. This is normal. This Workflow uses some definitions that caused it to become linked to other Workflows. When this happens, all the linked Workflows must be loaded along with the requested Workflow.

When you are finished with all your setups, the Applications DBA can load the Workflow back into the database. If any PL/SQL Procedures are modified which are attached to Function or Notification activities or to Document Attributes, then the modified Packages must be compiled. Make sure this code is migrated with the Workflow as testing is completed and the Workflow is moved to production. Once any changes to the definition of the Workflow have been made, in addition to saving the Workflow to the database, a .wft should be created and stored under your $CUSTOM_TOP directory. This copy of the file should be used when making any additional changes instead of the poxwfpoe.wft file. Note that the name of the .wft file is not limited to 8 characters.

Note that you cannot use the Document Types window to specify a different Workflow or a different top Process. Therefore, all changes must be made directly to this Workflow.

Item Attributes

To change the Attributes, perform the following steps in the Workflow Builder (after loading 'PO Approval Error' from the database). Double click the Item Attribute indicated. The 'Properties' page will open. Select or enter the desired value in the 'Value' field. Do not change anything else. Click Apply, and then click OK. After all changes are made, save the Workflow back to the database.

The Attribute 'System Administrator User Name' is a Role. Therefore, use 'Load Roles from Database' to assign a Role to this Attribute. How to use this feature is described in *Chapter 3, Builder Basics*.

Setting a value for 'System Administrator User Name' is not optional. The Workflow will error if no value is specified. It is highly recommended to set values other than 0 for the other three Attributes. Each organization will have to find the values that work best for the organization. Recommended starting values are 10 for 'Auto Retry Count for Document Manager', .04 for 'Relative Time of Auto Entry for Document Manager' and 10 for 'Timeout Value'.

Attribute Display Name	Purpose	Allowable Values	Seeded Value
Timeout Value	For Error Types of 1 or 2, if the Notification to 'System Administration User Name' times out, if the error is still active, an automatic retry will be executed	Any whole number 0 or greater	0
Relative Time of Auto Entry for Document Manager	Length of time, in days, Processes will have to wait before getting picked up again	Any number 0 or greater, for example, entering .04 equates to a wait time of 60 minutes	0
Auto Retry Count for Document Manager	Number of attempts to get document manager for approval.	Any whole number 0 or greater	0
System Administrator User Name	Application user who will receive Notifications for document manager related errors in status 1 and 2. THIS VALUE MUST BE SPECIFIED or the Workflow will error.	Any valid user or responsibility9	<null>

TABLE 12. 11

Performers

There are no requirements for setting up Performers for this Workflow (other than specifying a value for the Item Attribute 'System Administrator User Name'). However, many people find it confusing that two of the Notifications are sent to the document preparer rather than the administrator. Changing the Performer for these Notifications is a very simple task. Double-click on the Process to open the Process in the Diagrammer window. Then double-click the activity in the Diagrammer window to open the 'Properties' page. Click the Node tab. Either specify a different Item Attribute as the Performer or assign a constant (after using Load Roles from Database to load the desired Role).

This Performer is used in the following activities.

Process	Notification Display Name	Action That Must be Taken by Performer	Attribute Used as Performer	Potential Substitutes
Document Manager Error	Document Manager Failed	The Document Manager Failed and the Error Number is 3, indicating the error is not a Timeout or inactive error. The Error Message gives more details of the error	Preparer User Name	System Administrator User Name
PL/SQL Error Notification	PL/SQL Error Occurs	The error wasn't related to the document manager but to an error in the PL/SQL code.	Preparer User Name	System Administrator User Name

TABLE 12. 12

Activity Attributes

At the beginning of this chapter, the warning was given that you should only change the value of activity Attributes when directed to by the implementation guide or Oracle Support. This Workflow is one of the exceptions. The 'Document Manager Error' Process has a Wait activity that is configured to wait until an absolute date, but the date is not specified.

To configure this activity, double-click the Process name to open the Diagrammer window. Then double-click the Wait activity to open the 'Properties' page. Click the 'Node Attributes' tab. Change 'Wait Mode' to Relative Time. Change Relative Time to be an Item Attribute and select 'Relative Time of Auto Entry for Document Manager' as the Item Attribute value. See FIGURE 12.18.

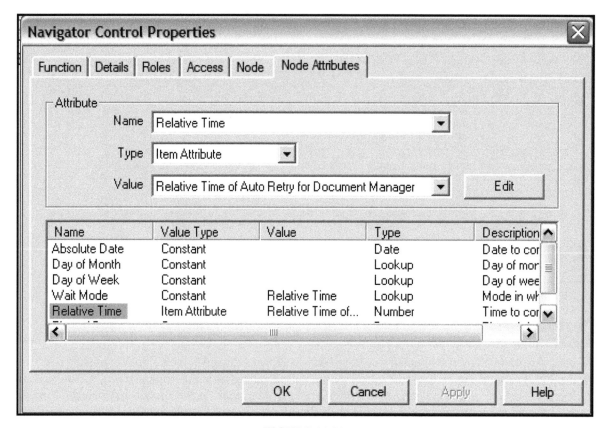

FIGURE 12.18

Possible Customization

Many organizations find that even when the Document Manager is reporting an error code of 3, answering the Notification with Retry will clear the error and the 'Approval' Workflow will progress. Therefore, some have customized the Workflow to utilize the autoretry functionality used for error codes 1 and 2. A sample customized Process is shown in FIGURE 12.19. If you decide to try this customization, remember to configure the Wait Node as shown above.

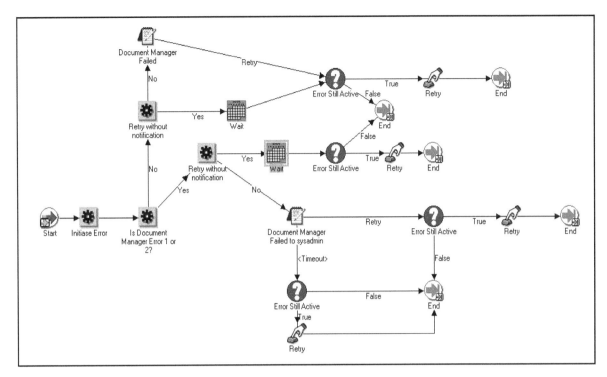

FIGURE 12.19

PO SEND NOTIFICATIONS

This Workflow is started from the Concurrent Program 'Send Notifications for Purchasing Documents'. There are no required setups that utilize the Workflow Builder. The documentation states that starting this Concurrent Program is a required step. It isn't. This Workflow simply checks for documents waiting human action and reminds the human. These reminders require a response. Many organizations find this Workflow to be very annoying. If you do wish to utilize this Workflow, you might wish to schedule the Concurrent Program to only run once/week.

If you do schedule this program, make sure that your Background Engines will include this Workflow. If you run Background Engines without specifying an Item Type, this Workflow is automatically included. If you run Background Engines for each Item Type, then you must schedule one for this Workflow also.

OM ORDER HEADER – OEOH AND OM ORDER LINE – OEOL

There are no required setups that require the Workflow Builder for the Order Management Workflows. However, many organizations have order Processes that require adding customizations to handle the unique needs of their order headers or lines processing. This type of modification is not covered in this book as it is unique to each organization. Oracle provides a guide that discusses the requirements for adding custom Processes. The Release 11.5.10 version is *Oracle Order Management, Using Oracle Workflow in Oracle Order Management, Release 11i,* Part No. A96689-02 April 2005. The Release 12 version is *Oracle Order Management, Using Oracle Workflow in Oracle Order Management, Release 12,* Part No. B31586-01 December 2006.

You cannot substitute the Workflow, but you can specify the Process to use both for the header and each line type. The assigned Processes must be designed to work together, i.e., if the 'OM Order Header' Process has a 'Wait for Flow' activity, then the 'OM Order Line' Process must have a 'Continue Flow' activity. Using the 'Order Management Super User' responsibility, choose Setup → Transaction Types → Define. See FIGURE 12.20.

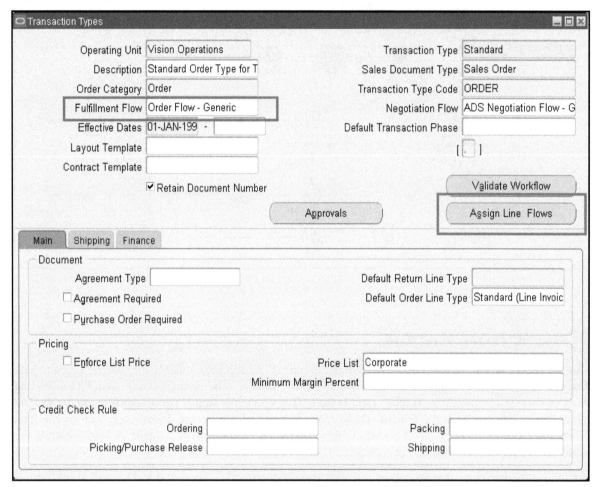

FIGURE 12.20

The Process for the order header is specified in Fulfillment Flow. To specify the Process for each line type associated with the Transaction Type, click 'Assign Line Flows'. See FIGURE 12.21.

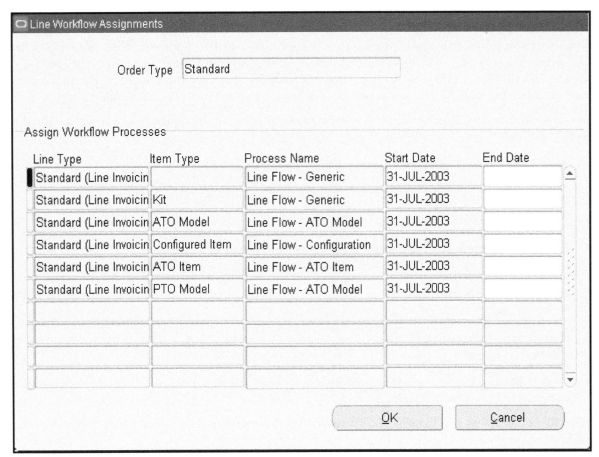

FIGURE 12.21

OTL WORKFLOWS FOR EMPLOYEES – HXCEMP

Oracle Time and Labor allows for the submission and approval of time cards using many methods: Auto Approve, HR Supervisor, Formula, Project Manager, Specific Person, and Custom Workflow. The application uses the Workflow 'OTL Workflows for Employees (HXCEMP)' to manage the Approval Process.

This Workflow requires that all the setup steps be done for Oracle Time and Labor. These steps are documented in the *Oracle Time and Labor Implementation and User Guide*. This manual is over 275 pages. Thus, this book will only cover settings that affect the Workflow.

The applicable sections and manuals are *Approval Styles, Workflow Approval Styles, Defining Approval Styles, Preferences, Oracle Time and Labor Implementation and User Guide*. The Release 12 manual is *Part No. B31652-03, June 2007* and the Release 11.5.10 manual is *Part No. B15865-03, September 2006*.

Use one of the OTL Administrator responsibilities to define the approval styles that the Workflow will use. Then assign these styles to various criteria that ultimately decide which style an individual will use.

Define Approval Style

To define the approval style, the navigation path is Approval → Define Approval Styles. Name the style. This name will be used in the 'Preferences' screen. Use the 'Approval Rules' (Release 12) or the 'Data Interdependency Rules' zone to specify Time Entry Rules that determine when a timecard needs approval. Defining these Rules is not covered in this book. This section can be left blank.

The 'Approval Style Components' zone assigns approval types to an application. The values for the 'Type' field are:

- **Auto Approve** – the timecard is approved when submitted

- **HR Supervisor** – the timecard must be approved by the employee's supervisor

- **Person** – the timecard must be approved by the person entered in the 'Identifier' field

- **Entry Level Approval** – the approval style will be determined by a specific field in the timecard; use the 'Entry Level Approval Component' zone to specify the field and the Approval Type

- **Formula (Selects Mechanism)** – the Approval Process uses the formula identified in the 'Identifier' field

- **Workflow** – the custom Workflow Process specified in Identifier will be used to approve the timecard

- **Project Manager** – this style is only an option for the Projects application; available in Release 12 and Release 11.5.10 with 11*i*.HXT.I

FIGURE 12.22 shows the Release 11.5.10 version of the screen and the Person and HR Supervisor methods of approval.

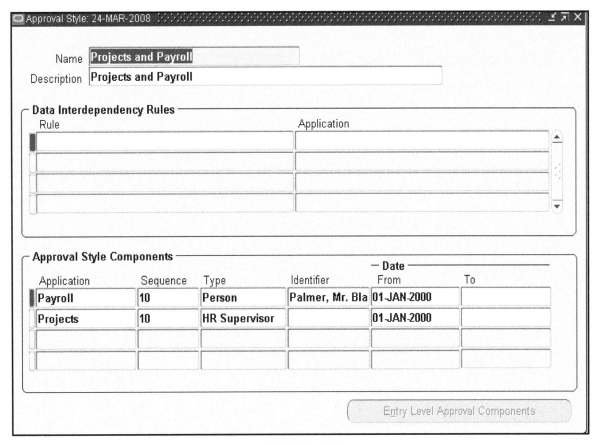

FIGURE 12.22

FIGURE 12.23 shows the Release 12 version of the screen and the 'Entry Level Approval' method of approval. Note that for this style the zone 'Entry Level Approval Components' is used.

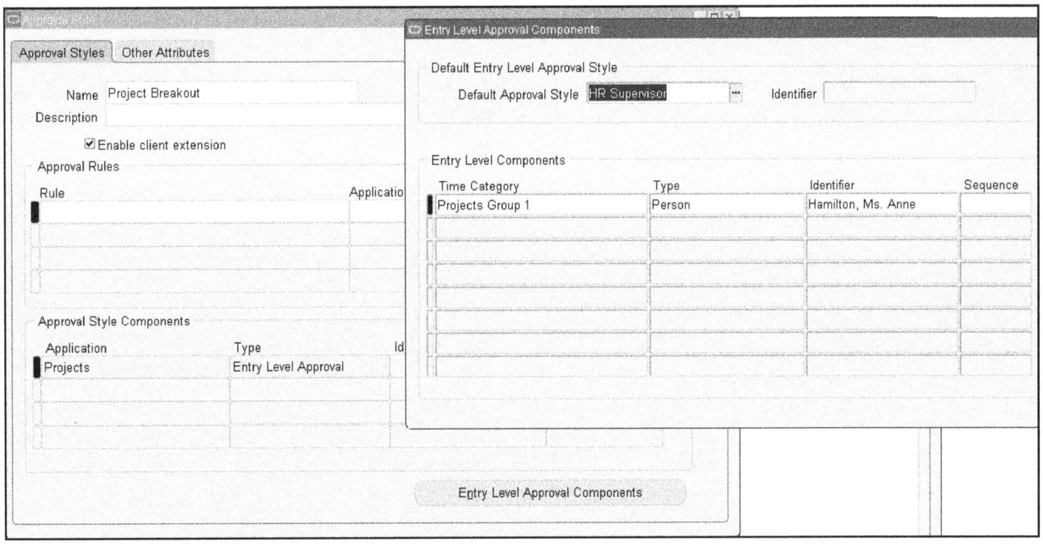

FIGURE 12.23

FIGURE 12.24 shows the 'Project Manager', 'Workflow', 'Auto Approve' and 'Formula (Selects Mechanism)' methods of approval.

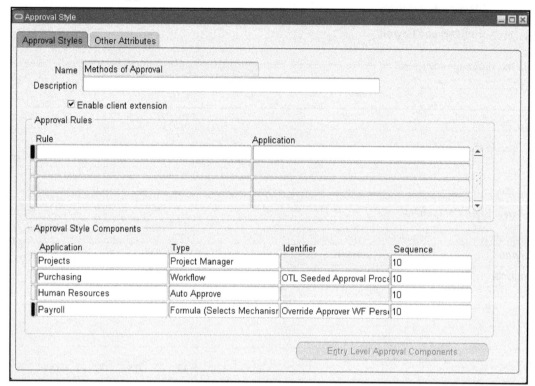

FIGURE 12.24

Note that the Release 12 version of this screen has a tab 'Other Attributes'. See FIGURE 12.25. This tab allows the configuration of the following:

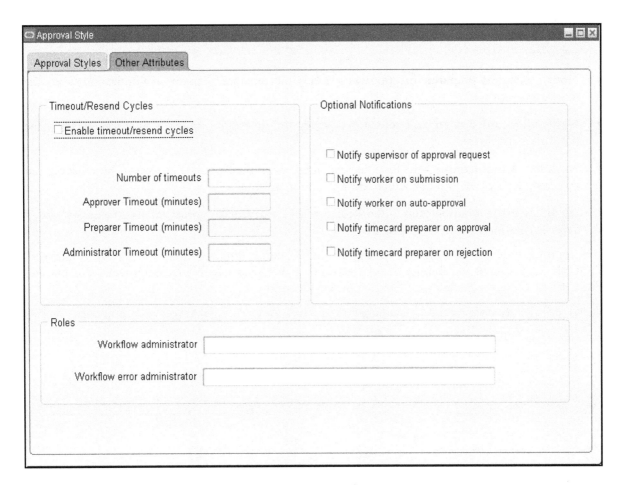

FIGURE 12.25

- **Enable timeout/resend cycles** – clicking this opens the next four fields and allows configuration of the Notification Timeouts

    ♦ **Number of timeouts** – number of times the Notification will be sent to the same person before it notifies the next person; applies to all Timeout and resend cycles

    ♦ **Approver Timeout (minutes)** – how long the Notification to the approver is active before timing out and is either resent or sent to the next approver

    ♦ **Preparer Timeout (minutes)** – how long the Notification to the preparer is active before timing out and is resent

    ♦ **Administrator Timeout (minutes)** – how long the Notification to the preparer is active before timing out and is resent

- **Notify supervisor of approval request** – sends a copy of the approvers' Notifications to the worker's direct supervisor

- **Notify worker on submission** – sends a Notification to the worker whose timecard is submitted by another person

- **Notify worker on auto–approval** – sends a Notification to the worker that the timecard was auto–approved

- **Notify timecard preparer on approval** – sends the timecard preparer a Notification when the timecard is approved

- **Notify timecard preparer on rejection** – sends the timecard preparer a Notification when the timecard is rejected

- **Workflow Administrator** – the Role that can intervene in the Approval Process if the approver and timecard preparer fail to act on a timecard waiting for approval

- **Workflow error administrator** – the Role that can intervene to correct Workflow errors, and if necessary, re–initialize the Workflow

The approval style matches one of the legs in the Workflow Process 'Find and Notify Approvers'. FIGURE 12.26 shows the Release 11.5.10 version of the 'Find and Notify Approvers' Process and FIGURE 12.27 shows the Release 12 version of this Process.

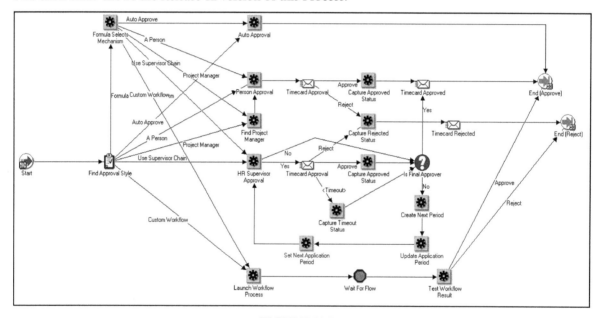

FIGURE 12.26

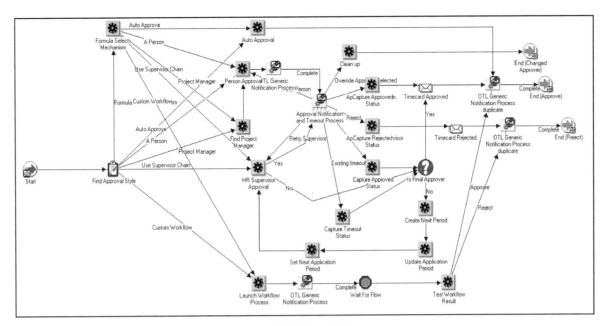

FIGURE 12.27

Assign Approval Styles Using Preference

Once the approval styles are defined, they must be assigned using the 'Preferences' screen. This is not the 'Preferences' screen used to set passwords or individual Mailer preferences. The navigation path is simply 'Preferences'. When the screen opens, and the + next to 'Preference' tree' is clicked, it looks like FIGURE 12.28.

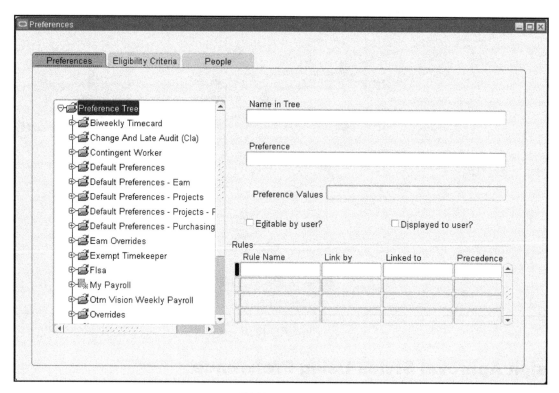

FIGURE 12.28

The 'Default Preferences and Overrides' branch are delivered by Oracle Corporation. The definitions in 'Default Preferences' cannot be changed. So if 'OTL Auto Approve' is not the desired approval style, then create a custom branch. In each branch multiple preferences can be defined, but the one that affects the approval styles is 'Time Store Approval Style'. FIGURE 12.29 shows a sample definition of this preference. Note that 'Approval Style' and 'Override Approval Style' match 'Name' from FIGURE 12.22, not Type.

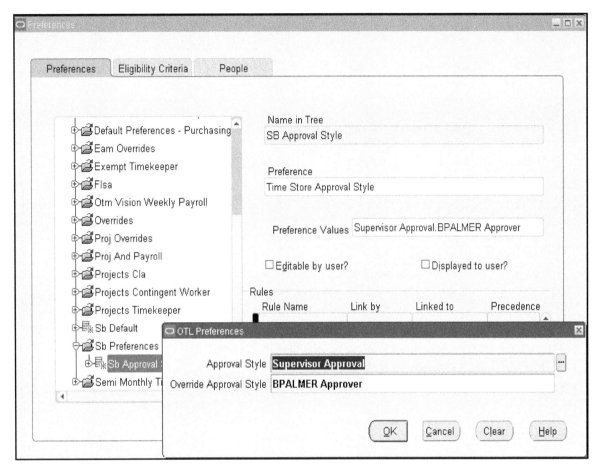

FIGURE 12.29

Once all the various combinations of Approval Styles are defined, the next step is to create a Rule that links this Name in Tree/Preference to an Eligibility Criteria Type.

FIGURE 12.30 shows the creation of this Rule and some of the Eligible Criteria Types.

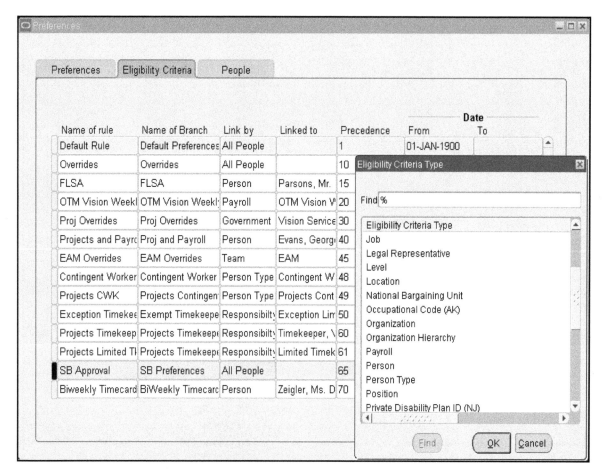

FIGURE 12.30

The Eligible Criteria Type becomes the Link by. The Linked to LOV is determined by the Link By. Except for Link by = All People, a value must be specified in order for the Rule to be applied. Precedence determines the order of applying the Rule. The highest number is applied first. MetaLink Doc. ID: 339158.1, *Can I use Preference Eligibility Criteria linked by a Responsibility* and MetaLink Doc. ID: 377097.1, *Some Preference Linked to Employees Using Eligibility Criteria of 'Responsibility' Cannot be Detected* explain that Rules should only use the links 'All People or Person' or 'Primary Assignment Attribute' as the other links are dependent on context and will not function as designed except through on–line submission and then only if the timecard is submitted by the employee, not a timekeeper.

The 'People' tab allows you to see how the Rules would be applied to a specific person and whether your Rules are context dependent. FIGURE 12.31 shows that the Rule from FIGURE 12.30 showed up in the hierarchy and that it always governs the Approval Style as it has the highest Precedence number.

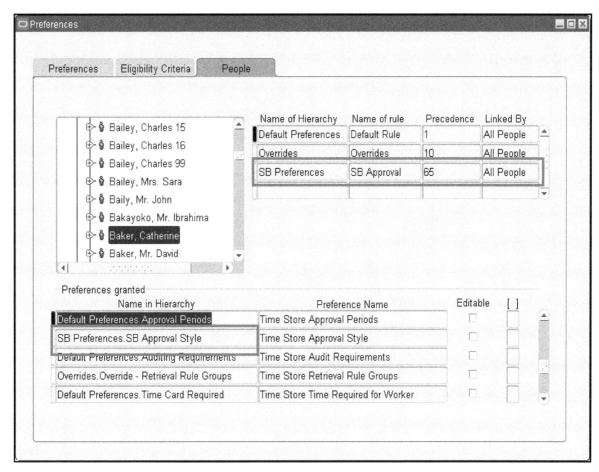

FIGURE 12.31

FIGURE 12.32 shows the application of a Rule that is only applicable to a specific responsibility. Note that 'SB Default' shows as the highest ranking hierarchy but that is not the evaluated hierarchy for the Preference Name 'Time Store Approval Style'. This is because the hierarchy evaluation is based on the current responsibility, which isn't the responsibility named in the Rule.

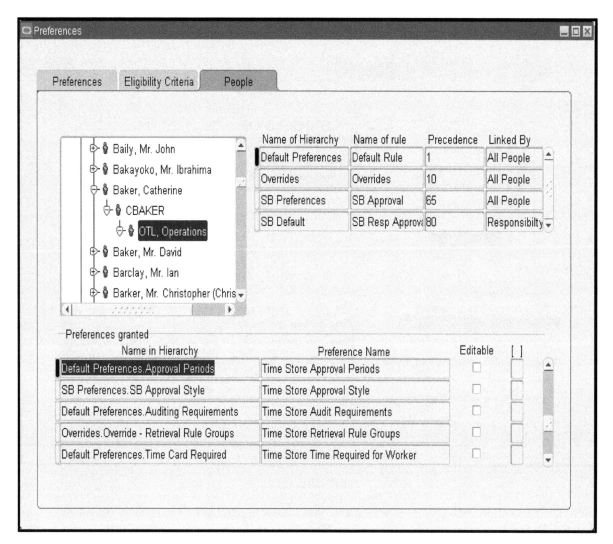

FIGURE 12.32

The Builder Part

In Release 11.5.10, this Workflow has optional setups that can only be performed using the Workflow Builder. Note that Release 12 uses the 'Other Attributes' tab shown in FIGURE 12.25 to configure these Attributes. The Internal Name of the 'OTL Workflows for Employees' Workflow is HXCEMP. If your Applications DBA is sending you the file from the UNIX/LINUX file system, the file is $HXC_TOP/patch/115/import/US/hxcempwf.wft. If the Applications DBA has used the Builder to create the .wft file it will also contain 'Standard' and 'Standard Flexfield' Workflow. This is normal.

When you are finished with all your setups, the Applications DBA can load the Workflow back into the database. If any PL/SQL Procedures are modified which are attached to Function or Notification activities or to Document Attributes, then the modified Packages must be compiled. Make sure this code is migrated with the Workflow as testing is completed and the Workflow is moved to production. Once any changes to the definition of the Workflow have been made, in addition to saving the Workflow to the database, a .wft should be created and stored under your $CUSTOM_TOP directory. This copy of the file should be used when making any additional changes instead of the poxwfpoe.wft file. Note that the name of the .wft file is not limited to 8 characters.

Item Attributes

These Item Attributes function as the Timeouts in the activities listed in Purpose. To change the Attribute, perform the following steps in the Workflow Builder (after loading 'OTL Workflows for Employees' from the database). Double click the Item Attribute indicated. The 'Properties' page will open. Select or enter the desired value in the 'Value' field. Do not change anything else. Click Apply, and then click OK. After all changes are made, save the Workflow back to the database.

Attribute Display Name	Purpose	Allowable Values	Seeded Value
Approval Timeout	This Attribute serves as the Timeout value (in minutes) for the activities 'Timecard Approval' (both occurrences), 'Approver Inaction(Person Approval), 'Approver Inaction', 'Administrator Notification' in the Process 'Approval Notification and Timeout Process.	Any whole number 0 or higher. 0 functions as 'No Timeout'	0
Default Timeout	This Attribute serves as a Timeout value (in minutes), but is not currently used in any activities.	Any whole number 0 or higher. 0 functions as 'No Timeout'	2880

TABLE 12. 13

Validation Errors for HXCEMP

This Workflow as seeded by Oracle for both Release 11.5.10 and Release 12 has validation errors. The Error Messages imply that the Workflow will not function. It will function, but seeing errors makes everyone nervous and can cause companies to ignore Error Messages that will cause problems. The validation screen looks like FIGURE 12.33.

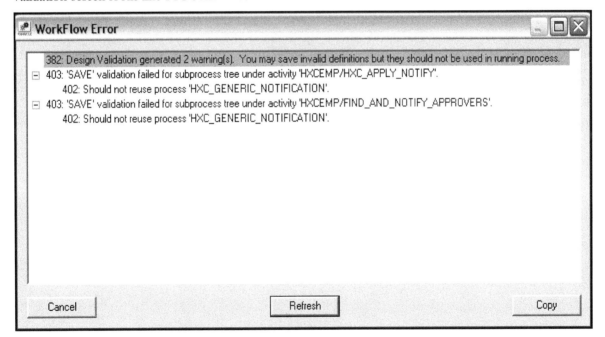

FIGURE 12.33

To fix the errors, right-click the Process 'OTL Generic Notification Process duplicate'. Select 'Copy'. Right-click 'Processes' and select 'Paste'. When the 'Properties' page opens, add a 2 to the end of both the Internal Name and Display Name. Repeat 3 times but add a 3, then a 4, then a 5. FIGURE 12.34

shows the list of Processes before doing this step and FIGURE 12.35 shows the list of Processes after finishing this step.

FIGURE 12.34

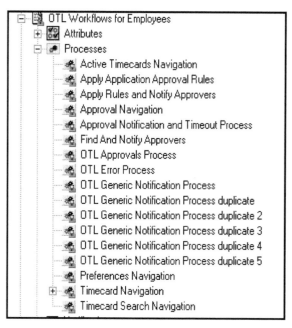

FIGURE 12.35

Double-click the Process 'Apply Rules and Notify Approvers' so that the Diagrammer window opens. Drag in the new 'OTL Generic Notification Process duplicate 2' you just created. Right-click 'OTL Generic Notification Process' noting the labeled legs running in and out of the Process. Select 'Delete Selection'. Drag 'OTL Generic Notification Process duplicate 2' to the place formerly occupied by 'OTL Generic Notification Process'. Redraw the in and out legs, making sure to choose the correct labels. FIGURE 12.36 shows the Process before doing this step and FIGURE 12.37 shows the Process after doing this step.

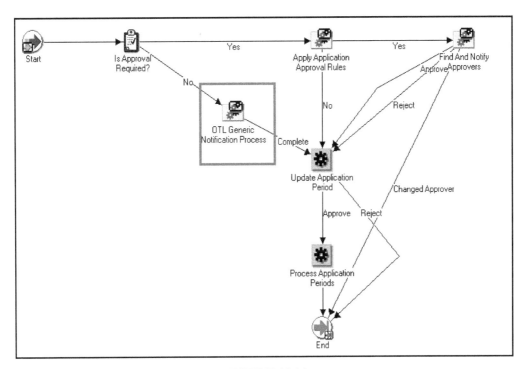

FIGURE 12.36

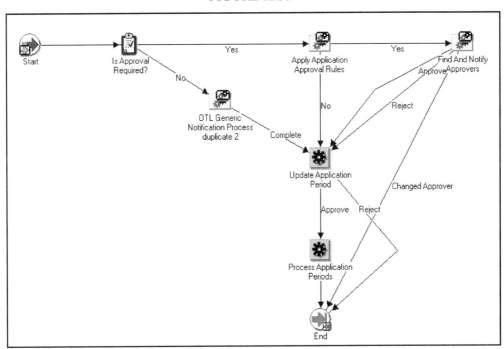

FIGURE 12.37

Next double-click the Process 'Find and Notify Approvers' so that the Diagrammer window opens. Look at FIGURE 12.38 and notice there are two 'OTL Generic Notification Process' nodes and two 'OTL Generic Notification Process duplicate' nodes (only half the Process is shown so that the node labels are readable).

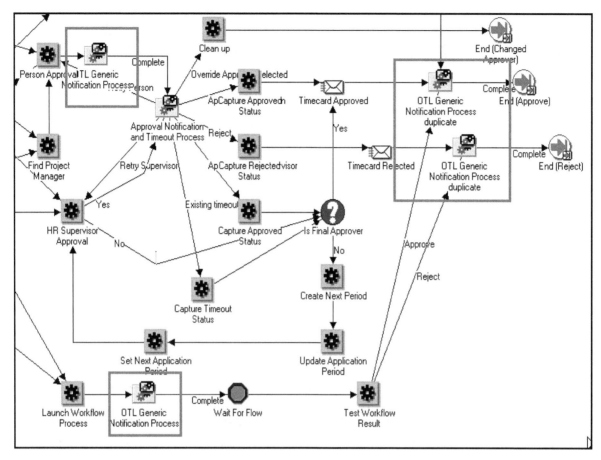

FIGURE 12.38

Drag in the new 'OTL Generic Notification Process duplicate 3', 'OTL Generic Notification Process duplicate 4' and 'OTL Generic Notification Process duplicate 5' you just created. Pick one of the 'OTL Generic Notification Process' nodes and right-click it noting the labeled legs running in and out of the Process. Select 'Delete Selection'. Drag 'OTL Generic Notification Process duplicate 3' to the place formerly occupied by the just deleted 'OTL Generic Notification Process'. Redraw the in and out legs making sure to choose the correct labels. Repeat the process for the other 'OTL Generic Notification Process' replacing it with 'OTL Generic Notification Process duplicate 4'. Now choose one of the 'Notification Process duplicate' nodes. Using the same process, replace one of them with 'OTL Generic Notification Process duplicate 5'. The Workflow will now validate successfully. FIGURE 12.39 shows the changed Process.

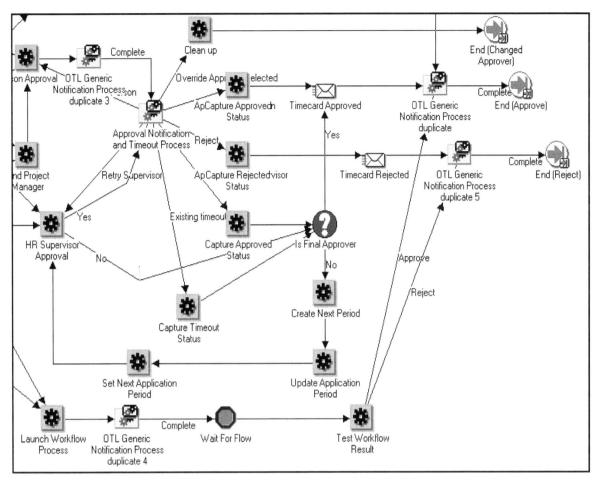

FIGURE 12.39

Note that the replacement of both OTL Generic Notification Process in this diagram is required because this process is used in 'Approve Notification and Timeout' Process, which is called by this Process. The reason all the replacements are recommended is that Oracle Workflow does not recommend a sub-process using a Process already used in the calling Process.

Approval Style of Workflow Requires Workflow Builder and Custom Workflow

If the chosen style is Workflow, this Workflow has setups that can only be performed using the Workflow Builder. It also requires creating a custom Workflow or customizing the Oracle-provided template 'OTL Seeded Approval' Workflow (HXCSAW). If your Applications DBA is sending you the file from the UNIX/LINUX file system, the file is $HXC_TOP/patch/115/import/US/hcseedaw.wft. If the Applications DBA has used the Builder to create the .wft file it will also contain the 'Standard' and 'Standard Flexfield' Workflow. This is normal.

When you are finished with all your setups, the Applications DBA can load the Workflow back into the database. If any PL/SQL Procedures are modified which are attached to Function or Notification activities or to Document Attributes, then the modified Packages must be compiled. Make sure this code is migrated with the Workflow as testing is completed and the Workflow is moved to production. Once any changes to the definition of the Workflow have been made, in addition to saving the Workflow to the database, a .wft should be created and stored under your $CUSTOM_TOP directory. This copy of the file should be used when making any additional changes instead of the hcseedaw.wft file. Note that the name of the .wft file is not limited to 8 characters.

The requirements for the custom Workflow are:

- The starting Process must have an Internal Name that begins with OTC_APPROVAL (note: the documentation says OTL_APPROVAL, it is wrong – see MetaLink Doc. ID: 338758.1, *Create a custom Workflow and get it to appear under the 'Identifier' column in Define Approval Style Form?*)

- The Workflow must contain two Attributes, one with the Internal Name PARENT_ITEM_TYPE and one with the Internal Name PARENT_ITEM_KEY

- The Workflow must set the Item Attribute Workflow Approval Result (Internal Name WF_APPROVAL_RESULT) in the corresponding HXCEMP Workflow

- The last node in the starting Process (before the End Node) must be a 'Continue Flow' node with the 'Node Attributes' tab set as:

    ◆ Attribute Name 'Waiting Activity Label' must be the Type 'Constant' and have the value 'WAITFORFLOW'.

    ◆ Attribute Name 'Waiting Flow' must be the Type' Constant' and have the value 'Master'

The 'OTL Seeded Approval' Workflow (HXCSAW) complies with the first three requirements, but not the last. FIGURE 12.40 shows the Workflow as delivered by Oracle.

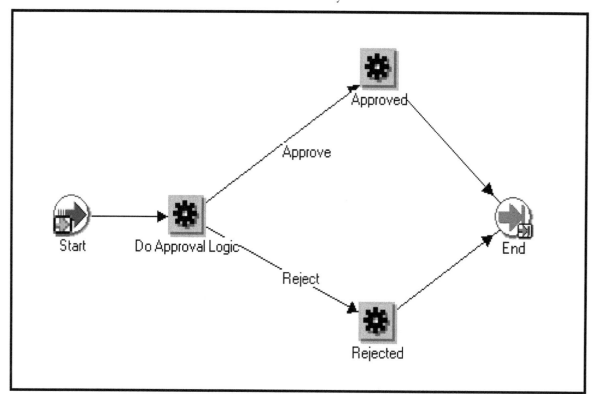

FIGURE 12.40

The 'Do Approval Logic' node should be replaced with your custom Function or sub-process to approve the timecard. As seeded it will return Reject. The Approved and Rejected legs correctly set the status of the Item Attribute 'Workflow Approval Result' in the parent 'HXCEMP' Workflow. However, the 'Continue Flow' node should be added as shown in FIGURE 12.41.

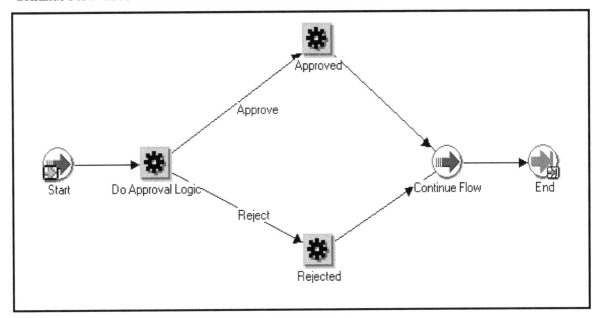

FIGURE 12.41

SOME NOTES ON PROJECTS WORKFLOWS

PASYSADMIN

There are four Workflows that use PL/SQL to set the value of an Item Attribute to PASYSADMIN. This Attribute is then used as the Performer in Notifications. These Workflows are 'PA: CRM Workaround Workflow (PACRMUPD)', 'PA Forecast Item Generation Workflow (PARFIGEN)', 'PA Budget Integration Workflow (PAWFBUI)', and 'PA: HR Related Updates Workflow (PAXWFHRU)'. If you are using any of these Workflows you must define PASYSADMIN as a user. You can then use the same techniques as used for SYSADMIN to provide access to the Notifications sent to this user.

PA: HR Related Updates Workflow – PAXWFHRU

This Workflow is initiated when updates or inserts are made to the HR tables. It is supposed to be dependent on the value of the Profile Option 'PA: Licensed to use Project Resource Management'. However, the code that initiates the Workflow also checks if any records exist in PA_UTILIZATION_OPTIONS_ALL. This table has a record for each org for which Project Resource Management has been set up. If any records exist in this table (the ORG_ID is not checked), this Workflow is initiated regardless of the setting of the Profile Option.

SUMMARY AND WHAT'S NEXT

This chapter has barely scratched the surface of all the Workflows that exist. The examples discussed illustrate how the Workflow is dependent on setups entered both through the Workflow Builder and through the normal application setup screens. In addition to reading the user and implementation guides, implementers should research MetaLink for white papers and other notes that either impact the Workflow setups or that point to additional patches that should be applied to avoid problems. The best way to search for a particular Workflow is to simply enter the Workflow's Internal Name.

Workflow, like any Oracle product, is constantly changing. New releases and new patches provide additional functionality designed to facilitate Workflow development and administration. The next chapter will discuss the new functionality introduced specifically for Release 12 and functionality back-ported to Release 11.5.10 through 11i.ATG_PF.H.delta.5 (Rollup 5) and 11i.ATG_PF.H.delta.6 (Rollup 6).

Chapter

New Features

This chapter will discuss most of the functionality released in 11i.ATG_PF.H.delta.5 (Rollup 5) and 11i.ATG_PF.H.delta.6 (Rollup 6) including some significant one-off patches and MetaLink Doc. IDs. As a bonus, this chapter will also explain how to set up Worklist Flexfields, a feature introduced in 11i.ATG_PF.H.delta.3 (Rollup 3).

PATCHING CURRENT IS IMPORTANT

There have been six major patches (rollups) released for E-Business Suite Release 11i that contain significant updates to Workflow, and a seventh is announced but not released. The code in these patches is part of the base functionality in Release 12. The fourth patch, 11i.ATG_PF.H.delta.4 (Rollup 4), was released August 6, 2006 and is required to install security patches and Diagnostics (from July 2007 through January 2008). The fifth patch, 11i.ATG_PF.H.delta.5 (Rollup 5) was released May 3, 2007 and is required to install the April 2008 security patches. Rollup 4 remains the base level for the April 2008 Diagnostics.

E-Business Suite Release 11.5.10 has been available since December 2004 and Release 12 has been available since January 2007. The four Release Update Packs (RUPs) for Release 12 contain bug-fixes, performance improvements, and limited (usually regulatory) new functionality. Rollups for Release 11.5.10 contain new functionality as well as bug-fixes and performance improvements. This new functionality for Release 11.5.10 allows customers of this release to enjoy the same features native to Release 12.

The Release 12 Release Update Packs (RUPs) apply to all products; however, Oracle has released patches for just ATG. These Release Update Packs are released quarterly in January, April, July, and October. Oracle did not release an April 2008 Release Update Pack. Instead, customers can monitor the Oracle Workflow Known Issues section of MetaLink Doc. ID: 396314.1, *Oracle Workflow Documentation Resources, Release 12,* for critical patches.

ATG patches include the following products: Application Object Library (FND), Oracle Applications Manager (AOM), Workflow (OWF), Oracle Applications Framework (FWK), CRM Technical Foundation (JTT), Oracle Common Application Components (JTA), Oracle Applications Technology Stack (TXK), BI Publisher (formerly XML Publisher) (XDO), Oracle XML Gateway (ECX), Oracle e-Commerce Gateway (EC), Application Install (AK), Oracle Alert (ALR), Oracle User Management (UMX), Web ADI (BNE), and Oracle Report Manager (FRM).

As one can see from this list, these patches affect the underlying structure of all the applications, and thus, when applied, require testing of all the applications. Oracle has also instituted a policy for Release 11.5.10 requiring at least ATG_PF.H.delta.<n-1> as the basis to apply security patches. An exception to this policy was made for the January 2008 patches. There is no formal policy to date for Release 12.

Workflow is also dependant on patches found in HR and AME (Approvals Management Engine). Even if running HR as a shared product, these patches are critical to the smooth operation of Workflow as they contain patches necessary to sync employee changes into the Workflow Directory Services tables. The current patch for HR in Release 11.5.10 is 11i.HR.K.2. The latest AME patch, 11i.AME.B.2, is included in the HR patch. However, AME also requires two additional one-off patches, 4629194 and 5305176.

Although not required to run Workflow, Oracle Diagnostics provides many scripts that enhance the ability to administer Workflow. These scripts do not perform any updates, so application of these patches does not require testing. Diagnostic patches are released at least quarterly. As of May 2008, the latest Release 11*i* patch is 11i E-BUSINESS SUITE DIAGNOSTIC PACK APRIL 2008 (6991179). The latest Release 12 patch is R12.IZU.A.delta.4 January 2008 (6497339).

MetaLink provides scripts to determine what patches you have installed in your environment. These scripts do not test for many of the one-offs, however. If you are responsible for administering these applications, you should visit the Knowledge Browser on MetaLink and peruse the new notes for each product. You can also configure your headlines to display new notes for these products. The scripts are found in the following MetaLink Doc. IDs:

- 461431.1 – *Script to Check What Workflow Related Patches Are Installed in EBusiness Suite R12*

- 336843.1 or 275379.1 – *Oracle Workflow Diagnostic Script wfreleases.sql (Release 11i), Script to Check What Workflow Related Patches Are Installed In EBusiness Suite 11i*

- 368280.1 – *How Can Version of AME Be Determined?*

- 342459.1 – *eBusiness Support Diagnostics Overview*

Click R12 Catalog or R11i Catalog to get the current patch

- 135266.1 – *Oracle HRMS Product Family – Release 11i and 12 Information*

Information about the features discussed in this book can be found in the *Oracle Workflow Administrator's Guide, Release 12, Part No. B31431-02, June 2007*, and the following MetaLink Doc. IDs:

- 412709.1 – *Oracle Workflow Documentation Updates for 11i.ATG.PF.H.delta.5 (RUP 5)*

- 431219.1 – *Oracle Workflow Documentation Updates for 11i.ATG.PF.H.delta.6 (RUP 6)*

- 444524.1 – *About Oracle Applications Technology ATG_PF.H Rollup 6* – Lists all changes to Workflow (New Features, New/Changed Programs, New/Changed Profile Options, New/Changed Public APIs, New Business Events, New/Changed User Interfaces, New/Changed Scripts) from CU1 through 11i.ATG_PF.H.delta.6 (Rollup 6).

Unless otherwise indicated, the functionality discussed is available in both releases (assuming that Release 11.5.10 is patched through 11i.ATG_PF.H.delta.6 (Rollup 6)).

RETRY ERRORED WORKFLOW ACTIVITIES

11i.ATG_PF.H.delta.6 (Rollup 6) introduced a new Concurrent Program, 'Retry Errored Workflow Activities'. This program can be run as a one-time program or scheduled periodically.

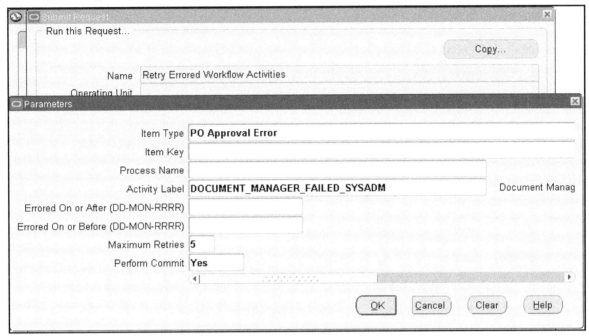

FIGURE 13.1

The program utilizes the following parameters:

- **Item Type** – the Display Name of the errored Workflow

- **Item Key** – this parameter only displays if Item Type is specified and is used to retry a specific Workflow

- **Process Name** – this parameter only displays if Item Type is specified and is used to limit retries to a specific Process containing an errored activity

- **Activity Label** – this parameter only displays if Item Type is specified and is used to limit retries to a specific activity. If the activity occurs in multiple Processes, specify the Process Name to further limit the retries. Although the Activity Label is the same as the Internal Name of the activity in most cases, the Activity Label is actually the value found on the Node tab of the 'Properties' page of the activity in the Diagrammer window in Workflow Builder. This field is used to uniquely identify an activity (such as multiple End Nodes)

- **Errored On or After (DD-MON-RRRR)** – this parameter allows you to limit retries to activities that errored on or after a specific date (and thus avoid restarting old Workflows)

- **Errored On or Before (DD-MON-RRRR)** – this parameter allows you to limit retries to activities that errored before a specific date

- **Maximum Retries** – the number of times the program should retry this activity. The maximum value is 99

- **Perform Commit** – whether to issue a commit after each retry ('Yes') or wait until all retries for all Workflows are attempted ('No'). Choosing 'Yes' reduces rollback size and increases performance

JUNIOR ADMINISTRATOR

Oracle refers to this feature as "Granting Restricted Access to Workflow Monitoring Data". This feature allows companies to set up administration of Workflow by Item Type or by Item Attribute name and value. In addition companies can also restrict the actions performed on the allowed Workflows. An additional restriction is that users accessing this feature cannot administer Workflows they own. Ownership is determined by the field WF_ITEMS.OWNER_ROLE. Some Workflows, such as APINV (AP Invoice), may not set an owner, so no "cannot administer Workflows they own" restriction would exist for these Workflows.

To enable this feature requires the following one-time setups:

- Create 'Object Instance Set' for Item Types

- Create 'Object Instance Set' for Item Attributes

- Create Permission Sets for Workflow Actions

- Create Roles for Workflow Actions and Assign Permission Sets

- Once these setups are finished, grants and Role assignments must be created for each user, responsibility, or organization. These grants include:

  - Grant 'Object Instance Set' values for Item Types and/or Item Attribute Values

  - Assign Roles for Workflow Actions

One-Time Setups

Restrict by Item Type – Create Object Instance Set

This step creates an 'Object Instance Set' that allows the restriction of Workflow access by Item Type. It must be performed from the 'Functional Developer' responsibility. When the form opens, enter WORKFLOW_ITEMS in the 'Name' field and click Go. When the result of the query is returned, click on the 'Workflow Items' link. Do not click the pencil in the 'Update' column. See FIGURE 13.2.

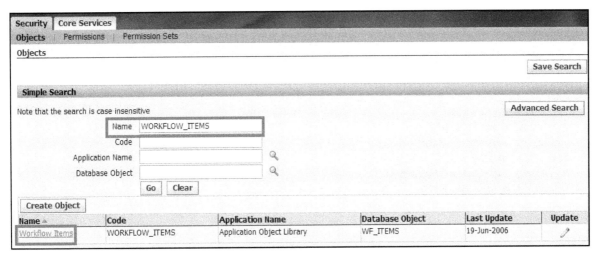

FIGURE 13.2

When the following screen appears, click on the 'Object Instance Sets' tab. See FIGURE 13.3.

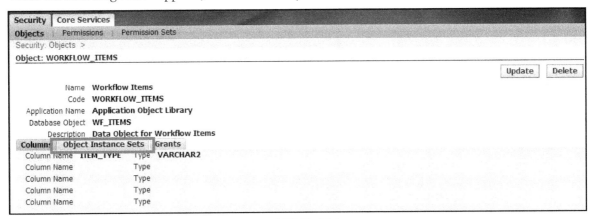

FIGURE 13.3

When the following screen appears, click the 'Create Instance Set' button. See FIGURE 13.4.

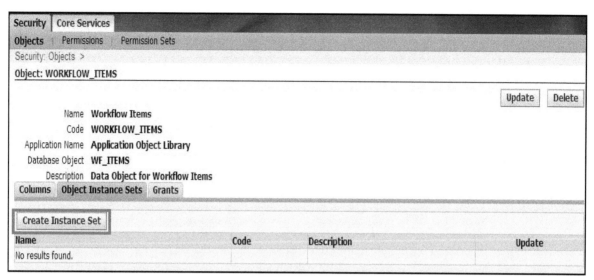

FIGURE 13.4

When the next screen displays, enter the following information. See FIGURE 13.5.

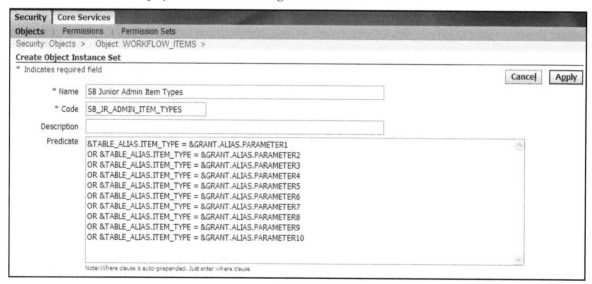

FIGURE 13.5

- **Name** – Enter text to identify this instance set

- **Code** – Enter an Internal Name to identify this instance set. This field cannot be updated once saved. Limit characters to alphabetics, numbers, hyphens, and underscores

- **Predicate** – Enter the following text exactly as it is shown in the above diagram. The Oracle documentation only lists &TABLE_ALIAS.ITEM_TYPE = &GRANT_ALIAS.PARAMETER1. However, if entered like this, you can only grant access to a single Workflow. Entering the following parameters allows granting access to 1-10 Workflows (10 is the number of allowable parameters for this definition)

```
&TABLE_ALIAS.ITEM_TYPE = &GRANT_ALIAS.PARAMETER1
```

```
OR  &TABLE_ALIAS.ITEM_TYPE  =  &GRANT_ALIAS.PARAMETER2
OR  &TABLE_ALIAS.ITEM_TYPE  =  &GRANT_ALIAS.PARAMETER3
OR  &TABLE_ALIAS.ITEM_TYPE  =  &GRANT_ALIAS.PARAMETER4
OR  &TABLE_ALIAS.ITEM_TYPE  =  &GRANT_ALIAS.PARAMETER5
OR  &TABLE_ALIAS.ITEM_TYPE  =  &GRANT_ALIAS.PARAMETER6
OR  &TABLE_ALIAS.ITEM_TYPE  =  &GRANT_ALIAS.PARAMETER7
OR  &TABLE_ALIAS.ITEM_TYPE  =  &GRANT_ALIAS.PARAMETER8
OR  &TABLE_ALIAS.ITEM_TYPE  =  &GRANT_ALIAS.PARAMETER9
OR  &TABLE_ALIAS.ITEM_TYPE  =  &GRANT_ALIAS.PARAMETER10
```

- Click Apply. Note that 'Object Instance Sets' may not be deleted.

Restrict by Item Attribute Value – Create Object Instance Set

This step creates an 'Object Instance Set' that allows the restriction of Workflow access by the value of a specific Item Attribute. Item Attributes are specific to a particular Item Type. There are no universal Item Attributes. Even ORG_ID only appears in 130 out of over 1000 Workflows. There are over 10,000 distinct Item Attributes. Thus, restricting access by Item Attribute value has limited value. In addition, if access by Item Type is granted to a user as well as access by Item Attribute, the combination of the grants may produce no viewable Workflows.

For example: access is granted to the Workflows APEXP and APINV. Access is also granted to Workflows with the Attribute ORG_ID = 204. APINV does not use this Attribute and thus the user will be unable to see any APINV Workflows.

Like the previous 'Object Instance Set', the work must be performed from the 'Functional Developer' responsibility. When the form opens, enter WORKFLOW_ITEM_ATTRIBUTE_VALUES in the 'Name' field and click Go. When the result of the query is returned, click on the 'Workflow Item Attribute Values' link. See FIGURE 13.6.

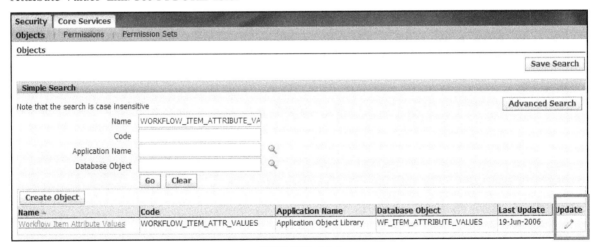

FIGURE 13.6

This seeded 'Object Instance Set' allows referencing two columns from the table ITEM_ATTRIBUTE_VALUES: NAME (the Internal Name of the Item Attribute) and TEXT_VALUE (the value of the Item Attribute when the type is not DATE, NUMBER, or EVENT). The columns ITEM_TYPE and NUMBER_VALUE are not included. Thus, the Predicate cannot limit by Item Type nor can any Attribute declared NUMBER be referenced (like ORG_ID). However, additional columns can be added. Click the pencil icon in the 'Update' column

When the 'Update' screen appears, add the columns ITEM_TYPE and NUMBER_VALUE. The 'Type' column autofills based on the definition of the column in the table WORKFLOW_ITEM_ATTRIBUTE_VALUES. See FIGURE 13.7.

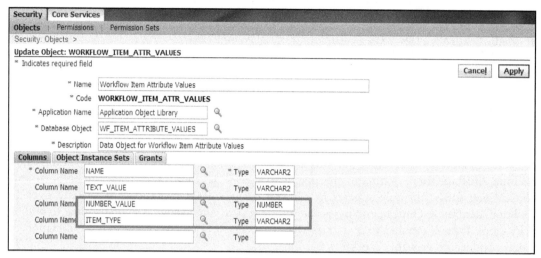

FIGURE 13.7

When finished, click Apply. This returns you to the screen where you can now click the 'Workflow Item Attribute Values' link. Click the 'Object Instance Sets' tab. When the following screen appears, click the 'Create Instance Set' button. See FIGURE 13.8.

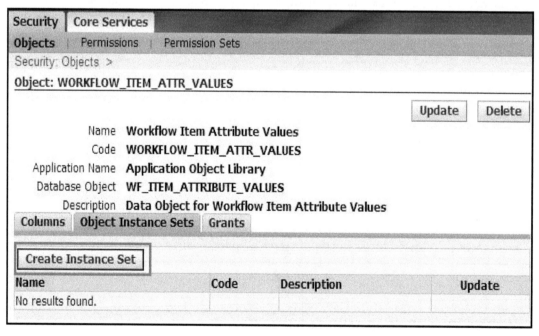

FIGURE 13.8

When the next screen displays, enter the 'Name' and 'Code'. In the example shown in FIGURE 13.9, the 'Predicate' field allows for viewing any Workflow with the Item Attribute ORG_ID that has the value '204'. Click Apply.

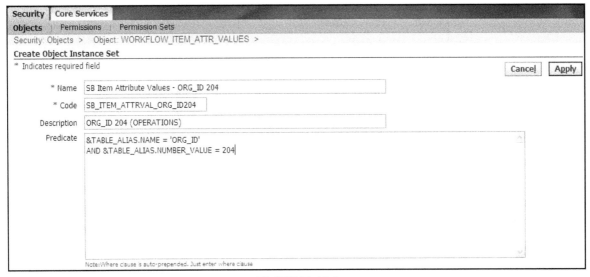

FIGURE 13.9

Notice that the 'Predicate' for the Item Attribute 'Object Instance Set' did not include any &TABLE_ALIAS.<column> = &GRANT_ALIAS.PARAMETER<n> statements. This construct is not available for these 'Object Instance Sets'. Thus, unlike the Item Type 'Object Instance Set' where one instance set is defined and the restricting values will be defined as the grant is made, all restricting values must be part of the definition. This can result in the requirement to define multiple Item Attribute 'Object Instance Sets'.

The Oracle documentation provides two examples of coding this Predicate. The example for ORG_ID is incorrect as the value for ORG_ID is stored in NUMBER_VALUE, not TEXT_VALUE. The Oracle examples (corrected) are:

```
&TABLE_ALIAS.NAME = 'CURRENT_PERSON_ID'
AND EXISTS (SELECT 'Y' FROM per_people_f
WHERE person_id = &TABLE_ALIAS.NUMBER_VALUE
AND TRUNC(SYSDATE) BETWEEN effective_start_date
AND effective_end_date

&TABLE_ALIAS.NAME = 'ORG_ID'
AND &TABLE_ALIAS.NUMBER_VALUE IN (204,1731,2541)
```

Only one Workflow, HRSSA, utilizes the Item Attribute CURRENT_PERSON_ID. Thus, assigning this 'Object Instance Set' would restrict someone to administering HRSSA Workflows for active employees.

The second example restricts access to all Workflows (130 of them) that utilize the Attribute ORG_ID and ORG_ID is set to any of the values in the IN clause.

There is no limit to the number of Item Attribute 'Object Instance Sets' that can be created.

Restrict by Action – Create Action Permission Sets

After defining the 'Object Instance Sets' that limit which Workflows can be administered, 'Action Permission Sets' must be created. 'Action Permission Sets' limit what actions can be performed on the Workflows. Oracle has predefined the following actions as shown in FIGURE 13.10.

Action	Permission Name	Permission Code
Skip	Skip Workflow Activity	WF_SKIP
Retry	Retry Activity	WF_RETRY
Rewind	Rewind Workflow	WF_REWIND
Suspend	Suspend Workflow	WF_SUSPEND
Cancel	Cancel Workflow	WF_CANCEL
Update	Update Workflow Item Attributes	WF_UPDATE_ATTR
Monitor	Monitor Data	WF_MON_DATA

FIGURE 13.10

Oracle has pre-seeded the Role 'Workflow Admin Role' that has access to all of the above actions, so if you only need to limit which Workflows can be administered and not the actions, skip to the next section.

In order to be able to view the Workflows, the Action 'Monitor' must be allowed. Since you have to be able to view the Workflow to perform any other Action, 'Monitor' is the minimum permission that can be assigned. Now companies only need to consider what other Actions will be permitted.

 It is certainly possible to create 'Action Permission Sets' that contain any combination of the above actions. This leaves 720 possible combinations of the other 6 actions. Rather than try to create that many 'Action Permission Sets', Solution Beacon recommends creating an Action Permission Set that contains a single permission. This results in the need for only 7 sets. Then per user (or responsibility) companies can decide which 'Action Permission Sets' to assign.

Unlike 'Grant Object Sets', assigning multiple 'Action Permission Sets' results in the ability to perform the actions contained in all sets.

'Action Permission Sets' are created using the 'Functional Administrator' responsibility. This responsibility contains a single form. When the form opens, enter the following data:

- **Name** – Enter text to identify this instance set

- **Code** – Enter an Internal Name to identify this instance set. This field cannot be updated once saved. Limit characters to alphabetics, numbers, hyphens, and underscores

Click 'Add Another Row' (see FIGURE 13.11).

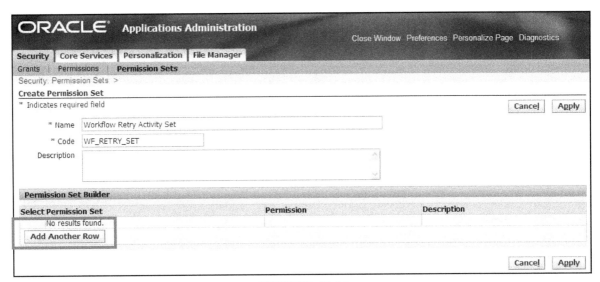

FIGURE 13.11

Use the List of Values to pick the appropriate 'Permission'. Use the values from the column 'Permission Name' in FIGURE 13.10. See FIGURE 13.12 for an example of assigning the ability to retry activities.

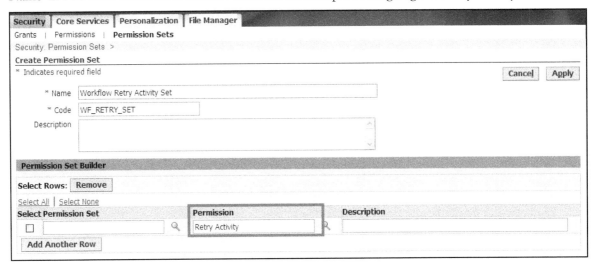

FIGURE 13.12

Click Apply.

Repeat this process until a 'Permission Set' is created for all 7 actions.

Restrict by Action – Create Role

Now that the Permission Sets are created, Roles must be created that contain these Permission Sets.

 Solution Beacon recommends creating 7 Roles, one for each Permission Set.

Roles must be created from the responsibility 'User Management'. This responsibility can be assigned to anyone, but it will only function if the user has been assigned the Role 'Security Administrator'. And to grant the Role 'Security Administrator', the responsibility 'User Management' must be used. Since initially the only user that has the Role 'Security Administrator' is the user SYSADMIN, the first step is to log in as SYSADMIN and grant the Role 'Security Administrator' to other users.

Once the 'Security Administrator' Role and the responsibility 'User Management' is assigned to a user, login as that user and choose the 'User Management' responsibility. This responsibility has four menu options, but only has one screen. 'Select Roles and Role Inheritance'. When the screen opens, verify you are on the 'Roles and Role Inheritance' tab, then click the 'Create Role' button (see FIGURE 13.13).

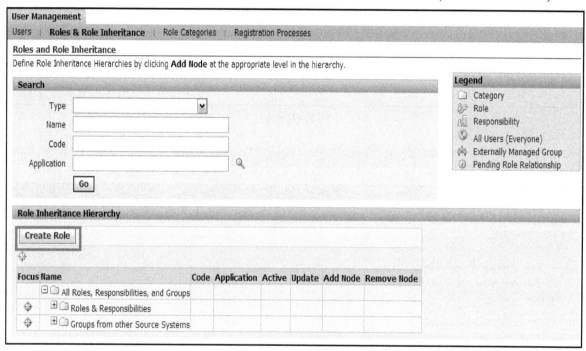

FIGURE 13.13

Enter the following information (see FIGURE 13.14):

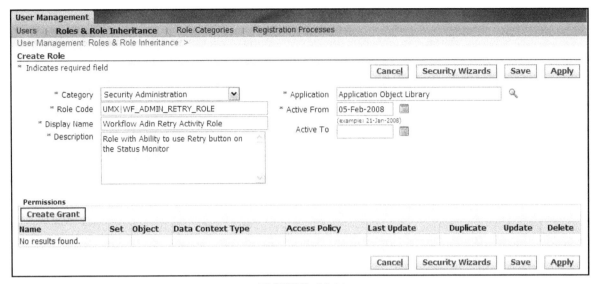

FIGURE 13.14

- **Category (Required)** – Use the List of Values to select a 'Category'. Since this Role will restrict access, the category 'Security Administration' was selected. If desired, the 'Role Categories' tab can be used to create a custom category

- **Application (Required)** – Use the List of Values to select an 'Application'. Since security belongs to the Application Object Library, this value was selected

- **Role Code (Required)** – The value entered cannot contain any spaces. Characters should be restricted to alpha, numbers, hyphen, underscore and the pipe characters. The value created will be added to WF_LOCAL_ROLES with PARTITION_ID set to 13. This partition belongs to the application User Management (UMX) and all Roles already there start with 'UMX|'. Therefore, it is recommended to continue this naming convention.

- **Display Name (Required)** – Enter the name of the Role. Any characters can be used

- **Description (Required)** – Enter a description for the Role

- **Active From (Required)** – Defaults to current date but can be changed

- **Active To (Optional)** – This field is only used to end-date a Role

After all the fields are entered, click 'Save' (not Apply). If Apply is clicked the form returns blank and you will have to re-query the Role to create the grants.

Once the top of the form is saved, click the 'Create Grant' button. This opens a 4-step form.

Step 1 – Enter the name of the grant and click Next (see FIGURE 13.15).

Step 2 – Does not display, the form proceeds directly to Step 3.

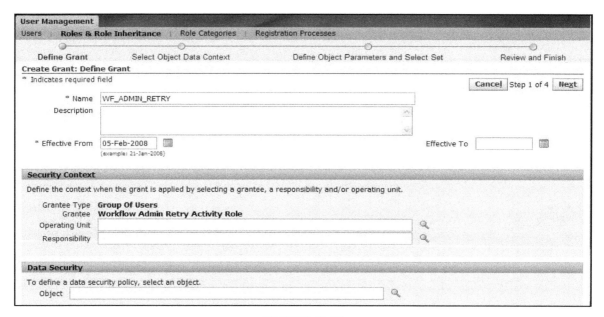

FIGURE 13.15

Step 3 – Select one of the Permission Sets just created. In our example, we created a Role that allows users to Retry activities, so the Permission Set 'Workflow Retry Activity Set' containing the permission 'Retry Activity' is selected. Click Next (see FIGURE 13.16).

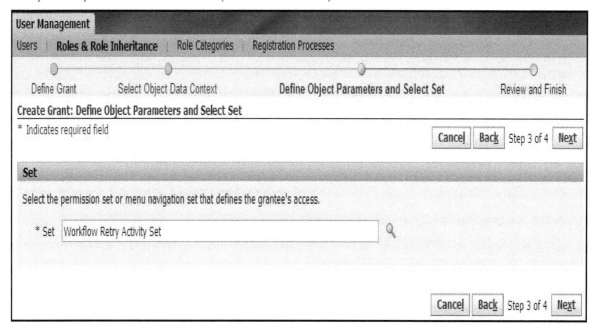

FIGURE 13.16

Step 4 – Review and either click 'Back' to make corrections or 'Finish' to accept the entry. The next screen states the Role is created. Click OK. Repeat these steps to create all 7 Roles. FIGURE 13.17 shows the definition for the Action 'Monitor Data'.

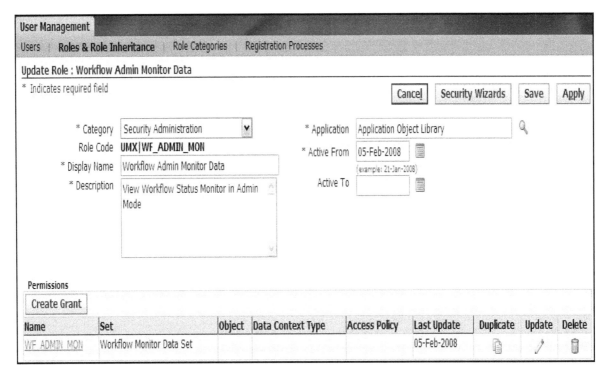

FIGURE 13.17

User/Responsibility Setup

Grant Object Instance Set

Now that all the 'Object Instance Sets' and Roles are created, the next task is to grant the correct combination to various users and/or responsibilities.

As mentioned earlier, when granting Item Attribute 'Object Instance Sets', make sure that the combination of grants still allows access to the desired Workflows. If a grant is made for an 'Object Instance Set' that references the Attribute CURRENT_PERSON_ID (which is only found in the Workflow HRSSA) and a second grant is made to the user for an 'Object Instance Set' that references the Attribute CURRENCY (which is not found in the Workflow HRSSA), then this user will not be able to view any Workflows as there are no Workflows that contain both the Item Attribute CURRENCY and the Item Attribute CURRENT_PERSON_ID.

However, if a grant is made for an 'Object Instance Set' referencing the Attribute CURRENCY=USD and another grant is made for an 'Object Instance Set' referencing the Attribute ORG_ID=204, then any Workflow that satisfies both conditions will be listed twice. Thus, the combination of grants needs to be carefully planned.

Making grants of the 'Object Instance Set' that restricts by Workflow Name is performed somewhat differently than the grant for any of the Item Attribute 'Object Instance Sets' due to the need to specify the parameter values.

Grants are made from the 'Functional Administrator' responsibility. This is a single screen responsibility, so when the form opens, click the 'Create Grant' button.

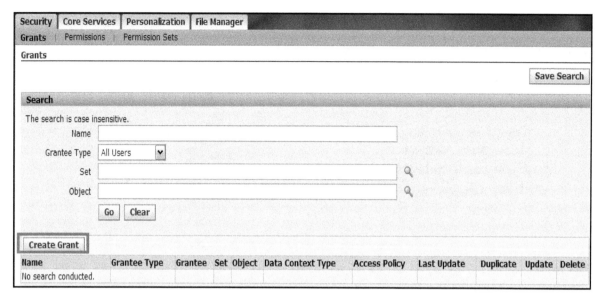

FIGURE 13. 18

Creating grants is a four-step process. First we will show how to create the grant for the Item Attribute 'Object Instance Set'. For Step 1, enter the following information (See FIGURE 13.19):

- **Name (Required)** – enter a descriptive name

- **Description (Optional)** – enter a description of the grant

- **Effective From (Required)** – current date defaults in

- **Security Context (Required)** – select 'Grantee Type'

    o **Specific User** – select the 'User' in the field 'Grantee'

    o **Operating Unit** – select the 'Operating Unit'

    o **Responsibility** – select the 'Responsibility'

- **Data Security Object (Required)** – Select 'Workflow Items' (this is an Oracle seeded value, not any object created earlier)

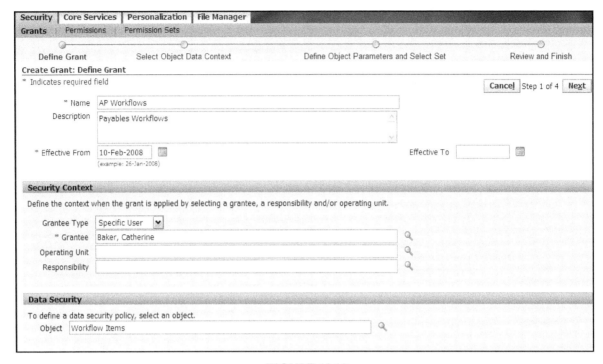

FIGURE 13.19

Click Next. For Step 2, set 'Data Context Type' to 'Instance Set' and select the 'Instance Set' created earlier. Click Next (see FIGURE 13.20).

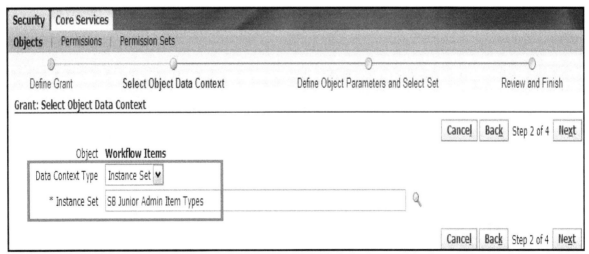

FIGURE 13.20

Step 3 specifies the Workflows to which access will be granted. Enter up to 10 Workflows. The Internal Name of the Workflow must be used. Select the set 'Business Workflow item permission set'. See FIGURE 13.21 for an example of restricting the Workflows to APINV and APEXP. Click Next.

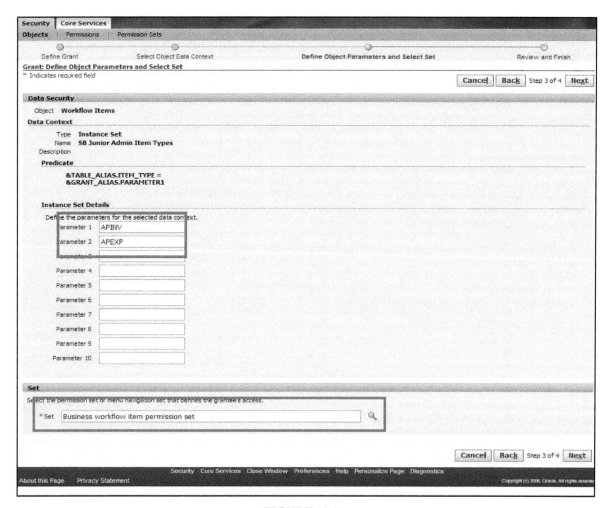

FIGURE 13.21

For Step 4, review the results. Click 'Back' to make corrections or click 'Finish' to accept the setup. See FIGURE 13.22.

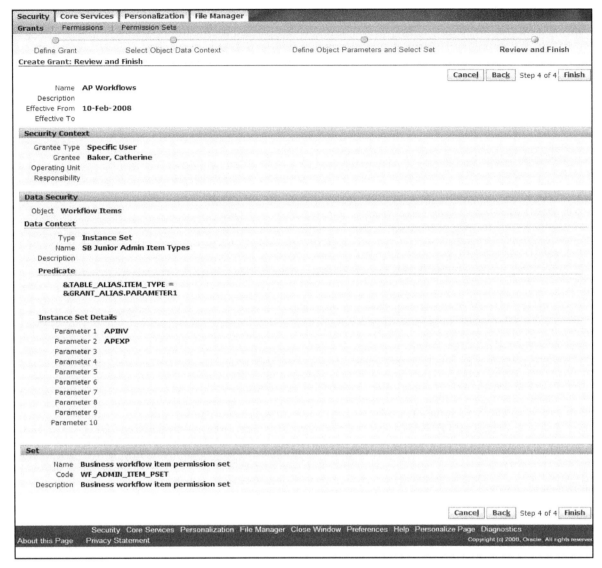

FIGURE 13.22

Granting an 'Object Instance Set' to restrict access by Item Attribute Value is similar. Use the 'Functional Administrator' responsibility and click the 'Create Grant' button when the form opens. Enter the name of the grant and the name of the user or responsibility to which the grant is made. The object name is now 'Workflow Item Attribute Values'. Click Next to advance to page 2 (see FIGURE 13.23).

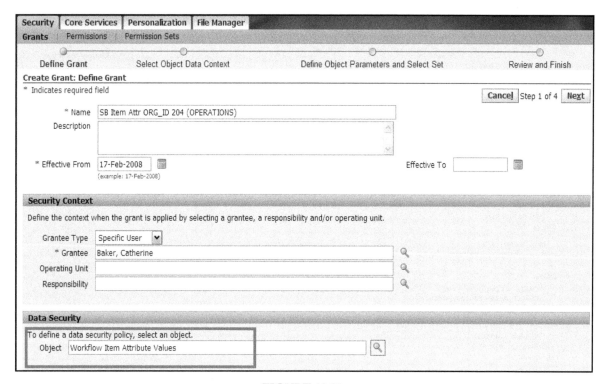

FIGURE 13.23

The Data Context Set is still 'Instance Set', but this time use the name of the Instance Set that was created for the Item Attributes. Click Next to advance to the next step (see FIGURE 13.24).

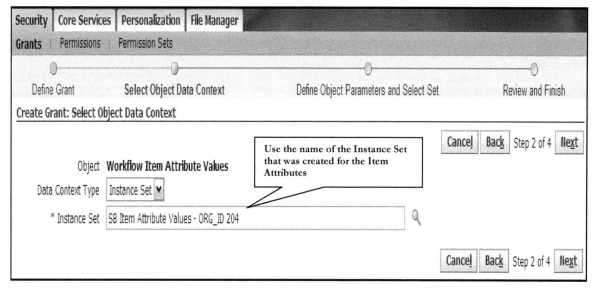

FIGURE 13.24

There are no parameters for an Item Attribute 'Object Instance Set', but the Set 'Business workflow item attribute permission set' must be specified (see FIGURE 13.25). Click Next.

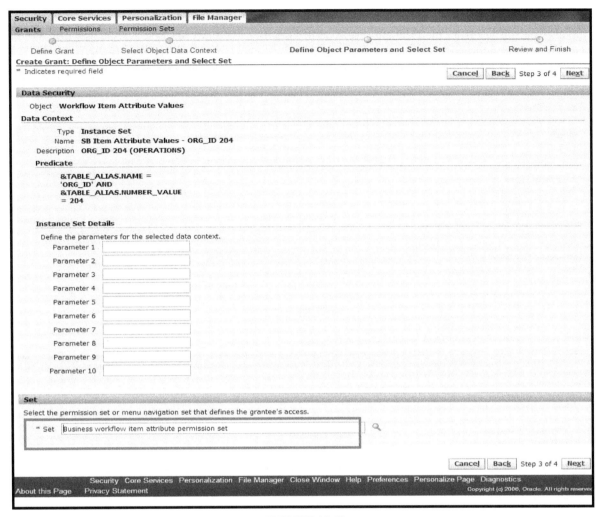

FIGURE 13.25

The next screen is the 'Review and Finish' screen. Click 'Back' to make any corrections or 'Finish' to accept all the values. Repeat for any additional grants.

Assign Roles

This step assigns the Roles that determines the actions allowed in the 'Status Monitor' screen. Unlike grants on 'Object Instance Sets', which can either cause duplicates or be too restrictive, grants of Roles are cumulative. Remember that the Role for monitoring must always be granted. Since our Roles are set up so that each Role represents an action, assign the Roles that match the desired action(s).

Grants of Roles must be made from the 'User Management' responsibility. This responsibility only functions if the user has first been assigned the Role 'Security Administrator'. Initially only the user SYSADMIN has this Role, so either the following steps must be performed as the user SYSADMIN or the user SYSADMIN must grant the 'Security Administrator' Role to additional users (after assigning the 'Security Administrator' Role, remember to assign the 'User Management' responsibility).

Navigate to the 'Users' screen by either selecting this menu choice, or selecting any other menu choice and clicking this tab from the resulting screen. Enter the user to whom the Role will be assigned. When the user name is returned, click the pencil icon in the 'Update' column (see FIGURE 13.26).

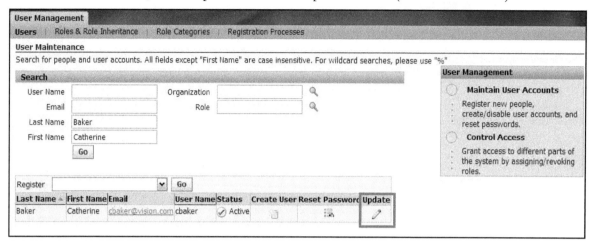

FIGURE 13.26

Click the 'Assign Roles' button (see FIGURE 13.27).

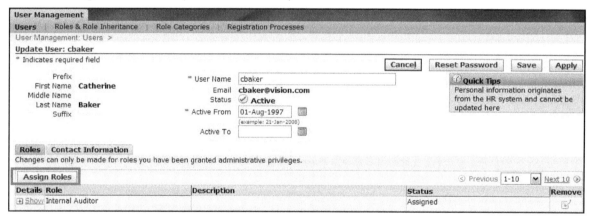

FIGURE 13.27

Since we started all our Role names with Workflow, query by Workflow%. Click the box beside each desired Role. Remember that the Role 'Workflow Admin Role' assigns all actions, so if this Role is clicked, no other Roles are needed. When all desired Roles are checked, click the Select button in the upper right-hand corner (see FIGURE 13.28).

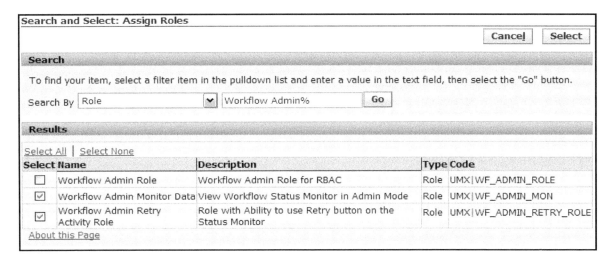

FIGURE 13.28

For each Role assigned, a 'Justification' must be entered. This is a comment field and therefore can be anything. To save your changes but still display the same data, click 'Save'. To save your changes and return to a blank form, click Apply (see FIGURE 13.29).

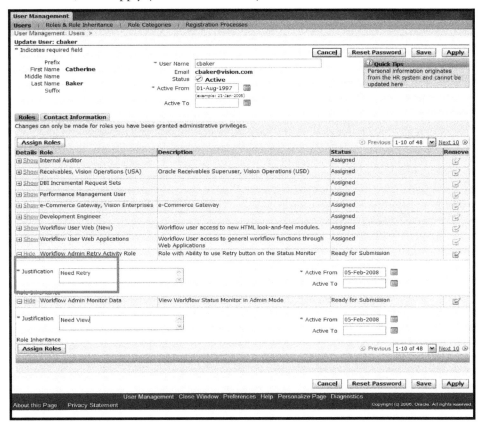

FIGURE 13.29

Final Step

Once all the grants and Roles are defined and assigned, the user who will be the Junior Administrator must be assigned a responsibility containing the Workflow Administration screens. Do not select the responsibility assigned as the Workflow Administrator. For example, if the responsibility 'Workflow Administrator Web Applications' is assigned as the Workflow Administrator, then use the responsibility 'Workflow Administrator Web (New)' or create a responsibility with the Workflow Administrator menus.

Note that if the grants were made to a responsibility and not to a user, then the Workflow Administration menus should be added to that responsibility.

The entire Workflow Administration menus can be granted. All the screens in this menu function in query mode except the 'Notification Worklist', the 'Status Monitor' and the 'Notification Search' screens. The 'Notification Worklist' and the 'Notification Search' screens restrict the user to his/her own Notifications. The 'Status Monitor' restricts access based on the assigned grants and Roles.

The Item Types that can be accessed are limited by the Object Instance Grants. If both our examples from above are assigned, the user will only be able to access APEXP Workflows where the ORG_ID Item Attribute has a value of 204. APINV Workflows do not have an Item Attribute ORG_ID and therefore cannot be accessed if this example is implemented.

Opening the 'Activity Statuses' screen from the 'Workflow Status Monitor' for one of these Workflows yields a screen similar to FIGURE 13.30. Note there is no Skip, Update Attributes, Rewind, Suspend Workflow, or Cancel Workflow button. Only the Retry button is available.

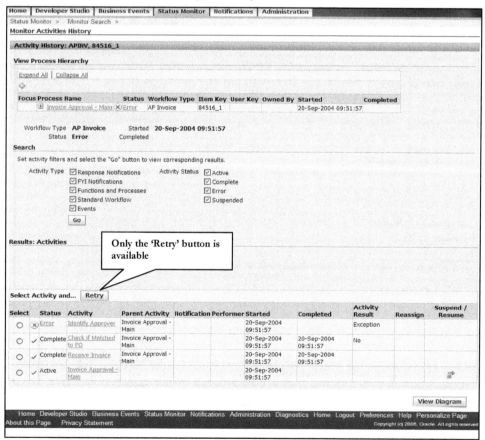

FIGURE 13.30

NEW LOOK FOR ACTIVITY HISTORY

11i.ATG_PF.H.delta.5 (Rollup 5) introduced some new features for the 'Activity History' screen. These new features are also in Release 12 regardless of the Rollup Pack applied. The first change is the addition of a section at the top of the screen that allows the Administrator to see all child Workflows and even to click into the 'Activity History' for these Workflows (see FIGURE 13.31). Click the + box next to the 'Process Name' to see any children Workflows. Double-click on the 'Process Name' to open the Activity History for that Process.

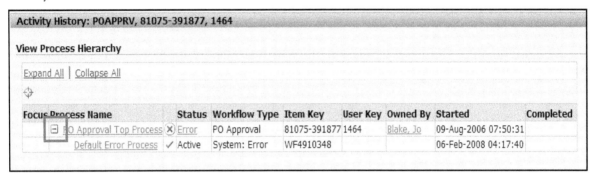

FIGURE 13.31

A new column, 'Notification', has been added to the bottom of the 'Activity History' screen. This allows the Administrator to open and view the Notification (and respond) without having to click the 'Activity' link, note the NOTIFICATION_ID and navigate to the 'Notification Search' screen. See FIGURE 13.32.

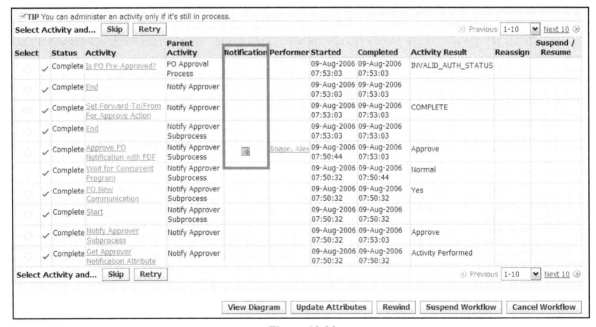

Figure 13.32

If you open the Notification, you can return to the 'Activity History' screen by clicking the 'Monitor Activities History' link at the top of the screen.

NOTIFICATION SEARCH SCREEN AVAILABLE FOR END USERS

Users have always had access to their Notifications through the 'Notification Worklist'. However this screen does not allow searching for specific Notifications. Now the 'Function Workflow Notification Search' (WF_WORKLIST_SEARCH) can be added to any menu. This screen is the same screen used by Administrators to search for Notifications. However when assigned to a non-Administration responsibility, this screen limits users to searching only for their own Notifications.

WORKFLOW MAILER NOW REQUIRED FOR ORACLE ALERT

As of Release 11i.ATG_PF.H.delta.4.(Rollup 4), the Workflow Mailer must be initiated in order to send Alerts or process responses from Oracle Alert. The Oracle Alert Response Processor can continue to be used to process responses for Alerts sent prior to upgrading to Release 11i.ATG_PF.H.delta.4 (Rollup 4).

WORKFLOW MAILER PARAMETER CHANGES

Changes instituted in Family Pack OWF.H and subsequent ATG_PF.H rollups have introduced issues. Some of the issues include accessing links to OA Framework pages, inability to read emails sent to SYSADMIN, and the Notification Mailer inexplicably refusing to send emails. This section will cover the MetaLink Doc. IDs that address these issues.

New Patches

MetaLink Doc. ID: 405970.1, *Oracle ATG Newsletter – December 2007, Volume 6* contains the latest recommended notes and actions for Workflow and other ATG products. This newsletter recommends that if 11i.ATG_PF.H.delta.5 (Rollup 5) has been installed, then the one-off patches 6412999 and 6441940 should be applied. These patches have not been superseded. Additionally there is a Java bug that prohibits saving the time Events should be scheduled. This bug is described in MetaLink Doc. ID: 463783.1, *Schedule Events Page Resets the Submit Time to 00 00*. This note recommends Patch 6399304.

For Release 12 users, you must have applied Patch 6435000, *12.0.4 Release update Pack (RUP4)* to receive the equivalent patches.

Setting the Workflow Mailer Framework User (and Other Selected Mailer Parameters)

There must be a user account and responsibility assigned to the Workflow Mailer so that the Notification Mailer may access the Applications. By default this user is SYSADMIN and the responsibility is 'System Administrator'. This user can be changed as long as:

- The user assigned is active and is either the Workflow Administrator or is assigned the responsibility assigned as the Workflow Administrator

- The responsibility assigned to the Workflow Mailer must match a responsibility assigned to this user; this responsibility does not have to be the responsibility assigned as the Workflow Administrator, but it must contain the Workflow Administrator menus

- The APPLICATION_ID assigned to the Workflow Mailer must be the same as that of the responsibility assigned to the Workflow Mailer

MetaLink Doc. ID: 344936.1, *Email Body Contain: ORA-20002: 3207: User 'SYSADMIN' does not have access to Notification* describes how to change this user, responsibility, and APPLICATION_ID. While we are navigating through the Notification Mailer parameter screens, we will make all the other required changes as well.

- First you need to obtain the USER_ID, RESPONSIBILITY_ID, and APPLICATION_ID to be used. To obtain the USER_ID, execute the following SQL. Substitute the desired user name for <name>.

```
SELECT user_id,user_name FROM fnd_user
 WHERE user_name = upper ('<name>');
```

- To obtain the RESPONSIBILITY_ID and APPLICATION_ID, execute the following SQL. Substitute the desired responsibility name for <resp_name>.

```
SELECT responsibility_id,application_id,responsibility_name
  FROM fnd_responsibility_tl
 WHERE upper(responsibility_name =  upper('<resp_name>')
   AND language = 'US';
```

- Now navigate to the 'Workflow Manager' page of Oracle Applications Manager (OAM). From the 'System Administrator' responsibility, the navigation path is Workflow → Oracle Applications Manager → Workflow Manager.

- In the Dashboard at the top of the page, click the icon to the right of 'Notification Mailers' (see FIGURE 13.33).

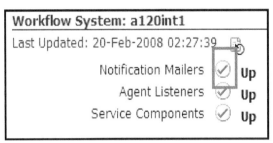

FIGURE 13.33

- If the status of the Workflow Notification Mailer is Running, select 'Stop' in the Actions box and click Go. Click the Browser Refresh Button until the status changes to 'User Deactivated'. Then click the 'Edit' button (see FIGURE 13.34).

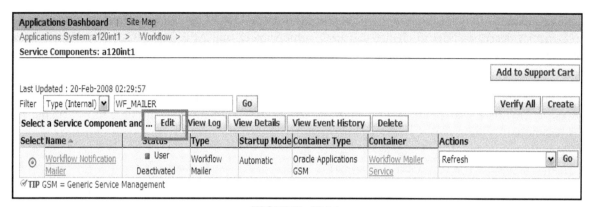

FIGURE 13.34

- Click the 'Advanced' button. Click the Next button until Step 2 of 8 appears. Per MetaLink Doc. IDs 422870.1, *Java Mailer not Removing Processed Emails from Inbox after Folder ATG.H Rup4*, 437986.1, *E-Mail Notifications Are Not Getting Processed, Remain Sitting In The Inbox*, 418077.1, *Workflow Notification Mailer Stops Processing*, and 332152.1, *OWF.H Diagnostics and Solutions*, the parameter Processor Close on Read Timeout should be checked (see FIGURE 13.35).

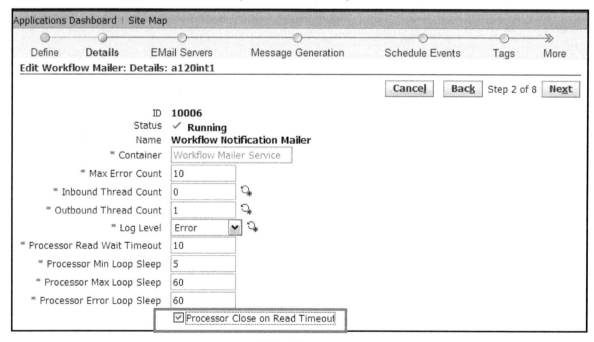

FIGURE 13.35

- Click the Next button so that Step 3 of 8 appears. Per MetaLink Doc. ID 422870.1, *Java Mailer not Removing Processed Emails from Inbox after Folder ATG.H Rup4*, ensure the 'Expunge Inbox on Close' box is checked (see FIGURE 13.36).

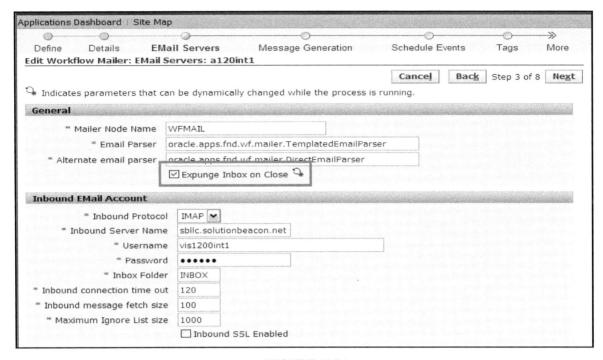

FIGURE 13.36

- Click the Next button so that Step 4 of 8 appears. Per MetaLink Doc. ID: 414376.1, *You Have Insufficient Privileges For The Current Operation On Reqapprv Notif*, set Framework URL Timeout to 120.

Set 'Framework User', 'Framework Responsibility', and 'Framework Application ID' to the values from the select statements run earlier in this section. The default values are 0 (SYSADMIN), 20420 (System Administrator), and 1 (System Administration). Remember, as long as SYSADMIN is not end-dated and the Workflow Administrator is set to SYSADMIN or to a responsibility and SYSADMIN is assigned this responsibility, these values may be left as is (see FIGURE 13.37).

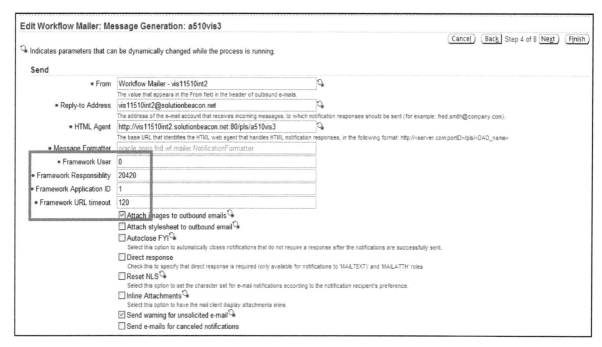

FIGURE 13.37

- Click the Next button so that Step 5 of 8 appears. The next section describes how to schedule Events so that the Notification Mailer will shutdown (briefly) and restart once per week. This step is not necessary unless your Applications run 24x7. If the database is shut down at least weekly, this shutdown also stops and restarts the Notification Mailer.

Schedule Startup and Shutdown of Mailer

The next steps are from MetaLink Doc. IDs 443643.1, *How To Automatically Restart the Workflow Mailer Processes Regularly* and 414376.1, *You Have Insufficient Privileges For The Current Operation On Reqapprv Notif.*

- Step 5 of 8 looks like FIGURE 13.38 (no Events may be scheduled, this is OK).

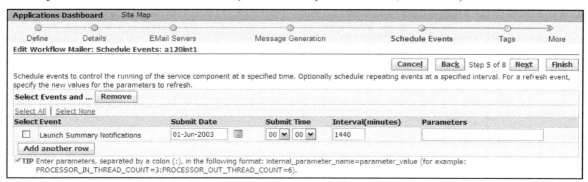

FIGURE 13.38

- Click 'Add another row'. For the 'Event', select 'Stop'. Enter the date and time you wish the Notification Mailer to stop. For example, to have the Notification Mailer stop every Friday at 11:00 PM, enter the next Friday and select the time as 23:00.

Click 'Add another row'. For the 'Event', select 'Start'. Enter the date and time you wish the Notification Mailer to start. Allow at least 5 minutes between the stop and start times. For example, to have the Notification Mailer re-start every Friday at 11:15 PM, enter the next Friday and select the time as 23:15.

The value entered for 'Interval\Resubmit' is in minutes. 10080 is equivalent to 7 days (see FIGURE 13.39).

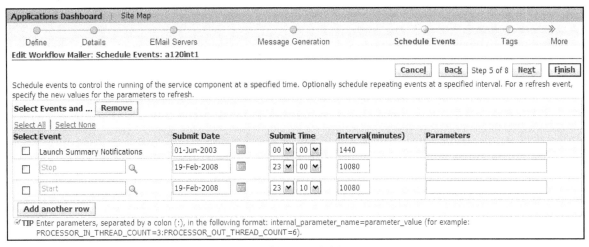

FIGURE 13.39

- Click the 'Finish' button. This takes you a page that displays the current settings. Scroll down to review the Scheduled Events. If the 'Submit Time' shows all zeros, you are experiencing the error described in MetaLink Doc. ID 463783.1, *Schedule Events Page Resets the Submit Time to 00 00* (see FIGURE 13.40). This note recommends Patch 6399304. Apply this patch, then re-enter the time for the Events.

Note that if you are running Release 12, the equivalent patch is included in 11i.ATG_PF.H.delta.4 (Rollup 4).

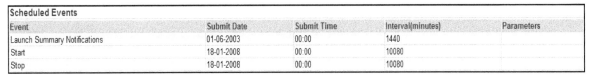

FIGURE 13.40

- If Patch 6399304 (Release 11*i*) or 6435000 (Release 12) has been applied, then the Scheduled Events section of screen 8 of 8 should look similar to FIGURE 13.41. Notice that 'Submit Time' matches the time entered in screen 5 of 8 (see FIGURE 13.39).

Scheduled Events				
Event	Submit Date	Submit Time	Interval(minutes)	Parameters
Launch Summary Notifications	01-Jun-2003	00:00	1440	
Start	19-Feb-2008	23:10	10080	
Stop	19-Feb-2008	23:00	10080	

FIGURE 13.41

- Click the 'Finish' button. This returns you to the first 'Edit' page. Do not click Apply. This might automatically restart the Notification Mailer. If this happens, the 'Submit Time' is reset to the current time. Instead, click on the Service Components link at the top of the page. This will return you to the page where the Notification Mailer can be re-started.

- Before restarting the Notification Mailer, perform the following query:

```
SELECT * FROM fnd_svc_comp_requests_v;
```

FND_SVC_COMP_REQUESTS_V is a view is across the table FND_SVC_COMP_REQUESTS and the synonym WF_ALL_JOBS. WF_ALL_JOBS is a synonym for SYS.USER_JOBS, which is a view across DBA_JOBS, which is a view across SYS.JOB$.

Based on the 'Scheduled Events' example in FIGURE 13.41, the query returned the results shown in FIGURE 13.42:

COMPONENT_ID	COMPONENT_REQUEST_ID	CREATED_BY	EVENT_DATE	EVENT_DISPLAY_NAME	EVENT_FREQUENCY
10006	10000	1	6/1/2003	Launch Summary Notifications	1440
10006	10043	0	2/19/2008 23:00	Stop	10080
10006	10044	0	2/19/2008 23:10	Start	10080

EVENT_NAME	EVENT_PARAMS	FAILURES	INTERVAL	JOB_ID
oracle.apps.fnd.wf.mailer.Mailer.notification.summary	null	0	SYSDATE + (1440/(24*60))	685
oracle.apps.fnd.cp.gsc.SvcComponent.stop	null	null	SYSDATE + (10080/(24*60))	22390
oracle.apps.fnd.cp.gsc.SvcComponent.start	null	null	SYSDATE + (10080/(24*60))	22391

LAST_DATE	NEXT_DATE	OBJECT_VERSION_NUMBER	REQUESTED_BY_USER	THIS_DATE
2/19/2008 20:44	2/20/2008 20:44	18	null	null
null	2/19/2008 23:00	1	SYSADMIN	null
null	2/19/2008 23:10	1	SYSADMIN	null

WHAT
FND_SVC_COMPONENT.EXECUTE_REQUEST (p_component_request_id => 10000);
FND_SVC_COMPONENT.EXECUTE_REQUEST (p_component_request_id => 10043);
FND_SVC_COMPONENT.EXECUTE_REQUEST (p_component_request_id => 10044);

FIGURE 13.42

- Check the values in NEXT_DATE. If they are missing the time entered (see FIGURE 13.43), verify that Patch 6399304 (Release 11i) or 6435000 (Release 12) is applied. Apply the patches, delete the Events and re-enter them.

LAST_DATE	NEXT_DATE	OBJECT_VERSION_NUMBER	REQUESTED_BY_USER	THIS_DATE
	1/18/2008	2	SYSADMIN	
	1/18/2008	2	SYSADMIN	
1/16/2008 13:54	1/17/2008 13:54	30		

FIGURE 13. 43

- Return to OAM and in the 'Action' column, select 'Start' then click Go. A page displays stating 'Action Start has been performed on Workflow Notification Mailer'. Click OK. OAM returns to the Service Components page. Click the Browser 'Refresh' button until the status changes to 'Running'.

If Apply was clicked, or the changes were made while the Notification Mailer was still running, the Notification Mailer will restart automatically and execute the new Events. Unfortunately, this will also reset 'Next Time' for both Events. So after the Notification Mailer has re-started, perform the query again on FND_SVC_COMP_REQUESTS_V. If the time changed, stop the Notification Mailer, navigate to page 5, delete the Events and re-enter them. This time remember not to click Apply. Restart the Notification Mailer.

SET PROFILE OPTION VALUES FOR THE USER ASSIGNED TO THE MAILER

Several Profile Options govern how long a user may stay logged into the applications. For security reasons, these Profile Options are set so that inactive sessions will time out and so that regardless of the activity, users are required to periodically log in.

However, when the session expires for the user assigned to the Notification Mailer, then Notification recipients cannot open links attached to framework regions. This problem is described in MetaLink Doc. ID: 414376.1, *You Have Insufficient Privileges For The Current Operation On Reqapprv Notif*. The recommendation is to set the following Profile Options at the user level for the user assigned as the Notification Mailer framework user:

- **ICX:Session Timeout** – 12000

- **ICX: Limit connect** – 1000000

- **ICX: Limit time** – 192

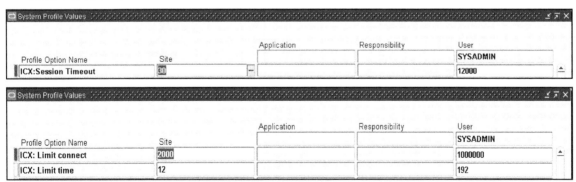

FIGURE 13. 44

RESPONSE VALUE DELIMITER

Another new feature introduced in 11i.ATG_PF.H.delta.5 (Rollup 5) is the ability to specify the delimiter character for email responses. By default the Notification Mailer uses the single apostrophe (') as the delimiter. This has caused issues with some Blackberries and also causes comments containing a single apostrophe (such as using the word "don't") to be truncated. The following choices are supported:

- **DEFAULT** – single quote (')

- **APOS** – same as DEFAULT (')

- **QUOTE** – double quote (")

- **BRACKET** – [for opening and] for closing

Note that Microsoft Outlook Express does not support QUOTE. Presently the only way to set this parameter globally is via SQL*Plus. Use the following query to find the parameter_id for the parameter HTML_DELIMETER:

```
SELECT c.parameter_id, c.parameter_name,a.parameter_value
  FROM fnd_svc_comp_param_vals a, fnd_svc_comp_params_vl c
 WHERE c.parameter_id = a.parameter_id
   AND c.parameter_name = 'HTML_DELIMITER';
```

This query returns the component_id for the Notification Mailer:

```
SELECT component_id, component_name FROM fnd_svc_components c
 WHERE component_name LIKE 'Workflow Notification Mailer'
 ORDER BY component_id;
```

Then run afsvcpup.sql. Enter the component_id, parameter_id from the above queries and the desired value for parameter_value. The parameter value MUST match one of the four delimiter values above. The value is all uppercase.

If you only wish to override this value for specific Notifications, add the Message Attribute #WFM_HTML_DELIMETER and set it to the desired parameter value.

ADDITIONAL MAILER FEATURES

11i.ATG_PF.H.delta.5 (Rollup 5) also introduced some additional Workflow Mailer features. Additional Mailers can be defined and those Mailers can be dedicated to specific Item Types or even specific Messages from a specific Item Type. On page 1 of Advanced Setups enter the Item Type or the Item Type and Message name combination in the 'Correlation ID' field (see FIGURE 13.45) . The format of the entry is:

```
<item_type_internal_name>
<item_type_internal_name>:<Message_internal_name>
```

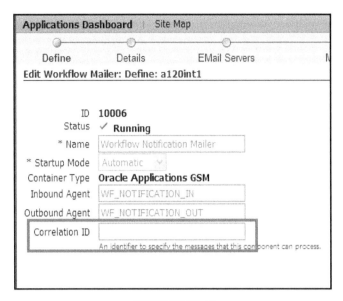

FIGURE 13.45

Another new feature is the Notification to SYSADMIN when email Notifications fail. In addition to the Notification to SYSADMIN, the Notification Mailer will now set the recipient's Mailer preference to DISABLED and the MAIL_STATUS of the Notification to FAILED. Once the cause of the failed Notification is diagnosed (usually a missing or invalid email address), the recipient's Mailer preference can be reset and the Notification re-sent through the Concurrent Program 'Resend Failed Workflow Notifications'.

Unfortunately, resetting an individual's Mailer preference is one of the few things the Workflow Administrator cannot do through any of the administration screens. Individual Mailer preferences are stored in the table FND_USER_PREFERENCES where MODULE_NAME = 'WF' and PREFERENCE_NAME = 'MAILTYPE' and USER_NAME = <user name>. To reset an individual's Mailer preference value to the global Mailer value, use the following SQL:

```
UPDATE fnd_user_preferences fup
   SET fup.preference_value =
           (SELECT fup1.preference_value FROM fnd_user_preferences fup1
              WHERE fup1.user_name = '-WF_DEFAULT-'
                AND fup1.module_name = 'WF'
                AND fup1.preference_name = 'MAILTYPE')
   WHERE fup.module_name = 'WF'
     AND fup.preference_name = 'MAILTYPE'
     AND fup.user_name = '<username>';
```

WORKFLOW DIRECTORY SERVICES USER/ROLE VALIDATION

This program was delivered via the one-off Patch 4719658 and bundled into 11i.ATG_PF.H.delta.5 (Rollup 5). The program will repair any corrupt data in WF_LOCAL_ROLES and WF_LOCAL_USER_ROLES. MetaLink Doc. ID: 418765.1, *What parameters Should be Passed for Workflow Directory Services User/Role Validation Program*, recommends running the program twice. The first run should set the parameter 'Fix dangling user/roles to Yes and Add missing user/role assignments to No'. The second run should reverse the values for these parameters.

If the parameter 'Update WHO columns in WF tables' is set to 'Yes', any Roles changed will reflect 'Last Updated By' as the person running the program and 'Last Update Date' as the execution date of this program.

OTHER DIRECTORY SERVICES NOTES

Numerous issues have been noted with changing responsibilities assigned to users and the changes not being reflected in the user's list of responsibilities without running the above program or bouncing Apache. Oracle now states in MetaLink Doc. ID: 433473.1, *Unable to Activate a User Responsibility Assignment that Existed Before Upgrade,* that this is due to an error in the AP_WEB_PROXY_ASSIGN_PKG.proxy_assignments Subscription for the oracle.apps.fnd.wf.ds.userRole.updated Event. According to this Doc. ID, this Subscription should be disabled.

MetaLink Doc. ID: 406892.1, *Missing/Corrupted User-Role Responsibilities,* recommends several patches (which are included in 11i.ATG_PF.H.delta.5 (Rollup 5) and also recommends scheduling the following Concurrent Programs (in the following order):

* Sync responsibility Role data into the WF table.

* Synchronize WF LOCAL tables

* Workflow Directory Services User/Role Validation

ADDITIONAL SECURITY FEATURE FOR GRANT WORKLIST

Grant Worklist has always been part of Release 11*i* and Solution Beacon has recommended using this feature to control access to the SYSADMIN's Notifications and to grant one's supervisor access to Notifications.

In 11i.ATG_PF.H.delta.5 (Rollup 5), Oracle added the ability to restrict the grant by Item Type. To restrict by Item Type, select 'Selected Item Types', then highlight the desired 'Item Type(s) and click the 'Move' link. Access can be revoked by clicking the 'Remove' link (see FIGURE 13.46).

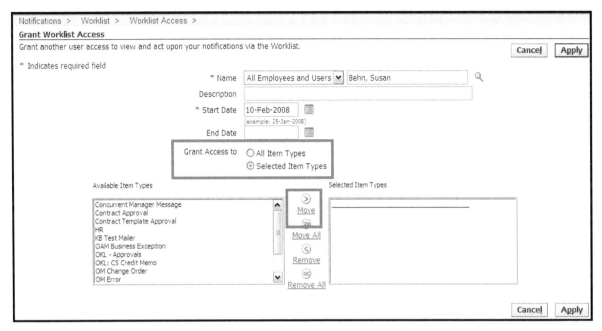

FIGURE 13. 46

WORKLIST FLEXFIELDS

This feature was actually introduced in 11i.ATG_PF.H.delta.3 (Rollup 3), but it has not been widely used or understood. Worklist Flexfields allow the display of Message Attributes that appear in the body of a Message to be seen in the Notification Worklist without opening the Notification.

Once set up, the data is stored in WF_NOTIFICATIONS and available for display from the 'Personal Worklist'. Oracle provides five Date, Form, URL, or Number fields and ten Text fields. The same number of Protected fields are reserved for Oracle use.

Since Message Attributes are specific to a particular Message, this functionality is best used when creating a Worklist View for a specific Workflow.

Assign Personal Worklist to a Menu

Since Worklist Flexfields are only available from the Personal Worklist, the first step is to assign this Function to any desired menus (see FIGURE 13.47).

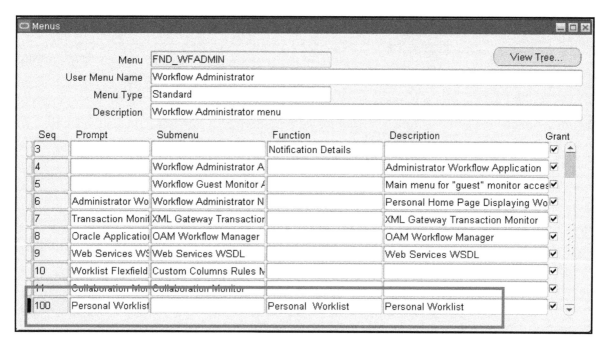

FIGURE 13. 47

Oracle documentation says you must also set the Profile Option Personalize Self_service Defn to Yes. This is not true.

Create Flexfield Rule(s)

The next step involves assigning the Message Attributes to the special WF_NOTIFICATION fields. This functionality is available from the Workflow Administration menus. The navigation is Worklist Flexfields Rules → Worklist Flexfields Rules. When the 'Search' screen opens, click the 'Create Rule' button (see FIGURE 13.48).

The Rule shown in FIGURE 13.48 will be used to add the errored Item Type or Event, Error Message and Error Stack from the Workflow WFERROR. The Workflow Administrator will then be able to see which Workflow errored and the complete Error Message and Error Stack when viewing the Notification Worklist for this Workflow. If the 'Export' button has been enabled for the 'Personal Worklist' screen, the information can even be exported to Excel.

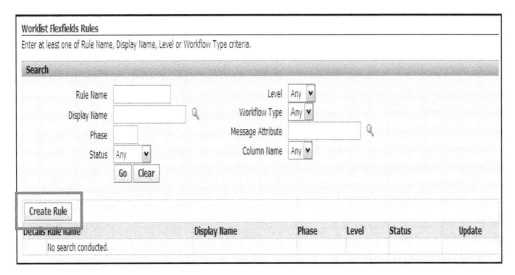

FIGURE 13.48

Enter the following information:

- **Rule Name (Required)** – enter a name for the Rule, no restrictions on characters or case

- **Display Name (Required)** – enter a Display Name for the Rule

- **Status (Required with default)** – defaults to Enabled

- **Phase (Required)** – must be a number 100 or higher.

- **Description (Optional)** – description of the Rule

- **Owner Name (Required)** – the Display Name of an installed application, must match DISPLAY_NAME in FND_APPLICATION_TL

- **Owner Tag (Required)** – the application short name for the application listed in Owner Name, must match APPLICATION_SHORT_NAME in FND_APPLICATION

Note that the Level defaults to User and cannot be changed (see FIGURE 13.49).

THE ABCS OF WORKFLOW

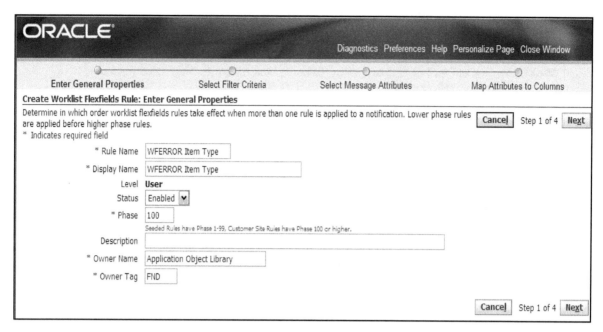

FIGURE 13. 49

Select the Workflow that owns the Message Attributes using the Workflow's DISPLAY_NAME (see FIGURE 13.50). Click Next.

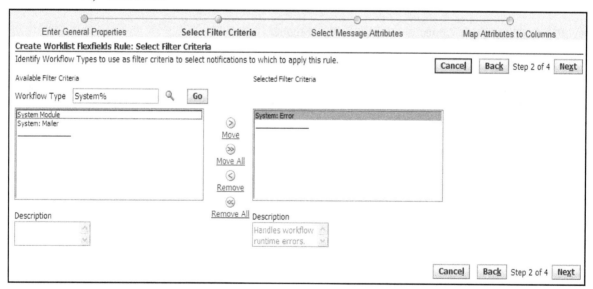

FIGURE 13. 50

Select the desired Message Attributes. The List of Values will be limited to Messages Attributes from the Workflows selected in Step 2 (see FIGURE 13.51). Click Next.

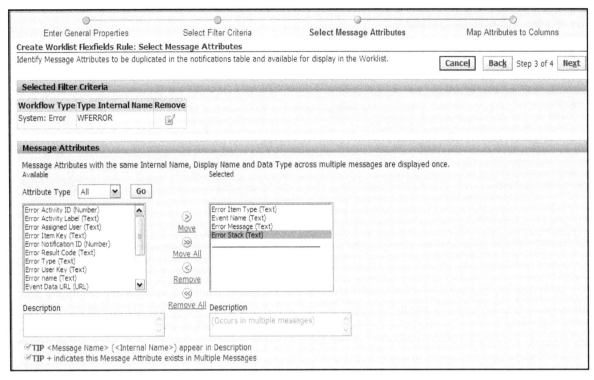

FIGURE 13. 51

The selected Attributes need to be assigned to Flexfield Columns. Remember that you are limited to five Numeric, Date, URL, or Form Attributes and ten Text Attributes (see FIGURE 13.52).

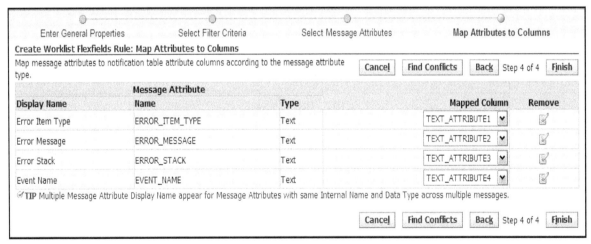

FIGURE 13. 52

After mapping the Attributes, click the 'Find Conflicts' button. This will identify if multiple Message Attributes have been assigned to the same Flexfield Attribute. Conflicts are OK as long as the Message Attributes belong to different Workflows. Click 'Finish'.

Create Worklist View

Now that the Personal Worklist Function is assigned and the Message Attributes are assigned to a Workflow Flexfield, the view to display these Attributes must be created. Open the 'Personal Worklist' form and click 'Personalize' (see FIGURE 13.53).

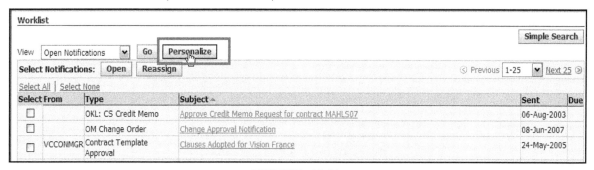

FIGURE 13.53

Either select an existing view and click 'Duplicate' or click 'Create View'. For our example, since Messages from WFERROR require a response, we will duplicate the 'To Do Notifications' view (see FIGURE 13.54).

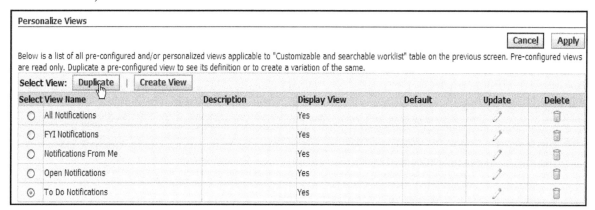

FIGURE 13.54

Enter a name for the View, select the number of rows to display (25 is the highest value allowed), click whether you want this view to be the view used when Personal Worklist is opened, or (optionally) give the view a Description.

Refer back to the mapping of Message Attributes to Flexfield Columns and add the appropriate Flexfield Columns by highlighting the fields in 'Available Columns' and using the 'Move' link or arrow to move these fields to 'Columns Displayed'. Highlight any undesired fields in 'Columns Displayed' and use the 'Remove' link or arrow to remove these fields from the view. Use the 'Rename Columns / Totaling' button to rename the columns from 'Text Attribute<n>' to a name that describes the mapped Message Attribute. Use the re-order arrows to arrange the order of the selected fields (see FIGURES 13.55 and 13.56).

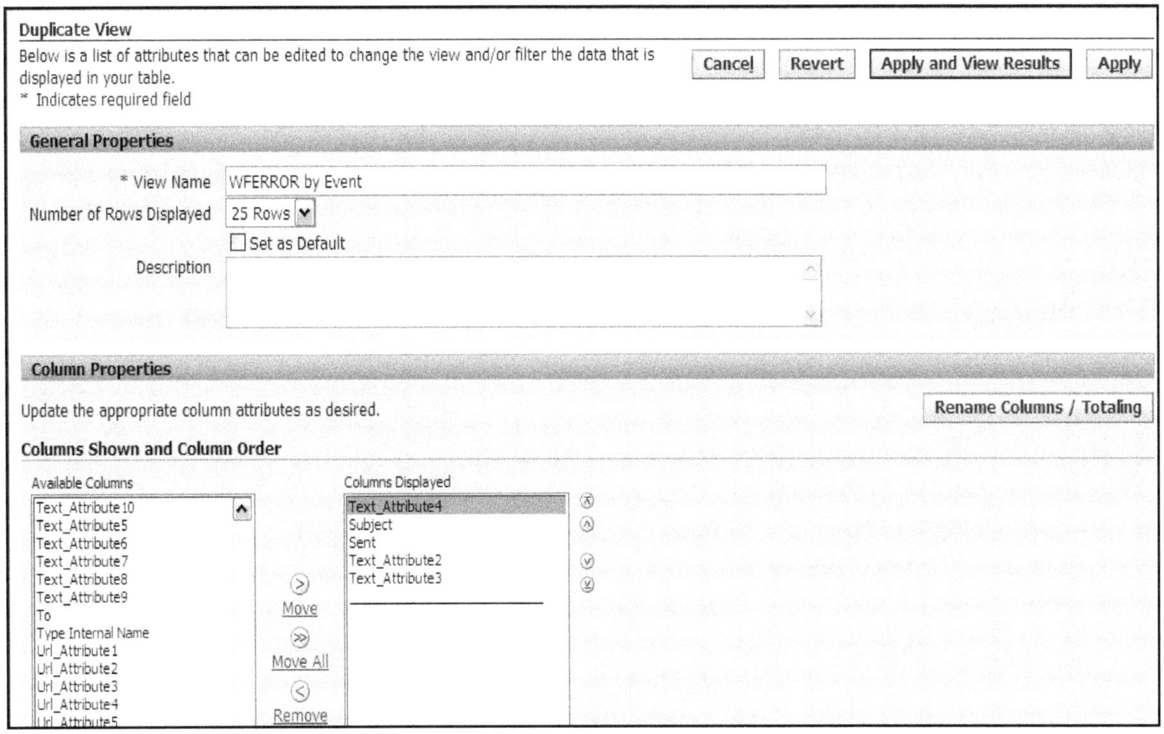

Duplicate View

Below is a list of attributes that can be edited to change the view and/or filter the data that is displayed in your table.
* Indicates required field

| Cancel | Revert | Apply and View Results | Apply |

General Properties

* View Name	WFERROR by Event
Number of Rows Displayed	25 Rows ⌄
	☐ Set as Default
Description	

Column Properties

Update the appropriate column attributes as desired.

| Rename Columns / Totaling |

Columns Shown and Column Order

Available Columns

```
Text_Attribute10
Text_Attribute5
Text_Attribute6
Text_Attribute7
Text_Attribute8
Text_Attribute9
To
Type Internal Name
Url_Attribute1
Url_Attribute2
Url_Attribute3
Url_Attribute4
Url_Attribute5
```

⊘ Move
⊛ Move All
⊘ Remove

Columns Displayed

```
Text_Attribute4
Subject
Sent
Text_Attribute2
Text_Attribute3
```

FIGURE 13.55

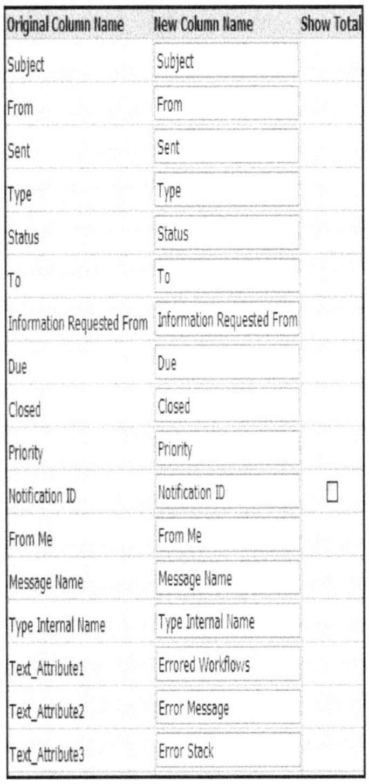

Original Column Name	New Column Name	Show Total
Subject	Subject	
From	From	
Sent	Sent	
Type	Type	
Status	Status	
To	To	
Information Requested From	Information Requested From	
Due	Due	
Closed	Closed	
Priority	Priority	
Notification ID	Notification ID	☐
From Me	From Me	
Message Name	Message Name	
Type Internal Name	Type Internal Name	
Text_Attribute1	Errored Workflows	
Text_Attribute2	Error Message	
Text_Attribute3	Error Stack	

FIGURE 13.56

Move to the bottom of the form to set the 'Sort Settings' and 'Filter Criteria'. For our example, two views were created, 'WFERROR by Item Type' and 'WFERROR by Event'. FIGURE 13.57 shows the sort settings and filter criteria for 'by Item Type' and FIGURE 13.58 shows the settings for 'by Event'.

Be aware that you can later update any of these settings except the filter criteria. New criteria can be added, existing criteria can be changed, but there is no way to remove criteria except by deleting the view and recreating it.

When all the data is entered, click the Apply and 'View Results' button to see the resulting view of Notifications.

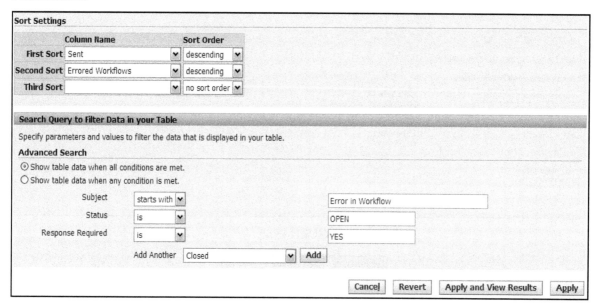

FIGURE 13.57

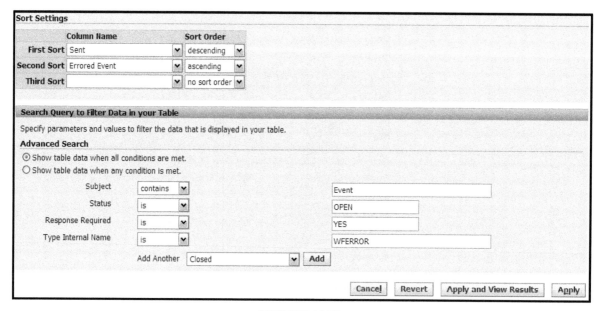

FIGURE 13.58

FIGURE 13.59 shows the resulting view for errors from Item Types.

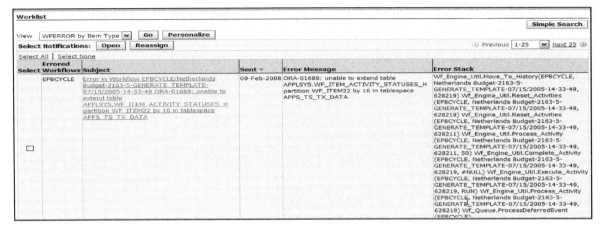

FIGURE 13.59

FIGURE 13.60 shows the resulting view for errors from Events.

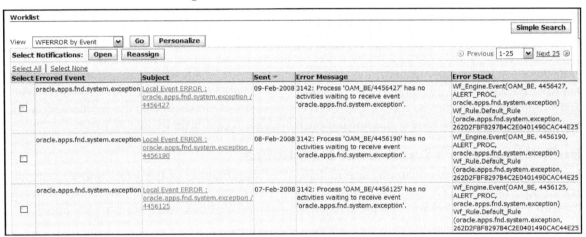

FIGURE 13.60

It should be noted that Error Message and Error Stack contain carriage returns, so when exported to Excel, these columns spill over to other lines. The following queries will display the same information with the carriage returns removed.

WFERROR – Errored Item Type Query

```
SELECT Wf_Notification.GetAttrText(notification_id,
        'ERROR_ITEM_TYPE') errored_workflow
    ,Wf_Notification.GetAttrText(notification_id,
        'ERROR_ACTIVITY_LABEL') errored_activity
    ,begin_date sent
    ,REPLACE (subject, CHR (10), '; ') subject
    ,REPLACE (Wf_Notification.GetAttrText
        (notification_id, 'ERROR_MESSAGE')
        , CHR (10), '; ') error_message
    ,REPLACE (Wf_Notification.GetAttrText
```

```
            (notification_id, 'ERROR_STACK')
            , CHR (10), '; ') error_stack
     FROM wf_notifications
    WHERE MESSAGE_TYPE = 'WFERROR' AND message_name = 'RESET_ERROR_MESSAGE'
      AND status = 'OPEN'
  ORDER BY 1 ASC, 2 ASC, 3 DESC;
```

WFERROR – Errored Event Query

```
  SELECT   Wf_Notification.GetAttrText(notification_id,
              'EVENT_NAME') error_event
          ,Wf_Notification.GetAttrText(notification_id,
              'EVENT_KEY') event_key
          ,begin_date sent
          ,REPLACE (Wf_Notification.GetAttrText
              (notification_id,'ERROR_MESSAGE')
              , CHR (10), '; ')error_message
          ,REPLACE (Wf_Notification.GetAttrText
              (notification_id,'ERROR_STACK')
              , CHR (10), '; ') error_stack
     FROM wf_notifications
    WHERE MESSAGE_TYPE = 'WFERROR' AND message_name = 'DEFAULT_EVENT_ERROR'
  ORDER BY 1 ASC, 3 DESC;
```

TWO IMPORTANT ONE-OFF PATCHES

Both these patches require a password to download the patch. If the described functionality is desired, and you have applied the prerequisite rollup, then file a Service Request (SR) with Oracle Support to get a password. Solution Beacon has applied and tested the patches and can testify that the functionality works as described below. At the time of this publication, there was no equivalent Release 12 patch.

Bulk Close of FYI and Bulk Response

Patch 6722406 enables the ability to close multiple 'FYI' Notifications at the same time. Prior to this patch, 'Bulk Close of FYI' has been limited to the 'Personal Worklist'. Now it can be used from the standard 'Notification Worklist'. This patch requires that 11i.ATG_PF.H.delta.6 (Rollup 6) be applied.

To close multiple 'FYI' Notifications, the Notifications must be open and must not require a response. To ensure that this requirement is met, use the view 'FYI Notifications'. Click the Select button next to each 'Notification', then click the Close button. A confirmation page appears. Click Apply. FIGURE 13.61 shows the selection of the Notifications and FIGURE 13.62 shows the confirmation page.

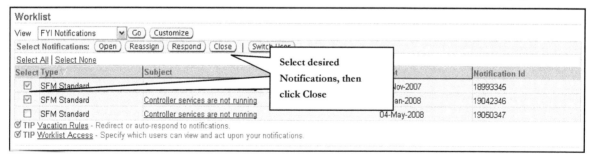

FIGURE 13. 61

FIGURE 13. 62

In order to respond to multiple Notifications with a single response, the Notifications must be open and must originate from the same node in the workflow. For example, you can use this feature to approve multiple requisitions simultaneously, but not a mix of requisitions and expense reports. This feature is enabled through the Profile Option 'WF: Enable Bulk Notification Response'. If this Profile Option is set to Yes, then the Respond button is added to the Notification Worklist. Click the Select button next to each Notification then click the Respond button. A new page opens with all the selected Notifications and a single set of Response buttons. Clicking the desired response answers all shown Notifications. FIGURE 13.63 shows the new Respond to Notifications as Group page.

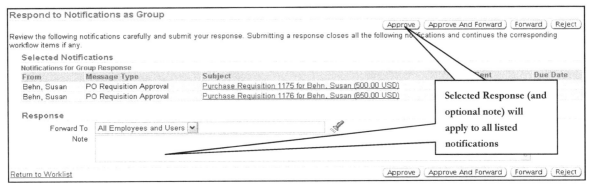

FIGURE 13. 63

Blackberry HTML Response Fix

Patch 6802716 enables the ability to answer Notifications sent to a Blackberry using the Notification preference 'HTML Mail' or 'HTML Mail with Attachments'. This patch requires that 11i.ATG_PF.H.delta.5 (Rollup 5) be applied. The patch replaces the spaces in the HTML code with %20. Prior to this patch, highlighting the HTML response only transmitted through the first space and so the response was incomplete. The procedure still requires a couple of extra steps. Open the message and scroll down so that the HTML under the desired response is highlighted and then click the trackball. Click the trackball again to accept the response. This opens a response email. Click the trackball, highlight Send, then click. FIGURE 13.64 shows the various steps.

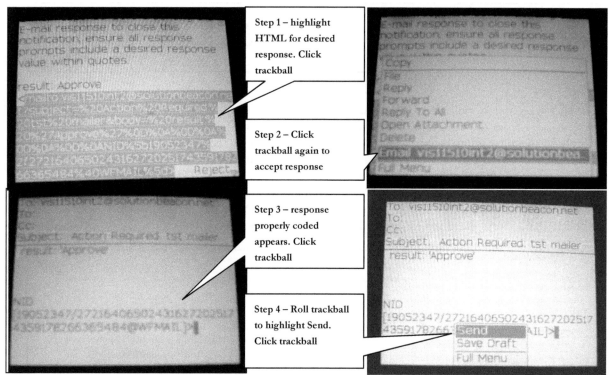

FIGURE 13. 64

SUMMARY AND WHAT'S NEXT

We started this chapter talking about the need to keep current with patches. The myriad changes covered in this chapter show that Workflow continues to be enhanced both in Release 11*i* and Release 12. The 11*i*.ATG_PF.H RUPs mirror the functionality added to Release 12. However, to gain the new functionality, one must apply the current patches. This puts the onus on Workflow Administrators to keep current with the notes published in MetaLink, discern what needs to be applied, and to test the results.

One of the most exciting new features is the Approvals Management Engine (AME). The next chapter will discuss how to set up and use AME and provide some example Workflows where it can be utilized.

Approvals Management Engine (AME)

Oracle defines Oracle Approvals Management, otherwise referred to as AME, as a self-service application that allows users to define business rules that govern the Approval Process for transactions in Oracle Applications integrated with AME. In other words, AME provides the opportunity for an organization to transform their unique business cases into Approval Routing Rules for a particular transaction.

This chapter discusses how AME can be utilized to create both simple and complex business cases involving the approval of Oracle Payables (AP) Invoices, Purchase Requisitions (PO) and Human Resources (HR). It also discusses the basic components of the AME application (i.e., Attributes, Conditions and Rules) that are required as part of AME setup for any integrating application. Finally, it discusses how Workflow has been integrated with AME to drive invoice approval routings. The Oracle Approvals Management Implementation Guide provides more in-depth information on the AME engine and other advanced features that are outside the scope of this chapter.

This chapter assumes that the current environment is using E-Business Suite Release 12.0.4 or Release 11.5.10.2 with Oracle Approvals Management patched to Mini-Pack B.2 (11i.AME.B.2 – Patch 57085760).

AME BASICS

AME is used to develop specific business cases within the framework of the application to facilitate how a transaction will be routed to required approvers. An organization's business cases involving approval routing are translated into Rules within AME. Sometimes, these Rules are simple. For example, a simple Rule regarding approval of AP invoices may require any invoice greater than $100 to be approved by the requester's immediate manager or supervisor. Many organizations have more complex Rules regarding approval routings pertaining to AP invoices. An example of a complex approval routing requirement could be an organization requiring any invoice greater than $10,000 that is matched to a purchase order including computer equipment items to be approved by the IT Manager, along with the requester's two immediate supervisors. AME's flexibility allows this type of unique approval requirement to be developed. Whenever Approval Rules are developed in AME for an application such as Payables, it identifies all of the necessary approvers for a given transaction (invoice) and notifies them through Workflow Notifications.

AME is integrated with multiple business applications and is expanding with each subsequent release of Oracle Applications. APIs are also provided that allow AME to integrate with third party applications.

Advantages of AME

The AME application provides many advantages for the business user looking to develop Approval Rules for various applications. The most obvious advantage of an automated Approval Process is to speed up the approval cycle. Another advantage is that business rules can be set up in AME without writing additional programming code or customizing the application. Another advantage of AME is that the approval routing can leverage some of the hierarchical structures that already exist in Oracle Applications, such as HR employee/supervisor or HR position hierarchies. Additionally, if an organization requires that an invoice be routed to a particular individual or group of individuals, AME provides the business user the ability to set up their own specific approval routing hierarchies.

One of the unique features of AME is its ability to respond to any changes that may occur in an organization during the transaction's Approval Process. The changes can include organizational hierarchy changes (i.e., supervisor/manager), modifications to an AME Rule or even changes to the values of the current transaction.

How does AME do this? Whenever an identified approver for a transaction responds with an approval, AME constructs a new approver list based on the most current Conditions in the application, including the current AME Rules for the transaction. This includes the current values of the application and any changes to the approval hierarchy upon which the Transaction Rule is based. For example, if the original Rule in AME requires an invoice greater than $1,000 to be approved by the requester's two immediate supervisors, the approval for an invoice is initially sent to the most immediate supervisor. If a new Rule is created prior to the final approval by the second supervisor that requires the review and approval by a tax accountant, a new approver list is built that includes the tax accountant approver after the first approval.

AME Components

In order for a business user to develop business scenarios in AME that determine approval routings, it is important to understand the different setup components within AME. These components often must be created or modified as part of the development of business cases. A brief description of these components will be discussed in the next several sections.

Transaction Types

A Transaction Type describes the transaction for which AME Approval Routing Rules will be based. This can include Oracle Applications transactions such as purchase requisitions, credit limits or salary changes. Oracle provides many seeded Transaction Types to satisfy many of the common transactions that are created within a particular E-Business module. Since the Transaction Type represents a given transaction occurrence, one application can have several defined Transaction Types in AME. For example, the Payables application comes seeded with three Transaction Types; Payables Invoice Approval, OIE Expense Reports and Payables Holds Resolution. These Transaction Types can be configured to control approval routing for Payables invoices, Payables expense reports and release of invoice holds respectively.

Business users that want to integrate custom applications with AME can create new Transaction Types. Some instances necessitate the creation of a new Transaction Type such as for *i*Recruitment Vacancy Approval where Oracle actually recommends creating a new Transaction Type if the user chooses not to use the available seeded Rules. The difference in this case is that the Vacancy Approval Process is already integrated with AME and the Transaction Type name is a parameter. Any decision to integrate AME and a custom application hinges upon whether or not the custom application can recognize AME Approver

Type Return Values. In Release 11*i*, the seeded Approver Types in the AME application only return either the ID of an Oracle Applications user, or the ID of an HR employee (represented by USER_ID and PERSON_ID respectively). In Release 12, the HR Position is also a valid approver type. As long as the custom application can identify either ID, the integration should behave the same as it does with the E-Business module integration. Creation of a new Transaction Type can only be accessed from the 'Approvals Management Administrator' responsibility (which will be discussed later in this chapter). Transaction Types can be thought of as AME's cornerstone component, since all other component setups and/or configurations are based on a specific Transaction Type.

Configuration Variables

Configuration Variables are system parameters that determine the runtime behavior of AME. The value of a Configuration Variable can dictate how AME and the calling application's Workflow interact with one another during the Approval Process. This interaction includes the initial point when AME attempts to build an approver list, or could be after an individual responds to an approval Notification and any time in between. Configuration Variables help to determine runtime behavior such as whether AME responds to 'FYI' Notifications, how often duplicate approvers should appear in an approver list, or who to notify when an AME error occurs. A set number of Configuration Variables in AME are seeded with default values; however, they can be configured by Transaction Type to override the default value. FIGURE 14.1 shows the 'Configuration Variables' page in AME.

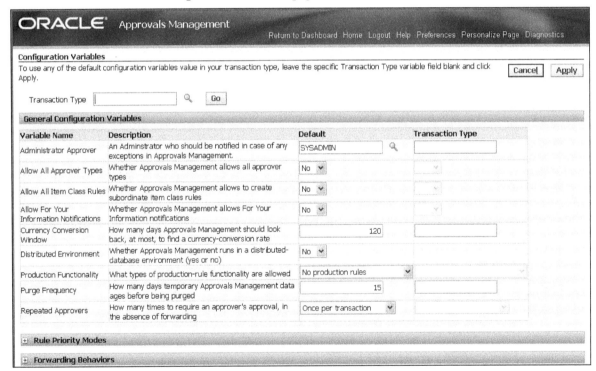

FIGURE 14.1

The following gives a brief description of the seeded Configuration Variables.

- **Administrator Approver** – identifies the Oracle user account notified if an error occurs while AME attempts to generate an approver list.

- **Allow All Approver Types** – indicates (either with 'Yes' or 'No') whether or not all Approver Types are available to the Transaction Type when creating Rules and determining recipients of Approval Notifications. An Approver Type defines the type of entity that can receive Notifications for approval. AME comes seeded with two Approver Types in 11*i*: 'FND user' and 'HR employees' plus 'HR Positions' in Release 12.

- **Allow All Item Class Rules** – indicates (either with 'Yes' or 'No') whether Rules can be created for a Transaction Type at the transaction's header (parent) level only or also at the subordinate (child) level.

- **Allow For Your Information Notifications** – indicates (either with 'Yes' or 'No') whether AME recognizes 'FYI' Notifications generated by a Transaction Type.

- **Currency Conversion Window** – a numeric value that indicates the maximum number of days in the past AME should look for a currency conversion rate. When a Currency Attribute is defined, AME uses a user-supplied currency rate to retrieve the value of the Attribute. When the Attribute is associated with a Condition, AME has to determine whether the Condition is true or false by finding the current or any previous currency rates that might impact the result.

- **Distributed Environment** – indicates (either with 'Yes' or 'No') whether AME is currently run in a distributed database environment. This variable is important because it impacts how AME logs exceptions. In a non-distributed environment, AME can create its own internal log as well as update Workflow logs to indicate an error has occurred. However, in a distributed environment, AME cannot create its own internal log. Therefore, exceptions can only be viewed by querying Workflow directly, which in turn could impact performance.

- **Production Functionality** – indicates which kinds of Productions are allowed within a given Transaction Type. Productions assign a value to a variable name. The possible values are 'All production rules', 'Per-approver production rules', 'No production rules', or 'Per-item production rules'.

- **Purge Frequency** – a numeric value that determines how long AME should save temporary data in its database tables. During the process of generating approver lists for transactions, AME creates temporary records in multiple tables of its schema. The records are updated whenever a user responds to an approval Notification. AME uses this data to determine where it is in the approval stage of a single transaction. When the data is purged, the Approval Process in starts over. It is important to assess the average amount of time (days) that a typical AME transaction will take to receive all necessary approvals. This variable should be set high enough to ensure that all required approvals can be received and processed by AME before the records are purged.

- **Repeated Approvers** – indicates how often an approver should appear on an approval list. Some transactions may satisfy multiple AME Rule configurations that result in an approver appearing more than once on an approver list. The variable tells AME whether or not the approver should receive only one approval Notification or multiple Approval Notifications for each occurrence on the approver list.

- **Rule Priority Modes** – inform AME how to prioritize Rule Types for a given Transaction Type. When Rule Priorities are enabled for a Rule Type, the Priority Mode must also be followed by a positive numeric value. This value represents the priority threshold for an AME Rule created using the enabled Rule Type. For a given transaction that satisfies one or more Rules, AME determines which Rules can be kept and acted upon and which can be discarded. Any Rule that falls outside of the priority's threshold will be discarded. Rule Priority Modes can be set to either Absolute or Relative.

An absolute Rule Priority Mode can be further explained with the following example.

The Rule Priority for the 'Pre List Approver Group' Rule Type in the Payables Invoice Approval Transaction Type has been set to 10. Three Pre List Approver Group Rules have been setup as follows:

Rule 1: If the Invoice is PO matched, require pre-approval from the Purchasing Manager and the requester's supervisor. Priority 5

Rule 2: If the Invoice is Project matched, require pre-approval from the Project Manager and the requester's supervisor. Priority 5

Rule 3: Require pre-approval from an AP Senior Clerk. Priority 15

In this example, if either Rule 1 or 2 are active in AME, Rule 3 would never be considered. Although the Rule might be satisfied by an invoice transaction, because the Rule Priority mode has been set to 10 and there is at least one active Rule with a priority within this threshold, any other Rules outside the threshold will be discarded.

A relative Rule Priority mode will include the number of satisfied rules in order of priority up to the number of rules allowed by the threshold. For example, if the threshold is 3, and five rules are applicable, the 3 rules with the lowest priority will apply and the remaining two rules will be discarded.

- **Forwarding Behaviors** – informs AME how to handle various forwarding scenarios for the approver list generated for the current transaction. These scenarios can include situations such as:

  - Was the approval request forwarded to another approver further along in the current approver list?

  - Was the approval request forwarded to a previous approver in the current list who has already submitted an approval?

  - Was the approval request forwarded to an individual not in the approver list?

  Depending on the forwarding scenario, this Configuration Variable allows you to inform AME of the action that is amending the current approver list. These actions could determine whether to extend or shorten the current approver list based on who the approval was forwarded to. Additionally, AME could build a new list with a new set of approvers for a fowardee outside the current approver list and in a different approval hierarchy. There are many different possibilities for how AME can be configured to handle forwarded Approval Notifications.

One caveat regarding Configuration Variables is that it is best to consult with the Oracle product group for the integrating application Workflow to make sure it recognizes all of the possible values of the Configuration Variable. Modifying the value of a Configuration Variable to a value not recognized by the integrating application can lead to undesirable results. Some options, such as 'Allow FYI Notification', are not allowed for some transaction types, such as Requisition Approval. Refer to Oracle MetaLink Doc. ID: 338508.1, *Error "Oracle Approvals Management has found parallelization configuration…"* for more details.

Attributes

Attributes are business variables that represent the value of a data element of a given transaction. In the case of an AP invoice transaction, typical Attributes are invoice amount or supplier name. Attributes can be thought of as the 'building blocks' of business case development. The value of an Attribute(s) for a transaction can ultimately determine whether a business case (Approval Rule) has been met because Approval Rules use Conditions that in turn use Attributes. Most Attributes needed to create business rules are seeded with the Transaction Type. Additional Attributes can be created when necessary as long as they can be linked to the source transaction.

Attributes in AME can be either static or dynamic. Static Attributes have a constant value that remains the same for each and every transaction associated with the Attribute's Transaction Type. Dynamic Attributes use a SQL query to retrieve the value of an Attribute at runtime whenever a transaction is created. Most Attributes in a Transaction Type are Dynamic. The ability to use a SQL query to retrieve an Attribute value is a powerful feature in AME. The Attribute's SQL query can be any syntactically valid query, including a query that calls a database object such as a Package that might include more complicated programming logic. The only requirement is that the database object must return a single value, such as is the case with a function.

Consider an Attribute that needs to retrieve a value that represents the number of supervisor levels needed to be traversed to find a supervisor with sufficient signing authority. A database Package could be developed to loop through an HR hierarchy, retrieve signing authority, and determine whether or not sufficient authority exists that could return the number of HR levels encountered to AME. The AME Attribute's SQL query value could call the Package as follows:

```
SELECT <custom package name>.signing_limit_levels (:transactionId) from dual;
```

Attribute Types

Several different Attribute Types exist within AME:

- **String Attributes** – are alphanumeric and can have a total length of 100 characters.

- **Numeric Attributes** – any numeric value that is acceptable in PL/SQL. This includes numbers containing decimal or sign operators (+/-). AME requires that any dynamically generated numeric Attribute be converted to a canonical form. This can be done by using the fnd_number.number_to_canonical function as part of the dynamic SQL query:

```
SELECT fnd_number.number_to_canonical(:requester_id)
  FROM ap_invoices_all WHERE invoice_id = :transactionId;
```

- **Currency Attributes** – are used whenever an organization's transactions involve multiple currency values. This allows Oracle to use currency conversion between denominations when retrieving the value of an Attribute. AME requires that any dynamic Attribute setup as a currency Attribute must include the following columns as part of the SQL query: numeric column, currency and conversion method. The following is an example of a SQL query of a Currency Attribute:

```
SELECT  fnd_number.number_to_canonical(ai.INVOICE_AMOUNT),
        nvl(ai.Invoice_Currency_Code,asp.Invoice_Currency_Code),
        nvl(ai.Exchange_Rate_Type,'Corporate')
  FROM  ap_invoices_all ai, ap_system_parameters_all asp
 WHERE  ai.invoice_id = :transactionId AND ai.org_id = asp.org_id;
```

Any AME Conditions developed using a Currency Attribute must include a Condition for every currency the Transaction Attribute value might have.

- **Boolean Attributes** – have only two allowable values: true and false. AME provides a format string that can be used in the SQL query of a Dynamic Boolean Attribute. The syntax format is in the form of either 'ame_util.booleanAttributeTrue' or 'ame_util.booleanAttributeFalse'.

- **Date Attributes** – are commonly used on transaction data that contains a date value, such as invoice date. AME requires that Date Attributes be returned in the format 'YYYY:MON:DD:HH24:MI:SS'. AME provides a format string that can be used in the SQL query of a Dynamic Date Attribute. The format string 'ame_util,versionDateFormatModel' can be used to return the proper date format at runtime.

AME also allows a user to inherit any previously defined Attributes seeded with AME (Mandatory and Required) as well as those previously defined for any Transaction Type. In FIGURE 14.2, click on 'Use Existing Attribute' on the Attributes summary page to select from a list of all defined Attributes in AME and choose any that are applicable to your Transaction Type:

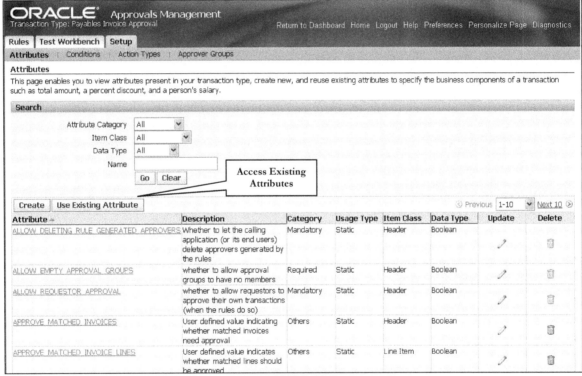

FIGURE 14.2

Mandatory Attributes

All Transaction Types currently defined in AME use several Mandatory Attributes that can be thought of as runtime parameters, because they often determine various aspects of AME runtime behavior, such as whether to allow a requester to approve his/her own transactions (e.g., invoices) or how to handle approval rejections. The following Mandatory Attributes are defined in AME for all Transaction Types:

- **ALLOW_DELETING_RULE_GENERATE_APPROVERS** – determines whether the integrating application can delete any approvers from the default generated approver list

- **ALLOW_REQUEST_APPROVAL** – determines whether the requester of a transaction can be included as an approver and approve their own transaction

- **AT_LEAST_ONE_RULE_MUST_APPLY** – determines whether every transaction in the integrating application must be satisfied by at least one defined Rule in AME. If this value is set to 'Yes' and a transaction is not satisfied by at least one Rule, AME will raise an exception and write to its internal log

- **REJECTION_RESPONSE** – determines how AME handles any approval request that was rejected by the recipient. Possible responses include whether AME should discontinue notifying any additional required approvers, or resume sending Notifications to all other approvers

- **USE_RESTRICTIVE_ITEM_EVALUATION** – applies to any Rule that uses line-level (subordinate) Conditions. It informs AME if one line-level item has to satisfy all the Conditions of a Rule for the Rule to satisfy a transaction. An example is if a Rule has two line-level Conditions and a transaction has two lines and the first line satisfies the first Rule Condition and the second line satisfies the second Rule Condition. If the value of this Attribute is set to False, this Rule would apply and be satisfied by the transaction, because both Conditions have been met, albeit by different lines. If the value of the Attribute is True, the Rule is not satisfied by the transaction because at least one line would have to satisfy both Conditions of the Rule

- **EFFECTIVE_RULE_DATE** – AME uses the value of this Attribute to determine which Rules are active and in effect as of this date. The default is the current date

- **EVALUATE_PRIORITIES_PER_ITEM** – determines whether AME should evaluate the Rule Priorities of a Rule

- **USE_WORKFLOW** – determines whether AME should log any exception errors to Workflow's exception stack in addition to its own

- **WORKFLOW_ITEM_KEY** – uses either the integrated application Workflow's Item Key or internal Transaction ID when logging errors to Workflow's exception stack.

- **WORKFLOW_ITEM_TYPE** – uses the Item Type of the integrated application's Workflow when logging errors to Workflow's exception stack.

- **REPEAT_SUBSTITUION** – determines whether AME should process Substitution Rules at the end of an approval cycle in the event that any ad-hoc approvers were added to the original approver list. Substitution Rules will be discussed later in the chapter.

Whenever a new Transaction Type is created in AME, these Attributes will be added to the Transaction Type automatically.

Required Attributes

Like Mandatory Attributes, Required Attributes determine AME runtime behavior, but they are defined specific to a Transaction Type. AME is seeded with the following Required Attributes. Any of these Attributes can be inherited and modified to meet the needs of a specific Transaction Type.

- **ALLOW_EMPTY_APPROVAL_GROUPS** – The value of the Attribute (True or False) determines whether AME will raise an exception for any Approver Groups that do not contain any members at runtime. This typically applies to any Approver Groups that dynamically select its members. Approver Groups are discussed later in the chapter.

- **FIRST_STARTING_POINT_PERSON_ID/SECOND_STARTING_POINT_PERSON_I D** – When Dual Chains of Authority are used as part of a Rule's action, AME must determine which individuals should be included as the first approver for each approver list. The value of these two Attribute determine the starting approvers.

- **INCLUDE_ALL_JOB_LEVEL_APPROVERS** – determines whether or not AME will include all approvers with the same job level on an approver list. When AME traverses a hierarchy to generate an approver, it must decide whether to include all approvers (True) with the same required job level or only include the first one encountered (False).

- **TRANSACTION_REQUESTER_PERSON_ID** – the person requesting the Transaction Type's transaction. AME uses this as the starting point for traversing the hierarchy. An example of a transaction's requester is REQUESTER_ID in the Payables invoice transaction.

- **TRANSACTION_REQUESTER_POSITION_ID** – the position of the person requesting the Transaction Type's transaction. AME uses this as the starting point for traversing the position hierarchy.

- **JOB_LEVEL_NON_DEFAULT_STARTING_PERSON_POINT_ID** – This Attribute is null by default. When populated, this Attribute determines the starting point used by AME to generate an approver list. A value in this Attribute overrides the value in the Required Attribute TRANSACTION_REQUESTER_PERSON_ID. This only applies to Action Types that depend on employee job levels.

- **NON_DEFAULT_STARTING_POINT_POSITION_ID** – This Attribute is null by default. When populated, this Attribute determines the starting point used by AME to generate an approver list. A value in this Attribute overrides the value in the Required Attribute TRANSACTION_REQUESTER_POSITION_ID. This only applies to Action Types that depend on HR positions.

- **SUPERVISORY_NON_DEFAULT_STARTING_POINT_PERSON_ID** – This Attribute is null by default. When populated, this Attribute determines the starting point used by AME to generate an approver list. A value in this Attribute overrides the value in the Required Attribute TRANSACTION_REQUESTER_POSITION_ID. This only applies to Action Types that depend on Supervisory levels.

- **TOP_SUPERVISOR_ID** – is the person at the top of a hierarchy, such as the CEO of an organization. Whenever AME traverses a supervisor hierarchy and encounters a NULL supervisor value, it determines whether it has reached the top of the hierarchy or if a problem exists due to a gap in the hierarchy setup. If this value is null or AME reaches a NULL value and the current supervisor does not equal the value of this Attribute, AME will raise an exception.

- **TOP_POSITION_ID** – is the same as the TOP_SUPERVISOR_ID Attribute except that the value is represented by a position, rather than an employee id (PERSON_ID).

- **NON_DEFAULT_POSITION_STRUCTURE_ID** – determines which HR position structure AME will use when traversing a position hierarchy. It is null by default, which informs AME to use the position structure assigned to the current business group.

Both Mandatory and Required Attributes are seeded with default values. They can be modified to meet the needs of a specific Transaction Type. FIGURE 14.3 shows some of the Required Attributes for Payables Invoice Approval. Clicking on the pencil in the 'Update' column will yield FIGURE 14.4, where changes to the Attribute can be made.

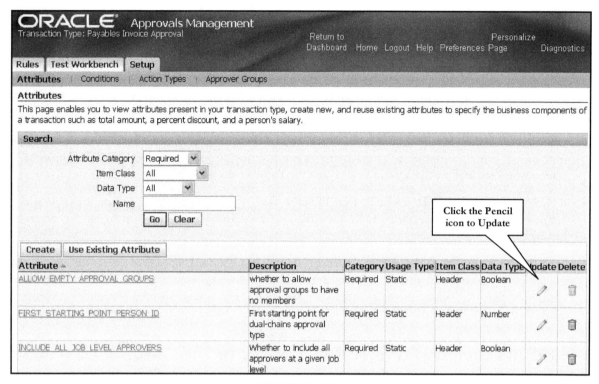

FIGURE 14.3

FIGURE 14.4

Conditions

The next major AME setup component is Conditions. Conditions evaluate an Attribute's value for a given transaction. The result of a Condition can either be true or false. Conditions are precursors to AME business rules. The result of a Condition helps to determine whether a business case (Rule) has been satisfied. The Conditions within AME represent the 'if' part of an Approval Rule. For example,

> If invoice supplier is Vendor A, then require approvals from Approver A, Approver B

In this example, AME will retrieve and evaluate the value of the Attribute invoice_supplier to determine if the value was equal to Vendor A.

Types of Conditions

There are three different types of Conditions that exist in the AME application: Ordinary-Regular, Ordinary-Exception and List Modifier.

Ordinary-Regular and **Ordinary-Exception Conditions** - while similar in how they are defined, they differ because they are limited to the Rules to which they can be associated based on the type of the Rule (discussed later in the chapter). Ordinary-Exception Conditions are often used to suppress a similar Ordinary-Regular Condition when creating a Rule.

List Modifier Conditions - are used to check for the presence of a specific approver in a generated list. A List Modifier Condition can verify whether the target approver exists anywhere in the approver list or only as the final approver in the list. If the designated approver appears in the approver list, the Condition is considered to be true. List Modifier Conditions are often used in Approval Rules to modify an AME-generated approver list. This type of condition can substitute one approver for another, or suppress/extend an approver list based on the presence of a target approver. An example of a List Modifier Condition could be:

> If Approver B is final approver, then require approver up 1 level

This Condition would evaluate to true if Approver B was the last approver in an approver list built by AME at runtime. FIGURE 14.5 shows an example of a List Modifier Condition. In this case, the Condition would evaluate to 'True' if Susan Behn is any approver in the list.

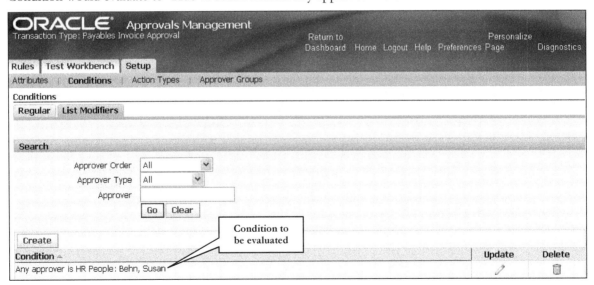

FIGURE 14.5

Condition Definition Formats

When a new Condition is created, the format of the Condition builder will differ based on the data type of the Attribute to be associated with the Condition.

- Conditions based on a Numeric Attribute can define a lower and upper limit in the Condition such as:

```
lower_limit <{=} attribute_name <{=} upper_limit
```

- Conditions based on string Attributes are defined in the format:

```
attribute_name in {value1, value2.....}
```

- Conditions based on Date Type Attributes are defined in the format:

```
lower_limit <{=} attribute_name <{=} upper_limit
```

- Conditions based on Currency Attributes are defined in the format:

```
lower_limit <{=} attribute_name <{=} upper_limit
```

- Conditions based on Boolean Attributes are defined in the format:

```
attribute_name is {True or False}
```

For any Conditions where lower and/or upper bound limits are allowed, either one or both can be populated. When only one of the limits is populated, the null limit constitutes an unbound limit to AME.

For example:

```
If {null} <= supplier_invoice_amount < 5000
```

This Condition indicates that if the invoice amount for a supplier is less than $5000, the Condition is considered true. This would include any invoices with negative invoice values. When defining Conditions with an unbound limit, it is important to understand the types of transactions that might satisfy the Condition.

Since Conditions are the basis of AME Rules creation, it is important that you define your Conditions carefully to ensure that use of the Condition in an Approval Rule applied to a transaction will generate the proper approvers.

Action Types and Actions

Actions within AME describe what should be done if a Condition and Rule is satisfied by a transaction. It is the Actions that dictate the approver list generated by AME for a given transaction. Actions not only provide instruction as to who the approvers are, but how many approvers are required for a given transaction and in what order they should be notified.

Action Types are groupings of actions with similar functionality, such as the approval hierarchy, that should be traversed when building an approver list. For example, Actions pertaining to building an approval based solely on the supervisor tree in HR are grouped into an Action Type. The multiple actions for this Action Type would all pertain to traversal of the supervisor hierarchy, but would be expressed in terms of how many levels to traverse.

Although Oracle does provide a means via the application to add new Actions and Action Types, they don't encourage the creation of new Action Types. The programming logic involved in communicating to AME how Action Types and Actions work to construct an approver list is quite extensive and complex. Instead, Oracle recommends using AME's predefined Action Types. A variety of Action Types are provided that should satisfy most approval requirements of an organization. The only requirement is that you have to inform AME of any actions that you want made available to you at the time you set up your Rules. This is done by enabling the Action Type grouping associated with the actions you will need.

The 'Action Types' self-service page in AME displays all the Action Types available to any Rules created for the current Transaction Type. The 'Use Existing Action Type' button (See FIGURE 14.6) allows you to choose from a list of predefined AME Action Types by selecting via a checkbox those required for the Transaction Type (See FIGURE 14.7).

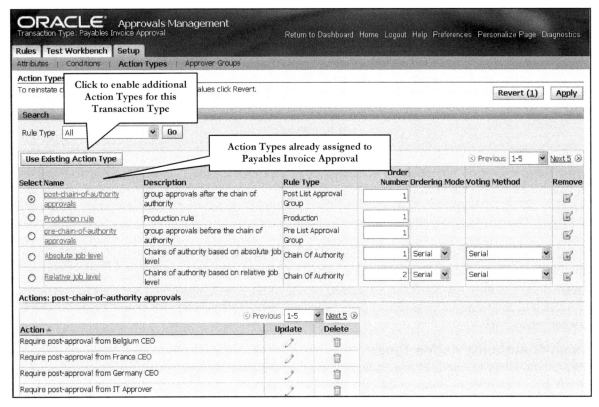

FIGURE 14.6

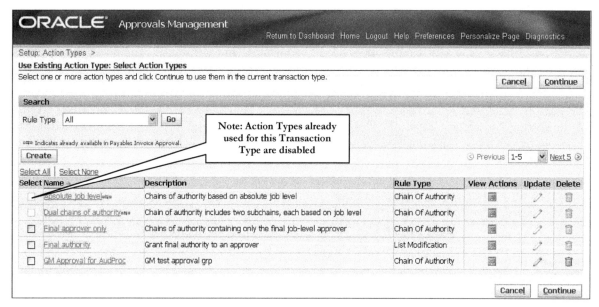

FIGURE 14.7

AME only allows you to select Action Types that have not been previously enabled for the Transaction Type. There is no harm in enabling all available Action Types for a given Transaction Type to ensure that any actions required while creating Rules are available.

Action Type Hierarchies

Action Types categorized and into six different types of hierarchies: Chain-of-Authority, List Modification, Substitution, Pre List Approver Groups, Post List Approver Groups and Production.

Action types and their associated actions tend to be one of the more complicated concepts to understand in AME. The following tables are intended to provide a basic understanding of Action Types as they are categorized in AME.

Chain-of-Authority Action Types

The Action Types in Table 14.1 typically utilize either the supervisor or position hierarchy defined in Oracle HR to generate an approver list for a given transaction.

Action Type	Description	Example
Absolute job level	Ascends the HR supervisor hierarchy until an approver with the appropriate job level is found	Require approvals up to job level 6
Relative job level	Ascends the HR supervisor hierarchy until an approver is found with a job level <n> levels higher than the requestor of a transaction	Require approvals at least 4 levels up
Approval-Group Chain of Authority	Chain-of-authority list is built in the same manner as the List-Creation or List-Modification Action Types. However, instead of using the HR supervisor or position structure, it uses a predefined Approver Group list to generate the chain-of-authority	If transaction item contains building material, require approvals from Mark, then Chris and then Sharon.
Manager then Final-Approver	Ascends the HR supervisor hierarchy, but only the immediate supervisor and final approver on the	Require approval up to first supervisor and CEO only

Action Type	Description	Example
	approval list are required to approve	
Final Approver Only	Ascends the HR supervisor hierarchy, but only requires approval from the person that is last on the approver list	Require approval from division manager only
Dual Chains of Authority	Ascends the HR supervisor hierarchy and builds two separate chains of approvers. An Action for each chain must be provided.	Require approval from previous employee supervisor and current employee supervisor (i.e., during employee transfer)
Line-Item Job-Level	Ascends the HR supervisor hierarchy. Enables approval chains to be built based on a line level item in a transaction	Require approval from manager of an accounting code cost center distribution segment on an Invoice Distribution line
Supervisory Level	Ascends the HR supervisor hierarchy based on a fixed number of required approvers. There is no correlation or dependency on job level.	Require approvals up to 3 supervisors
HR Position	Ascends the HR position hierarchy up to a specified position	Require approvals up Accounting Manager
HR Position Level	Ascends the HR position hierarchy up a specified number of positions	Require approvals up to position at level 4

TABLE 14. 1

FIGURE 14.8 shows an example of Chain of Authority Action Types with the Actions for the Supervisory Level Action Type. Click the 'Use Existing Action Type' button to activate an Action Type for a specific Transaction Type such as Payables Invoice Approval.

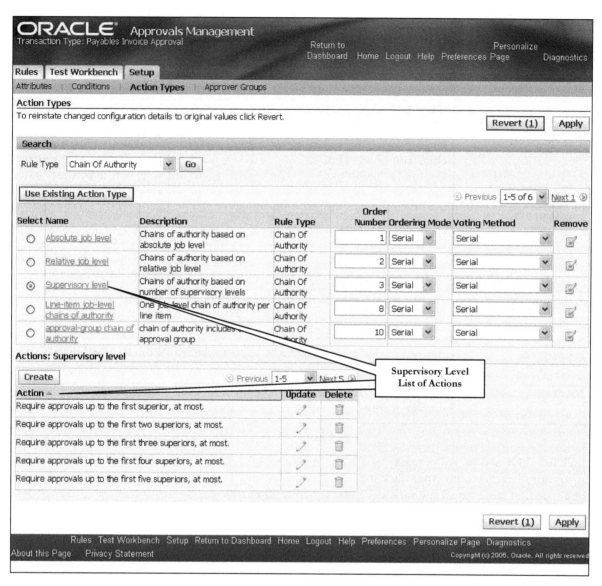

FIGURE 14. 8

List-Modification Action Types

Like the Chain-Of-Authority Action Type, the List-Modification Action Type also traverses the HR supervisor hierarchy structure. However, its intent is to modify the approver list either by granting or revoking authority limits. It accomplishes this by either extending or removing individuals from an approver chain that might normally be built for a transaction. This modification of the approver chain is based on the target approver specified when using the Action Type. An example is allowing an IT manager to be the final approver of a computer purchase even though the amount of the transaction might normally require approval up to the CFO level. Because the IT manager may be more knowledgeable of the purchase, the approval list is shortened to allow him to be the final approver of the transaction. See Table 14.2.

Action Type	Description	Example
Final Authority	Grants final authority to an approver that typically does not have signing authority by ending the approval chain when the approver chain reaches the designated approver	If Approver is IT Manager, allow final approval
Nonfinal Authority	Revokes final approval authority from an approver that normally has sufficient signing authority by extending an approval chain beyond the final approver until a targeted or designated approver is reached	If Approver is Harry, require approval up one supervisor

TABLE 14.2

Substitution Action Types

Substitution Action Types allow a target approver to be replaced by another designated approver whenever a transaction generates an approval chain involving the target approver. An example is routing approvals to an employee in the absence of another. A Substitution Action Type might be used to replace a potential transaction approver that will be absent from the office for an extended period of time (e.g., vacation, leave of absence).

Pre List and Post List Approver Group Action Types

Approver Group Action Types allow an approver list to be built based on a predefined list of members that are part of the approval group. Approval Groups are discussed in more detail later in this chapter. This list can be static, containing the specific names of individuals responsible for approvals of a given transaction or it can be dynamically built based on a SQL statement. See Table 14.3.

Action Type	Description	Example
Approval-group Chain-of-Authority	Chain-of-authority list is built in the same manner as the List-Creation or List-Modification Action Types. However, instead of using the HR supervisor or position structure, it uses a predefined Approver Group list to generate the chain-of-authority	If transaction item contains building material, require approvals from Mark, then Chris and then Sharon.
Pre and Post Chain-Of-Authority	Inserts an approver list either before or after the normal approver chain that might be generated for a given transaction.	If transaction includes sales tax, require approval by Sales Tax group, then require approval up to job level 3

TABLE 14. 3

Approver Groups

AME Approver Groups are a customized list of one or more individuals required to approve a transaction. Why is it referred to as a custom list of approvers? Many of the pre-defined actions in AME that build an approver list do so using standard Oracle hierarchy structures such as HR supervisor or HR position hierarchies. Other times, the hierarchy (or path) of required approvers for a transaction does not follow one of Oracle's standard hierarchies. Also, if a business scenario requires additional approvers outside of the standard approver list built using a standard Oracle hierarchy, an approval group could be utilized. Typically, approvers would be added either before or after building the standard list. These would be known as pre and post list approvers. Pre and post list approvers will be discussed shortly. In either case, the creation of Approver Groups allows you to inform AME how to construct an approver list when it does not follow an Oracle standard hierarchy.

Static and Dynamic Approver Groups

Approver groups in AME can be created statically or dynamically. A Static Approver Group is one in which the members of the Approver Group are specifically identified. In other words, as the Approver Group is being created, you identify the members by name. FIGURE 14.9 shows the setup for a Static Approver Group.

Static Approver Groups

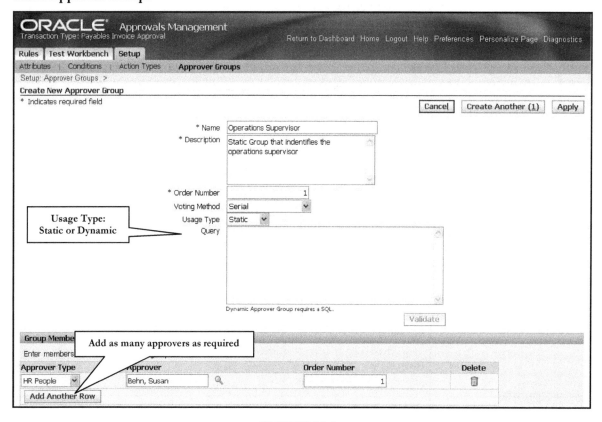

FIGURE 14. 9

When defining a Static Approver Group in AME, the members of the group can be defined in the following ways (Approver Type):

- **HR People** –by choosing their employee name as it exists in Oracle's HR schema

- **FND User** – by choosing their username as it exists in the FND schema

- **Nested Group** – by choosing the member's current Approver Group. Using nested groups as an Approver Type is beneficial whenever there is a need to combine several smaller, separate Approver Groups into a larger approver. For example, if there were two separate Approver Groups that included supervisors from the Payables and Accounting departments respectively, you could create an Approver Group that represented all finance supervisors by combining these two groups together. This is much more efficient and faster than defining each supervisor member of the finance department again in this new Approver Group.

- **HR Positions (Release 12 only)** – by choosing a specific position in HR

The 'Add Another Row' button allows you to continue to add as many members to the Approver Group as are necessary.

Keep the following in mind when using Static Approver Groups:

1. Members of a Static Approver Group will always be the same unless you update the Approver Group setup. When you associate a Static Approver Group with an AME Rule, the same approvers will appear for all transactions that satisfy the Rule. While this may seem obvious, it is noteworthy to point out, especially for Approver Groups that include multiple members.

2. AME assumes that Approver Group members will either be Oracle HR employees, Oracle Applications users (FND) or HR positions. The 'HR People' and 'FND Users' Approver Types are defined to only retrieve data from the HR or FND schemas. If Approver Group members exist in another repository (e.g., PeopleSoft schema) a workaround would be to either define a Dynamic Approver Group or to nest Approver Groups that in themselves are dynamic. Even if you use this method, AME would still need to know how the entity from the other repository corresponds to either an HR employee or FND user. .

3. The order number associated with each Approver Group member identifies the order in which the members of the Approver Group will receive Approval Notifications. If there is a need for members to be notified in a certain sequence, adjust the order number for each member accordingly.

Dynamic Approver Groups

A Dynamic Approver Group is similar to the Static Approver Group in that you inform AME of the members that the group consists of. However, instead of specifically identifying members by name or position, you must use a SQL script to identify the Approver Group members. Dynamic Approver Groups are particularly useful in cases where the specific members of the group are not known or can change often. For example, consider the following approver requirement for Payables invoices.

> If invoice is associated with an Oracle project, then require approval from the project manager and project director.

In this example, for an organization that has multiple simultaneous projects running, it would be difficult to identify each project manager and director for each project. If the individual assigned to either Role changes during the life of the project, a Static Approver Group would have to be modified each time a Role change took place. Using a Dynamic Approver Group prevents this sort of maintenance because the associated SQL would be written in such a way as to retrieve the current individual assigned to each Role.

The ability to use SQL provides power and flexibility when identifying Dynamic Approver Group members. The associate SQL query can be as simple or complex as is required. The only requirement from an AME perspective is that the SQL has to either return the ID of an HR employee (PERSON_ID), an Oracle Applications user (user_id) or HR position (position id). This is similar to choosing the Approver Type for Static Approver Group members. FIGURE 14.10 shows the setup of a Dynamic Approver Group.

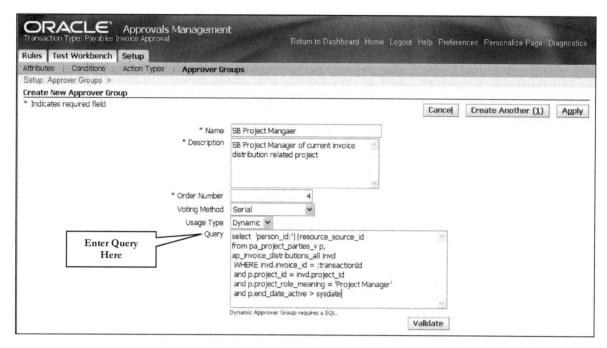

FIGURE 14.10

The following shows the syntax required to retrieve each Approver Type.

For an HR Employee:

```
SELECT    'PER:'||(id related to person_id in PER_ALL_PEOPLE_F)
    from (transaction table) WHERE (transacton_id) = :transactionId
```

Example:
```
SELECT 'PER:'||requester_id FROM AP_INVOICES_ALL
    WHERE invoice_id = :transactionId
```

For an FND User

```
SELECT    'USR:'||(id related to user_id in FND_USER)
        from (transaction table) WHERE (transaction_id) = :transactionId
```

Example:
```
SELECT 'USR:'||created_by FROM PO_REQUISITION_HEADERS_ALL
    WHERE requisition_header_id = :transactionId
```

Empty Approver Groups

It is possible to have Dynamic Approver Groups with no members. Situations may exist where the SQL query associated with an Approver Group returns no records for a particular transaction satisfying a Rule. When this occurs, AME needs to know how to proceed with building an approver list. If AME encounters an empty Approver Group, should it raise an exception or should it do nothing and continue trying to build other parts of the approver list? The answer could be based on several factors.

- Is the Approver Group being used as the sole means of building the standard approval list for a transaction? In this case, AME should raise an exception because the integrating Workflow might conclude the transaction is approved because no approvers were found (auto-approval). This may not be acceptable to some organizations.

- Is the Approver Group being used to generate a list of additional approvers (pre/post list) that represent knowledge experts required to review the transaction? Again, if it is imperative that the additional approvers review the details of a transaction, AME should raise an exception if no members are found.

As discussed earlier in the chapter in the section on Attributes, AME provides the required Attribute ALLOW_EMPTY_APPROVER_GROUPS to control how AME responds to an empty Approver Group situation. The value of this Attribute can be either True or False. A value of True informs AME to do nothing and allow the transaction approval build to continue. A value of False informs AME to raise an exception for any required Approver Group that finds no members. It is important to set this Attribute properly based on the needs of the organization.

Approver Group Properties

Whether creating a Static or Dynamic Approver Group, there are several properties that pertain to both types of groups.

- **Name** – Unique name of the Approver Group. Approver group names are unique across all Transaction Types in AME.

- **Description** – Text that describes that should describe the purpose of the Approver Group

- **Order Number** – Identifies the order in which the Approver Group members will appear on a transaction's approver list. This is particularly important when a transaction satisfies a Rule that uses actions associated with multiple Approver Groups.

- **Voting Method** – Identifies how Approver Group members will be notified as well about how their responses will be processed by AME. There are currently four different voting methods options.

  - **Serial** – Members are identified in a sequential order based on the order they are retrieved either from the Dynamic SQL query or as ordered in the Static Approver Group member listing. AME determines that a transaction is approved when all members of the group approve the transaction.

  - **Consensus** – Members of the group are identified at the same time. Order number or Order By (SQL) are irrelevant. All members of the group must approver the transaction to be considered fully approved by AME.

  - **First-Responder-Wins** – Similar to consensus voting, members of the group are notified at the same time. However, the response of the overall group is determined by the first response received. All subsequent responses are recorded, but ignored by AME.

  - **Order-Number** – The members of the group are notified based on their assigned order number, which is more relevant to Static Approver Groups than Dynamic. Any members of the group with the same order number will be notified at the same time. As is the case with serial and consensus voting, all members of the group must approve in order for AME to consider the transaction to be approved by the Approver Group.

One caveat regarding the use of voting methods – not all Transaction Types in AME support the use of all voting method types. The serial voting method is supported by all Transaction Types in AME. However, because the other methods have the ability to notify potential approvers in parallel, they are not supported by all AME Transaction Types. Before deciding to use one of these voting types for an Approver Group, consult the appropriate Oracle product group and verify that it is supported by the current Transaction Type. Failure to do so will cause undesirable results.

- **Usage Type** – whether the Approver Group members will be static or retrieved dynamically.

- **Query** – If the Approver Group is Dynamic, AME expects this field to be populated with a SQL statement. Use the Validate button to verify that the SQL syntax is correct.

Pre/Post List Approver Lists

AME allows Approver Groups to be used as the foundation for constructing a standard approval list. However, organizations using AME tend to use Approver Groups as a means to identify approvers that need to be added either before or after the standard approver list built by AME. Typically, an organization's standard approval list requirements for transactions can be satisfied by using one of Oracle's standard hierarchies, such as HR supervisor. Yet, some specific transactions require one or more additional individuals to review the transaction before it is deemed fully approved. These additional approvers are usually knowledge experts or someone whose position in the organization requires him or her to have a vested interest in the transaction itself.

For example, an organization may require that all of its invoices that exceed $5000 be reviewed and approved by two supervisor levels above the requester of the invoice. However, if the invoice exceeds $5000 and is matched to a purchase order related to computer equipment, the organization may require that the director of IT also be included as an approver in addition to the two supervisors. The appearance of the additional approvers before or after the standard list is based on how the Action used when a Rule that uses the Approver Group is defined. AME provides two different actions (grouped by Action Type) that inform AME whether to include the additional approvers before or after any standard list that is built.

Rules

The final setup component to discuss in this chapter is the AME Rule. The Rule is the most direct representation of an organization's approval business case requirement in AME. It merges the various setup components discussed so far (e.g., Conditions, Actions, and Approver Groups) in such a way as to tell AME *when this situation occurs, this is what should be done.*

Whenever a transaction is initiated, all current, active Rules defined for the Transaction Type are evaluated to determine what Rules the transaction satisfies and ultimately what approval path the transaction will follow when submitted for approval. Rules are defined by associating one or more Conditions to determine if a particular business case has been satisfied. Additionally, Rules are associated with Action Types to determine the approval Action and, therefore, the approver list that should be generated for the transaction. Generally when defining business cases in AME, the setup of the Rule will be the last step in this process.

Rule Types

Similar to Action Types, Rules use Rule Types to determine the type of list to build if all of the associated Conditions of the Rule are true. The associated Rule Type determines which Action Types are available when assigning actions to the Rule. FIGURE 14.11 shows the 'Update Rule' screen:

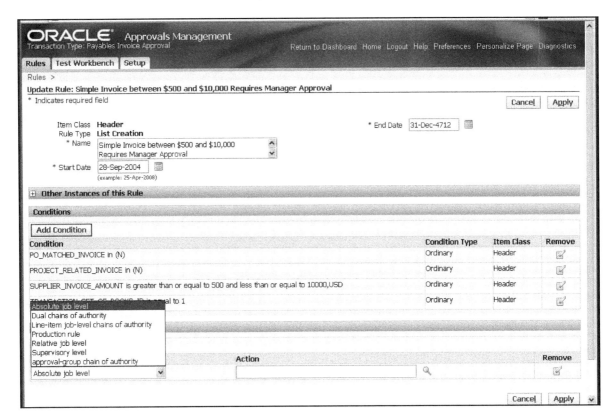

FIGURE 14.11

In the current version of AME, there are eight different Rule Types. Table 14.4 lists each Rule Type along with a brief description of the type of approver lists that can be generated.

Rule Type	Description
List-Creation	Used to build standard chain-of-authority list of approvers that ascend some organizational hierarchy to generate the chain of approvers. Probably the most commonly used Rule Type. List creation allow the following Action Types to be used: Absolute job level, Relative Job Level, Dual Chains of Authority, Final Approver Only, Manager Then Final Approver, Supervisory Level, Approver Group Chain of Authority, Line-Item Job-Level Chains of Authority, HR Position, Position Level.
List-Creation Exceptions	Similar to the List Creation Rule Type in that it builds a chain-of-authority list of approvers as well. However, it is often used to suppress a list-creation Rule so as to require approvals from a certain group of approvers if an additional Condition is met. An example is a Rule to force approval by a particular group of approvers based on cost center of an Invoice Distribution account. Requires the use of at least one exception Condition when defining the Rule. Allowable Action Types are the same as List Creation.
List Modification	Allows a Rule to grant or revoke final approval based on a target approver. Allowable Action types are Final Authority and Non Final Authority
Substitution	Allows for delegation of an approval authority to another approver. Similar to Workflow Vacation Rules. Whenever a targeted approver is supposed to appear on an approval list, they are substituted with a given approver. Allowable Action Type is substitution.
Pre/Post Approval Rules	Allows for additional approvers outside of a transaction's generated chain-of-authority to be added to the list of approvers. Allowable Action Types are Pre-Chain-of-Authority and Post-Chain-of-Authority.
Combination Rules	Allows a combination of Action Types of different allowable Rule Types to be used on the same Rule. For example, a Rule Type that allows for only list-creation actions could be combined with a Rule Type that only allows for substitution actions. The most common use of this is in business cases that require pre or post list approvers to be included in an approver list. For example, suppose there was a requirement to include the operations manager as a pre-approver for all purchase orders with a specific deliver-to location. In theory, two Rules could be defined; one that builds the standard list (List-Creation) and the other that includes the operations manager (Pre-List Approver Group). However, the more efficient and recommended approach would be to create one Rule that uses the combination Rule Type and includes multiple actions. Each Action would build the necessary part of the overall approver list
Production Rules	Outputs runtime values to a particular integrating transaction. Not available for all Transaction Types. It is the responsibility of the integrating application to interpret and use the Production output

TABLE 14. 4

FIGURE 14.16 shows a simple Rule that requires manager approval for invoices between $500 and $10,000. Click on the pencil in the 'Update' column to update this Rule or click the Create button to create a new Rule. Creating a Rule is logically broken down into four pages. FIGURE 14.12 and FIGURE 14.13 show the update page for this simple Invoice Rule, which is the same as the final confirmation page displayed when creating a Rule.

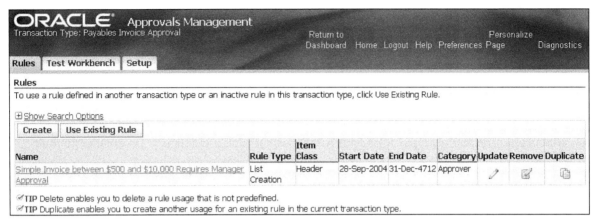

FIGURE 14.12

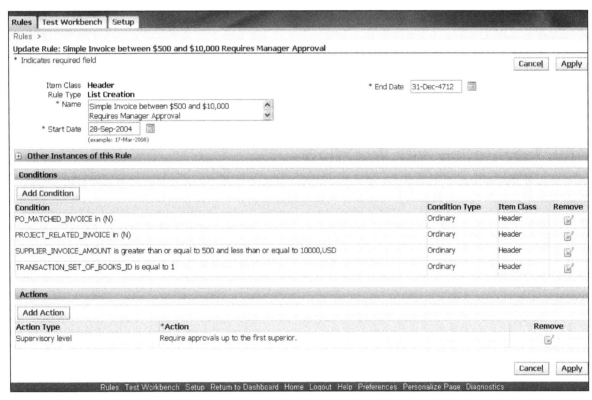

FIGURE 14.13

Rule Priorities

The concept of Rule Priorities was discussed earlier in the chapter under the Configuration Variables section. The only additional item to mention here regarding Rule Priorities is that if the Rule Priority Mode Configuration Variable has been enabled for a given Transaction Type, then all Rules created after the variable is enabled must assign a Rule Priority. The Configuration Variable could also be enabled for all Transaction Types. If this is the case, but priorities for a particular Transaction Type are irrelevant, set the priority for all Rules to the same number. However, be sure that this number equals or is greater than the integer assigned to the Configuration Variable.

Rule Properties

All Rules in AME have the following properties in common.

- **Name** – must be unique across all Transaction Types. A Rule created under one Transaction Type can be inherited under another Transaction Type. Since the pool of Rules is available system wide, the name of the Rule must be unique

- **Rule Type** – defines the type of approver list that will be built if the transaction satisfies the Rule

- **Description** – the description of the Rule can contain up to 100 characters

- **Item Class** – determines whether the Rule is evaluated at a transaction's header level or for each item level associated with a transaction. For example, a Rule could be defined and evaluated at the purchase requisition header only, or for each purchase requisition line.

- **Start / End Dates** – determines the active dates of the Rule. By default, when a Rule is defined, AME assigns the current date and time to the start date. The standard Oracle practice of using December 31, 4712 is assigned to the end date. These dates can be modified as needed. Note that a Rule's start date cannot be retroactive (begin in the past).

The discussion of several Business Case examples later in the chapter will demonstrate how to define Rules in AME

AME Integration with Workflow

The beginning of the chapter mentioned that AME is not synonymous with Oracle Workflow, nor is it a by-product or extension of Workflow. Yet, the two are increasingly thought of in tandem because of the dependency of more and more Workflows on AME's ability to generate an approver list. Although Workflows themselves are designed to perform various activities, the primary reason for designing a Workflow is to notify an individual when an event occurs in the application or database.

Prior to AME, the underlying code of a Workflow would have to be fully written in such a way as to determine the Notification list recipients. If the Notification list only included approvers in a standard hierarchy such as the HR supervisor, the code was pretty straightforward. However, if the Notification list did not follow a standard hierarchy or required additional individuals outside the standard hierarchy to be notified, more complicated code would be required to address the approval needs of the Workflow. The use of AME in Workflow reduces the need for much of this code because AME contains the logic that determines the list of recipients.

In reviewing Workflows utilizing AME, typically there will be a node in the Workflow responsible for calling a PL/SQL Package in the database. At some point in the Package's code, there is a call to one of AME's API Packages. The purpose of the AME API is to return the ID of the next approver on the approver list, which is the next individual to be notified by Workflow. The following code snippet is an example of a call to one of AME's API Packages.

```
AME_API.GetNextApprover(200, substr(itemkey, 1, instr(itemkey,'_')
   - 1),'APINV', l_next_approver);
```

This call to the GetNextApprover Procedure uses the 'Payables Invoice Approval' Transaction Type. It communicates with AME to determine whether there is another approver for the current Payables invoice transaction. If there is an additional approver that has not been previously notified, the Procedure returns information about the approver and stores it in the variable l_next_approver. This variable is a PL/SQL record variable that contains information about the approver such as name, user_id (FND_USER) and/or PERSON_ID (HR). Workflow uses this information to send the appropriate Notification Message. Let us review the 'Payable Invoice Approval' Workflow to get a better understanding of how AME integrates with Workflow.

Invoice Approval Workflow and AME

The objective of the 'Invoice Approval' Workflow is to notify individuals required to review and approve Payables invoices. Whenever AP is configured to use Workflow for approvals via the 'Payables Options' form (discussed later), all invoices are subject to invoice approval. Payables will automatically set the approval status of each invoice to Required. Once the invoice is validated and approval is initiated for the invoice either online or via the 'Invoice Approval Workflow' Concurrent Program, the invoice falls into the Workflow cycle. The approval logic can best be explained by reviewing the path of the Workflow.

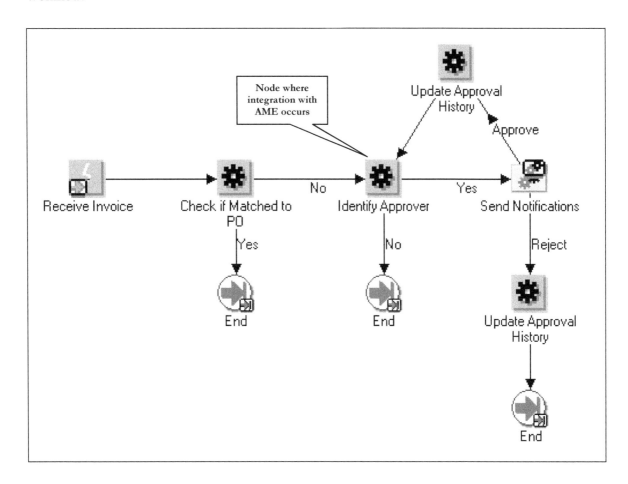

FIGURE 14.14

Approval Logic

When an invoice transaction falls into the 'Invoice Approval' Workflow, the Workflow determines if the invoice transaction is fully matched to a purchase order. If it is, then the Workflow ends and the approval status of the invoice is updated to 'Not Required'. However, if the invoice is not matched to a purchase order, then the Workflow tries to identify the first or next individual responsible for review and approval of the invoice. The Workflow node 'Identify Approver' is where AP and AME are integrated. It is at this point that the Workflow calls AME to determine if the invoice initially meets any of the currently defined Rules in AME for invoice approvals, or if any additional approvers are left on the approval chain hierarchy.

For any AME Rule satisfied by the invoice transaction, AME attempts to build an approver list based on the applied Rule, the associated Action Type, and the actions that define the appropriate approvers. If a successful approver list is built, then Workflow sends a Notification to the first approver in the list. The Workflow remains active and continues to call AME as long as:

- More approvers are left on the approver chain

- The transaction has not been rejected by any approver

- The Workflow Notification has not expired due to the non-responsiveness of an approver

The components defined in AME, especially the business rules, have a direct impact on the approval routings within the 'Payables Invoice Approval' Workflow. It is very important to plan and define Rules carefully to ensure that the organizational approval requirements are met and approval routings flow as intended.

It is important to note the behavior of AME and Workflow for invoices that do not satisfy any predefined Rule. By default, the approval status of any new invoices is set to Required. Once the invoice is sent for approval either manually by the user online or via the 'Invoice Approval Workflow' Concurrent Program, the approval status of the invoice changes to Initiated. When the Workflow begins, if the invoice is not matched to a purchase order transaction and does not initially satisfy any Approval Rules in AME, the Workflow ends and the status of the invoice remains Initiated. This is the behavior of the Payable Invoice Workflow delivered with Oracle. Furthermore, invoices cannot be paid until the invoice is approved. So for any invoices that fall into the category of not satisfying any Approval Rules, this could potentially prevent these invoices from ever being paid.

A couple of alternatives could be used to resolve this issue. First, the Payables Invoice Workflow could be modified to deal with any invoices that do not initially meet the Conditions of an Approval Rule. The second alternative is to set the Mandatory Attribute AT_LEAST_ONE_RULE_MUST_APPLY. Setting the value of this attribute to True will cause the Workflow to raise an exception for any invoice transactions that do not satisfy at least one defined Rule. In this case, organizations could at least be aware that their Rules defined in AME do not cover all business cases that exist for invoices transactions.

Finally, some of the newer Oracle-delivered Workflows such as the 'Payables Invoice Approval' exclusively use AME to derive the approver list Notification recipients. In other words, when the decision is made to enable the Workflow in a production environment, AME must be used in order to indicate to whom the Workflow should send Notifications. In other traditional Workflows such as the 'Purchase Requisition Approval', users can choose either to use AME to build the approval list or to use the standard HR supervisor hierarchy to build the approval list. Choosing AME versus the standard hierarchy is typically done by setting a profile option or a system level option in the integrating application. These specific setups will be discussed in more detail in the next section.

AME Implementation

To implement AME:

1. Download and install the latest AME patchset

2. Assign and configure AME security

3. Enable the use of AME for the integrated application Workflow

4. Configure the appropriate AME Transaction Type

AME Installation

The first step to implementing AME is to install the AME application. As of E-Business Suite Release 11.5.9, AME comes seeded with the Oracle Applications software and is installed as part of the overall product install. As of the writing of this chapter, the latest version of the AME application is 11i.AME.B RUP (Roll-Up Patch).

You can find the most recent patch for AME by using the 'Simple Search Function' under the 'Patches & Updates' tab on MetaLink (see FIGURE 14.15).

FIGURE 14.15

AME Security Setup

AME security setup is the process of giving privileges to the appropriate user or group of users to provide them the ability to setup and configure the AME application. Prior to the current RUP release of

AME, granting access to the AME application was done using Oracle's traditional method of assigning the necessary responsibility to the user account. However, the current version of AME (AME.B) uses a two-step process to provide access to the AME application. The first step involves assigning the appropriate role to the applications user. This step provides access to the various functions within AME. Version 11.AME.B uses the Oracle Role Based Access Model (RBAC), which is part of the new User Management model (UMX), to provide access to the AME.

Predefined Roles

The following roles are predefined in Patchset 11i.AME.B.

- **Approvals Management Business Analyst** – provides view access to the Business Dashboard, as well as access to Attributes, Conditions, Groups, Test Workbench, and Rules, with create, update, and delete permissions. This role has access to the 'Setup Report' page and the 'Configuration Variables' page, with permission to change Transaction Type configuration values. This role can create, update, and delete Actions and can create, update, and delete Action Type configuration values, but it cannot create, update, or delete Action Types. This is the most commonly used role because it provides the ability to configure Transaction Types in AME.

- **Approvals Management System Administrator** – provides access to the Admin Dashboard, the Setup Report, the exceptions log, and Configuration Variables, with permission to define Transaction Type values. This role can create, update, and delete Transaction Types.

- **Approvals Management Administrator** – has all the access rights of both the Business Analyst and System Administrator roles. This role can create, update, and delete Action Types and can modify default configuration values.

- **Approvals Management System Viewer** – has view only access to the Admin dashboard and Setup Report.

- **Approvals Management Process Owner** – has view only access to the Business Dashboard, Attributes, Conditions, Action Types, Approver Groups, Test Workbench, and Rules. This role also has access to the 'Setup Report' page.

Custom Roles

Oracle does provide the ability to create custom AME roles. Custom roles may be necessary to limit the AME setup functions to which a user has access. Oracle provides a Permission Set to specifically define those functions that a role should have access to as well as the type of access (e.g., insert, update, delete) granted to the role. The details of all of the predefined Permission Sts are outside the scope of this chapter. For more information regarding the specifics of all permission sets and the type of access each grants, please refer to *Oracle Approvals Management Implementation Guide, Release 12, Part No. B31622-02, December 2006*.

Assigning Roles

When assigning an AME role to a user, you must login to Oracle Applications as the SYSADMIN user and use the 'User Management' responsibility to grant the necessary role(s) to the user. Following are the steps to grant an AME role to an Oracle user:

1. Login to the Oracle Applications as user SYSADMIN
2. Choose the 'User Management' responsibility
3. Choose the 'Users' menu function (from list of functions on the right-hand side of the responsibilities page)

4. From the User Management search page, enter criteria to search for the user or group of users requiring access. For example, enter the Oracle Applications user name. Press the Go button to initiate the search and review the results to make sure you have the correct user(s). Once you verify that you have the user(s) you want, click on the 'Update' button for each user for whom you wish to assign AME roles (see FIGURE 14.16).

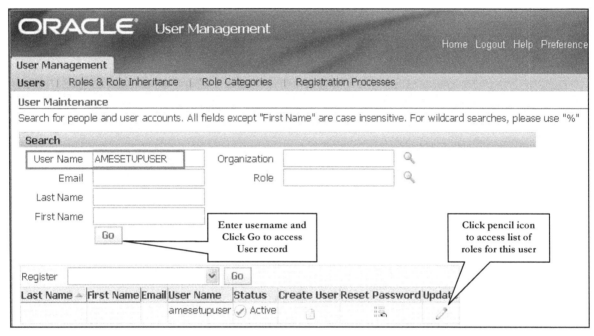

FIGURE 14.16

5. From the 'Update User' page, click on the 'Assign Roles' button (see FIGURE 14.17).

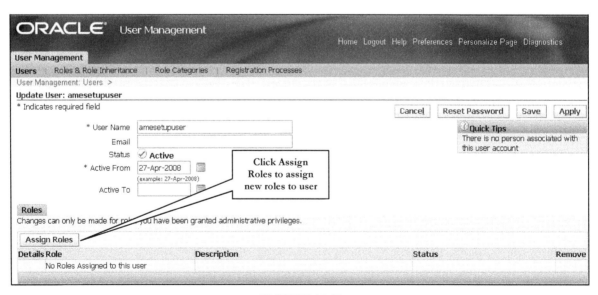

FIGURE 14.17

6.   When the 'Search and Select: Assign Roles' page appears, type 'Approvals Management%' as the search criteria. Be sure that the 'Search By' is 'Roles and Responsibilities'. Press the Go button to initiate the search. Once the results are displayed, place a check mark next to each role you want to assign the user. Press the Select button to accept the selections and return to the 'Update User' page (see FIGURE 14.18).

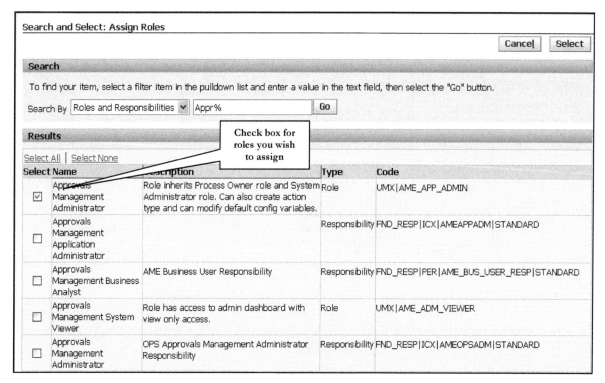

FIGURE 14.18

7.   From the 'Update User' page, select the Apply button to update the role assignments for the user.
8.   Once the roles have been selected, AME requires that the individual assigning the Rule provide a justification for assigning the specific role(s) to the intended user. The justification reason is free form text so any reason can be provided in the 'Justification' field. Click the Apply button to save changes (see FIGURE 14.19).

FIGURE 14.19

After the roles have been assigned, access must be granted to AME Transaction Type data. Data Security Access allows an organization to segregate the configuration of different Transaction Types. For example, an organization may have Functional SuperUsers responsible for defining Rules for Transaction Types related to only their departments.

The following describes each step required to grant AME Transaction Type data access to an Oracle user.

1. Login to Oracle Applications as SYSADMIN
2. Choose the 'Functional Administrator' responsibility
3. From the 'Grant Search' page, click on the 'Create Grant' button (see FIGURE 14.20)

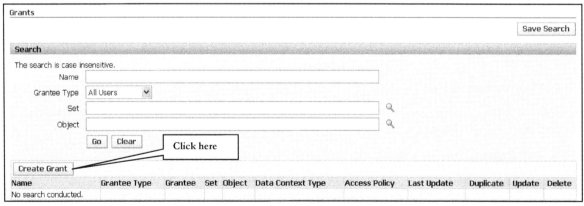

FIGURE 14.20

4. From the 'Create Grant' screen, enter data in the following fields (see FIGURE 14.21)
   ♦ **Name** – Unique name of the grant. Ex. (Username) Data Grant

- **Description** – Enter descriptive text regarding the grant such as the reason or purpose of the grant

- **Effective From/To Dates** – If the grant is for a specific period of time, enter the appropriate dates. The 'Effective From' date field is populated with the current date and time by default. If the grant is not time sensitive, leave these fields as is

- **Security Context** – The 'Security Context' section allows you to enter the user or group of users being granted the current access. Entering the correct user information in this section can sometimes be tricky. As a recommendation, performing grants for a single user at a time appears to be most successful. To perform a single grant, do the following: if the Oracle user assignee has an HR employee name associated with their FND user account, enter the employee name in the 'Grantee' field. If the user does not have an associated HR employee record, enter the Oracle username in the 'Grantee' field. Additionally, change the 'Grantee Type' drop down option to 'Specific User'.

- **Data Security** - Under 'Data Security', enter 'AME Transaction Types' in the 'Object' field

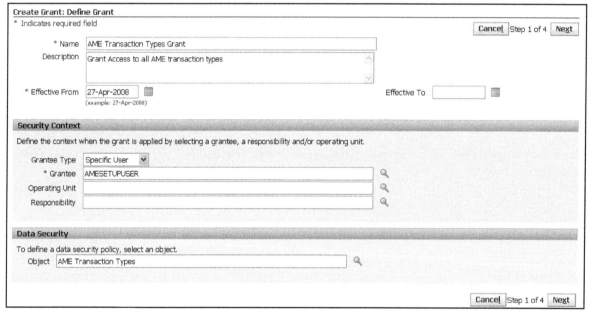

FIGURE 14.21

5. Click on the Next button

6. On the 'Select Object Data Context' page (see FIGURE 14.22), choose the appropriate level of access

- **All Rows** – Provides access to all AME Transaction Types

- **Instance** – Provides access to a specific AME Transaction Type

- **Instance Set** – Provides access to one or more AME Transaction Types based on a predefined instance set. Creating an instance set is outside the scope of this book.

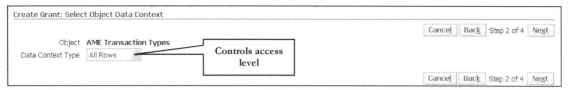

FIGURE 14.22

7. Click on the Next button

8. On the 'Define Object Parameters and Select Set' page, enter 'AME Calling Applications' in the 'Set' field under the 'Set' section (see FIGURE 14.23)

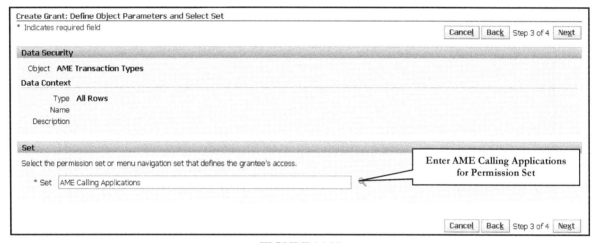

FIGURE 14.23

9 Click on the Next button

10. On the 'Review and Finish' page, verify that all of the information entered is correct. Click on the 'Finish' button to save the changes to the database.

The previous setup steps describe the process of granting access to AME functionality for all current Transaction Types in the application. If the goal is to limit the access to specific Transaction Types and overall functionality, adjust the setting for the data security object, context type and permission set accordingly. Refer to *Oracle Approvals Management Implementation Guide, Release 12, Part No. B31622-02, December 2006* or contact Oracle support for more information regarding specific settings.

Integrated Application AME Setup

As mentioned earlier in the chapter, many Workflows use AME to get the list of approvers. Some of these Workflows use AME by default whenever the specific module begins using the Workflow. Other Workflows use a decision point node (inside the Workflow) to determine whether to use AME or another means to find Notification recipients. In either case, there is usually some setup feature in the integrated applications that has to be set in order to indicate that AME should be used for approvals. Unfortunately, the manner in which the setup is done sometimes differs not only by application module, but even by individual Workflows within an application.

The following examples demonstrate different ways in which Workflow is setup or enabled to use AME for approvers.

AP Invoice Approval Workflow

The 'AP Invoice Approval' Workflow by default only uses AME to generate a list of Notification approvers. In order to enable Workflow to control invoice approval, setups must be completed through the 'Payables Options' form.

Three options shown in FIGURE 14.24 dictate how Invoice Approval is facilitated in the Payables application.

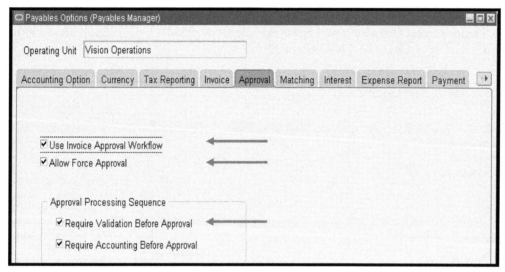

FIGURE 14.24

The first option, 'Use Invoice Approval Workflow', is the primary option because it informs the Payables application to force all invoices to go through the 'Invoice Approval' Workflow. As mentioned previously, when this option is enabled, all invoices are set to Required and must initially move into the Workflow cycle. The next option is 'Allow Force Approval'. This allows a user to automatically set the approval status of an invoice to Approved, which allows an invoice to be automatically approved without going through the Workflow cycle. The last option, 'Require Validation Before Approval', requires an invoice to be fully validated before it can be placed in the Workflow approval cycle.

Payables Expense Report Approval Workflow

This Workflow is responsible for sending Approval Notifications for AP expense reports. It can selectively use AME to build the list of approval Notification recipients by retrieving the value of the Profile Option 'AME:Installed' (see FIGURE 14.25). If the value of the Profile Option is set to 'Yes' at the Payables Application level, the Workflow will use AME for approvals. If it is set to No, the Workflow will not use AME for its approval hierarchy list. The Profile Option can be set from the standard Oracle 'Profile Options' form (Read the *Oracle Applications System Administrator's Guide – Maintenance, Release 11i, Part No. B13924-04, July 2006* for more information).

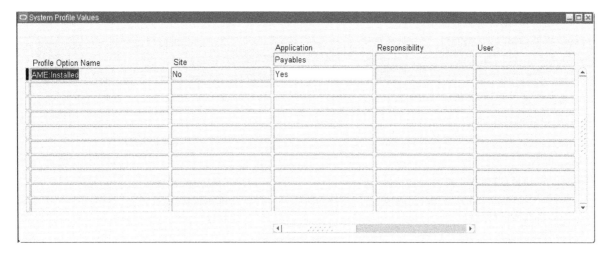

FIGURE 14.25

Purchase Requisition Approval Workflow

This Workflow sends Notifications to individuals who must review and approve purchase requisitions. Like the 'Payables Expense Report' Workflow, this Workflow also has built-in functionality that allows the Workflow to either use AME or another method for retrieving the list of Notification recipients. However, the Workflow does not look at a Profile Option to determine the approval path. Instead it looks at the Purchase Requisition Document Type Setup in Purchasing (see FIGURE 14.26). If the value of the 'Approval Transaction Type' field on the 'Document Types Setup' form is set to PURCHASE_REQ then the 'Purchase Requisition Approval' Workflow will use AME for approval routing.

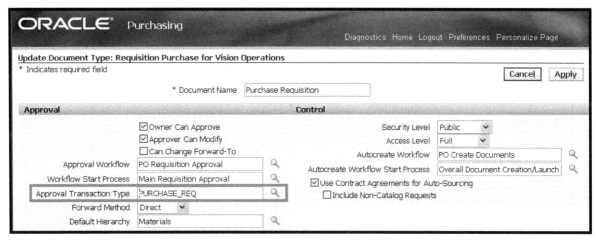

FIGURE 14.26

iRecruitment Vacancy Approval Setup

Vacancy Approval is one of the few exceptions where creation of a new Transaction Type is expected. The 'iRecruitment Vacancy Approval' Transaction Type is delivered with seeded Rules so unless the seeded Rules work for your organization, you will want to follow the instructions in the user guide for iRecruitment to create a new Transaction Type for this Approval Process.

In the 'Approvals Management Administrator' responsibility, click the 'Create Transaction Type' button (see FIGURE 14.27).

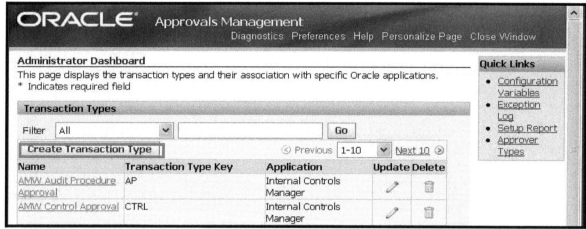

FIGURE 14.27

Create a Transaction Type with a unique key and name. Accept the default values on Step 2 of the setup flow. On Step 3 of the Creation Process flow, update the Static Usage to Dynamic for the Workflow Item Key and update the query to

```
SELECT item_key FROM hr_api_transactions WHERE transaction_id = :transactionId.
```

Also, update the Workflow Item Type to HRSSA. The summary page for the Transaction Type Creation Process is shown in FIGURE 14.28.

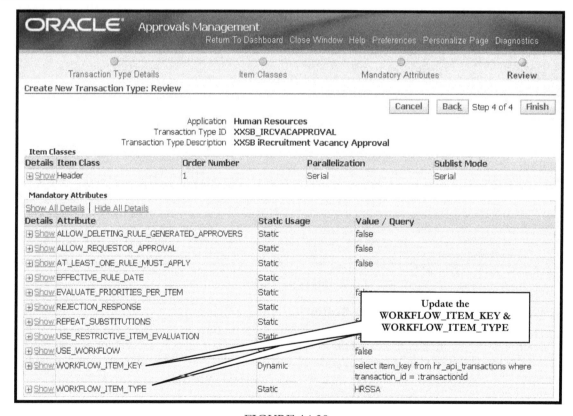

FIGURE 14.28

Then go to the 'Approvals Management Business Analyst' responsibility and create the AME components as needed.

Next, set the Profile Option 'IRC: Vacancy Approval Transaction Type' to the Internal Name of the Transaction Type to be used for Vacancy Approval (see FIGURE 14.29):

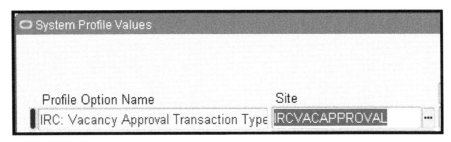

FIGURE 14.29

Finally, go to Application Developer Responsibility → Application → Function, search for IRC_VAC_DETS_NET, go to the 'Form' tab and change the value for the AMETranType to the new Transaction Type name in the Parameters field as shown in FIGURE 14.30

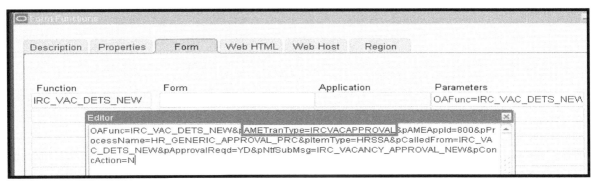

FIGURE 14.30

It is important to note that enabling AME for a particular integrated application Workflow differs between applications and Workflows. You should consult either the appropriate Oracle User's Guide or Oracle Support for more information on the specific setup required to enable the AME feature for a particular Workflow.

Configuring AME Transaction Types

So far this chapter has focused on the AME basics, as well as how to prepare the application to be used and integrated with other E-Business Suite applications. Now the focus shifts to the actual development of Rules in AME. Each of the examples in this section will demonstrate the creation of not only the AME Rule itself, but any supporting component development (e.g., Attribute, Conditions, Approver Group, etc.). However, before we begin setting up Rules in AME, a couple of points need to be mentioned regarding Transaction Types and Rule development planning.

AME Configuration Dashboard

In Patchset AME.B, the Approvals Management Business Analyst Role provides access to the Business Analyst Dashboard (see FIGURE 14.31).

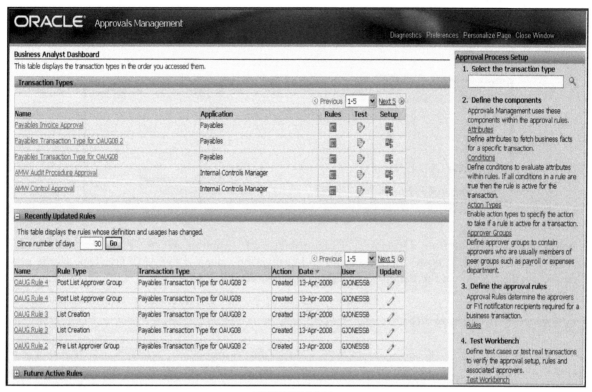

FIGURE 14.31

The Dashboard provides a "birds eye view" of the different setup components in the AME application.

Along with displaying an overview of the various currently defined Transaction Types, the Dashboard also displays any Rules that have recently been defined, updated or deleted along with any Rules that are slated to become active at a future date. More importantly, the Dashboard provides links to all of the setup components required when defining new business case Rules in AME, including Attributes, Conditions, Approver Groups and Rules.

Transaction Type Analysis

Whenever a business user begins the process of defining Rules to represent organization business cases, it is important to have an understanding of the Transaction Types upon which the business rules will be based. As part of this understanding, a user should determine two important elements of the Transaction Type:

- What does the Transaction Type's Transaction ID represent?

- How does the Transaction Type determine the requester of a transaction?

The answer to the first question would require some research (i.e., MetaLink, Application-specific guides, etc.) to discover what value in a particular transaction is used to represent the Transaction ID. In the case of the Payables Invoice Approval Transaction Type, the INVOICE_ID in AP_INVOICES_ALL is used as the Transaction Type. The importance of knowing the value of the Transaction ID lies in the fact that all Dynamic Attributes use the Transaction ID as part of the WHERE clause of the SQL statement used to retrieve their value.

The other important item to consider is the starting point AME will use to build an approver list. Typically, the individual requesting a particular transaction, such as an invoice or expense report, will represent the approver list starting point. To determine the requester initiating a transaction, a required Dynamic Attribute is defined for most, if not all, Transaction Types that contains the logic to retrieve this value. The required Attribute is TRANSACTION_REQUESTOR_PERSON_ID. In the Payables Invoice Approval Transaction Type for example, the value of this Attribute is retrieved by the following SELECT statement:

```
SELECT requester_id
FROM ap_invoices_all
WHERE invoice_id = :transactionId;
```

This means that the person populated in the 'Requester' field on the Invoice Header in Payables will be flagged as the initiator of the transaction. Any approver lists that are built from an invoice transaction will begin using the Requester ID as the basis. However, if the approver list is required to start from another data element in the transaction, there are other AME Attributes that can be set at runtime to force AME to build the list using another starting point. Review the "Attribute(s)" section of this chapter for more information.

AME Rule Development Planning

Prior to beginning the process of defining AME Rules and any supporting components, several planning procedures should be followed and considered.

- **Component Requirements** – This means determining whether there are any additional setup components that need to be defined in order for the Rule to be defined. To make this determination, some of the following questions should be answered:

  1. Are there any new Conditions that need to be defined and used on the Rule? Can a previously created Condition be reused?

  2. For any new Conditions that need to be defined, are there any additional associated Attributes that need to be defined for the Condition?

  3. Are there any non-standard hierarchy approvers that need to be added to the approval list? If so, are there new Approver Groups that need to be defined or can a previously defined list be used?

  4. Have all of the necessary Action Types been enabled for the current Transaction Type to allow the appropriate Action to be used when defining a new Rule?

  There are other questions that could be considered as well. These represent some of the more common questions that should be answered prior to Rule development.

- **Use Decision Trees (or similar diagram)** – A pictorial representation of the different approval scenarios can aid in the Rule development in AME. Primarily, the decision tree diagram helps to outline the beginning and end results of an approval scenario without the unnecessary detail. Decision trees can also provide the following benefits:

  1. Help gain support from management and users because they can quickly identify and understand what events initiates the approval scenario and who all the potential approvers will be

2. Provide a basis for creating a testing document

3. Improve overall logic by identifying all possible combinations of transaction events and approvers

4. Identify any approver alternatives that should be considered

5. Identify any problems with the initiating transaction event or potential approvers

FIGURE 14.32 is an example of a decision tree outlining an approval scenario:

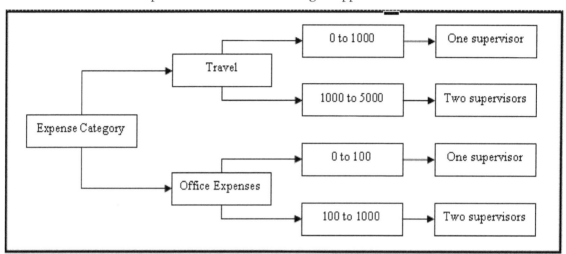

FIGURE 14.32

- **Develop Test Cases** – As is the case with other Oracle product implementations, documenting the specific business case requirements along with the expected results helps to ensure AME Rules are evaluated properly. AME provides a function that allows Rules to be tested prior to installation in a production environment. The Testing Workbench feature will be discussed later in this chapter.

Business Case #1

For each of the following Business Case demonstrations, the HR supervisor hierarchy is used as the basis for building approval lists. Additionally, we assume that only one currency (USD) is used.

The first business case is a simple approval requirement for the Payables application. Although it is a very basic example, the intent is to introduce the method of developing a Rule and its supporting components from the ground up. Additionally, the goal is to show some of the different AME self-service pages encountered during this process.

Business Requirement: For any invoice greater than or equal to five hundred dollars, require approval one supervisor level up from the requester.

The first step prior to the development of any AME Rule is to determine what supporting components need to be defined along with the Rule. Based on our business case requirement, we assume that the following components need to be defined.

- Attribute: Total Invoice Amount – This will retrieve the total amount of the invoice

- Condition: Total Invoice Amount >= $500 – This Condition will ensure that the associated Rule will only be satisfied by the appropriate invoice total amount

- Rule: If Total Invoice Amount >= $500, then require approvals up to the first supervisor

Now it is time to set up the AME components.

1. Login to Oracle Applications using the 'Approval Management Business Analyst' responsibility (see FIGURE 14.33):

Approvals Management Administrator	Approvals Management Business Analyst
Approvals Management Application Administrator	Business Analyst Dashboard
Approvals Management Business Analyst	
CRM HTML Administration	

FIGURE 14.33

2. From the Business Analyst Dashboard, enter Payables Invoice Approval in the Select Transaction Type field located on the right hand side of the Dashboard (see FIGURE 14.34). Click on the magnifying glass icon, which will display the Search and Select window (see FIGURE 14.35). The Payables Invoice Approval Transaction Type should be the only Transaction Type displayed. Click on the Quick Select icon. This will query all of the data related to this Transaction Type and make it active in AME.

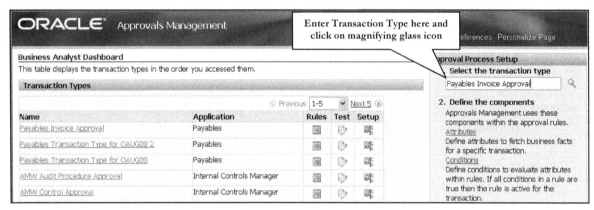

FIGURE 14.34

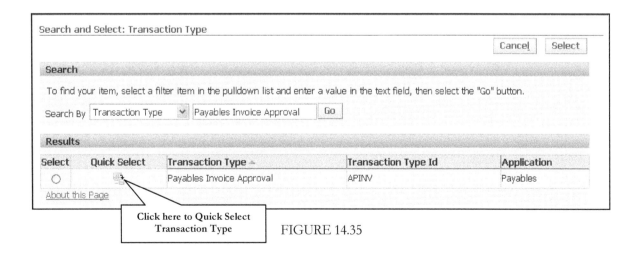

FIGURE 14.35

3. The first component we need to create is the Attribute to retrieve the total invoice amount. From the 'Business Analyst Dashboard', click on the 'Attributes' link to navigate to the 'Attributes Listing' page (see FIGURE 14.36).

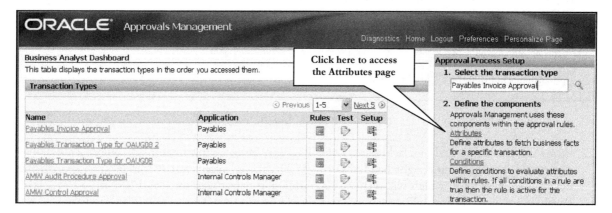

FIGURE 14.36

4. The 'Attributes' page provides a listing of all previously defined Attributes for the current Transaction Type. For the purposes of this example, a new Attribute will be defined. Click on the Create button (see FIGURE 14.37).

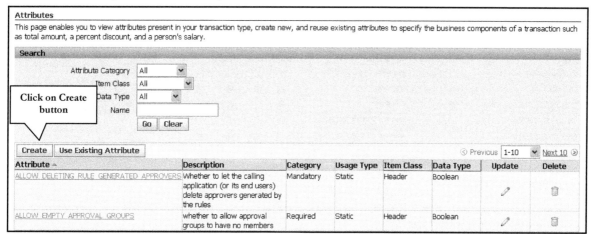

FIGURE 14.37

5. From the 'Create New Attribute' page, enter the following values for the listed fields (see FIGURE 14.38).

♦ Name: INVOICE_TOTAL_AMOUNT

♦ Item Class: Header

♦ Description: Retrieve the total amount of the invoice from the invoice header

♦ Data Type: Number

♦ Usage Type: Dynamic (since the value of the Attribute is real-time, we need to define as a Dynamic Attribute)

♦ Value: SELECT invoice_amount FROM ap_invoices_all WHERE invoice_id = :transactionId;

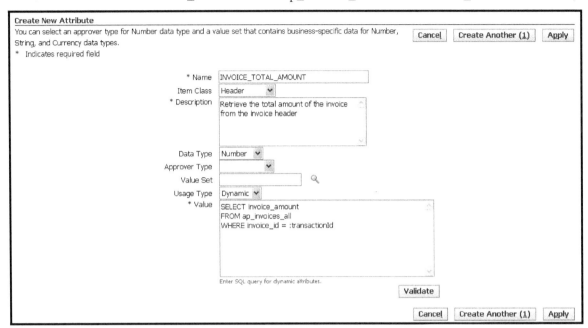

FIGURE 14.38

Click on the Validate button to verify the SQL syntax is correct. Click on the Apply button to save the changes to the database. Attributes are listed in alphabetical order. Verify the Attribute was created successfully.

6. Now that the necessary Attribute has been created, a Condition needs to be defined that will set the lower limit for the invoice amount in accordance with the Business Rule (>= $500). From the 'Attributes' listing page, click on the 'Conditions' link located at the top of the page (see FIGURE 14.39).

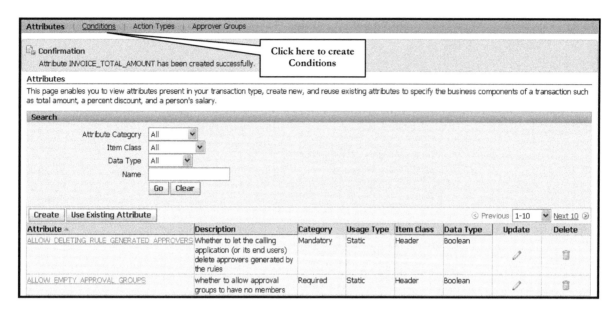

FIGURE 14.39

7. The 'Conditions' page, like the 'Attributes' page, provides a listing of all currently defined Conditions for the current Transaction Type. Unlike the Attributes functionality however, you cannot inherit predefined Conditions from other Transaction Types. You can only define new Conditions or update previously defined Conditions. For the purpose of this example, we need to define a new Condition. Click on the Create button to begin defining a new Condition (see FIGURE 14.40).

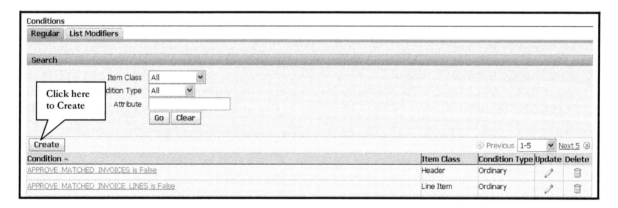

FIGURE 14.40

8. From the 'Create New Condition' page, perform the following steps (see FIGURE 14.41):

    ♦ If not already set, change Condition Type to Ordinary

    ♦ Enter INVOICE_TOTAL_AMOUNT in the Attribute field. Press the 'Tab' key

    ♦ Once the 'Expression' section appears, change the expression drop down to 'is greater than or equal to'

    ♦ In the field next to the drop down, enter '500' in the lower bound region

♦ The 'Create New Condition' page should look like the following

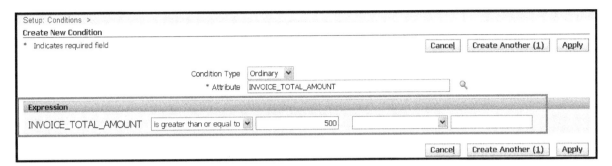

FIGURE 14.41

♦ Click on the Apply button to save the changes. Conditions are listed in alphabetical order based on the associated Attribute name. Verify that the Condition was created successfully.

9. Once the supporting AME components have been created, the Rule is ready to be defined. However, before doing that we need to verify that we have the necessary Action Type available to the Rule. Since this approval requirement specifies approval from the invoice requester's supervisor, the standard supervisory level Action Type should be available. To verify this, click on the 'Action Types' link located at the top of the 'Conditions' page (see FIGURE 14.42).

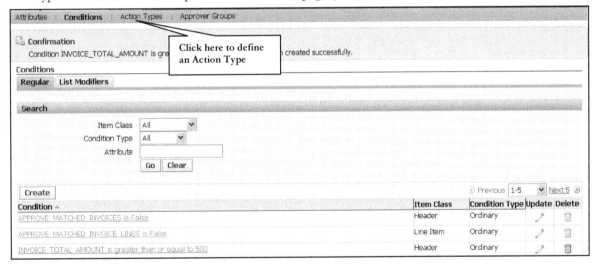

FIGURE 14.42

10. The 'Action Types' screen provides a listing of all Action Types currently available to this Transaction Type. Search through this list to verify that the Action Type(s) required for any Rules you will create is listed. If the Action Type is not listed, click on the 'Use Existing Action Type' button (see FIGURE 14.43). This will allow you to pick any number of Action Types which are not currently available and add them accordingly (see FIGURE 14.44).

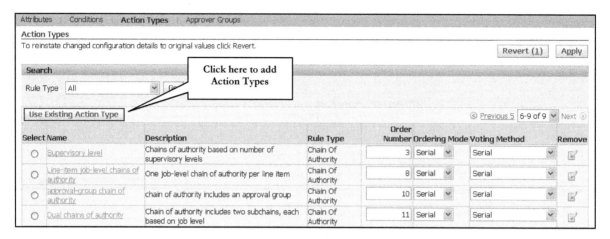

FIGURE 14.43

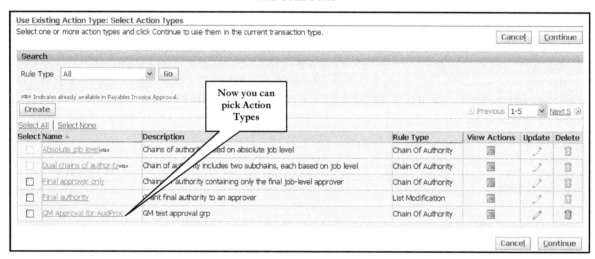

FIGURE 14.44

11. To define the overall Approver Rule, click on the 'Rules' tab located in the upper left hand portion of the current page (see FIGURE 14.45).

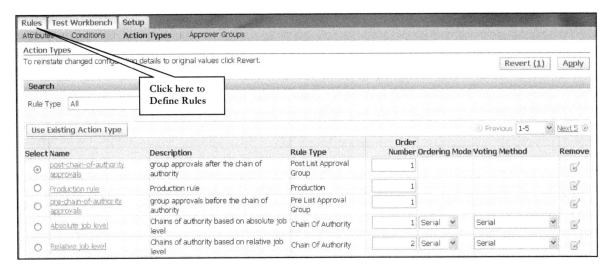

FIGURE 14.45

12. Like the other AME components, the 'Rules' page gives a listing of all defined, active Rules for the current Transaction Type. A new Rule is defined for this example. Click on the Create button to begin defining a new Rule (see FIGURE 14.46).

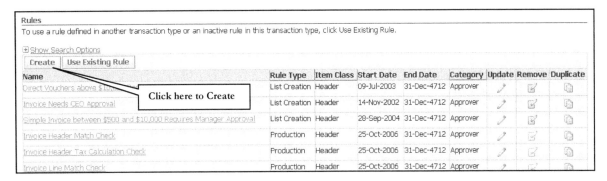

FIGURE 14.46

13. On the first page of the Rule Creation Process, enter the following information for each field (see FIGURE 14.47):

♦ Name: Invoices Greater than 500 require 1 supervisor approval

♦ Rule Type: List Creation (Choose from drop down list)

♦ Leave default values for start and end dates. Click the Next button

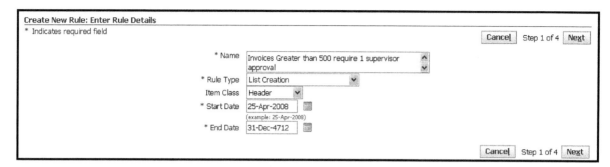

FIGURE 14.47

14. On the next page, the required Condition needs to be added to the Rule. Click on the 'Add Condition' button (see FIGURE 14.48).

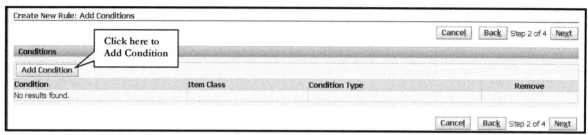

FIGURE 14.48

15. The next page that appears is the listing of all current Conditions defined for the Transaction Type. Multiple Conditions can be selected at the same time. For this particular Rule, choose the Rule 'INVOICE_TOTAL_AMOUNT is greater than or equal to 500'. Place a check mark next to the Condition. Click on the 'Continue' button (see FIGURE 14.49).

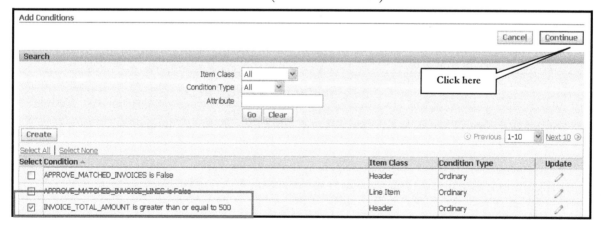

FIGURE 14.49

16. Click on the Next button.

17. On the next page, the required actions of the Rule need to be added. In the Action Type field, AME provides a list of all Action Types currently available to the transaction. Choose supervisory level from the list. Press the 'Tab' key.

18. In the 'Action' field, enter a % and then click the magnifying glass icon. This will cause AME to display a window that lists all of the actions associated with the chosen Action Type. For this example, choose the 'Require approvals up to the first superior action' from this window. Using the 'Quick Select' icon will select and close the window simultaneously (See FIGURE 14.50).

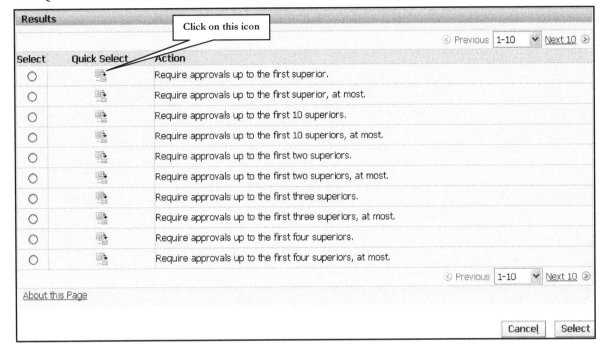

FIGURE 14.50

19. Verify that the 'Add Actions' page looks like FIGURE 14.51:

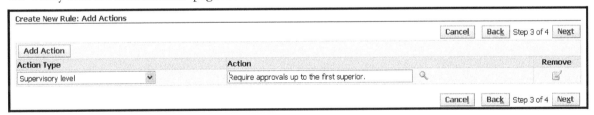

FIGURE 14.51

20. Click on the Next button.

21. The next page provides an overview of the new Rule including all associated Conditions and Actions. Review this page and verify all information is correct. Click on the 'Finish' button to save changes to the database (see FIGURE 14.52).

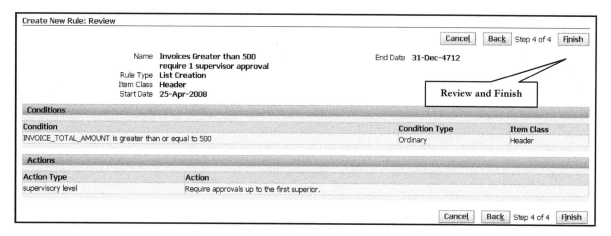

FIGURE 14.52

22. The 'Rules' listing page provides a listing of all Rules sorted by the date they were created. Verify that the Rule was created successfully (see FIGURE 14.53):

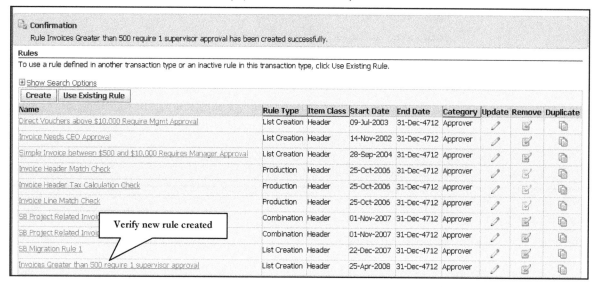

FIGURE 14.53

The business requirement has now been turned into a Rule in the AME application. In the Testing Workbench later in this chapter, the Rule will be tested to verify that it works as expected. Hopefully, this exercise has demonstrated that the actual process of defining AME Rules and components does not have to be a complex procedure. If proper analysis and planning has been done, most Approval Rules can be defined with similar ease regardless of the complexity of the business approval requirement.

Business Case #2

The second business case example is a little more complex for a couple of reasons. First, it involves multiple approver requirements based on the amount of a Payables invoice. Second, the approval requirement will require defining a new AME component type which is a new Approver Group.

Business Requirement 1: For any invoice less than or equal to $5000, require approval from the supervisor of the invoice requester

Business Requirement 2: For any invoice greater than $5000, require approval from two supervisor levels above the invoice requester.

Business Requirement 3: If the supplier of any invoice is DELL, require pre-approval from IT Manager.

Again, the first thing that should be done is determine what supporting components need to be defined along with any Rules that need to be defined. Based on our business case requirement, we are assuming that the following components need to be defined.

> Attribute: Invoice Supplier Name – This will retrieve name of the supplier on the invoice record
>
> Condition(s): Total Invoice Amount <= $5000
>
> > Total Invoice Amount > 5000
> >
> > Invoice Supplier Name = 'DELL'
>
> Approver Group: IT Manager
>
> Rule 1: If Total Invoice Amount <= $5000, then require approvals up to the first supervisor
> Rule 2: If Total Invoice Amount > $5000 then require approvals up to the first two supervisors
> Rule 3: If Invoice Supplier Name = 'DELL', require pre-approval from IT Manager

Next, the AME components need to be defined. The procedures to setup the components are the same as described in the first Business Case example. For this example, many of the procedures will only include the data that should be entered into the appropriate fields on the definition page. Please see the first business case example for specifics on navigating to the various self-service pages.

1. Login to Oracle Applications as the 'Approvals Management Business Analyst' responsibility.

2. Activate the 'Payables Invoice Approval' Transaction Type from the Business Analyst Dashboard.

3. Click on the 'Attributes' link. From the 'Attributes' listing page, click on the Create button.

4. From the 'Create New Attribute' pages, enter the following values for the new Attribute

   ♦ Name: INVOICE_SUPPLIER_NAME

   ♦ Item Class: Header

   ♦ Description: Retrieve the name of the supplier of the invoice from the invoice header

   ♦ Data Type: String

   ♦ Usage Type: Dynamic (since the value of the Attribute is real-time, we need to define as a Dynamic Attribute)

   ♦ Value: `SELECT vendor_name FROM po_vendors pv, ap_invoices_all ai WHERE ai.invoice_id = :transactionId AND ai.vendor_id = pv.vendor_id`

5. Click on the Validate button to verify the SQL syntax. Click on the Apply button to save changes to the database.

6. From the 'Attributes' listing page, click on the 'Conditions' link located at the top of the page.

7. Three new Conditions need to be created based on the business approval requirements. Click on the Create button. Enter the first Condition as follows.

   ♦ If not already set, change Condition Type to Ordinary

   ♦ Enter INVOICE_TOTAL_AMOUNT in the 'Attribute' field. Press the 'Tab' key

   ♦ Once the 'Expression' section appears, change expression drop down to 'is less than or equal to'

   ♦ In the field next to the drop down, enter '5000' in the lower bound region

8. Click on the Apply button to save the changes.

9. The second Condition needs to be created. Click on the Create button. Enter the second Condition as follows.

   ♦ If not already set, change Condition Type to Ordinary

   ♦ Enter INVOICE_TOTAL_AMOUNT in the 'Attribute' field. Press the 'Tab' key

   ♦ Once the 'Expression' section appears, change the expression drop down to 'is greater than'

   ♦ In the field next to the drop down, enter '5000' in the lower bound region

10. Click on the Apply button to save changes.

11. The last Condition that needs to be defined is different from the first two Conditions because it uses a String Attribute (INVOICE_SUPPLIER_NAME) instead of a Numeric Attribute. The procedures to define the Condition are similar as demonstrated. Click on the Create button.

    From the 'Create New Condition' page, perform the following steps
    ♦ Change 'Condition Type' to 'Ordinary'

    ♦ Enter INVOICE_SUPPLIER_NAME in the 'Attribute' field. Press the 'Tab' key

    ♦ Once the 'String Values' section appears, enter 'Dell Computers' in the 'String Value' field. This is case sensitive so enter the value exactly as it appears in the supplier name field in the supplier record

    ♦ The 'Create New Condition' page should look like FIGURE 14.54:

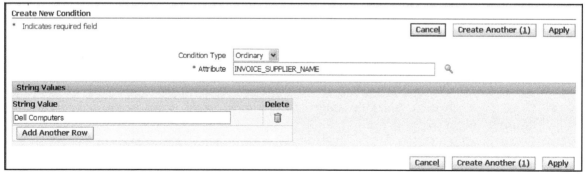

FIGURE 14.54

12. Click on the Apply button to save changes. Verify that the Condition was created successfully by reviewing the list of Conditions (scc FIGURE 14.55):

Condition	Item Class	Condition Type	Update	Delete
APPROVE_MATCHED_INVOICES is False	Header	Ordinary		
APPROVE_MATCHED_INVOICE_LINES is False	Line Item	Ordinary		
INVOICE_SUPPLIER_NAME in (Dell Computers)	Header	Ordinary		
INVOICE_TOTAL_AMOUNT is greater than 5000	Header	Ordinary		
INVOICE_TOTAL_AMOUNT is greater than or equal to 500	Header	Ordinary		

FIGURE 14.55

13. The next component to define is the Approver Group. The purpose of this Approver Group is to retrieve the current IT Manager of the organization. This must be an Approver Group because this approver is outside an Oracle standard hierarchy. A couple of different approaches can be used to define the Approver Group. The Approver Group could be created as a Static Approver Group by specifically naming an individual at the time the Approver Group is defined. The Approver Group could also be defined dynamically by writing a SQL statement that retrieves the id of the employee currently assigned to the IT Manager job within the organization. For simplicity sake in this example, a Static Approver Group will be defined. From the 'Setup' tab, click on the 'Approver Groups' link at the top of the page (see FIGURE 14.56).

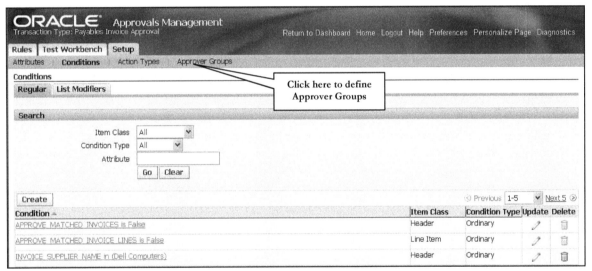

FIGURE 14.56

14. The 'Approver Groups' listing page displays all of the pre-defined Approver Groups for the current Transaction Type. You can define a new Approver Group, inherit an Approver Group defined in another Transaction Type or update an existing Approver Group on this page. For this example, a new Approver Group will be defined. Click on the Create button (see FIGURE 14.57).

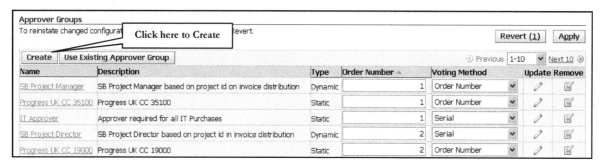

FIGURE 14.57

15. On the 'Create New Approver Group' page, enter the following for the necessary fields.

♦ Name: IT Manager Approver Group

♦ Description: Static Approver Group Naming IT Manager

♦ Order Number: 1

♦ Voting Method: Serial

♦ Usage Type: Static

16. Once this data has been entered, navigate to the 'Group Members' section and click on the 'Add Another Row' button.

17. Change the 'Approver Type' field to 'HR People'. This will allow entry of a current HR employee in the 'Approver' field.

18. In the 'Approver' field, enter the name of an employee in your organization's HR schema. (Ex. Jones, Gerald). You can also use the magnifying glass icon and enter criteria in the 'Search and Select' window to display a list of current HR employees. Choose an employee from this list.

19. The 'Order Number' field should have a '1'. If it does not, enter a '1' in this field. The 'Create New Approver Group' page should look similar to FIGURE 14.58.

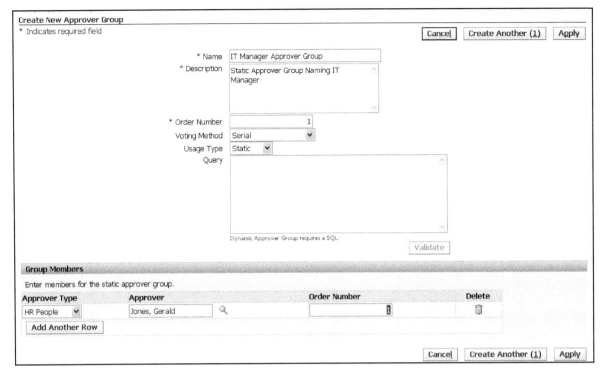

FIGURE 14.58

20. Click on the Apply button to save changes.

21. The 'Approver Groups' listing page orders Approver Groups by their assigned Order Number. Verify that the Approver Group was created successfully (see FIGURE 14.59).

FIGURE 14.59

22. Since the business requirement calls for both standard HR supervisor lists to be built along with a pre-approver list, be sure that the following Action Types are available to the Transaction Type.

♦ Supervisory Level

♦ Pre-Chain-of-Authority Approvals

Refer to the first business case example for more information on enabling Action Types for a Transaction Type

23. Now that the supporting components have been defined, the actual AME Rules need to be defined in the application. Two of the Rules will build the standard HR supervisor approver list based on invoice amount. The other Rule will build the pre-approver list, if applicable, based on supplier. The defining of each Rule follows the same procedures as described in the first Business Case.

24. From the current self-service page, click on the 'Rules' tab.

25. From the 'Rules' listing page, click on the Create button.

26. The first Rule should be defined with the following values for the necessary fields.

   - Name: Invoice less or equal to 5000 require 1 supervisor approver

   - Rule Type: List Creation

   - Start / End Dates: (Leave the default dates in each field)

   - Condition: INVOICE_TOTAL_AMOUNT is less than or equal to 5000

   - Action Type: Supervisory Level

   - Action: Require Approvals up to the first superior

   Click on the 'Finish' button to save changes

27. The second Rule should be defined with the following values for the necessary fields

   - Name: Invoice greater than 5000 require 2 supervisor approvers

   - Rule Type: List Creation

   - Start / End Dates: (Leave the default dates in each field)

   - Condition: INVOICE_TOTAL_AMOUNT is greater than 5000

   - Action Type: Supervisory Level

   - Action: Require Approvals up to the first two superiors

   Click on the 'Finish' button to save changes

28. The final Rule should be defined with the following values for the necessary fields

   - Name: DELL invoices require IT Manager approval

   - Rule Type: Pre List Approver Group

   - Start / End Dates: (Leave the default dates in each field)

   - Condition: INVOICE_SUPPLIER_NAME in (DELL)

   - Action Type: pre-chain-of-authority approvals

   - Action: Require pre-approval from IT Manager Approver Group

   Click on the 'Finish' button to save changes

29. Remember, the 'Rules' listing page orders the current Rules by the date the Rule was defined in AME. Verify that each Rule was created successfully

Business Case #3

Requirement 1: For any purchase requisition less than or equal to $25,000, require approval from the supervisor of the requisition buyer

Requirement2: For any purchase requisition greater than $25,000 and less than or equal to $50,000, require approval from two supervisor levels above the requisition buyer

Requirement3: For any purchase requisition greater than $50,000 and less than or equal to $100,000, require approval from three supervisor levels above the requisition buyer

Requirement4: For any purchase requisition greater than $100,000 require approval from four supervisor levels above the requisition buyer

Requirement 5: Vehicle purchases require director level or above approval and IT purchases require pre-approval from the IT Manager.

For this case, the following components need to be defined:

Attributes: No new Attributes are required. All necessary Attributes are seeded.

Conditions:

REQUISITION_TOTAL >= $0 and <= $25,000

REQUISITION_TOTAL > $25,000 and <= $50,000

REQUISITION_TOTAL > $50,000 and <= $100,000

REQUISITION_TOTAL > $100,000

Condition ▲	Item Class	Condition Type
REQUISITION_TOTAL is greater than 100000,USD	Header	Ordinary
REQUISITION_TOTAL is greater than 25000 and less than or equal to 50000,USD	Header	Ordinary
REQUISITION_TOTAL is greater than 50000 and less than or equal to 100000,USD	Header	Ordinary
REQUISITION_TOTAL is greater than or equal to 0 and less than or equal to 25000,USD	Header	Ordinary

FIGURE 14.60

Conditions:

ITEM_CATEGORY = AUTOMOTIVE.VEHICLE

ITEM_CATEGORY in (COMPUTER.PC, COMPUTER.SERVER)

Condition ▲	Item Class	Condition Type
ITEM_CATEGORY in (425.00, AUTOMOTIVE.VEHICLE)	Line Item	Ordinary
ITEM_CATEGORY in (COMPUTER.PC, COMPUTER.SERVER)	Line Item	Ordinary

FIGURE 14.61

Approver Group: IT_APPROVER

The Approver Group shown in FIGURE 14.62 is a Static Approver Group. Approvers can be people defined in HR or users defined in the 'Create User' form. Users not linked to employees are the only records available as FND User Approver Types. If a user is linked to an employee, that user will only appear in the HR People List of Values. This allows for significant flexibility in AME. One way to meet a requirement to send an approval request to a distribution list is by assigning a user with an email address that is a distribution list.

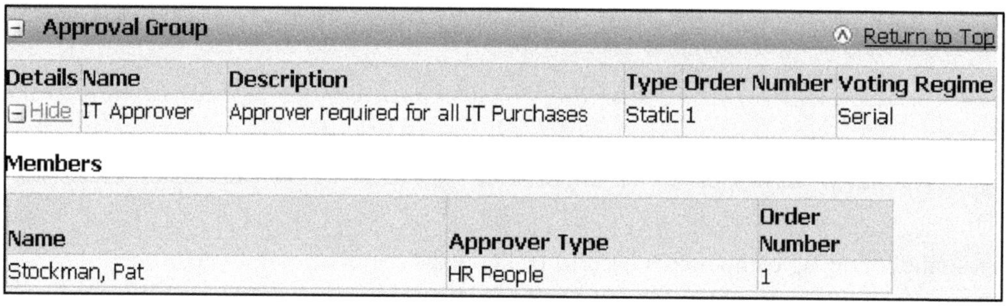

Approval Group					⊛ Return to Top
Details Name	**Description**		**Type**	**Order Number**	**Voting Regime**
⊟Hide IT Approver	Approver required for all IT Purchases		Static	1	Serial

Members

Name	Approver Type	Order Number
Stockman, Pat	HR People	1

FIGURE 14.62

Rules 1-4: – Supervisor level Rules are created for each requisition total range as shown in FIGURE 14.63:.

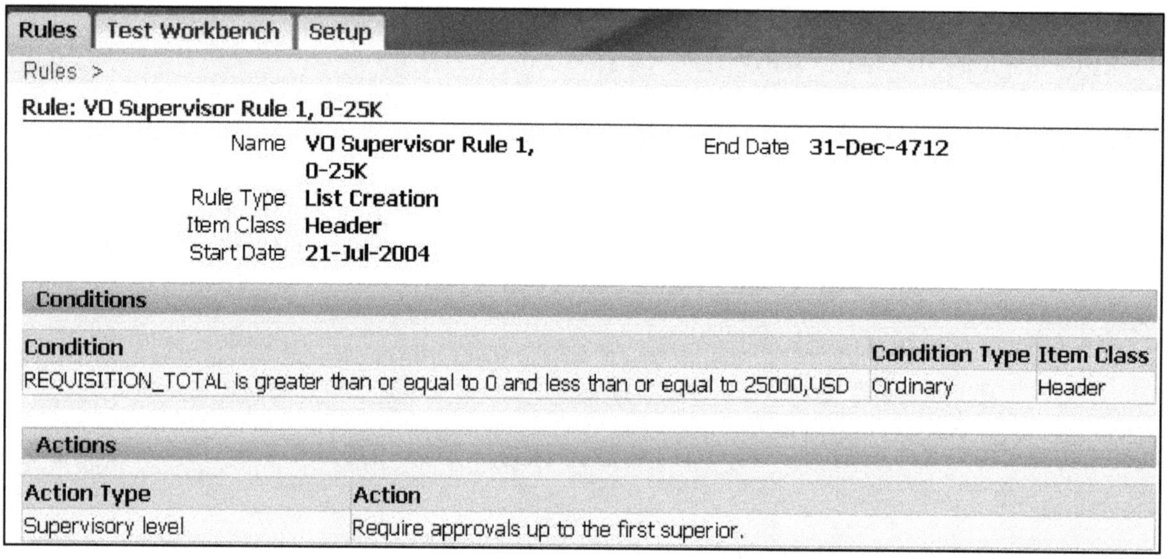

Rules	**Test Workbench**	**Setup**

Rules >

Rule: VO Supervisor Rule 1, 0-25K

Name	**VO Supervisor Rule 1, 0-25K**	End Date	**31-Dec-4712**
Rule Type	**List Creation**		
Item Class	**Header**		
Start Date	**21-Jul-2004**		

Conditions

Condition	Condition Type	Item Class
REQUISITION_TOTAL is greater than or equal to 0 and less than or equal to 25000,USD	Ordinary	Header

Actions

Action Type	Action
Supervisory level	Require approvals up to the first superior.

FIGURE 14.63

Rule 5: A pre-Approval Rule as shown in FIGURE 14.64 is created to require pre-approval based on any line item with the category COMPUTER.PC or COMPUTER.SERVER.

FIGURE 14.64

Rule 6: The final Rule for the purchase requisition case is for the job level approval. Job levels are based on the approval authority for the employee's job. This is set via the 'Job' form available in Purchasing at Setup → Personnel → Jobs. FIGURE 14.65 shows the job level for a director and the Rule requiring at least a job level of 5 or higher for the purchase of a vehicle. AME will include all approvers in the supervisor chain until an employee is found with a level 5 or higher.

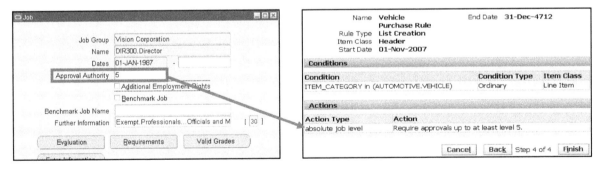

FIGURE 14.65

Business Case #4

For all HR Vacancy Approvals, the following approvals are required:

Requirement 1: Send an FYI Notification to the hiring manager

Requirement 2: Require approval from the hiring manager's VP

Requirement 3: If there is no VP, then require approval from the Division Controller

Requirement 4: Require approval from the Controller for this hiring manager

Requirement 5: Require approval from the Hiring Manager's SVP which is based on the people group

Requirement 6: If there is no SVP, then go to the next level

Requirement 7: Require approval from the Hiring Manager's EVP or CFO, COO or President also identified by the people group

Custom Approver Groups were used to determine the various VPs and controllers needed to approve vacancies. Otherwise, the setup of Rules is similar to those shown in earlier examples. Key custom Approver Groups are shown in the Table 14.5.

Group Name	Desc	Usage Type	Order #	Voting	Dynamic Query
XXSB_IRC_HIRING_MANAGER	This group will contain the personId for the hiring manager of the vacancy	Dynamic	1	Serial	SELECT 'person_id:'||XXSB_irc_notificationspkg.get_irc_manager_id(:transactionId) FROM dual
XXSB_IRC_HIRING_MGR_VP	Hiring manager's Vice President	Dynamic	3	Serial	SELECT 'person_id:'||XXSB_IRC_NOTIFICATIONS_PKG.GET_IRC_VP_PERSON_ID(:transactionId) FROM DUAL
XXSB_IRC_DIVISION_CONTROLLER	Get the division controllers of the hiring manager	Dynamic	4	Serial	SELECT 'user_id:'||user_id FROM FND_USER where USER_NAME = (SELECT DECODE(PAF.ASS_ATTRIBUTE5, '001', 'IRC_DIV_001', '002', 'IRC_DIV_002', '003', 'IRC_DIV_003', '005', 'IRC_DIV_005','IRC_DIV_003') FROM PER_ALL_ASSIGNMENTS_F PAF WHERE PERSON_ID = XXSB_IRC_NOTIFICATIONS_PKG.get_irc_manager_id(:transactionId) AND SYSDATE BETWEEN PAF.EFFECTIVE_START_DATE AND PAF.EFFECTIVE_END_DATE AND paf.PRIMARY_FLAG = 'Y')

| XXSB_IRC_FINAL_VAC_APPROVAL | This group will contain the final approver list for Vacancy Approval | Dynamic | 5 | Serial | SELECT person_id FROM   ((SELECT 'person_id:' \|\| ppf.person_id person_id, ppf.full_name,ind_level,ppg.group_name   FROM per_all_assignments_f paf2, per_all_people_f ppf, pay_people_groups ppg , (SELECT   paf1.person_id ,LEVEL ind_level FROM   per_all_assignments_f paf1   START   WITH   paf1.person_id   = XXSB_irc_notifications_pkg.get_irc_manager_id   (:transactionid) AND   paf1.primary_flag = 'Y' AND SYSDATE   BETWEEN   paf1.effective_start_date AND   paf1.effective_end_date   CONNECT   BY PRIOR paf1.supervisor_id = paf1.person_id AND paf1.primary_flag = 'Y'   AND LEVEL > 1 AND   SYSDATE   BETWEEN paf1.effective_start_date   AND paf1.effective_end_date AND LEVEL > 1) loc WHERE   paf2.person_id = loc.person_id AND SYSDATE   BETWEEN   paf2.effective_start_date AND   paf2.effective_end_date   AND paf2.people_group_id = ppg.people_group_id AND SYSDATE BETWEEN ppf.effective_start_date AND ppf.effective_end_date AND   paf2.person_id = ppf.person_id AND   ppg.group_name = 'Senior Vice President') UNION ALL (SELECT * FROM   (SELECT   'person_id:'   \|\| ppf.person_id person_id,ppf.full_name, ind_level, ppg.group_name FROM per_all_assignments_f paf2, per_all_people_f ppf,   pay_people_groups   ppg,(SELECT paf1.person_id ,LEVEL   ind_level   FROM per_all_assignments_f   paf1   START   WITH paf1.person_id   = XXSB_irc_notifications_pkg.get_irc_manager_id   (:transactionid) AND paf1.primary_flag = 'Y' AND SYSDATE   BETWEEN   paf1.effective_start_date AND   paf1.effective_end_date   CONNECT   BY PRIOR paf1.supervisor_id = paf1.person_id AND paf1.primary_flag = 'Y' AND LEVEL > 1 AND SYSDATE   BETWEEN   paf1.effective_start_date AND paf1.effective_end_date AND   LEVEL > 1) loc WHERE   paf2.person_id = loc.person_id AND SYSDATE   BETWEEN   paf2.effective_start_date AND   paf2.effective_end_date   AND paf2.people_group_id = ppg.people_group_id AND SYSDATE BETWEEN ppf.effective_start_date AND ppf.effective_end_date AND   paf2.person_id = ppf.person_id AND ppg.group_name IN ('Executive Vice President' ,'COO','CFO','President') ORDER BY loc.ind_level ASC) WHERE ROWNUM = 1)) |

TABLE 14. 5

The defining of these Rules along with the supporting components really demonstrates the flexibility of the AME application when defining complex or unique approvals.

The topic of discussion in the next and last section in the chapter, Testing Workbench, will include a section to test whether the first Business Case Rule builds the expected approver lists.

AME Testing Workbench

The ability to define both simple and complex Approval Rules for various E-Business transactions makes AME a very useful Oracle application. However, one of the great features in the AME application is the ability to verify whether the defined Rule setups satisfy your business approval needs. Furthermore, you can perform this verification prior to actually deploying the setups into a production environment. The Test Workbench allows you to evaluate defined Rules against both test as well as 'real' transactions in the integrating application. A test application is one in which the values of various Attributes which have been defined for the Transaction Type are manually entered by the user and submitted to the workbench. However, depending on the number of Attributes and particularly those that are essential based on referenced Conditions, this could be a cumbersome task. Evaluating Rules against real transactions in the appropriate integrated application is often the preferred method of testing. For the purposes of this chapter, use of the workbench using real transactions will be discussed.

Although the Testing Workbench is primarily used as a tool during the Rules development process, it can also be a very useful production support tool. The reason for this is because when the workbench evaluates Rules against actual application transactions, it allows you to preview certain aspects, such as:

• Are Attribute values, particularly custom Attributes retrieving values correctly?

• Are the appropriate Rules being applied or satisfied by the transaction?

• Is the proper approver chain(s) being generated for the transaction based on the Rule(s) chosen?

As is the case with the other AME definition components, access to the Testing Workbench occurs from the AME Business Analyst Dashboard. The workbench can also be accessed via a tab within the setup pages. FIGURE 14.66 shows the link to the 'Test Workbench' from the 'Dashboard' page.

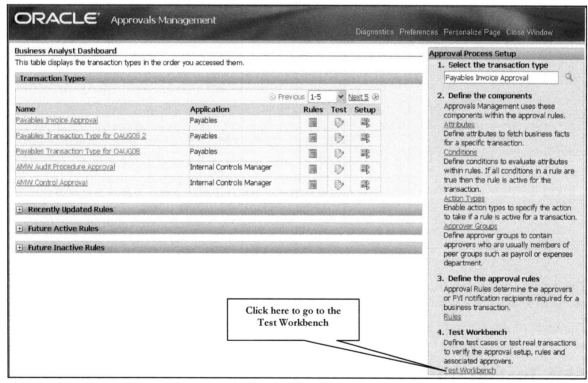

FIGURE 14.66

Executing a Test

The execution of a test in the workbench basically involves a three step process.

1. Retrieve the id of the transaction to be evaluated and enter it in the workbench parameter

2. Review the values of the Transaction Type's Attributes populated by the workbench. The values are based on the current transaction

3. Review the approver list generated by the workbench after the defined Rules have been evaluated against the Attribute values

To demonstrate the use of the workbench, let's refer to Business Case #2 defined in the previous section of this chapter. To recap, the Payables business case involved three Rules to accomplish the following approval requirements.

- Invoices <= $5000 require approval from one supervisor above the requester

- Invoices > $5000 require approval from two supervisors above the requester

- If the supplier of an invoice was DELL, require approval from the IT Manager approval group

For the purpose of this example, a DELL invoice that exceeds $5000 will be assumed. Based on this assumption, the results of the executing the workbench should generate three approvers with one being the individual identified as the IT Manager.

In Payables, the FIGURE 14.67 shows the invoice transaction:

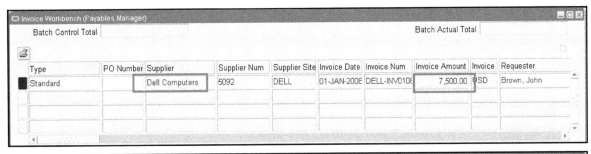

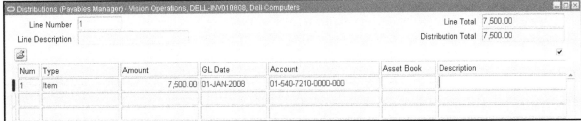

FIGURE 14.67

Notice the requester of this invoice is John Brown. In Human Resources, the reporting structure has John Brown reporting to Mike Stanley. Mike Stanley reports to Mary Renola. It is expected that based on the amount of the invoice, both of these individuals should be listed as required approvers. Additionally, in the previous section the IT Manager Approver Group included one member, Gerald Jones. He should also be included as a required approver because the invoice is from Dell Computers.

Now, let's run this transaction through the workbench to verify whether the proper approver list is generated.

To execute a test against this invoice, navigate to the Test Workbench. On the first page of the 'Test Workbench', notice that you have several options pertaining to managing or executing a test in AME. The 'Test Cases' section allows you to either create, copy or run a previously defined Test Case transaction. However, since our scenario involves testing an actual transaction in the database, the 'Run Real Transaction Test' option should be chosen to execute our test. Click on this button to begin the test. See FIGURE 14.68.

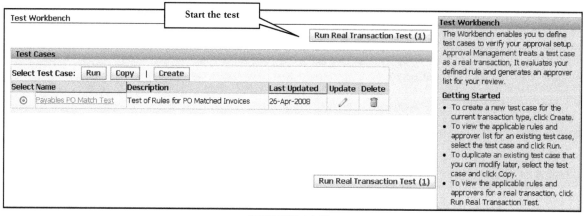

FIGURE 14.68

The next screen prompts the user for the 'Transaction ID' that AME will use to evaluate against the defined Rules of the Transaction Type. It is important to mention that the Transaction ID is the unique database id of the current transaction. In the case of a Payables invoice, the Transaction ID is represented by the INVOICE_ID from AP_INVOICES_ALL. For this example, the Invoice ID for the invoice created earlier is 156015. Enter the appropriate Invoice ID in the 'Transaction Id' field and click the Go button (see FIGURE 14.69).

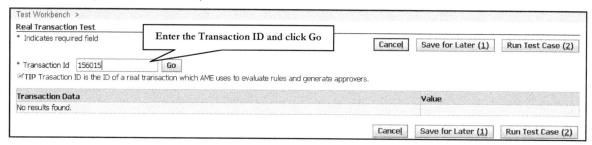

FIGURE 14.69

AME will then populate the values of all Attributes defined for the current Transaction Type (Payables Invoice Approval) based on the setup and Dynamic SQL code (if applicable) associated with the an Attribute. FIGURE 14.70 shows the values of the Header Attributes of the Transaction Type for the invoice. These values should be consistent with the data entered for your invoice transaction. After reviewing the values retrieved for the various Attributes of the transaction, choose the 'Run Test Case' button to execute and evaluate the Rules and actions defined for the transaction.

Focus Transaction Data	Value
⊟ Parameters	
⊟ Mandatory Attributes	
⊟ Transaction ID:156015	
ALLOW_DELETING_RULE_GENERATED_APPROVERS	false
ALLOW_REQUESTOR_APPROVAL	true
AT_LEAST_ONE_RULE_MUST_APPLY	false
EFFECTIVE_RULE_DATE	
EVALUATE_PRIORITIES_PER_ITEM	false
REJECTION_RESPONSE	STOP_ALL_ITEMS
REPEAT_SUBSTITUTIONS	false
USE_RESTRICTIVE_ITEM_EVALUATION	false
USE_WORKFLOW	true
WORKFLOW_ITEM_KEY	156015_
WORKFLOW_ITEM_TYPE	APINVAPR
⊟ Header Attributes	
⊟ Transaction ID:156015	
ALLOW_EMPTY_APPROVAL_GROUPS	true
APPROVE_MATCHED_INVOICES	true
FIRST_STARTING_POINT_PERSON_ID	
INCLUDE_ALL_JOB_LEVEL_APPROVERS	true
INVOICE_SUPPLIER_NAME	Dell Computers
INVOICE_TOTAL_AMOUNT	7500
JOB_LEVEL_NON_DEFAULT_STARTING_POINT_PERSON_ID	
PO_MATCHED_INVOICE	N
PROJECT_RELATED_INVOICE	N
REQUIRE_TAX_CALCULATION	false
SB_CHAR_MIGRATION_ATTRIBUTE	D
SB_MIGRATION_ATTRIBUTE2	1
SB_SALES_TAX_PRESENT	0
SECOND_STARTING_POINT_PERSON_ID	
SUPERVISORY_NON_DEFAULT_STARTING_POINT_PERSON_ID	
SUPERVISORY_NON_DEFAULT_STARTING_POINT_PERSON_ID	
	Currency Code **USD**
	Value **7500**
SUPPLIER_INVOICE_AMOUNT	Conversion Type **Corporate**
SUPPLIER_INVOICE_ATTRIBUTE CATEGORY	
SUPPLIER_INVOICE_ATTRIBUTE1	
SUPPLIER_INVOICE_ATTRIBUTE10	
SUPPLIER_INVOICE_ATTRIBUTE11	
SUPPLIER_INVOICE_ATTRIBUTE12	
SUPPLIER_INVOICE_ATTRIBUTE13	
SUPPLIER_INVOICE_ATTRIBUTE14	
SUPPLIER_INVOICE_ATTRIBUTE15	
SUPPLIER_INVOICE_ATTRIBUTE2	
SUPPLIER_INVOICE_ATTRIBUTE3	
SUPPLIER_INVOICE_ATTRIBUTE4	
SUPPLIER_INVOICE_ATTRIBUTE5	
SUPPLIER_INVOICE_ATTRIBUTE6	
SUPPLIER_INVOICE_ATTRIBUTE7	
SUPPLIER_INVOICE_ATTRIBUTE8	
SUPPLIER_INVOICE_ATTRIBUTE9	
SUPPLIER_INVOICE_BASE_AMOUNT	
SUPPLIER_INVOICE_CREATION_DATE	26-Apr-2008
SUPPLIER_INVOICE_CURRENCY_CODE	USD
SUPPLIER_INVOICE_DATE	01-Jan-2008
SUPPLIER_INVOICE_DESCRIPTION	
SUPPLIER_INVOICE_EXCHANGE_RATE_TYPE	
SUPPLIER_INVOICE_EXPENDITURE_ORGANIZATION_NAME	
SUPPLIER_INVOICE_GLOBAL_ATTRIBUTE1	
SUPPLIER_INVOICE_GLOBAL_ATTRIBUTE10	
SUPPLIER_INVOICE_GLOBAL_ATTRIBUTE11	
SUPPLIER_INVOICE_GLOBAL_ATTRIBUTE12	
SUPPLIER_INVOICE_GLOBAL_ATTRIBUTE13	
SUPPLIER_INVOICE_GLOBAL_ATTRIBUTE14	
SUPPLIER_INVOICE_GLOBAL_ATTRIBUTE15	

583

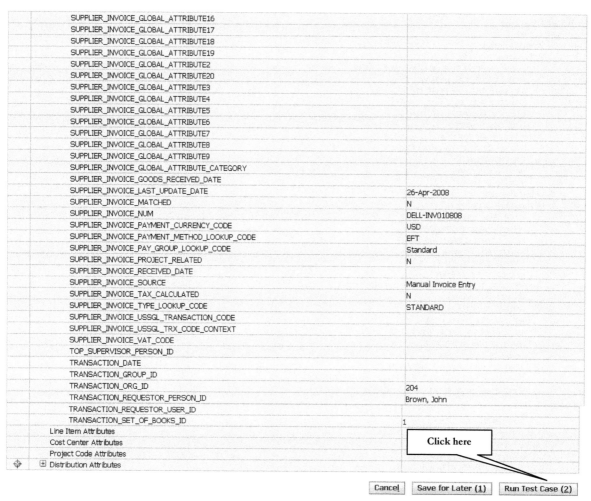

FIGURE 14.70

The next page displays the results of AME's evaluation of the transaction against the current defined Rules. The results page is divided into two sections; 'Applicable Rules' and 'Final Processed Approver List'.

The 'Applicable Rules' section displays information about the Rules satisfied when the transaction was evaluated.

The 'Final Processed Approver List' section displays a list of all of the approvers required to review and approve the invoice transaction. This list represents a list of approvers after AME has evaluated and suppressed any repeated approvers that may have appeared on the original list.

Based on the Rules previously defined and the actions associated with the Rules, the approver list contains the list of expected approvers (see FIGURE 14.71).

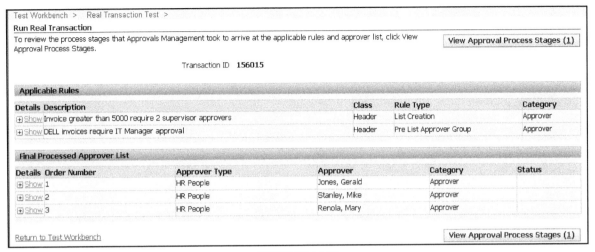

FIGURE 14.71

In both the 'Applicable Rules' and 'Final Processed Approver List', each item line has a 'Show' link. This link allows the user to view the details of the item. For example, the 'Show' link in the 'Applicable Rules' section shows details of why the Rule was considered to be satisfied by the current transaction. It lists properties of the Rules such as the Conditions and actions associated with the Rule. Subsequently in the 'Final Processed Approver List', the 'Show' link displays details that explain why the individual appears on the approver list.

FIGURE 14.72 shows the 'Dell Invoice Rule' details and the IT Manager approver

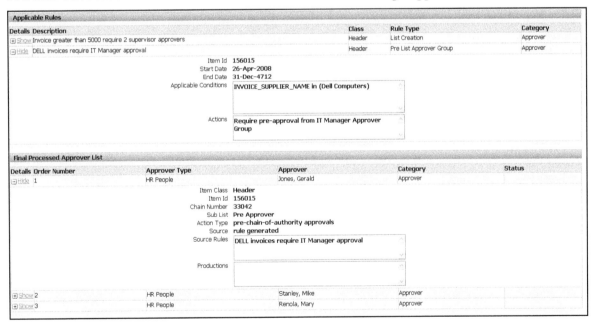

FIGURE 14.72

The 'View Approval Process Stages' button allows the user to review the various stages of the approver list generation and how AME arrived at the final approver list (see FIGURES 14.73 and 14.74).

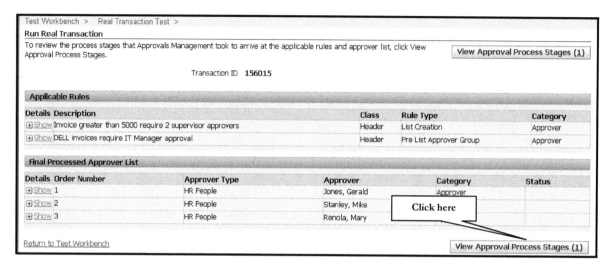

FIGURE 14.73

Applicable Rules

Final Applicable Rules

Details Description	Class	Rule Type	Category
⊞ Show Invoice greater than 5000 require 2 supervisor approvers	Header	List Creation	Approver
⊞ Show DELL invoices require IT Manager approval	Header	Pre List Approver Group	Approver

Item Productions

Item Class	Item Id	Variable Name	Variable Value
No results found.			

Default Approver List

Details Approver Type	Approver	Category	Status
⊞ Show HR People	Jones, Gerald	Approver	
⊞ Show HR People	Stanley, Mike	Approver	
⊞ Show HR People	Renola, Mary	Approver	

Approver List After Supressing Repeated Approvers

Details Approver Type	Approver	Category	Status
⊞ Show HR People	Jones, Gerald	Approver	
⊞ Show HR People	Stanley, Mike	Approver	
⊞ Show HR People	Renola, Mary	Approver	

Final Approver List

Details Order Number	Approver Type	Approver	Category	Status
⊞ Show 1	HR People	Jones, Gerald	Approver	
⊞ Show 2	HR People	Stanley, Mike	Approver	
⊞ Show 3	HR People	Renola, Mary	Approver	

FIGURE 14.74

As previously stated, the Testing Workbench can be a very useful during the process of implementing and developing AME Rules for invoice approval routing. Having the ability to evaluate and see the results of your AME setups using *real* transaction prior to implementation in a production environment is quite valuable.

Migrating AME Components

FNDLOAD is an Oracle tool that can be used to migrate configuration data from one database instance to another to avoid having to manually re-enter tested configurations . We tested the FNDLOAD commands for AME in a Release 11.5.10.2 Vision database, and they appear to function correctly as designed. However, we encourage extensive testing, particularly for these entities, since they were recently added and documentation is limited.

The following AME setup components can be migrated with FNDLOAD:

- Transaction Types

- Attributes

- Conditions

- Approver Groups

- Action Type Configurations

- Rules

- Approver Types

- Item Classes

The following sections provide the commands necessary to download setup data from a source database into a flat file and upload the data from the flat file to a target database. Additional notes describe the commands and setup recommendations. Transaction Types, Attributes, Conditions, Approver Groups, Action Type Configurations and Rules are discussed.

Transaction Types

Download

```
FNDLOAD apps/<apps pwd> 0 Y DOWNLOAD amescvar.lct <download file name>.ldt
AME_CALLING_APPS APPLICATION_SHORT_NAME=<FND application short name>
TRANSACTION_TYPE_ID=<AME transaction type short name>
```

Example:

```
FNDLOAD apps/apps 0 Y DOWNLOAD amescvar.lct sbtrantype.ldt AME_CALLING_APPS
APPLICATION_SHORT_NAME=SQLAP TRANSACTION_TYPE_ID=SBTRANSTYPE
```

Upload

```
FNDLOAD apps/<apps pwd> 0 Y UPLOAD amescvar.lct <download file name>.ldt
```

Example:

```
FNDLOAD apps/apps 0 Y UPLOAD amescvar.lct sbtrantype.ldt.ldt
```

Attributes

Downloading Attributes requires executing two scripts. One script downloads the attribute structure itself and the other downloads the data contained in the Value field of the Attribute. Both scripts allow you to download all of the current Attributes for a given AME Transaction Type. Additionally, you can download a single Attribute or multiple Attributes using a pattern string (e.g., SB%).

Solution Beacon recommends that if you are creating Attributes for an existing Transaction Type, name any new or custom Attributes starting with the same prefix. This will allow for them to be singled out and downloaded as a group at migration time. If creating a new Transaction Type, download all Attributes using only the application short name and Transaction Type parameters.

Download

Attributes

```
FNDLOAD apps/<apps pwd> 0 Y DOWNLOAD amesmatt.lct <download file name>.ldt
AME_ATTRIBUTES APPLICATION_SHORT_NAME=<FND application short name>
TRANSACTION_TYPE_ID=<AME transaction type short name>
[ATTRIBUTE_NAME=<attribute_name>]
```

Example:

```
FNDLOAD apps/apps 0 Y DOWNLOAD amesmatt.lct sbattributes.ldt AME_ATTRIBUTES
APPLICATION_SHORT_NAME=SQLAP TRANSACTION_TYPE_ID= SBTRANSTYPE
ATTRIBUTE_NAME=SB_CUST_ATTRIBUTE
```

Attribute Usages

```
FNDLOAD apps/<apps pwd> 0 Y DOWNLOAD amesmatr.lct <download file name>.ldt
AME_ATTRIBUTE_USAGES APPLICATION_SHORT_NAME=<FND application short name>
TRANSACTION_TYPE_ID=<AME transaction type short name>
[ATTRIBUTE_NAME=<attribute_name>]
```

Example:

```
FNDLOAD apps/apps 0 Y DOWNLOAD amesmatr.lct sbattribute_usages.ldt
AME_ATTRIBUTE_USAGES APPLICATION_SHORT_NAME=SQLAP
TRANSACTION_TYPE_ID=SBTRANSTYPE ATTRIBUTE_NAME=SB_CUST_ATTRIBUTE
```

Upload

Attributes

```
FNDLOAD apps/<apps pwd> 0 Y UPLOAD amesmatt.lct <download file name>.ldt
```

Example:

```
FNDLOAD apps/apps 0 Y UPLOAD amesmatt.lct sbattributes.ldt
```

Attribute Usages

```
FNDLOAD apps/<apps pwd> 0 Y UPLOAD amesmatr.lct <download file name>.ldt
```

Example:

```
FNDLOAD apps/apps 0 Y UPLOAD amesmatr.lct sbattribute_usages.ldt
```

Conditions

• The script that downloads AME Conditions allows you to download all conditions for a given Transaction Type or only those associated with a particular Attribute or group of Attributes.

- If creating a new Transaction Type, you can download all conditions using only the Application Short Name and Transaction Type parameters.

 If you are creating conditions on Attributes for an existing Transaction Type, name any new or custom Attributes starting with the same prefix. This will allow for the associated conditions to be singled out and downloaded as a group at migration time.

Download

```
FNDLOAD apps/<apps pwd> 0 Y DOWNLOAD amesconk.lct <download file name>.ldt
AME_CONDITIONS APPLICATION_SHORT_NAME=<FND application short name>
TRANSACTION_TYPE_ID=<AME transaction type short name>
[ATTRIBUTE_NAME=<attribute_name>]
```

Example:

```
FNDLOAD apps/apps 0 Y DOWNLOAD amesconk.lct sbconditions.ldt AME_CONDITIONS
APPLICATION_SHORT_NAME=SQLAP TRANSACTION_TYPE_ID=SBTRANSTYPE
```

Upload

```
FNDLOAD apps/<apps pwd> 0 Y UPLOAD amesconk.lct <download file name>.ldt
```

Example:

```
FNDLOAD apps/apps 0 Y UPLOAD amesconk.lct sbconditions.ldt
```

Approval Groups

Two scripts must be executed to migrate custom Approver Groups. One script downloads the structure of the Approver Group, including the SQL query used to select members for any dynamic queries. The other script downloads data regarding the order number and voting regime of the Approver Group. There are several notes of interest regarding downloading Approver Groups:

- The download script only works for Dynamic Approver Groups. It does not work for Static Approver Groups.

- The script does not recognize Approver Group names containing spaces. If the Approver Group(s) contains spaces, add the '%' wildcard symbol between each word of the Approver Group to ensure it is downloaded properly

- The primary Approver Group script does not download all Approver Groups for a given Transaction Type unless you supply the name of an Approver Group or some matching pattern of multiple groups if the naming convention of the groups is similar.

- The Approver Group configuration script allows all Approver Group configurations for a given Transaction Type to be downloaded at one time.

 To download multiple Approver Groups at one time (instead of having to create multiple download files), use a common prefix when naming the Approver Group. For example, use <application short name>_cust + the name of the Approver Group as the prefix for custom Approver Groups.

Download

Approval Group

```
FNDLOAD apps/<apps pw> 0 Y DOWNLOAD amesappg.lct <download file name>.ldt
AME_APPROVAL_GROUPS APPROVAL_GROUP_NAME=<Approval Group Name>
```

#Need to use wildcards if Approval Group name has spaces

Example:

```
FNDLOAD apps/apps 0 Y DOWNLOAD amesappg.lct sbappgrps.ldt AME_APPROVAL_GROUPS
APPROVAL_GROUP_NAME=SB%Cust%Grp%
```

Approval Group Configuration

```
FNDLOAD apps/<apps pw> 0 Y DOWNLOAD amesaagc.lct <download file name>.ldt
AME_APPROVAL_GROUP_CONFIG APPLICATION_SHORT_NAME=<FND application short name>
TRANSACTION_TYPE_ID=<AME transaction type short name>
[APPROVAL_GROUP_NAME=<Approval Group Name>]
```

#Need to use wildcards if Approval Group name has spaces

Example:

```
FNDLOAD apps/apps 0 Y DOWNLOAD amesaagc.lct sbappgrpscon.ldt
AME_APPROVAL_GROUP_CONFIG APPLICATION_SHORT_NAME=SQLAP
TRANSACTION_TYPE_ID=SBTRANSTYPE APPROVAL_GROUP_NAME=SB%Cust%Grp%
```

Upload

Approval Group

```
FNDLOAD apps/<apps pw> 0 Y UPLOAD amesappg.lct <download file name>.ldt
```

Example:

```
FNDLOAD apps/apps 0 Y UPLOAD amesappg.lct sbappgrps.ldt.ldt
```

Approval Group Configuration

```
FNDLOAD apps/<apps pw> 0 Y UPLOAD amesaagc.lct <download file name>.ldt
```

Example:

```
FNDLOAD apps/apps 0 Y UPLOAD amesaagc.lct sbappgrpscon.ldt
```

Action Type Configurations

Action Type configurations refers to the download of Action Types that have been enabled and configured for a given Transaction Type. You can migrate these Action Types from one instance to another. The download allows all configurations for a given Transaction Type to be downloaded at one time using the Application Short Name and Transaction Type parameters of the script. You can also download by specific Action Type or a group of Action Types using a specific string pattern to match against.

Download

```
FNDLOAD apps/<apps pw> 0 Y DOWNLOAD amesaatc.lct <download file name>.ldt
AME_ACTION_TYPE_CONFIG APPLICATION_SHORT_NAME=<FND application short name>
TRANSACTION_TYPE_ID=<AME transaction type short name> [ACTION_TYPE_NAME=<action
type name>]
```

#Need to use wildcards if Action Type name has spaces

Example:

```
FNDLOAD apps/apps 0 Y DOWNLOAD amesaatc.lct sbacttconf.ldt
AME_ACTION_TYPE_CONFIG APPLICATION_SHORT_NAME=SQLAP
TRANSACTION_TYPE_ID=SBTRANSTYPE
```

Upload

```
FNDLOAD apps/<apps pw> 0 Y UPLOAD amesaatc.lct <download file name>.ldt
```

Example:

```
FNDLOAD apps/apps 0 Y UPLOAD amesaatc.lct sbacttconf.ldt
```

Rules

Downloading AME Rules requires two scripts to be executed. The first script downloads information about the rule (e.g., name, description, etc.) along with the associated Conditions and Rule Type. The second script downloads all associated Actions for the Rule. Both scripts allow all Rules for a given Transaction Type to be downloaded. You can also download a specific Rule. However, unlike some of the previous components, you cannot download a group of Rules using a string of wildcards. The reason for this is that the FNDLOAD scripts use the Oracle generated Rule Key as a parameter to download a specific Rule.

 Solution Beacon recommends downloading all rules for a Transaction Type unless only a handful of new rules have been created that need to be migrated.

Download

Rules

```
FNDLOAD apps/<apps pw> 0 Y DOWNLOAD amesrulk.lct <download file name>.ldt
AME_RULES APPLICATION_SHORT_NAME=<FND application short name>
TRANSACTION_TYPE_ID=<AME transaction type short name> [RULE_KEY=<Rule Key>]
```

Rule Key is found in AME_RULES table

Example:

```
FNDLOAD apps/apps 0 Y DOWNLOAD amesrulk.lct sbrules.ldt AME_RULES
APPLICATION_SHORT_NAME=SQLAP TRANSACTION_TYPE_ID=SBTRANSTYPE
```

Rule Actions

```
FNDLOAD apps/<apps pw> 0 Y DOWNLOAD amesactu.lct <download file name>.ldt
AME_ACTION_USAGES APPLICATION_SHORT_NAME=<FND application short name>
TRANSACTION_TYPE_ID=<AME transaction type short name> [RULE_KEY=<Rule Key>]
```

Rule Key is found in AME_RULES table

```
Ex. FNDLOAD apps/apps 0 Y DOWNLOAD amesactu.lct sbrulesact.ldt
AME_ACTION_USAGES APPLICATION_SHORT_NAME=SQLAP TRANSACTION_TYPE_ID=SBTRANSTYPE
```

Upload

Rules

```
FNDLOAD apps/<apps pw> 0 Y UPLOAD amesrulk.lct <download file name>.ldt
```

Example:

```
FNDLOAD apps/apps 0 Y UPLOAD amesrulk.lct sbrules.ldt
```

Rule Actions

```
FNDLOAD apps/<apps pw> 0 Y UPLOAD amesactu.lct <download file name>.ldt
```

Example:

```
FNDLOAD apps/apps 0 Y UPLOAD amesactu.lct sbrulesact.ldt
```

CONCLUSION

It was the intent of this chapter to provide the reader with enough high level understanding of AME functionality and how organizations can use AME to control their approval requirements for invoice approval routing in Oracle Payables. As with any other Oracle application, mastery of the application comes through practice and experimentation. Hopefully, the chapter has demonstrated how thorough planning of Business Case Rules and further understanding of AME can allow business users to develop their most unique or complex approval requirements in this powerful application.

What's on the Horizon?

We've ended each chapter with a "What's Next" section. Now we're near the end of the book and the "What's Next" is that Workflow is slowly being replaced with Business Process Execution Language (BPEL). Oracle started talking about replacing Workflow with BPEL two years ago. On August 11, 2006, a formal Product Obsolescence / Desupport notice was emailed to all customers. The current version of this document is MetaLink Doc. ID: 391546.1, *Oracle Workflow Cartridge 2.6.X* with the sub-title *Oracle Corporation Product Obsolescence Desupport Notice*. Additionally, Oracle Technology Network contains a 'statement of direction Oracle Workflow' page. This page can be found at :

http://www.oracle.com/technology/products/ias/Workflow/Workflow_sod.html.

WHAT DESUPPORT ENTAILS

Error Correction Support for Oracle Workflow ended September 11, 2007. Oracle Workflow is not included in the 11*g* database. But unless you are using "Standalone Workflow" and are planning to upgrade to the 11*g* database, don't panic. Read the entire note. The exceptions are:

- A restricted use of Oracle Workflow components will be embedded in Oracle Warehouse Builder for customers licensed to use Oracle Warehouse Builder for Oracle Database Version 11*g*R1.

- Oracle Workflow is included in Oracle E-Business Suite Release 11*i* and Release 12. It is part of the Applications Technology Group (ATG) suite.

- Error correction support for Workflow will continue as long as you are using a product with which Workflow is bundled. For example, Release 11.5.10 customers and Release 12 customers (even those on the 11*g* database) will receive error correction support for Workflow until error correction support ends for Release 11.5.10 and/or Release 12.

To continue to receive support under the exceptions, the customer must be on Release 2.6.X of Workflow. Earlier releases are already de–supported, with no exceptions (see MetaLink Doc. ID: 169458.1, *Oracle Workflow Cartridge 2.0.x & 2.5.x*).

Note that Fusion is not the E-Business Suite. As of the publication date of this book, Oracle stated that Workflow will not be part of the Fusion Applications. Per *Oracle BPEL, How to Get Ready For It* (located at http://jrpjr.com/paper_archive/collab07_wf_bpel.ppt and presented at the COLLABORATE 07 Workflow SIG, Sunday April 15, by John Peters, Workflow SIG Coordinator and President of JRP JR,

Inc., after conversations with Oracle Workflow Development), the following Workflow areas will be replaced:

- Process Navigator Flows

    ♦ Migrated to ADF Task Flows

    ♦ In Oracle AS11 a new feature, Activity Guides, is planned to target these use cases

- Page Flows

    ♦ Migrated to ADF Task Flows

- Simple Deferred Activities (DML activities)

    ♦ Database Events

    ♦ BPEL can also be used

- XML Transaction Flows

    ♦ Transformations capabilities of E-Business Suite

    ♦ BPEL can also be used

- Business Processes

    ♦ Orchestration of system services and human tasks

    ♦ BPEL can also be used

At the Workflow SIG meeting at Open World 2007, Oracle stated the Account Generators would move to Subledger Accounting (SLA). *Chapter 7, Account Generators*, lists the Workflows in Release 12 where using Subledger Accounting instead of an Account Generator has already been implemented as an option.

WHAT HAPPENS TO MY EXISTING WORKFLOWS?

MetaLink Doc. ID: 394387.1, *How To Migrate Workflow Processes To Oracle BPEL Process Manager* states that there will be no automated migration of Business Processes from Workflow to BPEL. Oracle will migrate all the standard Workflow Processes as part of an upgrade process. However, all customizations to Oracle Workflows will be lost. Customers will be responsible for re-developing all their custom Workflows in BPEL or another technology.

Oracle recommends that any new development use BPEL Process Manager instead of Oracle Workflow and customers should plan to start migrating existing custom Workflows to Oracle BPEL Process Manager.

Yet, as we all have experienced, changes in the table structures usually force changes to customizations and custom Workflows, so until the new table structures are known, existing custom Workflows can be left as is. What is important is documentation. To prepare to migrate to BPEL, completely document existing customizations and custom Workflows. Include in the documentation the business reasons for the customizations. You may find that later E-Business Suite releases have negated the need for a customization, and thus it won't need to be migrated.

If you do choose to migrate, Oracle Technology Network has an excellent paper called *Migrating to BPEL from Oracle Work Flow*. The paper is dated January 2007. It is available from the following link:

http://www.oracle.com/technology/products/ias/bpel/pdf/owf2bpel.pdf

This paper is also an excellent source for practicing with BPEL, as it explains how to relate Workflow structures with the equivalent BPEL constructs.

Jerry Ireland wrote *Chapter 16, BPEL for Workflow Developers*. This chapter describes how to use BPEL to implement a variation of the Workflow used throughout this book.

WHAT ABOUT THE APPROVALS MANAGER ENGINE (AME)

Plans for replacing Oracle Approvals Manager Engine (AME) have not been formally announced. All Oracle Workflow Development has said is that it "will not be replaced by the Oracle Rules Engine, but by a successor that will use BPEL and the Human Workflow components".

SHOULD I PANIC?

No. Error correction support ends November 2013 for Release 11.5.10 and January 2015 for the current version of Release 12. These dates are inclusive of Extended Support, which require additional support fees. Additional versions of Release 12 (such as Release 12.1) will include error correction support for 8 years from the application release date. To see further details about Oracle's Lifetime Support policies, see the following links:

http://www.oracle.com/support/lifetime-support-policy.html

http://www.oracle.com/support/library/brochure/lifetime-support-applications.pdf

http://www.oracle.com/support/library/brochure/lifetime-support-technology.pdf

http://www.oracle.com/support/library/oracle-lifetime-support-policy-faq.pdf

Oracle has already stated that even when Release 11.5.10 and/or Release 12 are certified for the 11*g* database, Workflow error correction will continue until error correction ceases for the E-Business Suite release.

SHOULD I MAKE PLANS TO LEARN AND USE BPEL?

Yes. Regardless of the Workflow implications, BPEL is a powerful tool that encompasses a standard that enables assembling discrete services across multiple dissimilar databases at multiple organizations into end-to-end process flows.

BPEL is part of the Oracle Fusion Middleware product set also known as Application Server. Since Application Server is required for all E-Business Suite installations, BPEL can be installed in any existing Release 11.5.10 or Release 12 installation. BPEL is an extra-cost option, so it will require buying the appropriate software license.

How Do I Learn More About BPEL?

There are many resources available to learn BPEL. One of the best is Oracle Technology Network (OTN). The BPEL page is located at:

http://www.oracle.com/technology/products/ias/bpel/index.html.

This page contains links for white papers, tutorials, webinars, downloads and others.

There are two books that provide an excellent introduction to BPEL. The first is *BPEL Cookbook: Best Practices for SOA Based Integration and Composite Applications* The second is *Business Process Execution Language for Web Services*. Both books are published by PACKT Publishing and are available from www.amazon.com.

The OTN page provides a link whereby BPEL can be downloaded and installed on your PC. Note that this download does NOT allow users to deploy any developed BPEL Business Processes in a production environment. It is provided as a self-learning tool.

Additionally, when BPEL is loaded on your PC, it loads several demos that are very useful for learning the product. MetaLink Doc. ID: 376688.1, *BPEL PM Quick Start Tutorial* gives a list of all these demos.

The Oracle Documentation for BPEL can be found from the 'Oracle Documentation' page http://www.oracle.com/technology/documentation/index.html. BPEL is not directly listed, but if you click 'Search Oracle Documentation' and then type 'BPEL' in the 'Enter a word or phrase' box, you will be directed to a page that looks similar to FIGURE 15.1.

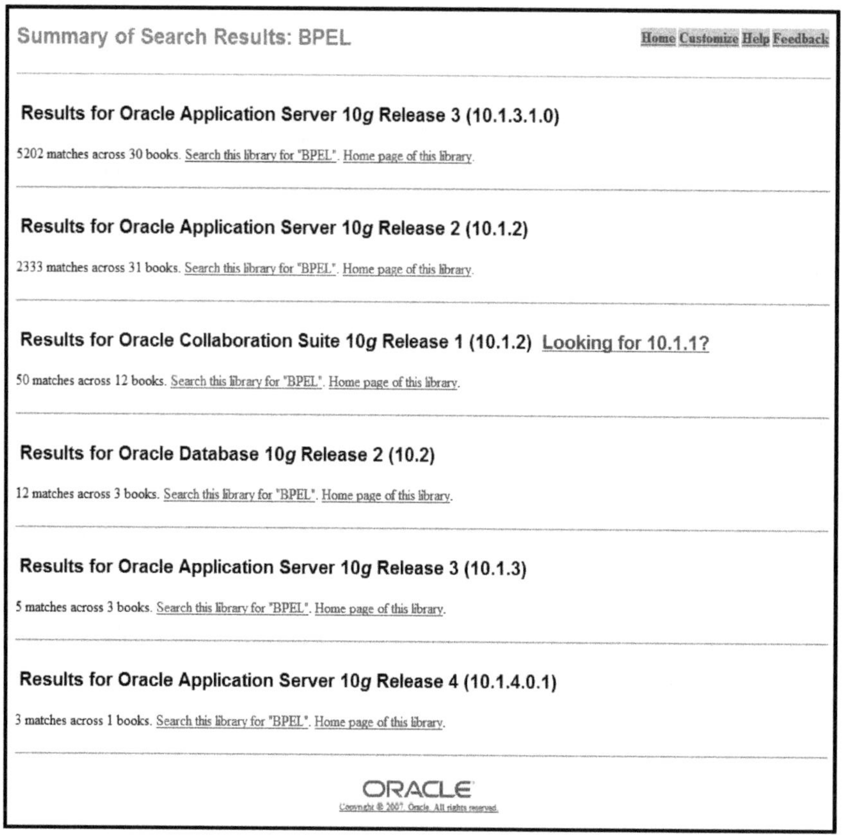

Summary of Search Results: BPEL   Home Customize Help Feedback

---

Results for Oracle Application Server 10g Release 3 (10.1.3.1.0)

5202 matches across 30 books. Search this library for "BPEL". Home page of this library.

Results for Oracle Application Server 10g Release 2 (10.1.2)

2333 matches across 31 books. Search this library for "BPEL". Home page of this library.

Results for Oracle Collaboration Suite 10g Release 1 (10.1.2) Looking for 10.1.1?

50 matches across 12 books. Search this library for "BPEL". Home page of this library.

Results for Oracle Database 10g Release 2 (10.2)

12 matches across 3 books. Search this library for "BPEL". Home page of this library.

Results for Oracle Application Server 10g Release 3 (10.1.3)

5 matches across 3 books. Search this library for "BPEL". Home page of this library.

Results for Oracle Application Server 10g Release 4 (10.1.4.0.1)

3 matches across 1 books. Search this library for "BPEL". Home page of this library.

ORACLE
Copyright © 2007 Oracle. All rights reserved.

FIGURE 15.1

Select your version of the Application Server and click the 'Search this library for "BPEL"' link. You will then have the opportunity to view the documentation on-line or as a PDF that can be saved to your hard drive.

Another great resource is the Oracle Applications Users Group – OAUG. The web site contains links to papers presented at the conferences and to the SIGs. Currently BPEL is part of the OAUG Middleware SIG. Information about migrating Workflow to BPEL will be addressed by the Workflow SIG.

WHAT OTHER SKILLS ARE NECESSARY?

Oracle recommends that those learning BPEL should learn the following as well:

- JDeveloper – BPEL was designed to work with this application

- Java/J2EE

- SOA Knowledge – SOA is Service Oriented Architecture and BPEL is part of this. General knowledge will suffice, at least in the beginning

- Oracle Application Server Knowledge – everyone should know the pieces of this architecture and the strengths and weaknesses of each piece so that the correct technology is selected for the Business Process

- XML – A defined BPEL Process is actually a structured XML Document. So knowing XML will enable reading the BPEL definitions.

If you are wondering whether your SQL and PL/SQL skills were just made obsolete, the answer is no. BPEL has the capability to use PL/SQL routines. However the format for a BPEL PL/SQL Procedure will look very different from a Workflow PL/SQL Procedure.

WHAT NOW?

The last chapter of this book, *Chapter 16, BPEL for Workflow Developers*, leads readers into the future by showing how to convert a Workflow into a BPEL.

In the meantime, Oracle continues improving Workflow. Each ATG rollup patch contains Workflow improvements. Workflow will continue to be used for several more years, but only for E-Business Suite. Oracle has not replaced any of the existing product Workflows with BPEL – yet. Nor do we know when that will happen. Oracle is legally constrained from releasing definitive future product directions and dates. So our recommendations are:

- Continue to use Workflow (as long as you are on Release 11.5.10 or the current release of Release 12 you have no choice)

- Continue to ensure that the Workflow technology functions correctly in your environment

- Monitor new ATG rollup patches for Release 11.5.10 and new rollups or Point Releases for Release 12. Utilize the new Workflow functionality these patches deliver.

- Read the Readme documents and the Release Content Documents carefully. Whenever a Workflow is replaced by a BPEL, study the BPEL, comparing it to the old Workflow. Compare the old code and new code.

- Read the paper found from the link in the section *What Happens to My Existing Workflows*

- Make sure all your current customizations to Oracle Workflows and your custom Workflows are documented

- Examine your custom code and try to separate the calls to Workflow APIs and the use of Workflow tables from the code referencing the Applications module tables and APIs. This will make moving the code to BPEL easier.

- Learn BPEL. Practice using it.

- Become familiar with the functionality delivered in the various components of Fusion Middleware. Know which piece is best for what use.

- Include the purchase of BPEL and other pieces of the Fusion Middleware in your next capital budget.

And relax. In the Preface, we stated that Workflow had put the fun back in the Applications. It hasn't left. BPEL is different, but it will be equally as exciting. Enjoy!

BPEL for Workflow Developers

As a key enabler for SOA development, it will be essential to understand how to build Business Processes using BPEL (Business Process Language). BPEL has been a standard for describing Business Processes for several years. Oracle has embraced it fairly recently as an important building block to their SOA Suite strategy and for Fusion. Most importantly it is a key part of the future E-Business Suite Applications. E-Business Suite Processes prior to the Fusion Applications are built on Oracle's own proprietary tool, Workflow. The use of Workflow has grown to the point where every Applications module utilizes it in some way.

With the latest E-Business Suite versions, Release 11.5.10 and now Release 12, BPEL is an important part of the pre-built Process Integration Packs (PIPs) that are delivered through Oracle's Application Integration Architecture (AIA). These PIPs connect the E-Business Suite to Siebel, Retek, etc. Oracle no longer delivers Workflow with the database and has desupported it outside of the E-Business Suite (where, like Application Object Library (AOL), it is one of the Application Technology Group (ATG) products) and Warehouse Builder.

Because Fusion Middleware includes BPEL as the glue that holds SOA together, its usage will grow over time. So how do the two Workflow solutions compare? This chapter assumes, particularly since it comes after 15 chapters about Workflow, a certain familiarity with Workflow, and so will concentrate more on BPEL. This chapter does not claim to be a complete tutorial or reference for the BPEL product. See *Chapter 15, What's on the Horizon*, for a list of references to learn more about BPEL.

The major difference in the two Business Process tools is in their original design goals. Workflow was designed to manage a flow within a single database, and to communicate with people. The Event system was added around 2002 to begin to address the need for communication outside the database. BPEL was designed to address the need to perform complex integration scenarios between disparate systems via web-services. Workflow is mostly PL/SQL-based, with portions in the database kernel. BPEL is primarily XML and Java -based, and resides in the middle tier. BPEL is based on industry-wide standards while Workflow is more proprietary. The other major difference is that Workflow was delivered as part of the database and is used with no extra charge as part of the E-Business Suite, while BPEL has a separate license fee. The expectation is that it will be licensed in the same way that forms and reports are - bundled with E-Business Suite as run-time only with a requirement to pay a license fee for any type of development use.

WHAT IS BPEL?

So what is BPEL and how does it work? First, BPEL makes use of XML and Web Services; it uses an XML-based language that supports the Web Services technology stack. To run BPEL code that has been generated, the code is parsed by a BPEL engine, which does the same kind of parsing job as other XML interpreters. Each Process that is run is defined by a Web Services Description Language (WSDL) document, and its Messages are transmitted across the Web by the Simple Object Access Protocol (SOAP). Processes that look up available Web Services can use the Universal Description, Discovery and Integration (UDDI) directory.

To define how Processes should be executed, BPEL has XML definitions or commands that specify the order of operations, the looping of operations, and synchronous and asynchronous requirements for operations. Synchronous operations block requesters until a request is either fulfilled or denied. Asynchronous operations allow requesters to continue without waiting for a response. BPEL also has commands to take care of fault conditions and commands to undo or reverse operations. These capabilities take XML beyond its traditional definitional role into the role of an executable language.

The examples in this document use Oracle SOA Suite 11*g* Technology Preview 3

BPEL PROCESS MANAGER COMPONENTS

The tool set that helps to define, orchestrate and manage Business Processes is currently referred to as BPEL Process Manager. It has several parts to it (see FIGURE 16.1).

The BPEL Designer provides a graphical and user-friendly way to build BPEL Processes. It uses BPEL as its native format. This means that Processes built with the Designer are portable and it enables developers to view and modify the BPEL source at any time.

The core BPEL engine provides an implementation of a BPEL Server. The Oracle BPEL Process Manager executes standard BPEL Processes and provides a "dehydration" capability so that the state of long-running flows is automatically maintained in a database. The BPEL Server uses an underlying J2EE application server, with support for most major commercial application servers and a bundled version available.

The built-in integration services enable developers to easily access advanced connectivity and transformation capabilities from standard BPEL Processes. These capabilities include support for XSLT and XQuery transformation as well as bindings to hundreds of legacy systems through JCA adapters and native protocols. Human Workflow, which was initially an important missing capability, is provided as a built-in BPEL Service to enable the integration of people and manual tasks into BPEL flows. The JDeveloper BPEL Designer provides wizards to build these complex Workflows and a simple GUI to map Transformations.

The extensible WSDL binding framework enables connectivity to protocols and Message formats other than SOAP. Bindings are available for Java, JMS, email, JCA, HTTP GET and POST and many other protocols enabling simple connectivity to hundreds of back-end systems. Web Services Invocation Framework (WSIF) allows binding directly and transparently to any backend protocol or programming construct in order to get the benefits of a loosely-coupled Web Services architecture with the performance and transactionality of native protocols.

The SOA Console provides a mature web-based interface for management, administration and debugging of Processes deployed to the BPEL server. Audit trails and Process history/reporting information is automatically maintained and available both through the SOA Console and via a Java API.

Most of the work takes place on the middle tier (See FIGURE 16.1).

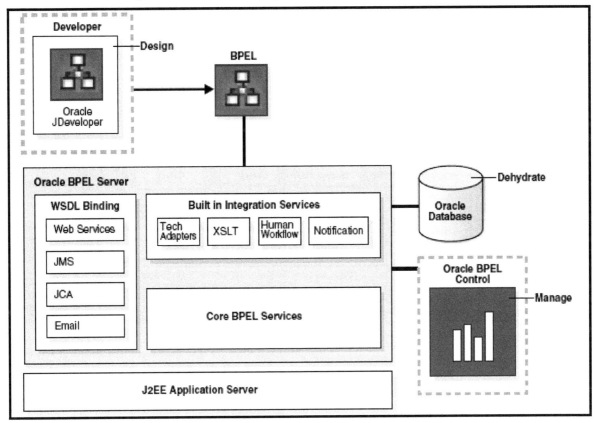

FIGURE 16. 1 – BPEL PROCESS MANAGER COMPONENTS

WORKFLOW COMPONENTS

Although the two tools have similar functionality for the components, Workflow, in contrast, has the majority of its components residing in the database server. Its designer is a client-based tool with a proprietary file format that has to be loaded into database tables for execution. The middle tier is utilized only as a base for email and access from the Worklist, analysis and monitoring tools. FIGURE 16.2 shows the Workflow Components:

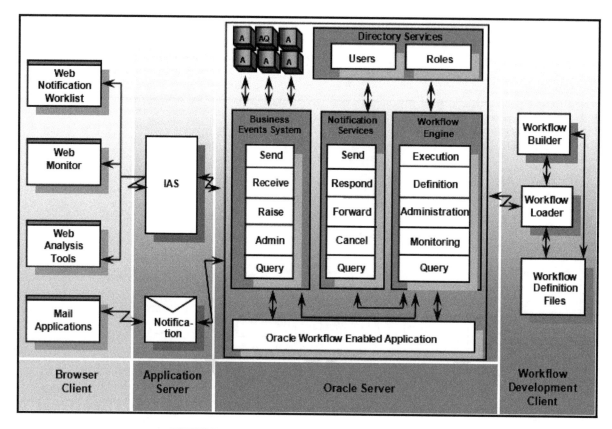

FIGURE 16. 2 – WORKFLOW COMPONENTS

BPEL DESIGNER (JDEVELOPER)

The design environment (Oracle JDeveloper) provides a rich Integrated Development Environment where BPEL Processes can be designed and deployed. BPEL Processes can be designed by dragging and dropping elements (known as activities) into the Process and editing their 'Properties' pages. There are also a number of wizards that make some of the steps easier. BPEL Processes can be integrated with external services that can also be designed and edited (known as Partner Links). Also many technology adapters and services such as Workflows, Worklists, Transformations, Notifications, Sensors, and Business Rules can be integrated with the Process. Processes are organized into Projects within Applications.

JDeveloper has many sections that allow you to perform various tasks. FIGURE 16.3 shows these sections. These sections stay in sync with each other to show different views of an object.

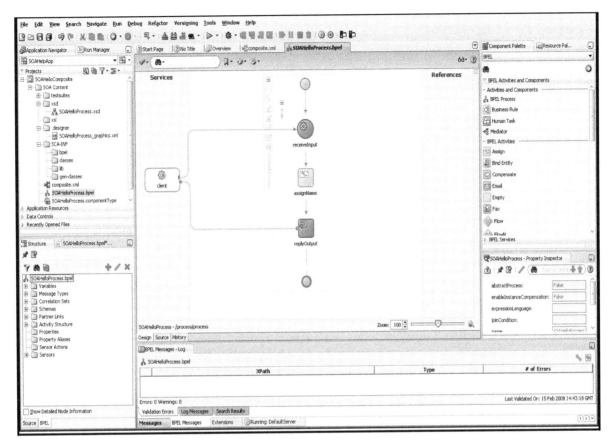

FIGURE 16. 3 – JDEVELOPER SECTIONS

Application Navigator

This section displays the Applications and Projects along with the various files that they contain. Double-clicking on any object will cause that object to be displayed in the other sections. Right-clicking on an object shows a context-sensitive menu of commands relevant to the object.

Diagram Window

The Diagram window provides a visual view of an object. FIGURE 16.3 shows a BPEL Process. This window can be toggled back and forth between the visual view and the underlying source as they are always kept in sync no matter where changes are made. The window also has a handy 'History' tab that compares two versions of the source in a side-by-side display.

Structure Window

The Structure window displays a tree structured representation of the object that is displayed in the diagram window. It also will toggle to a 'Source' tab to stay in sync with the diagram window. It is particularly handy for finding a place in the source code or diagram. Clicking on an object in the structure window will highlight that portion on the appropriate 'Source' tab or 'Design' tab of the diagram window.

Component Palette

The Component Palette window is a context sensitive list of objects that can be dragged and dropped onto the diagram window. The Process Activities palette (shown in FIGURE 16.3) and the Services Palette are the building blocks of a BPEL Process.

Property Inspector

The Property Inspector displays the details of an object. A single click on an object in either the Diagram window or the Structure window will cause that object to be displayed. Objects can also be modified using the Property Inspector and all the other views will be kept in sync.

Log Window

This window displays progress and errors from the various tasks the designer is asked to do. If errors are found during deployment of a Process, double-clicking the error will navigate directly to the offending line in the source file referenced.

SOA CONSOLE

After a Process is completed it can be compiled and deployed to the Server. Deployment sends a set of files with a directory structure similar to the Project directory structure to the Server.

Oracle SOA Console provides an interface to run, monitor, and administer composite Processes. Starting up the console brings up a list of the Applications on the left. Clicking on a Process brings up a Dashboard. FIGURE 16.4 shows the Dashboard on the SOA Console:

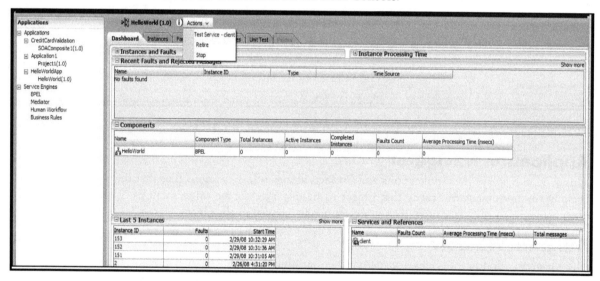

FIGURE 16. 4 – SOA CONSOLE – DASHBOARD

Dashboard

FIGURE 16.4 shows the 'Dashboard' tab that displays the list of components along with the last five Faults and Instances either currently running or completed. Click on an instance ID to see instance detail or on a component to view Instances of the component. The Action drop down at the top can be used to test the Service, retire it or stop it.

Component Details

Clicking on a component shows the last five Faults for the component and the last five Instances of the component along with the State and Start and Last Modified Times. Clicking on an instance shows the instance component detail. FIGURE 16.5 shows the Component Details on the SOA Console:

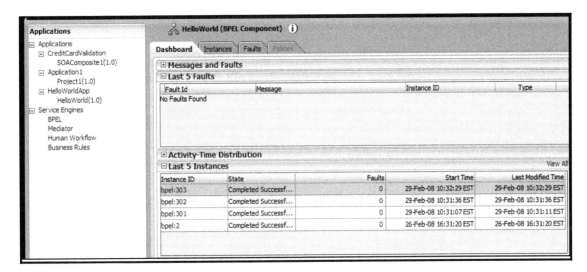

FIGURE 16. 5 – SOA CONSOLE – COMPONENT DETAILS

Instances Detail

On the 'Instance Detail' page (see FIGURE 16.6), the 'Audit' tab shows the detailed steps of the Process. Clicking on a <payload> will show complete details for the payload contents. Clicking on the 'Flow-Debug' tab displays a graphic view of the Process. Double-clicking one of the steps shows the step details.

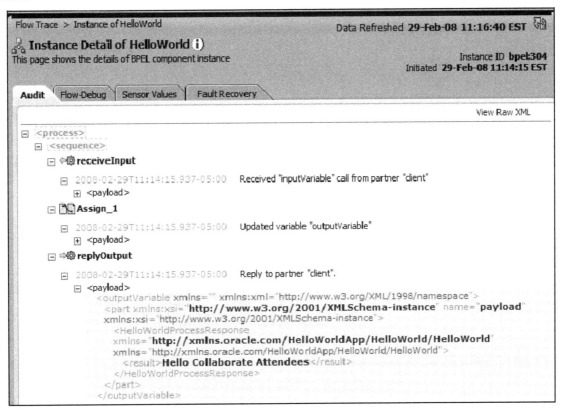

FIGURE 16. 6 – SOA CONSOLE – INSTANCE DETAIL

PROCESS OVERVIEW

To show the differences in the two Process Modelers, this section contrasts the implementation of a single flow in the two systems. When a new employee is entered, it is helpful to have a Process validate that everything is set up correctly for an employee and notify the proper personnel if they are not. The BPEL version does not do everything it would need to do in order to interface with the E-Business Suite, but provides the same basic steps. This flow actually highlights some of the strengths of Workflow so it is a somewhat unfair comparison. We've included this example because this is the type of transition that will have to be made from existing Workflows to BPEL.

Workflow

The Workflow version is a little more concise and readable, mostly because there is both an Internal and a Display Name and the flows are easily labeled. The Process in FIGURE 16.7 first goes to the database to look up and initialize some variables. It then checks to see if everything is in order for the employee. If everything is OK, the Process ends, just waiting for the System Administrator to be notified. If things are not OK, email is sent to HR to repair the setup and the Process waits for the HR person to respond. If HR does not respond in a timely manner, an email is sent to a supervisor with no wait for a response. A wait is introduced to prevent looping before the supervisor has had a chance to light a fire under someone. The loop at the bottom is just a way to limit the number of times the Process sends a Notification to the System Administrator.

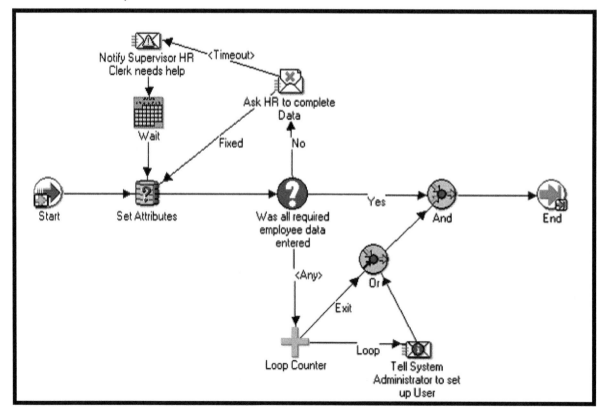

FIGURE 16. 7 – WORKFLOW DIAGRAM

BPEL

Two diagrams display views of the Applications. The first is the Composite View (see FIGURE 16.8). This shows the major components and their connections to external services. Exposed Services are displayed on the left swim lane. Components are shown in the middle lane. In this case there is a BPEL orchestration Process and a Human Workflow task to ask HR to fix the employee data. The External References are on the right. InitializeEmp retrieves employee information from the database. CheckEmp checks the database for valid data. The two Notification Services send email to the System Administrator and the HR manager.

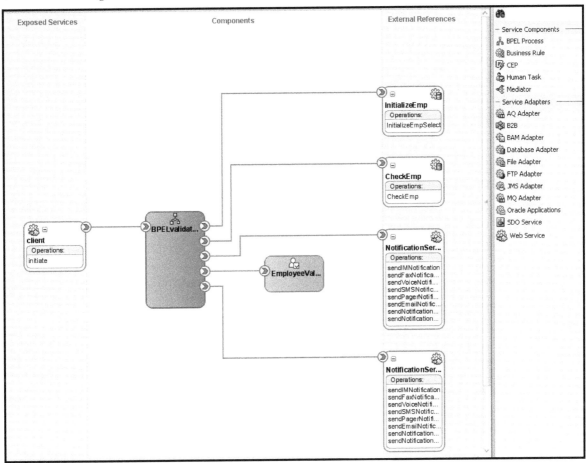

FIGURE 16. 8 – COMPOSITE DIAGRAM

The BPEL Process itself is laid out such that it needs to be looked at it in pieces.

The swim lane on the left contains the Client Service that starts the Process and receives the result. The References swim lane on the right contains Services called by the Process. It contains the 'EmployeeValidation TaskService' to do "Human Workflow" and two 'NotificationServices' to send email. The other two Services interact with the database, one for initializing variables and the other for checking to see if everything is set up for the employee. The actual flow (see FIGURE 16.9) shows the basic steps. There is an 'InitializeEmp' scope that does some initial setup (see FIGURE 16.11 for details). The next step is to send an email to the System Administrator. The final step is a while loop that does most of the major work invoking the 'CheckEmp' database adaptor and then performing a switch activity based on the return (See FIGURE 16.10 for details).

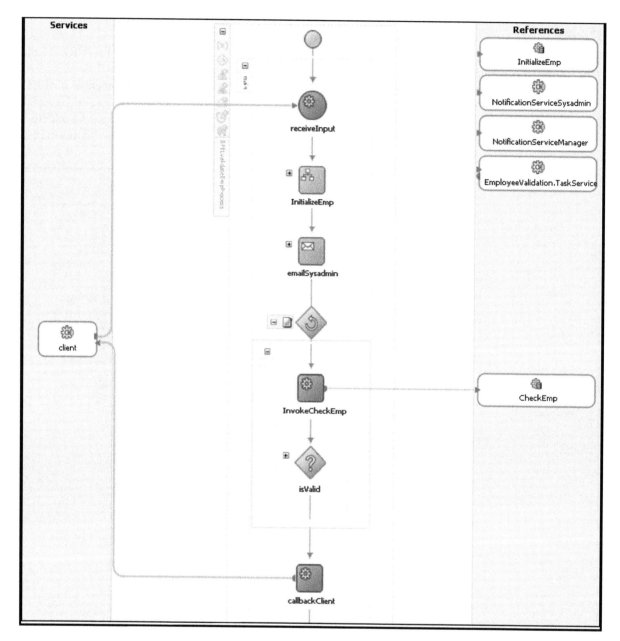

FIGURE 16. 9 – MAIN BPEL FLOW

The expanded switch activity splits the flow based on a return from the InvokeCheckEmp activity. If the return value is VALID, an appropriate return value for the Process is assigned and the Process ends. If the employee is not valid, a Notification is sent to HR that there is work to be done. This Notification expects a response of OK when everything is ready to check again. If for some reason a response is not received, the other branch of the second switch activity is taken and a 'notification without response' is sent to a manager. Like the Workflow example, a wait is introduced to allow work to be done before checking again.

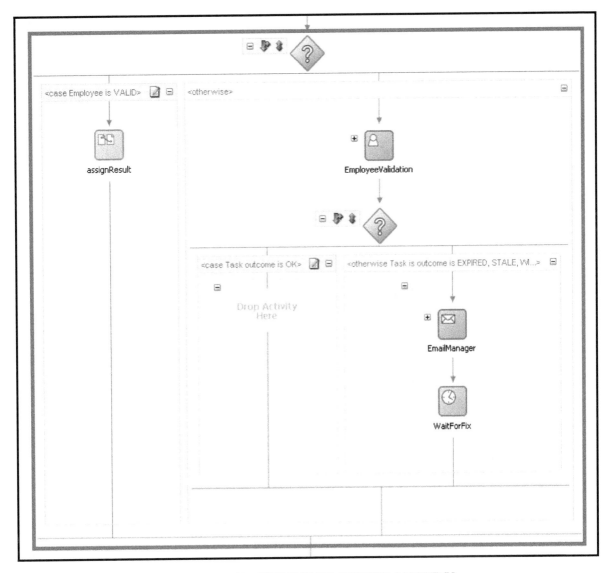

FIGURE 16. 10 – EXPANDED SWITCH ACTIVITY

FIGURE 16.11 shows that the InitializeEmp scope, shown in FIGURE 16.10, assigns some initial values to some internal variables and then invokes the InitializeEmp database adapter to retrieve additional information about the employee.

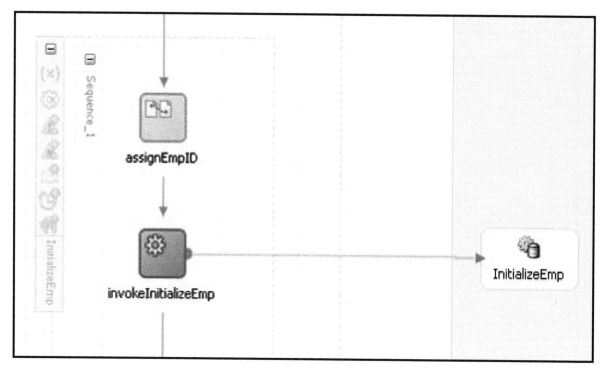

FIGURE 16. 11 – EXPANDED INITIALIZEEMP SCOPE

PROCESS DETAILS

To get started with a BPEL Process you need an application and a Process to hold all the pieces.

Create an Application to Contain the Process from the Application Navigator

Left-click the current Applications in the Application Navigator (see FIGURE 16.3) and choose 'New Application'.

Type 'myApplication' for the 'Application Name', accept the defaults for the rest, and click OK (see FIGURE 16.12).

FIGURE 16. 12

Create a BPEL Project for a Process

1. Type SOAvalidateEmpComposite as the Name (see FIGURE 16.13).

2. Click OK.

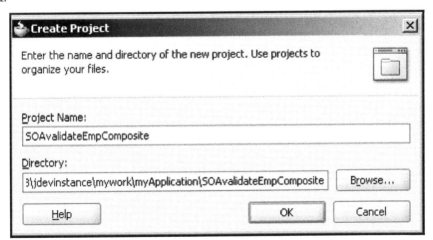

FIGURE 16. 13

3. Right-click on the new Project, 'SOAvalidateEmpComposite', now displayed in the Application Navigator section and select 'New'.

4.   Select 'SOA Tier' then 'SOA Composite' (see FIGURE 16.14).

5.   Click OK.

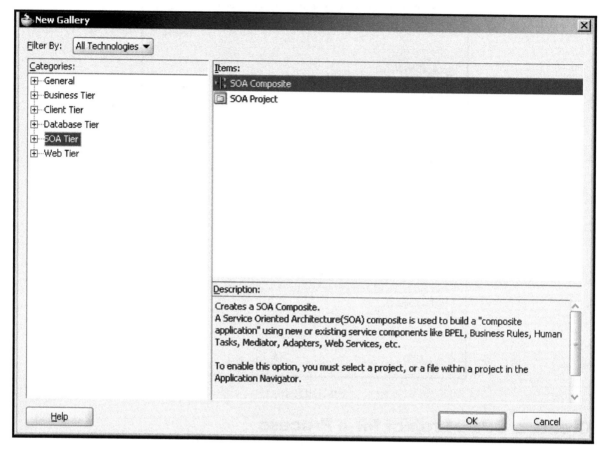

FIGURE 16. 14

6.   Select Composite with BPEL in Create Composite dialog (see FIGURE 16.15).

7.   Click OK.

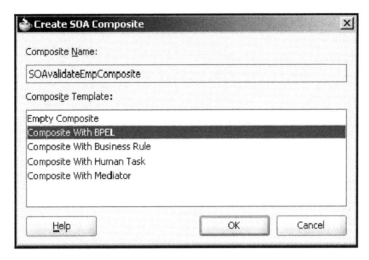

FIGURE 16. 15

8. Type 'BPELvalidationEmpProcess' as Name (see FIGURE 16.16).

9. In the Template field, choose 'Asynchronous BPEL Process'.

10. Be sure 'Expose as Composite Service' is checked.

11. Click OK.

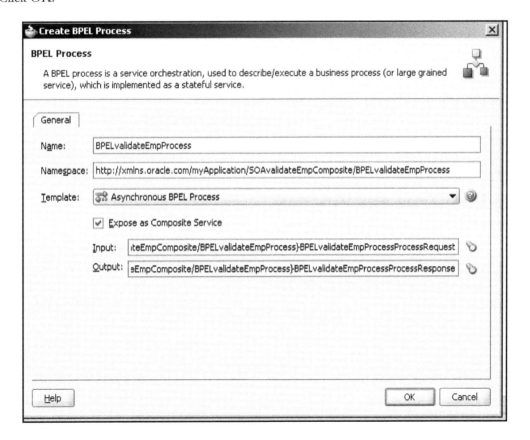

FIGURE 16. 16

The screen should now look like FIGURE 16.17 after you expand everything in the Application Navigator and click on the diagram:

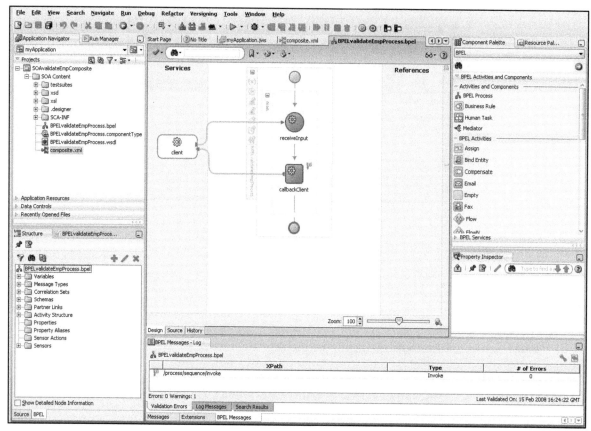

FIGURE 16. 17 – INITIAL BPEL PROCESS

To get started with Workflow you need an Item Type and Process:

Create Item Type and Process

- From the File menu choose Quick Start Wizard

- Enter 'XXEMP' as the Internal Name (see FIGURE 16.18)

- Enter 'Validate New Employee' as Display Name

- Enter 'XXVALEMP' as New Process Internal Name

- Enter 'Validate New Employee Data' as Display Name

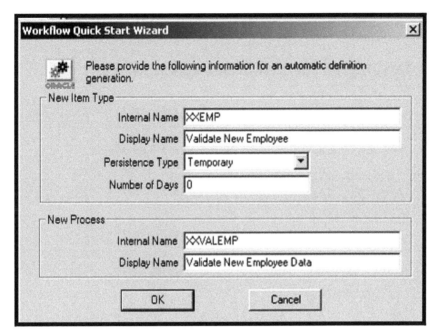

FIGURE 16. 18

Your screen should look like FIGURE 16.19.

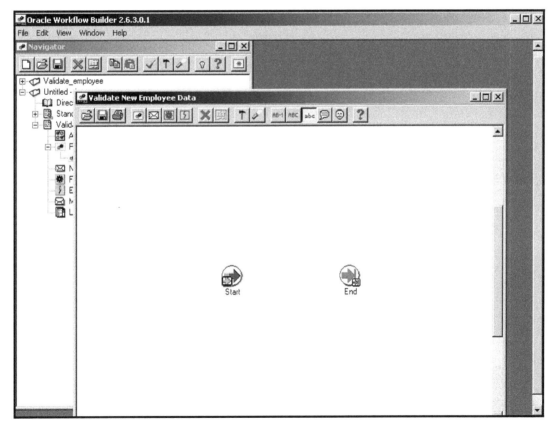

FIGURE 16. 19 – INITIAL WORKFLOW PROCESS

So far things are similar, but let's look at a couple of activities. We will look in more detail at the check employee call to the database and the step that notifies HR with an expected response.

Check the Employee for Valid Setup for BPEL

Add a Database Connection

BPEL needs to have a database connection defined in order to interact with a database.

1. Bring up the 'Database Navigator' view from the View drop down menu

2. Right-Click 'myApplication' and choose New Connection

3. Enter '10g' for Connection Name (see FIGURE 16.20)

4. Enter Username and Password

5. Check 'Deploy Password'

6. Enter the appropriate Host Name, JDBC Port and SID for the database

7. Click 'Test Connection' to be sure everything is set up correctly

8. Click OK

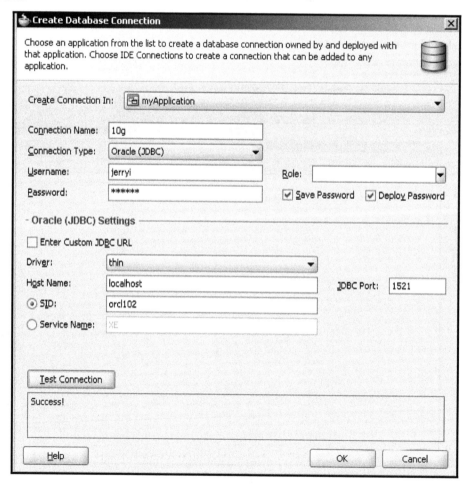

FIGURE 16. 20

Add Database Adaptor Service

Define the interaction with the database.

1. In the Component Palette, switch to the Services selection

2. Drag and drop the Database Adaptor into the right swim lane of the Diagram

3. Click Next on the Welcome page

4. Enter a Service Name of 'CheckEmp' and click Next (see FIGURE 16.21)

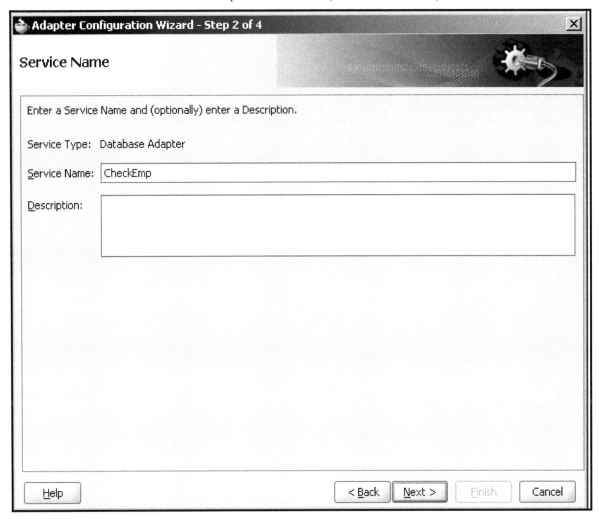

FIGURE 16. 21

5. Select the Database Connection you just created in Figure 16.20 (see Figure 16.22).

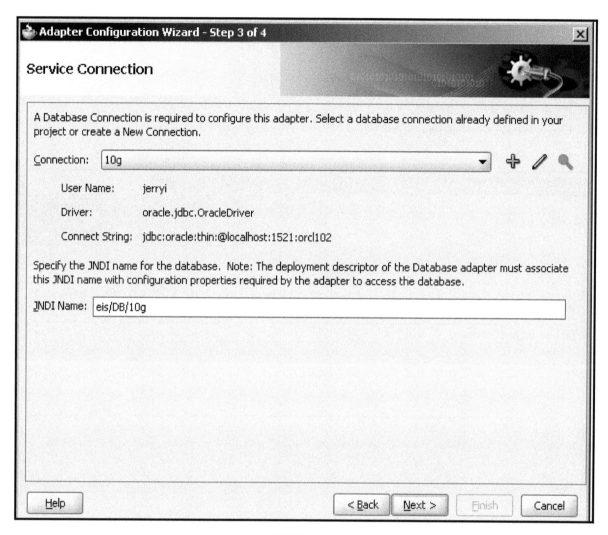

FIGURE 16. 22

6. Leave the default of 'Call a Stored Procedure or Function' and click Next

7. Select Schema JERRYI from the drop down list and click Browse (see FIGURE 16.23)

8. Choose CHECK_EMP to display the IN and OUT parameters and click OK

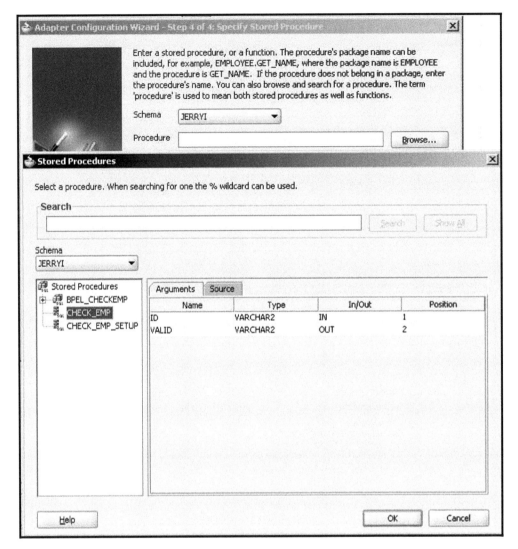

FIGURE 16. 23

9. Click Next and then Finish to complete

Add Invoke Activity to Diagram

1. In the Component Palette, switch to the BPEL Activities selection (see FIGURE 16.24)

2. Drag and drop the Invoke activity onto the diagram

3. Double-click the new activity

4. Enter 'InvokeCheckEmp' as the 'Name' and click the flashlight icon at the end of 'Partner Link'

5. Choose 'CheckEmp' that you just created. It is expanded to show the details in the example

6. Click on the Create Variable icon to the right of Input Variable and Output Variable and accept the default variables

7. Click OK.

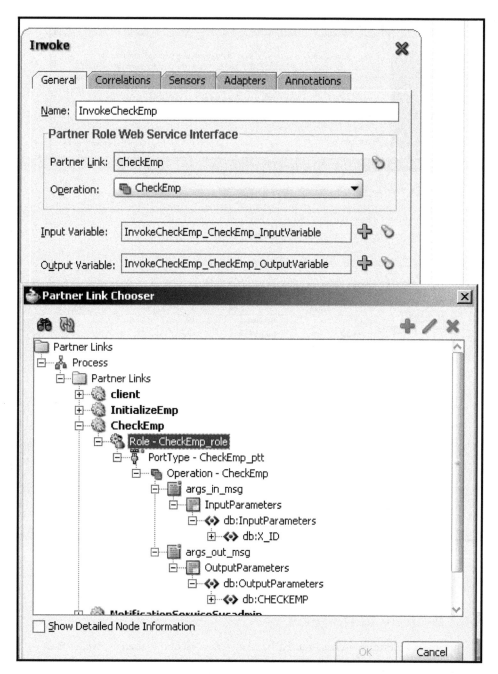

FIGURE 16. 24

Check the Employee for Valid Setup for Workflow

Things are a little simpler for Workflow. It is already connected to the database because that is where it runs. We just need to tell it what Procedure to call. The Procedure itself would have to be written differently to conform to Workflow.

Add Function to Call Procedure

1. Click the 'Function' icon at the top of the Diagram (see FIGURE 16.25).

2. Click the diagram where you want the Function to be.

3. Enter the following data in the pop-up:

   a. **Internal Name** – XXVALEMP

   b. **Display Name** – 'Was all required employee data entered'

   c. **Function Name** – WF_VALEMP.check_emp

   d. **Result Type** – Yes/No

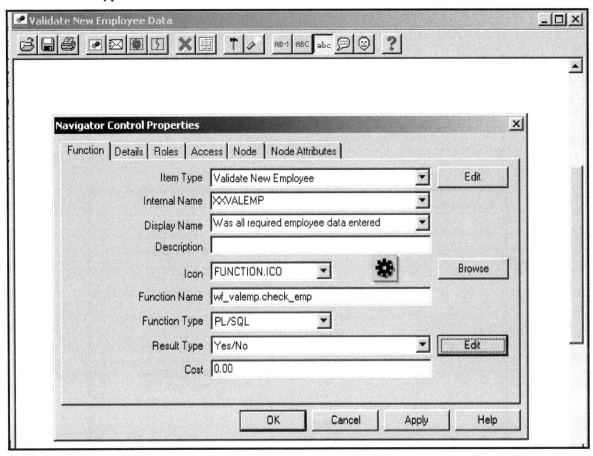

FIGURE 16. 25

While the Workflow step is simpler to set up, the code in the Package is more rigid in its format and it is not clear what variables are being returned to the Workflow Process because it returns values by calling APIs that set the variables defined in the flow. BPEL, on the other hand, is very clear about what is returned and also accepts Functions, custom SQL and allows for polling for changes in a table.

HR Validation Notification for BPEL

Add a Human Task to the Employee Validation Process

There are several ways to accomplish adding a human task to the 'Employee Validation' Process. In past versions of the SOA Suite, it was necessary to create the Human Task Definition first when you used different outcomes than the standard default outcomes of APPROVE and REJECT. This problem is fixed in the RDBMS 11*g* version, but our example uses a method that creates the definition first, since it shows the relationship of the human task within the composite structure.

1. Switch to the composite.xml tab of the Diagram Window.

2. Drag and drop Human Task from the Service Components section of the Component Palette onto the Components lane.

3. Enter EmployeeValidation, do not check 'Expose as Composite Service', and click OK.

4. Wire the BPEL Process to the Human Task by clicking on the BPEL Process arrow and dragging it to the Human Task arrow.

5. Double-click the Human Task to bring up the Human Task Editor (see FIGURE 16.26).

6. In the Human Task Editor enter 'Employee Validation' for Title.

7. Click the flashlight icon next to the Outcomes field.

8. Uncheck APPROVE and REJECT and check OK and click OK button.

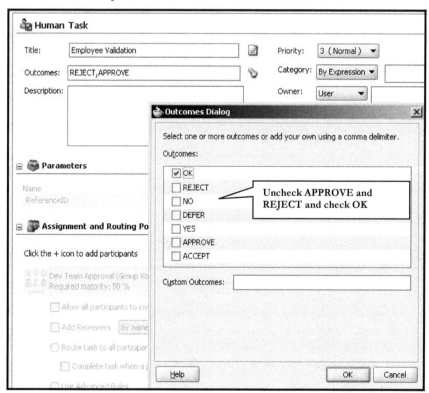

FIGURE 16. 26

9. For Parameters click the + icon on the right side (see FIGURE 16.27).

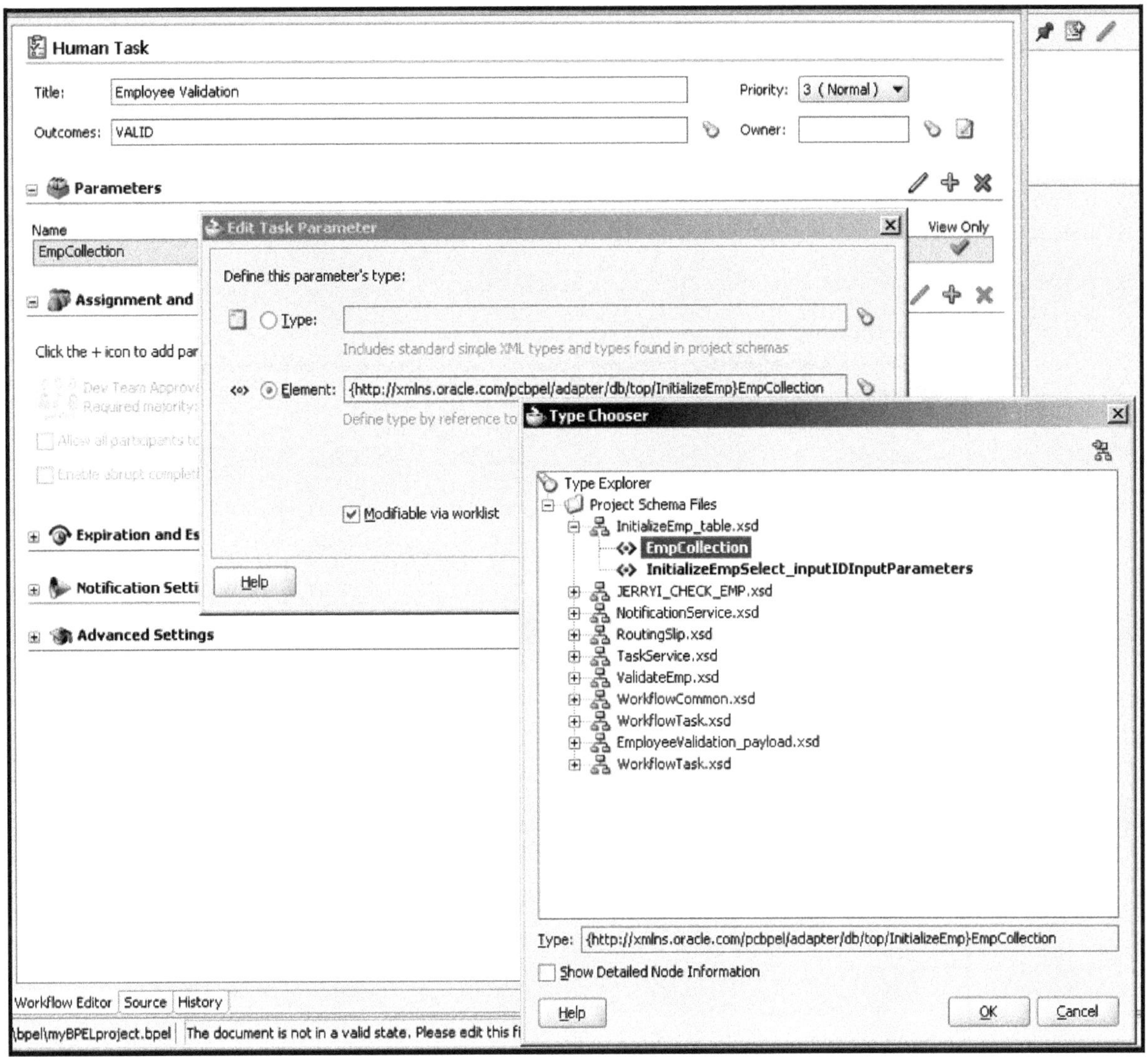

FIGURE 16. 27

10. In the Add Task Parameter window click Element and then the flashlight icon.

11. In the Type Chooser window, expand and select 'Project Schema Files > InitializeEmp_table.xsd > EmpCollection', and click OK. This is the schema that was defined as part of the InitializeEmp database adaptor and supplies basic employee information to the task.

12. Click OK twice to get back to the Human Task Editor.

13. In the 'Assignment and Routing Policy' section, click the + icon on the right side of the window (see FIGURE 16.28).

14. In the Add Participant Type window, for Type, select Single Approver.

15. For Label, enter 'Employee Validators'.

16. Click 'By name' and then the flashlight icon to the right of User Id(s) to display the Identity lookup dialog window. Ensure that your integration server connection is selected.

17. Ensure that Oracle BPEL Server is running and click Lookup to see a list of all users currently in the system.

18. Select 'jcooper' and click the Hierarchy just to see what that looks like.

19. Click 'jcooper' again to highlight it and click Select, and click OK.

20. Click the + icon next to 'Expiration and Escalation Policy'.

21. Select 'Expire after' from the drop down.

22. Enter a '1' in 'Day to have the notification expire after a day'.

23. Close and Save the Human Task editor.

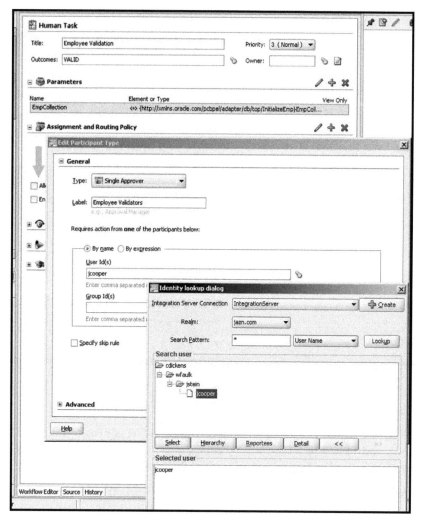

FIGURE 16. 28

Add Human Task to Diagram

1. Double-click the BPEL Process to get to the BPEL diagram.

2. Drag and drop a Human Task activity from the Process Activities in the Component Palette on to the diagram.

3. Choose 'EmployeeValidation' from the drop down next to Task Definition (see FIGURE 16.29).

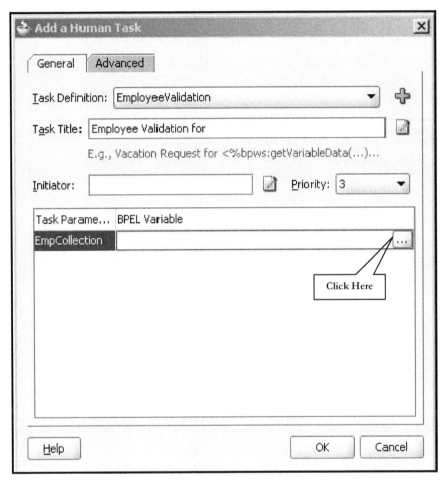

FIGURE 16. 29

4. Click the ... icon to the right of 'EmpCollection' in the BPEL Variable column.

5. In the 'Task Parameters' window, expand and select Variables > 'invokeInitialize_InitializeEmpSelect_inputID_OutputVariable' > 'EmpCollection' > 'ns2.EmpCollection' and click OK.

6. Click 'OK' in the Human Task window.

The result of all this work is the creation of many objects within the Process. Take a look at the number of additional objects in the Application Navigator. Also, expand the EmployeeValidation task and the Switch activity following it on the diagram. Fortunately, most of these objects can be manipulated using the Human Task Editor. The one thing that does not edit gracefully in the Task Editor is the Outcomes field. The switch activity that follows the email task does not get changed with the new values. There are default steps in each of the options of the switch activity. The proper steps for each response has to be added to complete the Process.

HR Validation Notification for Workflow

Create a Lookup Type

The Notification is going to return a value that is not currently defined as a Lookup Type so a new one has to be created.

1. Right-click the Lookup Type entry in the tree and select New Lookup Type.

2. Enter an Internal Name of 'XXXVALEMP_FIXED' and a Display Name of 'Fixed' (see FIGURE 16.30).

3. Click OK.

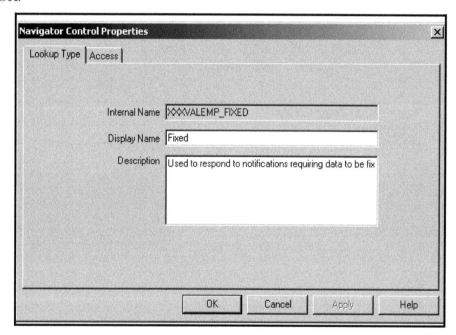

FIGURE 16. 30

4. Right-click the resulting 'Fixed' Lookup Type and select New Lookup Code.

5. Enter an Internal Name of 'FIXED' and a Display Name of 'Fixed' (see FIGURE 16.31).

6. Click OK.

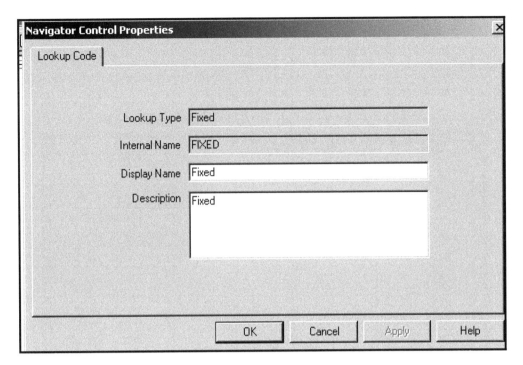

FIGURE 16. 31

Create Message

A Message for the Notification has to be created separately.

1. Right-click the Message entry in the tree and select New Message

2. Enter 'ASK_HR_TO_COMPLETE_DATA' as the Internal Name and 'Ask HR to Complete Data' as the Display Name (see FIGURE 16.32).

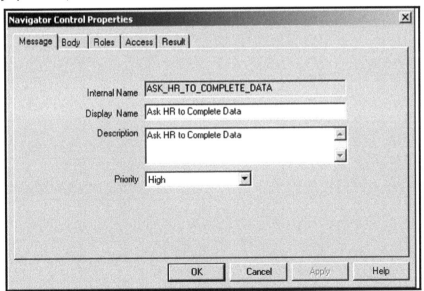

FIGURE 16. 32

3. Click the Body tab (see FIGURE 16.33)

4. Enter 'Employee data for employee &EMPLOYEE_NAME is not complete' in the Subject line. The &<attribute_name> substitutes the value of the Attribute.

5. Enter 'Please check information for &EMPLOYEE_NAME' in the Text Body.

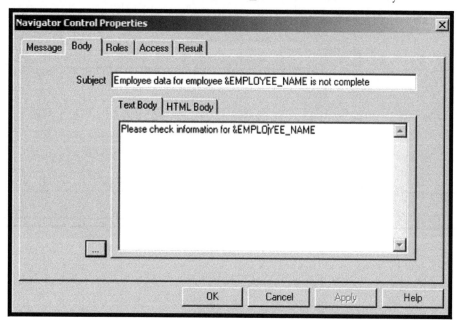

FIGURE 16. 33

6. Click the Result tab (see FIGURE 16.34).

7. Enter Result in the Display Name.

8. Choose 'Fixed' from the drop down list in the Lookup Type field.

9. Click OK.

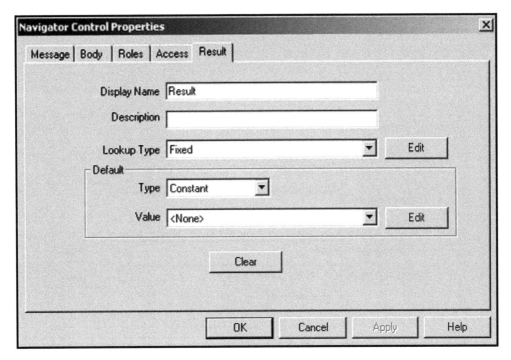

FIGURE 16. 34

Create the Notification on the Diagram

1. Click the New Notification icon ⊠ at the top of the Diagram.

2. Click on the Diagram where you want it placed.

3. Enter the following data into the form (see FIGURE 16.35):

   a. **Internal Name** – ASK_HR_TO_COMPLETE_DATA

   b. **Display Name** – 'Ask HR to complete Data'

   c. **Description** – 'Send notification to HR'

   d. **Result Type** – Fixed

   e. **Message** – 'Ask HR to Complete Data'

4. Click OK.

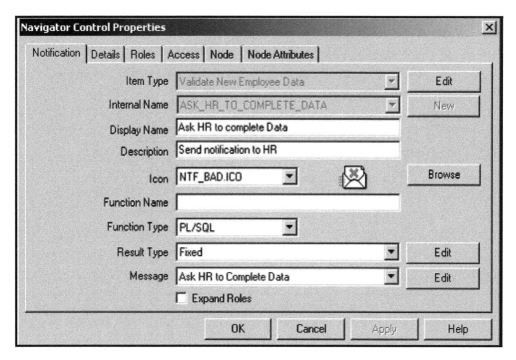

FIGURE 16. 35

5. Click on the Node tab.

6. For Performer Value enter 'HR003.HR GENERALIST' (see FIGURE 16.36).

7. Choose Relative Time from the Timeout Type drop down list.

8. Enter '1' in the days field.

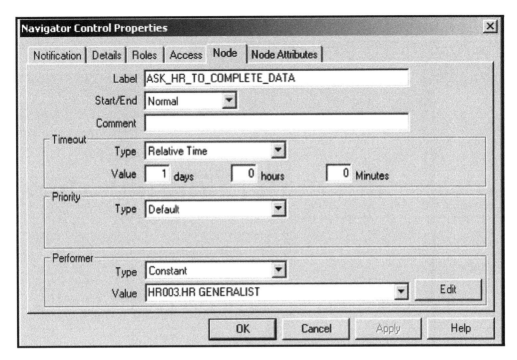

FIGURE 16. 36

Again, Workflow provides a much simpler setup for a Notification with a response. A Notification without a response is actually simpler in BPEL because the Notification and Message are not separate pieces. But BPEL provides many more automatic capabilities that would have to be built into the logic of a Workflow Process. It can automatically escalate a Notification up a management chain based on a time out setting, it can automatically send reminders if an item hasn't been responded to yet, and there are many more options.

VALIDATING AND RUNNING THE EMPLOYEE VALIDATION PROCESS IN BPEL

Validating the Process

1. Right-click the 'myApplication' Applications in the Application Navigator.

2. Select 'Deploy' > ' oar_myApplication' > 'to' > 'BundledOC4JServer'.

3. Click OK to accept default Deployment Plan.

4. Check for and repair errors.

Running the Process

1. Bring up the Oracle SOA Console by going to http://localhost:8988/SOAConsole/ (see FIGURE 16.37).

2. When the list of Applications appears, click on 'SOAvalidateEmpComposite' under 'myApplication' to bring up detail. You may have to expand the size of the left lane in order to click it.

3. Click 'Test Service – client' from the drop down Actions list at the top of the page.

4. Enter an ID for an Employee under Payload and click Invoke.

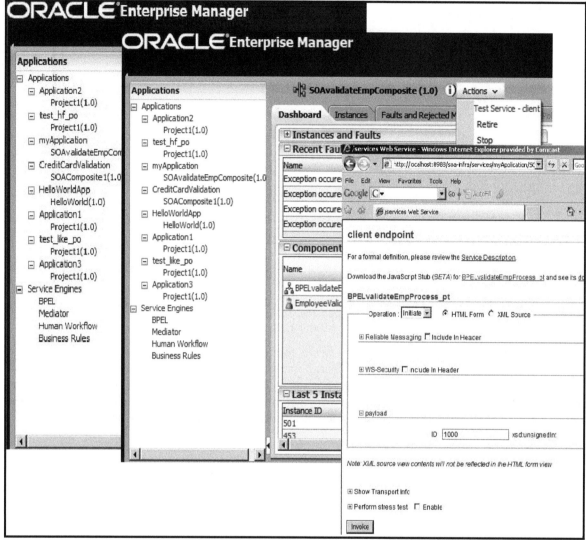

FIGURE 16. 37 – RUN EMPLOYEE VALIDATION

5. Return to the detail page and click on 'Refresh' at the top to bring up the latest instance

6. Click on the instance ID to bring up the Flow Trace page

7. Click on BPELvalidateEmpProcess to see the Audit detail of the BPEL Process.

8. Click on 'Flow-Debug' tab to see a graphical list of activities

In FIGURE 16.38, you can see that the Process has progressed to the point of waiting for a response from the validators. You can expand any of the audit step payloads to see more detail. You can also click on any of the nodes of the Flow to view the underlying code.

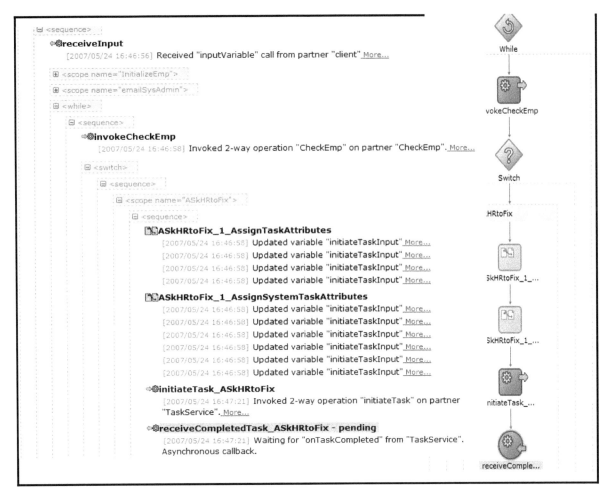

FIGURE 16. 38 – PROCESS PROGRESS

9. As a response to the request, start the Oracle Worklist Applications at http://localhost/integration/worklistapp and log in as jcooper/welcome1.

10. The Worklist is displayed (see FIGURE 16.39). Click on the task you want to respond to. Select OK from the drop down Actions list.

11. Click the circle with an arrow in it to the right of the Action chosen to respond.

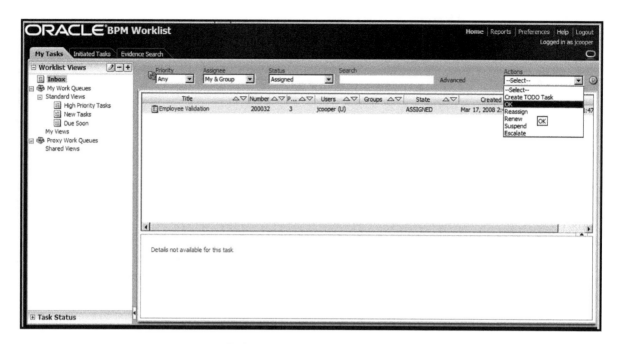

FIGURE 16. 39 – TASK LIST

12. Go back to the 'SOA Console' page and re-query the Process instance. It has now progressed.

DEPLOYING THE EMPLOYEE VALIDATION PROCESS IN WORKFLOW

In order to deploy a Workflow Process it has to be loaded into the database.

1. Select 'Save as' from the File menu.

2. Click Database.

3. Enter the APPS user, password and SID.

4. Click OK.

5. Any errors in logic will be reported and must be corrected before the Process is loaded.

6. The Workflow Process is then launched from a program via the Workflow API.

ADDITIONAL OBSERVATIONS

Both Workflow and BPEL have a detailed log of activities that are stored in their own respective set of tables in a database. Both require vigilant purging of these tables because they can grow very quickly and effect performance. Both have extensive error logging capabilities and methods for reversing earlier steps when a Process is not completed. In both cases this reversing or compensating can be a very tricky thing to implement. JDeveloper has a nice capability to switch back and forth between source code and diagrams. This capability provides a great learning tool and if you are handy with XML you can sometimes be more efficient working directly with the code. Workflow Builder has no underlying language to look at. Both tools have been known to get themselves in a confused state where they report a general error with no real clue as to where it exists and how to fix it. BPEL is better at creating test scenarios and storing them with the Applications.

CONCLUSIONS

Workflow and BPEL both have their strengths and weaknesses. Not surprisingly, they are best in the areas they were designed for and look a little awkward in areas they were not designed for but have been forced to supply. It will be interesting to see how the two play out and how the vast number of Workflows in E-Business Suite can be transitioned from Workflow to BPEL.

Sample BR110

This Appendix shows an example of documentation for a custom Workflow. The format used is a combination of an AIM *BR110 – Application Setup*, *MD060 – Module Functional Design* and *MD070 – Module Technical Design*. AIM is Oracle's Application Implementation Methodology, which combines a project management methodology with a set of documentation templates designed specifically to support the life cycle of implementing Oracle E–Business Suite. When AIM was released, Workflow didn't exist, so AIM does not contain a template specifically for Workflow. What is presented in this appendix is a documentation design that has evolved over several years with the input of many people who have used the results.

This Document is labeled BR110 to emphasize that individual Workflows require setup both in the applications as well as in the Builder. The version of the Workflow used in this chapter is the version that exists after *Chapter 5, Business Events*. Thus, any changes introduced in *Chapter 11, Advanced Builder and PL/SQL* are not reflected here. Everything following this paragraph is the documentation.

OVERVIEW AND JUSTIFICATION

Basic Business Need

Certain fields entered on the 'Employee' and 'Assignment' screens are crucial to the correct operation of 'Approval' Workflows. The fields are optional. This Workflow will validate that these fields are entered.

Business Process

Whenever a new employee is entered, a Workflow will be initiated that will ensure the email, position, supervisor, and default accounting has been entered. If the email address is missing a Notification will be sent to the email administrator requesting the email address. If any other information is missing, a Notification will be sent to the responsibility used to create the employee requesting the additional information. If this Notification is ignored, another Notification will be sent the following day. If the data is still incomplete after two reminder Notifications, a Notification will be sent to the responsibility used by HR Management requesting them to ensure the data is complete. The cycle of Notifications will continue until the data is complete.

Notification Layout – Email Address is Missing

The following is a sample Notification received by the email administrator when a new employee is created. This Notification is sent to the user listed in the Profile Option 'XXHR: Email Administrator'. If this Profile Option is blank, the Notification is sent to SYSADMIN.

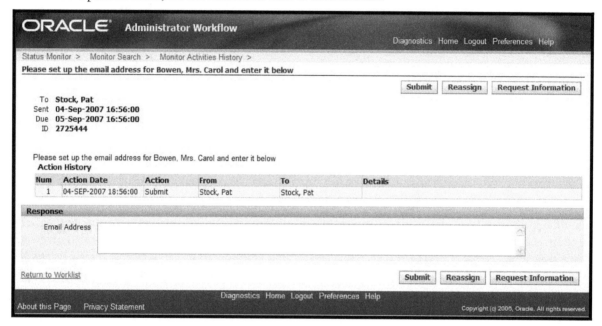

FIGURE A. 1

The recipient should provide the Email Address in the box provided and then click the 'Submit' button.

The recipient can also choose to reassign the Notification or request additional information by clicking on the 'Reassign' button or the 'Request Information' button at the bottom of the form.

Notification Layout – HR Data is Incomplete

The following is a sample Notification received when an employee is created and the primary assignment does not contain a position, a supervisor and/or the default accounting used in *i*Procurement. The Notification will be sent to the responsibility that created the employee.

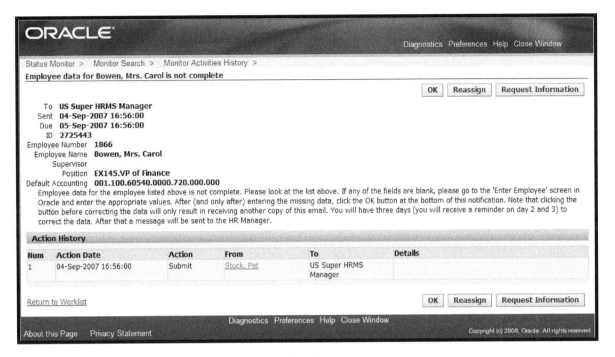

FIGURE A. 2

Since this notification is sent to a responsibility, all users assigned this responsibility will receive the notification. When the Notification is received, the employee and/or assignment record should be corrected and then the OK button pressed. If the Notification remains unanswered after 1 day, the Workflow will check whether the data was completed. If not, another Notification will be sent.

The recipient can also choose to reassign the Notification or request additional information by clicking on the 'Reassign' button or the 'Request Information' button at the bottom of the form.

Notification Layout – Escalation to HR Manager

The above Notification is sent three times. If no Action has been taken to correct the data, an escalation notice is sent to all holders of the 'US Super HRMS Manager' responsibility (see FIGURE A.3). The Workflow will then pause for a day and repeat the cycle of Notifications until the employee data is completed. Although no response is needed, if viewed through the Notification Worklist, the recipient must click OK to close the notification.

The recipient can also choose to reassign the Notification or request additional information.

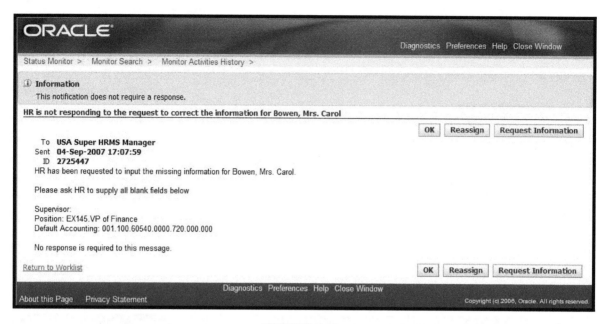

FIGURE A. 3

IMPLEMENTATION (INCLUDING REQUIRED SETUPS)

Resources Needed

1. Workflow and code delivered with this document requires Oracle developer skilled in Workflow and PL/SQL

2. Oracle Database Administrator to move code to various instances

3. HR Resource to validate results

4. System Administrator with access to create Profile Options and set Profile Option values.

Compile Program

1. Move Package spec/body XXHREMP to database

2. Compile Package spec XXHREMP

3. Compile Package body XXHREMP

Install Workflow

The Workflow can be installed by loading the XXHRVEMP.wft file into the Workflow Builder and then saving the Workflow to the <database name> database. Or you can use the Workflow loader program.

- Using Builder – the .wft file must be stored on a PC or fileserver drive, not the database server

  Load Workflow into Builder

  File → Open

  Click the Browse button and select the directory where the .wft file resides. Select XXHRVEMP.wft. Click OK. The Workflow will load into the builder

  Save Workflow to the database

  File → Save As

  Click the Database button. User Name = APPS, password = <apps password>, connect = <database name>. Click OK

- Using Loader (from a Unix command line) – the .wft file must be stored on the database server.

  ```
  WFLOAD apps/<password> 0 Y UPLOAD @<application_short_name>:<path>\XXHRVEMP.wft
  ```

Create Profile Options

Description:	A new Profile Option, 'XXHR: Email Administrator' is used to store the user who is the email administrator. Using Profile Options allows changes to the Roles as employees change without changing the underlying code.
Navigation:	(From Application Developer) Application → Profile
Note:	If "cut and paste" is used to enter the SQL Validation statement, delete the pasted " and ' marks and retype them. Oracle does not recognize the slanted ' and/or ".
Note:	Oracle is really picky on the SQL validation. It doesn't seem to recognize cut and paste on this one at all. If you want to cut and paste, copy the value from <development instance> and paste into the next instance.
Note:	The " are necessary characters. There is a space between user_name and \

Name	XXHR_EMAIL_ADMINISTRATOR	
Application	Custom Applications	
User Profile Name	XXHR: Email Administrator	
Description		
Active Dates – Start	<current date>	
Active Dates – End	<leave blank>	
SQL Validation	SQL="SELECT user_name \"User Name\",user_name INTO :visible_option_value,:profile_option_value FROM fnd_user" COLUMN="\"User Name\"(15)"	
Hierarchy Type	Security	
User Access – Visable	√	
User Access – Updatable		
Program Access – Visable	√	
Program Access – Updatable	√	
Hierarchy Type Access Level	Visible	Updatable
Site	√	√
Application	<unchecked>	<unchecked>
Responsibility	<unchecked>	<unchecked>
Server	<unchecked>	<unchecked>
Organization	<unchecked>	<unchecked>
User	<unchecked>	<unchecked

TABLE A. 1

Assign Value to New Profile Options

Description: In order to be effective, the new Profile Option needs to have a value

Navigation: (From System Administration) Profile → System – query up the Profile Options desired and the level of update.

Option	Level	Application / Responsibility / User	Value
XXHR: Email Administrator	Site		<employee name for email administrator>

TABLE A. 2

TECHNICAL OVERVIEW

Overview of Process

The Workflow starts whenever a new employee is created

FIGURE A.4 shows the Workflow:

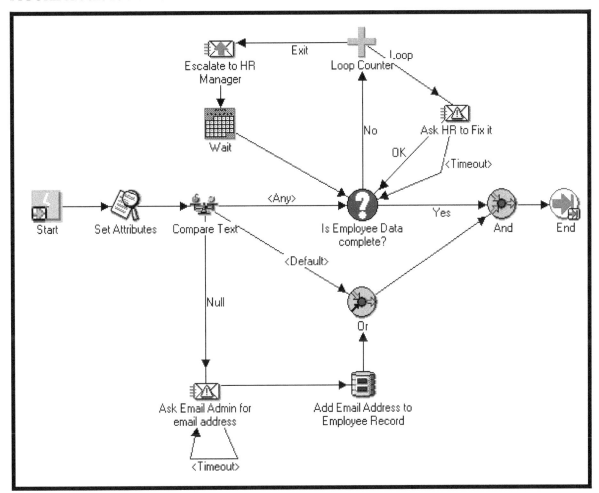

FIGURE A. 4

The first node, 'Set Attributes' calls the Package XXHRVEMP.SET_ATTRIBUTES. This Package retrieves the employee name, number, email address of the created employee. The owner of the Workflow is set to the individual who created the employee. The email administrator is retrieved from the Profile Option. All retrieved values are set into Item Attributes. If the Profile Option is missing or not set, the email administrator is set to the Workflow Administrator.

The next node, 'Compare Text', checks whether the Attribute containing the email address is null. If so a Notification is sent to the email administrator requesting the email address. This Notification will time out and repeat once a day until it is answered. Once the Notification is answered, the Workflow moves to the node 'Add Email Address to Employee Record' where the Procedure XXHRVEMP.ADD_EMAL_ADDRESS_TO_EMP_REC is executed. This Procedure updates the employee record with the value furnished as a response to the Notification. The Workflow then proceeds through the 'Or' node to wait at the 'And' node for the rest of the employee data to be declared complete.

If the email address is not null, the Workflow precedes through the 'Or' node to wait at the 'And' node for the rest of the employee data to be declared complete.

Regardless of the email address, the Workflow moves to the node 'Is Employee Data complete?'. This node executes the Procedure XXHRVEMP.IS_EMPLOYEE_DATA_COMPLETE. This Procedure gets the primary assignment record (if one exists) and retrieves the position, supervisor, and default accounting. If all of these fields have values, the Workflow proceeds to the 'And' node and waits for the email address to be found complete or added.

If any of the data is blank, a notification is sent to the responsibility used to create the employee. All users assigned to the responsibility receive a copy of the Notification. Any of these users can update the employee record and answer OK to the Notification (or just let the Timeout expire). When either the Notification is answered or times out, the data values are re-checked. If they are complete, the Workflow proceeds to the 'And' node. If not, another Notification is sent. This cycle is repeated 3 times. After that, a Notification is sent to the responsibility assigned to the HR Managers. This Notification does not require a response. The Workflow then waits 1 day for the managers to take action, then returns to check the employee values. The whole cycle of 3 Notifications to the responsibility that created the employee, then an escalation to the manager continues until all the data is complete.

Create Workflow from Scratch

If the Workflow had to be recreated from scratch, the following steps should be followed:

Verify Access Level

Description: This step verifies the Access Level of the Builder is set to 100

Navigation: Help → About Oracle Workflow Builder <version>

Set Access Level to 100
Uncheck 'Allow modifications of customized objects'

QuickStart Wizard

Description: This step creates the initial Item Type (Workflow), initial Process, and adds the 'Standard' Item Type and Directory Services

Navigation: File → QuickStart Wizard

New Item Type Internal Name	XXHRVEMP
Display Name	XXHR Validate New Employee
Persistence Type	Temporary

Number of Days	0
New Process Internal Name	VALIDATE_NEW_EMPLOYEE_TOP
Display Name	Validate New Employee Top Process

TABLE A. 3

Click OK, the Navigator tree appears, and the Diagrammer window opens with a Start and End Node

Define Lookup Types / Codes

Description: This step creates any custom Lookup Types and Codes that are not provided in 'Standard'

Navigation: To add a Lookup Type, right click 'Lookup Types' in the Navigator window, select 'New'

To add a Lookup Code, right click the specific Lookup Type, select New Lookup Code

Special Notes: Lookup Types must be unique across the entire database, so always preface the name with the ItemType Internal Name.

Lookup Type

Internal Name	XXHRVEMP_OK
Display Name	XXHRVEMP_OK
Description	

TABLE A. 4

Lookup Codes

Internal Name	Display Name	Description
OK	OK	

TABLE A. 5

Define Attributes

Description: This step creates the Attributes used in Messages, Performers, configuration of standard activities.

Navigation: To add an Attribute, right click the 'Attribute' tree in the Navigator window and select 'New Attribute'

What Attributes are Used For

Internal Name	Purpose
EMPLOYEE_NAME	Stores the employee name – used in Notifications
EMPLOYEE_NUMBER	Stores the employee number – used in Notifications
SUPERVISOR	Stores the employee's supervisor – used in Notifications
POSITION	Stores the employee's position – used in Notifications
DEFAULT_ACCOUNTING	Stores the employee's default accounting – used in Notifications

EMAIL_ADDRESS	Stores the employee's email address – used in Notifications and stores the value returned by the email administrator
EMAIL_ADMINISTRATOR	Either the user assigned to the Profile Option 'XXHR: Email Administrator' or the Workflow Administrator
HR	Responsibility of the user who created the new employee
HR_MANAGER	Responsibility used by HR Managers
EMPLOYEE_ID	Stores the employee id – used to access the employee records
EMAIL_ADMIN_ERROR	If the Profile Option 'XXHR: Email Administrator' is missing or blank, used to tell the Workflow Administrator why they are receiving the Notification instead
EVENT_NAME	Required Attribute to start the Workflow from an Event
EVENT_KEY	Required Attribute to start the Workflow from an Event
EVENT_DATA	Required Attribute to start the Workflow from an Event

TABLE A. 6

Setup

Internal Name	Display Name	Des-crip-tion	Type	Length / Format /	Default Type	Default Value
EMPLOYEE_NAME	Employee Name		Text		Constant	
EMPLOYEE_NUMBER	Employee Number		Text		Constant	
SUPERVISOR	Supervisor		Text		Constant	
POSITION	Position		Text		Constant	
DEFAULT_ACCOUNTING	Default Accounting		Text		Constant	
EMAIL_ADDRESS	Email Address		Text		Constant	
EMAIL_ADMINSTRATOR	Email Administrator		Text		Constant	
HR	HR		Role		Constant	
HR_MANAGER	HR Manager		Role		Constant	
EMPLOYEE_ID	Employee ID		Number		Constant	
EMAIL_ADMIN_ERROR	Email Admin Error Message		Text		Constant	
EVENT_NAME	Event Name		Text		Constant	
EVENT_KEY	Event Key		Text		Constant	
EVENT_DATA	Event Data		Event			

TABLE A. 7

Define Messages

Description: This step creates the Messages that are assigned to the Notifications. Messages contain the actual text sent.

Navigation: To add, right click the 'Messages' tree in the Navigator window and select New Message

Messages – Message tab

Internal Name	Display Name	Description	Priority
ASK_EMAIL_ADMIN_FOR_EMAIL_ADDR	Ask Email Admin for email address		Normal
ASK_HR_TO_FIX_IT	Ask HR to Fix it		Normal
ESCALATE_TO_HR_MANAGER	Escalate to HR Manager		Normal

TABLE A. 8

Messages – Result tab

Message Display Name	Result Display Name	Description	Lookup Type	Default Type	Default Value
Ask HR to Fix it	Result		XXHRVEMP_OK	Constant	<None>

TABLE A. 9

Messages – Body tab

Message Display Name	Subject	Text Body	HTML Body
Ask HR to Fix it	Employee data for &EMPLOYEE_NAME is not complete	WF_NOTIFICATION (ATTRS,EMPLOYEE_NUMBER,EMPLOYEE_NAME,SUPERVISOR,POSITION,DEFAULT_ACCOUNTING) Employee data for the employee listed above is not complete. Please look at the list above. If any of the fields are blank, please go to the 'Enter Employee' screen in Oracle and enter the appropriate values. After (and only after) entering the missing data, click the OK button at the bottom of this Notification. Note that clicking the button before correcting the data will only result in receiving another copy of this email.	
Ask Email Admin for email address	Please set up the email address for &EMPLOYEE_NAME and enter it below	&EMAIL_ADMIN_ERROR Please set up the email address for &EMPLOYEE_NAME and enter it below	
Escalate to HR Manager	HR is not responding to the request to correct the information for &EMPLOYEE_NAME	HR has been requested to input the missing information for &EMPLOYEE_NAME. Please ask HR to supply all blank fields below Supervisor: &SUPERVISOR Position: &POSITION Default Accounting: &DEFAULT_ACCOUNTING No response is required to this Message.	

TABLE A. 10

After the Messages are defined, any Attribute referenced by the Message must either be drag and dropped from the Item Attribute definitions to the specific Message (not to the Messages folder) or created.

If there is an asterisk ('*') next to the Attribute, after dragging and dropping, right-click the 'Attribute', select 'Properties'. When the 'Properties' page opens, change the value in the 'Source' field from 'Send' to 'Respond'.

Attributes to be copied for 'Ask Email Admin for email address' (listed using the Attribute Display Name).

- Employee Name

- *Email Address

- Email Admin Error Message

Attributes to be copied for 'Ask HR to Fix it' (listed using the Attribute Display Name)

- Employee Name

- Employee Number

- Supervisor

- Position

- Default Accounting

Attributes to be copied for 'Escalate to HR Manager' (Listed using the Attribute Display Name)

- Employee Name

- Supervisor

- Position

- Default Accounting

Define Functions / Notifications/Events

Description: This step creates the Functions and Notifications

Navigation: To add, right click in the white space on the Diagrammer window and select either 'New Function' or 'New Notification' or 'New Event'

Functions/Notifications Created

Type	Display Name	Purpose
Event	Start	Replace start node with an Event start node
Function	Set Attributes	Uses the Item Key to find the employee record and set values for the email address, employee number, employee name, owner (person who created the employee),and responsibility that created the employee. Get value for the email admin Profile Option. Get responsibility name used by HR managers
Function	Is Employee Data complete?	Check the primary assignment and verify if the position, supervisor, and default accounting have been specified.
Function	Add Email Address to Employee Record	Take the email address returned by the email administrator and update the employee record
Notification	Ask Email Admin for email address	Notify the email administrator that an email address is needed. Requires administrator to enter the address and answer OK
Notification	Ask HR to Fix it	Notify the users of the responsibility used to create the employee that the information is not complete.
Notification	Escalate to HR Manager	Notify the users of the selected HR Manager responsibility that requests to complete the employee definition are being ignored

TABLE A. 11

Event Tab

Internal Name	Display Name	Descrip-tion	Icon	Event Action	Event Filter	Cost
START	Start		EVENT ICON	Receive	sb.apps.xxhr.employee.create	0.00

TABLE A. 12

Function Tab

Internal Name	Display Name	Descrip-tion	Icon	Function Name	Function Type	Result Type	Cost
ADD_EMAIL_ADDRESS_TO_EMP_RECOR	Add Email Address to Employee Record		DB_UPD_ICO	XXHRVEMP.ADD_EMAIL_ADDRESS_TO_EMP_REC	PL/SQL	Yes/No	0.00
IS_EMPLOYEE_DATA_COMPLETE?	Is Employee Data complete?		QUESTION.ICO	XXHRVEMP.IS_EMPLOYEE_DATA_COMPLETE	PL/SQL	<None>	0.00
SET_ATTRIBUTES	Set Attribute		REVIEW.ICO	XXHRVEMP.SET_ATTRIBUTES	PL/SQL	<None>	0.00

TABLE A. 13

Notification Tab

Internal Name	Display Name	Des-crip-tion	Icon	Function Name	Function Type	Result Type	Message	Expand Roles
ASK_EMAIL_ADMIN_FOR_EMAIL_ADDR	Ask Email Admin for email address		NTF_URG.ICO		PL/SQL	<None>	Ask Email Admin for email address	

Internal Name	Display Name	Des-crip-tion	Icon	Function Name	Function Type	Result Type	Message	Expand Roles
ASK_HR_TO_FIX_IT	Ask HR to Fix it		NTF_URG.ICO		PL/SQL	XXHRV EMP_O OK	Ask HR to Fix it	
ESCALATE_TO_HR_MANAGER	Escalate to HR Manager		NTF_HIGH.ICO		PL/SQL	<None>	Escalate to HR Manager	

TABLE A. 14

Add Timeouts, Performers, Messages, Event Details, Node Attributes to Functions/Notifications/Events

Description: This step adds Timeouts, Performers and Messages to individual nodes in the Diagrammer window.

Navigation: Right click on the Node and choose 'Properties', or double-click the Node. The 'Properties' page opens. When all the data is entered, click the OK button.

Node Display Name	Tab	Field Name	Value
Start	Event Details	Event Name	Event Name
		Event Key	Event Key
		Event Message	Event Data
	Node	Start/End	Start
Compare Text	Node Attributes	Attribute Name	Test Value
		Type	Item Attribute
		Value	Email Address
		Attribute Name	Reference value
		Type	Constant
		Value	@
Ask Email Admin for email address	Node	Timeout Type	Relative Time
		Timeout Value	1 days
		Performer Type	Item Attribute
		Performer Value	Email Administrator
	Notification	Message	Ask Email Admin for email address
Loop Counter	Node Attributes	Attribute Name	Loop Limit
		Type	Constant
		Value	3
Ask HR to Fix it	Notification	Message	Ask HR to Fix it
	Node	Performer Type	Item Attribute
		Performer Value	HR
		Timeout Type	Relative Time
		Timeout Value	1 days

Escalate to HR Manager	Notification	Message	Escalate to HR Manager
	Node	Performer Type	Item Attribute
		Performer Value	HR Manager
		Timeout Type	No Timeout
Wait	Node Attributes	Attribute Name	Wait Mode
		Type	Constant
		Value	Relative Time
		Attribute Name	Relative Time
		Type	Constant
		Value	1

TABLE A. 15

Transitions

Description: This step completes the drawing of the Process

Navigation: To add a Transition, hold the cursor over the 'Starting Node' and click the right mouse button. With the right mouse button held down, drag the cursor to the 'Ending Node' until the ⫯ symbol appears at the bottom of the cursor. Then let go of the mouse button. If a list of results appears, select the appropriate result.

Step 1: Delete the 'Start Node' that looks like a green arrow

Step 2: Draw the following lines

Starting Node Display Name	Ending Node Display Name	Result
Start	Set Attributes	
Set Attributes	Compare Text	
Compare Text	Ask Email Admin for email address	Null
Compare Text	Or	<Default>
Compare Text	Is Employee Data complete?	<Any>
Ask Email Admin for email address	Add Email Address to Employee Record	
Ask Email Admin for email address	Ask Email Admin for email address	<Timeout>
Add Email Address to Employee Record	Or	
Or	And	
Is Employee Data complete?	Loop Counter	No
Loop Counter	Ask HR to Fix it	Loop
Ask HR to Fix it	Is Employee Data complete?	OK
Ask HR to Fix it	Is Employee Data complete?	<Timeout>
Loop Counter	Escalate to HR Manager	Exit
Escalate to HR Manager	Wait	
Wait	Is Employee Data complete?	
Is Employee Data complete?	And	Yes

And	End	

TABLE A. 16

Code for Program

The code is a set of Procedures inside the Package XXHREMP.

Package Spec

The current version and date of this Package Spec is denoted in the $Header section. Ensure this section looks like

```
/* $Header:  XXHRVEMP.pls 1.0 <date> $ */
```

Package Body

The current version and date of this Package Body is denoted in the $Header section. Ensure this section looks like

```
/* $Header:  XXHRVEMP.plb 1.0 <date> $ */
```

Index

6399304, 494, 499, 500

6441940, 494

AB-1 icon, 109

abc icon, 109

ABC icon, 109

About Oracle Workflow Builder 2.6.3.<x>, 360

Abstract DataType, 345

   SYS.AQ$_JMS_TEXT_MESSAGE, 171, 341, 342, 343

   WF_AGENT_T, 341, 342

   WF_DEFERRED_TABLE_M, 172, 254, 340, 343

   WF_EVENT_T, 171, 188, 341, 342, 344

   WF_PARAMETER_LIST_T, 341

   WF_PARAMETER_T, 188, 341

Access Level, xxiv, 3, 70, 222, 301, 360, 361, 362, 363, 364, 421, 424, 429, 436, 438, 440, 442, 642, 644

Account Generators, xxiv, 223, 225, 226, 227, 229, 234, 236, 237, 238, 239, 294, 405, 594

   AR: Substitute Balancing Segment, 226

   FA Account Generator, 226

   FTE: Generate Distribution Account, 226

   Generate Cost of Goods Sold Account, 226, 238

   IAC Account Generator, 225

   IGC Budget Account Generator, 226

   IGC Charge Account Generator, 226

   Inventory Cost of Goods Sold Account, 226

   ITR Account Generator, 225

   MHCA Account Generator, 225

   OKL Account Generator, 226, 239

   OM: Generate Cost of Goods Sold Account, 225

   OZF: Account Generator, 226

   PO Account Generator, 226, 236

   PO Requisition Account Generator, 226

   Project Budget Account Generation, 226

   Project Supplier Invoice Account Generation, 226, 227

   Project Web Employees Account Generator, 226

   PSB Account Generator for OLD Integration, 225

Action Permission Sets, 478

Action Type

   Custom, 185

   Launch Workflow, 182

   Send Notification, 186

Activity, 3, 4, 166, 298, 312, 324, 326, 332, 333, 437, 439

   Customizable: Does Journal Batch Need Approval, 420, 423

   Customizable: Is Journal Batch Valid, 420, 422

   Customizable: Is Preparer Authorized to Approve, 420, 423

   Customizable: Verify Authority (activity), 420

   Customizable: Verify Authority (process), 420

   Submit Concurrent Program Activity, 392

   Wait for Concurrent Program Activity, 392

Activity Attributes, 3, 210, 230, 231, 232, 233, 237, 312, 392, 412, 424, 445

Activity Guides, 594

ADF Task Flows, 594

Administration Workflow Tests, 289

Administrator, 1, 5, 22, 23, 41, 87, 110, 134, 140, 144, 149, 150, 170, 173, 194, 196, 217, 242, 257, 267, 268, 409, 426, 427, 428, 445, 453, 461, 478, 480, 483, 487, 489, 492, 493, 494, 519, 549, 606, 638, 641, 642, 646, 649, 650

ADT, 341

Advanced Builder and PL/SQL, xxiv, 68, 71, 100, 105, 127, 129, 138, 146, 154, 194, 239, 301, 311, 355, 357, 403, 637

Agent Activity, 6, 8, 242, 248, 253, 255, 284, 337

Agent Listener Container, 203

Agent Listeners, 3, 5, 10, 39, 40, 60, 170, 172, 244, 245, 254

Agent(s), 2, 3, 170, 171, 172, 173, 181, 244, 258, 292, 337

AME, 405, 423, 426, 432, 434, 436, 441, 443, 444, 470, 516, 517, 518, 595

   canonical form, 522

   Chain-of-Authority Action Types, 530

   Conditions

Ordinary-Exception, 527
Ordinary-Regular, 527
format string, 523
List-Modification Action Types, 530, 532, 533
runtime parameters, 523
Testing Workbench, 558, 568, 579, 580, 586
AME Components, 518, 586
AP_WEB_UTILITIES_PKG.logProcedure, 160, 161, 162, 165
API, 1, 132, 135, 136, 138, 140, 141, 146, 147, 149, 150, 158, 159, 162, 177, 184, 185, 186, 187, 200, 201, 205, 213, 215, 216, 229, 341, 342, 378, 383, 388, 397, 398, 399, 400, 401, 542, 634
AdHoc, 350
WF_CORE.Context, 135, 136, 147, 150, 153, 154, 155, 158, 213, 378, 379, 380, 383, 384, 388, 389
WF_DIRECTORY.UserActive, 149
WF_ENGINE.CompleteActivity, 228, 397, 398
WF_ENGINE.CompleteActivityInternalName, 397, 398
WF_ENGINE.CreateForkProcess, 398
WF_ENGINE.CreateProcess, 140, 184, 229, 392
WF_ENGINE.HandleError, 146
WF_ENGINE.LaunchProcess, 140
WF_ENGINE.SetItemAttr<type>, 150, 158, 184, 327
WF_ENGINE.SetItemOwner, 149
WF_ENGINE.SetItemUserKey, 149
WF_ENGINE.StartForkProcess, 398, 399
WF_ENGINE.StartProcess, 140, 184, 200, 230, 392
WF_EVENT.GetValueForParameter, 186
WF_EVENT.Raise, 177, 183, 186, 187
WF_EVENT.Raise3, 186
WF_NOTIFICATION.GetAttr<type>, 186, 383
WF_STANDARD.ContinueFlow, 396, 397
WF_STANDARD.WaitForFlow, 394, 397
Application Object Library Group, 29
Approvals Management Engine (AME), iii, xxv, 405, 423, 432, 436, 441, 516, 517
approver, 97, 134, 141, 156, 366, 418, 422, 423, 426, 427, 428, 434, 435, 437, 438, 440, 453, 454, 518, 519, 520, 521, 523, 524, 525, 527, 528, 529, 530, 531, 532, 533, 534, 535, 536, 537, 538, 539, 540, 542, 544, 557, 558, 568, 571, 573, 574, 579, 580, 581, 584, 585
AR: Substitute Balancing Segment, 226
Assign Roles, 472, 489, 490, 547, 548
Asynchronous operations, 600
ATG rollup patch, 597
ATG rollup patches, 597
Attribute(s), xxiii, 2, 3, 67, 69, 76, 78, 99, 101, 103, 104, 105, 106, 110, 116, 140, 147, 149, 150, 153, 161, 162, 165, 184, 188, 190, 192, 200, 216, 217, 225, 229, 230, 231, 264, 306, 311, 318, 342, 364, 366, 367, 368, 369, 372, 382, 386, 391, 392, 397, 402, 409, 412, 413, 424, 427, 436, 441, 442, 444, 466, 492, 509, 517, 522, 523, 524, 537, 546, 556, 557, 560, 561, 562, 569, 575, 580, 581, 582, 587, 588, 589, 645, 648
Activity, 311, 312, 412, 445
Boolean, 523, 528
Currency, 522, 528
Date, 100, 523, 528
Document, 129, 355, 371, 373, 419, 424, 438, 440, 442, 444, 460, 465
Document Types, 433
Dynamic, 557
Form, 158, 160, 370
Hidden, 236, 238, 391
Item, 413, 475
Item Type, 100, 210
Mandatory, 523, 524
Message, 21, 101, 108, 150, 186, 207, 329, 331, 364, 369, 371, 372, 505, 506, 508, 510
Node, 116, 119, 120, 123, 210, 312, 393, 650, 651
Numeric, 522
Reporting, 229, 233
Required, 524, 525
String, 522, 528
URL, xxiv, 370
Voting Option, 386
Black Ball, 386
Jury, 386
Popularity, 386
Require All Votes, 386
Simple Majority, 386
Simple Majority with Default, 386
Simple Majority with Multiple Defaults, 386
Tally on Every Vote, 386
Wait for All Votes, 386

AutoConfig, xxvii, 5, 7, 10, 267, 268, 269, 272, 273

Background Engine(s), 3, 6, 8, 34, 35, 36, 124, 125, 130, 131, 132, 138, 140, 146, 158, 159, 172, 201, 227, 241, 245, 254, 333, 340, 341, 343, 384, 429, 432, 436, 437, 439, 447

BES Clone Test, 292

Block, 92, 116, 134, 147, 228, 397

Body tab, 103, 123, 150, 300, 317, 628, 647

BPEL, iv, xxv, 66, 129, 593, 594, 595, 596, 597, 598, 599, 600, 601, 602, 603, 606, 607, 608, 610, 611, 612, 613, 614, 616, 621, 622, 624, 625, 631, 632, 634, 635

  Application Navigator, 603, 610, 611, 614, 625, 631

  Component Palette, 603, 617, 619

  Diagram Window, 603, 622

  Structure Window, 603

BPEL Activities, 619

BPEL Designer, 600, 602

BPEL engine, 600

BPEL Process Manager, 594, 600, 601

BPEL Processes, 600

Browser Look and Feel (BLAF), 257

Browser Signing DLL Location, 26

Builder, xxiii, xxiv, 1, 2, 7, 13, 15, 18, 59, 67, 68, 70, 71, 72, 78, 80, 85, 90, 109, 110, 113, 123, 124, 126, 130, 136, 140, 142, 147, 149, 150, 151, 155, 156, 162, 165, 166, 169, 175, 187, 195, 198, 205, 210, 214, 222, 225, 227, 264, 295, 301, 306, 311, 321, 355, 357, 360, 362, 363, 364, 372, 381, 382, 402, 403, 412, 413, 419, 421, 423, 424, 427, 429, 432, 435, 436, 437, 438, 440, 442, 444, 460, 465, 593, 637, 641, 644

  Diagrammer window, 4, 68, 70, 73, 76, 77, 80, 82, 87, 89, 109, 110, 116, 166, 188, 189, 231, 298, 302, 312, 323, 357, 358, 360, 362, 363, 386, 408, 412, 420, 424, 426, 436, 438, 445, 462, 463, 471, 645, 648, 650

  Navigator window, 68, 69, 70, 71, 76, 78, 80, 87, 89, 101, 109, 189, 298, 312, 323, 358, 361, 362, 420, 645, 646

Builder tool, xxiii, 68, 130, 169, 225

built-in integration services, 600

Business Analyst Dashboard, 556, 559, 560, 569, 580

Business Event Local System, 24

Business Event Naming Standard, 173

Business Event System, xxiii, xxiv, 2, 24, 40, 41, 42, 169, 170, 292, 294, 342

Business Event(s), xxiii, xxiv, 3, 8, 25, 41, 68, 76, 87, 100, 138, 148, 167, 169, 170, 171, 172, 173, 175, 176, 193, 201, 203, 244, 257, 340, 470, 637

Business Process Execution Language (BPEL), 593

Business Processes, 1, 2, 7, 67, 76, 141, 357, 594, 596, 599, 600

business rules, 3, 67, 68, 225, 404, 422, 437, 517, 518, 522, 527, 544, 556, 602

business users, 67, 592

Buttons

  Create Transaction Type, 553

  Delete Selection, 85, 358, 462, 464

  Developer Mode, 358

  Diagrammer Display, 357

  Help, 358

  New Event, 174, 188, 358, 648

  New Function, 77, 358, 648

  New Notification, 82, 358, 629, 648

  New Process, 358, 614, 645

  Open File, 358

  Opens, 358

  Print Diagram, 358

  Properties, 358

  Run Real Transaction Test, 582

  Run Test, 287

  Run Test Case, 582

  Save File, 358

  Show Comments, 358

  Show Display Name, 358

  Show Instance Labels, 358

  Show Internal Name, 358

  Show Performers, 358, 408

  View Approval Process Stages, 585

Capicom.dll, 26

Choose Icons, 123

cloned instance, 5, 7, 8, 10, 244, 268, 270

Comment(s), xxviii, 26, 186, 357, 358

Compare Date, 87

Component Palette, 622, 625

Components, 51, 70, 450, 451, 469, 600, 601, 602, 607, 622

Composite View, 607

Concurrent Programs

  Control Queue Cleanup, 6, 8, 41, 245, 248

  Invoice Approval Workflow, 543, 544, 552

Purge Obsolete Workflow Runtime Data, 42, 141, 221, 247

Workflow Background Process, 35, 245, 248, 343

Workflow Control Queue Cleanup, 257

Workflow Definitions Loader, 222

Workflow Directory Services User/Role Validation, 349, 503, 504

Container, 4, 66, 170, 244, 245

context, xxviii, 129, 130, 136, 145, 153, 155, 158, 159, 160, 161, 162, 163, 164, 165, 186, 268, 383, 389, 390, 391, 393, 458, 551, 603

Control Queue Cleanup, 6, 8, 41, 245, 248

Cost, 3

Create Worklist View, 510

custom icons, 59

customize logo, 59

database, xxvii, 1, 2, 3, 4, 5, 6, 8, 10, 14, 15, 18, 20, 24, 27, 29, 41, 42, 43, 60, 61, 69, 75, 76, 80, 81, 87, 100, 112, 113, 115, 123, 124, 125, 138, 146, 150, 154, 157, 158, 165, 166, 167, 169, 175, 191, 193, 198, 205, 210, 213, 216, 222, 223, 234, 244, 248, 254, 272, 273, 274, 276, 279, 282, 285, 292, 293, 295, 298, 299, 301, 302, 305, 306, 321, 323, 337, 362, 364, 367, 371, 380, 402, 403, 405, 419, 423, 424, 426, 427, 429, 436, 438, 440, 441, 442, 444, 445, 460, 461, 465, 498, 520, 522, 542, 551, 561, 567, 569, 582, 586, 587, 593, 594, 595, 599, 600, 601, 606, 607, 609, 616, 617, 620, 623, 634, 640, 641, 645

Database Adaptor, 617

Database Administrator, 10, 27, 29, 42, 640

Database Connection, 616, 617

Database Parameters
  aq_tm_processes, 41, 61, 248
  job_queue_processes, 41, 61, 248

Datastore, 3, 69

DBA, xxvi, 7, 8, 9, 10, 18, 41, 43, 112, 123, 213, 214, 227, 241, 248, 268, 279, 285, 419, 423, 424, 435, 436, 437, 438, 440, 442, 444, 460, 465, 500

DBMS_AQADM.Alter_Queue, 171

DEFAULT_ERROR Procedure, 126, 147

DEFAULT_EVENT_ERROR Procedure, 126

Deferred Activity, 3

definitions, xxiii, 2, 87, 222, 229, 244, 292, 299, 306, 311, 318, 323, 345, 352, 419, 423, 433, 436, 438, 440, 442, 444, 456, 597, 647

design tables, 218, 295, 296, 298, 301, 334

designer, 17, 67, 69, 76, 91, 92, 93, 102, 116, 117, 123, 138, 147, 149, 154, 166, 214, 218, 226, 378, 383, 388, 600, 601, 604

Desupport, 593

Developer, xxv, 1, 6, 7, 8, 9, 10, 11, 13, 67, 97, 100, 115, 129, 130, 132, 133, 140, 146, 151, 158, 165, 169, 173, 183, 192, 193, 195, 199, 202, 205, 209, 210, 212, 213, 215, 216, 217, 218, 219, 221, 222, 227, 230, 261, 285, 357, 362, 364, 382, 385, 403, 436, 595, 597, 599, 600, 640

Developer Studio, xxiv, 193, 195, 196, 199, 200, 202, 203, 205, 258

Diagnostics, xxiii, xxiv, 2, 6, 9, 21, 29, 60, 238, 241, 279, 284, 285, 286, 287, 289, 295, 336, 469, 470, 496

  BES Clone Test, 292

  Duplicate User Test, 291

  Event Diagnostic Test, 292, 293

  Grouping
    Activity, 287
    Data Collection, 287
    Setup, 287
    Workflow Tests, 287

  GSC Control Queue Test, 292

  GSM Setup Test, 292

  Mailer Component Parameter Test, 292

  Mailer Component Test, 292

  Notification Preference Validation Test, 29, 291

  Rule Function Validation Test, 292

  Workflow Advanced Queue Rule Validation Test, 292

  Workflow Agents/AQ Status Test, 292

  Workflow Directory Services, 29, 293, 349, 470, 503, 504

  Workflow Java Mailer, 292

  Workflow Objects Validity Test, 292

  Workflow Performance, 293

  Workflow Queues, 272, 292, 293

  Workflow Status and Purgeable Items, 293

  XML Parser Installation Test, 292

diagram, 2, 4, 67, 78, 99, 109, 123, 195, 230, 237, 264, 296, 298, 323, 324, 326, 333, 357, 406, 465, 474, 557, 603, 614, 619, 621, 625

Diagrammer window, 4, 68, 70, 73, 76, 77, 80, 82, 87, 89, 109, 110, 116, 166, 188, 189, 231, 298, 302, 312, 323, 357, 358, 360, 362, 363,

386, 408, 412, 420, 424, 426, 436, 438, 445, 462, 463, 471, 645, 648, 650

Directory
  FND_TOP/sql, 29, 59, 72, 222, 282, 283, 285, 286, 293, 401

Directory Services, xxiv, 2, 3, 4, 6, 7, 8, 9, 10, 11, 20, 24, 28, 29, 69, 75, 110, 112, 115, 198, 291, 293, 345, 365, 399, 400, 504, 644

Directory Services Tables, 345

Disabled, 25, 26, 27, 179, 181

Display Names, 72, 101, 154, 182, 295, 358

DML activities, 594

Do not send me mail, 26, 269, 270, 279, 367

Document Approval Manager, 435, 443

Duplicate User Test, 291

electronic signatures, 26, 43

electronic signing, 27

Email Administrator, 87, 90, 91, 149, 150, 382, 637, 638, 641, 642, 643, 644, 646, 649

email parser, 46

email server, 6, 9, 44, 171

Engine, 2, 3, 4, 34, 63, 90, 104, 124, 125, 126, 131, 132, 137, 138, 140, 146, 147, 148, 151, 154, 158, 159, 165, 167, 182, 184, 187, 206, 207, 210, 218, 230, 245, 333, 346, 369, 377, 380, 382, 423, 429, 432, 436, 437, 439, 441, 470, 595

Error Handling, 126, 134, 147, 378, 383, 388
  g_pkg, 136, 145, 153, 155, 377, 383, 388
  g_proc, 143, 145, 152, 153, 154, 155, 375, 377, 383, 387, 388
  g_trace, 136, 139, 141, 143, 144, 145, 152, 153, 155, 156, 157, 187, 375, 376, 377, 383, 387, 388

Errors
  ORA-1652, 29

eTRM, 296, 299

Event, 277

Event Data, 3

Event Diagnostic Test, 292, 293

Event Filter, 181, 189, 204, 205, 649

Event Groups, 177, 258, 338

Event Key, 3, 169, 181, 183, 184, 187, 188, 191, 202, 205, 315, 646, 650

Event Manager, 172, 173, 186, 337, 342

Event Subscription, 3

Events, xxiv, 2, 7, 9, 10, 38, 40, 41, 51, 69, 76, 141, 147, 167, 169, 170, 172, 173, 174, 175, 176, 177, 178, 179, 184, 186, 188, 191, 203,

204, 210, 223, 244, 248, 251, 253, 254, 258, 278, 292, 306, 332, 337, 338, 340, 341, 342, 344, 345, 494, 498, 499, 500, 501, 513, 542, 557, 558, 594, 648, 650

execution engine, 285

Exposed Services, 607

External Java Functions, 3

External References, 607

FA Account Generator, 226

File
  $FND_TOP/admin/template/afadmprf.sql, 268
  $FND_TOP/patch/115/sql/wfntfqup, 274
  fndwfaol.wft, 391
  init.ora, 41, 248
  SID.xml, 268

final approval, 518, 533, 540

FND: Notification Reassign Mode, 27

FND_FLEX_MESSAGE, 229, 233, 235

FND_FLEX_WORKFLOW.GENERATE, 230

FND_FLEX_WORKFLOW.INITIALIZE, 229

FND_GLOBAL API, 130

FND_USER_PREFERENCES, 269, 270, 345, 348, 354, 503

FNDLOGOS.gif, 59

Form Function, 201, 271

FTE: Generate Distribution Account, 226

Function, 3, 4, 63, 343
  AME
    ame_util.booleanAttributeFalse, 523
    ame_util.booleanAttributeTrue, 523
  FND_FLEX_WORKFLOW.INITIALIZE, 229
  IRC_VAC_DETS_NET, 555
  Personal Worklist, 365, 505, 506, 510, 514
  Wait for Resubmission, 426, 427
  WF_PREF. GET_PREF('<user_name>', '<preference_name>'), 348

Function Activity Procedure, 388

Function Mode, 135, 154, 162, 165, 213, 389

Function Security, 440

Function Tree, 87

Function(s), xxiv, 1, 2, 11, 58, 69, 72, 76, 78, 87, 89, 90, 92, 95, 98, 99, 110, 115, 119, 122, 123, 124, 125, 126, 129, 130, 132, 137, 146, 151, 154, 158, 159, 161, 173, 176, 184, 186, 188, 192, 200, 201, 209, 210, 223, 229, 230, 231,

232, 235, 237, 238, 257, 260, 261, 292, 293, 306, 311, 312, 314, 321, 333, 348, 357, 358, 362, 381, 382, 383, 385, 386, 390, 391, 412, 419, 424, 426, 436, 437, 438, 439, 440, 442, 444, 460, 465, 467, 494, 505, 510, 546, 618, 621, 648, 649, 650

'Add Email Address to Employee Record', 115

'Is Employee Data complete?', 115

'View my Reqs Change Order', 440

'View Reqs Change Order History', 440

Account Generator, 357

Activity, 132

Advanced Workflow Worklist, 58

AP Validate Expense Report, 134

Attribute, 365

Block, 426, 427

Compare, 260

Compare Text, 87

Concurrent Manager, xxiv, 391

Find Approver, 418, 424

Loop Counter, 93, 94, 95, 96, 97, 98, 123, 126, 156, 157, 158, 166, 194, 195, 311, 425

Message, 105

Notification, 389

post-Notification, xxiv, 146, 154, 331, 368, 381, 385, 386, 387

Responsibility, 58

Rule, 292

Selector, 140, 158, 159, 160, 199, 391, 397

Set Attributes, 115

Wait, 116

WF_NOTIFICATION, 64, 65, 105, 172, 186, 245, 247, 254, 256, 269, 270, 274, 282, 283, 383, 384

Functional SuperUsers, 8, 11, 549

Fusion, xxiii, 66, 593, 595, 598, 599

Fusion Middleware, 595, 598, 599

FYI Notification, 208, 281, 514, 521, 578

g_pkg, 136, 145, 153, 155, 377, 383, 388

g_proc, 143, 145, 152, 153, 154, 155, 375, 377, 383, 387, 388

g_trace, 136, 139, 141, 143, 144, 145, 152, 153, 155, 156, 157, 187, 375, 376, 377, 383, 387, 388

Generate Cost of Goods Sold Account, 226, 238

Generate Function, 230

Generic Services Manager, 2, 22, 26, 65, 292

Global Preferences, 25, 26, 267
    Browser Signing DLL Location, 26

Grant Object Sets, 478

GSC Control Queue Test, 292

GSM, 22, 26, 65, 292

GSM Setup Test, 292

GUID, 170, 184, 272, 337, 339, 340, 344

hierarchies, 7, 9, 10, 405, 432, 518, 530, 533, 538

hierarchy, 27, 76, 345, 350, 418, 422, 424, 427, 428, 434, 435, 458, 459, 518, 521, 522, 525, 528, 530, 531, 532, 533, 540, 542, 544, 552, 557, 558, 571

hourglass, 113

HTML Body tab, 105

HTML mail, 26, 269, 367

HTML mail with attachments, 26, 367

HTML summary mail, 26

Human Task Definition, 622

Human Task Editor, 622, 623, 625

Human Workflow, 595, 600, 607

IAC Account Generator, 225

icons, 39, 40, 41, 44, 59, 68, 69, 70, 74, 76, 87, 101, 103, 106, 109, 115, 122, 123, 124, 166, 173, 174, 179, 180, 182, 193, 195, 197, 211, 221, 242, 244, 245, 246, 248, 260, 263, 289, 394, 396, 408, 416, 424, 426, 434, 436, 438, 475, 490, 495, 559, 567, 572, 619, 623, 624, 625

AB-1, 109

abc, 109

ABC, 109

Copy, 69, 232, 233, 234, 289, 398, 432, 461

datastore, 69

Delete, 69, 85, 89, 94, 173, 176, 179, 191, 247, 358, 402, 462, 464, 651

Event, 76, 205

flashlight, 180, 619, 622, 623, 624

Function, 76, 78, 123, 237, 555, 621

green, 245, 246, 248

Help, 11, 44, 69, 70, 301, 358, 360, 363, 421, 424, 436, 438, 440, 442, 557, 644

New Notification, 629

Notification, 27, 40, 47, 72, 76, 96, 101, 123, 156, 214, 218, 260, 275, 328, 332, 366, 367, 371, 382, 383, 385, 387, 390, 493

Open, 28, 69, 70, 87, 109, 115, 122, 150, 268, 289, 334, 358, 364, 421, 444, 510, 515, 594, 641

Paste, 69, 234, 461

Process, 72, 76, 78, 123, 134, 147, 166, 184, 185, 199, 236, 258, 323, 357, 359, 363, 398, 422, 423, 432, 465, 565, 604, 644

red X, 208, 212, 244, 260

Save, 69, 74, 84, 86, 112, 113, 115, 358, 364, 429, 430, 481, 491, 624, 634, 641

Validate Design, 122

*i*Expense, 226, 370

IGC Budget Account Generator, 226

IGC Charge Account Generator, 226

Inbound Agent, 40, 65, 181, 244, 245

Installing, Upgrading and Maintaining Oracle E-Business Suite Applications Release 11.5.10+, xxiii

Internal Names, xxvi, 72, 101, 103, 109, 154, 182, 402

Inventory Cost of Goods Sold Account, 226

*i*Procurement, 294, 432, 434, 435, 440, 638

*i*Recruitment Vacancy Approval, 518, 553

Item Attributes, 3, 99, 106, 110, 120, 142, 150, 155, 158, 166, 184, 186, 193, 202, 215, 216, 232, 233, 235, 264, 306, 311, 327, 369, 371, 372, 405, 408, 409, 413, 427, 432, 436, 438, 441, 442, 444, 461, 472, 475, 488, 643

Item Key, 3

Item Type(s), 3, 21, 34, 42, 43, 58, 59, 69, 70, 71, 72, 73, 75, 78, 80, 81, 87, 89, 99, 101, 112, 115, 122, 123, 126, 129, 130, 135, 140, 147, 158, 159, 162, 167, 186, 187, 199, 222, 223, 227, 246, 250, 251, 258, 274, 278, 280, 291, 299, 302, 311, 321, 323, 329, 335,□ 353, 358, 362, 364, 391, 393, 397, 398, 402, 403, 406, 412, 424, 426, 430, 436, 438, 447, 471, 472, 475, 477, 492, 502, 504, 506, 512, 513, 524, 554, 614, 644

J2EE application server, 600

Java API, 601

Java Function, 176, 185

Java Function Activity Agent, 3

Java Mailer, xxiii, 20, 21, 46, 279, 292, 496

Java Mailer setup, 279

Java/J2EE, 597

JavaScript, 22

JDeveloper, 597, 600, 602, 603, 634

JDeveloper BPEL Designer, 600

Junior Administrator, xxv, 5, 8, 11, 472, 492

Label(s), 85, 109, 166, 189, 323, 357, 358, 396, 466, 471, 624

LDAP, 24

List of Values, 3, 58, 72, 78, 82, 101, 114, 120, 175, 199, 217, 231, 365, 419, 479, 481, 508, 576

Listeners, 2, 6, 8, 38, 170, 171, 172, 203, 244

Loader, 2, 70, 125, 641

Local System, 60, 169, 171, 181, 292, 337

Log Window, 604

Lookup Codes, 3, 78, 80, 87, 364, 398, 645

Lookup Type(s), 3, 4, 58, 69, 78, 80, 81, 82, 85, 87, 122, 123, 166, 205, 210, 321, 322, 330, 364, 386, 389, 391, 398, 402, 422, 626, 628, 645, 647

Loop Counter node, 93, 94, 95, 96, 97, 98, 123, 126, 156, 157, 158, 166, 194, 195, 311, 425

Loop Limit, 97, 119, 156, 195, 425, 650

Mailer Component Parameter Test, 292

Mailer Component Test, 292

Message(s), 2, 3, 6, 8, 9, 10, 17, 41, 46, 48, 49, 51, 53, 67, 69, 76, 85, 87, 99, 101, 102, 103, 104, 105, 106, 107, 108, 109, 110, 122, 123, 126, 134, 135, 136, 140, 146, 148, 150, 158, 166, 170, 171, 173, 177, 181, 182, 183, 184, 185, 186, 187, 188, 189, 191, 206, 210, 211, 213, 214, 217, 230, 234, 239, 248, 253, 254, 260, 278, 280, 300, 316, 318, 329, 333, 335, 340, 341, 342, 343, 345, 352, 353, 355, 364, 365, 366, 367, 369, 370, 371, 372, 373, 374, 377, 379, 380, 383, 384, 386, 387, 390, 402, 426, 428, 430, 445, 502, 506, 508, 509, 513, 543, 600, 627, 629, 631, 645, 646, 647, 648, 650, 651

Error, 122, 214, 229, 230, 384, 430, 443, 461, 510

Event, 337

JMS Text, 244

Queue, 41, 248

Web Services, 171, 245

MetaLink, xxviii, 1, 6, 8, 10, 11, 13, 15, 18, 20, 21, 22, 23, 26, 27, 28, 43, 45, 46, 59, 60, 92, 131, 132, 133, 149, 165, 226, 238, 239, 247, 253, 260, 267, 268, 270, 278, 279, 280, 282, 285, 286, 290, 292, 293, 296, 298, 336, 337, 340, 343, 349, 363, 372, 391, 405, 412, 432, 437, 440, 443, 458, 466, 468, 469, 470, 494, 495, 496, 497, 498, 499, 501, 503, 504, 516, 521, 545, 556, 593, 594, 596

MHCA Account Generator, 225

Microsoft Outlook Express, 367, 502

Monitor, 2, 4, 6, 8, 10, 11, 27, 59, 78, 123, 205, 211, 216, 220, 221, 230, 248, 252, 253, 478, 482, 492, 493, 597

Navigator Tree, 3

Navigator window, 68, 69, 70, 71, 76, 78, 80, 87, 89, 101, 109, 189, 298, 312, 323, 358, 361, 362, 420, 645, 646

New Item Type Internal Name, 72, 644

No Commits, 131

Node, 4
  End, 358
  Event, 184
  Start, 182, 184, 189, 358

node comment, 323

node label, 323, 398, 463

Notification, 3, 4, 26, 122, 147, 254, 256, 270, 287, 329, 331, 332, 344, 348, 349, 384, 388, 493, 639, 644
  AME Expense Report Approval Notification, 426
  AP Custom Default Error Notification, 427, 429
  Inform Individual of Expense Allocation Failure, 426
  Inform Preparer – No Manager Response, 427
  Inform Preparer of Auditor Requesting More Information, 427
  Inform preparer of Policy Non-Compliance for Missing Receipts, 427
  Inform Sys Admin of Custom Validation Failure, 426, 428
  Inform Sys Admin of Payables Validation Failure, 426
  Inform System Administrator – No Approver, 426, 428
  Inform System Administrator – No Vendor, 426, 428
  Request Approval from APPROVER, 427
  Request Individual's Approval, 427
  Verify With Mgr the Amt Approved With Policy Violations, 427

Notification Details, 26, 366

Notification Mailer, xxiii, xxv, 2, 4, 5, 6, 8, 9, 10, 25, 40, 44, 46, 47, 51, 52, 56, 208, 214, 242, 243, 244, 254, 255, 269, 270, 271, 274, 279, 280, 284, 292, 328, 330, 336, 345, 349, 366, 369, 372, 384, 494, 495, 498, 499, 500, 501, 502, 503

Notification Preference Validation Test, 29, 291

Notification Search, 275, 492, 493, 494

Notification Style, 25
  Disabled, 25, 26, 27, 179, 181
  Do not send me mail, 26, 269, 270, 279, 367
  HTML mail, 26, 269, 367
  HTML mail with attachments, 26, 367
  HTML summary mail, 26
  Plain text mail, 26, 367
  Plain text mail with HTML attachments, 26, 367
  Plain text summary mail, 26

Notification System, 2, 270

Notifications, xxiv, 1, 2, 6, 7, 8, 9, 10, 11, 20, 25, 26, 27, 34, 37, 38, 40, 43, 46, 49, 56, 69, 76, 79, 81, 89, 99, 101, 109, 110, 113, 125, 126, 132, 147, 150, 154, 172, 206, 208, 210, 218, 223, 227, 234, 235, 241, 242, 244, 245, 247, 254, 255, 256, 257, 263, 264, 266, 267, 269, 270, 274, 275, 276, 279, 280, 281, 282, 284, 293, 300, 306, 311, 312, 314, 321, 328, 329, 330, 332, 333, 335, 336, 337, 349, 353, 355, 365, 366, 367, 374, 379, 383, 387, 398, 426, 427, 436, 437, 438, 445, 447, 453, 467, 492, 494, 496, 502, 503, 504, 510, 512, 514, 515, 517, 519, 520, 521, 524, 535, 544, 552, 553, 602, 638, 639, 644, 645, 646, 648, 649, 650
  AP Custom Default Error Notification, 427, 429
  Inform AP Expense Report They Reviewed Is Mgr Rejected, 428
  Inform AP Mgr Approvd ShortPay with Missing Receipts, 428
  Inform AP Mileage Rate Has Been Adjusted, 428
  Inform Individual of Expense Allocations Failure, 428
  Inform Sys Admin of Custom Validation Failure, 426, 428
  Inform SysAdmin of Payables Validation Failure, 428
  Inform System Administrator – No Vendor, 426, 428
  Request AP to Review for Spending Policy Compliance, 428

OA Framework, 20, 26, 368, 370, 372, 494

OA_MEDIA, 59

OAM, xxiii, xxiv, xxvii, 2, 13, 20, 21, 34, 36, 39, 40, 41, 44, 56, 239, 241, 242, 245, 248, 249,

251, 254, 270, 279, 284, 286, 292, 294, 354, 495, 501

OAUG, iii, iv, v, viii, 597

Object Instance Set, 472, 473, 475, 476, 477, 478, 483, 484, 487, 488, 489

OKL Account Generator, 226, 239

On Revisit, 34, 125, 126, 146, 151, 228, 332, 333

ORA-1652, 29

Oracle Alert, xxvii, 20, 271, 328, 469, 494

Oracle Alert Response Processor, 494

Oracle Application Server Knowledge, 597

Oracle Applications Manager, xxiii, xxiv, xxvii, 2, 13, 20, 21, 34, 36, 39, 40, 41, 44, 56, 239, 241, 242, 245, 248, 249, 251, 254, 270, 279, 284, 286, 292, 293, 294, 303, 334, 354, 469, 495, 501

Oracle Diagnostics, 2, 5, 10, 238, 279, 285, 286, 289, 293, 294, 470

Oracle Internet Expenses Implementation and Administration Guide, 423

Oracle Order Management, Using Oracle Workflow in Oracle Order Management, Release 12, 447

Oracle Purchasing Users Guide Release 11i, 432

Oracle Purchasing Users Guide Release 12, 432

Oracle Role Based Access Model (RBAC), 546

Oracle SOA Console, 604, 631

Oracle SOA Suite 11g Technology Preview 3, 600

Oracle Technology Network, 593, 595, 596

Oracle Time and Labor Implementation and User Guide, 449

Oracle User Management, 345, 351, 469

Oracle Workflow, iii, ix, xxvii, 1, 2, 15, 18, 20, 21, 22, 27, 28, 29, 43, 70, 72, 125, 127, 132, 169, 222, 244, 257, 270, 279, 282, 285, 292, 293, 295, 299, 301, 336, 342, 345, 350, 360, 363, 364, 377, 386, 391, 403, 404, 421, 424, 432, 436, 438, 440, 442, 447, 465, 469, 470, 494, 496, 542, 593, 594, 595, 598, 644

Oracle Workflow Administrator's Guide, 2, 72, 295, 299, 345, 403, 470

Oracle Workflow API Reference, 342, 350, 403

Oracle Workflow Developer's Guide, 116, 125, 127, 364, 377, 386, 403

Orphaned Notifications, 247

OWF, xxvii, 18, 20, 21, 27, 29, 43, 279, 282, 336, 469, 494, 496

OWF.G, 20, 21, 29, 43

OWF.H, 21, 27, 282, 336, 494, 496

Owner, 61, 130, 148, 149, 150, 175, 181, 182, 186, 199, 235, 275, 401, 434, 507, 546

OZF: Account Generator, 226

Package

    WF_EVENT, 63, 124, 125, 138, 140, 146, 149, 150, 158, 162, 184, 186, 200, 215, 217, 228, 229, 230, 327, 331, 382, 383, 388, 389, 390, 391, 392, 393, 397, 398

Packages

    GL_WF_CUSTOMIZATION_PKG, 422

    GL_WF_JE_APPROVAL_PKG, 422

Page

    Confirmation, 202, 514, 540

    Function Properties, 77

    Node Attributes, 184, 231, 324, 362, 386, 391, 392

    Properties, 429

    Service Components, 245, 501

Page Flows, 594

partitioning, 42, 43

Patches

    11i.ATG_PF.H.delta.5 (RUP 5), 21, 330

    AME

        11i.AME.B.2, 470, 517

        4629194, 470

        5305176, 470

    AME.B, 545, 546, 556

    ATG_PF.H Rollup 3, 21, 257, 280

    Diagnostics

        R12.IZU.A.delta.4 January 2008 (6497339), 470

    HR

        11i.HR.K.2, 470

    One-off

        6399304, 494, 499, 500

    One-Off

        4719658, 503

        6412999, 494

        6441940, 494

PC, 2, 6, 8, 10, 28, 67, 74, 75, 112, 115, 122, 124, 295, 299, 575, 577, 596, 641

Performer(s), 4, 69, 110, 122, 149, 150, 198, 199, 202, 345, 346, 349, 358, 363, 405, 408, 409, 411, 413, 424, 427, 428, 445, 645, 650

Personal Home Page, 27, 266, 269

PHP, 27

pivot activity, 125, 126

PL/SQL, xxiv, xxv, 1, 2, 3, 7, 9, 10, 11, 29, 30, 34, 60, 61, 62, 65, 66, 67, 70, 76, 97, 123, 124,

125, 126, 129, 130, 131, 132, 138, 142, 154,
156, 158, 166, 167, 171, 176, 182, 184, 185,
186, 192, 193, 198, 199, 200, 201, 208, 210,
212, 213, 215, 217, 227, 232, 235, 261, 264,
271, 292, 355, 357, 371, 372, 377, 379, 381,
391, 403, 419, 420, 422, 424, 432, 438, 440,
442, 444, 445, 460, 465, 467, 522, 542, 543,
597, 599, 640, 649, 650
PL/SQL BLOB, 371
PL/SQL CLOB, 371, 377
PL/SQL functions, 115
Plain text mail, 26, 367
Plain text mail with HTML attachments, 26, 367
Plain text summary mail, 26
PO Account Generator, 226, 236
PO Requisition Account Generator, 226
pragma autonomous_transaction, 132
Procedure
  DBMS_AQADM.Alter_Queue, 171
  DEFAULT_ERROR, 126, 147
  DEFAULT_EVENT_ERROR, 126
  RETRY_ONLY, 126
Process Diagrammer, 4
process flow, 595
Process Integration Packs (PIPs), 599
Process Name, 219, 471, 493
Process Navigator Flows, 594
Processes, 2, 3, 4, 6, 8, 11, 26, 29, 34, 42, 69, 72,
  76, 87, 92, 127, 129, 130, 173, 199, 210, 225,
  226, 227, 234, 245, 248, 258, 306, 321, 340,
  363, 392, 398, 406, 420, 423, 429, 433, 437,
  439, 445, 447, 448, 461, 471, 498, 594, 599,
  600, 601, 602, 604
  AME Approval Process, 426
  AME Request Approval Process, 426
  AP Custom Default Error Process, 427, 429
  AP Rejection Process, 427
  AP Request More Info, 427
  Bothpay Process, 426, 428
  Manager (Shortpay) Approval Process, 425
  Manager (Shortpay) Approval Subprocess, 427
  Manager (Spending) Approval Process, 424,
    428
  Missing Receipt Policy Non-Compliance
    Process, 427
  No Manager Response Process, 425
  No Manager Response Process 2, 425
  Non AME Approval Process, 424, 426
  Policy Non-Compliance Process, 427

Rejection Process, 426, 428
Request Approval Process, 420, 427
Return Expense Report Process, 426
Server Side Validation Process, 426, 428
Third Party Expense Report, 425, 427
Third Party Expense Report Process, 427
Withdraw Expense Report Process, 426
Profile Options, 26, 165, 212, 239, 405, 413,
  418, 423, 470, 501, 552, 640, 641, 642
  AME:Installed, 552
  Concurrent: GSM Enabled, 26
  FA: Use Workflow Account Generator, 239
  FND: Notification Reassign Mode, 27
  ICX: Limit connect, 501
  ICX: Limit time, 501
  ICX:Session Timeout, 501
  IRC: Vacancy Approval Transaction Type,
    555
  OKL: Use Account Generator Workflow, 239
  PSB:Use Account Generator for Data Extract,
    239
  Server Timezone, 27
  Socket Listener Port, 27
  WF: GUEST Access to Notification, 27
  WF: ICX Session Mode, 27
  WF: Notification Reassign Mode, 27, 365
  WF: Plain text sign-on, 27
  WF: Routing Rules – Allow All, 27
  WF: Vacation Rules – Allow all, 27
  WF: Workflow Mailer Framework Web
    Agent, 27
Project Budget Account Generation, 226
Project Supplier Invoice Account Generation,
  226, 227
Project Web Employees Account Generator,
  226
propagate, 171
propagation, 248, 254
Properties, 15, 80, 87, 92, 101, 103, 106, 109,
  110, 114, 115, 116, 122, 123, 124, 125, 126,
  130, 147, 150, 158, 166, 195, 205, 231, 234,
  237, 298, 302, 311, 358, 359, 360, 364, 366,
  370, 412, 421, 436, 438, 441, 442, 444, 445,
  461, 471, 537, 542, 602, 647, 650
Property Inspector, 604
Protection Level, 3, 4
PSB Account Generator for OLD Integration,
  225
Purge, 42, 141, 221, 241, 242, 246, 247, 278, 520

Purge and Control Queue Cleanup tools, 241

Purge Obsolete Workflow Runtime Data, 42, 141, 221, 247

Queue Propagation, 254

queues, xxiv, 8, 244, 254

Quick Start Wizard, 71, 78, 614

Reference Value, 120

Related Links, 254

Relative Time, 92, 117, 118, 119, 195, 426, 436, 438, 445, 630, 650, 651

Release 11.5.10, xxiii, xxv, xxvii, 1, 2, 5, 13, 14, 23, 27, 28, 72, 80, 97, 110, 115, 138, 169, 171, 172, 173, 175, 193, 220, 225, 252, 257, 268, 279, 282, 283, 291, 296, 330, 331, 349, 351, 364, 414, 417, 418, 423, 424, 427, 432, 433, 447, 449, 450, 454, 460, 461, 468, 469, 470, 517, 586, 593, 595, 597, 599

Release 11.5.6, 27

Release 11.5.9, 20, 28, 169, 226, 252, 545

Release 11i, xxvi, xxvii, xxviii, 1, 22, 160, 165, 226, 270, 285, 414, 431, 447, 469, 470, 494, 499, 500, 504, 516, 519, 552, 593

Release 12, xxiii, xxiv, xxv, xxvii, xxviii, 1, 2, 5, 13, 15, 21, 22, 28, 66, 72, 97, 115, 116, 125, 127, 160, 162, 165, 169, 171, 173, 193, 225, 231, 239, 270, 295, 296, 299, 329, 330, 345, 350, 364, 377, 403, 414, 415, 418, 423, 424, 426, 427, 428, 432, 434, 447, 449, 450, 451, 452, 454, 460, 461, 468, 469, 470, 493, 494, 499, 500, 514, 516, 517, 519, 520, 535, 546, 551, 593, 594, 595, 597, 599

Request Groups, 58

Responsibility
  Application Developer, 58, 555
  Approvals Management Administrator, 519, 546, 553
  CRM HTML Administration, 286
  Database Administrator, 10, 27, 29, 42, 640
  Oracle Diagnostics Tool, 286
  Order Management Super User, 448
  OTL Administrator, 449
  System Administrator, 7, 8, 9, 10, 22, 23, 41, 67, 87, 196, 267, 286, 349, 350, 418, 422, 426, 444, 445, 494, 495, 497, 546, 552, 606, 607, 640
  Workflow Administrator Web (New), 22, 257, 492
  Workflow System Administrator, 23, 267

Restrict Assignee, 419

Result Code, 4, 123, 134, 233, 353, 379, 389, 397, 398

Result Type(s), 4, 76, 78, 80, 84, 85, 90, 105, 106, 108, 109, 150, 151, 154, 155, 193, 194, 205, 206, 207, 359, 385, 392, 422, 621, 629

Result Value, 4

RETRY_ONLY Procedure, 126

Role, 4, 23, 30, 144, 268, 326, 329, 331, 344, 345, 350, 351, 353, 355, 366, 390, 472
  Approvals Management Business Analyst, 546, 555, 556, 569

Rule Function Validation Test, 292

Running Diagnostic Tests, 287

run-time tables, 298

RUP3, xxvii

RUP4, 494

Sample Procedures
  tally_vote, 387

Sample Queries
  Activity Attribute Values, 413
  Constant Timeout with 0 or NULL value, 406
  Convert to canonical form, 522
  Errored Workflow Counts, 335
  Get TRANSACTION_REQUESTOR_PERSON_ID, 557
  Mailer component_id, 502
  No Time Attribute, 406
  Non-existent or Inactive Performers, 409
  Notification Counts, 336
  Open and Closed Workflow Counts, 334
  parameter_id for HTML Delimiter, 502
  Performer set to Item Attribute with NULL value, 410, 411
  To Count Errors by Error Message, 276
  WFERROR – Errored Event Query, 514
  WFERROR – Errored Item Type, 513
  WFERRORs Still Not Closed, 278

Sample Workflow, 67

savepoint, 131, 132, 138

Screen
  Notification Search, 275, 492, 493, 494
  Notification Worklist, 207, 208, 242, 244, 329, 372, 389, 400, 492, 494, 505, 506, 514, 515, 639
  Status Monitor, 5, 72, 99, 101, 146, 162, 184, 201, 203, 204, 205, 208, 213, 216, 241, 250, 258, 262, 287, 333, 489, 492

security group, 23, 113, 349

selector function, 131
Server Timezone, 27
Service Component Container, 4
Service Components, 3, 4, 39, 51, 65, 242, 244, 245, 254, 292, 500, 501, 622
Service Name, 617
Service Request, xxviii, 29, 34, 60, 167, 279, 284, 289, 293, 514
  SR, 34, 60, 167, 279, 284, 289, 514
session, 27, 76, 130, 158, 161, 349, 399, 400, 501
Set Attributes, 76, 78, 89, 115, 142, 148, 154, 193, 216, 643, 649, 651
SET_CTX mode, 164
Simple Object Access Protocol (SOAP), 600
SMTP, 20, 45, 46, 47, 172
SOA, 596, 597, 599, 604, 612, 622
SOA Console, 601, 604, 605, 634
Socket Listener Port, 27
SQL
  afsvcpup.sql, 502
  bde_wf_clean_worklist.sql, 247, 278
  wfbesdbg.sql, 293
  wfbkgchk.sql, 293
  WFCHACT.sql, 402
  WFCHACTA.sql, 402
  WFCHITA.sql, 402
  WFCHITT.sql, 402
  WFCHLUC.sql, 402
  WFCHLUT.sql, 402
  WFCHMSG.sql, 402
  WFCHMSGA.sql, 402
  wfdirchk.sql, 29, 293
  wfmlrdbg.sql, 293
  WFNTFPRG.sql, 247
  wfprot.sql, 364
  WFPROT.sql, 301
  WFRMALL.sql, 403
  WFRMITMS.sql, 403
  WFRMITT.sql, 403
  WFRMITT.SQL, 222
  WFRMTYPE.sql, 403
  WFRMTYPE.SQL, 222
  wfsmrdbg.sql, 293
  wfstatus.sql, 293
  wfver.sql, 59, 60, 66, 293
  wfverchk.sql, 293
SQL scripts, 59, 285, 286
Standard Activities, 116, 123, 192, 228, 239, 357, 645

Compare Date, 87
Compare Number, 87
Compare Text, 87, 89, 90, 120, 193, 323, 357, 644, 650, 651
Standard Flexfield Workflow, 234
Standard item type, 1, 69, 70, 71, 78, 80, 87, 89, 91, 93, 94, 95, 98, 101, 116, 123, 146, 192, 202, 215, 227, 230, 232, 234, 244, 245, 257, 311, 358, 362, 385, 386, 412, 424, 429, 460, 465, 644, 645
Status Monitor, 5, 72, 99, 101, 146, 162, 184, 201, 203, 204, 205, 208, 213, 216, 241, 250, 258, 262, 287, 333, 489, 492
subscription(s), xxiv, 2, 3, 4, 64, 170, 172, 173, 174, 175, 176, 177, 179, 180, 181, 182, 187, 244, 248, 253, 258, 270, 292, 293, 337, 339, 340, 344
supervisor, 11, 67, 136, 142, 148, 151, 152, 153, 217, 374, 375, 376, 377, 418, 423, 424, 450, 453, 504, 517, 518, 521, 522, 525, 528, 530, 531, 532, 533, 535, 538, 542, 544, 558, 559, 563, 565, 569, 573, 574, 575, 577, 581, 606, 637, 638, 644, 645, 649
surrogate, 130
synchronize, 6, 8, 28, 41, 173, 175, 349, 504
Synchronize Product Licenses and BES, 6
Synchronous operations, 600
SYS.AQ$_JMS_TEXT_MESSAGE, 171, 341, 342, 343
SYSADMIN, 6, 9, 26, 144, 149, 177, 189, 196, 204, 218, 221, 247, 267, 268, 269, 276, 280, 284, 335, 427, 428, 467, 480, 489, 494, 495, 497, 503, 504, 546, 549, 638
system, ii, 1, 2, 3, 4, 15, 23, 28, 31, 32, 60, 67, 112, 115, 122, 169, 170, 222, 241, 254, 268, 271, 272, 273, 287, 292, 337, 342, 346, 399, 400, 401, 419, 423, 435, 437, 440, 442, 444, 460, 465, 519, 522, 542, 544, 594, 599, 624
System Administrator, 7, 8, 9, 10, 22, 23, 41, 67, 87, 196, 267, 286, 349, 350, 418, 422, 426, 444, 445, 494, 495, 497, 546, 552, 606, 607, 640
Tab
  Administration, 267
  Body, 103, 123, 150, 300, 317, 628, 647
  Business Events, 258
  composite.xml, 622
  Developer Studio, 258
  Event, xxiv, 337
  Event Details, 210

Function, 429, 649

Home Page, 257

HTML Body, 105

Message, 647

Node, 92, 110, 122, 166, 189, 195, 227, 323, 329, 357, 359, 366, 397, 398, 421, 426, 436, 438, 445, 471, 630

Node Attributes, 87, 116, 192, 195, 231, 237, 298, 311, 312, 385, 391, 392, 412, 421, 424, 445, 466

Notifications, 266

Other Attributes, 452, 460

Result, 647

Status Monitor Tab, 258

Vacation Rules Tab, 274

Table

AQ$, 62, 340, 343

design tables, 218, 295, 296, 298, 301, 334

Directory Services, 345

  WF_DIRECTORY_PARTITIONS, 345

  WF_DIRECTORY_PARTITIONS_TL, 345

  WF_LOCAL_ROLES, 28, 110, 113, 114, 148, 149, 150, 198, 269, 270, 326, 345, 346, 349, 350, 351, 353, 355, 389, 399, 400, 401, 481, 503

FND_USER_PREFERENCES, 269, 270, 345, 348, 354, 503

Notification History, 331, 365

PA_UTILIZATION_OPTIONS_ALL, 467

PER_ALL_PEOPLE_F, 69, 137, 140, 148, 160, 187, 199, 269, 348, 349, 536

Queue, 340

run-time tables, 298

WF_ACTIVITIES, 278, 295, 296, 298, 306, 323

WF_ACTIVITY_ATTR_VALUES, 296, 298, 311, 312, 315

WF_ACTIVITY_ATTRIBUTES, 296, 298, 311, 312

WF_ACTIVITY_STATUSES, 295

WF_ACTIVITY_TRANSITIONS, 296, 324, 326

WF_AGENTS, 269, 272, 337

WF_COMMENTS, 248, 295, 330, 331

WF_EVENT_GROUPS, 339

WF_EVENTS, 338, 340

WF_ITEM_ACTIVITY_STATUSES, 43, 247, 298, 324, 329, 332, 333, 388

WF_ITEM_ACTIVITY_STATUSES_H, 43, 298, 324, 332

WF_ITEM_ACTIVITY_STATUSES_H, 248

WF_ITEM_ATTRIBUTE_VALUES, 162, 184, 215, 216, 230, 247, 269, 272, 298, 323, 327

WF_ITEM_ATTRIBUTE_VALUES, 43

WF_ITEM_ATTRIBUTE_VALUES, 295

WF_ITEM_ATTRIBUTE_VALUES, 298

WF_ITEM_ATTRIBUTES, 162, 215, 216, 230, 296, 298, 305

WF_ITEM_ATTRIBUTES, 295

WF_ITEM_ATTRIBUTES, 296

WF_ITEM_TYPES, xxvi, 295, 296, 298, 302, 311, 318, 329

WF_ITEMS, 43, 247, 298, 303, 326, 327, 329, 472

WF_ITEMS, 295

WF_LOCAL_ROLES, 326

WF_LOCAL_ROLES, 28, 110, 113, 114, 148, 149, 150, 198, 269, 270

WF_LOCAL_ROLES, 399

WF_LOCAL_USER_ROLES, 28, 345, 350, 351, 503

WF_LOOKUP_TYPES_TL, 296, 298, 321

WF_LOOKUPS_TL, 295, 296, 322

WF_MESSAGE_ATTRIBUTES, 295, 296, 298, 318, 331

WF_MESSAGES, 295, 296, 298, 300, 316, 317, 329, 365, 367

WF_NOTIFICATION_ATTRIBUTES, 247, 269, 273, 295, 331

WF_NOTIFICATION_OUT, 64, 65, 172, 245, 254, 269, 270, 274, 282, 283, 329, 336

WF_NOTIFICATIONS, 247, 256, 269, 270, 274, 295, 298, 327, 329, 331, 332, 349, 367, 374, 505

WF_PROCESS_ACTIVITIES, 157, 166, 296, 298, 302, 323, 324, 327, 331, 332, 343, 357

WF_RESOURCES, 268, 355, 384

WF_ROLE_HIERARCHY, 351

WF_ROLES, 31, 32, 350

WF_ROUTING_RULE_ATTRIBUTES, 345, 352, 353

WF_ROUTING_RULES, 345, 352

WF_SUBSCRIPTIONS, 339

WF_SYSTEMS, 269, 272, 273, 337, 340

WF_USER_ROLE_ASSIGNMENTS, 345, 351

WF_USER_ROLES, 33, 350

TABLES

WF_ACTIVITY_STATUSES_H, 295

Tables WF_ACTIVITY_TRANSITIONS, 298

Test Mailer, 279

test repository, 285

Test Value, 120, 650

Testing, xxiv, 76, 141, 147, 167, 193, 218, 221, 258, 403, 558, 568, 579, 580, 586

Throughput, 255

Timeout, 4, 34, 46, 85, 87, 92, 93, 94, 95, 96, 97, 146, 194, 195, 206, 207, 314, 326, 329, 332, 333, 382, 386, 388, 389, 391, 406, 407, 408, 419, 420, 422, 423, 426, 427, 436, 437, 438, 445, 453, 461, 465, 496, 497, 630, 644, 650, 651

Top Process, 71, 72, 130, 182, 645

Transition, 4

trigger, 110, 132, 133, 194

Universal Description, Discovery and Integration (UDDI) directory, 600

user interface, 257, 285

UserKey, 150

Vacation Rules, 6, 7, 9, 10, 11, 27, 58, 222, 257, 267, 274, 284, 329, 332, 345, 352, 353, 365, 540

Validate Design, 122

Versioning, 158, 166, 167, 210, 293

View Concurrent Programs, 245

Viewing Test Results, 289

Wait, 41, 98, 101, 116, 117, 118, 119, 123, 147, 194, 195, 218, 228, 244, 248, 311, 386, 392, 393, 394, 397, 398, 426, 427, 445, 446, 448, 651

Wait for Flow, 147, 228, 393, 394, 448

Wait Mode, 117, 118, 195, 445, 651

Warehouse Builder, 593, 599

web services, 171, 185

Web Services Description Language (WSDL), 600

web-services, 599

WF: GUEST Access to Notification, 27

WF: ICX Session Mode, 27

WF: Notification Reassign Mode, 27, 365

WF: Plain text sign-on, 27

WF: Routing Rules – Allow All, 27

WF: Vacation Rule Item Types, 58

WF: Vacation Rules – Allow all, 27

WF: Workflow Mailer Framework Web Agent, 27

WF_ACTIVITY_TRANSITIONS, 298, 324, 326

WF_CORE.Context, 135, 136, 147, 150, 153, 154, 155, 158, 213, 378, 379, 380, 383, 384, 388, 389

WF_DIRECTORY.UserActive, 149

WF_ENGINE.CreateProcess, 140, 184, 229, 392

WF_ENGINE.HandleError, 146

WF_ENGINE.LaunchProcess, 140

WF_ENGINE.SetItemAttr<type>, 150, 158, 184, 327

WF_ENGINE.SetItemOwner, 149

WF_EVENT_T, 171, 188, 341, 342, 344

WF_ITEM_ACTIVITY_STATUSES, 43, 247, 298, 324, 329, 332, 333, 388

WF_ITEM_ACTIVITY_STATUSES_H, 43, 248, 298, 324, 332

WF_ITEM_ATTRIBUTE_VALUES, 43, 162, 184, 215, 216, 230, 247, 269, 272, 295, 298, 323, 327

WF_ITEMS, 43, 247, 295, 298, 303, 326, 327, 329, 472

WF_LOCAL_ROLES, 28, 110, 113, 114, 148, 149, 150, 198, 269, 270, 326, 345, 346, 349, 350, 351, 353, 355, 389, 399, 400, 401, 481, 503

WF_LOCAL_USER_ROLES, 28, 345, 350, 351, 503

WF_NOTE, 365, 389

WF_NOTIFICATION, 64, 65, 105, 172, 186, 245, 247, 254, 256, 269, 270, 274, 282, 283, 383, 384, 506

WF_PROCESS_ACTIVITIES, 157, 166, 296, 298, 302, 323, 324, 327, 331, 332, 343, 357

wfdirchk.sql, 29, 293

WFERROR, 126, 127, 146, 147, 189, 204, 211, 218, 220, 221, 247, 277, 278, 326, 327, 335, 345, 380, 427, 430, 443, 506, 510, 512, 513, 514

WFLOAD, 222, 223, 362, 364, 641

WFRMITT.SQL, 222

WFRMTYPE.SQL, 222

WFSTD.wft, 6, 8

wfver.sql, 59, 60, 66, 293

Work Items, 6, 8, 43, 242, 246, 247, 248, 249, 251, 252, 255, 284, 303

Workflow Administration menus, 241, 242, 492, 506

Workflow Administrator, xxiii, xxiv, 1, 2, 5, 6, 7, 9, 10, 11, 20, 21, 22, 23, 25, 34, 41, 134, 144, 149, 150, 169, 170, 172, 195, 196, 241, 257, 260, 264, 268, 285, 286, 294, 333, 355, 426, 427, 428, 429, 454, 492, 494, 497, 503, 506, 516, 643, 646

Workflow Administrator Web (New), 22, 257, 492

Workflow Advanced Queue Rule Validation Test, 292

Workflow Agent Listener Service, 38, 39, 40, 66, 282, 284

Workflow Agents/AQ Status Test, 292

Workflow Background Process, 35, 245, 248, 343

Workflow Builder, xxiii, xxiv, 2, 4, 7, 9, 11, 13, 14, 15, 16, 18, 20, 34, 43, 59, 66, 67, 70, 127, 188, 199, 204, 210, 214, 216, 222, 225, 227, 247, 264, 298, 299, 301, 302, 305, 306, 311, 312, 314, 315, 318, 321, 322, 324, 357, 358, 360, 362, 364, 391, 403, 405, 406, 408, 413, 421, 423, 424, 426, 429, 435, 436, 437, 438, 440, 441, 442, 444, 447, 460, 461, 465, 468, 471, 634, 641

Workflow Builder Client, 13, 15

Workflow Configuration, 22, 23, 241, 267, 268, 337

Workflow Configuration for Cloned Database Instances, 268

Workflow Definitions Loader, 222

Workflow Directory Services, 29, 293, 349, 470, 503, 504

Workflow Document Web Services, 66, 244

Workflow error administrator, 454

Workflow Java Mailer, 292

Workflow Mailer, 6, 8, 9, 10, 20, 40, 45, 46, 47, 48, 51, 66, 242, 244, 282, 284, 494, 498, 502

Workflow Mailer Service, 40, 66, 244, 282, 284

Workflow Manager, xxiv, 2, 241, 242, 245, 303, 334, 495

Workflow Metrics, 248, 255

Workflow Notification Mailer, 13, 20, 26, 40, 244, 495, 496, 501, 502

Workflow Objects Validity Test, 292

Workflow Performance, 293

Workflow Queues, 272, 292, 293

Workflow Release 2.6.X, 593

Workflow Status and Purgeable Items, 293

Workflow System Administrator, 23, 267

Workflow Tests, 29, 287, 293, 294

Workflows
APINV, 472, 475, 485, 492
Expenses (APEXP), 134, 140, 160, 215, 405, 412, 423, 430, 475, 485, 492
HRSSA, 278, 430, 477, 483, 554
Journal Approval Workflow (GLBATCH), 413, 419
OTL Workflows for Employees (HXCEMP), 278, 449, 460, 461, 466, 467
PA: HR Related Updates Workflow (PAXWFHRU), 467
PASYSADMIN, 467
PO Approval, 270
PO Approval (POAPPRV), 431, 444
PO Approval Error (POERROR), 278, 443, 444
PO Approval Error (POERROR), 431
PO Approval Error (POERROR), 435
PO Change Approval for Requestor (PORPOCHA), 431, 440
PO Change Request Tolerance Check (PORCOTOL), 431, 440
PO Create Documents (CREATEPO), 431
PO Requisition Approval (REQAPPRV), 431, 443
PO Send Notification, 447
Requestor Change Order Approval (POREQCHA), 431, 433, 440, 443

WSDL binding framework, 600

WSIF, 600

XML, xxvii, 3, 17, 38, 61, 172, 173, 192, 244, 285, 292, 341, 469, 594, 597, 599, 600, 634

XML definitions, 600

XML interpreters, 600

XML Parser Installation Test, 292

XML reports, 285

XML Transaction Flows, 594

CPSIA information can be obtained
at www.ICGtesting.com
Printed in the USA
BVHW01s1047201117
500905BV00012B/1073/P